191 ZIS

137

1949

משנה

ArtScroll Mishnah Series®

A rabbinic commentary to the Six Orders of the Mishnah

Rabbis Nosson Scherman / Meir Zlotowitz

General Editors

the mishnah

ARTSCROLL MISHNAH SERIES / A NEW TRANSLATION WITH A COMMENTARY **YAD AVRAHAM** ANTHOLOGIZED FROM TALMUDIC SOURCES AND CLASSIC COMMENTATORS.

Published by

Mesorah Publications, ltd.

ששה סדרי **מִשְׁנָה**

ERUVIN
First Edition . . . February 1983

BEITZAH
First Edition . . . December 1982

COMBINED EDITION
Five Impressions . . . April 1986 — June 2000
Sixth Impression . . . August 2002

Published and Distributed by
MESORAH PUBLICATIONS, Ltd.
4401 Second Avenue
Brooklyn, New York 11232

Distributed in Europe by
LEHMANNS
Unit E, Viking Industrial Park
Rolling Mill Road
Jarrow, Tyne & Wear NE32 3DP
England

Distributed in Australia & New Zealand by
GOLDS WORLD OF JUDAICA
3-13 William Street
Balaclava, Melbourne 3183
Victoria Australia

Distributed in Israel by
SIFRIATI / A. GITLER — BOOKS
6 Hayarkon Street
Bnei Brak 51127

Distributed in South Africa by
KOLLEL BOOKSHOP
Shop 8A Norwood Hypermarket
Norwood 2196, Johannesburg, South Africa.

THE ARTSCROLL MISHNAH SERIES®
SEDER MOED Vol. I(b)-I(c); *ERUVIN / BEITZAH*

© *Copyright 1982, 1983, 1986, by* MESORAH PUBLICATIONS, Ltd.
4401 Second Avenue / Brooklyn, N.Y. 11232 / (718) 921-9000 / www.artscroll.com

---

ISBN
0-89906-262-8 (hard cover)

Typography by Compuscribe at ArtScroll Studios, Ltd.
4401 Second Avenue / Brooklyn, NY 11232 / (718) 921-9000

Printed in the United States of America by Moriah Offset
Bound by Sefercraft, Quality Bookbinders, Ltd. Brooklyn, N.Y.

✺§ Seder Moed Vol. I(b):

מסכת עירובין

Tractate Eruvin

✺§ Seder Moed Vol. I(c):

מסכת ביצה

Tractate Beitzah

The Publishers are grateful to

TORAH UMESORAH

and

YAD AVRAHAM INSTITUTE

for their efforts in the publication of the

ARTSCROLL MISHNAH SERIES

We proudly dedicate this tractate

in honor of our parents

Judge and Mrs. Gustave G. Rosenberg עמו״ש

ר׳ גרשון בן ר׳ יהודה — *born April 23, 1900*

מרת שרה שיינא בת דוב בעריל —*born February 15, 1901*

who were among the original founders of the

Fifth Avenue Synagogue;

and in honor of the Synagogue's

twenty-five years of unexcelled service

to the Jewish community

תשי״ח־תשמ״ג / 1958-1983.

May the Torah studied from this volume

be a source of merit

for the souls of our brother and sister

אברהם דוד ודבורה חאשא חוה

בני ר׳ גרשון

       Mr. and Mrs. Lawrence M. Rosenberg

הסכמה

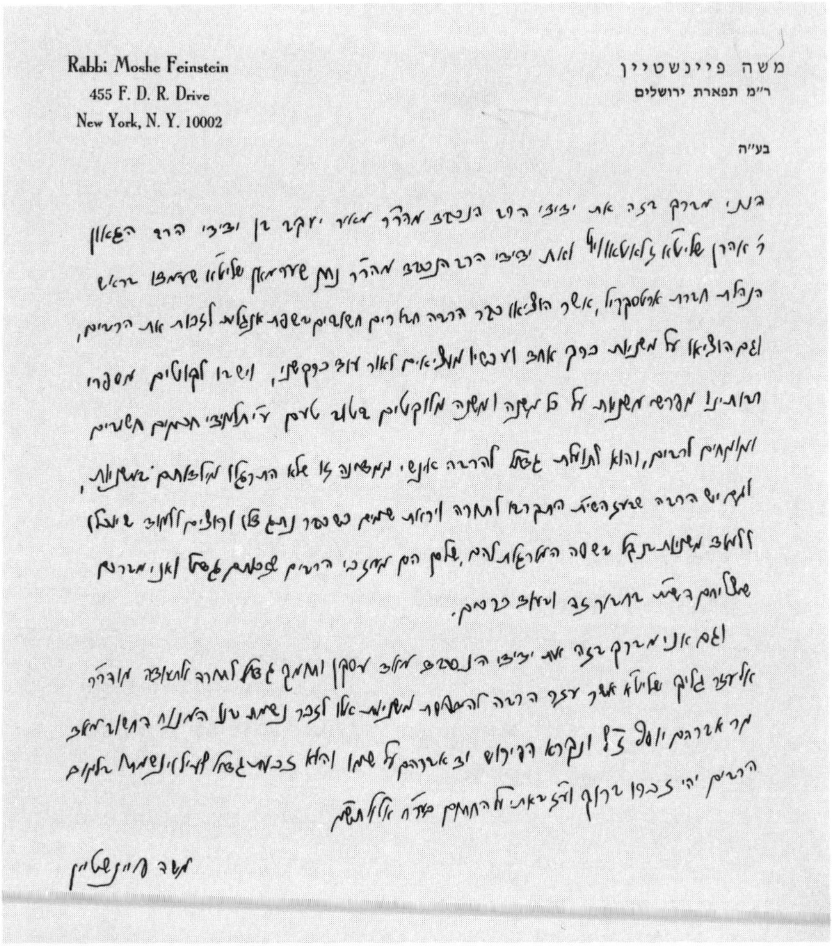

Rabbi Moshe Feinstein
455 F. D. R. Drive
New York, N. Y. 10002

משה פיינשטיין
ר"מ תפארת ירושלים

בע"ה

[handwritten letter]

אבי שלמה זלמן [signature]

בע"ה

הנני מברך בזה את ידידי הרב הנכבד מהר"ר מאיר יעקב בן ידידי הרב הגאון ר' אהרן שליט"א
זלאטאווייץ ואת ידידי הרב הנכבד מהר"ר נתן שערמאן שליט"א שעמדו בראש הנהלת **חברת ארטסקרול**,
אשר הוציאו כבר הרבה חבורים חשובים בשפת אנגלית לזכות את הרבים, וגם הוציאו על משניות כרך
אחד ועכשיו מוציאים לאור עוד כרך שני, ויש בו לקוטים מספרי רבותינו מפרשי משניות על כל משנה
ומשנה, מלוקטים בטוב טעם ע"י תלמידי חכמים חשובים ומומחים לרבים, והוא לתועלת גדול להרבה
אינשי ממדינה זו שלא התרגלו מילדותם במשניות, וגם יש הרבה שבעזהשי"ת התקרבו לתורה ויראת
שמים כשכבר נתגדלו ורוצים ללמוד, שיוכלו ללמוד משניות בנקל בשפה המורגלת להם, שלכן הם ממזכי
הרבים שזכותם גדול ואני מברכם שיצליחם השי"ת בחבור זה ובעוד כרכים.

וגם אני מברך בזה את ידידי הנכבד מאד עסקן ותומך גדול לתורה ולתעודה מוהר"ר אלעזר גליק
שליט"א אשר עזר הרבה להדפסת משניות אלו לזכר נשמת בנו המנוח החשוב מאד מר **אברהם יוסף** ז"ל
ונקרא הפירוש **יד אברהם** על שמו והוא זכות גדול לעילוי נשמתו בלמוד הרבים. יהי זכרו ברוך. וע"ז
באתי על החתום בער"ח אלול תש"מ.

משה פיינשטיין

מכתב ברכה

RABBI J. KAMENECKI
38 SADDLE RIVER ROAD
MONSEY, NEW YORK 10952

בע"ה

יום ה' ערב חג השבועות תשל"ס, פה מאנסי.

כבוד הרבני איש החסד שוע ונדיב מוקיר רבנן מר אלעזר נ"י גליק
שלו' וברכת כל טוב.

מה מאד שמחתי בהודעי כי כבודו רכש לעצמו הזכות שייקרא ע"ש
בנו המנוח הפירוש מבואר על כל ששת סדרי משנה ע"י "ארטסקראל"
והנה חברה זו יצאה לה מוניטין בפירושה על תנ"ך, והבה נקוה שכשם
שהצליחה בתורה שבכתב כן תצליח בתורה שבע"פ. ובהיות שאותיות
"משנה" הן כאותיות "נשמה" לפיכך טוב עשה בכוונתו לעשות זאת לעילוי
נשמת בנו המנוח אברהם יוסף ע"ה, ומאד מחאים השם "יד אברהם" לזה
הפירוש, כדמצינו במקרא (ש"ב י"ח) כי אמר אין לי בן בעבור הזכיר
שמי וגו'. ואין לך דבר גדול מזה להפיץ ידיעת תורה שבע"פ בקרב
אחינו שאינם רגילים בלשון הקדש. וד' הטוב יהי' בעזרו ויוכל לברך
על המוגמר. וירוה רוב נחת מכל אשר אתו כנפש מברכו.

[signature]

מכתב ברכה

בע״ה — ד׳ בהעלותך — לבני א״י, תשל״ט — פה קרית טלז, באה״ק

מע״כ ידידי האהובים הרב ר׳ מאיר והרב ר׳ נתן, נר״ו, שלום וברכה נצח!

אחדשה״ט באהבה ויקר,

לשמחה רבה היא לי להודיע שהרחבתם גדול עבודתכם בקודש לתורה שבע״פ, בהוצאת המשנה בתרגום וביאור באנגלית, וראשית עבודתכם במס׳ מגילה.

אני תקוה שתשמימו לב שיצאו הדברים מתוקנים מנקודת ההלכה, וחזקה עליכם שתוציאו דבר נאה ומתוקן.

בפנותכם לתורה שבע״פ יפתח אופק חדש בתורת ה׳ לאלה שקשה עליהם ללמוד הדברים במקורם, ואלה שכבר נתעשרו מעבודתכם במגילת אסתר יכנסו עתה לטרקלין חדש וישמשו להם הדברים דחף ללימוד המשנה, וגדול יהי׳ שכרכם.

יהא ה׳ בעזרכם בהוספת טבעת חדשה באותה שלשלת זהב של הפצת תורת ה׳ להמוני עם לקרב לב ישראל לאבינו שבשמים בתורה ואמונה טהורה.

אוהבכם מלונ״ח,
מרדכי

Approbation/מכתב ברכה   [x]

מכתב ברכה

RABBI SHNEUR KOTLER
BETH MEDRASH GOVOHA
LAKEWOOD, N. J.

בע"ה

שניאור קוטלר
בית מדרש גבוה'
לייקוואוד, נ. דז.

בשורת התרחבות עבודתם הגדולה של סגל חבורת ,,ארטסקרול'', המעתיקים ומפרשים, לתחומי התושבע"פ, לשים אלה המשפטים לפני הציבור ערוך ומוכן לאכול לפני האדם [ל' רש"י], ולשימה בפיהם — לפתוח אוצרות בשנות בצורת ולהשמיע בכל לשון שהם שומעים — מבשרת צבא רב לתורה ולימודה [ע' תהלים ס"ח י"ב בתרגום יונתן], והיא מאותות ההתעוררות ללימוד התורה, וזאת התעודה על התנוצצות קיום ההבטחה ,,כי לא תשכח מפי זרעו''. אשרי הזוכים להיות בין שלוחי ההשגחה לקיומה וביצועה.

יה"ר כי תצליח מלאכת שמים בידם, ויזכו ללמוד וללמד ולשמור מסורת הקבלה כי בהרקת המים החיים מכלי אל כלי תשתמר חיותם, יעמוד טעמם בם וריחם לא נמר. [וע' משאחז"ל בב"מ ושמרתם זו משנה — וע' חי' מרן רי"ז הלוי עה"ת בפ' ואתחנן] ותהי' משנתם שלמה וברורה, ישמחו בעבודתם חברים ותלמידים, ,,ישוטטו רבים ותרבה הדעת'', עד יקויים ,,אז אהפוך אל העמים שפה ברורה וגו' '' [צפני' ג' ט', עי' פי' אבן עזרא ומצודת דוד שם].

ונזכה כולנו לראות בהתכנסות הגליות בזכות המשניות כל' חז"ל הכתוב ,,גם כי יתנו בגוים עתה אקבצם'', בגאולה השלמה בב"א.

הכו"ח לכבוד התורה, יום ו' עש"ק לס' ,,ויוצא פרח ויצץ ציץ ויגמול שקדים'', ד' תמוז התשל"ט

יוסף חיים שניאור קוטלר
בלאאמו"ר הגר"א זצוק"ל

מכתב ברכה

ב״ה

לכבוד ידידי וידיד ישיבתנו, מהראשונים לכל דבר שבקדושה
הרבני הנדיב המפורסם ר' אליעזר הכהן גליק ני״ו
אחדש״ה באהבה,

בשורה טובה שמעתי שכב' מצא את המקום המתאים לעשות יד ושם להנציח זכרו של בנו **אברהם יוסף ע״ה** שנקטף בנעוריו. ״ונתתי להם בביתי ובחומתי יד ושם״. אין לו להקב״ה אלא ד' אמות של הלכה בלבד. א״כ זהו בית ד' לימוד תורה שבע״פ וזהו המקום לעשות יד ושם לנשמת בנו ע״ה.

נר ד' נשמת אדם אמר הקב״ה נרי בידך ונרך בידי. נר מצוה ותורה אור, תורה זהו הנר של הקב״ה וכשישומרים נר של הקב״ה שעל ידי הפירוש ״יד אברהם״ בשפה הלעזית יתרבה לימוד ושקיעת התורה בבתי ישראל. ד' ישמור נשמת אדם.

בנו אברהם יוסף ע״ה נתברך בהמדה שבו נכללות כל המדות, לב טוב והיה אהוב לחבריו. בלמדו בישיבתנו היה לו הרצון לעלות במעלות התורה וכשעלה לארצנו הקדושה היתה מבוקשו להמשיך בלימודיו. ביקוש זה ימצא מלואו על ידי הרבים המבקשים דרך ד', שהפירוש ״יד אברהם״ יהא מפתח להם לים התלמוד.

התורה נקראת, ״אש דת״, ונמשלה לאש ויש בה הכח לפעפע ברזל לפעוד כוחות האדם, הניצוץ שהאיר רבנו הרב שרגא פייוועל מנדלוביץ זצ״ל שמרת עליו, ועשה חיל. עכשיו אתה מסייע להאיר נצוצות בנשמות בני ישראל שיעשה חיל ויהא לאור גדול.

תקוה עזה שכל התלמידי חכמים שנדבה רוחם להוציא מלאכה ענקית זו לפרש המשניות כולה, יצא עבודתם ברוח פאר והדר ויכוונו לאמיתה של תורה ויתקדש שם שמים על ידי מלאכה זו.
יתברך כב' וב״ב לראות ולרוות נחת רוח מצאצאיו.
הכו״ח לכבוד התורה ותומכיה עש״ק במדבר תשל״ט

אלי' שווי

מכתב ברכה

דוד קאהן

ביהמ״ד גבול יעבץ
ברוקלין, נוא יארק

בס״ד כ״ה למטמונים תשל״ט

כבוד רחימא דנפשאי, עושה ומעשה
ר׳ אלעזר הכהן גליק נטריה רחמנא ופרקיה

שמוע שמעתי שכבר תקעת כפיך לתמוך במפעל האדיר של חברת ארטסקרול — הידוע בכל קצווי
תבל ע״י עבודתה הכבירה בהפצת תורה — לתרגם ולבאר ששה סדרי משנה באנגלית. כוונתך להנציח
זכר בנך הנחמד אברהם יוסף ז״ל שנקטף באבו בזמן שעלה לארץ הקודש בתקופת התרוממות הנפש
ושאיפה לקדושה, ולמטרה זו יכונה הפירוש בשם ״יד אברהם״; וגם האיר ה׳ רוחך לגרום עילוי לנשמתו
הטהורה שעי״ז יתרבה לימוד התורה שניתנה בשבעים לשון, על ידי כלי מפואר זה.

מכיוון שהנני מכיר היטב שני הצדדים, אוכל לומר לדבק טוב, והנני תקוה שיצליח המפעל הלזה לתת
יד ושם וזכות לנשמת אברהם יוסף ז״ל. חזקה על חברת ארטסקרול שתוציא דבר נאה מתוקן ומתקבל
מתחת ידה להגדיל תורה ולהאדירה.

והנני מברך אותך שתמצא נוחם לנפשך, שהאבא זוכה לברא, ותשבע נחת — אתה עם רעיתך תחיה —
מכל צאצאיכם היקרים אכי״ר

ידידך עז
דוד קאהן

מסכת עירובין
Tractate Eruvin

Translation and anthologized commentary by
Rabbi Hersh Goldwurm

Contributing editors:
Rabbi Yehezkel Danziger / Rabbi Avie Gold

Mesorah Publications, ltd.

General Introduction to Eruvin

by Rabbis Yehezkel Danziger / Hersh Goldwurm

One of the 39 primary labor categories (אֲבוֹת מְלָאכוֹת) prohibited Biblically on the Sabbath is transferring objects from a private to a public domain or vice versa. [See ArtScroll Mishnah *Shabbos* — General Introduction.] The Sages added several prohibitions against transferring even in private domains which might be confused with public domains. These prohibitions, and the adjustments to the domain required by the Sages to remove them, take up the greater part of tractate Eruvin. In order to provide an adequate understanding of this sometimes very complex tractate, a basic understanding of the many concepts which underlie it and definitions of the terms used in it are necessary.

◆§ I. The Four Domains and the Labor of Transferring

The rules governing the labor of הוֹצָאָה, *transferring*, take into account four domains. These are:

1. רְשׁוּת הָרַבִּים — *public domain*.

The *Talmud (Shabbos* 6a) defines a public domain as any commonly used street, public area, or highway at least sixteen cubits wide and open at both ends (מְפוּלָּשׁ). According to some *(Rashi, Eruvin* 6a, s.v. רשות הרבים), it must be used by at least 600,000 people (the counted population of the Jewish 'encampment' during their sojourn in the desert).[1]

2. רְשׁוּת הַיָּחִיד — *private domain*.

Any area measuring at least four fists (טְפָחִים) by four fists and enclosed by partitions at least ten fists high. The partitions may take the form of either conventional walls rising from ground level to a height of ten fists, the ten fist high walls of a ditch, or the nearly perpendicular walls surrounding a plateau. According to most opinions it need only be enclosed on three sides to qualify as a private domain.[2] Private ownership is *not* a prerequisite.

3. כַּרְמְלִית — *karmelis*.[3]

---

1. A lengthy halachic exposition on this topic is to be found in *Beur Halachah* to *Orach Chaim* 345:7. As to whether most *Rishonim* agree with *Rashi* or not, see the correspondence between the authors of *Beis Ephraim*, (vol. *Orach Chaim*, responsa 26-27), and *Mishkenos Yaakov* (vol. *Orach Chaim* responsa 120-122). This question has serious halachic implications, the most notable of which is the efficacy of a צוּרַת הַפֶּתַח, *form of a doorway* (colloquially referred to as an *eruv*), to permit carrying on city streets (this device is not effective for a true public domain). See *Orach Chaim* 303:18, 345:7, and 346:3 with commentaries.

2. This is the opinion of most authorities. However, *Rambam (Hil. Shabbos* 17:9) and *R' Chananel*, based on a variant reading of *Eruvin* 12b, hold that an area enclosed only on three sides is a *karmelis* and that in order to be classified as a private domain the area must be enclosed on all four sides. However, a לְחִי, *pole*, suffices to 'close off' the fourth side; see *Beur Halachah* 363:1.

3. This area is named for its intermediate halachic status, i.e., it is neither a public nor a private domain. *Yerushalmi* [*Shabbos* 1:1, cited by *Tos. (Shabbos* 6a) and *Aruch* (s.v. כרמלית)] derives this term from the Hebrew כַּרְמֶל (*Lev.* 23:14), *fresh grain*, i.e., grain which retains its natural moistness but is dry enough to be reaped — an intermediate state. *Sifra* (to *Lev.* 23:14) and *Yerushalmi* observe that כַּרְמֶל is composed of two words, רַךְ, *soft*, i.e., not yet dry or brittle, and מָל or מְלֵא, *full*, i.e., ripe and not overly moist. *Rambam (Comm.* to *Mishnah, Shabbos* 1:1) believes that כַּרְמְלִית is a shortened form of כְּאַרְמְלִית, *as a widow*. A widow conforms to neither of the basic marital states of a woman — she is neither a virgin nor a married woman. Similarly, a *karmelis* conforms to neither of the basic states of a domain — it is neither a public nor a private domain.

Any area at least four fists square which cannot be classified as either a public domain (because it is not set aside for public use[4]) or a private domain (because it does not have the required partitions), e.g., a field, empty lot, or an elevation at least three fists above the ground level of a public domain which has a minimum area of four by four fists.

4. מָקוֹם פְּטוּר — *exempt area.*

An area not part of either a public or private domain and also lacking the necessary dimensions to qualify as a *karmelis* (its width or length is less than four fists).

❧ ❧ ❧

On a Biblical level, the prohibition against transferring objects on the Sabbath concerns only the private and public domains. The primary labor of transferring (see *Shabbos* 7:2), [lit. *taking out*, i.e., from the private into the public domain], includes also הַכְנָסָה, *taking in*, from the public into the private domain (see *Shabbos* 2b and 96b).

[Another form of this labor which is known through הֲלָכָה לְמֹשֶׁה מִסִּינַי, *the Oral Tradition received by Moses on Mount Sinai,* is מַעֲבִיר אַרְבַּע אַמּוֹת בִּרְשׁוּת הָרַבִּים, *moving an object four cubits in the public domain.*]

On a Biblical level, these prohibitions apply only to the private and public domains. However, because the *karmelis* resembles both the public domain (being unenclosed) and the private domain (being that it is not used by the public) the Sages decreed that it be treated with all the strictures applicable to either of these two domains. Consequently, one may not carry an object four cubits in a *karmelis* or carry from a *karmelis* into a private domain or vice versa (thus treating it as a public domain). At the same time, one may not carry from a *karmelis* into a public domain or vice versa (thus treating it as a private domain).

❧ II. Partitions

The distinguishing features of a private domain are the partitions which surround it. The minimum requirements for partitions are: (a) a height of at least ten fists (if the sides of a mound or a ditch are ten fists high, they qualify as partitions); and (b) they must enclose an area of four fists square.

Obviously, every enclosure must have openings through which people can enter the enclosed area. Since this is an inherent feature of every enclosure, it follows that a partition is not necessarily disqualified because of openings in it. The Sages differentiated between an opening which is classified as an *entrance* (פֶּתַח) and an opening which is merely a *breach* (פִּרְצָה) — an entrance does not invalidate a partition while a breach does. Furthermore, not only does an entrance not invalidate a partition, it itself is considered a partition. Therefore, even the area opposite the entrance is also considered enclosed. This rule has many ramifications and a great many leniencies in the laws of partitions can be attributed to it.

A) Rules governing entrances

(a) פִּרְצָה יְתֵירָה מֵעֶשֶׂר אַמּוֹת — *a breach wider than ten cubits.*

An entrance may not be wider than ten cubits. Any opening greater than ten cubits is automatically classified as a breach.

(b) פָּרוּץ מְרֻבֶּה עַל הָעוֹמֵד — *the breaches exceed the standing sections.*

The amount of open space classified as entrances in any partition may not exceed the standing segments (see 1:8). This applies to openings which are merely

---

4. The definition of 'public' is subject to the dispute mentioned above. According to *Rashi*, any area not subject to use by 600,000 people is a *karmelis*, while according to others there is no specific number defining 'public.'

classified as entrances. Actual doorways, or even makeshift devices which have the form of doorways, are considered to be completely closed and are valid as partitions even if they form the entire partition. See (d) below.

(c) פַּסֵּי בִּירָאוֹת, שֶׁם ד׳ מְחִיצוֹת — *double posts, semblance of four walls.*

On a Biblical level, if the corners of the partitions are in place, the partitions are valid even if the open sections exceed the standing sections (see diagram in 2:1). Furthermore, these are valid even if the entire enclosure consists only of four corners and even if the openings are wider than ten cubits. [This is only valid if all four walls are outlined, i.e., if all four corners are marked off. If only three walls are outlined, the area is considered open even on the Biblical level.] Such an enclosure, however, is Rabbinically invalid (see 2:1).

In one instance, though, the Sages decreed that these Rabbinic rules of partitions be relaxed. This was to allow the pilgrims going up to Jerusalem to draw water from water holes [private domains] in the public domain. In this instance the Sages ruled that the area outlined by four corner-like double posts be considered a private domain (ibid.).

(d) צוּרַת הַפֶּתַח — *form of a doorway.*

A structure shaped in the form of a doorway is also effective as a partition and is in many respects even more effective than the general entrances. The form of a doorway consists of two posts to whose tops[5] a connective bar (or string or wire) is attached. According to most opinions, this is effective even if the entire enclosure is made up only of forms of doorways (provided a *reshus harabim* does not run through them). This device is widely used nowadays to convert an open area into a private domain.

B) Leniences regarding partitions

The Oral Law handed down from Sinai provides for a whole array of leniencies in regard to partitions (see *Gem.* 4b and *Rashi, Succah* 4b). They are:

(a) לָבוּד — *lavud.*

This provision allows us to consider two solid surfaces separated by a space measuring less than three fists as connected. For this reason, if there is a gap in a wall or partition measuring less than three fists, the open space is considered closed. This provision applies even to the thinnest surfaces. Thus a partition composed only of stakes separated from each other by less than three fists is valid as a partition. Similarly, a series of horizontal ropes or wires arrayed one over the other and separated from each other by less than three fists serve as a partition if they reach a height of ten fists (see 1:8,9).

(b) גּוּד — *extend.*

This provision allows us to (imaginarily) extend partitions conforming to the ten fist minimum to areas which they do not reach. This takes two forms:

1) גּוּד אֲחִית מְחִיצָתָא, *extend the partition downward*, e.g., a partition ten fists high on a balcony may be extended downward to convert the open area below it into a private domain (see diagram in 8:8). Although in theory this principle applies to all types of areas, its effectiveness is limited by the rule that where small goats can pass through (בְּקִיעַת גְּדָיִים) this imaginary partition, the partition is invalidated (*Gem.* 12a). The Gemara defines this as a gap of three fists or more. The main application of this principle is where the partition is over a body of water (where animals cannot pass) and renders the part of the sea enclosed by the extended partition a private domain. The free passage of fish through the partitions does not concern us (בְּקִיעַת דָּגִים לֹא שְׁמָהּ בְּקִיעָה; ibid.).

2) גּוּד אַסִּיק מְחִיצָתָא — *extend the partition upward*

---

5. However, if the string is attached to the *side* of the pole it is not valid to serve as a form of a doorway (see *Gem.* 11b; *Orach Chaim* 362:11).

A partition ten fists high can be extended upward and be considered as a partition for the area above.

(c) פִּי תִקְרָה יוֹרֵד וְסוֹתֵם — *the edge of a roof is considered to extend downward to serve as a partition.*

The downward extension of the roof is *not* invalidated by the passage of animals. It thus renders the area beneath the roof a private domain.

'Roof' is defined as any overhead board which measures at least four fists in width (*Tos.* 86b, s.v. קורה; *Rama* and *Beur Halachah*, *Orach Chaim* 361:2). This rule is applicable, however, only where the area is already partitioned off by at least two proper partitions set at right angles to each other. Where there are only two parallel walls the remaining two walls cannot be supplied by this provision (see *Gem.* 94b with *Tos.*; *Rama* loc. cit.).[6] Only flat roofs qualify for this provision, not slanting ones (*Gem.* 25b, *Orach Chaim* 361:1).

III. Private Domains Prohibited by Rabbinic Decree

Most of this tractate deals with the laws of transferring objects in areas which are private domains on a Biblical level but to which the Sages assigned certain prohibitions of carrying. Three types of areas were prohibited: private domains not fully enclosed; private domains which have not been enclosed for residential purposes; and private domains which more than one person has the right to use (see section IV).

A) Private domains not fully enclosed — courtyards and alleys

On a Biblical level, areas enclosed on three sides are considered private domains even though they are open on the fourth side.[7] The Sages decreed, however, that carrying be prohibited in such areas unless the open side is *adjusted* to set it off — at least symbolically — from the area outside the enclosure. This prohibition applies most commonly to a מָבוֹי, *alley*, and a חָצֵר, *courtyard*. In Talmudic parlance this is termed נִפְרָץ בִּמְלוֹאוֹ לְמָקוֹם הָאָסוּר, *entirely breached to a prohibited area*. A wall is considered entirely breached if the breach is wider than ten cubits (ibid.).

To understand much of this tractate, it is necessary to understand the layout of streets and houses in mishnaic times. In those times, and even up to modern times in many places, several houses would open into a courtyard and several courtyards would, in turn, lead into an alley through which the people would pass to get to the street.

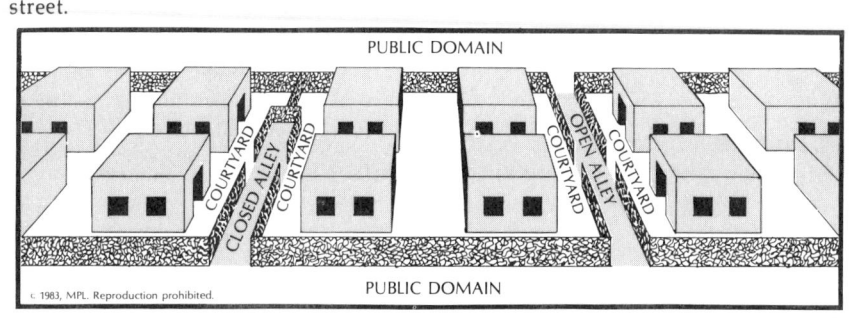

Typically, such an alley was a dead-end alley, closed on three sides and open only

6. *Rashi* (94b) maintains that the rule regarding the edge of a roof is applicable even in situations where there is only one proper partition.

7. Even according to the opinion of *Rambam* and *R' Chananel* mentioned above in footnote 2, such an area is, Biblically speaking, an exempt area and carrying in it, or from it to private and public domains, is permitted.

on the fourth side where it met the public domain. Such an alley is known as a מָבוֹי
סָתוּם, *closed alley*.

The closed alley is, Biblically speaking, a private domain and on a Biblical level one is permitted to carry in it. The Sages, however, were apprehensive that people might confuse the public domain with an alley, and extend the practice of carrying in an alley to the public domain as well.[8] Consequently, they decreed that in order to carry in an alley the open side must be adjusted *(Rav; Rashi)*.[9] Alternatively, without an adjustment to the fourth side people might erroneously conclude that the alley was part of the public domain (or *karmelis*) abutting it and would carry from the alley to the public domain, and vice versa *(R' Yehonasan; Meiri; R' Yeshayah HaAcharon* to 2a; see *Geon Yaakov, Sfas Emes* there). Whatever the consideration, the adjustment must serve to demonstrate that the two areas are to be viewed as separate entities.

◄§ Adjustment of an alley

Naturally, the open end of the alley can be adjusted by erecting a partition, or any of the legal equivalents of it described above, across the opening. However, such a

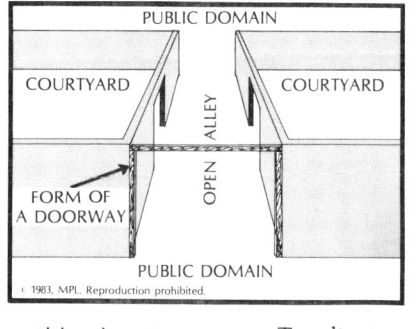

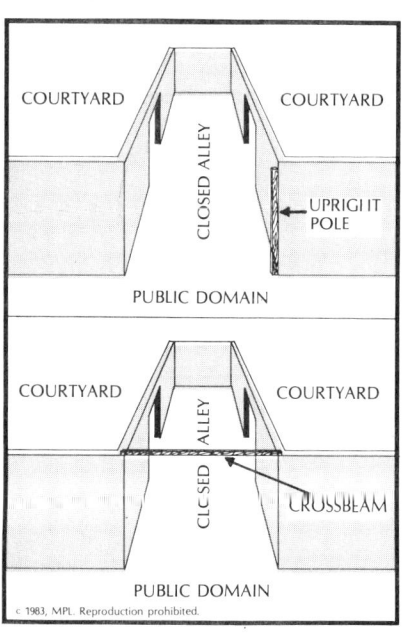

partition is not necessary. To adjust an alley it is sufficient to lay a קוֹרָה, horizontal *crossbeam* across the top of the opening of the alley at a height of at least ten fists, or to stand a לְחִי, vertical pole measuring ten fists high next to one of the walls at the opening of the alley. The crossbeam serves as a reminder (הֶכֵּירָא) that the alley ends at that point and that it is distinct from the public domain outside it. The pole also serves

8. R' Nissim Gaon (in *Mafteach Manulei HaTalmud* in the margin of *Talmud*, ed. Vilna 2a; see also R' Hai Gaon's responsum in *Teshuvos HaGeonim Mosafia* 76; *Sha'arei Teshuvah* 44; *Sefer Halttim* 29) believes this decree to be part of King Solomon's institution of *eruv* as related in the *Gem.* (21b).

9. Almost all *Rishonim* agree that the decree necessitating an adjustment to the fourth side of an alley is Rabbinic. See *Rashi* to 2a; *Rashi, Rashba* and *Ritva* to 11b; *Rambam Hil. Shabbos* 17:2, *Tur* and *Orach Chaim* 363:2. For a dissenting view see R' Yehonasan (11b) and *Meiri* (there and 2b).

As pointed out above in footnote 2, *Rambam's* view is that such an area is not Biblically a private domain. Accordingly, no new prohibition was needed to prohibit carrying in such an area since it in any case came under the general classification of *karmelis* — being neither a private nor a public domain. However, a special enactment was necessary to allow for the pole or crossbeam to remove the *karmelis* prohibition.

as such a reminder or, according to some opinions, as minimal type of partition (מְחִצָּה) [see *Gem.* 12b]. The dimensions and construction of the crossbeam and pole are discussed at length in chapter 1.[10]

⊸§ Adjustment of a courtyard

Just as an alley must be adjusted on its open side before carrying in it can be permitted, so too, a courtyard which is completely open to a public domain or *karmelis* must have its opening adjusted before carrying in it can be permitted. Here, a crossbeam or pole is insufficient; either two poles placed on opposite sides of the opening are required or a פַּס, *board*, four fists wide and ten fists high must be placed at one of the sides *(Gem.* 12a).

B) Private domains not enclosed for residential purposes

Some areas are given *karmelis* status although they are enclosed within partitions conforming to the rules set down for private domains. If an area not intended to be used for purposes related to daily living was surrounded with partitions, the partitions are not valid and the area retains its *karmelis* status. In Talmudic terminology this is called a קַרְפֵּף שֶׁלֹּא הוּקַף לְדִירָה, *karpeif* [enclosed area] *enclosed for purposes not related to daily living.* A common example of this is an enclosed garden which is not adjacent to a dwelling (2:3). The Sages decreed that such an area should have *karmelis* status because its size (more than 5,000 square cubits) renders it similar to a public domain and *karmelis (Levush* and *Mishnah Berurah* to *Orach Chaim* 358). Even if the area later becomes used for residential purposes its status is not changed — the determining factor is the use intended at the time the partitions were erected *(Gem.* 24a). This classification is limited to areas greater in area than 5,000 square cubits; enclosed areas of 5,000 square cubits or less have private domain status regardless of the use intended for them (2:4). The 5,000 cubit limit is based on the dimensions of the Tabernacle Courtyard which was fifty by one hundred cubits.

The *karmelis* status of such an area is Rabbinical; on a Biblical level it has private domain status *(Gem.* 67b). Nevertheless it is permissible to transfer objects from this area to a regular *karmelis* (provided they are moved less than four cubits), although on a Biblical level this should be viewed as transferring from a private domain to a *karmelis (Gem.,* loc cit.). A concept related to this is that dealing with some marginally adequate partitions. One of the concepts frequently used in regard to partitions is that of *lavud,* which allows one to erect a partition composed of only vertical stakes or horizontal ropes which are separated by less than three fists of air space. However, such a partition is valid only for areas measuring 5,000 square cubits or less. For areas greater in size, the partition must consist of both vertical and horizontal sections (1:10). However this limitation is relaxed for some extenuating circumstances (see 1:9,10).

⊸§ IV. Communal Courtyards and Alleys

Aside from the prohibitions on carrying in an alley or courtyard resulting from its being open on one side, there is yet another prohibition resulting from the laws of *eruvei chatzeiros* [merging of the courtyards] and *shitufei mevo'os* [incorporation of the alleys].

The law of *eruvei chatzeiros* which was enacted by King Solomon and the Sages of his generation *(Gem.* 21b) is composed of two elements: A) The prohibition against carrying into communal courtyards; and B) *eruv* and *shituf,* or the procedures by which one removes the prohibition

10. *Rama (Orach Chaim* 363·26) records that it is customary nowadays to adjust alleys and streets only by means of a form of a doorway.

A) The prohibition against carrying into communal courtyards

The law of *eruv* decreed that carrying from one person's private domain to one owned by another is to be treated as transferring from domain to domain. This was instituted to safeguard the prohibition against carrying between the Biblically prohibited domains — public and private — by prohibiting carrying even between private domains. A corollary of this law is that a courtyard which is owned and shared by the residents of the houses which open into it is considered under a different ownership than any of the houses that open into it *(Rashi* 2b).[11] As a result, one may not carry from his house to the courtyard (or vice versa) since that constitutes carrying from one private domain to another.

Rambam explains that the primary decree did not concern carrying from one house to another but concerned the alleys (which are also private domains). The Sages were concerned that in a town surrounded by walls (as many old towns were) in which all the streets become private domains, the prohibition against transferring from a public to private domain would be forgotten. With time people would begin to assume that just as one is allowed to carry objects from the courtyards [private domains] to the streets [ostensibly public domains] so, too, one is permitted to carry objects from the town streets to public domains beyond the town and that transferring is not a prohibited labor. Therefore, the Sages legislated that wherever there is a semblance of transferring from a public to a private domain, e.g., from a private domain owned by an individual to one owned by a consortium of people, it should be considered transferring and prohibited *(Rambam, Hil. Eruvin* 1:4-5).[12]

The determining factor here is not legal ownership, but occupancy as defined by halachah. One may carry into a courtyard which he shares with other owners who are not living there presently. It is only if the other houses are considered occupied on that particular Sabbath that carrying from house to courtyard or vice versa is prohibited (see 8:5). For this reason, in the terminology of this tractate, people living jointly in a courtyard are said to *restrict* (אוסרין) each other, i.e., each restricts the other's use of the courtyard by disallowing the carrying of objects between the houses and the courtyard.

All the members of one household are reckoned as one unit and do not restrict, nor do guests. A household in this regard is a place where one eats; if the house is used only for sleeping its residents do not restrict *(Orach Chaim* 370:5).

The power of restricting a courtyard is not limited to residents of that courtyard. Even the residents of a neighboring courtyard, whose only access to the alley is through a courtyard, restrict because they have the *right of passage.* There are certain limitations to this type of restriction; see 6:9,10.

Gentiles, although they do not have the power of restricting per se, were nevertheless given this power, for reasons which will be discussed in 6:1. The result of the special status given gentiles is that the law is defined differently in regard to them (see there).

There is one major qualification of the prohibition against carrying in the

---

11. See *Avnei Neizer, Responsa Orach Chaim* 301 who makes the point that *Rashi* sees the prohibition of the communal courtyard to be merely a special case of the basic prohibition which is (in contradistinction to *Rambam's* view which is presented further) to carry from one privately owned property to another. It would seem *Rashba* in *Avodas HaKodesh* 3:9 (cited by *Beur Halachah* to 370:3) also subscribes to this view.

12. Thus, according to *Rambam* the primary concern was for the alley and the prohibition of the courtyard derives from that. Some commentators argue that it follows from *Rambam's* explanation that no *eruv* is necessary for carrying from one individually owned private domain to another while others maintain that even *Rambam* admits that this case warrants an *eruv* (see *Tos. Yom Tov* and *Shoshanim L'David* to 7:1; see also *Be'ur Halachah* and *Daas Torah* to *Orach Chaim* 370:3).

courtyards. According to the halachically accepted view it applies *only* to כֵּלִים שֶׁשָּׁבְתוּ בְּבַיִת, objects which began the Sabbath in a house. Objects which at the onset of the Sabbath were already in the courtyard (כֵּלִים שֶׁשָּׁבְתוּ בְּחָצֵר) may be carried from courtyard to courtyard or even to an alley. They may not, however, be carried into a house. Additionally, if an object was brought from a house into the courtyard even permissibly (e.g., an article of clothing which was removed in the courtyard) it may not be carried from courtyard to courtyard or alley (*Tos.* 91b; cf. *Beur Halachah* 372:1).

B) Eruv and Shituf

Along with the prohibition, the Sages provided procedures by which the prohibition against carrying can be removed.

⋖§ עֵירוּבֵי חֲצֵירוֹת [eruvei chatzeiros] — merging courtyards

This procedure allows us to view all the houses opening into the courtyard as owned by a single consortium (composed of all the residents of the courtyard). This is accomplished by collecting a loaf of bread (or matzah) before the Sabbath from each of the dwellings which open into that yard and placing it in one of those dwellings for the duration of the Sabbath. This then symbolizes that all the contributing residents are legally residing in one dwelling (the place where they left their bread)[13] and the yard is therefore the province of only one dwelling (the one in which they have merged) rather than several. Since the yard and the house are all the property of one ownership, there is no prohibition to carry from one to the other.

It should be noted that the courtyard must still be enclosed on all four sides by a proper wall or one of the proper substitutes enumerated above. *Eruvei chatzeiros* removes only the prohibitions arising from communal use; it is not a remedy for prohibitions resulting from structural inadequacies.

⋖§ Joining two courtyards

Where courtyards open directly into each other they may join together in one *eruv*, thus enabling the residents to carry from one courtyard to the other.

Courtyards cannot join in one *eruv* unless there is a proper door or window through which they have access to each other. Without such access they cannot make an *eruv* for the purpose of passing objects over the wall between them (see 7:1-4), but each courtyard may make its own *eruv* to permit carrying in its own area. In the language of the Mishnah this is referred to as *they may make two* eruvin, *but may not make one* eruv (7:1).

Courtyards which do have a proper door or window between them have an option to either join in one *eruv* — in which case they will be permitted to carry even from one to another — or make two separate *eruvin* — in which case carrying will be permitted within the confines of each courtyard but not from one courtyard to the other. This is referred to as, *they may make two* eruvin, *or if they wish, they may make one* eruv (7:1).

Courtyards which are completely open to each other (i.e., no wall separates them), or have an opening in the wall between them which is more than 10 cubits wide, cannot make separate *eruvin* to permit carrying in each individual courtyard, but must join in one *eruv* or forfeit the chance to make any *eruv* at all. In the language of the mishnah, *they make one* eruv *but may not make two* (7:3).

---

13. The above is the halachically accepted view of *Rabbah*. *Shmuel* holds that eruv symbolizes a formal transfer of ownership (קִנְיָן) from the individual to the collective unit composed of all the courtyard residents (*Gem.* 49a).

◆§ שִׁתּוּפֵי מְבָאוֹת [shitufei mevo'os] — incorporating alleys

A provision similar to *eruvei chatzeiros* was instituted to permit carrying from a courtyard into an alley. Since the alley is the joint property of all of the courtyards opening into it, all the courtyards must incorporate into one unit in order for carrying to be permitted between the courtyards and it. [It follows, therefore, that all the individual *eruvei chatzeiros* made for each courtyard do not suffice for the alley since each *eruv* merged only the residents of that one courtyard with each other but not with the residents of the other courtyards (see *Tos.* 71b, s.v. בכת; *Rama* in *Orach Chaim* 387:1).] To do this, a separate merging called *shitufei mevo'os* is required. This differs from *eruvei chatzeiros* only in some particulars (see 8:6).

◆§ Blessing upon making an eruv or shituf

The making of an *eruv* or *shituf* is a mitzvah and one should see that it is made, wherever possible (*Gem.* 68a). When making an *eruvei chatzeiros* one recites the blessing עַל מִצְוַת עֵרוּב and declares:

בַּהֲדֵין עֵירוּבָא יְהֵא שָׁרֵי לָן לְאַפּוּקֵי וּלְעַיּוּלֵי מִן הַבָּתִּים לֶחָצֵר וּמִן הֶחָצֵר לַבָּתִּים וּמִבַּיִת לְבַיִת לְכָל הַבָּתִּים שֶׁבֶּחָצֵר

Through this eruv let it be permissible for us to take [objects] out and to bring in from the houses to the courtyard and from the courtyard to the houses, and from house to house for all of the houses in the courtyard (Orach Chaim 366:14,15).[14]

Similarly when making a *shitufei mevo'os* one recites the blessing עַל מִצְוַת עֵרוּב (*shituf* is merely a variant of *eruvei chatzeros*) and says:

בְּזֶה הַשִּׁתּוּף יִהְיֶה מֻתָּר לְכָל בְּנֵי הַמָּבוֹי לְהוֹצִיא וּלְהַכְנִיס מֵחֲצֵירוֹת לְמָבוֹי בַּשַּׁבָּת

Through this shituf let it be permissible for all the residents of the alley to take [objects] out and bring in between the courtyards and the alley on the Sabbath (Rambam, Hil. Eruvin 1:17).

Rama (Orach Chaim 387:1) endorses the prevalent custom to make only an *eruvei chatzeiros* to permit carrying in a town enclosed with partitions (and to dispense with an additional *shituf;* see comm. to 6:8). In light of this, *Mishnah Berurah* (there) proposes that in the formula said for such an *eruv*, the permission to bring and take between the alleys and courtyards be mentioned explicitly (see *Mishnah Berurah* 366:83).

◆§ בִּטוּל רְשׁוּת [bitul reshus] — nullification of rights

Both *eruv* and *shituf* must be made before the Sabbath begins. If any of the residents of the courtyard or alley forgot to join, the area is prohibited because it is still the property of two owners — the corporation of those who joined and the individual who did not. The forgetful person is therefore said to *restrict* the use of the courtyard by prohibiting everyone from carrying in it. Once the Sabbath begins, it is too late for him to join. The Sages, however, provided one other remedy for the courtyard, namely, *nullification of rights.*

This is a formal renunciation of one's rights to use the courtyard or his rights to his house. This renunciation is accomplished with an oral declaration which may be made even on the Sabbath (6:4).

By nullification, one gives up his rights to carry objects from his house into the courtyard (for that Sabbath) and is therefore no longer reckoned a partner in it. Consequently, if there is only one other resident in the courtyard it becomes, in effect, the sole domain of that resident and carrying between his house and the courtyard is permitted. Similarly, if all the residents except one merged in an *eruvei chatzeiros*, the one person who did not join in the *eruv* — and who therefore restricts

---

14. Many variations of this formula may be found in the *siddurim*. If the *eruv* is made for the entire year this is explicitly mentioned in the formula.

everybody else — can nullify his rights, thereby leaving only those who joined in the *eruv* as legal owners of the courtyard and therefore permitted to carry into it.

✥§ Renting a gentile's rights

A gentile who lives in a courtyard also restricts it under certain circumstances. However, neither of the two methods outlined above can remove that restriction. The only way to remove the restriction of a gentile is to rent his rights to the courtyard. The terms of this rental need not imply that the Jew actually take possession of the gentile's dwelling and prevent him from using the courtyard. Rather, it is a [symbolic *(Rambam, Hil. Eruvin 2:12)]* legal act, made solely for the purposes of *eruv*, and does not deprive the gentile of anything *(Gem. 62a)*.

✥§ V. Techum and Eruvei Techumin

The other major Rabbinic prohibition discussed in this tractate is the restriction of תְּחוּם שַׁבָּת [*techum Shabbos*], *the Sabbath boundary*, and its remedy, the עֵרוּבֵי תְחוּמִין [*eruvei techumin*], lit. *merging of boundaries*.[15]

A) Techum

On the Sabbath or festivals, a person is forbidden to go more than 2,000 cubits from his halachically defined place of dwelling at the onset of that day. This limit is called the *techum* or *boundary*. R' Akiva *(Sotah 27b)* maintains that this is a Biblical prohibition, but the Sages consider it a Rabbinic prohibition. The halachah follows the Sages.[16] Nevertheless, hints (אַסְמַכְתּוֹת) are cited from Scripture to buttress both the Rabbinic prohibition and the relevant dimensions (see *Gem. 51a, Ritva* there; *Rashi, Shabbos 34a*).

When speaking of a person's place (at the onset of the Sabbath) a legal concept is meant. This 'place' is referred to as his מְקוֹם שְׁבִיתָה, *place of dwelling for the Sabbath*. [The commentary will shorten this to 'place of dwelling' or 'Sabbath dwelling.']

Generally, a person's actual residence is assumed to be his halachic place of dwelling. However, if this cannot be assumed, e.g., the person is on a journey and will not spend the Sabbath at his home, or even if at the onset of the Sabbath he finds himself outside of the *techum* as determined by taking his home as the focal point, then his place of dwelling is identical with his physical location, i.e., wherever he happened to be at the onset of the Sabbath. The size of this place varies. A person's basic place of dwelling is four cubits. [According to some opinions this means an area of four cubits by four cubits while according to others it means four cubits to each side of him, in effect, an area of eight cubits by eight cubits (see 4:5).]

This base place of dwelling applies only when he was in a completely open area at

---

15. The word עֵרוּב, *eruv*, lit. *mixture* or *merging*, is used to indicate that the *eruv*'s purpose is to merge, as it were, the regular *techum* with areas beyond it. Alternatively, this word means, halachic remedy, a meaning borrowed from *eruvei chatzeiros* where its primary definition, merging, is clearly applicable *(Maggid Mishneh to Hil. Yom Tov 6:2* explaining the opinions of *Ravad* and *Rambam)*.

16. There is however a major controversy among the early commentators whether there is a Biblical *techum* extending twelve *mil* [one *mil* is 2,000 cubits — a conventional *techum*] from one's dwelling. *Talmud Yerushalmi (3:6)* states that even the Sages admit that the twelve *mil techum* is Biblically prohibited. *Rif* (end of ch. 1) assumes that *Talmud Bavli* agrees with this and finds an allusion there (17b). *Rambam (Hil. Shabbos 27:1* and *Sefer HaMitzvos, Lo Saaseh 321)* adopts this view and *Maggid Mishneh* reports that it is also the view of the Geonim. *Baal HaMaor* (end of ch. 1), however, disputes the contention that *Talmud Bavli* accepts *Talmud Yerushalmi's* distinction and *Ramban (Milchamos* and *Chiddushim* there) doubts whether even *Rif* accepted this as a halachic conclusion. Many authorities follow *Ramban's* view (see *Rosh, Rashba*, et al.) but *Rif's* view is mentioned by *Rama (Orach Chaim 404:1)* as a halachic possibility (see *Mishnah Berurah* there).

the onset of the Sabbath. If he was in a building, the entire building is considered his place of dwelling. If he was in a city, the entire city is considered his place of dwelling, or, in the language of the *Gemara* (see 5:8), 'the entire city is considered as his four cubits.'

B) Eruvei techumin

It is possible, however, for a person to formally establish his place of dwelling in a place other than where he actually is. This is done by making an *eruvei techumin*[17] and it enables one to go to a location up to 4,000 cubits away from where he actually is at the beginning of the Sabbath. In effect what this does is establish his place of dwelling somewhere between his actual location and the place to which he wants to go on the Sabbath. This does not give him more than the 2,000 cubit limit, it merely shifts the point from which it is measured. For example, if one sets the *eruv* at a point 2,000 cubits away from where he will actually spend the Sabbath, he will be able to travel 4,000 cubits in that direction — 2,000 cubits to the point of the *eruv* and 2,000 more beyond that. He cannot, however, go anywhere in the opposite direction since that would put him beyond a 2,000 cubit distance from his place of dwelling — the place of the *eruv*. Thus, whatever he gains in one direction comes at the expense of the opposite direction (5:7). He cannot set the *eruv* more than 2,000 cubits away from where he is spending the Sabbath, because if it were valid, then he himself would not be within the *techum* — in which case he would be forbidden to go anywhere (see 4:1). If he actually does set his *eruv* more than 2,000 cubits away, his *eruv* is invalid and the center point of his *techum* reverts to where he is *(Orach Chaim* 408:3).

There are two ways to set an *eruvei techumin:* (a) By going to a location within the 2,000 cubit limit and staying there until the Sabbath begins; thereby legally establishing his place of dwelling at this new location (see 4:9, *Orach Chaim* 409:7); (b) if he does not wish to spend the beginning of the Sabbath at the place from where he wants the *techum* to be measured, he can accomplish the same goal by placing a specified amount of food at that location before the Sabbath — the place where the food has been placed is then viewed as his place of dwelling. [For this reason, the food must remain there at least until the beginning of the Sabbath (see 3:4).] In either of these two methods, the person is viewed as (symbolically) residing at the location where his *eruv* is. In addition, there are special dispensations for establishing a place of dwelling for travelers. These are discussed in 4:7.

An *eruv* may be instituted only for the purpose of a mitzvah (e.g. to console mourners, to go to a wedding feast, to greet one's Torah teacher), as set forth in halachah *(Orach Chaim* 415:1 based on *Gem.* 31a; see 8:1).

The installation of an *eruv* where permitted is itself a mitzvah, and the blessing עַל מִצְוַת עֵרוּב is recited for it. This is followed by a short declaration [in a language understood by the person setting the *eruv*] of the *eruv's* purpose:

בְּזֶה הָעֵרוּב יְהֵא מֻתָּר לִי לֵילֵךְ מִמָּקוֹם פְּלוֹנִי אַלְפַּיִם אַמָּה לְכָל רוּחַ

With this eruv *let it be permitted for me to go from this place*[18] (i.e., the place of the eruv) *two thousand cubits in any direction (Orach Chaim* 415:4).

If this declaration is omitted the *eruv* is invalid *(Mishnah Berurah* 415:15).

17. According to *R' Hai Gaon* (in a responsum found in *Teshuvos HaGeonim Mosafia* 76, *Shaarei Teshuvah* 44, and *Sefer Halttim* 29; see *Ittim L'Binah* there), the institution of *eruvei techumin* is part of King Solomon's eruvin legislation (see *Gem.* 21b). *Rashi* (there) and *Rambam (Hil. Eruvin* 1:2 and 6:1), however, understand that King Solomon's legislation was restricted to the prohibition against carrying from one private domain to another and its remedy, *eruvei chatzeiros.*

18. The wording of *Shulchan Aruch*, מִמָּקוֹם פְּלוֹנִי, literally means *from that* (unspecified) place. But, as pointed out by *Mishnah Berurah*, in this case the phrase means *from this place.* Indeed, the formula recorded by *Rambam (Hil. Eruvin* 6:24) uses the phrase מִמָּקוֹם הַזֶּה, *from this place.*

◄§ VI. Units of Measure

Many of the laws discussed in this tractate deal with units of measure and are expressed in terms of cubits, fists and so on. The *Gemara* (3b) concludes that the cubit consists of six fists (טְפָחִים). However, fists can be measured either with the fists relaxed (שׁוֹחֲקוֹת) or compressed (עוֹצְבוֹת).[19] The difference is the width of half a finger for each cubit *(Rashba* in *Avodas HaKodesh* 1:3 cited by *Maggid Mishneh, Hil. Shabbos* 17:36).[20] The *Talmud (Menachos* 41b) states that a fist is as wide as four thumbs (of an average man) side by side at their widest point, which is equal to five forefingers or six little fingers side by side. (See also *Rambam, Comm.* to *Kelayim* 6:6; *Hil. Shabbos* 17:36.)

The general rule is that in any given case the more restrictive measure is used. Thus, the twenty cubits in our mishnah should be measured with compressed cubits. [*Rashba's* opinion is that with regard to the measurements of an alley or succah the compressed measurement is always used, even when that measure is more lenient.]

The codifiers do not agree on the translation of the Mishnaic measurements into contemporary terms. For example, views range from eighteen inches to a bit less than twenty-three for a cubit. Accordingly, the twenty-cubit height given in mishnah 1 could be from as little as thirty to almost forty feet. For the convenience of the reader, we present the following table which presents the three most prevalent views for the fist and cubit. It should be noted, however, that many authorities recommend that slightly larger measurements be used for safety's sake when performing a mitzvah that is required by the Torah.

	טפח — Fist	אמה — cubit	20 cubits
Chazon Ish	3.8 in./9.65 cm.	22.8 in./58 cm.	38 ft./11.60 m.
Igros Moshe	3.58 in./9.1 cm.	21.5 in./54.6 cm.	35.83 ft./10.92 m.
R' A.C. No'eh	3.15 in./8cm.	18.9 in./48 cm.	31.5 ft./9.6 m.

19. In the compressed fist the fingers are held together tightly; in the relaxed fist, loosely *(Rashi* 3b; *Rambam, Comm.).* Alternatively compressed and relaxed refers to the manner in which the fists are placed next to one another and not to the fingers of the fists *(Rambam, Hil. Shabbos* 17:36).

20. The context (in *Avodas HaKodesh*) suggests that *Rashba* means half an index finger, i.e., 1/10 of a fist. However, *Even HaOzer* (to 19a-b) understands this to be half a thumb, or 1/8 of a fist.

מסכת עירובין

Tractate Eruvin

עירובין [א] **מָבוֹי** שֶׁהוּא גָבוֹהַ לְמַעְלָה מֵעֶשְׂרִים
אַמָּה, יְמַעֵט. רַבִּי יְהוּדָה אוֹמֵר:
אֵינוֹ צָרִיךְ.
וְהָרָחָב מֵעֶשֶׂר אַמּוֹת, יְמַעֵט. וְאִם יֶשׁ לוֹ צוּרַת
הַפֶּתַח, אַף עַל פִּי שֶׁהוּא רָחָב מֵעֶשֶׂר אַמּוֹת, אֵין
צָרִיךְ לְמַעֵט.

יד אברהם

Chapter 1

Understanding the first two chapters of this tractate presupposes an understanding of the layout of streets and houses in mishnaic times. In those times, and even up to modern times in many places, several houses would open into a חָצֵר, *courtyard*. Several courtyards would, in turn, lead into a מָבוֹי, *alley*, through which the people would pass to get to the street. [See General Introduction for a fuller discussion of these concepts.]

This chapter deals with the dimensions of the opening between the alley and the street, and with the Rabbinically required adjustments to permit carrying objects in the alley. Mishnah 2 describes these adjustments as the laying of a קוֹרָה, *crossbeam*, across the opening, or the erection of a לְחִי, *pole*, next to one of the walls at the opening. Thus, mishnah 2 should have preceded mishnah 1 which discusses such technicalities of the halachah as the disqualifications of the pole or crossbeam. However, in compiling this tractate, R' Yehudah HaNassi ordered the topics in a way that would highlight the similarity between the laws of *Eruvin* and *Succah*; in either case a height of twenty cubits results in a disqualification, in the former for the crossbeam and in the latter for the *schach* (covering of the succah). Tractates *Eruvin* and *Succah* both begin with this law and both halachos are phrased in almost the identical language (*Tos.* 2a).

1.

מָבוֹי שֶׁהוּא גָבוֹהַ לְמַעְלָה מֵעֶשְׂרִים אַמָּה, — **An** [entrance of an] *alley that is higher than twenty cubits*

[The mishnah speaks of an alley whose entrance may be adjusted with a crossbeam, e.g., a closed alley.] This does not refer to the alley opening itself but to the crossbeam placed across the top of the open side (*Rashi; Rav*). The components or adjustments of an alley are sometimes referred to simply as *alley*, just as the parts of objects are sometimes given the name of the whole (*Meiri*).

The crossbeam was placed across the top of the open side of the alley at a height of more than twenty cubits.

יְמַעֵט. — *must be lowered* [lit. *he must diminish it*].

[That is, if one wishes to carry within the alley.] This is accomplished either by lowering the beam (*Rav; Rashi*), or by raising the ground level of the entrance directly under the crossbeam (*Rashba* and *Ran* from *Yerushalmi; see Gem.* 4b).

The function of the crossbeam is to serve as a reminder that the alley is to be viewed as distinct from and different than the public domain. A beam placed higher than twenty cubits is not prominent and does not serve this purpose (*Rav* from *Gem.* 3a).

It is not necessary that the crossbeam be

1. **A**n alley that is higher than twenty cubits must be lowered. R' Yehudah says: He need not.

And one which is wider than ten cubits must be narrowed. However, if it has the form of a doorway, even if it is wider than ten cubits, it need not be narrowed.

YAD AVRAHAM

within the twenty cubit limit. The mishnah means that the entrance — i.e., the space between the floor and the crossbeam — cannot exceed twenty cubits, but the crossbeam itself may be placed so that its bottom demarcates a height of exactly twenty cubits (*Tos. R' Akiva* from *Gem.* 3b).

Most of the commentators (*Tos., Rashba, Ritva, Ran, Meiri*) concur that the twenty cubit limit refers only to the crossbeam. Where the alley has been adjusted with an upright pole there is no such limit. As pointed out by *Maggid Mishneh* (*Hil. Shabbos* 17:14), the height of the doorway should have no effect on the pole whose bottom end reaches the ground [*Orach Chaim* 363:26; but see *Rambam* (*Hil. Shabbos* 17:14); *Tur* (*Orach Chaim* 363) with *Beis Yosef; Shulchan Aruch* (363:23) and *Beur Halachah* there].

רַבִּי יְהוּדָה אוֹמֵר: אֵינוֹ צָרִיךְ. — *R' Yehudah says: He need not* [lower it].

According to R' Yehudah the crossbeam does not function as a reminder or sign (thus there is no need for prominence), but as a legal partition which is effective even at heights greater than twenty cubits (*Rav; R' Yehonasan; Meiri*).

Others, however, (based on the *Gem.* 3a) explain that R' Yehudah also considers the crossbeam as a reminder except that he considers even one placed above twenty cubits as sufficiently noticeable to serve as a reminder (*Tos. R' Akiva; cf. Geon Yaakov, Tif. Yis.,* and *Sfas Emes* to 3a).

וְהָרְחָב מֵעֶשֶׂר אַמּוֹת, יְמַעֵט. — *And one which is wider than ten cubits must be narrowed* [lit. *he must diminish it*].

He must fence off the excess width until an opening of only ten cubits is left (*Rashi*). [The fence will then serve both to narrow the width of the opening, and

as the required pole.]

[Since every enclosure must have an entrance, the presence of such an opening does not detract from the area being considered completely enclosed. Consequently, if the unwalled side of an alley meets the halachic definition of an entrance, the alley is considered enclosed. Such an alley may be adjusted with a pole or crossbeam. However, an opening which is so wide that it can only be viewed as a gap or breach must be narrowed before it can be adjusted in this manner.]

Therefore, since entrances are generally not wider than ten cubits, the maximum opening adjustable by a pole or crossbeam is ten cubits. An alley whose opening is wider than that is not viewed as an entrance but as completely breached on its fourth side (see mishnah 8) and it cannot be adjusted unless its width is first reduced (*Rav; Rashi*).

וְאִם יֵשׁ לוֹ צוּרַת הַפֶּתַח, — *However, if it has the form of a doorway,*

I.e., the opening is framed with a doorway, two upright poles at the two sides of the entrance with a pole placed horizontally on top of them (*Rav; Rashi*).

The form of a doorway is considered by halachah as a valid partition in many situations. [See General Introduction.]

The crossbeam (קוֹרָה) discussed earlier does not qualify as a *form of a doorway* because it is placed on the walls of the alley, and not on poles which serve as doorposts (see *Magen Avraham* 363:28 and *Da'as Torah* there).

אַף עַל פִּי שֶׁהוּא רָחָב מֵעֶשֶׂר אַמּוֹת, אֵין צָרִיךְ לְמַעֵט. — *even if it is wider than ten cubits, it need not be narrowed.*

הַכְשֵׁר [ב] מָבוֹי — בֵּית שַׁמַּאי אוֹמְרִים:
לֶחִי וְקוֹרָה. וּבֵית הִלֵּל אוֹמְרִים:
לֶחִי אוֹ קוֹרָה. רַבִּי אֱלִיעֶזֶר אוֹמֵר: לְחָיַיִן.
מִשּׁוּם רַבִּי יִשְׁמָעֵאל אָמַר תַּלְמִיד אֶחָד לִפְנֵי
רַבִּי עֲקִיבָא: ,,לֹא נֶחְלְקוּ בֵּית שַׁמַּאי וּבֵית הִלֵּל
עַל מָבוֹי שֶׁהוּא פָּחוֹת מֵאַרְבַּע אַמּוֹת שֶׁהוּא אוֹ
בְלֶחִי אוֹ בְקוֹרָה. עַל מַה נֶחְלְקוּ? עַל רָחָב
מֵאַרְבַּע אַמּוֹת וְעַד עֶשֶׂר, שֶׁבֵּית שַׁמַּאי אוֹמְרִים:

יד אברהם

The mishnah distinguishes between the different types of legal partitions and their levels of effectiveness. Although halachically even an upright pole is considered a partition, it is considered so only to a lesser degree and it is therefore effective only where the space itself can be construed an entrance by virtue of its dimensions alone, i.e., a width of ten cubits or less. However, if one actually makes a form of doorway it is effective even in situations where the space itself exceeds the halachic dimensions of an entrance.

Likewise, if an entrance higher than twenty cubits is framed with the form of a doorway it need not be diminished (*Gem.* 11a).

2.

הֶכְשֵׁר מָבוֹי — *The adjustment of an alley* —

The mishnah now lists the mechanisms by which the fourth, open side of an alley may be adjusted so that the area within is rendered fit for carrying (*Rav; Rambam*).

The *Gem.* (11b) points out that our mishnah refers to a closed alley, i.e., one closed on three sides and open only on the fourth side. An alley open on two sides would first need to be upgraded with the form of a doorway at one of the open sides before the other open side could be adjusted with a pole or crossbeam (*Gem.* 6b; *Orach Chaim* 364:1).

בֵּית שַׁמַּאי אוֹמְרִים: לֶחִי וְקוֹרָה. וּבֵית הִלֵּל אוֹמְרִים: לֶחִי אוֹ קוֹרָה. — *Beis Shammai say:* [Is accomplished by placing] *a pole and a crossbeam. But Beis Hillel say:*

[Either] *a pole or a crossbeam.*[1]

Beis Shammai and Beis Hillel disagree over the stringency of the adjustment that the Rabbis require for the fourth side. According to Beis Shammai *both* a pole and a crossbeam are needed while according to Beis Hillel only one of the two is necessary, the choice being left to the individual.

Beis Shammai, however, agree with Beis Hillel that on a Biblical level an area enclosed on three sides qualifies as a private domain (*Rashi; Rashba; Ran*).[2]

The alley discussed here must be longer than it is wide, and must contain a minimum of two courtyards each of which has two or more houses opening into it. Otherwise it is categorized not as an alley, but as a courtyard which has more stringent rules for its

---

1. According to the opinion accepted by the *Poskim* (see *Gem.* 12b and 15a; *Rambam, Hil. Shabbos* 17:9,22; *Orach Chaim* 363:11; *Tos. R' Akiva*) a pole helps because it is considered a מְחִצָּה, *partition*, whereas a crossbeam serves merely as a הֶכֵּירָא, *reminder*, that this area is not to be confused with a public domain.

2. This is the opinion of most *Rishonim. Rambam* and *R' Chananel*, however, consider this area to be a *karmelis*. See General Introduction.

2. The adjustment of an alley — Beis Shammai say: A pole and a crossbeam. But Beis Hillel say: A pole or a crossbeam. R' Eliezer says: Two poles.

A disciple — in the presence of R' Akiva — stated in the name of R' Yishmael: 'Beis Shammai and Beis Hillel did not differ concerning an alley which is narrower than four cubits that it may be [adjusted] with a pole or a crossbeam. Concerning which did they differ? Concerning one which is wider than four cubits and up to ten cubits. Beis Shammai say: A pole

YAD AVRAHAM

adjustment.[1] A courtyard can only be adjusted with a partition measuring four fists (פס ד׳) or two poles (Rav from Gem. 12b and Tos.). Our streets and alleys are categorized as courtyards (see General Introduction) because they fail to meet some of the specifications of an alley as defined by halachah and cannot be adjusted with a mere pole or beam. Furthermore, it is customary not to avail oneself of the adjustment effective for a courtyard and to require that a form of a doorway be set up (see Orach Chaim 363:26 and Mishnah Berurah there: 111).

רַבִּי אֱלִיעֶזֶר אוֹמֵר: לְחָיַיִן. — R' Eliezer says: Two poles.

The Gemara (11b) leaves unresolved the question of whether R' Eliezer means two poles and a crossbeam (i.e., he is interpreting Beis Shammai's requirement of a pole and crossbeam, explaining the term pole in the plural; Yerushalmi; Chidushei HaRan), or whether he means two poles without a crossbeam. The halachah does not follow R' Eliezer (Rav; Rambam).

The Gemara (12a) points out that the Sages concur with R' Eliezer with regard to a courtyard which, in contrast to the alley discussed here, must be adjusted with two poles or with one single board (פס) measuring four fists.

מִשׁוּם רַבִּי יִשְׁמָעֵאל אָמַר תַּלְמִיד אֶחָד לִפְנֵי רַבִּי עֲקִיבָא: — A disciple — in the

presence of R' Akiva — stated in the name of R' Yishmael:

The Gemara (13a) relates that the disciple mentioned here was the famous R' Meir. As a young man he sought to enter R' Akiva's yeshivah but could not follow R' Akiva's deep discourses. He then went to study under R' Yishmael, from whom he acquired extensive knowledge, and then returned to R' Akiva to absorb the latter's profound method of analysis. The discussion cited in the mishnah occurred, evidently, after he returned to R' Akiva.

,,לֹא נֶחְלְקוּ בֵּית שַׁמַּאי וּבֵית הִלֵּל עַל מָבוֹי שֶׁהוּא פָּחוֹת מֵאַרְבַּע אַמּוֹת שֶׁהוּא אוֹ בְלֶחִי אוֹ בְקוֹרָה. — 'Beis Shammai and Beis Hillel did not differ concerning an alley which is narrower than four cubits that it may be [adjusted] with [either] a pole or a crossbeam.

Since the opening is so narrow, either one is by itself conspicuous enough to serve as a demarcation. It is only when the opening is wider than four cubits that two demarcations are needed (R' Yehonasan).

עַל מַה נֶּחְלָקוּ? עַל רָחָב מֵאַרְבַּע אַמּוֹת וְעַד עֶשֶׂר, — Concerning which [alley] did they differ? Concerning one which is wider than four cubits and up to ten cubits.

1. A courtyard is meant to be more private than an alley and its required adjustment reflects this difference and must provide a greater degree of separation from the outside than the adjustment of an alley (Beis Yosef to Tur, Orach Chaim 363 citing Rashba; Mishnah Berurah 363:102).

עֵירוּבִין לֶחִי וְקוֹרָה. וּבֵית הִלֵּל אוֹמְרִים: אוֹ לֶחִי אוֹ קוֹרָה."

אָמַר רַבִּי עֲקִיבָא: "עַל זֶה וְעַל זֶה נֶחֱלָקוּ."

[ג] הַקּוֹרָה שֶׁאָמְרוּ — רְחָבָה כְּדֵי לְקַבֵּל אָרִיחַ; וְאָרִיחַ חֲצִי לְבֵנָה שֶׁל שְׁלֹשָׁה טְפָחִים. דַּיָּה לַקּוֹרָה שֶׁתְּהֵא רְחָבָה טֶפַח כְּדֵי לְקַבֵּל אָרִיחַ לְאָרְכּוֹ.

יד אברהם

An alley wider than ten cubits cannot be adjusted at all unless the opening is narrowed to ten cubits (see mishnah 1).

שֶׁבֵּית שַׁמַּאי אוֹמְרִים: לֶחִי וְקוֹרָה. וּבֵית הִלֵּל אוֹמְרִים: אוֹ לֶחִי אוֹ קוֹרָה." — *Beis Shammai say:* [Both] *a pole and a crossbeam* [are required]. *But Beis Hillel say:* [Either] *a pole or a crossbeam* [are sufficient].'

[This is precisely the same dispute as above. R' Yishmael, however, restricts it to the case of an alley which is between four and ten cubits wide only.]

אָמַר רַבִּי עֲקִיבָא: "עַל זֶה וְעַל זֶה נֶחֱלָקוּ." — *Said R' Akiva: 'They differed in both cases* [lit. *about this and about that they differed*].'

The *Gemara* (13a) notes that R' Akiva's view ostensibly coincides with the first opinion stated in the mishnah. If this were so, however, R' Akiva's opinion would already be included in that of the *Tanna kamma* (anonymous first *Tanna*), rendering the restatement of his opinion here superfluous. The *Gemara* concludes that the difference between their positions must be in regard to an alley whose opening is narrower than four fists, whether it requires any adjustment at all. However, the *Gemara* does not find any hint in the mishnah as to which *Tanna* holds the stringent view and which the lenient

one.

All agree, however, that when the opening is less than three fists wide no adjustment at all is needed; any such opening is subject to the general halachic principle of לָבוּד, *lavud*, which states that two surfaces separated by a gap of less than three fists are considered as joined (with regard to the rules of partitions) [see Gen. Intro.]. Consequently, the open side of such an alley is legally considered closed and no further adjustment is necessary (*Meiri*).

There is a question, however, as to how to understand the opinion that even a width of between three and four fists does not require an adjustment. According to some, it is based on the opinion of Rabban Shimon ben Gamliel (*Gem.* 9a) that the rule of *lavud* is to be applied to all gaps of less than four fists, not three. Accordingly, since the accepted halachah is that the rule of *lavud* applies only to gaps of less than three, it should follow that an alley which is between three and four fists wide is not legally considered closed and must therefore be adjusted. This indeed is the ruling of *Rambam (Hil. Shabbos 17:9* as understood by *Meiri;* for other explanations of *Rambam's* view see *Even HaOzer, Eruvin* 5a and *Beur HaGra* to *Orach Chaim* 363:28).

Others maintain that the basis of this opinion is that any opening narrower

and a crossbeam. But Beis Hillel say: A pole or a
crossbeam.'

Said R' Akiva: 'They differed in both cases.'

3. The crossbeam of which they spoke — it is wide
enough to hold an *ariach*; an *ariach* is half a
brick measuring three fists. It is sufficient for the
crossbeam to be one fist wide to hold an *ariach*
lengthwise.

YAD AVRAHAM

than four fists is not legally considered
an entrance and as such is exempted
from any adjustment (*Rashba; Rosh;* et
al.). These authorities adopt the lenient
view as the halachah. [Since it is not
based on the dispute concerning *lavud* it
is not affected by the stringent ruling

there.] *Shulchan Aruch (Orach Chaim
363:28 see Mishnah Berurah)* cites both
views without rendering a decision, but
indicates that one should' adopt the
stricter view that between three and
four fists wide the alley opening does
require an adjustment.

3.

הַקּוֹרָה שֶׁאָמְרוּ — רְחָבָה כְּדֵי לְקַבֵּל אָרִיחַ;
— *The crossbeam of which they spoke* [in
mishnah 2] — *it is wide enough to hold
an* ariach;

An *ariach* is a brick with the
dimensions specified below. The
crossbeam must be wide enough to hold
an *ariach* so that it will have a semblance
of permanence; as if it were placed there
to serve as the support for a wall to be
made of *arichim* (*Rav; Rashi*).

Rashba quoting *Ravad* explains that
it should resemble an archway over the
entrance.

וְאָרִיחַ חֲצִי לְבֵנָה שֶׁל שְׁלֹשָׁה טְפָחִים. — *an*
ariach *is half a brick measuring* [lit. *of*]
three fists.

I.e., a square of three fists by three
fists (*Rambam; Rashi*).

Consequently the *ariach*, which is the
standard brick, measures three by one
and a half fists (*Rav; Rashi*).

The Talmud (*Bava Basra* 3b) explains
that the dimensions of the standard brick had to
be articulated because there were two stand-

ard sizes. The mishnah specifies that the
larger size is referred to here.

דַּיָּה לַקּוֹרָה שֶׁתְּהֵא רְחָבָה טֶפַח כְּדֵי לְקַבֵּל
אָרִיחַ לְאָרְכּוֹ. — *It is sufficient for the
crossbeam to be one fist wide to hold an*
ariach *lengthwise.*

The *ariach's* length, which is three
fists, can be accommodated by aligning
the *ariach's* length with the beam's
length (*Rambam*).

Although the width of the *ariach* is a fist
and a half, a crossbeam one fist wide is
considered sufficient to hold an *ariach*. The
edges of the *ariach* which overlap the beam
by one quarter of a fist on each side will be
covered with the mortar which will be part of
any wall built upon the beam (*Rav* from
Gem. 14a).

The above is based on the version found in
most editions of the Mishnah. The reading of
this mishnah in our editions of the Talmud
(see *Tos. Yom Tov* and *Shinuyei Nuschaos*)
is, לְקַבֵּל אָרִיחַ לְרָחְבּוֹ, *to hold an ariach
widthwise.* Thus this phrase explains how a
fist wide beam can hold a three fist long
ariach; namely by the *ariach's* width which is
only a fist and a half (see *Rashi*).

[ד] **רְחָבָה** כְּדֵי לְקַבֵּל אָרִיחַ, וּבְרִיאָה כְּדֵי לְקַבֵּל אָרִיחַ. רַבִּי יְהוּדָה אוֹמֵר: רְחָבָה אַף עַל פִּי שֶׁאֵין בְּרִיאָה.

[ה] **הָיְתָה** שֶׁל קַשׁ וְשֶׁל קָנִים, רוֹאִין אוֹתָהּ כְּאִלּוּ הִיא שֶׁל מַתֶּכֶת; עֲקֻמָּה, רוֹאִין אוֹתָהּ כְּאִלּוּ הִיא פְּשׁוּטָה; עֲגֻלָּה, רוֹאִין אוֹתָהּ כְּאִלּוּ הִיא מְרֻבַּעַת.

יד אברהם

4.

רְחָבָה כְּדֵי לְקַבֵּל אָרִיחַ, וּבְרִיאָה כְּדֵי לְקַבֵּל אָרִיחַ. — [It must be both] *wide* [enough] *to hold an* ariach *and strong* [enough] *to hold an* ariach.

[This mishnah elaborates on the phrase stated in the previous mishnah. The first *Tanna* here understands the phrase *to hold an ariach* to refer both to the width of the beam (as explained in the previous mishnah), and to its sturdiness — it must be strong and thick enough to actually support an *ariach*.]

It must be strong enough to support a row of *arichim* across its entire length (R' Yehonasan; Ravad based on Yeru-

shalmi, cited by Rashba).

רַבִּי יְהוּדָה אוֹמֵר: רְחָבָה אַף עַל פִּי שֶׁאֵין בְּרִיאָה. — R' Yehudah says: Wide [enough], *even if it is not strong* [enough].

[Even if it is not strong enough to actually support an *ariach* it is nevertheless valid as a crossbeam, and may be used to adjust an alley. R' Yehudah maintains that the rule that a crossbeam be sufficient *to hold an ariach* refers only to its width, not to its strength.] The halachah does not follow R' Yehudah's opinion (Rav; Rambam; Orach Chaim 363:17).

5.

R' Yehudah proceeds to give an example of his opinion that the crossbeam need only be wide enough to support an *ariach* but need not actually be strong enough (Rav, Rashi).

הָיְתָה שֶׁל קַשׁ וְשֶׁל קָנִים, רוֹאִין אוֹתָהּ כְּאִלּוּ הִיא שֶׁל מַתֶּכֶת; — *If it was* [made] *of straw or of reeds we view it as if it were* [made] *of metal;*

[The crossbeam had the required width but it lacked the strength to hold an *ariach*. Yet since this width would be sufficient to support a row of *arichim* if the crossbeam were made of metal, it is effective even when the crossbeam is

made of straw or reeds.]

The Gemara (14a) adds that the example offered here makes a point not deducible from R' Yehudah's general statement of his view. It teaches us that the crossbeam can even be made of a material which can never, under any circumstances, support an *ariach*.

עֲקֻמָּה, רוֹאִין אוֹתָהּ כְּאִלּוּ הִיא פְּשׁוּטָה; — [if it was] *bent, we view it as if it were straight;*

If it was curved and thus unfit to hold an *ariach* in its present state (Rav; Rashi) it is still effective as long as its width would be capable of supporting the *ariach* in a straightened shape.

4. **W**ide to hold an *ariach* and strong to hold an *ariach*. R' Yehudah says: Wide, even if it is not strong.

5. **I**f it was [made] of straw or of reeds we view it as if it were [made] of metal; bent, we view it as if it were straight; rounded, we view it as if it were squared.

YAD AVRAHAM

עֲגֻלָּה, — [if it was] *rounded*,

[Its surfaces were rounded (like a pole) not squared and flat (like a beam).] As a result, any *ariach* placed on it will roll off *(Rav; Rashi)*. It is wide enough, however, that if it were smoothed or split, its width would still be a fist *(Rashi)*.

רוֹאִין אוֹתָהּ כְּאִלּוּ הִיא מְרֻבַּעַת. — *we view it as if it were squared* [i.e., rectangular].

We consider it as if it had been planed down until it presented a flat surface [wide enough for an *ariach* (Rashi; see *Rashash*)].

Most commentators assume that even the Sages who dispute R' Yehudah (mishnah 4) and require that the beam actually be strong enough to support an *ariach* concur in the cases of the bent and the rounded beam *(Rambam, Hil. Shabbos 17:28; Rashba; et al.)*. As *Rashba* explains, where the crossbeam is made of straw, it is intrinsically too weak to support an *ariach*. Where the beam is bent or rounded, however, it is inherently strong enough (thus meeting the Sages' requirement) but its shape is a hindrance to placing *arichim* on it. Since this obstacle can be removed without adding anything to the beam — by bending it back to a straight shape or by planing the rounded part into a flat shape — it is valid in its present shape even according to the Sages.

It follows then, that where the curvature is such that it cannot be straightened or planed sufficiently for a brick to be placed on it, the beam will be valid only according to R' Yehudah. Accordingly, the halachah, which follows the Sages, would disqualify such a crossbeam (see *Ran*).

Others, however, maintain that even bent and rounded beams are valid only according to R' Yehudah, and not according to the Sages *(R' Yehonasan; Ran; cf. Even HaOzer and Geon Yaakov)*.

This case of the bent crossbeam refers even to one which is bent at an angle which leaves part of the beam outside the alley or above twenty cubits.[1] [Indeed, *Meiri* understands it to refer to this case specifically.] If removal of the segment extending outside the alley would result in a gap of less than three fists between the remaining segments of the beam, the beam is valid because of the principle of *lavud* [see mishnah 2, s.v. אוֹמֵר עֲקִיבָא ר׳] *(Gem. 14a)*.

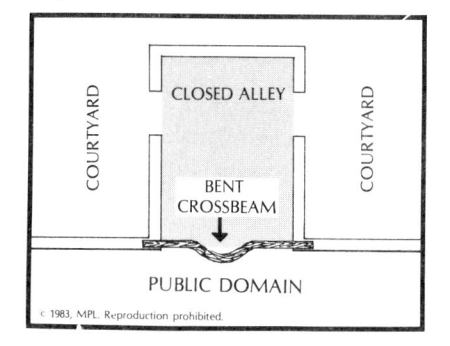

CLOSED ALLEY

COURTYARD

COURTYARD

BENT CROSSBEAM

PUBLIC DOMAIN

1. *Even HaOzer* and *Geon Yaakov* point out that even if the Sages dispute the validity of a bent crossbeam (the opinion of *R' Yehonasan* and *Ran* cited above) they do agree that if the bent beam can support the *ariach* but the bend carries beyond the alley that it is valid if it meets the above condition (see *Mishnah Berurah* 363:66).

כָּל שֶׁיֵּשׁ בְּהֶקֵפוֹ שְׁלֹשָׁה טְפָחִים, יֵשׁ בּוֹ רוֹחַב טֶפַח.

[ו] לְחָיַיִן שֶׁאָמְרוּ — גָּבְהָן עֲשָׂרָה טְפָחִים, וְרָחְבָּן וְעוֹבְיָן כָּל שֶׁהוּא. רַבִּי יוֹסֵי אוֹמֵר: רָחְבָּן שְׁלֹשָׁה טְפָחִים.

[ז] בַּכֹּל עוֹשִׂין לְחָיַיִן, אֲפִלוּ בְּדָבָר שֶׁיֵּשׁ בּוֹ

יד אברהם

כָּל שֶׁיֵּשׁ בְּהֶקֵפוֹ שְׁלֹשָׁה טְפָחִים, יֵשׁ בּוֹ רוֹחַב טֶפַח. — *Anything* [round] *which has a circumference of three fists has a diameter* [lit. *has a width*] *of one fist.*

The mishnah now explains how one is to ascertain whether a round beam has the required width of one fist (*Rav; Rashi*). [Since it is impractical to measure the diameter of a solid round object directly, the mishnah explains how to derive it from its circumference, which can be easily measured.]

The *Gemara* (14a) derives this rule from a verse in Scripture[1] describing the pool King Solomon made for the Temple — *And he* (Solomon) *made the pool*[2] *of cast metal, ten cubits from rim to rim, circular all around ... and a line of thirty cubits would encompass it ... (I Kings 7:23). Rambam (Comm.)* comments: ... the (exact) ratio of the diameter of a circle to its circumference

is irrational ... but it is possible to approximate it ... and the approximation used by scientists is the ratio of one to three and one seventh ... Since it is impossible to arrive at a perfectly accurate ratio, ... they (the Sages) assumed a round number and said: 'Anything which has a circumference of three fists has a diameter of one fist.' And they relied on this for all the measurements they needed.

Maggid Mishneh (Hil. Shabbos 17:26) points out that in our case this use of round numbers is a leniency, since a beam measuring three fists in circumference will not actually have a width of one fist — only a beam measuring at least 3 1/7 fists has such a width. Nevertheless, the beam is valid because the requirement for a beam measuring one fist across is Rabbinical (consequently, the Sages allowed a slightly narrower beam in this case).[3]

Another approach is taken by R' Shimon ben Tzemach (Tashbetz 1:165). He argues

1. *Rosh (Teshuvos 2:19)*, in an inquiry addressed to *Rashba*, wonders why the Talmud needs to derive from Scripture a matter easily ascertainable through measurement. [*Rashba's* response to this query has been lost *(Cheshek Shlomo).*] *Rosh* addresses this question in his *Tosafos* and answers that since the ratio given in the mishnah is only a practical approximation a Scriptural precedent for such an approximation is useful. This also solves the problem raised by *Tosafos* (14a) that the numbers given in this verse cannot be mathematically accurate. Although this is true, the verse uses these (approximate) numbers to teach the above halachah, that this approximation is the one adopted by the Torah.

2. This pool (יָם) was used as a *mikveh* by the *Kohanim* to cleanse themselves of *tumah*-contamination. Scripture alludes to this and states *(II Chronicles 4:6): ... but the pool was for the Kohanim to wash* (לְרָחְצָה). *Yerushalmi (Yoma 3:8)* explains how the construction of the pool conformed to the laws of *mikveh.*

3. Others suggest a reconciliation of the two ratios. The mishnah speaks of both relaxed and compressed fists (see General Introduction) — thus: 'Anything which has a circumference of three *relaxed* fists has a diameter of one *compressed* fist' (Hon Ashir; Lechem Shamayim; cf. Tashbetz).

Anything which has a circumference of three fists has a diameter of one fist.

6. The poles of which they spoke — their height is ten fists, while their width and thickness are any size. R' Yose says: Their width is three fists.

7. We may use anything as poles, even a living be-

YAD AVRAHAM

that this ratio derives from the oral law handed down to Moses on Sinai (הֲלָכָה לְמשֶׁה מִסִּינַי). When the *Gemara* (4a) reports that שִׁעוּרִין, *measures*, were included in this Sinaitic law, this ratio, too, is included. Thus

we were directed by the Giver of the Torah to disregard the small discrepancy between the mathematically known actual measurement of the diameter and that assumed because of the ratio given in the mishnah.[1]

6.

לְחָיַיִן שֶׁאָמְרוּ — *The poles of which they spoke* [in mishnah 2 as the adjustment of an alley] —

By using the plural form *poles*, the *Tanna* seems to indicate that the halachah follows R' Eliezer who requires two poles (see mish. 2). The *Gemara* (14b) explains, however, that the *Tanna* of our mishnah, wishing to avoid deciding in favor of any of the views stated in mishnah 2, refers to *the* [disputed] *poles*, of which at least one is necessary according to everyone (see *Rav* and *Rambam*).

גָּבְהָן עֲשָׂרָה טְפָחִים, — *their height is ten fists*,

The poles must be at least as tall as the minimum height of the other walls of the alley. [The minimum height for any partition is ten fists (*Succah* 5b).]

This is especially true according to the halachically accepted view that a pole is effective because it serves as a legal partition (see first footnote to mish. 2). Consequently it must be of the minimum height required for a partition (*Meiri*). However, even if the walls of the alley are higher it is sufficient for the pole to be ten fists high (*Rav; Rambam*).

וְרָחְבָּן וְעוֹבְיָין כָּל שֶׁהוּא. — *while their width and thickness are any size* [lit. *whatever it is*].

Even as thin as a thread (*Gem.* 14b).

רַבִּי יוֹסֵי אוֹמֵר: וְרָחְבָּן שֶׁל שָׁו, שְׁעָווּוּוּ. — R' Yose says: Their width is three fists.

He requires a more substantial partition (*Rav* from *R' Yehonasan*; see *Tos. Yom Tov* and *Tos. R' Akiva*). The halachah does not follow R' Yose (*Rav; Ramban* from *Gem.* 14b).

7.

בְּכֹל עוֹשִׂין לְחָיַיִן, אֲפִלּוּ בְּדָבָר שֶׁיֵּשׁ בּוֹ רוּחַ חַיִּים; — *We may use anything as poles* [lit. *we may make poles of anything*], *even a living being* [lit. *even with

something which has life*];

I.e., even an animal may be placed at the alley entrance to serve as a pole. The Talmud (*Succah* 23a-b) concludes

1. *Tashbetz*, in another approach, suggests that the ratio in the mishnah was meant to be used only as a rough figure, to be used only in learning (so as not to confuse the issue with fractions). In actual practice, one has to respect the mathematical reality; the beam has to measure 3 1/7 fists. But the silence of the *Poskim* on this matter indicates their disagreement.

עירוּבִין רוּחַ חַיִּים; וְרַבִּי יוֹסֵי אוֹסֵר.

וּמְטַמֵּא מִשּׁוּם גּוֹלֵל; וְרַבִּי מֵאִיר מְטַהֵר.

וְכוֹתְבִין עָלָיו גִּטֵּי נָשִׁים; וְרַבִּי יוֹסֵי הַגְּלִילִי פּוֹסֵל.

[ח] שַׁיָּירָא שֶׁחָנְתָה בְּבִקְעָה וְהִקִּיפוּהָ בִּכְלֵי בְהֵמָה — מְטַלְטְלִין בְּתוֹכָהּ, וּבִלְבַד שֶׁיְּהֵא גָדֵר גָּבוֹהַּ עֲשָׂרָה טְפָחִים, וְלֹא יִהְיוּ פְרָצוֹת יְתֵרוֹת עַל הַבִּנְיָן.

יד אברהם

(concerning a parallel case) that this is true only when the animal is tied up in such a manner that it can neither move from its place nor lie down (thus diminishing its height to less than ten fists), since either of these two circumstances would invalidate the pole (*R' Yehonasan; Orach Chaim* 363:3).

וְרַבִּי יוֹסֵי אוֹסֵר. — *but R' Yose forbids* [this].

R' Yose forbids using a living creature as a pole because of the possiblity that it may die. Although the animal is tied and cannot lay itself down, it will nevertheless sag upon death and may drop to below ten fists. The *Tanna kamma*, however, feels that we need not be concerned for the unlikely occurrence of a sudden death (*Succah* 23a-b). The halachah follows the *Tanna kamma* (*Rav; Rambam*).

וּמְטַמֵּא מִשּׁוּם גּוֹלֵל; — *And it transmits* tumah-*contamination as a tomb cover;*

[If an animal is used as a covering for a tomb[1] it is categorized as a גּוֹלֵל (*gollel*), tomb cover. As such it is classified as an אַב הַטּוּמְאָה, *primary* tumah and is subject to special laws of tumah-contamination (see *Ohalos* 2:4 and 15:8).]

Rav states that once an object has been classified as a *gollel*, it retains this stringent status forever, even after it ceases to serve this function. This is the view of *Rashi* and others (see *Tos. Kesubos* 4b).

Rambam (comm. to *Ohalos* 15:9; *Hil. Tumas Meis* 2:15) indicates that the status of *gollel* persists only as long as the object serves in that capacity.

[The translation of גּוֹלֵל presented here is that adopted by *Rav*, and is based on *Aruch* (s.v. גּוֹלל), *R' Chananel, Ravad* (cited by *Ramban* in *Toras HaAdam*), et al. See other interpretations in *Rashi* (*Chullin* 72a, s.v. גולל), *Rambam* (*Hil. Tumas Meis* 2:15), and *Tosafos* (*Shabbos* 152b, s.v. עד).

וְרַבִּי מֵאִיר מְטַהֵר. — *but R' Meir considers it uncontaminated* [lit. *cleanses it*].

R' Meir maintains that a living thing cannot serve as a legal partition and can thus not be given the status of a tomb cover (*Rav; Rashi* from *Succah* 24a). According to R' Meir's view a living thing can also not serve as a pole for this reason. He thus disputes the first ruling of the mishnah, too (*Tos. Yom Tov*).

Many texts, including the mishnah found in the *Gemara*, actually have R' Meir in place of R' Yose in the case of the pole, too. Thus, the disqualification of a living being as a pole is not based on the concern that it may die but on the inherent disqualification of a living being as a partition of any sort (*Rashi* 15b). The explanation offered above is based

---

1. *Tosafos* (*Shabbos* 152b and *Kesubos* 4b) points out that a *Tanna* will often choose an unlikely circumstance to illustrate a halachic principle.

ing; but R' Yose forbids [this].

And it transmits *tumah*-contamination as a tomb cover; but R' Meir considers it uncontaminated.

And we may write bills of divorce on it; but R' Yose HaGlili invalidates [it].

8. **A** caravan which made camp in a valley and surrounded it with animal trappings — they may carry within it provided that the barricade is ten fists high, and the gaps do not exceed the walled portion.

YAD AVRAHAM

on the version found in our mishnayos which ascribes the invalidating view to R' Yose.

וְכוֹתְבִין עָלָיו גִּטֵּי נָשִׁים; — *And we may write bills of divorce* [lit. *women's divorces*] *on it;*

[I.e., upon a live animal. The entire animal must then be given to the woman as if it were a regular bill of divorce.]

וְרַבִּי יוֹסֵי הַגְּלִילִי פּוֹסֵל. — *but R' Yose HaGlili invalidates* [it].

The disagreement between R' Yose and the Sages stems from their differing interpretations of the term סֵפֶר, *sefer,*

used by Scripture to denote the bill of divorce [*And he shall write for her a sefer of divorce ... (Deut.* 24:3)]. R' Yose takes *sefer* in its usual sense, scroll (or book). Since a scroll is usually written on parchment — an inanimate object — the word *sefer* inherently excludes all living things. The Sages interpret *sefer* in its alternative meaning of *a recounting of events,* i.e. *he shall write for her an account of divorce ...* Accordingly, no exclusion of living things is indicated (*Rav from Gem.* 15b).

8.

שֶׁיָּרָא שֶׁחָנְתָה בְּבִקְעָה — *A caravan which made camp in a valley*

[I.e., in a valley of open fields, which is classified as a *karmelis* (see *Shabbos* 6a and *Rashi* there).]

וְהִקִּיפוּהָ בִּכְלֵי בְהֵמָה — *and surrounded it with animal trappings —*

They used the saddles and other trappings to build a barricade around the camp but gaps remained open in many places, e.g., between one saddle and the next (*R' Yehonasan; Meiri*).

מְטַלְטְלִין בְּתוֹכָהּ, — *they may carry within it*

If they were camped there over the Sabbath, they are permitted to carry within the confines of the barricade they erected. Although the trappings were

placed around the camp only on a temporary basis, they are still considered a valid partition (*Tif. Yis.*).

וּבִלְבַד שֶׁיְּהֵא גָדֵר גָּבוֹהַּ עֲשָׂרָה טְפָחִים, — *provided that the barricade is ten fists high,*

Ten fists is the minimum height for any partition (*Succah* 5b).

וְלֹא יִהְיוּ פְּרָצוֹת יְתֵרוֹת עַל הַבִּנְיָן. — *and the gaps do not exceed the walled portion* [lit. *the building*].

Even if no individual gap exceeds ten cubits, if the gaps collectively exceed the walled part, the entire partition is invalid (*Rav; Rashi*). [Since more of the perimeter is open than closed, the area as a whole cannot be considered enclosed.]

כָּל פִּרְצָה שֶׁהִיא כְּעֶשֶׂר אַמּוֹת מֻתֶּרֶת, מִפְּנֵי שֶׁהִיא כְּפֶתַח; יָתֵר מִכַּאן אָסוּר.

[ט] **מַקִּיפִין** שְׁלֹשָׁה חֲבָלִים, זֶה לְמַעְלָה מִזֶּה וְזֶה לְמַעְלָה מִזֶּה, וּבִלְבַד שֶׁלֹּא יְהֵא בֵין חֶבֶל לַחֲבֵרוֹ שְׁלֹשָׁה טְפָחִים. שִׁעוּר חֲבָלִים עוֹבְיָן יָתֵר עַל טֶפַח, כְּדֵי שֶׁיְּהֵא הַכֹּל עֲשָׂרָה טְפָחִים.

[י] **מַקִּיפִין** בְּקָנִים, וּבִלְבַד שֶׁלֹּא יְהֵא בֵין קָנֶה לַחֲבֵרוֹ שְׁלֹשָׁה טְפָחִים. בְּשַׁיָּרָא

יד אברהם

[If the walled part exceeds the gaps the partition is valid and one may carry even opposite the gaps. Since most of the perimeter is closed the entire area is considered enclosed, and the gaps are viewed as entrances.]

This rule applies whether the gaps are in the height or in the width (*Orach Chaim* 362:9 from *Gem.* 16b).

כָּל פִּרְצָה שֶׁהִיא כְּעֶשֶׂר אַמּוֹת מֻתֶּרֶת, מִפְּנֵי שֶׁהִיא כְּפֶתַח; — *Any gap which is ten cubits wide is permitted for it is [considered] as an entrance;*

[The mishnah now explains why gaps do not invalidate a partition. All partitions must have openings to serve as entrances in them, so that gaps of less than ten cubits may be considered entrances.] However, even if the gaps are ten cubits or less they must not exceed the walled part. If they do, the partition is invalidated although each

gap could, in itself, be considered an entrance (*Rav; Rashi*).

יָתֵר מִכַּאן אָסוּר. — *greater than this is prohibited.*

If one gap is greater than ten cubits the entire partition is invalid, even though the walled part exceeds the gaps. Moving objects in the alley is prohibited. Since a gap of this size exceeds the maximum for an entrance it is considered a breach and invalidates the partition. [Because of the breach, the walled section cannot be considered as enclosing the area and the area as a whole therefore remains open.] However, if the gap was adjusted with the *form of a doorway* (see mishnah 1), it is considered a partition even when the opening is greater than ten cubits (*Rav; Rambam*).

In an instance where the gaps exactly equal the walled part, the partition is still valid (*Orach Chaim* 362:9; *Gem.* 16b).

9.

מַקִּיפִין שְׁלֹשָׁה חֲבָלִים, זֶה לְמַעְלָה מִזֶּה וְזֶה לְמַעְלָה מִזֶּה, וּבִלְבַד שֶׁלֹּא יְהֵא בֵין חֶבֶל לַחֲבֵרוֹ שְׁלֹשָׁה טְפָחִים. — *They may [also] surround [the camp] with three ropes, one above the other [lit. this above this,*

and this above this], provided that there not be three fists between one rope and the other.

This is done by driving pickets at least ten fists tall into the ground and

Any gap which is ten cubits wide is permitted for it is as an entrance; greater than this is prohibited.

9. They may surround [the camp] with three ropes, one above the other, provided that there not be three fists between one rope and the other.

The thickness of the ropes is more than a fist, in order that the total should be ten fists.

10. They may surround [the camp] with pickets provided that [the space] between one picket and the other is not three fists. They spoke of a

YAD AVRAHAM

attaching ropes to them. The lowest rope is hung within three fists of the ground, the next rope within three fists of the first, and the third within three fists of the second.

Through the principle of *lavud* [see General Introduction] two objects less than three fists apart are considered joined to each other. Consequently, the open areas measuring less than three fists are considered closed and part of the walled section. However, since the minimum height required for a partition is ten fists, and the three spaces between the ropes measure in total slightly less than nine fists, the difference must be made up by the thickness of the ropes, as explained below (Rav).

שִׁעוּר חֲבָלִים עוֹבְיָין יָתֵר עַל טֶפַח, — The thickness of the ropes [lit. the measure

of the ropes — their thickness] is more than a fist,

The average thickness of each rope must be slightly more than one third of a fist so that all three ropes taken together add up to just over a fist (Rav).

[The text as adopted is that proposed by R' Yeshayah Pick in Masores HaShas (16b) and found in many versions (see Shinuyei Nuschaos) and in Rambam (ed. Kafich). The regular versions have שִׁעוּר חֲבָלִים וְעוֹבְיָין יָתֵר עַל טֶפַח.]

כְּדֵי שֶׁיְהֵא הַכֹּל עֲשָׂרָה טְפָחִים. — in order that the total [height of the fence] should be ten fists.

[So that when the thickness of the ropes is added to the maximum allowable gaps between ropes, the total will come to ten fists (the minimum size of a partition).]

10.

מַקִּיפִין בְּקָנִים, — They may [also] surround [the camp] with pickets

[The pickets are each longer than ten fists so that when they are driven into the ground their exposed length measures ten fists. They are placed at a short distance from each other to serve as a partition. However, they are not

tied one to the other.]

וּבִלְבַד שֶׁלֹּא יְהֵא בֵּין קָנֶה לַחֲבֵירוֹ שְׁלֹשָׁה טְפָחִים. — provided that [the space] between one picket and the other is not three fists.

[The principle of *lavud* described in the General Introduction is effective here too.]

עירובין דִּבְּרוּ — דִּבְרֵי רַבִּי יְהוּדָה. וַחֲכָמִים אוֹמְרִים: לֹא
א/י דִּבְּרוּ בְּשַׁיָּירָא אֶלָּא בַּהוֹוֶה.
כָּל מְחִצָּה שֶׁאֵינָהּ שֶׁל שְׁתִי וְשֶׁל עֵרֶב אֵינָהּ
מְחִצָּה — דִּבְרֵי רַבִּי יוֹסֵי בְּרַבִּי יְהוּדָה. וַחֲכָמִים
אוֹמְרִים: אֶחָד מִשְּׁנֵי דְבָרִים.
אַרְבָּעָה דְבָרִים פָּטְרוּ בְּמַחֲנֶה: מְבִיאִין עֵצִים

יד אברהם

בְּשַׁיָּירָא דִּבְּרוּ — דִּבְרֵי רַבִּי יְהוּדָה. [When stating this rule] they spoke [only] of a caravan — [these are] the words of R' Yehudah.

[R' Yehudah does not dispute the ruling of this mishnah, but he does qualify it. His qualification applies to the ruling of the previous mishnah as well.]

R' Yehudah is of the opinion that the dispensation to erect such a flimsy partition (consisting only of stakes or of ropes) was permitted only in difficult circumstances, such as a caravan camping for the Sabbath in an open space. Individuals, however, are not allowed this leeway and must erect a proper and complete partition — one running both vertically and horizontally[1] (Rav; Rashi).

The Gemara (16b) defines a caravan as a group consisting of at least three persons. One or two travelers do not qualify for this dispensation, according

to R' Yehudah. The Gemara (16b) explains, additionally, that R' Yehudah does not completely deprive an individual of availing himself of the dispensations afforded a caravan. He only limits the amount of space an individual may enclose with such a flimsy partition. Members of a caravan may enclose as much area as they see fit for their needs with a partition of stakes or ropes; an individual (or two people) who uses this type of partition is limited to an area of 5,000 square cubits (see 2:5).[2]

Most of the commentators (Rashba, Ritva et al.; see also Rambam, Hil. Shabbos 16:13, Orach Chaim 360:1) hold that a group of two is also entitled to only 5,000 square cubits, but R' Yehonasan maintains that each of them is allowed 5,000 cubits for a total of 10,000 square cubits for the pair.

וַחֲכָמִים אוֹמְרִים: לֹא דִּבְּרוּ בְּשַׁיָּירָא אֶלָּא בַּהוֹוֶה. — But the Sages say: They spoke of a caravan only because it is common.

1. Ritva and Rashba (Avodas HaKodesh 3:3) assume that R' Yehudah's limitation refers not only to partitions composed of horizontal or vertical sections (mish. 9-10) but also to a partition which had gaps totalling less than the majority of that partition (mish. 8). Thus, R' Yehudah understands the word caravan to exclude other circumstances from the leniencies of mish. 8-10, while the Sages understand the term to be used loosely.

Other authorities disagree. In their view, R' Yehudah concurs that the word caravan is used loosely in the initial context (mish. 8) and that a partition with gaps is valid in all circumstances. He maintains, however, that this term would not have been used if it were not exclusive in at least the last two cases — a partition composed of stakes or ropes (Geon Yaakov; Mishnah Berurah 360:3).

Rambam's (Hil. Shabbos 16:12) interpretation (apparently) differs from that of all other commentators in that he assigns the differentiation between an individual and a caravan even to a complete partition which was erected on a temporary basis (see Keren Orah to 16b, Mirkeves HaMishneh).

2. The halachic requirements concerning partitions are not uniform; for an area of more than 5,000 square cubits the definition of an effective partition is more stringent than for a lesser area (see further 2:5). Since a partition such as described here is viewed by R' Yehudah as flawed, he rules it effective for an area of 5,000 square cubits, but invalid for a greater area.

caravan — [these are] the words of R' Yehudah. But the Sages say: They spoke of a caravan only because it is common.

Any partition not consisting of a warp and a weft is not [considered] a partition — [these are] the words of R' Yose ben R' Yehudah. But the Sages say: Either of the two.

Four obligations were waived in a camp: They may

YAD AVRAHAM

[In illustrating the rules of such a partition, the Sages chose the example of a caravan only because it was common for a caravan to put up such partitions around their camp and not because their use is restricted to caravans. Thus the Sages permit even an individual to enclose an area greater than 5,000 cubits if necessary.]

However, even the Sages permit such a partition only for an individual camping in a wilderness (similar to a caravan). In an inhabited area, he must put up a proper partition composed of both vertical and horizontal sections (*Gem.* 17a with *Rashi*).

כָּל מְחִצָּה שֶׁאֵינָהּ שֶׁל שְׁתִי וְשֶׁל עֵרֶב אֵינָהּ מְחִצָּה — דִּבְרֵי רַבִּי יוֹסֵי בְּרַבִּי יְהוּדָה. — *Any partition not consisting of a warp and a weft* [i.e., vertical and horizontal sections] *is not [considered] a partition — [these are] the words of R' Yose ben R' Yehudah.*

R' Yose is even more stringent than his father, R' Yehudah, and forbids such partitions even for a caravan (*Rav; Rashi*).

However, as before, this limitation applies only to areas greater than 5,000 square cubits. For less than that R' Yose and R' Yehudah agree with the Sages that even an individual may use this type of partition. Moreover, in the case of a caravan R' Yose permits an area of 15,000 square cubits (5,000 square cubits for each member). He disagrees only with the ruling allowing a caravan as much area as needed (*Gem.* 16b; *Rashba; Ritva*)

וַחֲכָמִים אוֹמְרִים: אֶחָד מִשְּׁנֵי דְבָרִים. — *But*

the Sages say: Either of the two [is sufficient].

[I.e., a partition need only consist of either horizontal or vertical sections.]

The *Gemara* (17a) points out that the Sages here do not hold a view identical with the Sages who dispute R' Yehudah in the first part of our mishnah. If they did, a restatement of their opinion would be redundant. They differ with the previous Sages concerning an individual camping (or living) in a settled area. The previous Sages had permitted such an individual to enclose only 5,000 square cubits with this flimsy partition (see above), but the latter Sages permit him to enclose as much as he needs.

The halachah follows R' Yehudah regarding an individual; i.e., one or two individuals are given a maximum total of 5,000 square cubits. Concerning a caravan, however, the halachah follows the latter Sages; a group of three or more is allotted as much space as it needs even in a settled area (see *Rif; Rambam, Hil. Shabbos* 16:12; *Orach Chaim* 360:1).

אַרְבָּעָה דְבָרִים פָּטְרוּ בְּמַחֲנֶה: — *Four obligations* [lit. *matters*] *were waived* [lit. *they exempted*] *in a* [military] *camp:*

[Because the mishnah has mentioned a dispensation granted (according to R' Yehudah) only to a caravan, the mishnah goes on to list, tangentially, four instances where other exceptions are made for camps.]

These obligations were waived for a Jewish military camp on a campaign, even during מִלְחֶמֶת הָרְשׁוּת, *an optional war* (i.e., a war for territorial expansion,

עֵירוּבִין מִכָּל מָקוֹם; וּפְטוּרִים מֵרְחִיצַת יָדַיִם; וּמִדְּמַאי;
וּמִלְּעָרֵב. א/י

יד אברהם

even if sanctioned by the Sanhedrin), and certainly during מִלְחֶמֶת מִצְוָה, *a war ordained by God*, such as the wars waged by Joshua for the conquest of *Eretz Yisrael (Rav; Rashi;* from *Gem.* 17a).

Ritva notes that various opinions are listed in *Talmud Yerushalmi* as to what constitutes a camp. The opinions range from a low of ten, to 100 and 12,000. *Ritva* states that the authorities rule that ten soldiers are sufficient. R' Moshe Goldstein, editor of the Jerusalem edition of *Ritva*, demonstrates that this is what *Rambam* actually wrote in *Hil. Melachim* 6:13 (וְאֵין מַחֲנֶה פְּחוּתָה מֵעֲשָׂרָה) instead of (וְאֵין מֶחֱצָה פְּחוּתָה מֵעֲשָׂרָה).

מְבִיאִין עֵצִים מִכָּל מָקוֹם; — *They may bring wood from anywhere;*

They have the right to requisition wood belonging to others, even if the wood had been cut and bundled, and it is not considered robbery (*Rav; Rashi*). This is based on the principle of הֶפְקֵר בֵּית דִּין הֶפְקֵר, *the court may declare a property ownerless*, where it is deemed necessary (*Rav*).

וּפְטוּרִים מֵרְחִיצַת יָדַיִם; — *(and) they are exempt from washing hands;*

They may eat bread without first washing their hands as prescribed in halachah (*Gem.* 17b). R' Yehonasan adds that they are also exempted from washing their hands before prayer and may rely instead on other methods to cleanse their hands.

The *Gemara* (17b) states that they are, nevertheless, not exempted from the obligation to wash after eating (מַיִם אַחֲרוֹנִים). This obligation, based on health considerations (i.e., the residue of the salt used in Mishnaic times could damage the eyes on contact; it was therefore necessary to wash the hands before leaving the table; see *Tos.* 17b; *Orach Chaim* 181:1), cannot be waived even in a camp.

וּמִדְּמַאי; — *(and) from demai;*

Because many of the common people were lax in tithing their produce, Yochanan *Kohen Gadol* (together with

his *beis din*) decreed that all tithes (except for *terumah*) must be separated from produce bought from a Jew unless the seller is a חָבֵר, *chaver*, i.e., an individual known to be careful in the performance of these *mitzvos*. Since this obligation is only Rabbinic [on a Torah level one can rely on the fact that the majority of common people do separate the necessary tithes; see *Shabbos* 23a] it is relaxed in some circumstances (*Gem.* 17b; see prefatory note to 3:2).

Rav (Demai 3:1; cited by *Tos. Yom Tov* here) states (based on an opinion given in *Yerushalmi* there) that this dispensation is granted only on a temporary basis. When the camp stays in a place overnight they must separate tithes from the *demai*. However, *Rambam (Hil. Melachim* 6:13; *Ma'asros* 10:11) does not mention this restriction (see *Tos. Yom Tov* here and *Tos. Anshei Shem Demai* 3:1).

וּמִלְּעָרֵב. — *and from making an* eruv.

[In order to carry objects (on the Sabbath) from the private domain of one person to that of others an *eruvei chatzeiros* must be established (see General Introduction). For a military camp this Rabbinic stricture was relaxed so that the soldiers be permitted to carry from one tent to the other without restraint. Of course, only the requirement for *eruvei chatzeiros* was relaxed, not that necessitating partitions before carrying is permitted. The camp must be surrounded with adequate partitions as outlined in the previous mishnayos. (Obviously, this applies only when there is no battle under way, otherwise all Sabbath prohibitions are waived, as in any other life-threatening situation.)]

The *Gemara* (17b) notes that the requirement for *eruvei techumin* [for one who wishes to go beyond the maximum permitted distance (see Gen. Intro.)] is not relaxed for military camps (*Rav; Rambam;* from *Gem.* 17b).

The *Gemara* explains that this distinction is due to the Biblical status of the *techum*

bring wood from anywhere; they are exempt from washing hands; from *demai;* and from making an *eruv.*

prohibition. Now, as is stated several times in Talmud (see *Gem.* 79b, 103a; *Sotah* 5:3), there is a dispute between R' Akiva and the Sages whether the *techum* prohibition is Biblical or Rabbinic. As pointed out by *Tosafos* here, the Talmud itself assumes that the halachah is according to the Sages that it is only Rabbinic. Consequently, the halachah should be that soldiers in a camp are *not* required to make an *eruvei techumin.* This indeed is the opinion of most authorities (*Ramban* in *Milchamos;* *HaMaor;* *Tos.* 17b; *Rashba;* *Rosh;* and others).

Rambam (Hil. Melachim 6:11), however, rules that they are obligated to make an *eruvei techumin.* The explanation is given (by *Rashba* here and others) that in *Rambam's* view (see *Hil. Shabbos* 27:1) all *Tannaim* concur that there is a Biblical prohibition of *techumin.* They only disagree

with the length of that *techum.* The Sages maintain that it is 24,000 cubits (the length of Israel's camp in the wilderness). The Rabbis, however, limited the *techum* to 2,000 cubits. R' Akiva, however, considers 2,000 cubits to be the Biblical maximum. This view is based on a passage in *Yerushalmi* (*Eruvin* 3:4). Although, according to the Sages, the device of *eruvei techumin* is applicable only to a Rabbinical restriction, it is nevertheless viewed in a more stringent light, because it is modeled after a Biblical law. Consequently it is not waived even for a camp. The obligation for *eruvei chatzeiros,* however, has no Biblical counterpart, and is waived.

[The fact that the view cited in *Talmud Yerushalmi* is nowhere mentioned in *Talmud Bavli* is taken by most authorities as proof that this view is rejected by the (more authoritative) *Talmud Bavli.*]

Chapter 2

◄§ Public Wells

In Mishnaic times almost all public wells and springs were situated in the public domain (or *karmelis*). The springs and wells themselves were usually at least ten fists deep and four fists in length and width and thus qualified as private domains (see General Introduction). Obviously, then, it would be prohibited to draw water on the Sabbath from the well (a private domain) to the surface (a public domain or *karmelis*). This prohibition caused difficulty for the pilgrims en route to Jerusalem for the festivals. These pilgrims camped by the roadside for the Sabbath and it was difficult for them to prepare water for the Sabbath before it began. To alleviate this hardship the Sages decreed that the stringency of Rabbinic strictures concerning the validity of partitions be suspended around wells and springs and that only minimal partitions need be built. Thus minimum, makeshift partitions consisting of slats were erected around water sources and the pilgrims were permitted to draw water from them. However, it is clearly assumed (*Gem.* 20a) that the area surrounding the water source had to be considered a private domain on a Biblical level. The dispensation for pilgrims raises questions among the commentators as to the Biblical status of many of the strictures governing partitions. Two of these have already been mentioned (above 1:8): (a) In a partition the gaps may not exceed the walled portions; and (b) no gap may exceed ten cubits. Neither of these rules are observed in erecting slats. For a discussion of the halachic principles underlying these dispensations see commentary at end of mishnah 1.

The scope and extent of this dispensation is disputed. The *Gemara* (20b, 21a) states that the dispensation of slats outlined in the mishnah here was only for the livestock of the festival pilgrims (עוֹלֵי רְגָלִים); a person wishing to drink must climb into the well and drink his fill there. *Tosafos* (21a) explains that the *Gemara* means

עוֹשִׂין [א] פַּסִּין לְבֵירָאוֹת, אַרְבָּעָה דְיוּמְדִין
נִרְאִין כִּשְׁמוֹנָה — דִּבְרֵי רַבִּי
יְהוּדָה. רַבִּי מֵאִיר אוֹמֵר: שְׁמוֹנָה נִרְאִין כִּשְׁנֵים
עָשָׂר, אַרְבָּעָה דְיוּמְדִין וְאַרְבָּעָה פְּשׁוּטִין.
גּוֹבְהָן עֲשָׂרָה טְפָחִים, וְרוֹחְבָּן שִׁשָּׁה, וְעוֹבְיָין
כָּל שֶׁהוּא; וּבֵינֵיהֶן כִּמְלֹא שְׁתֵּי רְבָקוֹת שֶׁל שָׁלֹשׁ

יד אברהם

that one may not erect slats except where a need for pilgrims' livestock exists, and
that a partition of slats erected in the absence of such a need is invalid. Thus a
pilgrim traveling without any animals may not erect such a partition. But once such
a partition has been erected for valid reasons, all carrying, including drawing water
for a person, is permitted within that enclosure. This opinion seems to have been
accepted by *Rashba*, *Ritva* and *Ran* as well.

Furthermore, if the well is too wide for a person to climb in and out of, these slats
may also be erected for people (*Gem.* 21a).

1.

עוֹשִׂין פַּסִּין לְבֵירָאוֹת, — *They may erect
slats around wells,*

They refers to pilgrims going up to
Jerusalem for the festivals (*Gem.* 20b).[1]

The Sages permitted pilgrims to erect
a flimsy partition of slats around the
wells to enable them to draw water for
their animals. This is necessary because
the interior of a well is [usually] a
private domain whereas the area
surrounding it is either a public domain
or a *karmelis* (see prefatory note to this
chapter). By erecting a partition they
render the area within it a private
domain, and are permitted to draw
water from the well, bring their
livestock into the enclosure, and water
them there (*Rav*; *Rashi*).

אַרְבָּעָה דְיוּמְדִין נִרְאִין כִּשְׁמוֹנָה — דִּבְרֵי רַבִּי
יְהוּדָה. — *four double-posts which seem
like eight — [these are] the words of R'
Yehudah.*

[The slats which the Sages validated
as partitions for the wells are, at a

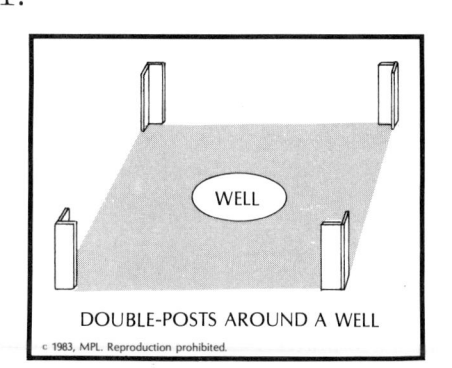

WELL

DOUBLE-POSTS AROUND A WELL

© 1983, MPL. Reproduction prohibited.

minimum, *four double-posts ...*]

A double-post is made by joining two
upright slats at right angles (see
diagram). Four such double-posts are
placed at the four corners of the area
surrounding the well. In this manner
each side is framed by two slats and is
considered a partition with a wide
entrance (*Rav*; *Rashi*).

The word דְיוֹמָד is a contraction of two
words, דְיוֹ, two (dyo is two in Greek; the
Gemara gives numerous examples where this

1. The definition of pilgrims is subject to debate. *Rashi* (21a), followed by *Ohr Zarua* (2:129),
Ritva and *Meiri*, broadens this to include all whose travel is for the purpose of a *mitzvah*.
However, the silence of all the later authorities (including *Tur* and *Shulchan Aruch*) on the
subject of slats for wells indicates that they accepted a strict interpretation of the term pilgrim.
Consequently, this halachah has no practical application in post-Temple times.

1. **T**hey may erect slats around wells, four double-posts which seem like eight — [these are] the words of R' Yehudah. R' Meir says: Eight which seem like twelve, four double-posts and four single ones.

Their height [is] ten fists, their width six, and their thickness any size whatsoever; and between them [is]

YAD AVRAHAM

Greek prefix was used in Talmudic phraseology), and עֲמוּד, post, i.e., double-posts (Gemara 18a).

רַבִּי מֵאִיר אוֹמֵר: שְׁמוֹנָה נִרְאִין כִּשְׁנֵים עָשָׂר, אַרְבָּעָה דְיוֹמְדִין וְאַרְבָּעָה פְּשׁוּטִין. — R' Meir says: Eight which seem like twelve, four double-posts and four single [lit. plain] ones.

R' Meir maintains that the open space allowed by R' Yehudah between the double-posts is too great and requires that an additional, single slat be placed in the middle of the open space to break up the breach (Rav; Rashi).

[The mishnah will outline further the size of the open space disputed by R' Meir and R' Yehudah. Surely when the double-posts are moved closer together, thus lessening the gap, no additional single slats are required even according to R' Meir. Conversely, when they are moved too far apart even R' Yehudah will require additional slats. The mishnah refers to a case where the gap is between ten and thirteen and one-third cubits. R' Meir holds that a gap of more than ten cubits disqualifies the partition and additional slats are needed, whereas R' Yehudah allows gaps up to 13⅓ cubits.]

Although the mishnah does not at this point make clear the size of the gap allowed by each Tanna, it does teach us that an oversize gap between the double-posts may be remedied with a single slat even according to R' Meir (Tos. Yeshanim and Tos. HaRosh).

גּוֹבְהָן עֲשָׂרָה טְפָחִים, — Their height [is] [i.e., must be] ten fists,

[This is the minimum height for any partition.]

וְרוֹחְבָּן שִׁשָּׁה, — (and) their width six, [I.e., one cubit.]

It is logical to assume that some minimum width is necessary to establish a partition. However, the requirement that the slats be at least a cubit wide is, in respect to the laws of Sabbath, only a Rabbinical stricture. In a parallel case concerning a succah a width of a fist suffices (Tos., Succah 4b, cited by Gilyon HaShas).

The dimensions given here refer to the double-posts mentioned earlier, leaving unclear the dimensions required of the single slats referred to by R' Meir. Obviously, these slats must conform to the ten fist minimum height because this height is fixed for all partitions without exception. There is a disagreement, however, concerning their width. Rashi, R' Yehonasan and Meiri (in Beis HaBechirah) assume that these slats, too, must each be six fists wide. Other authorities state that the requirement of six fists in width does not refer to these slats (Rashba, Ran, Meiri in Chidushim). Ritva asserts that this is the opinion accepted by most commentators who, however, disagree, as to what width is required for these slats. Some hold that they must be at least three fists wide (Ritva), while others assume that there is no minimum width at all (Rashba; Ran).

וְעוֹבְיָין כָּל שֶׁהוּא; — and their thickness any size whatsoever;

There is no reason for us to consider their thickness as long as their width defines a line of demarcation (Meiri).

וּבֵינֵיהֶן — and [the open space] between them

[The mishnah now specifies the maximum gap permitted for this enclosure, and will restate the disagreement between R' Meir and R' Yehudah in terms which clarify the maximum dimensions each one allows for a gap.]

עֵירוּבִין שָׁלֹשׁ בָּקָר — דִּבְרֵי רַבִּי מֵאִיר. רַבִּי יְהוּדָה
ב/ב אוֹמֵר: שֶׁל אַרְבַּע אַרְבַּע.
קְשׁוּרוֹת וְלֹא מֻתָּרוֹת; אַחַת נִכְנֶסֶת וְאַחַת
יוֹצֵאת.

[ב] מֻתָּר לְהַקְרִיב לַבְּאֵר, וּבִלְבַד שֶׁתְּהֵא
פָרָה רֹאשָׁהּ וְרֻבָּהּ בִּפְנִים וְשׁוֹתָה.

יד אברהם

כִּמְלֹא שְׁתֵּי רְבָקוֹת שֶׁל שָׁלֹשׁ שָׁלֹשׁ בָּקָר —
דִּבְרֵי רַבִּי מֵאִיר. — [is] [not more than] *the equivalent of two teams of three oxen each — [these are] the words of R' Meir.*

The *Gemara* (19a,b) cites a *baraisa* which clarifies this further. The average size of an ox is taken as one and two-thirds cubits in width so that one team of three oxen is five cubits wide and two teams are ten cubits wide. This is the maximum allowable width according to R' Meir. Therefore, in the first case given in the mishnah, where the gap is thirteen and one-third cubits, R' Meir requires a slat to be inserted to break up the gap (leaving two gaps — each less than ten cubits).

Thus, according to R' Meir no dispensation is given as far as the width of the gap is concerned (see above 1:1 and 1:8), whereas R' Yehudah feels that the ten cubit restriction on gaps was relaxed here. However, according to the view of *Rashi* and *Ramban* (see below, s.v. אַחַת יוֹצֵאת) here, too, a dispensation was granted — the fists used in measuring may be 'relaxed' ones (שׁוֹחֲקוֹת; see *Yad Avraham* to 1:1, s.v. מְעֻשָּׂרִים).

Meiri (Chiddushim) indicates that the disagreement between R' Yehudah and R' Meir extends to all facets of the laws of partitions. R' Yehudah allows gaps of thirteen and one-third cubits for all partitions but the mishnah (and the halachah) accepts his opinion only for wells where the need for leniency is indicated, not for regular partitions.

רַבִּי יְהוּדָה אוֹמֵר: שֶׁל אַרְבַּע אַרְבַּע. — *R' Yehudah says: [Two teams of] four [oxen] each.*

[Each team is six and two-thirds cubits wide and the maximum gap allowed measures thirteen and one-third

cubits across. In the first case of the mishnah, where R' Yehudah permitted the enclosure to be erected with only four double-posts, the gap was clearly not more than this maximum.]

R' Yehonasan explains that the standard is given of oxen (rather than cubits) because they are the basis for this halachah. The slats have to be sufficiently far apart to allow the passage of two teams between them because it frequently occurs that one team of oxen is entering the enclosure while another is exiting and we wish to avoid having the slats constantly knocked down and the necessity of setting them up every Friday. The typical team of oxen consisted of three oxen so that R' Meir felt that a gap greater than ten cubits need not be permitted, whereas R' Yehudah provided for teams of even four oxen.

קְשׁוּרוֹת וְלֹא מֻתָּרוֹת; — *Tied* [together] *but not loose;*

[The mishnah now returns to a description of the teams of oxen used by the *Tannaim* as their standard of measurement.] The oxen must be tied together so that they take up less space. A space measuring the equivalent of two loose teams of oxen disqualifies the partition (*Rav; Rashi*).

The *Gemara* (19a) explains that the mishnah reiterates *not loose* to stress that *tied* is meant literally. Otherwise, it might have been argued that tied means only closely grouped in contrast to widely spaced.

אַחַת נִכְנֶסֶת וְאַחַת יוֹצֵאת. — *one* [team] *enters and one exits.*

In this manner they require more room than two teams going in the same direction (*Rav; Rashi*).

Rashi (see also *Ritva*) and *Rambam* (*Comm.*) define this further and state that the

the equivalent of two teams of three oxen each — [these are] the words of R' Meir. R' Yehudah says: Four each.

Tied but not loose; one enters and one exits.

2. It is permitted to place [the slats] close to the well, provided that a cow has its head and most of its body within while drinking.

YAD AVRAHAM

difference between the two measurements is the difference between ten relaxed cubits (שׁוֹחֲקוֹת) and ten exact cubits (מְצוּמְצָמוֹת). If one makes the logical assumption that the exact cubit (being the antonym of 'relaxed') is the same as compressed cubit (עֲצוּבוֹת), one can clarify this further. As already mentioned (*comm.* to 1:1, s.v. מְעַשְׂרִים), *Rashba* holds that a cubit composed of relaxed fists is one half finger bigger (i.e., 1/60) than one with compressed fists. Thus, according to R' Meir the difference is 5 fingers, while according to R' Yehudah it is 6 2/3.

◆§ **Basis for Dispensation to Pilgrims**

The dispensation allowing minimum, makeshift partitions around water sources is based in the premise that Rabbinical restrictions should be relaxed because of the pilgrims' overriding need for water. However, it is clearly assumed that the area surrounding the water source has to be considered a private domain on a Biblical level (*Gem.* 20a). This dispensation raises questions regarding two strictures governing partitions: (a) gaps may not exceed the walled portion; and (b) no gap may exceed ten cubits. Neither of the rules is observed in erecting slats.

(a) Concerning the gaps exceeding walled parts there are two views. *Ravad* (cited in *Rashba* to 15b) maintains that on a Biblical level a partition can be formed even when the gaps exceed the walled portions and that its disqualification is strictly Rabbinic. [The statement in the *Gemara* (15b) that this rule is from the Oral Law given to Moses on Sinai is explained by *Ravad* in a novel manner. God, foreseeing Rabbinic legislation concerning partitions, informed Moses that the Sages would institute a rule invalidating a partition containing gaps exceeding the walled segments. Since, however, the rule did not take effect until the Rabbis decreed it, it was in their power to grant exceptions to it, as for pilgrims. A similar explanation is given by *Chachmas Shlomo* to 5b (see *Maharsha's* comments there).] Most commentators (*Tos.* 17b, *Rashba, Ritva* and others), however, understand it to be Biblical and they draw a distinction. Where the four corners of the enclosure are defined (as here), there is a semblance of four partitions (שָׁם אַרְבַּע מְחִצּוֹת; see *Gem.* 22a). This is sufficient to consider the area enclosed and the gaps therefore do not matter (Biblically). [The Rabbinic rule requiring that the gaps not exceed the walled segments in any case was relaxed here.] Where the corners are not defined, however, there is a Biblical rule disqualifying partitions whose gaps exceed the walled parts. The size of the gap allowed here is the subject of a disagreement between R' Meir and R' Yehudah (mish. 1).

(b) Concerning the disqualification of gaps greater than ten cubits, *Tosefos HaRosh* states that this, too, is only a Rabbinic rule (see *Tos. Shabbos* 6a-b and *Eruvin* 6b).

Chazon Ish (Orach Chaim 112:5-6) believes, however, that a gap of thirteen and one-third cubits does invalidate (on a Biblical level) a partition in a case where the gaps exceed the walled portions. However, *R' Yehonasan's* explanation for the determination of the thirteen and one-third cubit limit for the open space between the slats (cited above, s.v. רַבִּי יְהוּדָה) indicates that he views this limit as Rabbinic in any case.

2.

מֻתָּר לְהַקְרִיב לַבְּאֵר, — *It is permitted to place* [*the slats*] *close to the well,*

Thereby constricting the space within the enclosure (*Rav; Rashi*).

עירובין
ב/ג
מֻתָּר לְהַרְחִיק כָּל שֶׁהוּא, וּבִלְבַד שֶׁיַּרְבֶּה בְּפַסִּין.

[ג] **רַבִּי יְהוּדָה** אוֹמֵר: עַד בֵּית סָאתַיִם. אָמְרוּ לוֹ: ,,לֹא אָמְרוּ בֵּית סָאתַיִם אֶלָּא לְגִנָּה וּלְקַרְפֵּף. אֲבָל אִם הָיָה דִיר אוֹ סַהַר אוֹ מֻקְצֶה אוֹ חָצֵר, אֲפִלּוּ בֵּית חֲמֵשֶׁת כּוֹרִין, אֲפִלּוּ בֵּית עֶשְׂרָה כּוֹרִין, מֻתָּר. וּמֻתָּר

יד אברהם

domain to the public one (Rav; Rashi).

מֻתָּר לְהַרְחִיק כָּל שֶׁהוּא, — It is permitted to place [the slats] at any distance [from the well],

Thereby increasing the area inside the enclosure and the gap between the double-posts at the corners (Rav; Rashi).

וּבִלְבַד שֶׁיַּרְבֶּה בְּפַסִּין. — provided one increases the [number of] slats.

Single slats have to be placed at ten cubit intervals according to R' Meir (mish. 1) and thirteen and one-third cubit intervals according to R' Yehudah — the view accepted as halachah (Rav; Rashi).

וּבִלְבַד שֶׁתְּהֵא פָרָה רֹאשָׁהּ וְרֻבָּהּ בִּפְנִים וְשׁוֹתָה. — provided that a cow has its head and most of its body within [the enclosure] while drinking.

The Gemara (19a) defines this as two cubits, i.e., the distance from the openings between the slats to the rim of the well on all sides may not be less than two cubits. If the space is smaller there is concern that because of the narrowness of the space the animal will not actually enter the enclosure but will remain just outside it and the owner will then be drawn after the animal while carrying the water-filled bucket. He will thereby be carrying from the private

3.

רַבִּי יְהוּדָה אוֹמֵר: עַד בֵּית סָאתַיִם. — R' Yehudah says: Until [an area of] two beis-seah.

R' Yehudah disagrees with the previous mishnah that permits the slats to be placed at any distance. According to him, the area enclosed within these slats may not exceed two beis-seah [or fifty by one hundred cubits] (Rav; Rashi).

The seah is a volume measure and a בֵּית סָאה, beis-seah [lit. the house of a seah], is the area in which a seah of barley may be planted. The standard tract fit for planting a seah of barley seed is fifty cubits square and an area of

two beis-seah is therefore an area measuring fifty by one hundred cubits — which was the size of the courtyard of the מִשְׁכָּן, Tabernacle,[1] (Gem. 23b, see Ex. 27:18) — or 5,000 square cubits. This would make a square of slightly more than seventy cubits. [See first footnote to mishnah 5.]

אָמְרוּ לוֹ: ,,לֹא אָמְרוּ בֵּית סָאתַיִם אֶלָּא לְגִנָּה וּלְקַרְפֵּף. — They said to him: 'They did not state [the limit of] two beis-seah except in regard to a garden or a karpeif.

R' Yehudah's contemporaries agree that indeed the tradition recorded by R' Yehudah (from the Sages of an earlier

---

1. The two seah measurement was based on the Tabernacle dimensions obviously because of the general parallel drawn between the מְלָאכוֹת, labors, prohibited on the Sabbath and the construction of the Tabernacle (see ArtScroll Mishnah Shabbos, General Introduction).

2
3
It is permitted to place [the slats] at any distance, provided one increases the slats.

3. **R'** Yehudah says: Until two *beis-seah*.

They said to him: 'They did not state two *beis-seah* except in regard to a garden or *karpeif*. But if it was a fold, a corral, a backyard or a courtyard, even five *korin*, even ten *korin*, it is permissible. And

generation) concerning the difference between areas measuring two *beis-seah*, or less, and those of greater size, has validity. They disagree, however, with R' Yehudah's application of this rule. They argue that this rule applies only to gardens and *karpeifs* — not wells.

A garden or *karpeif* [a fenced-in area outside the town (such as those) used to store wood (*Rav; Rashi*)] is an area שֶׁלֹּא הוּקְפוּ לְדִירָה, *enclosed for purposes not related to (daily) living*, i.e., none of the routine functions of day-to-day life are performed in it. Such an area, if greater than two *beis-seah*, is Rabbinically viewed as a *karmelis* with all its attendant strictures (see General Introduction). A well, however, is considered as serving a purpose related to daily living because the water is used for human consumption (*Rav, Rashi from Gem. 22a*).[1] Consequently, the enclosure erected around it is considered as enclosed for living purposes, and therefore not subject to the limit of two *beis-seah*.

אֲבָל אִם הָיָה דִּיר — *But if it was a fold*, Tracts of land were enclosed and livestock were placed there temporarily so that their wastes would fertilize the fields (*Rav; Rashi*).

R' Yehonasan (and *Meiri*) stipulate that there be a hut for the herder (since the enclosure must be used by humans). Similarly, *Ritva* explains that the continuous

presence of the herder among his flock renders the area enclosed for (human) living, but he does not indicate that a hut is necessary.

או סַחַר — *(or) a corral*,
I.e., an enclosure for holding animals situated in town (*Rav, Rashi*).

Rambam (Comm.) has in his version סֹהַר, *a jail* (see *Rav* and *Tos. Yom Tov*). [Although a jail is a domicile of sorts it is nevertheless singled out for mention because it could have been argued that such forced habitation is not to be considered a habitation (see *Yoma* 10b and *Birkei Yosef, Yoreh Deah* 286:4 concerning a *mezuzah* for a jail).]

או מֻקְצֶה אוֹ חָצֵר, — *(or) a backyard or a courtyard*,
[In Talmudic times most houses faced a courtyard, and much of the daily business of living took place in the front courtyard. Some houses had an additional enclosed space in the back which was used mainly for storage. This backyard is not the same as a *karpeif* which is located at a distance from the house and entered only infrequently (see *Beur Halachah* to 358:1).]

אֲפִלּוּ בֵּית חֲמֵשֶׁת כּוֹרִין, אֲפִלּוּ בֵּית עֲשָׂרָה כּוֹרִין, מֻתָּר. — *even* [if it is an area of] *five* korin, *even ten* korin, *it is permissible* [to carry in it].

[A *kor* = 30 *seah*, thus a *beis-kor* covers 75,000 square cubits.]

The Sages reason that since even R' Yehudah agrees that the two *beis-seah*

---

1. The implication is that an area used exclusively for animals is not considered enclosed for living purposes (see *Beur Halachah* to 358:1, s.v. לדירה). *Rashi* (22a) adds the requirement that such an enclosure must be used for continual human traffic (i.e., not sporadically) in order to qualify as enclosed for living purposes.

עירובין לְהַרְחִיק כָּל שֶׁהוּא, וּבִלְבַד שֶׁיַּרְבֶּה בְּפַסִּין.״ ב/ד

[ד] רַבִּי יְהוּדָה אוֹמֵר: אִם הָיְתָה דֶרֶךְ הָרַבִּים מַפְסַקְתָּן, יְסַלְּקֶנָּה לַצְּדָדִין. וַחֲכָמִים אוֹמְרִים: אֵינוֹ צָרִיךְ. אֶחָד בּוֹר הָרַבִּים, וּבְאֵר הָרַבִּים, וּבְאֵר הַיָּחִיד, עוֹשִׂין לָהֶם פַּסִּין; אֲבָל לְבוֹר הַיָּחִיד, עוֹשִׂין לוֹ מְחִצָּה גְבוֹהַּ עֲשָׂרָה טְפָחִים — דִּבְרֵי רַבִּי עֲקִיבָא. רַבִּי יְהוּדָה בֶּן בָּבָא אוֹמֵר: אֵין עוֹשִׂין פַּסִּין אֶלָּא

יד אברהם

limitation does not apply to the circumstances cited here, it should not apply to a well surrounded with slats (Rashi, as interpreted by Ritva, 22a).

וּמֻתָּר לְהַרְחִיק כָּל שֶׁהוּא, — And it is permitted to place [the slats] at any distance,

The mishnah now concludes the Sages' argument. Having stated that a corral and the like are not subject to the two beis-seah limitation, they now explain that the enclosure of a well is similarly unlimited. Since the water in the well is fit for human consumption, it, too, is enclosed for living purposes (Rav; Rashi).

But R' Yehudah disagrees and points out that two types of enclosures are subject to the limitation of two beis-seah: (a) An area not enclosed for purposes of (human) living; (b) an area enclosed with partitions only marginally valid. (A similar example of this type of limitation is found in 1:10; see Yad Avraham there.) Although slats around a well cannot be made subject to the two beis-seah limit under the first qualifica-

tion, they are subject to it, according to R' Yehudah, under the second (Ritva to 22a).

Although the Sages agree to these two qualifications, they contend that the case of slats differs from that of a partition of ropes or stakes erected by the members of a caravan (above 1:9,10) in that it is permanent, whereas the partition erected by a caravan is temporary. Alternatively, here we are more lenient because of the needs of the festival pilgrims (Tos. 18a).

וּבִלְבַד שֶׁיַּרְבֶּה בְּפַסִּין.״ — provided one adds slats.'

[As one increases the size of the area being enclosed, the distance between the double-posts at the corners obviously increases, too. As a result, one must add as many slats as are needed so that no one gap is large enough to invalidate the partition. The maximum allowable gap is subject to the dispute in mishnah 1, R' Meir maintaining it is ten cubits while R' Yehudah holds it is thirteen and one-third cubits.]

The halachah follows the Sages (Rav; Rambam).

4.

רַבִּי יְהוּדָה אוֹמֵר: אִם הָיְתָה דֶרֶךְ הָרַבִּים מַפְסַקְתָּן, יְסַלְּקֶנָה לַצְּדָדִין. — R' Yehudah says: If the general traffic passes between them [lit. if the path of the public separates them], it must be diverted to the side.

If the flow of traffic passes between the slats, the enclosure is invalidated. To rectify this, we must set up the slats so that the traffic will not pass through them but be diverted around the enclosed area. R' Yehudah maintains it is permitted to place [the slats] at any distance, provided one adds slats.'

4. R' Yehudah says: If the general traffic passes between them, it must be diverted to the side. But the Sages say: It is unnecessary.

Whether a public cistern, a public well, or a private well — they may erect slats; but for a private cistern, they must erect a partition ten fists high — [these are] the words of R' Akiva. R' Yehudah ben Bava says: They may not erect slats except for a public well; but

YAD AVRAHAM

that the passage of traffic through any halachic partition invalidates that partition (Rav from Gem. 22a).

וַחֲכָמִים אוֹמְרִים: אֵינוֹ צָרִיךְ. — But the Sages say: It is unnecessary.

[The Sages disagree with R' Yehudah's premise and maintain that in this instance the partitions retain their validity even when the public passes through the gaps between them.] The halachah follows the opinion of the Sages (Rav, Rambam).

אֶחָד בּוֹר הָרַבִּים, וּבְאֵר הָרַבִּים, וּבְאֵר הַיָּחִיד, עוֹשִׂין לָהֶם פַּסִּין; — Whether a public cistern, a public well, or a private well — they may erect slats;

A well is fed from underground water sources; a cistern is a hole dug in the ground to collect rain water (Rambam).

אֲבָל לְבוֹר הַיָּחִיד, עוֹשִׂין לוֹ מְחִצָּה גְבוֹהָ עֲשָׂרָה טְפָחִים — דִּבְרֵי רַבִּי עֲקִיבָא. — but for a private cistern, they must erect a partition ten fists high — [these are] the words of R' Akiva.

Since the basis for the dispensation given for the use of slats was the need of the festival pilgrims for water, they are effective only as long as there is water. Therefore, a private cistern, which is apt

to run dry, is not granted this dispensation because it might lead to people needlessly carrying their utensils to draw water when the water has already been used up. Although this could happen at a public cistern as well, there is no need for concern there, since word of the non-availability of water at a public water hole spreads rapidly through a campsite. In contrast a private well is granted this dispensation because wells are not prone to dry up (Rav; Rashi).

רַבִּי יְהוּדָה בֶּן בָּבָא אוֹמֵר: אֵין עוֹשִׂין פַּסִּין אֶלָּא לִבְאֵר הָרַבִּים בִּלְבָד; — R' Yehudah ben Bava says: They may not erect slats except for a public well;

R' Yehudah ben Bava concurs with R' Akiva concerning a private cistern. He additionally excludes a public cistern because the dispensation was granted only for choice water (cistern water is generally unfit for human consumption — Gem. 21a; see Rashi),[1] and a private well, because the dispensation was granted to make water accessible to the broad public, and not for a chosen few who are given permission to use an individual's well (see Rav and Rashi).

Although in stating the dispensation of

---

1. Although the dispensation was granted primarily for the watering needs of animals, nevertheless the Sages stipulated that the water for which this dispensation is used be water fit for human consumption. This is because once dispensation was granted it was extended even to human needs. Therefore, R' Yehudah ben Bava argues, it is granted only where it will serve the needs of both humans and animals (Tos. 21a).

לְבְאֵר הָרַבִּים בִּלְבָד: וְלַשְׁאָר, עוֹשִׂין חֲגוֹרָה גְבוֹהַ
עֲשָׂרָה טְפָחִים.

[ה] **וְעוֹד** אָמַר רַבִּי יְהוּדָה בֶן בָּבָא: הַגִּנָּה
וְהַקַּרְפֵּף שֶׁהֵן שִׁבְעִים אַמָּה
וְשִׁירַיִים עַל שִׁבְעִים אַמָּה וְשִׁירַיִים מוּקֶפֶת גָּדֵר
גְּבוֹהַ עֲשָׂרָה טְפָחִים — מְטַלְטְלִין בְּתוֹכָהּ, וּבִלְבַד

יד אברהם

slats the *Tanna* of mishnah 1 speaks of wells and not cisterns, that mishnah cannot be cited in support of R' Akiva's view. The *Tanna* may have chosen this example merely to avoid having to differentiate between a public and private facility, which he would have had to do had he spoken about a cistern (*Gem.* 18a).

וְלַשְׁאָר, עוֹשִׂין חֲגוֹרָה גְבוֹהַ עֲשָׂרָה טְפָחִים. — *but for the others, they must erect an enclosure* [lit. *a belt*] *ten fists high.*

I.e., an enclosure made of ropes (see above 1:9-10) (*Rashi*). Others interpret the word חֲגוֹרָה simply as partition — not as ropes (*Tos.; R' Yehonasan*). *Meiri* assumes that it means a wall constructed of uprights and horizontals

(שְׁתִי וָעֵרֶב), and excludes a partition of ropes.

Ritva accepts *Rashi*'s interpretation but sees a disagreement here between R' Akiva, whose use of the term מְחִצָּה, *partition*, is seen to exclude a partition of ropes, and R' Yehudah ben Bava who does accept such a partition. It is, however, not explained why such a partition should not be valid, at least for an area less than two *beis-seah* (see *Tos. R' Akiva* to this mishnah and *Keren Orah* to 21a). *Tosefos HaRosh* also objects to reading into the text a disagreement between R' Akiva and R' Yehudah ben Bava concerning the type of partition needed. The halachah follows R' Yehudah ben Bava (*Rav, Rambam* from *Gem.* 23a).

5.

The mishnah now elaborates on a topic mentioned previously only incidentally (mish. 3) — the status of an area enclosed for a purpose not related to daily living. The mishnah will define precisely the dimensions of an area in this classification in which one may carry. As already mentioned, an area in this classification is given all the restrictions of a *karmelis*; i.e., one may not carry from it to either a public or private domain, nor further than four cubits within the area itself. *Rashi* (67b) explains that a large area which is uninhabited can be confused with a public domain. It is therefore given the strictures attendant to a public domain while retaining its Biblical status (and restrictions) as a private domain (*Gem.*

67b). [Thus, if one were to carry into it from a public domain, he would be liable for a sin offering.]

וְעוֹד אָמַר רַבִּי יְהוּדָה בֶן בָּבָא: — *Additionally, R' Yehudah ben Bava said:*

In addition to the stricture with regard to slats around a watering hole (previous mishnah), he stated yet another stricture (*Rav*, from *Gem.* 23a).

הַגִּנָּה וְהַקַּרְפֵּף — *A garden or a* karpeif

[As mentioned in mishnah 3 a garden or a *karpeif* is considered enclosed for a purpose other than living and is subject to the restrictions of this status.]

שֶׁהֵן שִׁבְעִים אַמָּה וְשִׁירַיִים עַל שִׁבְעִים אַמָּה וְשִׁירַיִים — *that is seventy cubits and a fraction* [lit. *remainder*] *by seventy*

for the others, they must erect an enclosure ten fists high.

5. Additionally, R' Yehudah ben Bava said: A garden or a *karpeif* that is seventy cubits and a fraction by seventy cubits and a fraction and is enclosed by a fence ten fists high — we may carry

YAD AVRAHAM

cubits and a fraction

This size is based on the dimensions of the Courtyard of the מִשְׁכָּן, *Tabernacle*, which is fifty by one hundred cubits (*Ex.* 27:18), or 5,000 square cubits. When squared out this comes to seventy cubits and a fraction by seventy cubits and a fraction.[1] Although the prohibition to carry in such an area is only Rabbinic, a Biblical allusion is cited in support of it (*Gem.* 23b).

The Courtyard of the Tabernacle was used as the standard for several reasons. Firstly, the structure and indeed the very identification of all of the מְלָאכוֹת, [primary] *labors*, is derived from the activities of the Tabernacle (see ArtScroll Mishnah *Shabbos*, General Introduction). Secondly, the Courtyard of the Tabernacle is itself an example of

a large area enclosed for a purpose other than living [and thus demonstrates that an area of such dimensions can yet be considered properly enclosed and an area in which one may carry; since this is the largest area in which permission to carry can be established, the Sages adopted it as the limit with anything larger being prohibited] (*Tos.*). The Sages did not want to prohibit carrying in an area equal to or less than the Courtyard of the Tabernacle because the *Kohanim* did carry objects within this enclosure on the Sabbath (*Shulchan Aruch HaRav* 358:3).

מוּקֶּפֶת גָּדֵר גָּבוֹהַּ עֲשָׂרָה טְפָחִים — *and is enclosed by a fence ten fists high —*

[The minimum height for a partition.]

מְטַלְטְלִין בְּתוֹכָהּ, — *we may carry* [lit. *move* (objects)] *within it,*

1. The method commonly used today for the derivation of square roots is a relatively recent mathematical innovation and differs greatly from the method used in earlier times. The calculations made by the Rishonim to find the square root of 5,000 is as follows:

Take the fifty cubits by which the length exceeds the width [i.e., of a rectangle 50x100 cubits] and surround the remaining fifty cubit square with them and you will have a square of seventy cubits and four fists. How is this so? Make [from the extra square] five strips, each ten cubits wide and fifty cubits long. Place one of these strips on the eastern border [of the remaining square] and one on the west. The dimensions are now seventy by fifty cubits. Place one strip on the north and another on the south. The configuration now measures seventy by seventy except that each corner is missing ten cubits square as a result of the additions to the original. Take from the fifty [i.e., the fifth strip of fifty by ten cubits cut from the extra square] four pieces, each ten by ten and fill the four corners with them. Now one strip ten by ten cubits, which equals sixty by sixty fists, remains. Cut this into thirty strips, each ten cubits long and two fists wide. The total length of these strips is three hundred cubits. Place seventy along each border. The configuration now measures seventy cubits and four fists by seventy cubits and four fists, except that the corners are each missing two fists by two fists. A strip twenty cubits long is left in your hand. Take eight fists from it and fill in the corners. You are now left with a length eighteen cubits and four fists by two fists. This amount is the slight difference [about which R' Akiva and the Sages are in disagreement, see below]. If you were to further divide this piece and surround [the square] with it, the addition would not even equal two-thirds of a fingerbreadth [to each side], for you would need a strip two hundred eighty-two cubits and four fists to surround the four sides (*Rashi* 23a).

עֵירוּבִין שֶׁיְּהֵא בָהּ שׁוֹמֵרָה, אוֹ בֵית דִּירָה, אוֹ שֶׁתְּהֵא
ב/ה סְמוּכָה לָעִיר.
רַבִּי יְהוּדָה אוֹמֵר: אֲפִלוּ אֵין בָּהּ אֶלָּא בּוֹר
וְשִׁיחַ וּמְעָרָה, מְטַלְטְלִין בְּתוֹכָהּ.

יד אברהם

[I.e., one may transport objects for distances greater than four cubits just as in any private domain.]

וּבִלְבַד שֶׁיְּהֵא בָהּ שׁוֹמֵרָה, — *provided it contains a watchman's hut,*

A hut (similar to a succah) which can be used night or day the year-round by herders or watchmen (R' Yehonasan cited by Tos. Yom Tov).

אוֹ בֵית דִּירָה, — *or a dwelling,*

A bona fide dwelling for the owner to live in, although it is used only sporadically (ibid; Meiri). [This explains why dwelling is listed after hut.]

אוֹ שֶׁתְּהֵא סְמוּכָה לָעִיר. — *or it is near a city.*

If the garden or *karpeif* is close to the city, neither a hut nor a dwelling is required to permit carrying within it, because the area is constantly used by the owner to walk and relax in (ibid.).

Near a city is defined as within the 2,000 cubit radius which is the Sabbath *techum* (R' Yehonasan).

Accordingly, the person to whom this prohibition applies either spent the Sabbath in the area of the garden or *karpeif* or arrived there on the Sabbath by having made an *eruvei techumin* (enabling him to walk beyond the *techum*; see Gen. Intro.).

Meiri quotes other opinions which hold that only the (approximately) seventy cubits immediately abutting the city [which are considered part of the city for the purpose of

measuring the *techum* (see 5:2)] are considered near the city.

R' Yehudah ben Bava refers not only to areas seventy cubits square but also to any area less than this. According to R' Yehudah ben Bava, this figure excludes only carrying in areas greater than this, even when they contain a watchman's hut, etc. (Tos. and others).

There are two opinions about why this should be so. *Rashi* and *Rav* state that the presence of a watchman's hut,[1] etc., does give the area the status of enclosed for living purposes. Nonetheless, R' Yehudah ben Bava prohibits carrying within *any* area if it is greater than seventy cubits square. This would mean that the seemingly unanimous statement (above mishnah 3) permitting carrying in an area enclosed for the purposes of living, even [if it is] an area of five *korin*, is actually subject to a disagreement, with R' Yehudah ben Bava (here) dissenting.

Tosafos, however, explains that this problem in *Rashi's* interpretation may be resolved by assuming that there are two levels of 'living,' each with its own set of rules. In an area enclosed for bona fide constant and continuous living, i.e., it adjoins a proper dwelling occupied permanently, one may carry even if the area is greater than the seventy cubit square limit. An area enclosed for a lesser degree of living, such as those mentioned here,[2] is subject to the seventy cubit square limitation. If it does not have

1. The criterion for determining the status of an enclosure is whether it was enclosed for the purposes of living. If an area was enclosed for a purpose other than living but was later converted to a function defined as for living purposes, its status as a *karmelis* remains unchanged. The determining factor is not the actual use of the area, but the purpose for which the partition enclosing it was intended (Gem. 24a). Ostensibly, *Rashi* understands that the watchman's hut, etc. mentioned here preceded the enclosure (פֶּתַח וּלְבַסּוֹף הוּקַף), thus satisfying this requirement (Tos. HaRosh and Tos. R' Peretz).

2. According to this interpretation, it is necessary to make a distinction between the fold and corral mentioned in mishnah 3, which are considered properly enclosed for living purposes (and in which one may carry even if it is more than seventy cubits square), and the watchman's

2
5

within it, provided it contains a watchman's hut, or a dwelling, or it is near a city.

R' Yehudah says: Even if it contains only a cistern, a ditch or a cave, we may carry in it.

YAD AVRAHAM

either of these qualities, carrying is prohibited in it even if the area is seventy cubit square or less.

A slightly differing approach is assumed by most authorities (*Tos., Rashba, Ritva, Ran* and *Meiri*). The presence of the conditions outlined here do not classify the area as enclosed for living purposes.[1] Furthermore, R' Yehudah ben Bava agrees with all the other *Tannaim* that in areas seventy cubits square or less the classification enclosed for living purposes is not necessary. However, he adds the requirement that even in such areas a token of living (such as listed here) is necessary; in areas greater than seventy cubits square these tokens of living are insufficient.

רַבִּי יְהוּדָה אוֹמֵר: — *R' Yehudah says:*

[Whenever R' Yehudah is mentioned in a mishnah without his father's name being given, it refers to R' Yehudah ben R' Ilai, not to be confused with the R' Yehudah ben Bava of the first part of our mishnah.]

אֲפִלּוּ אֵין בָּה אֶלָּא בּוֹר וְשִׁיחַ וּמְעָרָה, — *Even if it* [i.e., the enclosure] *contains only a cistern, a ditch or a cave,*

בּוֹר is a [circular] pit [dug for water], שִׁיחַ is a rectangular one (see *Bava Kamma* 50b), while מְעָרָה, cave, refers to a water hole inside a cave. Others

explain *cave* as having nothing to do with water holes. Rather, it refers to a cave in a field where people go to cool off from the sun (*R' Yehonasan*).

מְטַלְטְלִין בְּתוֹכָה. — *we may carry in it.*

R' Yehudah concurs with R' Yehudah ben Bava that even for an area seventy cubits square or less some type of living is necessary in order for carrying in it to be permitted. He differs, however, as to the level of living required. According to him a mere water hole is sufficient to serve as a token of living (*Meiri*).

This raises questions concerning *Rashi's* view (quoted above in mishnah 3, s.v. אָמְרוּ לוֹ) that an enclosure put up around a water hole is considered enclosed for living purposes, whereas our mishnah considers it only a token of living, and not valid to permit carrying in an area greater than seventy cubits square. Two answers offered by the commentators are: (a) Our mishnah's water hole is effective even when it is dry; it is then considered only a token of living. (b) A water source confers living status upon an area only when there is no other water source prepared for the festival pilgrims). Our mishnah, speaks of a place where other water is readily available [such as from a

hut discussed here, which is classified as only partially enclosed for living purposes (and which is therefore limited to seventy cubits square). In the former case, the area is used by the herder continually, whereas in the latter, the hut is used only sporadically (*Tos.;* see *Beur Halachah* to 362:1, s.v. כדי לשמור). It follows then that *Rashi* disagrees with *R' Yehonasan's* definition of שׁוֹמְרָה (as a hut used continually) mentioned earlier (s.v. שׁוֹמְרָה).

1. The reasons why the conditions mentioned here are not classified as for living purposes are different for each of the given conditions:

(a) A watchman's hut — *Tosafos* implies that actually such a hut should qualify as a living area. However, the mishnah speaks of a hut placed in the area that had already been enclosed (see above note 1 and *Gem.* 24a). *Rashba* and *Ran* argue that a watchman's hut is intrinsically not considered a living area because the watchman lives there only to watch the enclosure, not as his actual residence (see *Rashi* 15a, s.v. משום בית דירה).

(b) A dwelling — All concur that this is considered a proper living area. The mishnah speaks of a case where the enclosure preceded the dwelling.

(c) Near to the city — Nearness cannot confer a living status upon a place which is not actually used for living purposes.

רַבִּי עֲקִיבָא אוֹמֵר: אֲפִלּוּ אֵין בָּהּ אַחַת מִכָּל
אֵלּוּ, מְטַלְטְלִין בְּתוֹכָהּ, וּבִלְבַד שֶׁיְּהֵא בָּהּ שִׁבְעִים
אַמָּה וְשִׁירַיִם עַל שִׁבְעִים אַמָּה וְשִׁירַיִם.
רַבִּי אֱלִיעֶזֶר אוֹמֵר: אִם הָיְתָה אָרְכָּהּ יָתֵר עַל
רָחְבָּהּ אֲפִלּוּ אַמָּה אַחַת, אֵין מְטַלְטְלִין בְּתוֹכָהּ.
רַבִּי יוֹסֵי אוֹמֵר: אֲפִלּוּ אָרְכָּהּ פִּי שְׁנַיִם בְּרָחְבָּהּ,
מְטַלְטְלִין בְּתוֹכָהּ.

‏[ו] **אָמַר** רַבִּי אֶלְעָאי: ,,שָׁמַעְתִּי מֵרַבִּי
אֱלִיעֶזֶר: ,וַאֲפִלּוּ הִיא כְּבֵית כּוֹר.' וְכֵן

יד אברהם

brook passing in front of the enclosure] (Meiri; Rashba).

רַבִּי עֲקִיבָא אוֹמֵר: אֲפִלּוּ אֵין בָּהּ אַחַת מִכָּל אֵלּוּ, מְטַלְטְלִין בְּתוֹכָהּ, — *R' Akiva says: Even if it contains none of these, one may carry within it,*

[R' Akiva rejects the premise advanced by R' Yehudah ben Bava (and R' Yehudah) and rules that an area less than seventy cubits square does not need even a token of living in it in order to permit carrying within it. The prohibition against carrying in a *karpeif* applies only to an area greater than seventy cubits square and in that case only a true enclosure for living purposes suffices to remove the prohibition.]

The halachah follows R' Akiva (Gem. 23b).

וּבִלְבַד שֶׁיְּהֵא בָּהּ שִׁבְעִים אַמָּה וְשִׁירַיִם עַל שִׁבְעִים אַמָּה וְשִׁירַיִם. — *provided that its area is* [not greater than] *seventy cubits and a fraction by seventy cubits and a fraction.*

The *Gemara* (23b) remarks that essentially R' Akiva's view is the same as that of the Sages in mishnah 3 ('They said to him: They did not state [the limit of] two *beis-seah* ...') However, he differs slightly on the maximum area allowed for a *karpeif* enclosed for purposes other than living. The Sages give the maximum as two *beis-seah*, i.e., 5,000 square cubits, exactly as the

Tabernacle Courtyard. R' Akiva, however, holds that the maximum area allowed is the figure closest to 5,000 square cubits which can be made into a square whose sides are composed of whole large units. This comes to seventy cubits and four fists by seventy cubits and four fists (Rav; Rashi). The halachah follows the Sages rather than R' Akiva on this point (Rav).

Any calculation more exact would require us to include even fractions of fingerbreadths in the computation [see first footnote to this mishnah]. *Rambam (Comm.)* takes a different approach. He prefaces his commentary by saying that the exact square root of 5,000 is impossible to arrive at and only approximations are possible. Accordingly, R' Akiva uses the figure 70 2/3 cubits square [presumably because this fraction is the closest using an easily calculable number in the cubit system which does not exceed 5,000 square cubits]. The Sages pick the fraction 70 5/7 cubits [the closest fraction not falling below 5,000 square cubits, although it exceeds it by about half a square cubit].

[Rambam also offers the possibility that both R' Akiva and the Sages use smaller, more exact fractions. The disagreement seems to be whether one picks the closest fraction below 5,000 square cubits, or the fraction above this sum.]

רַבִּי אֱלִיעֶזֶר אוֹמֵר: אִם הָיְתָה אָרְכָּהּ יָתֵר עַל רָחְבָּהּ אֲפִלּוּ אַמָּה אַחַת, אֵין מְטַלְטְלִין בְּתוֹכָהּ. — *R' Eliezer says: If its length exceeds its width by even one cubit, we may not*

R' Akiva says: Even if it contains none of these, one may carry within it, provided that its area is seventy cubits and a fraction by seventy cubits and a fraction.

R' Eliezer says: If its length exceeds its width by even one cubit, we may not carry in it.

R' Yose says: Even if its length is double its width, we may carry in it.

6. **S**aid R' Ilai: 'I have heard from R' Eliezer, "Even if it is as a *beis-kor*." And I also heard from

YAD AVRAHAM

carry in it.

The *Gemara* (23b) demonstrates from a *baraisa* that what is really meant is that the length may not exceed double the width (see *Tos. R' Akiva's* comment on *Rav*). In the Tabernacle Courtyard (which serves as the model for the maximum size of the area) the ratio of the length to the width was two to one. R' Eliezer is of the opinion that just as the area must conform to the Tabernacle in total size, so, too, must it conform to its general dimensions. However, anything between a square and a rectangle of two to one ratio is permitted.

רַבִּי יוֹסֵי אוֹמְרוּ אֲפִלּוּ אָרְכָּה הוּ שְׁנַיִם בְּרָחְבָּה
בְּתוֹכָהּ. — *R' Yose says: Even if its length is double its width, we may*

carry in it.

[In contrast to R' Akiva who had spoken about an area seventy by seventy cubits, implying it must be a square, R' Yose states that even a rectangle (or a circular area; *Orach Chaim* 358:1) is permitted as long as the length does not exceed the width by more than double.]

The *Gemara* (23b) points out that although R' Yose's view seems identical with R' Eliezer's, there is a difference between them. R' Eliezer means that even the diagonal may not exceed double the width. R' Yose, however, holds that as long as the length does not exceed double the width one may carry within the area (*R' Chananel, Rif, Tos.* and *Rambam*; cf. *Rashi*). The halachah is as R' Yose (*Gem.* 23b).

6.

אָמַר רַבִּי אִלְעַאי: — *Said R' Ilai:*

[R' Ilai was the father of the R' Yehudah so frequently mentioned in the mishnah and a disciple of R' Eliezer (*Seder HaDoros*, in *Seder Tannaim VaAmoraim*).]

שָׁמַעְתִּי מֵרַבִּי אֱלִיעֶזֶר: וַאֲפִלּוּ הִיא כְּבֵית
כּוֹר. — *'I have heard from R' Eliezer, "Even if it is* [as large] *as a* beis-kor."

R' Ilai refers back to the disagreement in the previous mishnah concerning the limit of two *beis-seah* for an enclosed garden or *karpeif* (*Rav*).

[R' Ilai maintains that a *beis-kor* rather than two *beis-seah* is the limit and derives this from allusions in Scripture (see *Gem.* 26a). A *kor* is thirty *seah* and a *beis-kor* is therefore the area in which thirty *seah* can be planted. This translates into 75,000 square cubits (fifteen times the size of the other opinion) or a square of approximately 273 5/6 by 273 5/6 cubits.]

He disputes the version of R' Eliezer's opinion quoted in the previous mishnah, in

שָׁמַעְתִּי מִמֶּנּוּ: ,אַנְשֵׁי חָצֵר שֶׁשָּׁכַח אֶחָד מֵהֶן וְלֹא
עֵרֵב — בֵּיתוֹ אָסוּר מִלְּהַכְנִיס וּלְהוֹצִיא לוֹ, אֲבָל
לָהֶם מֻתָּר.' וְכֵן שָׁמַעְתִּי מִמֶּנּוּ שֶׁיּוֹצְאִין בְּעֵקְרַבְנִין

יד אברהם

which R' Eliezer seems to concur with the
figure of seventy cubits square as stated by
R' Yehudah ben Bava and R' Akiva and
disagrees only as to the shape this area may
take (Ritva).

[Cf. Tos. HaRosh and Shinuyei Nuschaos
note that some versions have R' Elazar (not
R' Eliezer).]

R' Yehonasan and Meiri suggest that even
according to R' Ilai the figure seventy cubits
square has halachic validity, but that he
restricts its application to a בִּקְעָה, valley,
whose partitions are not readily identifiable
as such. [Since its partitions are made up of
the slopes of the surrounding hills (over
which people travel), they are not readily
identified in the popular mind as being
partitions although they are legally valid as
such (see Shabbos, 100a הַמִּתְלַקֵּט).] A תֵּל
garden or a karpeif, although not enclosed
for living purposes, nevertheless has readily
identifiable partitions, and is therefore
subject only to the restriction of the greater
figure — beis-kor.

The halachah does not follow R' Ilai (Rav;
Rambam).

וְכֵן שָׁמַעְתִּי מִמֶּנּוּ: — And I also heard from
him,

[I.e., R' Ilai continued to list other
rulings he had heard from R' Eliezer.]

This segment of the mishnah and the
next have no relationship at all to the
subject matter of this chapter, and are
placed here only because their author
was the same as that of the opening
segment of this mishnah — R' Ilai
testifying in the name of R' Eliezer. For
an explanation of such groupings see
the Geonic responsum cited further in
chapter 3 (in a note to mishnah 1, s.v.
הַנּוֹדֵר). The topics treated here are
discussed in the mishnah each in its
appropriate place (Eruvin 6:3 and
Pesachim 2:6), but in neither case is R'
Ilai's opinion mentioned.

אַנְשֵׁי חָצֵר שֶׁשָּׁכַח אֶחָד מֵהֶן וְלֹא עֵרֵב, —
"If one of the residents of a courtyard
forgot and did not participate in the

eruv —

The first of these segments deals with
eruvei chatzeiros. As explained in the
General Introduction, if a courtyard is
shared by all the houses opening into it,
one may not, under Rabbinic law, carry
from the houses to the yard unless an
eruvei chatzeiros has been made. This
symbolically unites all the various
houses into one 'household' or 'family.'
It follows, however, that if one of the
houses forgets to contribute, even if all
the other residents of the courtyard
have contributed toward an eruv, none
of the people may carry. However, the
situation can be remedied even after the
Sabbath has begun (when an eruv
cannot be made) by employing the
device of בִּיטוּל רְשׁוּת, nullification of
rights, wherein the forgetful member
renounces, for the duration of the
Sabbath, his right to use of the
courtyard (see further 6:2-3). As a
result, the courtyard is viewed as
belonging only to those who had
participated in the eruv and carrying is
permitted; the resident who forgot to
join the eruv is now considered a guest
visiting the others. This procedure is
effective even on the Sabbath (Rav from
Gem. 26b).

בֵּיתוֹ אָסוּר מִלְּהַכְנִיס וּלְהוֹצִיא לוֹ, — his
house is forbidden to him with regard to
bringing into it [from the courtyard]
and taking out of it [into the courtyard],

If he carries from his house to the
courtyard, it is as if he has retracted his
nullification and is again treating this
domain as his own. The courtyard
thereby reverts back to its original
status wherein carrying was prohibited
(Rav; Rashi). [See also Ravad quoted by
Rashba for an alternate explanation.]

The principle that carrying from one's
home to the courtyard indicates a retraction
of the previous nullification is undisputed

him, "If one of the residents of a courtyard forgot
and did not participate in the *eruv* — his house is
forbidden to him with regard to bringing into it and
taking out of it, but it is permitted to them." And I
also heard from him that one fulfills his obligation on
Pesach with *akravnin*. But I made the rounds of all

YAD AVRAHAM

(see further 6:3). Ostensibly, the underlying
idea is that merely using one's house does not
indicate retraction because even under the
guest status one would use the house.
Transferring objects from the house to
another location, however, is regarded as a
demonstration of ownership and is thereby a
retraction; this is not the typical behavior of a
guest.

אֲבָל לָהֶם מֻתָּר. — *but it is permitted to them."*

It is permitted for the other members
of the courtyard to carry from the courtyard even into his house and from his
house into the courtyard.

Since they have an *eruv* and he — the
only resident not participating in the
eruv — has nullified his rights, all the
residents who retain rights have
participated in the *eruv*. The only
reason it is prohibited to the one who
nullified his rights is because that would
constitute a retraction of the nullification. This, obviously, applies only to
him.

The Gemara (26b) points out that R'
Eliezer assumes that one who nullifies his
rights to the domain relinquishes not only his
rights in the courtyard but also his rights in
the house. Consequently, both the house and
the courtyard are considered to be under the
sole control of those participating in the *eruv*
and they may, therefore, carry from one to
the other. The Sages (see further 6:3)
disagree and maintain that only the courtyard
is meant. Accordingly, while the courtyard is
considered the property of those participating in the *eruv*, the house remains the

property of its owner. As a consequence,
nobody may carry from the courtyard to the
house because they would be carrying from a
domain owned (solely) by the participants in
the *eruv* to one owned by someone else.

The *Gemara* concludes that if one
explicitly specifies that the house is not
included in the nullification, R' Eliezer agrees
with the Sages. Conversely, if one explicitly
nullifies his rights in the house, the Sages
agree to R' Eliezer's ruling. Their disagreement is only on how to interpret a general
statement of nullification.

The halachah follows the Sages (*Rav,
Rambam*). [See further in 6:3.]

וְכֵן שָׁמַעְתִּי מִמֶּנּוּ שֶׁיּוֹצְאִין בַּעֲקַרְבְּנִין בְּפֶסַח.
— *And I also heard from him that one
fulfills his obligation on Pesach with
akravnin.*

One can fulfill his obligation to eat
maror (bitter herbs) with the species
named *akravnin*.

The *Gemara* (26b) defines *akravnin*
as a vine which grows around (or near;
see *Tos. Chadashim*) date palms[1]
(*Rashi*). A gloss in *Rambam's* Commentary (see ed. Kafich) states that it owes
its name to the shape of its leaves which
look something like an *akrav* (עַקְרָב),
scorpion.

The mishnah in *Pesachim* (2:6) lists five
species of *maror*, omitting *akravnin*. Some
authorities maintain that the list of five
species enumerated in *Pesachim* (2:6) is not
meant to exclude other bitter vegetables
possessing the identifying characteristics
given by the Talmud (there 39a). Rather, the
fifth variety listed there, *maror*, is a generic

---

1. *Tosefos HaRosh* remarks, on the basis of *Pesachim* 39a, that *maror* must be a vegetable,
and concludes that this too is a vegetable which exhibits characteristics similar to a vine by
curling around the trunks of trees.
   This is not the same as *cherchavina* in *Pesachim* 2:6 which is also described in the *Gemara*
(there 39a) as a vine around the date palm. There are two such vines, the one mentioned in
Pesachim and the one mentioned here (*Tos.* 26b).

[א] בַּכֹּל מְעָרְבִין וּמִשְׁתַּתְּפִים, חוּץ מִן הַמַּיִם וּמִן הַמֶּלַח.

יד אברהם

term embracing all bitter herbs, and is not the name of a specific species (Meiri; R' Aharon HaLevi; Rama, Orach Chaim 473:5).

Consistent with this approach, Meiri explains the dispute between R' Eliezer and the Sages as based on the following:

Akravnin is intrinsically a bitter herb and as such should be valid as maror. However, because of its proximity to the date palm it absorbs a sweet taste. R' Eliezer upholds its validity on the basis of the intrinsic bitterness of the herb, while the Sages disqualify it because of its acquired sweetness.

However, there is another view that maror is a specific species, and that only the five species listed in Pesachim are valid [according to the Sages] (see Mishnah Berurah and Beur Halachah to 473:5). Accordingly, it is logical to assume that this premise is at the core of the disagreement. The Sages were the recipients of a tradition limiting the valid species to five, thus excluding akravnin. R' Eliezer either had a different tradition giving six valid species, or one that any bitter herb is valid, not just the five listed in the mishnah in Pesachim.

וְחָזַרְתִּי עַל כָּל תַּלְמִידָיו וּבִקַּשְׁתִּי לִי חָבֵר, — But I made the rounds of all his students and sought corroboration [lit. for a

comrade for myself],

[R' Ilai searched for a fellow student among R' Eliezer's disciples who also remembered hearing these three halachos from R' Eliezer.]

וְלֹא מָצָאתִי." — yet I did not find [anyone].'

[He found none that had any recollection of these statements being made by R' Eliezer.]

The Gemara (Pesachim 39a) records R' Ilai's statement, 'but I made the rounds ... and sought corroboration' with this addition, 'until I came to R' Eliezer ben Yaakov who concurred with my words.' This does not contradict the impression created in our mishnah that R' Ilai never did find corroboration among R' Eliezer's disciples. R' Eliezer ben Yaakov was not a disciple of R' Eliezer (see Seder HaDoros in Seder Tannaim VaAmoraim, s.v. רבי אליעזר בן יעקב). Furthermore, he sought someone who had actually heard R' Eliezer make these statements (as he had). R' Eliezer ben Yaakov did not profess to have heard them from R' Eliezer; he merely agreed that the halachos were true (Tos. 26b).

Chapter 3

⁕§ Techum and Eruvei Techumin

As explained in the General Introduction, a person may not go more than 2,000 cubits from his place of dwelling on the Sabbath or festivals. This 2,000 cubit limit is known as his techum, Sabbath boundary.

The מָקוֹם שְׁבִיתָה, place of dwelling, is generally defined as the place where the person happened to be at the onset of the Sabbath. However, as will be explained in the next two chapters, it can be changed to other places by the use of various legal devices.

One who finds it necessary to go to a location beyond this limit can do so by preparing an eruvei techumin[1] [or, for short, an eruv] before the Sabbath. In effect, what this does is to establish his legal מָקוֹם שְׁבִיתָה, place of dwelling, somewhere between his actual location and the place to which he wants to go on the next day.

his students and sought corroboration, yet I did not find.'

1. **A**ny [food] may be used to make an *eruv* or a *shituf*, except water and salt.

YAD AVRAHAM

This does not give him more than the 2,000 cubit limit; it merely shifts the point from which it is measured. For example, if one sets the *eruv* at a point 2,000 cubits away from where he is actually spending the Sabbath, he will be able to travel 4,000 cubits in that direction — 2,000 cubits to the point of the *eruv* and 2,000 more beyond that. He cannot, however, go anywhere in the opposite direction since that would put him beyond a 2,000 cubit distance from his legally established place of dwelling — the place of the *eruv*. Thus, whatever he gains in one direction comes at the expense of the opposite direction. He cannot set it at more than 2,000 cubits away from where he is spending the Sabbath because, if such an eruv were valid, he himself would not be within the *techum* — in which case he would be forbidden to go anywhere beyond four cubits (see

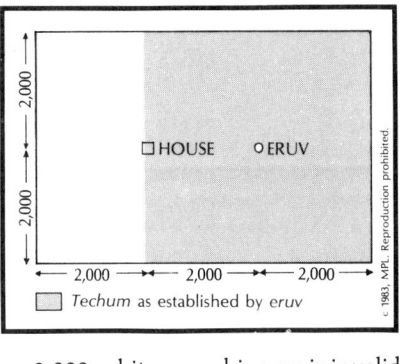

Techum as established by *eruv*

4:1). If he actually does set his *eruv* more than 2,000 cubits away, his *eruv* is invalid and the center point of his *techum* reverts to where he is (*Orach Chaim* 408:4).

There are two ways to set an *eruvei techumin:* (a) By going to a location within the limit of 2,000 cubits and staying there until the Sabbath begins; thereby legally establishing one's place of dwelling at this new location (see below 4:9; *Orach Chaim* 409:7); (b) if he does not wish to have to spend the beginning of the Sabbath at the place from where he wants the *techum* to be measured, he can accomplish the same goal by placing a specified amount of food at that location before the Sabbath; the place where the food has been placed is then viewed as his place of dwelling. [For this reason, the food must remain there at least until the beginning of the Sabbath.] In either of these two methods, the person is viewed as (symbolically) residing at the location where his *eruv* has been set.

1.

בְּכֹל מְעָרְבִין — *Any [food] may be used to make an* eruv

I.e., an *eruvei techumin* (*Rav; Rambam; Tos.;* et al.). As pointed out by *Tosafos* and others, *eruvei chatzeiros*

may be made only with bread (*Gem.* 81a).

Rashi, based on an alternate version of the Gemara (81a), has a slightly different explanation, although he agrees to the rule

1. According to *R' Hai Gaon* (in a responsum found in *Teshuvos HaGeonim Mosafia 76, Sha'arei Teshuvah 44,* and *Sefer Halttim 29;* see *Ittim L'Binah* there), the institution of *eruvei techumin* is part of King Solomon's *eruvin* legislation (see *Gem.* 21b). *Rashi* (there) and *Rambam* (*Hil. Eruvin* 1:2 and 6:1), however, understand that King Solomon's legislation was restricted to the prohibition to carry from one private domain to another and its remedy, *eruvei chatzeiros*.

עירובין
ג/א
וְהַכֹּל נִקָּח בְּכֶסֶף מַעֲשֵׂר, חוּץ מִן הַמַּיִם וּמִן
הַמֶּלַח.
הַנּוֹדֵר מִן הַמָּזוֹן מֻתָּר בְּמַיִם וּבְמֶלַח.
מְעָרְבִין לַנָּזִיר בְּיַיִן, וּלְיִשְׂרָאֵל בִּתְרוּמָה.

יד אברהם

stated here. This will be explained below in
7:10.

וּמִשְׁתַּתְּפִים, — *or a* shituf,

As explained in the General Introduction to this tractate, to permit carrying
from the many courtyards that open
into an alley, the courtyards must be
'merged' into one. The device for doing
this is called שִׁתּוּפֵי מְבוֹאוֹת [*shitufei
mevo'os*], *incorporation* [lit. *partnership*] *of the alleys. The* shituf *is made by
collecting a certain amount of food from
each of the concerned courtyards and
placing it all in one utensil (see 7:6-9).
Despite the similarity between *eruvei
chatzeiros* and *shitufei mevo'os*, the
former may only be made with bread,
while our mishnah teaches that any
kind of food is valid for the* shituf.

חוּץ מִן הַמַּיִם וּמִן הַמֶּלַח. — *except water
and salt.*

These substances are disqualified
because they do not nourish a person.
The essence of *eruvei techumin,
eruvei chatzeiros* and *shitufei mevo'os* is
that the primary residence of a person is
considered to be the place where he eats.
For this reason, the *techum* can legally
be measured from where the person
deposited his food prior to the Sabbath
(although he will not actually be eating
there). Similarly, the inhabitants of all
of the courtyards can legally be
considered as living (as one unit) in the
courtyard where the *shitufei mevo'os* —
their communal food — has been placed
(even though they will not actually be
eating there). This status can only be
conferred upon food which people
would actually use to make a meal, i.e.,
something nourishing. Water and salt
do not qualify as such (*Rashi*).
The *Gemara* (27a) adds mushrooms,
truffles and other fungi (כְּמֵהִין וּפְטָרְיוֹת); see

Aruch HaShalem, s.v. כמהין) to this list; they,
too, are similar to water and salt and are not
considered nourishment (*Rav; Rambam*).
Tosafos (27a) implies that only raw
mushrooms, etc., are excluded because they
are not fit for consumption in their present
state. *Rashba* and *Ritva* maintain that the
reason for disqualifying mushrooms is that
they in themselves cannot constitute a meal,
nor are they used by themselves as side
dishes (לִפְתָּן). See *Mishnah Berurah* 386:23.

וְהַכֹּל נִקָּח בְּכֶסֶף מַעֲשֵׂר, — *(And) any
[food] may be purchased with [second]
tithe funds,*

Among the tithes that must be taken
from all produce (grown in Eretz
Yisrael) is מַעֲשֵׂר שֵׁנִי, *second tithe.* This
tithe is set aside from the crops that
grow during the first, second, fourth
and fifth years of the seven-year
shemittah cycle. It must be brought to
Jerusalem to be eaten there by the owner
and his guests. [See prefatory remarks
to mish. 2.]
The Torah gives the owner the option
of redeeming the produce set aside as
second tithe. This redemption may only
be effected with minted coins of a value
equal to that of the produce, and such
redemption conveys the status of second tithe from the produce to the coins.
The coins must then be brought to
Jerusalem and used to purchase foods
which must be eaten within the walls of
the city in accordance with the laws of
the second tithe (*Deut.* 14:22-27). The
mishnah informs us that all foodstuffs
may be purchased with second tithe
funds as stated by Scripture: *And you
shall spend the money for whatever
[foods] your soul desires ... (Deut.
14:26) (Rav; Rashi).*

חוּץ מִן הַמַּיִם וּמִן הַמֶּלַח. — *except water
and salt.*

From the verse cited above the

Any [food] may be purchased with tithe funds, except water and salt.

One who vowed to abstain from nourishment is permitted water and salt.

One may make an *eruv* for a *nazir* with wine, or

YAD AVRAHAM

Gemara (27b) derives that foodstuff bought with second tithe funds must meet two criteria: It must be (a) פְּרִי מִפְּרִי, *a fruit* (this term is used in its broadest application and includes even meat) *which can propagate itself;* and (b) גִּדּוּלֵי קַרְקַע, *that which grows* [i.e., receives its ultimate nourishment from the earth] *from the ground;* this includes meat, since animals derive their sustenance from plants (see *Tos. Bava Metzia* 89 and *Shabbos* 73b). Water or salt conform to neither the first criterion (*Rav; Rashi*), nor the second (*R' Yehonasan; see Teshuvos Be'er Sheva* 3).

הַנּוֹדֵר מִן הַמָּזוֹן מֻתָּר בְּמַיִם וּבְמֶלַח. — *One who vowed to abstain from nourishment is permitted* [to partake of] *water and salt.*

[A person who vows to abstain from eating or deriving benefit from any object or class of object is required by the Torah to keep that vow (*Num.* 30:3). However, since water and salt do not nourish, the wording of the vow mentioned in our mishnah does not include them.][1]

The *Gemara* (30a) draws a fine distinction concerning the phraseology of the vow. If the vow used the noun מָזוֹן, *nourishment,* then only the five species of grain (wheat, barley, oats, rye and spelt) are included. Our mishnah speaks of a case where he said 'Let *anything* which nourishes be prohibited to me' (*Rav*).

The basis for this distinction is that all foodstuffs give temporary nourishment, but only the grains give proper long-term nourishment [thus the generalized term 'nourishment' refers only to them] (*Rav; R' Yehonasan*).

The vow referred to here was specified to be effective for only a short period, otherwise, it would not take effect at all. Vows that are impossible to fulfill do not take effect and since it is impossible to survive without nourishment, this vow is impossible to fulfill (*Shach, Yoreh Deah* 217:29; see *Tif. Yis.*).

מְעָרְבִין לְנָזִיר בְּיַיִן, — *One may make an eruv for a nazir with wine,*

One who has taken the vow of *nazir* may not drink wine (*Numbers* 6:3). Nevertheless, his *eruv* may be of wine since it may be drunk by others. Although in order to be valid the *eruv* must be permitted to be eaten, there is no requirement that the one using the *eruv* be able to eat it himself (*Rav*, from *Gem.* 28a, 30b).

וּלְיִשְׂרָאֵל בִּתְרוּמָה. — *or for an Israelite with terumah.*

1. The mishnah groups these three halachos (*eruv*, tithes, vow) together although their resemblance is only superficial (in each case an exception is made for water or salt), because the form of these mishnayos was cast by the *Tannaim* preceding 'Rabbi,' the editor of the Mishnah. In those pre-Mishnaic days, mishnayos were not arranged in a topical sequence by tractate, but several halachos having little in common except similar phraseology were often bunched together. (This was done to facilitate memorization; see e.g., *Chullin* 1:4-7.) Before 'Rabbi,' (and according to some even after him) the Mishnah was not written and had to be memorized in its entirety by all students. (It was thus often useful to order mishnayos by word association rather than by topic.) When 'Rabbi' incorporated these mishnayos into his Mishnah he did not disturb their grouping, but recorded them in the form he found them, based on the principle (*Eduyos* 1:3): חַיָּב אָדָם לוֹמַר בִּלְשׁוֹן רַבּוֹ, *a person is obligated to express himself using the phrasing of his mentor (Teshuvos Maharik* 174; *Meleches Shlomo* citing R' Yosef ibn Virga's *She'eiris Yosef*).

עירובין ג/א

סוּמְכוֹס אוֹמֵר: בְּחֻלִּין. וּלְכֹהֵן בְּבֵית הַפְּרָס. רַבִּי יְהוּדָה אוֹמֵר: אֲפִלּוּ בְּבֵית הַקְּבָרוֹת, מִפְּנֵי שֶׁיָּכוֹל לֵילֵךְ, לַחוּץ, וְלֶאֱכוֹל.

יד אברהם

Although *terumah* is forbidden to be eaten by a non-*Kohen* [see prefatory notes to next mishnah], he may derive benefit, such as setting an *eruv*, from it (*Pesachim* 23a with *Tos.*); additionally, the requirement that the *eruv* be edible is met, because it can be eaten by *Kohanim* (*Rav*).

סוּמְכוֹס אוֹמֵר: בְּחֻלִּין. — *Sumchos says:* [Only] *with non-terumah.*

Sumchos disagrees with the first *Tanna* and invalidates an *eruv* made for a non-*Kohen* with *terumah*. In his opinion, the *eruv* must be made from fully tithed produce which may be consumed by a non-*Kohen*. Sumchos rejects the premise that an *eruv* can be made for someone who cannot eat it himself on the basis of its being permissible to others. In his opinion, the maker of the *eruv* must himself be able to eat it (*Rav* from *Gem.* 30b).

The *Gemara* notes that Sumchos disagrees only in the case of *terumah* for a non-*Kohen* and not in the case of wine for a *nazir*. In the latter case it is possible for the *nazir* to have his vow annulled by a *beis din*. Ordinarily vows may not be annulled on the Sabbath unless their annulment is considered necessary for the Sabbath (*Shabbos* 157a). Nevertheless, since the *nazir's* vow prevents

him from drinking wine [in fulfillment of *oneg Shabbos*, Sabbath joy], its annulment is considered as necessary for the Sabbath (*Tos.* 30b). Although the declaration of *terumah* is also treated as a vow and is therefore also eligible for annulment, this recourse is of no use since the annulment of the *terumah* would cause the produce to revert to its previous state of *tevel* [see prefatory notes to next mishnah] and be prohibited to everyone (*Gem.* 30b). It would be impossible to separate other *terumah* from this produce because this prohibited on the Sabbath (*Beitzah* 5:2).

וּלְכֹהֵן בְּבֵית הַפְּרָס. — *(And) for a* Kohen *in a* beis-hapras.

A *beis-hapras* is a field in which a grave has been plowed over,[1] giving rise to the suspicion that bone fragments have been scattered all over the field. A *Kohen* may not walk over the *beis-hapras* [extending to one hundred cubits from the grave in every direction (*Ohalos* 17:1)] for fear he may touch or move[2] one of the bone fragments. This is a Rabbinical law (*Shabbos* 15a). On a Biblical level, one may rely on the knowledge that the plow rarely reaches as deep as the grave, leaving the bones intact in all probability (*Tos., Moed Katan* 5b; see *Mishnah Acharonah* to *Ohalos* 17:1).

1. Many suggestions have been offered for the origin of this name. *Rambam* (*Comm.* to *Ohalos* 17:1; see also *Rosh* there; *Tos., Niddah* 57a) relates it to וַיִּפְרשׂ אֶת הָאֹהֶל, *and he spread out the tent* (*Ex.* 40:19), i.e., a *beis-hapras* is an area in which bones have been spread or strewn. *Rashi* (*Niddah* 57a) derives פְּרָס from the Talmudic term פְּרוּסָה, *piece* (probably related to מַפְרֶסֶת in *Lev.* 11:3 [see *Rashi* there] and to פָּרוֹס לָרָעֵב in *Isaiah* 58:7), i.e., an area of bone fragments. *Tosafos* (*Niddah* 57a), in an alternate opinion, believes פְּרָס is from פַּרְסָה, *hoof* or *footsole* (see *Lev.* 11:3), i.e., an area where the *feet* of *Kohanim* may not tread.

Although a field in which a grave has been lost, i.e., the location of the grave has been forgotten, is also called a *beis-hapras* (*Ohalos* 18:3), it is not amenable to the type of examination described below and is not the subject of our mishnah. Our mishnah deals only with the case of a grave which has been plowed over but whose original site is still known (*Tos., Niddah* 57a).

2. Contamination is not transmitted to one passing over (מַאֲהִיל) bare bones; such contamination is only contracted when one passes over an entire skeleton or major parts of it (see *Ohalos* 2:1). Individual bones contaminate only by touch or by being moved (הֶסֵּיט).

for an Israelite with *terumah*. Sumchos says: With non-*terumah*.

For a *Kohen* in a *beis-hapras*. R' Yehudah says: Even in a graveyard, because he may go, make a partition, and eat.

YAD AVRAHAM

As seen below (mishnah 3), the *eruv* food must be in the place chosen to be the symbolic place of dwelling of the user of the *eruv*. A corollary of this principle is that the food must be accessible to the user in his symbolic place of dwelling.

This creates a problem for a *Kohen* if the *eruv* has been placed in a graveyard. [A *Kohen* is not permitted to become contaminated with the *tumah* of a corpse (Lev. 21:1). Since stepping on or over a grave would contaminate him, he is, in practical terms, forbidden to enter a cemetery.] Forbidden to enter the graveyard, the *Kohen* has no access to the food placed there as his *eruv*.[1] The *eruv* should be invalid.

An *eruv techumin* of a *Kohen*, which has been placed in a *beis-hapras*, then, should be invalid because of the provision stipulating that the *eruv* be in a place accessible to its user. However, the *eruv* is valid because the *Kohen* may enter the *beis-hapras* by carefully examining the ground in front of him for bones and proceed without becoming contaminated.[2] Any big bone will be immediately visible and a small bone can be checked for by blowing the loose dirt in front of him and seeing whether any small fragments become uncovered (Rav; Rashi).

רַבִּי יְהוּדָה אוֹמֵר: אֲפִלּוּ בְּבֵית הַקְּבָרוֹת, — R' *Yehudah says: Even in a graveyard,*

[Even if the *eruv* was placed in a graveyard it is valid although he must pass over graves to reach the *eruv*.]

מִפְּנֵי שֶׁיָּכוֹל לֵילֵךְ, לָחוֹץ, וְלֶאֱכוֹל. — *because he may go, make a partition, and eat* [*the* eruv].

He may have himself carried through the graveyard in a box, the bottom of which will act as an אֹהֶל, *tent,* separating between him and the *tumah,* thus preventing him from becoming contaminated. A tent or roof acts as a barrier against contamination if it is interposed between the corpse and the person (see *Ohalos* 8:1).

The first *Tanna* permits only a *beis-hapras*, not a graveyard. The *Gemara* (31a) explains that he invalidates an *eruv* in a graveyard not only for a *Kohen* but for anybody. This is because one derives benefit from the grave by leaving his *eruv* on it, and it is forbidden to derive benefit from a grave. The actual placement of the *eruv* on a grave is not considered a derivation of benefit because of the general rule that *mitzvos* were not given for the purpose of deriving benefit, i.e., the performance of a *mitzvah* is not legally viewed as having derived (personal) benefit (with regard to all instances where such

1. The person for whom the *eruv* is made need not actually place the food there himself; an agent of his may do it for him. Therefore, the *Kohen* could have had an agent who is not a *Kohen* — and who is therefore permitted to enter the cemetery — place the *eruv* there.

2. He is, however, considered *tamei* with regard to eating *terumah*, and may not eat *terumah* until he has cleansed himself. The prohibition against a *Kohen* who is *tamei* eating *terumah* is more stringent than that against a *Kohen* causing himself to become *tamei*. Consequently, although the Sages permitted him to enter the *beis-hapras* with such an inspection, they forbade him to eat *terumah* afterwards (Tos. 26b). Some authorities hold that a *Kohen* may rely on this inspection only for the performance of a *mitzvah*. Since an *eruv techumin* is only made to facilitate the performance of a *mitzvah*, a *Kohen* may rely on this inspection and place his *eruv* in a *beis-hapras* (Tos., Rashba; cf. Meiri).

benefit is prohibited). Since an *eruv techumin* can only be made for the purpose of performing a *mitzvah*, the making of the *eruv* is itself considered a *mitzvah* and the benefit one derives from having done so is therefore not a violation of the prohibition against deriving benefit from a grave. The first *Tanna* agrees with this in principle but argues that once the Sabbath has begun and the *eruv* has taken effect, its continued presence in the graveyard does not contribute to the *mitzvah*, and its safeguarding there should not be considered a *mitzvah*. Consequently, one is deriving forbidden benefit from the grave from the continued presence of the *eruv* on the grave. For this reason, one is forbidden to place the *eruv* there and it is invalid if one does. R' Yehudah feels that a person has no interest in his *eruv* once it has taken effect and its continued safeguarding is of no consequence and therefore of no benefit to him (*Rav* from *Gem.* 30b-31a).

From the fact that R' Yehudah permits the *eruv* only because there is a way for the *Kohen* to enter the graveyard (by being carried over the graves in a container of some sort), it is evident that he considers it necessary for the *Kohen* to actually have personal access to the *eruv*. This would seem to reflect only the opinion of Sumchos (see previous segment of mishnah), who holds that the person for whom the *eruv* is made must himself be able to eat the food in order for it to be effective. Accordingly, an *eruv* placed in a graveyard would be ineffective for a *Kohen* who personally lacks access to it and the fact that it is accessible to a non-*Kohen* is of no help to him. According to the *Tanna kamma*, who disputes Sumchos, the person for whom the *eruv* is made need not actually be able to eat the *eruv* himself as long as others may eat it. [For this reason he permits a non-*Kohen* to use *terumah* for his *eruv* even though only a *Kohen* may eat it.] It should follow then that a *Kohen* may have his *eruv* in a graveyard (even if there were no way for him to enter), since although it is inaccessible to him, it is accessible to others. This, indeed, is the understanding of *Rashi* and *Ritva* (30b).

Tosafos (27a) and *Rosh*, however, disagree. According to them, even the *Tanna kamma* agrees that the *eruv* must at least be accessible to the person for whom it is made, although he does not actually have to be able to eat it. In their opinion, therefore, the requirement that the *Kohen* be able to reach the *eruv* placed in a graveyard is accepted by both Sumchos and the *Tanna kamma*.

The halachah follows neither Sumchos nor R' Yehudah (*Rav, Rambam, Orach Chaim* 409:1). Thus even a non-*Kohen* may make an *eruv* with *terumah*, and an *eruv* placed in a graveyard is invalid, but in a *beis-hapras* it is valid (see *Beur Halachah* there).

2.

⊷§ **The Portions Separated from Produce**

The mishnah will now discuss some of the portions and tithes that must be separated from crops. The following terms are relevant to the discussion:

טֶבֶל — *Tevel.*

Tevel is the name given to every commodity that requires one or more tithes to be removed from it. Prior to the separation of the particular tithe the food is called *tevel*, a contraction of לֹא טַב, *not good*, meaning it is not yet fit for consumption (*Rav, Berachos* 7:1; *R' Manoach, Hil. Chametz* 6:7). Alternatively, the word may be derived from the word טַבְלָא, *board or table*, suggesting that this food is as inedible as a board (*Aruch*).

Before the proper tithes have been separated, the produce may not be eaten by anyone. But once they have been set aside, the remaining produce [called חֻלִּין, *chullin*, non-sanctified] may be eaten even if the tithes have not yet been distributed.

תְּרוּמָה — **Terumah**

The first portion separated is *terumah* (usually between a fortieth and sixtieth of the total) which is given to a *kohen* and is forbidden to a non-*kohen*. This portion is sometimes called תְּרוּמָה גְדוֹלָה, *great terumah*, to differentiate it from תְּרוּמַת מַעֲשֵׂר, *terumah from the* [first] *tithe*, described below, s.v. מַעֲשֵׂר מִן הַמַּעֲשֵׂר.

מַעֲשֵׂר רִאשׁוֹן — First Tithe

After *terumah* has been separated, the first tithe is taken from the remainder and presented to a Levite. This tithe is exactly a tenth of the crop.

מַעֲשֵׂר מִן הַמַּעֲשֵׂר — Tithe from the Tithe

From his first tithe, the Levite separates an additional *terumah* that he gives to a *kohen*. The amount of this *terumah* is exactly one tenth of his first tithe. It is also called תְּרוּמַת מַעֲשֵׂר, *terumah of the tithe*, and has all the laws of *terumah*. Before separation, the first tithe is called *tevel*, and like all produce before the separation of *terumah* it may not be eaten. Thus, before the first tithe may be eaten, two *terumos* are taken: The regular *terumah*, which was separated from the entire crop before the Levite's share was taken from it; the special tithe separated by the Levite. Consequently, if the original owner neglected to separate the regular *terumah* from the produce before giving the first tithe to a Levite, the Levite must separate both the *terumah* and the tithe from the tithe. However, in some cases (see below, s.v. וּבְמַעֲשֵׂר רִאשׁוֹן שֶׁנִּטְלָה) the obligation to separate the regular *terumah* from the first tithe is waived.

מַעֲשֵׂר שֵׁנִי — Second Tithe

In the first, second, fourth and fifth years of the seven-year Sabbatical cycle, a second tithe is separated from what remains of the produce after the *Kohen's* and Levite's shares have been removed. This tithe must be brought to Jerusalem by the owner and is eaten there by him, his household, and his guests. If this is not convenient, the owner may redeem the produce for money (only minted coins may be used for this purpose) which takes on the sanctity of the second tithe. He must take this money to Jerusalem and use it there to purchase food which assumes the sanctity previously resident in the produce and redemption money.

מַעֲשֵׂר עָנִי — Tithe of the Poor

In the third and sixth years of the Sabbatical cycle, a tenth of the produce is separated for distribution to the poor. It has no sanctity or special requirements, but the produce is *tevel* until this tithe is removed from it.

חַלָּה — Challah

Dough requires yet an additional *terumah*. This is called *challah*, literally *loaf*, and has all of the laws of *terumah*.

דְּמַאי — Demai

With the passage of time, it became apparent to the Sages that many עַמֵּי הָאָרֶץ, *ignorant people*, who, as a rule, were less than meticulous in their observance of the *mitzvos*, were becoming less scrupulous in the separation of the various tithes. Although they continued to separate *terumah* carefully and to treat it with the proper seriousness, and most of them were just as careful with the other tithes, significant numbers of them no longer separated any tithes except for *terumah*. As a result, anyone who purchased produce from an ignorant person — unless he was known to be fully observant — could not know whether or not the produce was *tevel*, and the seller could not be trusted to give an honest answer even if he were asked directly. Such a produce was called דְּמַאי, *demai*, a contraction of דָּא מַאי, *what is this?* In view of the possibility that the *demai* might be *tevel*, Yochanan *Kohen Gadol* and his *beis din* forbade purchasers to eat it unless they separated the doubtful tithes. However, they did *not* impose this burden upon poor people. In view of the compliance of *most* ignorant people with the laws of tithes and the great need of the poor, the Sages allowed them to use *demai* without tithing.

מְעָרְבִין [ב] בִּדְמַאי, וּבְמַעֲשֵׂר רִאשׁוֹן
שֶׁנִּטְּלָה תְרוּמָתוֹ, וּבְמַעֲשֵׂר שֵׁנִי
וְהֶקְדֵּשׁ שֶׁנִּפְדּוּ; וְהַכֹּהֲנִים בְּחַלָּה וּבִתְרוּמָה. אֲבָל
לֹא בְטֶבֶל, וְלֹא בְמַעֲשֵׂר רִאשׁוֹן שֶׁלֹּא נִטְּלָה
תְרוּמָתוֹ, וְלֹא בְמַעֲשֵׂר שֵׁנִי וְהֶקְדֵּשׁ שֶׁלֹּא נִפְדּוּ.

יד אברהם

מְעָרְבִין בִּדְמַאי, — *We may make an* eruv
with demai,

Although the Sages prohibited most
people to eat *demai*, they permitted poor
people to eat it. Consequently [ac-
cording to the *Tanna kamma* of mishnah 1], it may be used for *eruv* based on
the principle that an *eruv* which is
edible for some people is valid even for
those forbidden to eat it. Moreover,
even Sumchos, who disagrees with this
principle, agrees in the case of *demai*,
since even a rich man could renounce
his property and become poor, thus
exempting himself from the prohibition
against eating *demai* (Gem. 31a with
Tos.).

וּבְמַעֲשֵׂר רִאשׁוֹן שֶׁנִּטְּלָה תְרוּמָתוֹ, — *with*
first tithe whose terumah *has been*
taken,

If this statement, 'We may make an
eruv with first tithe food whose
terumah has been taken,' were taken at
face value it would be superfluous;
since *terumah* was separated, obviously
anyone may eat it, or make an *eruv* with
it. The *Gemara* (31b), therefore,
interprets the mishnah (in this case as
well as all the following ones) as
referring to a specific case of the general
rule. In the case of first tithe, the
mishnah refers to a situation where only
'its' *terumah*, i.e., the tithe from the
tithe which the Levite gives the *Kohen*,
was separated, but not the regular
terumah. Under normal circumstances
this produce would still be considered
tevel and forbidden, but here the
mishnah refers to a case where the first
tithe had been separated before the
grain had been threshed and prepared

for storage. Before threshing, the
obligation to separate *terumah* and the
other tithes is not yet in effect.
Therefore, when the obligation of
tithing takes effect, the produce already
has the status of first tithe and only the
tithe of the tithe, but not the regular
terumah, need be separated.

וּבְמַעֲשֵׂר שֵׁנִי וְהֶקְדֵּשׁ שֶׁנִּפְדּוּ; — *and with*
second tithe or consecrated produce that
were redeemed;

One may redeem his second tithe or
consecrated objects (הֶקְדֵּשׁ) with money.
The redeemed produce loses its sacred
status and may be consumed as *chullin*
(non-sanctified food), and the redemption money assumes the sacred status of
the second tithe or consecrated substance. If the redeemer is the original
owner, he must add a fifth to the value
of the item being redeemed. The mishnah speaks of a situation in which the
fifth was *not* added, and teaches that
although adding the fifth is an
obligation, the failure to add it does not
invalidate the redemption process.
Therefore, one may make an *eruv* with
such food even before paying the
additional fifth (Gem. 31b).

וְהַכֹּהֲנִים בְּחַלָּה וּבִתְרוּמָה. — *and Kohanim*
— with challah *or with* terumah.

The mishnah has recorded a difference of opinion earlier (mishnah 1)
whether even a non-*Kohen* may use
terumah and *challah* for an *eruv*. *Kohen*
is mentioned here only because the most
likely person to use *terumah* would be a
Kohen, but this does not imply that only
a *Kohen* may use *terumah* and *challah*
for this purpose.

Another reason our mishnah speci-

2. **W**e may make an *eruv* with *demai*, with first tithe whose *terumah* has been taken, and with second tithe or consecrated produce that were redeemed; and *Kohanim* — with *challah* or with *terumah*. But not with untithed produce, nor with first tithe whose *terumah* has not been taken, nor with second tithe or consecrated produce that were not redeemed.

YAD AVRAHAM

fies *Kohanim* is because this list is identical with the one given in *Pesachim* (2:5) in reference to the substance with which a person may fulfill his obligation to eat matzah on Pesach. There, of necessity, only a *Kohen* may discharge his obligation with matzah made of *terumah* or *challah* since only a *Kohen* is permitted to eat them. Consequently, in order to keep the lists identical, our mishnah mentions *Kohanim* with regard to *terumah* and *challah*, although its use as an *eruv* is not restricted to them (*Rosh*).

אֲבָל לֹא בְטֶבֶל, — *But* [one can] *not* [make an *eruv*] *with untithed produce,*

Ordinary *tevel* is obviously unfit for an *eruv* because it may not be eaten by anybody (even a *Kohen*). [Although the prohibition to eat it can be removed by tithing it, the act of tithing is itself prohibited on the Sabbath. Consequently, there is no permissible way to eat this food on the Sabbath and it is therefore unfit for an *eruv*.] Although this is obvious, the mishnah states this to include even Rabbinically forbidden *tevel*, e.g., grain grown in an unperforated flower pot. By Biblical law such grain is not considered produce of the earth and need not be tithed, but the Sages imposed the tithe obligation on it. Even though it is only *tevel* Rabbinically, it may not be used for an *eruv* (*Gem.* 31b).

וְלֹא בְמַעֲשֵׂר רִאשׁוֹן שֶׁלֹא נִטְלָה תְרוּמָתוֹ, — *nor with first tithe whose* terumah *has not been taken,*

First tithe from which its *terumah* has not been separated is *tevel*. Thus this statement, if taken at face value, is already included in the previous ruling invalidating untithed produce for an *eruv*. Besides, the invalidation of an *eruv* using bona fide *tevel* is obvious, since it may not be eaten by anyone, and need not be stated. The *Gemara* (31b) explains that the circumstances referred to by the mishnah include even a situation where one reversed the regular sequence and gave the first tithe to a Levite before separating the regular *terumah*. In this case, because the first tithe was taken off after threshing and storing, when the obligation to separate the regular *terumah* had already taken effect, the Levite must separate both *terumah* and the tithe from the tithe, as opposed to the instance above where the first tithe has been separated before the *terumah* obligation took effect (ibid.).

וְלֹא בְמַעֲשֵׂר שֵׁנִי וְהֶקְדֵּשׁ שֶׁלֹא נִפְדּוּ. — *nor with second tithe or consecrated produce that were not redeemed.*

Even if they were redeemed, but the redemption was not performed properly, e.g., second tithe was redeemed with uncoined metal, or consecrated produce was redeemed with land, they may not be used for an *eruv* (ibid.).

הַשּׁוֹלֵחַ עֵרוּבוֹ בְּיַד חֵרֵשׁ, שׁוֹטֶה, וְקָטָן, אוֹ בְּיַד
מִי שֶׁאֵינוֹ מוֹדֶה בָּעֵרוּב, אֵינוֹ עֵרוּב. וְאִם אָמַר
לְאַחֵר לְקַבְּלוֹ מִמֶּנּוּ, הֲרֵי זֶה עֵרוּב.

[ג] **נָתְנוּ** בְּאִילָן, לְמַעְלָה מֵעֲשָׂרָה טְפָחִים אֵין
עֵרוּבוֹ עֵרוּב; לְמַטָּה מֵעֲשָׂרָה טְפָחִים

יד אברהם

הַשּׁוֹלֵחַ עֵרוּבוֹ — *If one sends his* eruv
[To be deposited on the designated place.]

בְּיַד חֵרֵשׁ, — *with* [lit. *in the hand of*] *a deaf-mute,*

Technically חֵרֵשׁ signifies a deaf person. But throughout the Talmud (see *Chagigah* 2b-3a, *Terumos* 1:2) wherever חֵרֵשׁ is juxtaposed with שׁוֹטֶה וְקָטָן, *a deranged person or a minor,* it refers to a deaf person who is deemed mentally incompetent. As the *Gemara* (there) makes clear, this refers to a deaf-mute who, because of his condition, lacks the ability to communicate and is considered mentally incompetent. Such a person is not obligated in the performance of mitzvos. Hence one who was born deaf and is, as a result, a deaf-mute is in this category.[1]

שׁוֹטֶה, — *a mentally deranged person,*

One who is deranged to the extent that he is no longer halachically obligated to observe mitzvos (because he is not considered responsible for his actions). The exact criteria for judging a deranged person are discussed in the Talmud (*Chagigah* 3b) and at length in the *Poskim*, and do not lend themselves to synopsis (see *Rambam, Hil. Eidus*

9:9-10; *Even HaEzer* 121; *Yoreh Deah* 1:5; *Choshen Mishpat* 35:8-10). *Rambam* adds: 'The very feebleminded (הַפְּתָאִים בְּיוֹתֵר) ... are included under the category of deranged.'

וְקָטָן, — *or a minor,*

[A boy less than thirteen years old or a girl less than twelve.]

אוֹ בְּיַד מִי שֶׁאֵינוֹ מוֹדֶה בָּעֵרוּב, — *or with someone who does not accept* [the law of] *eruv,*

One who rejects the Rabbinical law of *eruv* is suspect of not fulfilling his chore, or, even if he is seen to place the *eruv* in its ordained site, may not have performed the act with the intent that it establish this site as the legal place of dwelling of the one who sent him (*R' Yehonasan*).

The *Gemara* (31b) explains that this term refers to the כּוּתִים, *Cuthites* (i.e., Samaritans).[2] Although the Cuthites observed many mitzvos zealously (see *Gittin* 10a), they did not bow to the authority of the Sages, and consequently did not recognize the prohibition against going outside the *techum*, nor the remedy of *eruv*.

[It would seem from the *Gemara's* identification that no other identifiable group

1. The halachic status of a deaf-mute who has been taught to talk by modern methods is extensively discussed in the responsa of the *Acharonim*. See *Teshuvos Divrei Chaim* II, *Even HaEzer* 72; *Maharam Schick, Even HaEzer* 79; *Maharsham* 2:140; *Teshuvos HaGri Steif* 239; *Igros Moshe, Even HaEzer* 3:33.

2. The *Cuthites* were one of the nations brought by the Assyrian king Shalmanesser to settle the part of *Eretz Yisrael* left desolate by the exile of the Ten Tribes (II *Kings* 17:24-41). This area was called שׁוֹמְרוֹן, *Samaria,* and this name is the source of the Cuthites' alternative designation as Samaritans. The term was later used to describe all of these nations. Although the *Cuthites* converted to Judaism (ibid.) they remained separated from the main body of the Jewish people; indeed they constituted a hostile force to the Jews and at many times a menace.

3
3

If one sends his *eruv* with a deaf-mute, a mentally deranged person, or a minor, or with someone who does not accept *eruv*, the *eruv* is not valid. But if he instructed another to receive it from him, the *eruv* is valid.

3. If he placed it on a tree, higher than ten fists his *eruv* is not valid; below ten fists his *eruv* is valid.

existed at that time that fit this description. As a rule, all the Jews living in that era accepted the principle of *eruv* and the authority of the Sages. It is puzzling, however, why the *Gemara* does not include the heretical *Tzedokim* (Sadducees) in the term 'someone who does not accept ...' *Rashba* and *Ritva* (to 61b) deduce from this that the Sadducees are to be considered among those 'accepting *eruv*.' *Rambam (Hil. Eruvin* 2:16, cf. his Comm. to 6:1 and *Rav* here) assumes that the Sadducees are to be categorized as 'not accepting an *eruv*' (see also *Orach Chaim* 385:1 and *Eliyah Rabbah* there). Perhaps the *Gemara* mentions only *Cuthites* because in the time this definition was offered, the Sadducees no longer existed as an identifiable group.]

אֵינוֹ עֵרוּב. — *the* eruv *is not valid* [lit. *it is not an* eruv].

The *Gemara* (31b) differentiates between an *eruvei techumin*, which is invalid under the conditions described here, and an *eruvei chatzeiros*, which is valid. *Rashi* and *R' Yehonasan* explain that this results from a basic difference between these two *eruvin* in regard to the legal significance of their placement. In the case of *eruvei techumin*, placing the *eruv* is a legal *act* establishing a legal place of dwelling for the maker of the *eruv*. This necessitates that someone act as a legal agent for him, a position which excludes those whose mental faculties are impaired [these are excluded from acting as agents in *any* legal transaction (see *Gittin* 23a)]. One

who does not accept *eruv* is disqualified because we suspect him of not intending to establish residence for the sender. When making an *eruvei chatzeiros*, however, it is not the *act* of placing the *eruv* food in one utensil, but the mere fact of its being there, which effects the *eruv*. Thus, even if we discount the agency of those who put the *eruv* in its place and do not consider their act as having legal standing, the *fact* of the *eruv* food being in the requisite place validates the *eruv per se*. Even if the food had been put there by a monkey the *eruv* would be valid (cf. *Tos.*, *Rashba*, and *Ritva*).

וְאִם אָמַר לְאַחֵר לְקַבְּלוֹ מִמֶּנּוּ, הֲרֵי זֶה עֵרוּב. — *But if he instructed another to receive it from him, the* eruv *is valid* [lit. *this is indeed an* eruv].

If the one sending the *eruv* instructed a qualified person to receive the *eruv* from the unqualified agent and properly place it, the *eruv* is valid. [It is only the actual placement of the *eruv* which needs to be done by a qualified agent.] However, the sender must see the deaf-mute, etc., actually give the *eruv* to the qualified agent before relying on the validity of the *eruv* (*Rav* from *Gem.* 31b; see *Ritva* and *Beur Halachah* 409:8). But after having witnessed the transfer, he may rely on the qualified agent to faithfully fulfill his assignment without further verification (*Gem.* 31b).

3.

נָתְנוּ בְּאִילָן, לְמַעְלָה מֵעֲשָׂרָה טְפָחִים — *If he placed it on a tree, higher than ten fists*

A person designated a spot in the public domain as his (symbolic)

עירובין עֵרוּבוֹ עֵרוּב. ג/ג

נְתָנוֹ בְּבוֹר, אֲפִלּוּ עָמֹק מֵאָה אַמָּה, עֵרוּבוֹ עֵרוּב.

נְתָנוֹ בְּרֹאשׁ הַקָּנֶה אוֹ בְּרֹאשׁ הַקֻּנְדָּס, בִּזְמַן שֶׁהוּא תָלוּשׁ וְנָעוּץ, אֲפִלּוּ גָבוֹהַּ מֵאָה אַמָּה, הֲרֵי זֶה עֵרוּב.

יד אברהם

below — לְמַטָּה מֵעֲשָׂרָה טְפָחִים עֵרוּבוֹ עֵרוּב.
ten fists his eruv is valid [lit. his eruv is an eruv].

In this case the tree branch is considered a karmelis (since it is less than ten fists high) and carrying from it to the public domain is subject to only a Rabbinical prohibition. Since the provision that a person be able to take the eruv to his legal place of dwelling refers only to the beginning of the Sabbath, i.e., בֵּין הַשְּׁמָשׁוֹת, the twilight period, and the rule is that during this period Rabbinic prohibitions, such as those against carrying from a karmelis to a public domain, may be superseded (for the purposes of a mitzvah),[1] he would have been allowed at that time to take the eruv from the tree and eat it. As a result, the eruv is valid (Rav from Gem. 32b).

The reason for this rule is that the twilight period is in a state of legal doubt, i.e., it is uncertain whether this period belongs to the previous day and is therefore considered a weekday, or to the following day and is part of the Sabbath.[2] Since it is not definitely part of the Sabbath, the Sages were lenient with regard to Rabbinically instituted prohibitions, allowing them to be superseded for the sake of a mitzvah.

dwelling but placed the eruvei techumin food on a nearby tree, on a branch measuring ten fists high [i.e., the branch had a vertical section ten fists in length (see Tos. 33a; Shabbos 101a)] and four fists square. The branch thus meets all the requirements for a private domain (Rav from Gem. 32b).

[See below, s.v. נְתָנוֹ בְּבוֹר, for Gra's interpretation of the mishnah as referring to a tree in a karmelis].

אֵין עֵרוּבוֹ עֵרוּב; — his eruv is not valid [lit. his eruv is not an eruv];

The underlying principle is that the eruv must be able to be eaten at the place of the symbolic dwelling at the moment when it takes effect, i.e., when the Sabbath begins. Since in order to do this he would have to take the eruv from its place on the tree (the private domain) to his place of dwelling in the public domain — a forbidden act on the Sabbath — he is not able to eat the eruv at the beginning of the Sabbath. As a result, the eruv is not valid (Rav from Gem. 32b).

[Although he could climb the tree and eat the eruv there, that is not his intended place of dwelling.]

1. Rambam (Hil. Shabbos 24:10; Hil. Eruvin 6:9) adds the provision that the superseding of the Rabbinical prohibition be necessary (cf. Rashi Shabbos 34a and Ritva there) to the performance of a mitzvah. [Since an eruvei techumin may be resorted to only for the purpose of a mitzvah, it, too, is considered a mitzvah (see Gem. 31a).]

Ravad (cited by Ritva) restricts this even further, and states that this dispensation is only a theoretical one in that it views Rabbinical prohibitions in the twilight period, regarding the validity of an eruvei techumin, as permitted and thus no obstacle to the validity of the eruv. In practice, however, one is not actually permitted to supersede the prohibition. Shulchan Aruch (Orach Chaim 342) rules according to Rambam.

2. The exact demarcation of this doubtful period and its duration are discussed at length in Shabbos 34a-35b (see Tos. there) and Orach Chaim 261:2 (see Beur HaGra, Mishnah Berurah and Beur Halachah there).

3

3

If he placed it in a ditch, even a hundred cubits deep, his *eruv* is valid.

If he put it atop a reed or atop a pole, so long as it is uprooted and is stuck [into the ground], even if it is a hundred cubits high, his *eruv* is valid.

נָתְנוֹ בְּבוֹר, אֲפִלּוּ עָמֹק מֵאָה אַמָּה, — *If he placed it in a ditch, even a hundred cubits deep,*

This ditch is at least four fists square and ten fists deep and thus conforms to the dimensions of a private domain. Furthermore, the ditch is situated in a *karmelis* and the *karmelis* had been designated the person's place of dwelling. Accordingly, to take the *eruv* to the dwelling entails transgressing only a Rabbinical prohibition (*Rav* from *Gem.* 35b).

By changing the circumstances of the case from a tree to a ditch the mishnah indicates that the surrounding area is a *karmelis*, for it is unusual to have an open ditch in a public domain (*Geon Yaakov*).

According to *Vilna Gaon* (cited in *Tosafos Chadashim*) and *Lechem Shamayim*, the *Gemara* understands that even the previous case of the tree refers to one standing in a *karmelis*. Where the branch is ten or more fists high (and is thus a private domain), two Rabbinic prohibitions have to be dealt with: (a) the prohibition against carrying from a private domain to a *karmelis;* and (b) the prohibition of removing something from a tree (see *Gem.* 32b). In face of the two-fold prohibition there is no permission to supersede Rabbinic laws and the *eruv* is therefore invalid. When the branch is below ten fists only one prohibition remains. (A branch less than ten fists high is only a *karmelis* and carrying from *karmelis* to *karmelis* within four cubits is permitted. Thus only the prohibition of removing something from a tree remains.) This is permitted in the twilight period. A ditch, by comparison, is never prohibited by more than one prohibition — carrying from a private domain to a *karmelis*. Thus, an *eruv* in a ditch is always valid.

עֵרוּבוֹ עֵרוּב. — *his* eruv *is valid.*

As in the previous case, since only a Rabbinic prohibition is involved, it is superseded in the twilight period when the *eruv* takes effect (*Rav, Gem.* 35b).

There is an additional principle to be learned from this mishnah. Even if the ditch is one hundred cubits deep, and consequently the time needed to actually bring it up from the bottom of the ditch to the place of dwelling is longer than the entire twilight period so that by the time someone climbing, eruv in hand, got to the top of the ditch it would already be night when Rabbinic prohibitions may no longer be superseded, nevertheless the *eruv* is valid. Only a *halachic* inaccessibility of the *eruv* invalidates it, not a technical one (*Hon Ashir*).

נָתְנוֹ בְּרֹאשׁ הַקָּנֶה אוֹ בְּרֹאשׁ הַקֻּנְדָּס, — *If he put it atop a reed or atop a pole,*

Since the pole or reed lacks the prerequisite dimensions of four fists square, its top is an exempt area (see General Introduction),[1] and there is no prohibition against taking an object from an exempt area to a public domain (*Rav; Rashi*).

בִּזְמַן שֶׁהוּא תָלוּשׁ — *so long as it* [the reed] *is uprooted*

[I.e., the reed or pole is no longer rooted in the earth.]

וְנָעוּץ, אֲפִלּוּ גָבוֹהַּ מֵאָה אַמָּה, הֲרֵי זֶה עֵרוּב. — *and is* [only] *stuck* [into the ground], *even if it is a hundred cubits high, his* eruv *is valid.*

If, however, the reed is still rooted, the *eruv* is not valid. Here there is an additional Rabbinical prohibition against removing something from atop

---

1. *Rav* (following *Rashi*, see also *Rashba* and *Ritva*), however, stipulates that the reed or pole must have a platform measuring four fists square at the top (only the reed or pole itself is less than four by four). The platform does not render the area a private domain because it lacks

נָתְנוּ בְּמִגְדָּל וְאָבַד הַמַּפְתֵּחַ, הֲרֵי זֶה עֵרוּב. רַבִּי אֱלִיעֶזֶר אוֹמֵר: אִם אֵינוֹ יוֹדֵעַ שֶׁהַמַּפְתֵּחַ בִּמְקוֹמוֹ, אֵינוֹ עֵרוּב.

יד אברהם

the reed — lest he break off a piece from the frail reed (*Rav; Gem.* 35b). Doing this to a rooted reed violates the forbidden labor of קוֹצֵר, *reaping,* a Biblical transgression (*Tos. HaRosh*). Because of the likelihood of its occurrence this Rabbinic apprehension is not waived even during twilight (*Rashi*).

This apprehension applies only to a rooted reed and not to a tree (since the mishnah above validated an *eruv* placed on a tree below ten fists). A reed is very frail so that the possibility that one may break off a piece is much greater than with a tree where breaking off a twig would require a greater effort (*Rav; Rashi*). Alternatively, it is not readily apparent whether a reed is rooted or not. Consequently, one may break off a piece

thinking that the reed was uprooted while in fact it was not (*Rav; Rambam*).

נָתְנוּ בְּמִגְדָּל וְאָבַד הַמַּפְתֵּחַ, הֲרֵי זֶה עֵרוּב. — *If he placed it in a locker and lost the key, the eruv is valid.*

The *Gemara* (35a), in the accepted interpretation (see *Beur Halachah* to *Orach Chaim* 394:3), explains that the locker and its lock were held in place by ropes, so that in order to open it without the key one must cut these ropes.[1] On a Rabbinical level this is considered akin to the forbidden labor of סוֹתֵר, *demolishing.*[2] However, this is no obstacle to the validity of the *eruv* for, as stated earlier, the mishnah holds that a Rabbinic prohibition standing in the way of using the *eruv* does not

partitions ten fists high. Even if it had such partitions but they extended downward it would still not be a private domain according to the halachah as long as the walls do not extend to within three fists of the ground (see *Gem.* 33b and *Shabbos* 101a; *Rambam Hil. Shabbos* 14:18). Only if it had walls ten fists high extending upward would it be a private domain.

The reason for this requirement is a general provision that the *eruv* be placed on a substantial surface; i.e., one measuring at least four fists square. However, many authorities (*Rosh* citing *Maharam of Rothenburg*) disagree and point out that though the *Gemara* (33b) states this provision in the name of R' Yehudah without giving a dissenting opinion, nevertheless, in *Tosefta* (2:9) the Sages disagree and the halachah should follow the majority. (*Rambam* and *Shulchan Aruch* also omit this stipulation.)

1. The option of breaking down the door of the locker is not considered at all by the *Gemara* because it comes under the category of סוֹתֵר, *demolishing,* a Biblically prohibited labor. The dictum, 'Building and demolishing do not apply to utensils' (*Gem.* 35a), applies only to minor changes made to the utensil. [The labors of building and demolishing apply primarily to structures attached to the ground. Slight adjustments to these structures are considered a violation of these labors (see *Shabbos* 12:1).] Making a new utensil or completely dismantling an existing one is considered a violation of the labors of building and demolishing, even in the case of utensils (*Tos., Rosh*).

Others explain that breaking down the door of the locker is considered demolishing only in the case of large utensils holding forty *se'ah* or more. Because of their size they are classified as structures even though they are not actually attached to the ground. It is to this size locker that the mishnah refers. Smaller utensils *are* subject to the dictum, 'Building and demolishing does not apply to utensils' (*Tos.* 34b; *Ran* to *Shabbos* 146a attributes this view to *Rashi*; cf. ArtScroll Mishnah *Shabbos* 22:3, p. 354).

Gra (to *Orach Chaim* 314:3) maintains that *Rashi's* view is that utensils are never categorized as being built or demolished with regard to the laws of the Sabbath. The locker discussed in our mishnah therefore refers to one built into the ground. Breaking such a structure can be classified as demolition.

2. The cutting of the ropes is categorized as a minor adjustment and is subject to the dictum, 'Building and demolishing do not apply to utensils,' according to all opinions.

3
3

If he placed it in a locker and lost the key, the *eruv* is valid. R' Eliezer says: If he does not know that the key is in its place, the *eruv* is not valid.

YAD AVRAHAM

invalidate the *eruv* (*Rav* following *Rashi* 35a).

In this case the actual place of the *eruv* poses no problem because the mishnah may be referring to a case where both the locker and the dwelling place are in the private domain (see *Rashi* 34b, s.v. אמאי) or to a case where the dwelling is in a *karmelis*. In any case the *eruv* is valid because the prohibition against carrying from private domain (the locker) to a *karmelis* is also only Rabbinic. However according to *Vilna Gaon's* view that a twofold Rabbinic prohibition does invalidate an *eruv* (see above, s.v. נִתְּנוּ בְּאִילָן) the mishnah speaks only of a case in which both the locker and the dwelling place were in a private domain. If one of them was in a *karmelis* the double prohibition — transferring from a private domain to a *karmelis* and demolishing — would invalidate the *eruv*.]

רַבִּי אֱלִיעֶזֶר אוֹמֵר: אִם אֵינוֹ יוֹדֵעַ שֶׁהַמַּפְתֵּחַ בִּמְקוֹמוֹ, אֵינוֹ עֵרוּב. — *R' Eliezer says: If he does not know that the key is in its place, the* eruv *is not valid.*

R' Eliezer maintains that an additional Rabbinic prohibition is involved here — that of *muktzeh* (objects not permitted to be moved on Shabbos or Yom Tov — see preface to ch. 17 of ArtScroll Mishnah *Shabbos*).

R' Eliezer agrees with the stringent view of R' Nechemiah that no utensil

may be moved on the Sabbath except for the purpose for which it is primarily used. The only knife available with which to cut the rope holding the door in place is a food knife, and may not, according to this view, be moved to cut a rope.[1] Thus, in addition to the prohibition against cutting the rope, we have yet another Rabbinic law to supersede — that of *muktzeh*, and as explained above, only one Rabbinic ordinance may be superseded in the twilight period — not two[2] (*Rav*; *Rashi*).

Tosefos (35a) points out that the solution of breaking the lock itself is not advanced as a means of getting at the *eruv* because it would constitute a transgression on a Biblical level (see *Shulchan Aruch, Orach Chaim* 314:7).

The halachah does not follow R' Eliezer (*Rav*; *Rambam*).

Rashba (citing *Ravad*; see also *Ritva*) draws a distinction from the phraseology used by the mishnah. The mishnah invalidates the *eruv* only if it is not known whether the key is in its place. If, however, it can be assumed that the key is in place but the owner forgot where he had placed it, the *eruv* is valid even according to R' Eliezer. *Mishnah Berurah* (394:8) explains that this is based on the probability that he will remind himself of the key's location. *Rashba* and

1. The above in *Rashi's* understanding of R' Nechemiah's view. According to R' Tam (*Shabbos* 36a), R' Nechemiah permits moving utensils for purposes other than their primary one as long as they are common uses of the utensil. Cutting ropes, however, does not qualify as a common use of a food knife. R' Chananel (cited by *Rashba* and *Ritva*) goes even further and believes that all cutting activities are considered proper uses of a knife. The mishnah refers here to a person who does not have any knife and must cut the rope with a hatchet or the like.

2. The differentiation between one and two Rabbinic prohibitions is not in *Rashi* but is added by *Rav* to explain why the Rabbinical prohibition against demolishing does not invalidate the *eruv* according to R' Eliezer without the introduction of the additional dimension of *muktzeh*. *Tosefos R' Akiva* points out that *Rav* and *Rashi* thus contradict their commentary to the case of an *eruv* placed on a tree 'below ten fists' in which there is also a two-fold prohibition — using a tree, and transferring from a *karmelis* to a public domain — but the *eruv* is nevertheless valid (see comm. to mishnah 3; cf. *Vilna Gaon* in s.v. נִתְּנוּ בְּבוֹר). *Tosefos* (35a) objects to *Rashi's* reasoning and believes that the mishnah speaks of a locker which is a utensil; cutting the rope that holds it closed transgresses no prohibition at all. R' Eliezer invalidates the *eruv* only because of *muktzeh* and does not accept the rule that Rabbinic ordinances should pose no obstacle to *eruv*.

[ד] **נִתְגַּלְגֵּל** חוּץ לַתְּחוּם, וְנָפַל עָלָיו גַּל, אוֹ נִשְׂרַף, אוֹ תְּרוּמָה וְנִטְמֵאת — מִבְּעוֹד יוֹם, אֵינוֹ עֵרוּב; מִשֶּׁחֲשֵׁכָה, הֲרֵי זֶה עֵרוּב. אִם סָפֵק — רַבִּי מֵאִיר וְרַבִּי יְהוּדָה אוֹמְרִים: הֲרֵי זֶה חַמָּר גַּמָּל. רַבִּי יוֹסֵי וְרַבִּי שִׁמְעוֹן אוֹמְרִים: סְפֵק עֵרוּב כָּשֵׁר.

יד אברהם

Ritva also point out that the phrase 'if he does not know' suggests that in case of doubt (as to whether the key is in place) the *eruv* is invalid. It thus follows that R' Eliezer accepts R' Meir and R' Yehudah's view (below, mishnah 4) invalidating a doubtful *eruv.* [This explains why the circumstance of the key is couched in different language by R' Eliezer. The mishnah could have said simply *R' Eliezer says: It is not a valid* eruv. But that would have given the erroneous impression that R' Eliezer invalidates the *eruv* only in the case stated by the first *Tanna,* i.e. if 'it was (definitely) lost.']

4.

נִתְגַּלְגֵּל חוּץ לַתְּחוּם, — *If it rolled beyond the* techum,

[The food for the *eruvei techumin* had been placed near where the boundary would have been had he not instituted an *eruv,* but before the beginning of the Sabbath it rolled to a point outside the boundary.] Since the *eruv* food is now beyond the 2,000 cubits allowed for the *techum* he cannot get to

it and it is therefore invalid (*Rav; Rashi*).

Although the reason he cannot get to his *eruv* is due only to the Rabbinic prohibition against walking beyond the *techum* and, as seen from the previous mishnah, Rabbinic prohibitions do not, as a rule, disqualify an *eruv,* the prohibition of *techum* is an exception to this rule (*Ritva*).[1]

The *Gemara* (35a) adds that only if

1. *Ritva* does not clarify how the prohibition of *techum* differs from other Rabbinic prohibitions so that it can invalidate an *eruv* which rolled beyond it. The following is suggested:

It is axiomatic that the *eruv* be in the same area as the selected place of dwelling as stated by the *Gemara* (32b). What constitutes the same area is open to definition. *Ritva* (s.v. באילן) maintains that an *eruv* removed more than four cubits from the dwelling is not valid, while *Tosafos* (s.v. הכא) seems to hold that an *eruv* in any area where it may be carried to the dwelling is considered to be in the same area as the dwelling. [*Ritva's* explanation here is obviously necessary only for *Tosafos'* view. According to *Ritva's* own view the *eruv* is disqualified on the grounds that it is four cubits removed from the dwelling.]

It may be postulated that the prohibition of *techum* may be regarded as definitive of the 'same area' rule. This supposition may be inferred from the fact that the *Gemara* (51a) finds a Scriptural allusion (אסמכתא) to the (Rabbinical) prohibition of *techum* (see *Ritva* there) in the verse *(Ex. 16:29) ... Let every person stay in his place* — his place being defined as the 2,000 cubit *techum.* Thus if at the onset of the Sabbath, a person's *eruv* is at a site where it would be outside his *techum* if the *eruv* were not valid, it is viewed as being in an area differing from that of the person. Furthermore the determination that the person is in the same area as the *eruv* must be made independently of the validity of the *eruv.* Thus, in the case under discussion, where the *eruv* is outside of the person's *techum* as determined by his regular dwelling, it is judged to be outside of the area designated to be the centerpoint of the *techum* as per *eruv,* although it would be within the *techum* if the *eruv* were valid (cf. *Beis Meir, Orach Chaim* 365:8; *Chazon Ish Orach Chaim* 80 p. 241 and 109:7).

Tosafos (35a, s.v. נתגלגל) seems to hold that the *eruv,* if effective, would have as its centerpoint the place it had rolled to, and not the spot where it had been placed initially. In this

4. If it rolled beyond the *techum,* or a heap fell on it, or it burned, or [it was] *terumah* which became contaminated — if it was still day, the *eruv* is invalid; if after dark, the *eruv* is valid. If it is in doubt — R' Meir and R' Yehudah say: He is caught in between. R' Yose and R' Shimon say: A doubtful *eruv* is valid.

YAD AVRAHAM

the *eruv* rolled to a point four cubits beyond the *techum* is the *eruv* invalid. If the distance is less than this the *eruv* is valid.[1]

וְנָפַל עָלָיו גַּל, — *or a heap* [of rubble] *fell on it,*

Since it is necessary to dig out the *eruv* (a Biblically forbidden labor), the *eruv* is considered inaccessible at the onset of the Sabbath *(Rav from Gem.* 35a).

אוֹ נִשְׂרַף, — *or it burned,*

I.e., it no longer exists.

אוֹ תְּרוּמָה וְנִטְמֵאת — — *or* [it was] terumah *which became contaminated* —

[*Terumah* — the portion separated from the produce to be given to a *Kohen* — may not be eaten by anyone if it contracted *tumah*-contamination.]

מִבְּעוֹד יוֹם, — *if* [any of these happened while] *it was still day,*

[I.e., before the twilight which marks the onset of the Sabbath.]

אֵינוֹ עֵרוּב; — *the* eruv *is invalid;*

[In order for the *eruv* to symbolically establish a person's dwelling place, it must be accessible and fit for consumption at the time it takes effect — the onset of the Sabbath.]

מִשֶּׁחֲשֵׁכָה, הֲרֵי זֶה עֵרוּב. — *if after dark, the* eruv *is valid.*

Once the *eruv* takes effect it remains in force for the entire Sabbath whether or not the food still exists *(Rav; Rashi).*

אִם סָפֵק — — *If it is in doubt* —

I.e., it is not known whether these events occurred before the onset of the Sabbath, when they would invalidate the *eruv,* or after nightfall *(Rashi).*

There is disagreement among the authorities regarding an *eruv* that was initially set at a time when its validity was in doubt, i.e., during twilight. *Rashi (Shabbos* 34a) and *Rambam (Hil. Eruvin* 6:13) see this case, too, as included here (and valid according to R' Yose). *Tosafos* (there) is of the opinion that such an *eruv* is invalid according to all the *Tannaim* mentioned here (see *Orach Chaim* 415:3 with *Mishnah Berurah*).

רַבִּי מֵאִיר וְרַבִּי יְהוּדָה אוֹמְרִים: הֲרֵי זֶה חַמָּר גַּמָּל. — *R' Meir and R' Yehudah say: He is caught in between* [lit. *He is a donkey driver who is also a camel driver*].

A donkey is guided from behind, while a camel is led from in front. A person driving a camel and a donkey would therefore walk between the two, dividing his attention between the donkey in front of him and the camel behind him. A similar situation pertains to the doubtful *eruv.* If the *eruv* was valid, the person's *techum* must be measured using the location of the *eruv* as the centerpoint. If the *eruv* was not valid, his *techum* is measured using his

view the explanation for the invalidation of the *eruv* is simple. If the *eruv* were valid at its present location, the person's house would be outside of his *techum* and prohibited to him for the duration of the Sabbath. In order to spare the person this unforeseen and uncomfortable consequence, the Sages invalidated the *eruv.* However, the basic premise of *Tosafos* (that the *eruv* is effective at the place it rolled to) needs further explanation.

1. It is uncertain whether this is so only for an *eruv* which was initially placed at the *techum* line or if it holds true even for one which rolled out from well inside the *techum* boundary. (See *Maggid Mishneh, Hil. Eruv* 6:11; *Beur Halachah* 409:5.)

עירובין
ג/ה
אָמַר רַבִּי יוֹסֵי: ,,אַבְטֹלְמוֹס הֵעִיד מִשּׁוּם
חֲמִשָּׁה זְקֵנִים עַל סָפֵק עֵרוּב שֶׁכָּשֵׁר.''

[ה] **מַתְנֶה** אָדָם עַל עֵרוּבוֹ וְאוֹמֵר: ,,אִם בָּאוּ
עוֹבְדֵי כּוֹכָבִים מִן הַמִּזְרָח, עֵרוּבִי
לַמַּעֲרָב; מִן הַמַּעֲרָב, עֵרוּבִי לַמִּזְרָח; אִם בָּאוּ
מִכָּאן וּמִכָּאן, לִמְקוֹם שֶׁאֶרְצֶה אֵלֵךְ; לֹא בָּאוּ לֹא

יד אברהם

home as the centerpoint. Therefore, the only area allowed to the person is that shared by both *techumin* (*Rav, Rashi*).

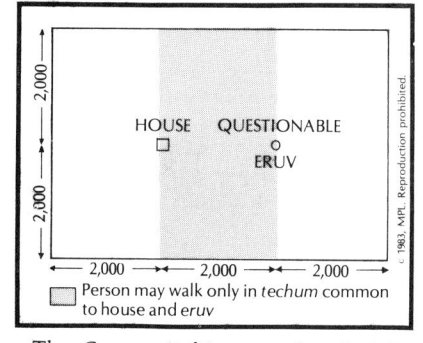

Person may walk only in *techum* common to house and *eruv*

The *Gemara* (35b) states that R' Meir follows R' Akiva's opinion that the prohibition of *techum* is Biblical. Accordingly, this case comes under the general rule that in a case of doubt concerning a Biblical prohibition one must follow the more stringent position.

**רַבִּי יוֹסֵי וְרַבִּי שִׁמְעוֹן אוֹמְרִים: סָפֵק עֵרוּב
כָּשֵׁר.** — *R' Yose and R' Shimon say: A doubtful eruv is valid.*

We may rely on the general principle of חֲזָקָה, *chazakah*, which states that in cases of doubt the halachah presumes that the status quo has been preserved. Since the *eruv* had originally been intact and properly placed before the Sabbath, we assume that the eruv was still valid at the time in question — the onset of the Sabbath. Consequently, although the

food is either no longer there or no longer usable, the *eruv* remains valid for the rest of the Sabbath (*Rav*). [As explained above, the *eruv* food need only be in place at the onset of the Sabbath for the *eruv* to be valid for the whole Sabbath.]

Rashi (36a) disagrees with this explanation, pointing out that in our mishnah there are two conflicting factors of status quo to consider: (a) the status quo of the *eruv* food, which should be presumed to have been in place and intact at the onset of the Sabbath and which therefore points to the *eruv* being valid; and (b) the status quo of the person's *techum* which, barring the institution of an *eruv*, is measured from his home. Since the validity of that *eruv* is in question, the status quo of his *techum* should be maintained, namely to reckon his *techum* from his home (rather than the place of his *eruv*). Thus the two status quo factors cancel each other out and we are left with a simple situation of a doubt without the consideration of status quo.

According to *Rashi*, the reason R' Yose is lenient in this situation (assuming the *eruv* to be valid) is because he holds the prohibition of *techum* to be only Rabbinical so that it is subject to the general rule that in cases of doubt concerning Rabbinical prohibitions the lenient position is adopted.

Tosafos (*Shabbos* 34a), however, asserts that R' Yose's ruling is based upon the premise of status quo (as does *Rav*). *Tosafos* (here 35b) implies that the principle of status quo cannot be applied to the person's *techum* (see *Leshon HaZahav*).[1]

1. It follows then, that in the opinion of *Tosafos* (and *Rav*) an *eruv* installed during twilight will not be valid (since the *eruv* never achieved a status of validity); whereas according to *Rashi* it would (because this is still a case of doubt relating to a Rabbinical prohibition).

Said R' Yose: 'Avtulmos attested in the name of five sages that a doubtful *eruv* is valid.'

5. A person may attach a condition to his *eruv* and say, 'If gentiles come from the east, my *eruv* is to the west; if from the west, my *eruv* is to the east; if they come from both directions, I shall go to the place I choose; if they do not come from either

YAD AVRAHAM

אָמַר רַבִּי יוֹסֵי: ,,אַבְטוֹלְמוֹס הֵעִיד מִשּׁוּם חֲמִשָּׁה זְקֵנִים עַל סָפֵק עֵרוּב שֶׁכָּשֵׁר." — *Said R' Yose: 'Avtulmos attested in the name of*

five sages that a doubtful eruv is valid.'
The halachah follows R' Yose (Rav, Rambam).

5.

מַתְנֶה אָדָם עַל עֵרוּבוֹ וְאוֹמֵר: ,,אִם בָּאוּ עוֹבְדֵי כּוֹכָבִים מִן הַמִּזְרָח, עֵרוּבִי לַמַּעֲרָב; מִן הַמַּעֲרָב, עֵרוּבִי לַמִּזְרָח; — *A person may attach a condition to his* eruv [techumin] *and say, 'If gentiles come from the east, my* eruv *is to the west; if* [they come] *from the west, my* eruv *is to the east;*

A person who fears a visit on the Sabbath from gentile tax collectors (*Rashi*) or assessors of fines (*Aruch*) and wishes to avoid a confrontation with them, may prepare an *eruvei techumin* so that he will be able to travel four thousand cubits on the Sabbath. However, since he does not know in which direction he will have to flee he places an *eruv* in two directions to enable himself to flee 4,000 cubits to either side of his home. Since one cannot have two valid *eruvin* at one time (see mishnah 6), he must make each *eruv* conditional. That *eruv* which will have its condition fulfilled will become valid retroactively (to the beginning of the Sabbath) while the other will become invalidated, thus leaving him with only one *eruv*. [The conditions must, of course, be mutually exclusive — that if one is fulfilled the other is automatically invalidated.] This he does by stating that only one of the

two *eruvin* should be valid, and that this be determined by the direction from which the gentiles come. If they come from the east, necessitating his fleeing towards the west, then the *eruv* to the west should be valid (while the one to the east is invalidated). If they come from the west, so that he must flee towards the east, then the *eruv* to the east should be valid (with the one to the west invalidated). This *Tanna* accepts the principle of בְּרֵירָה [*bereirah*], *retroactive clarification*, which holds that one may institute a legal process and make its present validation conditional upon events which have not yet taken place and whose outcome cannot now be predicted (*Rav; Rashi*).[1] [The validity of this principle is the subject of dispute among many *Tannaim* — see *Gem*. 36b-37b.]

On the subject of *bereirah* the Talmud (*Beitzah* 37b-38a) rules that this principle may be applied only with regard to Rabbinical, not Biblical, laws. Since the need for *eruvei techumin* is only Rabbinical, an *eruv* based on the use of the principle of *bereirah* is valid (*Maggid Mishneh to Hil. Eruvin* 8:3).

אִם בָּאוּ מִכָּאן וּמִכָּאן, לְמָקוֹם שֶׁאֶרְצֶה אֵלֵךְ; — *if they come from both directions* [lit. *from here and there*], I shall [be able to]

---

1. Conditions attached to an action are not in the category of *bereirah* if they can be fulfilled by either of the parties involved. Only conditions not fulfillable by the parties are categorized as *bereirah* (*Tos.* 37a).

מִכָּאן וְלֹא מִכָּאן, הֲרֵינִי כִּבְנֵי עִירִי.״

,,אִם בָּא חָכָם מִן הַמִּזְרָח, עֵרוּבִי לַמִּזְרָח; מִן
הַמַּעֲרָב, עֵרוּבִי לַמַּעֲרָב; בָּא לְכָאן וּלְכָאן, לְמָקוֹם
שֶׁאֶרְצֶה אֵלֵךְ; לֹא לְכָאן וְלֹא לְכָאן, הֲרֵינִי כִּבְנֵי
עִירִי.״

רַבִּי יְהוּדָה אוֹמֵר: אִם הָיָה אֶחָד מֵהֶן רַבּוֹ,
הוֹלֵךְ אֵצֶל רַבּוֹ. וְאִם הָיוּ שְׁנֵיהֶם רַבּוֹתָיו, לְמָקוֹם
שֶׁיִּרְצֶה יֵלֵךְ.

[ו] רַבִּי אֱלִיעֶזֶר אוֹמֵר: יוֹם טוֹב הַסָּמוּךְ
לַשַׁבָּת בֵּין מִלְּפָנֶיהָ וּבֵין

יד אברהם

go to the place I choose;
[I.e., the *eruv* of the side chosen at
that time should be retroactively valid.
This is a continuation of the previous
condition, taking all the possibilities
into consideration.]

לֹא בָאוּ לֹא מִכָּאן וְלֹא מִכָּאן, הֲרֵינִי כִּבְנֵי
עִירִי.״ — *if they do not come from either
direction* [lit. *not from here and not
from there*], *I am as my townspeople.'*
[I.e., if it happens that they do not
come from either side, then both *eruvin*
should be invalid and his *techum* should
be reckoned from his home. Such a
four-sided conditional *eruv* is valid,
with the actual site of the *eruv*
determined on the Sabbath by the
conditions set forth.]

,,אִם בָּא חָכָם מִן הַמִּזְרָח, עֵרוּבִי לַמִּזְרָח; מִן
הַמַּעֲרָב, עֵרוּבִי לַמַּעֲרָב; בָּא לְכָאן וּלְכָאן,
לְמָקוֹם שֶׁאֶרְצֶה אֵלֵךְ; לֹא לְכָאן וְלֹא לְכָאן,
הֲרֵינִי כִּבְנֵי עִירִי.״ — *[Or he may say] 'If a
scholar comes from the east, my* eruv *is
to the east; from the west, my* eruv *is to
the west; if one* [scholar] *comes to here
and* [one comes] *to there, I shall* [be able
to] *go to the place I choose; if to neither
direction, I am as my townspeople.'*
[It had been reported that a renowned
scholar would come to a point within

4,000 cubits of this town to deliver a
discourse but it was not known whether
this point would be to the east or west of
the town. To ensure his ability to attend
the discourse, the person may make two
eruvin, one to the east and one to the
west, and attach the conditions given
above.]

רַבִּי יְהוּדָה אוֹמֵר: אִם הָיָה אֶחָד מֵהֶן רַבּוֹ,
הוֹלֵךְ אֵצֶל רַבּוֹ. — *R' Yehudah says: If one
of the scholars was his teacher, he must
go to his teacher.*
R' Yehudah refers to the possibility
of two scholars arriving, in which case
the stipulation had been that he be able
to choose at that time which *eruv* was to
be valid. R' Yehudah maintains that we
assume that this condition was meant
only where neither of the scholars was
his teacher or both were. Otherwise, it is
assumed that at the time the condition
was made the person surely intended to
validate the *eruv* enabling him to listen
to his teacher's discourse. His decision
on the Sabbath to go to the other
scholar's discourse is viewed as one
reached subsequent to the imposition of
the conditions and is invalid. The Sages
dispute R' Yehudah's view, arguing that
it is not unusual for a person to want to
listen to another scholar and thus no

direction, I am as my townspeople.'

'If a scholar comes from the east, my *eruv* is to the east; from the west, my *eruv* is to the west; if one comes to here and [one comes] to there, I shall go to the place I choose; if to neither direction, I am as my townspeople.'

R' Yehudah says: If one of the scholars was his teacher, he must go to his teacher. But if both were his teachers, he may go to the place he chooses.

6. **R'** Eliezer says: If Yom Tov adjoins the Sabbath either before it or after it — a person

YAD AVRAHAM

assumptions should be made about his original intent (*Rav* from *Gem.* 36b).

וְאִם הָיוּ שְׁנֵיהֶם רַבּוֹתָיו, לִמְקוֹם שֶׁיִּרְצֶה יֵלֵךְ. — *But if both were his teachers, he may*

go *to the place he chooses* [i.e., he may attend the lecture of whichever scholar he chooses].

The halachah does not follow R' Yehudah (*Rav; Rambam*).

6.

A person may not have two *eruvin* at the same time. Since the *eruv* symbolically represents the person's dwelling place, he cannot be considered as residing in two places simultaneously. Similarly, one cannot have an *eruv* in one place for half the Sabbath and in another place for the second half of the day. The boundary is designated at the onset of the Sabbath so that the one *eruv* in effect then retains its validity for the entire day.

The mishnah now deals with the problem of a *Yom Tov* which immediately precedes or follows the Sabbath. Although each day is holy in its own right, it is possible that since they follow immediately one upon the other and since, with respect to laws such as *techumin*, they are identical, they are to be regarded as קְדוּשָׁה אַחַת, *one (fused) period of holiness*, i.e., one forty-eight hour period of holiness — with respect to the laws common to both. On the other hand, it may be that since *Yom Tov* and the Sabbath are basically separate and unrelated periods

of holiness, they are to be viewed as שְׁתֵּי קְדוּשׁוֹת, *two separate periods of holiness*, even when the coincidences of the calendar throw them together.

The practical significance of this question may be seen with regard to *eruvei techumin*. If the two days are viewed as one period of holiness, then an *eruv* made at the onset of the first day would be valid for both days. The second day would not need a separate *eruv* nor *could* one make a separate *eruv* for the second day. (This would be the equivalent of making a second *eruv* for the second half of the Sabbath.) If, however, each day is regarded as a separate period of holiness, then each day requires its own *eruv* and an *eruv* made for the first day alone is not valid for the second day.

רַבִּי אֱלִיעֶזֶר אוֹמֵר: יוֹם טוֹב הַסָּמוּךְ לַשַּׁבָּת בֵּין מִלְּפָנֶיהָ וּבֵין מִלְּאַחֲרֶיהָ — *R' Eliezer says: If Yom Tov adjoins the Sabbath either before it or after it —*

[I.e., Yom Tov is on Friday or on Sunday.]

מִלְאַחֲרֶיהָ — מְעָרֵב אָדָם שְׁנֵי עֵרוּבִין, וְאוֹמֵר:
„עֵרוּבִי הָרִאשׁוֹן לַמִּזְרָח, וְהַשֵּׁנִי לַמַּעֲרָב;"
„הָרִאשׁוֹן לַמַּעֲרָב, וְהַשֵּׁנִי לַמִּזְרָח;" „עֵרוּבִי
הָרִאשׁוֹן, וְהַשֵּׁנִי כִּבְנֵי עִירִי;" „עֵרוּבִי הַשֵּׁנִי,
וְהָרִאשׁוֹן כִּבְנֵי עִירִי."
וַחֲכָמִים אוֹמְרִים: מְעָרֵב לְרוּחַ אַחַת אוֹ אֵינוֹ
מְעָרֵב כָּל עִקָּר; אוֹ מְעָרֵב לִשְׁנֵי יָמִים, אוֹ אֵינוֹ

יד אברהם

מְעָרֵב אָדָם שְׁנֵי עֵרוּבִין, וְאוֹמֵר: „עֵרוּבִי הָרִאשׁוֹן
לַמִּזְרָח, וְהַשֵּׁנִי לַמַּעֲרָב;" — *a person may
make two* eruvin *and declare, 'My* eruv
[*for*] *the first* [day] *is to the east and*
[*for*] *the second* [day] *to the west;'*

If it was necessary for him to go 3,000
cubits in one direction on the first day
and 3,000 cubits in the other direction
on the second day, he may do so by
making two *eruvin*, one for each day. R'
Eliezer maintains that the two days are
to be considered as two separate periods
of holiness, and the *techum* of each day
is determined at the onset of that day.
Therefore, the *eruv* of the preceding day
does not influence the *techum* of the
following day and another *eruv*, in a
different location, may be instituted for
that day, taking effect at its onset (*Rav;
Rashi*).

The *eruv* for the second day may be placed
at the second location even before the first
day (if one is sure it will still be there at the
onset of the second day). In fact, this is the
procedure discussed here in the mishnah
(*Rav*). This is indeed the only possible way it
can be done when the *Yom Tov* follows the
Sabbath since one is not permitted to carry
the *eruv* through a public domain or *karmelis*

on the first day, namely the Sabbath (*Tos.
Yom Tov*). When the first day is *Yom Tov*,
one may put the *eruv* for the second day (the
Sabbath) in place on the *Yom Tov* day (it is
permissible to carry objects on *Yom Tov* for
the needs of the Sabbath). However, if this
procedure is used one must use the same food
used for the first *eruv* so that one need not
designate new food as an *eruv* on *Yom Tov*.
If other food were used, its designation as an
eruv would constitute הֲכָנָה, *preparing*, on
Yom Tov for the Sabbath (or vice versa),
which is forbidden,[1] (*Gem.* 39a) and the
eruv would therefore be invalid (*Rashba* cited
by *Maggid Mishneh, Hil. Eruvin* 8:9; see also
Sha'ar HaTziyun 416:15). [This interpretation follows the view of *Tosefos Yom Tov*
cited above.][2]

The *Gemara* (38b) points out that the
eruvin may not be placed more than 2,000
cubits apart; i.e., if one is placed 1,000 cubits
to the east of his home the other may not be
placed more than 1,000 cubits to the west of
his home (not the maximum 2,000). Thus,
each *eruv* enables the person to go only an
average of 3,000 cubits in each direction.
(This is only an average since he may place
one *eruv* 1,500 cubits away from his home
and the other 500 cubits in the opposite
direction — as long as they are within 2,000
cubits of each other. In this case, he would be

1. The device of *eruv tavshilin* which allows one to cook on *Yom Tov* for the Sabbath (see
Beitzah 2:1) is of no avail here. This device is effective only to permit preparations for the
Sabbath meal and not for matters unrelated to food needs (*Ran, Beitzah* 16b; *Magen Avraham*
and *Mishnah Berurah, Orach Chaim* 528:2; cf. *Hagahos R' Akiva Eiger* and *Da'as Torah*
there). See also *Beur HaGra* (loc. cit.) and *Yerushalmi, Beitzah* 2:1.

2. *Tosefos Yom Tov's* view is disputed by many authorities (see *Tos. R' Akiva*), who argue
that even if one used the same food for the second *eruv* it must still be redesignated as an *eruv*
because its location has been changed. Accordingly, even on *Yom Tov* before the Sabbath both
eruvin have to be put in place so as to avoid the problem of *preparing* (see below). *Mishnah
Berurah* (416:23; see *Sha'ar HaTziyun* there) points out that *Rashba* (38a and *Avodas
HaKodesh*) and *Ritva* (38a) both subscribe to the latter opinion, and accept it as halachah.

may make two *eruvin* and declare, 'My *eruv* [for] the first is to the east and [for] the second to the west;' '[for] the first to the west and [for] the second to the east;' 'My *eruv* is [for] the first, but [for] the second I am as my townspeople;' [or] 'My *eruv* is [for] the second, but [for] the first I am as my townspeople.'

But the Sages say: He makes an *eruv* to one direction or he makes no *eruv* at all; either he makes an *eruv* for both days or he makes no *eruv* at all. How

YAD AVRAHAM

able to travel 3,500 cubits in the first direction but only 2,500 cubits in the second direction.) If they were more than 2,000 cubits apart, the *eruv* for the second day would be inaccessible to the person before the time it takes effect at the onset of the second day (in the twilight period) and would therefore be invalid.

הָרִאשׁוֹן לַמַּעֲרָב, וְהַשֵּׁנִי לַמִּזְרָח; — '[for] the first [day] to the west, and [for] the second [day] to the east;'

[Or if he needs to go first to the west and then to the east, he should reverse the order of his declaration]

עֵרוּבִי הָרִאשׁוֹן, וְהַשֵּׁנִי כִּבְנֵי עִירִי;" "עֵרוּבִי הַשֵּׁנִי, וְהָרִאשׁוֹן כִּבְנֵי עִירִי." — 'My *eruv* is [effective only for] the first [day], but [for] the second [day] I am as my townspeople;' [or] 'My *eruv* is [effective for] the second [day], but [for] the first [day] I am as my townspeople.'

This segment refers to a new set of circumstances. The person needed an *eruv* on only one of the two days and wished to revert back to his normal *techum* (that of his town) on the other day. In such a case he makes one *eruv* and declares that the *eruv* be valid only for that day (*Rav; Rashi*).

וַחֲכָמִים אוֹמְרִים: מְעָרֵב לְרוּחַ אַחַת אוֹ אֵינוֹ מְעָרֵב כָּל עִקָּר; — But the Sages say: [Either] he makes an eruv to one direction or he makes no eruv at all;

[The ruling of the Sages is based on the premise that two holy days following each other are viewed as one period of holiness so that the two days are considered (for *eruv* purposes) as

one long day. Accordingly, one cannot make separate *eruvin* for each day.]

Rashba and *Ritva* deduce from the language of the mishnah ('or no *eruv* at all') that if one does make *eruvin* to two directions for one day both *eruvin* are invalid. Thus, if he is at home he automatically reverts to the *techum* of his home (this *techum* is his automatically and needs no designation), and if he was out in the field (hence his dwelling place and the corresponding *techum* need to be clearly designated; see further 4:5) he has no *techum* at all and may not budge from his four cubits.

אוֹ מְעָרֵב לִשְׁנֵי יָמִים, אוֹ אֵינוֹ מְעָרֵב כָּל עִקָּר. — either he makes an eruv for both days or he makes no eruv at all.

The *Gemara* (38a) points out that this segment is identical with the previous part of the Sages' argument. The phrase, 'Either he makes an *eruv* to one direction ...' essentially means that one can make only one *eruv* for both days. The *Gemara* explains that the first segment does not refer to the case of *Yom Tov* which falls immediately before or after the Sabbath, but to a single day of *Yom Tov* or Sabbath and is used to introduce the Sages' argument. The Sages argue that surely on one day 'one either makes an *eruv* to one direction or none at all,' i.e., one cannot make an *eruv* in one direction for the first half of the day and another, in a different direction, for the second half of the day. The same argument follows for two days, one right after the other — one must make one *eruv* for both days [because they are one period of holiness] or none at all (*Ritva*).

עירובין מְעָרֵב כָּל עִקָּר. כֵּיצַד יַעֲשֶׂה? מוֹלִיכוֹ בָּרִאשׁוֹן וּמַחְשִׁיךְ עָלָיו, וְנוֹטְלוֹ וּבָא לוֹ. בַּשֵּׁנִי, מַחְשִׁיךְ עָלָיו וְאוֹכְלוֹ. וְנִמְצָא מִשְׂתַּכֵּר בַּהֲלִיכָתוֹ, וּמִשְׂתַּכֵּר בְּעֵרוּבוֹ.

נֶאֱכָל בָּרִאשׁוֹן, עֵרוּבוֹ לָרִאשׁוֹן, וְאֵינוֹ עֵרוּב לַשֵּׁנִי. אָמַר לָהֶם רַבִּי אֱלִיעֶזֶר: "מוֹדִים אַתֶּם לִי שֶׁהֵן שְׁתֵּי קְדֻשּׁוֹת!"

יד אברהם

כֵּיצַד יַעֲשֶׂה? — *How should one proceed?*

This is a continuation of the Sages' statement. How does one proceed to make one *eruv* for both days?

The necessity for posing this question is due to the fact the Sages are really uncertain as to whether the two days should be considered one period of holiness or, as R' Eliezer asserts, two. [Their previous rejection of a separate *eruv* for each day is a result of the *possibility* that the two days are considered one period of holiness.] In practice, therefore, they require that one make the *eruv* in such a manner that it will satisfy both positions (*Gem.* 36a). According to the position that they are one period of holiness no problem exists since the *eruv* made on the eve of the first day is automatically valid (and binding) for the second day. However, according to the position that the two days are considered two separate periods, an *eruv* instituted for the first day is not automatically valid for the second unless it was (a) intended for both days and (b) is still in place at the onset of the second day. If one is not sure that it is still there at the onset of the second day the *eruv* is not valid for the second day. He cannot at that time take fresh food, designate it as an *eruv*, and put it in place just prior to the onset of the second day because the explicit designation of food as an *eruv* is considered הֲכָנָה, *preparing*, (see above, s.v. הָרִאשׁוֹן לַמְעָרֵב) and is forbidden on both the Sabbath and *Yom Tov*. Consequently, he must make the *eruv*

on the eve of the first day in such a manner that he is assured of its availability for the second day (*Gem.* 39a).

The food already used as an *eruv* for the first day (which therefore does not require designation as an *eruv*) may be used on the first day to serve as the *eruv* for the second day, but if he leaves it in an unsafe place how can he be sure that it will still be available to him on the next day? (*Rav*)

[Although the mishnah discusses this problem from the perspective of the Sages, the point made is equally true for R' Eliezer, since he too considers the two days two periods of holiness, requiring a separate *eruv* for the second day.]

מוֹלִיכוֹ בָּרִאשׁוֹן — *He should take it* [i.e., the *eruv*] *on* [the eve of] *the first* [day]

I.e., he should have the *eruv* put in its place by an agent before the onset of the first day (*Rav; Rashi*).

If he went himself he would not need an *eruv* of food, as will be explained below (4:9). Since the mishnah discusses going to place food there, it is obvious that the mishnah is referring to making an *eruv* through an agent (*Tos. Yom Tov*).

וּמַחְשִׁיךְ עָלָיו, — *and stay with it until nightfall,*

[He waits until it is definitely night (see *Rashi* and *Tos., Shabbos* 34a, *Orach Chaim* 415:2) and the *eruv* has taken effect.]

וְנוֹטְלוֹ וּבָא לוֹ. — *then take it and go.*

He should remove the *eruv* so that he can be sure of having it to use again on the next night (*Rav; Rashi*). [Once the *eruv* has taken effect — at nightfall — it need no longer be kept at that site.]

should one proceed? He should take it on the first and stay with it until nightfall, then take it and go. On the second, he should stay with it until nightfall, then eat it. Thus he benefits in his walking [area], and he benefits from his *eruv.*

If it was eaten on the first the *eruv* is valid for the first, but the *eruv* is not valid for the second. Said R' Eliezer: '[So] you agree with me that they are two [periods of] holiness.'

YAD AVRAHAM

Clearly this procedure is possible only when *Yom Tov* precedes the Sabbath so that the *eruv* may be carried home. If the Sabbath preceded *Yom Tov,* the *eruv* cannot be carried home that night and one must return to the *eruv* site on the next night before the onset of *Yom Tov* to inspect whether the *eruv* is still there *(Rav; Rashi).*

בַּשֵּׁנִי, מַחֲשִׁיךְ עָלָיו — *On the* [eve of the] *second* [day], *he should* [return with it and] *stay with it until nightfall,*

[Since it is still before the onset of the Sabbath, he is permitted to carry it back to the site.]

וְאוֹכְלוֹ. — [and he may] *then eat it.*

Since, as explained above, the mishnah discusses a case in which the second day was the Sabbath, he cannot carry it home after nightfall and if he wishes to eat it must do so at the site of the *eruv* *(Tif. Yis.).*

וְנִמְצָא מִשְׂתַּכֵּר בַּהֲלִיכָתוֹ, — *Thus he benefits in his walking* [area],

By going to and from the *eruv* site he assures himself of being able to use his *eruv* for the second day and thereby extends his *walking area* to include the goal of his journey *(Rav, Rashi).*

וּמִשְׂתַּכֵּר בְּעֵרוּבוֹ. — *and he benefits from his eruv.*

In that he gets to consume it *(Rav, Rashi)* [i.e., in a case where the owner himself went out on the eve of the second day to check on the *eruv*].

Galia Maseches (part 1 p. 158) proposes a novel interpretation for this segment of the mishnah. It has already been pointed out (see

prefatory note to this chapter) that an *eruvei techumin* does not extend the *techum,* but merely shifts it toward the direction one wants to go. Thus it can be said that one who makes an *eruv* does not really benefit. However, the case under discussion is an exception for, as stated in *Tosefta* (4:1) regarding the Sages' view, a person who makes an *eruv* for the *Yom Tov* preceding the Sabbath and neglects to do so for the Sabbath will be permitted to traverse only the area shared by the *techum* as fixed per his residence and that fixed per his *eruv.* (This is because the Sages are uncertain whether the Sabbath is to be viewed as a continuation of the *Yom Tov* period in regard to *eruv* or not. Accordingly, one must conduct himself in a manner which will satisfy both positions.) However, by renewing the *eruv* before the onset of the Sabbath one *benefits* in that he now has the benefit of a full *eruv* without having to subtract the possible *techum* of his house. This is true for both methods of *eruv* mentioned here — making an *eruv* with one's feet or with food. Thus *he benefits from his walking,* if he establishes an *eruv* with his feet, and *benefits* from his *eruv,* if he makes an *eruv* with food.

נֶאֱכַל בָּרִאשׁוֹן, עֵרוּבוֹ לָרִאשׁוֹן, וְאֵינוּ עֵרוּב לַשֵּׁנִי. — *If it was eaten on the first* [day] *the* eruv *is valid for the first* [day], *but the* eruv *is not valid for the second.*

[This is a continuation of the Sages' statement. If the *eruv* was eaten on the first day, and was therefore not in place at the onset of the second day, there is no valid *eruv* for the second day. Since the Sages consider it possible that the two days are to be considered as two separate periods of holiness in which case each day requires its own *eruv,* the

[ז] רַבִּי יְהוּדָה אוֹמֵר: רֹאשׁ הַשָּׁנָה שֶׁהָיָה
יָרֵא שֶׁמָּא תִּתְעַבֵּר —
מְעָרֵב אָדָם שְׁנֵי עֵרוּבִין, וְאוֹמֵר: ,,עֵרוּבִי בָּרִאשׁוֹן
לַמִּזְרָח, וּבַשֵּׁנִי לַמַּעֲרָב;" ,,בָּרִאשׁוֹן לַמַּעֲרָב,
וּבַשֵּׁנִי לַמִּזְרָח;" ,,עֵרוּבִי בָּרִאשׁוֹן, וּבַשֵּׁנִי כִּבְנֵי
עִירִי;" ,,עֵרוּבִי בַּשֵּׁנִי, וּבָרִאשׁוֹן כִּבְנֵי עִירִי." וְלֹא
הוֹדוּ לוֹ חֲכָמִים.

יד אברהם

second day must be considered as being without an *eruv*.]

אָמַר לָהֶם רַבִּי אֱלִיעֶזֶר: ,,מוֹדִים אַתֶּם לִי שֶׁהֵן שְׁתֵּי קְדֻשּׁוֹת!" — *Said R' Eliezer: '[So] you agree with me that they are two [periods of] holiness.'*

'Your ruling regarding an *eruv* eaten on the first [as well as that about returning the *eruv* to its place on the eve of the second] is based on the premise that they are two separate periods, and that is exactly my position on this matter' *(Rav, Rashi)*. [The Sages, however, are uncertain as to whether the two days are to be considered one period of holiness or two and as a result require that the *eruv* conform to both positions.]

The halachah follows R' Eliezer *(Rav, Rambam* from *Gem.* 39b).

7.

During most of the Talmudic era, neither the beginning of the month (Rosh Chodesh) nor the beginning of the year (Rosh Hashanah) was fixed by a static calendar, but by the actual sighting of the new moon by witnesses. Thus the first day of the month would fluctuate between thirty days after the previous Rosh Chodesh and thirty-one days, depending upon when witnesses arrived to testify before the *beis din*. This did not cause any problem with observing the festivals on their proper dates since, with the exception of Rosh Hashanah, they occur in the middle of the month by which time the exact day proclaimed as Rosh Chodesh was already known throughout *Eretz Yisrael*. (The Diaspora observed two days of *Yom Tov*, as we do today, because communications in those days were too slow to assure the transmission of the information regarding the day of Rosh Chodesh.) However, the Rosh Hashanah festival, which coincides with Rosh Chodesh, did present a problem. Even in Jerusalem (or any of the subsequent places where the *beis din* charged with declaring Rosh Chodesh had its seat), where the designation of the day as the first of the month (and the year) would immediately be known, there was no way of knowing on the previous evening whether the following day would be merely the thirtieth of *Elul* (if witnesses did not appear) or the first of Tishrei and Rosh Hashanah (if they did appear). Because of this, all of *Eretz Yisrael* had to celebrate both the thirtieth and the thirty-first days following Rosh Chodesh Elul as Rosh Hashanah. The mishnah now discusses the procedure to be followed by one who needs to go beyond the regular *techum* on one or both of these days. Are the two days of Rosh Hashanah to be considered as one period of holiness, or as two separate periods? (See ArtScroll Mishnah *Rosh Hashanah*, pp. 86, 109-114, for further discussion on this topic.)

רַבִּי יְהוּדָה אוֹמֵר: רֹאשׁ הַשָּׁנָה שֶׁהָיָה יָרֵא שֶׁמָּא תִּתְעַבֵּר — *R' Yehudah says: [If*

7. **R'** Yehudah says: [If before] Rosh Hashanah there was concern lest [Elul] be full, a person may make two *eruvin* and declare, 'My *eruv* for the first is to the east, and for the second to the west:' 'For the first to the west, and for the second to the east;' 'My *eruv* is for the first, but for the second [I am] as my townspeople;' [or] 'My *eruv* is for the second, but for the first [I am] as my townspeople.' But the Sages did not agree with him.

YAD AVRAHAM

before] Rosh Hashanah there was concern lest [Elul] be full [lit. *Rosh Hashanah when he was afraid lest it be full*],

[The expression *a full month* is the Mishnaic idiom for saying that the thirty-first day will be declared Rosh Chodesh, or in this case Rosh Hashanah.]

The problem was that this person needed to go beyond the *techum* in one direction on the thirtieth and in an opposite direction on the thirty-first (*Rav, Rashi*).

מְעָרֵב אָדָם שְׁנֵי עֵרוּבִין, וְאוֹמֵר: ,,עֵרוּבִי בָּרִאשׁוֹן לַמִּזְרָח, וּבַשֵּׁנִי לַמַּעֲרָב;'' ,,בָּרִאשׁוֹן לַמַּעֲרָב, וּבַשֵּׁנִי לַמִּזְרָח;'' — *a person may make two* eruvin *and declare, 'My* eruv *for the first* [day] *is to the east, and for the second* [day] *to the west;' 'For the first* [day] *to the west, and for the second* [day] *to the east;'*

The *eruv* made for the first day does not determine the *techum* for the second day; each is considered a distinct and separate period of holiness for itself and entitled to its own *techum* (*Rav; Rashi*).

,,עֵרוּבִי בָּרִאשׁוֹן, וּבַשֵּׁנִי כִּבְנֵי עִירִי;'' ,,עֵרוּבִי בַּשֵּׁנִי, וּבָרִאשׁוֹן כִּבְנֵי עִירִי.'' — *'My* eruv *is for the first* [day], *but for the second* [day I am] *as my townspeople;'* [or] *'My* eruv *is for the second* [day], *but for the first* [day I am] *as my townspeople.'*

[Or, needing an *eruv* for only one day he wishes to retain the *techum* of his home on the other day so as not to lose any of the 2,000 cubit distance allowed him on the side of his home opposite the direction in which the *eruv* was placed.]

The *Gemara* (39a) explains that even the Sages who disagreed with R' Eliezer in the previous mishnah, and considered the possibility that two consecutive days of holiness (the Sabbath and *Yom Tov*) should be viewed as one long period, may agree here with R' Yehudah that the two days of Rosh Hashanah must be viewed as two separate entities. It was only the Sages of the subsequent generation — that of R' Yehudah — who explicitly ruled that the two days of Rosh Hashanah be considered as one period of holiness. In the case of the Sabbath and *Yom Tov* each day has a definite holiness to it and, because they follow immediately one upon the other, the combined period of holiness may perhaps be legally viewed as one entity. In the case of Rosh Hashanah, however, there is essentially only one day of holiness, so that when two days are celebrated one of them is basically a weekday, celebrated as Rosh Hashanah only because of the uncertainty about the arrival of witnesses. Therefore, the *eruv* of the first day cannot determine the *techum* for the second, because consideration of the second day as Rosh Hashanah is based on the premise that the first day had been a weekday — and therefore a day on which an *eruv* does not take effect.

וְלֹא הוֹדוּ לוֹ חֲכָמִים. — *But the Sages did not agree with him.*

[The Sages maintain that only one *eruv* can be made for both days and that

וְעוֹד אָמַר רַבִּי יְהוּדָה: מַתְנֶה אָדָם עַל הַכַּלְכָּלָה בְּיוֹם טוֹב רִאשׁוֹן, וְאוֹכְלָהּ בַּשֵּׁנִי. וְכֵן בֵּיצָה שֶׁנּוֹלְדָה בָּרִאשׁוֹן, תֵּאָכֵל בַּשֵּׁנִי. וְלֹא הוֹדוּ לוֹ חֲכָמִים.

יד אברהם

the *eruv* made for the first day determines the *techum* for the second day as well.]

They argue that the two days are to be viewed as one period of holiness. This is based on the rule instituted by the Sages (*Rosh Hashanah* 4:4) that witnesses coming on the thirtieth day to testify to having seen the new moon were to be received by the *beis din* only until the *Minchah* period (i.e., *Minchah ketanah* — two and one half hours before sundown, see *Yad Avraham* there). Since witnesses coming after that hour were not received on that day, once that hour passed without any witnesses having come, *beis din* could no longer declare that day Rosh Chodesh (or Rosh Hashanah) and it was then known with certainty that the next day would be Rosh Hashanah. (If the thirtieth day is not declared Rosh Chodesh, the thirty-first day automatically becomes Rosh Chodesh even if witnesses do not appear before *beis din*.) Consequently, from the *Minchah* period and on it was known in Jerusalem (or wherever the seat of the *beis din* was at the time) with certainty that that day (the thirtieth) was not Rosh Hashanah, but a weekday.

Nevertheless, the Sages instituted

that the remaining segment of the day be celebrated as *Yom Tov* so that in future years the people not belittle the importance of observing the thirtieth day as Rosh Hashanah (during that portion of the day when the witnesses would still be accepted if they came). In this case, the Sages argue, the Rabbinic legislation ordering the celebration of the first day even when it was known that the second day would be the real Rosh Hashanah amounts to an order mandating a two-day celebration of the Rosh Hashanah festival, i.e., a two-day-long, single period of holiness. Consequently, every Rosh Hashanah is to be viewed as one extended period of holiness.

R' Yehudah, however, does not view the celebration of the first day in this instance as a Rabbinic observance of a bona fide *Yom Tov*, but only as a precaution instituted by the Sages to prevent future disregard for the celebration of Rosh Hashanah on the thirtieth day. Consequently, it is not to be considered one extended period of holiness, since only one of the days is inherently holy (*Rav* from *Gem.* 39a-b).

[The commentary at the end of mishnah 8 discusses which view is halachically accepted.]

8.

All produce grown in *Eretz Yisrael* must be properly tithed (see prefatory note to mish. 2) before it may be eaten. The Sages, however, prohibited the separation of tithes on *Yom Tov* and the Sabbath (*Beitzah* 5:2). The mishnah now discusses a possible way of circumventing this problem on Rosh Hashanah.

וְעוֹד אָמַר רַבִּי יְהוּדָה: — *Additionally, R'*

Yehudah said:

R' Yehudah, in accord with his premise that the two days of Rosh Hashanah are viewed as two separate periods of holiness, applied his view to other pertinent cases.

מַתְנֶה אָדָם עַל הַכַּלְכָּלָה בְּיוֹם טוֹב רִאשׁוֹן, וְאוֹכְלָהּ בַּשֵּׁנִי, — *A person may stipulate a condition concerning a basket [of produce] on the first day of Yom Tov*

8. **A**dditionally, R' Yehudah said: A person may stipulate a condition concerning a basket on the first day of Yom Tov and eat it on the second. And so also, an egg laid on the first may be eaten on the second. But the Sages did not agree with him.

[i.e., Rosh Hashanah] *and eat it on the second* [day].

R' Yehudah maintains that it is possible to circumvent the prohibition against tithing on Rosh Hashanah by attaching the proper conditions to the tithing process. This will result in the produce being considered tithed (and therefore edible) but only on the second day.

The condition, though not articulated in the mishnah, is self-evident. On the first day before removing the required tithe portions from the produce he makes the following declaration: 'If today is a weekday [i.e., if the *beis din* will not receive witnesses today] let these [the produce to be separated] be the tithes for the remaining produce, but if today is holy [i.e., if the *beis din* will or has already received testimony establishing today as Rosh Hashanah] my words are null and void [i.e., the tithing should not take effect].' He then removes the tithe portions and puts them aside. The result of this is that if the first day really is the holiday, no violation took place, since the tithing did not take effect. If the first day is not the holiday then the tithing is permissible and takes effect. However, at this point he may not yet eat from the produce because he has no way of knowing whether the first day is really a weekday (in which case the tithing took effect and the produce is permissible) or whether the first day is holy (in which case the tithing did not take effect and the produce is still forbidden).

On the second day, he takes the tithes separated conditionally on the first day and says the following: 'If yesterday was holy [so that yesterday's tithing was invalid] let these [the produce separated yesterday] become the tithes for the remainder of the produce; but if today is holy, then the tithes have already been consecrated yesterday[1] and the produce is already permissible.' Again no prohibition has been violated since the tithing only takes effect if the second day is not holy. What has happened, however, is that the produce has now become permissible. Since only one of these two days can be holy and the other is necessarily a weekday, one of these two tithings has to have taken effect. Yet no prohibition has been violated because the condition stipulated has ensured that the tithing takes effect on whichever of the two is really the weekday (*Rav; Rashi* from *Gem. 39b*).

וְכֵן בֵּיצָה שֶׁנּוֹלְדָה בָּרִאשׁוֹן, תֵּאָכֵל בַּשֵּׁנִי. — *And so also, an egg laid on the first* [day of Rosh Hashanah] *may be eaten on the second* [day].

An egg laid on the Sabbath or *Yom Tov* may not be eaten on that day (*Beitzah* 1:1). R' Yehudah, however, permits the egg laid on the first day of Rosh Hashanah to be eaten on the second day in accord with his view that one of the two days of Rosh Hashanah is in reality a weekday. Thus, if the egg laid on the first day is to be forbidden for consumption, it is only upon the premise that the first day was Rosh

1. *R' Yonasan* remarks that on the second day it would seemingly have been sufficient to say, 'If today is a weekday let these be the tithes,' without adding 'if today is holy, the tithes are already consecrated.' The necessity of mentioning this is to impress upon the person performing the separation, ostensibly a forbidden act, the possibility that today, the second day, may be *Yom Tov*.

[ט] **רַבִּי דוֹסָא** בֶּן הַרְכִּינַס אוֹמֵר: הָעוֹבֵר
לִפְנֵי הַתֵּבָה בַּיּוֹם טוֹב שֶׁל
רֹאשׁ הַשָּׁנָה אוֹמֵר: "הַחֲלִיצֵנוּ ה' אֱלֹהֵינוּ אֶת יוֹם
רֹאשׁ הַחֹדֶשׁ הַזֶּה, אִם הַיּוֹם אִם לְמָחָר;" וּלְמָחָר
הוּא אוֹמֵר: "אִם הַיּוֹם אִם אָמֶשׁ." וְלֹא הוֹדוּ לוֹ
חֲכָמִים.

יד אברהם

Hashanah and consequently it would be permitted on the second day — which would be a weekday. If the second day is in reality Rosh Hashanah, then the egg would in effect have been laid on a weekday (Rav).

וְלֹא הוֹדוּ לוֹ חֲכָמִים. — *But the Sages did not agree with him.*

They disagreed with R' Yehudah in both these cases for the same reason as in the previous mishnah — the Sages believe that the two days of Rosh Hashanah are to be viewed not as doubtful festivals of which only one is in reality holy, but as one extended period of holiness, i.e., one festival consisting of two days, both of which are equally holy according to Rabbinic law (Rav). [Since both days are definitely holy, tithing is forbidden on each of them, and the egg laid on the first day remains prohibited on the second because they are viewed as one extended day. (This is the primary application of the concept that the two days of Rosh Hashanah are to be viewed as יוֹמָא אֲרִיכְתָּא, *an extended day.*)]

The Gemara (39b) explains that the three instances used by the mishnah are all necessary to illustrate this disagreement in all its facets. Had the mishnah stated the dispute only in the case of eruv (mishnah 7) we might

have assumed that R' Yehudah's reason for ruling leniently (allowing two *eruvin*) is because no action must be taken on the *Yom Tov* which would even seem to be a violation of it. However, where he must separate tithes, an act normally prohibited on the *Yom Tov*, even if he does so through a conditional separation, thereby technically avoiding the prohibition, we might think that R' Yehudah agrees that this should not be permitted because it *appears* to be a prohibited act. Consequently, the mishnah must add this case, too. However, it could still be argued that in the case regarding the egg, R' Yehudah would agree with the Sages and opt for stringency because the prohibition to eat the egg is based on a Rabbinic ordinance instituted to avoid a Biblical transgression (see *Beitzah* 2b), whereas the rationale for the prohibition against separating tithes is merely because that act is similar to repairing, i.e., putting something unusable into a usable state.

The halachah follows the Sages regarding Rosh Hashanah. However, regarding the two days observed in the Diaspora for the festivals other than Rosh Hashanah, the Sages agree with R' Yehudah that the two days are considered as two separate periods, one of which is a weekday with regard to the laws of our mishnah (Rav; from Gem. Beitzah 4b Orach Chaim 416:1, 413:6, 427:22).[1]

9.

רַבִּי דוֹסָא בֶּן הַרְכִּינַס אוֹמֵר: הָעוֹבֵר לִפְנֵי
הַתֵּבָה בַּיּוֹם טוֹב שֶׁל רֹאשׁ הַשָּׁנָה — R' Dosa ben Harkinas says: He who leads the

prayers [lit. *he who passes before the Ark*] on the Yom Tov of Rosh Hashanah

1. [The terms *first day of Yom Tov* and *second day of Yom Tov* as used in the mishnah refer solely to the two day festival of Rosh Hashanah which was singled out for mention in the previous mishnah. The Mishnah, which was edited in *Eretz Yisrael*, primarily discusses circumstances applicable there. The two day festival as it is practiced in the Diaspora is not mentioned at all in the Mishnah.]

9. **R**' Dosa ben Harkinas says: He who leads the prayers on the *Yom Tov* of Rosh Hashanah says, 'Fortify us, O HASHEM, our God, on this Rosh Chodesh, whether [it is] today or whether [it will be] tomorrow;' and on the morrow he says, '... whether [it is] today or whether [it was] yesterday.' But the Sages did not agree with him.

YAD AVRAHAM

[I.e., the *chazzan* who stands before the Ark while leading the service (see ArtScroll Mishnah *Ta'anis* 2:1; cf. *Tur Orach Chaim* 148 and 150, *Beis Yosef* and *Bach*). When leading the prayer on the first day of Rosh Hashanah (when the actual date of Rosh Chodesh is not yet known) the *chazzan* faces the problem of mentioning that the day is possibly Rosh Chodesh.]

אוֹמֵר: ,,הַחֲלִיצֵנוּ ה' אֱלֹהֵינוּ אֶת יוֹם רֹאשׁ הַחֹדֶשׁ הַזֶּה, אִם הַיּוֹם אִם לְמָחָר'; — *says* [in his prayer], '*Fortify us, O HASHEM, our God, on this Rosh Chodesh, whether* [*it is*] *today or whether* [*it will be*] *tomorrow;*'

I.e., 'fortify us on this Rosh Chodesh day if it is indeed today, or if Rosh Chodesh is tomorrow then fortify us tomorrow' (*Rav; Rashi*). Without the clause making the prayer conditional, the prayer would seem to be a falsehood, since the actual date of Rosh Chodesh is not yet known (*R' Yehonasan*).

R' Dosa's view pertains not only to Rosh Hashanah, but to every Rosh Chodesh (*Gem.* 40a). He mentions Rosh Hashanah only because of the first aspect of his ruling — that Rosh Chodesh must be mentioned in the Rosh Hashanah prayer. Similarly, the conditional clause must, according to R' Dosa, also be appended to the mention of Rosh Hashanah in the prayer. The requirement is framed in terms of Rosh Chodesh only to highlight R' Dosa's view that Rosh Chodesh must be mentioned at all (*Geon Yaakov*).

[It seems that R' Dosa's version of the fourth blessing of the Rosh Hashanah She-

moneh Esrei prayer, where we thank God for His granting us the holiday (... וַתִּתֶּן לָנוּ הַחֲלִיצֵנוּ בְּיוֹם אֶת יוֹם הַזִּכָּרוֹן), had the formula, הַזִּכָּרוֹן הַזֶּה ..., 'Fortify us on this Day of Remembrance ...' R' Dosa's ruling is unique in two aspects: (a) that Rosh Chodesh, too, must be mentioned in this formula; and (b) that the doubtful status of Rosh Chodesh must be considered so that one beseeches God to fortify him on the Rosh Chodesh whenever it is.]

וּלְמָחָר הוּא אוֹמֵר: ,,אִם הַיּוֹם אִם אָמֶשׁ'. — *and on the morrow he says, '... whether* [*it is*] *today or whether* [*it was*] *yesterday.*'

[If he prayed in a place not near enough to the *beis din* to know whether yesterday had been designated Rosh Hashanah or not, and as a result he was forced to celebrate a second day Rosh Hashanah in a state of uncertainty, he must include a clause mentioning the doubtful status of Rosh Chodesh on the second day as well.]

וְלֹא הוֹדוּ לוֹ חֲכָמִים. — *But the Sages did not agree with him.*

They dispute both points made by R' Dosa. They maintain that the phrase used to commemorate Rosh Hashanah — 'the Day of Remembrance' (יוֹם הַזִּכָּרוֹן) — refers to Rosh Chodesh as well, as can be seen from the verse (*Numbers* 10:10): *And on ... your Roshei Chadashim you shall blow the trumpets ... and they shall be* **a remembrance** *for you ...* The Sages also dispute the second point and feel that explicit mention of the doubtful status of the *Yom Tov* would tend to weaken its observance by the people. [By extension they negate the use of a conditional clause even on Rosh

עירוּבִין [א] **מִי** שֶׁהוֹצִיאוּהוּ עוֹבְדֵי כּוֹכָבִים אוֹ רוּחַ
רָעָה, אֵין לוֹ אֶלָּא אַרְבַּע אַמּוֹת.
הֶחֱזִירוּהוּ, כְּאִלּוּ לֹא יָצָא.
הוֹלִיכוּהוּ לְעִיר אַחֶרֶת, נְתָנוּהוּ בְּדִיר אוֹ בְּסַהַר
— רַבָּן גַּמְלִיאֵל וְרַבִּי אֶלְעָזָר בֶּן עֲזַרְיָה אוֹמְרִים:
מְהַלֵּךְ אֶת כֻּלָּהּ. רַבִּי יְהוֹשֻׁעַ וְרַבִּי עֲקִיבָא אוֹמְרִים:
אֵין לוֹ אֶלָּא אַרְבַּע אַמּוֹת.

יד אברהם

Chodesh of other months.] *(Gem. 40a; Tos.).*

The halachah follows the Sages *(Rav; Rambam).*

Chapter 4

As mentioned previously, the *techum* assigned a person usually extends 2,000 cubits to all sides. However, this is so only if this *techum* had been so designated at the onset of the Sabbath or *Yom Tov.* This designation takes place in one of two ways. Either the *techum* surrounding one's home is automatically designated as long as no reason for negating it exists, or one can specifically designate for himself a different *techum* by making an *eruv* which symbolically establishes his place of dwelling for the Sabbath at that location, and from where his *techum* is measured. However, if one, for whatever reason, has no predesignated *techum*, he is allotted a minimal *techum* of four cubits. The following chapter will discuss instances in which either the minimal *techum* applies or the regular *techum* should be considered as predesignated, and various ramifications of these cases.

1.

מִי שֶׁהוֹצִיאוּהוּ עוֹבְדֵי כּוֹכָבִים — *One who was taken out* [of his *techum*] *by gentiles*

I.e., he was taken out forcibly on the Sabbath *(Rav).*

[The designation of a person's *techum* occurs only at the onset of the Sabbath and remains in effect for that entire Sabbath. When one leaves this *techum* on the Sabbath, even against his will, he cannot have a new regular *techum* assigned him. If he left the *techum* willfully (בְּמֵזִיד) the law differs in some details from that outlined here. This is explained below (s.v. כְּאִלּוּ לֹא יָצָא).]

או רוּחַ רָעָה, — *or by an evil spirit*

He suffered a bout of mental derangement during which he left his *techum.* Upon recovery, he found himself stranded outside his *techum (Rav; Rashi).*

The term evil spirit is used by the mishnah to describe any disorder of a person's power of perception, whatever its cause may be *(Rambam, Comm., ed. Kafich).*

אֵין לוֹ אֶלָּא אַרְבַּע אַמּוֹת. — *(he) has only four cubits.*

[He is given a new minimal *techum* of four cubits at his new location. This applies even to one who left the *techum* willfully *(Gem. 41b).* The way these four cubits are measured is discussed below (mishnah 5).]

הֶחֱזִירוּהוּ, — *If they brought him back,*

I.e., they brought him back forcibly to within his original *techum (Rav from Gem. 41b).* [On his own, he would be

4
1

1. **O**ne who was taken out by gentiles or by an evil spirit has only four cubits. If they brought him back, it is as if he never left.

If they took him to another town, [or] if they put him in a fold or in a corral — Rabban Gamliel and R' Elazar ben Azariah say: He may traverse its entirety. R' Yehoshua and R' Akiva say: He has only four cubits.

forbidden to leave his new four cubit *techum*.]

כְּאִלּוּ לֹא יָצָא. — *it is as if he never left.*

He may again traverse the entire city and 2,000 cubits beyond it as if he had never left (*Rav; Rashi*). [His unwilling departure and return on the Sabbath does not deprive him of the *techum* already assigned to him at the onset of the Sabbath.]

The above is true only if both the departure from the *techum* and the subsequent return occurred against the person's will. If either the departure or return was willful, he is allotted only the minimal four cubits even after he is again within his orginal techum (*Rav* from *Gem.* 41b). However, if he departed and returned inadvertently (בְּשׁוֹגֵג) he is accorded the same consideration as if he were forced to do so (*Orach Chaim* 405:5).

הוֹלִיכוּהוּ לְעִיר אַחֶרֶת, — *If they took him to another town,*

If the gentiles [or derangement] took him to a town surrounded by a wall (*Rav; Rashi*). [The wall serves to render the entire city as the legal equivalent of a four cubit square area and subject to the disagreement of *Tannaim* here.]

Many authorities (*Ramban* and others; see *Beur Halachah* 405:5) maintain that this rule applies even to a town not surrounded by a wall. They adduce the rule (see 5:1-3) that the regular 2,000 cubit *techum* is measured from the outskirts of an unwalled town, not from the individual's house, for the entire town is considered as the person's place of dwelling. In an open area one's personal place of dwelling would only include the four cubits around him. It is clear, therefore, that even an unwalled town is considered the equivalent of a person's four cubit place of

dwelling in this respect.

Those holding *Rashi's* view differentiate between the rules for measuring the *techum* in the first place, and those which apply to one who has lost his *techum* and is being assigned a new, minimal *techum*. In this latter case, only a walled city can be considered as four cubits. This view is adopted by *Shulchan Aruch* (*Orach Chaim* 405:5).

נְתָנוּהוּ בְדִיר אוֹ בְסַהַר — — *[or] if they put him in a fold or in a corral —*

Or they put him in a different enclosed area such as a fold or corral. These enclosures are all larger than four cubits (*Rav*).

Above (2:3) it was explained that corrals were located in the towns. Accordingly, the corral here is either in a town not surrounded by walls or situated just outside the town walls. For this reason the walls of the corral become significant [but see *Ramban; Ohr Zarua* 2:146].

רַבָּן גַּמְלִיאֵל וְרַבִּי אֶלְעָזָר בֶּן עֲזַרְיָה אוֹמְרִים: מְהַלֵּךְ אֶת כֻּלָּהּ. — *Rabban Gamliel and R' Elazar ben Azariah say: He may traverse its entirety.*

The entire enclosed area is considered as if it were a four cubit area and he may walk anywhere within the confines of the walls even though he has been allotted only a minimal *techum* (*Rav; Rashi*).

However, this is so only if he had been brought there against his will. If he willfully violated the *techum*, he is not accorded more than four cubits even within the walled area (*Orach Chaim* 405:6; see *Beur Halachah* there and *Tos. R' Akiva* here for a dissenting opinion).

רַבִּי יְהוֹשֻׁעַ וְרַבִּי עֲקִיבָא אוֹמְרִים: אֵין לוֹ אֶלָּא אַרְבַּע אַמּוֹת. — *R' Yehoshua and R'*

מַעֲשֶׂה שֶׁבָּאוּ מִפְּרַנְדִּיסִין, וְהִפְלִיגָה סְפִינָתָם
בַּיָּם. רַבָּן גַּמְלִיאֵל וְרַבִּי אֶלְעָזָר בֶּן עֲזַרְיָה הִלְּכוּ אֶת
כֻּלָּה; רַבִּי יְהוֹשֻׁעַ וְרַבִּי עֲקִיבָא לֹא זָזוּ מֵאַרְבַּע
אַמּוֹת, שֶׁרָצוּ לְהַחֲמִיר עַל עַצְמָן.

[ב] **פַּעַם** אַחַת לֹא נִכְנְסוּ לַנָּמָל עַד שֶׁחֲשֵׁכָה.

יד אברהם

Akiva say: He has only four cubits.

In their opinion the ruling that enclosed areas are considered the equivalent of four cubits refers only to instances in which the person began the Sabbath within the enclosure and not to where he arrived after the onset of the day (*Rav, Rashi,* following one view in *Gem.* 42b).

מַעֲשֶׂה שֶׁבָּאוּ מִפְּרַנְדִּיסִין, — *It once happened* [lit. *a happening*] *that they arrived from Prandisin*

[It once happened that the four *Tannaim* involved in this dispute arrived in *Eretz Yisrael* on the Sabbath eve from a journey originating in Prandisin.[1] Since the ship had entered port before the onset of the Sabbath, their *techum* was measured from the spot where their ship was anchored.]

וְהִפְלִיגָה סְפִינָתָם בַּיָּם. — *and their ship went* [back] *out to sea.*

Before they disembarked, a storm arose, broke their anchor and drove them out to sea. This happened after the onset of the Sabbath (*Meiri; Tif. Yis.*).

[In this instance one (i.e., the four Sages) was forced to leave his original *techum* (measured from the port) and found himself within an enclosure (the

ship). It is thus analogous to the case just discussed.]

רַבָּן גַּמְלִיאֵל וְרַבִּי אֶלְעָזָר בֶּן עֲזַרְיָה הִלְּכוּ אֶת כֻּלָּה; — *Rabban Gamliel and R' Elazar ben Azariah traversed its entirety;*

In accordance with their view that an enclosed area is considered the equivalent of four cubits, they permitted themselves to walk throughout the ship (*Rav; Rashi*).

רַבִּי יְהוֹשֻׁעַ וְרַבִּי עֲקִיבָא לֹא זָזוּ מֵאַרְבַּע אַמּוֹת, שֶׁרָצוּ לְהַחֲמִיר עַל עַצְמָן. — *R' Yehoshua and R' Akiva did not move out of* [their] *four cubits, because they wished to be strict with themselves.*

The Gemara (43a) infers from the last phrase of the mishnah that in reality the four *Tannaim* agree that on a moving ship one may move even beyond four cubits; since the ship is constantly in motion, a minimal *techum* of four cubits cannot be established, for there is no fixed point (where the ship is stationary) against which to measure. Hence, there can be no prohibition against moving beyond the four cubit *techum*. Alternatively, even if we were to fix a point (relative to the sea bottom) against which to measure, since the boat is in motion the person is continuously

---

1. *Mosaf HeAruch* speculates that Prandisin is identical with Brundisium [modern day Brindisi], a port in southern Italy. An allusion to a trip taken by these sages to Rome is found in the Talmud (*Makkos* 24a). The historian R' Isaac HaLevi (*Doros HaRishonim*, v. 3, pp. 348-352) feels that other allusions in the Talmud (*Succah* 23a and 41b; see also *Ma'aser Sheni* 5:9) to a trip taken together by these Sages refer to this voyage to Rome. HaLevi conjectures that this voyage took place during the short tenure of the emperor Nerva (96-98 CE) and was for the purpose of establishing a more congenial attitude in Rome toward the Jews after they had suffered greatly under the rule of Domitian (son of Vespasian and brother of Titus; 81-96 CE). History indeed records that Nerva abolished the special tax Jews had been forced to pay since the Destruction.

4
2

It once happened that they arrived from Prandisin and their ship went out to sea. Rabban Gamliel and R' Elazar ben Azariah traversed its entirety; R' Yehoshua and R' Akiva did not move out of four . cubits, because they wished to be strict with themselves.

2. **O**nce, they did not enter the harbor until night

being moved beyond his four cubit *techum* (as measured against the sea bottom) and is, as a result, constantly being allotted a new four cubits. Wherever he walks on the ship, therefore, is always within his 'new' minimal *techum* (*Rashi* 42b).

It would seem that there is another reason why R' Yehoshua and R' Akiva should have permitted themselves to walk through the entire ship — because they began the Sabbath within the enclosure (the walls of the ship). As explained above, everyone concurs that in such a case the entire enclosed area is considered as four cubits. However, R' Akiva holds that since the primary purpose of the walls of a ship is to keep the boat afloat, and not to serve as partitions, they do not qualify

as an enclosure with regard to this rule (*Tos.* 42b; see *Tos. R' Akiva*; cf. *Rashba* and *Ritva*).[1]

Despite all the above considerations, R' Yehoshua and R' Akiva were voluntarily stringent because of their concern lest the ship suddenly stop (thus fixing a specific four cubit space) without their realization (*Gem.* 43a with *Rashi*).[2]

The halachah follows Rabban Gamliel and R' Elazar ben Azariah in all the cases listed here (*Rambam; Rav*).

[The practical halachah as it applies to one arriving by boat on a Sabbath is too detailed and complicated to be outlined here. See *Orach Chaim* 248:1-3, 404, and 405:5 and commentaries.]

2.

— פַּעַם אַחַת לֹא נִכְנְסוּ לַנָּמֵל עַד שֶׁחֲשֵׁכָה.
Once, they did not enter the harbor until night had fallen.

On a different occasion, these Sages arrived by boat on Friday night not long after the Sabbath had begun. The question arose whether the ship had already reached a point within 2,000

cubits of the city before the onset of the Sabbath — in which case their *techum* would be that of the city (as will be explained below in mishnayos 4, 7) and they would be permitted to walk from the ship to the city, and even 2,000 cubits beyond the city (*Tos.* 43b) — or whether the city was more than 2,000

1. According to the view accepted as halachah (*Orach Chaim* 248:2, 404), laws of *techumin* do not apply to travel above the height of ten fists (from the ground), and one who is on a ship whose bottom floats more than ten fists above the sea or river bottom has no *techum* limit at all. Accordingly, it must be assumed that the ship of our mishnah floated in shallow water less than ten fists above the sea floor, otherwise there would have been no reason for R' Akiva to be strict (*Gem.* 43a).

2. There is another opinion in the *Gem.* (42b) which holds that R' Yehoshua and R' Akiva considered their actions mandated by their interpretation of the law. *Tosafos* (43a) explains that according to this opinion, the phrase 'they wished' means that they wished to act according to their interpretation. The opinion adopted in our commentary is the one which the Gemara, in its conclusion, seems to prefer.

עֵירוּבִין אָמְרוּ לוֹ לְרַבָּן גַּמְלִיאֵל: "מָה אָנוּ לֵירֵד?"

ד/ג אָמַר לָהֶן: "מֻתָּרִים אַתֶּם; שֶׁכְּבָר הָיִיתִי מִסְתַּכֵּל

וְהָיִינוּ בְּתוֹךְ הַתְּחוּם עַד שֶׁלֹּא חֲשֵׁכָה."

[ג] **מִי שֶׁיְּצָא** בִּרְשׁוּת וְאָמְרוּ לוֹ: "כְּבָר

נַעֲשָׂה מַעֲשֶׂה," יֵשׁ לוֹ אַלְפַּיִם

יד אברהם

cubits from the point where their ship had been at the onset of the Sabbath[1] — in which case they would be forced to remain within the four cubit minimal *techum* of one who finds himself outside his original *techum* (*Rav*; *Rashi*). [According to R' Yehoshua and R' Akiva this would restrict them to just four cubits on the ship, while according to Rabban Gamliel and R' Elazar ben Azariah they would be free to move throughout the ship (which is considered as four cubits) but forbidden to leave the ship.]

Rav (based on *Talmud Yerushalmi*) argues that the port could not have been surrounded by walls. If it had been, R' Gamliel would have permitted them to disembark regardless of their location at the onset of the Sabbath. For, in his opinion as recorded in mishnah 1, one who is taken out of his *techum* (in this case by the motion of the ship) and deposited in a walled area may traverse that entire area.

Rashba and *Ritva*, however, maintain that the *Talmud Bavli* disagrees with this argument and that the mishnah refers to even a walled port-city. They resolve the question in two ways. Either (a) Rabban Gamliel was responding to R' Akiva and R' Yehoshua and resolving the question for them in accordance with their view, or (b) the port area was not within the city walls. The question was not, as a superficial reading would suggest, whether they were permitted to disembark, but whether they would be permitted to traverse the entire city as well. If, at the onset of the Sabbath, the ship was within the *techum* of the city, they would be permitted to traverse the entire city, for it would be

considered their Sabbath place of dwelling (see mish. 7). If, however, the ship was not within the city's *techum*, they would be permitted to disembark (according to Rabban Gamliel) and traverse the entire port area, but would not be permitted even one cubit beyond it.

אָמְרוּ לוֹ לְרַבָּן גַּמְלִיאֵל: "מָה אָנוּ לֵירֵד?" — *They asked Rabban Gamliel [lit. they said to him, to Rabban Gamliel]: 'May we disembark [lit. what is regarding our going down]?'*

[The other three sages asked Rabban Gamliel to calculate their *techum* for them.]

The translation reflects the interpretation given the question by *Rav* (see above). According to the interpretation of *Rashba* and *Ritva* merely disembarking was never in doubt. [The port area may have been within 2,000 cubits of where their ship had been at the onset of the Sabbath and merely disembarking would be permitted even according to R' Akiva and R' Yehoshua.] The question was only whether they had the run of the whole city. Thus they asked, 'May we go down [into the entire town]?'

אָמַר לָהֶן: "מֻתָּרִים אַתֶּם; שֶׁכְּבָר הָיִיתִי מִסְתַּכֵּל וְהָיִינוּ בְּתוֹךְ הַתְּחוּם עַד שֶׁלֹּא חֲשֵׁכָה." — *He answered [lit. said to] them: 'You are permitted, for I had been observing and we were within the techum before dark.'*

Rabban Gamliel had been observing the horizon at the onset of the Sabbath to ascertain whether or not they had already arrived within the *techum* of the port-city (*Rav*).

1. Here, too [see footnote to mishnah 1, s.v. רַבִּי יְהוֹשֻׁעַ וְרַבִּי עֲקִיבָא לֹא זָזוּ], the *Gemara* (43a) explains that at the onset of the Sabbath the ship floated in shallow water within ten fists of the harbor bottom, so that the *techum* of the people on board is measured from that place (see *Tos. R' Akiva*).

had fallen. They asked Rabban Gamliel: 'May we disembark?'

He answered them: 'You are permitted, for I had been observing and we were within the *techum* before dark.'

3. **I**f one left with permission and they said to him: 'The act has already been done,' he has two thousand cubits in every direction. If he was within

YAD AVRAHAM

The *Gemara* (43b) relates that Rabban Gamliel had a tube calibrated to see 2,000 cubits and no further. *R' Hai Gaon* (*Teshuvos HaGeonim* 314; *Otzar HaGeonim*; see *Meiri*) explains that this tube was mounted at a fixed height (e.g., four cubits) and slanted at an angle coinciding with that of the upper angle of a right triangle whose upright arm measured that height (e.g., four cubits), and whose horizontal leg measured a *techum* — 2,000 cubits. A person whose line of sight was directed through this tube, at such an angle, would see along the hypotenuse of the triangle, and his line of sight would terminate at the 2,000 cubit mark (cf. *Rambam, Comm.*).

3.

מִי שֶׁיָּצָא בִּרְשׁוּת — *If one left* [the techum] *with permission*

He left the *techum*, to perform an activity for which halachah permits one to transgress the *techum* (*Rambam*). For example, one who had seen the new moon and went beyond the *techum* to testify before the *beis din;* or one who left to rescue a person from an attacking army or from a flood;[1] or a midwife who went to aid in delivering a baby (*Rav; Rashi;* see *Rosh Hashanah* 2:6).

וְאָמְרוּ לוֹ: ,,כְּבָר נַעֲשָׂה מַעֲשֶׂה‟, — *and they said to him: 'The act has already been done,'*

They said to him that Rosh Chodesh has already been proclaimed, or the people have already been saved, or the child has already been delivered, and there is no need for you to proceed further (*Rashi*). [The person now finds himself outside his *techum* and should, by right, be allotted only the minimal four cubit *techum.*]

יֶשׁ לוֹ אַלְפַּיִם אַמָּה לְכָל רוּחַ. — *he has* [a techum of] *two thousand cubits in every direction.*

He is awarded a new, full *techum,* centered at his location at the time he becomes aware that the act has been done (*Rav; Rashi*). A strict application of the law demands that he be given a *techum* of only four cubits. Indeed, this was the rule for most of the Second Temple era. As related in another mishnah: 'Originally they [the witnesses who had left their *techum* to testify about the sighting of the new moon] did not move from there [the courtyard called Beis Yaazek where witnesses to the new moon gathered] all day; [then] Rabban Gamliel the Elder enacted that they should [be permitted to] walk two thousand cubits in every direction. And not only these, but also a midwife who comes to aid a delivery ... have two thousand cubits in every direction' (*Rosh Hashanah* 2:5). [See also *Gem.* 45a.]

1. However, one may transgress the laws of the Sabbath only where danger to a life is present. Where only monetary loss is at stake, no dispensation is granted (*Gem.* 45a).

עירוּבִין אַמָּה לְכָל רוּחַ. אִם הָיָה בְּתוֹךְ הַתְּחוּם, כְּאִלוּ לֹא
יָצָא. שֶׁכָּל הַיּוֹצְאִים לְהַצִּיל חוֹזְרִין לִמְקוֹמָן.

ד/ד

[ד] מִי שֶׁיָּשַׁב בַּדֶּרֶךְ, וְעָמַד וְרָאָה וַהֲרֵי
הוּא סָמוּךְ לָעִיר, הוֹאִיל וְלֹא

יד אברהם

Even if they were actually needed to perform the task they set out to do the same rule applies. They are awarded a new *techum* of two thousand cubits and may not return, as spelled out in *Rosh Hashanah* (2:5). The mishnah informs us here that even though they did not actually accomplish anything by leaving their *techum*, it is not retroactively considered as if they left without permission, but they are still entitled to a new *techum* (*Tif. Yis.*).

אִם הָיָה בְּתוֹךְ הַתְּחוּם, — *If he was within the* techum,

[If at the time he was made aware of the situation he had not yet left his *techum*.]

כְּאִלוּ לֹא יָצָא. — *it is as if he did not leave.*
The *Gemara* (44b) remarks that this statement is puzzling as it seems to be a tautology. Surely if one did not leave the *techum* it is as if he never left. The accepted view interprets this segment as follows: if he had actually left the *techum* but the new *techum* given him partly overlaps his old *techum*, he may leave the new *techum* and return to his old *techum*.

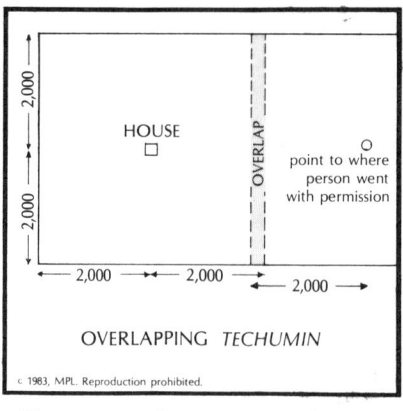

OVERLAPPING *TECHUMIN*

© 1983, MPL. Reproduction prohibited.

However, once he returns to within his old

techum he loses the new *techum* and may not return there. As long as he stays with the new *techum*, though, he is not required to return to his old *techum* (*Mishnah Berurah* 407:7).

שֶׁכָּל הַיּוֹצְאִים לְהַצִּיל חוֹזְרִין לִמְקוֹמָן. — [*And*] *all those leaving* [their techum] *to save* [*people*] *may return to their places.*

[This refers to an armed group of people who left their *techum* to save others. On their return, they may carry their weapons with them (but see below).]

The prefix שׁ (שֶׁכָּל) is usually rendered *because* or *for*. Here the word שֶׁכָּל is rendered as if it were written וְכָל, *and all*. A similar instance of this usage is found in *Beitzah* 1:2 שֶׁאֵמַר כִּירָה מוּכָן הוּא. Some versions (the mishnah in the Talmud and some manuscripts; see *Shinuyei Nuschaos*) have וְכָל or כָּל.]

Rav (based on *Rambam, Comm.*), however, explains the שׁ in a more literal manner. Just as we find another case of a halachic leniency for one who left their *techum* with permission, namely that those who went to save people may return with their weapons, likewise, in our case, do we apply a halachic leniency to one who left the *techum* with permission.

The *Gemara* (45a) demonstrates that even those going to save someone from an attack may *not* return to their original *techum*, contrary to the impression created by the simple reading of the mishnah. Rather the mishnah states that the Sages sanctioned yet another dispensation for those who leave with permission. They may return to the place where they will spend the rest of the Sabbath taking their weapons along with them, although this entails a seemingly unnecessary carrying in the public domain or *karmelis* (*Rav*).

The *Gemara* (45a) relates that this law was

the *techum*, it is as if he did not leave. [And] all those leaving to save [people] may return to their places.

4. **O**ne who sat down while on a journey, then stood up and saw that he was near a city, since

enacted in response to a tragic occurrence. 'At first they would leave their weapons in the first house near the [city] walls. Once, the enemy saw them do this and pursued them. [When] they [the Jews] entered [this house] to gather their weapons the enemy entered after them. [In the ensuing panic] they [the Jews] pushed each other and as a result killed one another in even greater numbers than did the enemy. At that time it was decreed that they be permitted to return to their places with their weapons.'

In another approach the *Gemara* takes the phrase 'may return to their places' to refer to their permission to return from beyond the *techum* to within it. The mishnah speaks of an instance in which the would-be rescuers were defeated and had to seek refuge. In that case, they may go beyond their present *techum* (see *Orach Chaim* 407:3).

4.

One who desires to designate a particular location as his place of dwelling for purposes of reckoning his *techum* may either (a) go to the designated place and stay there until the onset of the Sabbath, thus formally establishing his residence by his presence, or (b) have himself represented at that spot by food sufficient for two meals — i.e., an *eruvei techumin*. Additionally, the Sages allowed a special dispensation for the traveler. He may declare as his dwelling place for the Sabbath a definite area of four cubits square which is less than 2,000 cubits distance from him, without actually being there at the onset of the Sabbath (see mishnah 7). The next two mishnayos discuss cases in which such a declaration had not been made; however, it may reasonably be assumed that if the individual would have realized where he was he could have wanted that other site designated as his place of dwelling.

מִי שֶׁיָּשַׁב בַּדֶּרֶךְ, — *One who sat down while on a journey* [lit. *on the road*],

He was tired and sat down to rest, not realizing that he was within the *techum* of a nearby town (*Rav; Rashi*).

וְעָמַד — *then stood up*

I.e., because he had been sitting he had not realized his whereabouts. When he stood up and was able to see how close the city was, the Sabbath had already begun and it was too late to designate a *techum* (*Ritva*).

Thus the phrase *and stood up* is inserted merely to explain why the person did not realize his whereabouts.

Meiri however understands the word וְעָמַד in its alternative meaning, *he stopped*, and perceives it as referring to a separate case. *One who sat down during a journey or one who stopped*. According to *Meiri* the mishnah alludes to the fact that sitting down, or at least stopping, is a prerequisite for the designation of a spot as one's dwelling place. A person who is moving cannot designate a *techum* with his mere presence: *Rashba* (45b) and *Ritva* (46a) cite *Ravad* who concurs with this view. *Rashba* himself (*Avodas HaKodesh, Shaar* 5) disputes this principle and concludes that indeed one can designate a *techum* while walking. *Shulchan Aruch* and the later *Poskim* are silent on this question and presumably concur with the latter opinion.]

וְרָאָה וַהֲרֵי הוּא סָמוּךְ לָעִיר, — *and saw that he was near a city,*

He now realized that he was within the *techum* of a city (*Rav; Rashi*). [Had

עֵירוּבִין הָיְתָה כַּוָּנָתוֹ לְכָךְ, לֹא יִכָּנֵס — דִּבְרֵי רַבִּי מֵאִיר.

ד/ה רַבִּי יְהוּדָה אוֹמֵר: יִכָּנֵס.

אָמַר רַבִּי יְהוּדָה: "מַעֲשֶׂה הָיָה וְנִכְנַס רַבִּי טַרְפוֹן בְּלֹא מִתְכַּוֵּן."

[ה] **מִי שֶׁיָּשֵׁן** בַּדֶּרֶךְ וְלֹא יָדַע שֶׁחֲשֵׁכָה, יֵשׁ לוֹ אַלְפַּיִם אַמָּה לְכָל רוּחַ — דִּבְרֵי רַבִּי יוֹחָנָן בֶּן נוּרִי. וַחֲכָמִים אוֹמְרִים: אֵין לוֹ אֶלָּא אַרְבַּע אַמּוֹת.

יד אברהם

he realized this before he sat down to rest, he would have designated the city as his מְקוֹם שְׁבִיתָה, *dwelling place for the Sabbath*, and he would be allotted the same *techum* given to all the city's residents.]

הוֹאִיל וְלֹא הָיְתָה כַּוָּנָתוֹ לְכָךְ, — *since it had not been his intention,*

[I.e., he had not consciously intended to designate the city as his place of dwelling. During the time preceding the Sabbath, when one's *techum* is designated, he had not known that the city was near enough to be considered his place of dwelling and, as a result, he tacitly assigned that designation to the place where he was actually sitting.]

לֹא יִכָּנֵס — דִּבְרֵי רַבִּי מֵאִיר. — *he may not enter* [the city] — [*these are*] *the words of R' Meir.*

Since his intention had not been to designate the city as his place of dwelling, he may not enter the city and be considered as one of the residents, i.e., he is not allowed the same *techum* allowed to them. Instead, his 2,000 cubits are measured from his present place and cannot pass beyond this *techum* even if its boundaries end in the middle of the city (*Rav; Rashi*). [He may, of course, enter the part of the city which falls within his *techum*.]

Since in this case the exact limit of his *techum* has not been measured before the Sabbath, one may, as a rule of thumb, reckon

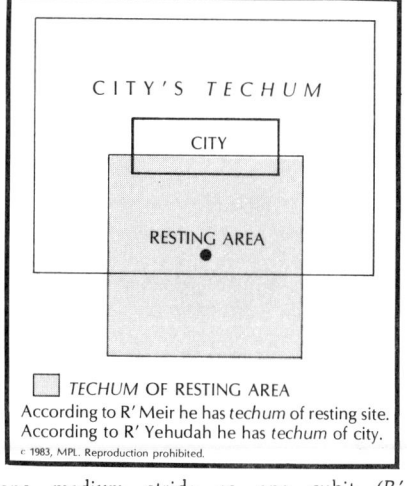

CITY'S TECHUM

CITY

RESTING AREA

☐ TECHUM OF RESTING AREA

According to R' Meir he has *techum* of resting site.
According to R' Yehudah he has *techum* of city.

© 1983, MPL. Reproduction prohibited.

one medium stride as one cubit (*R' Yehonasan from Gem.* 42a).

R' Meir contends that the person's tacit designation of his present location as his dwelling place, although based on the erroneous assumption that the city is yet far off, effectively denies him the city's *techum* (*Ritva*).

This case is not comparable to those described in mishnayos 1 and 2. There, the Sages had not yet given up hope of arriving at the seaport before the Sabbath (*Rashba; Ritva*).

רַבִּי יְהוּדָה אוֹמֵר: יִכָּנֵס. — *R' Yehudah says: He may enter.*

He may traverse the entire *techum* allotted the citizens. Although he had already tacitly designated his present

4
5

it had not been his intention, he may not enter — [these are] the words of R' Meir. R' Yehudah says: He may enter.

R' Yehudah said: 'It once happened that R' Tarfon entered without intent.'

5. **O**ne who slept while on a journey and did not know that it had become dark has two thousand cubits in every direction — [these are] the words of R' Yochanan ben Nuri. But the Sages say: He has only four cubits.

YAD AVRAHAM

location as his dwelling place, the city, nevertheless, assumes that designation. The presumption is that, had he realized prior to the Sabbath where he was, he would certainly have designated the city as his dwelling place. According to the halachah, this overrides his tacit designation which was based on a lack of information (Rashba; cf. Rif, Sha'ar HaTziyun 400:1).

This only applies when it is to the traveler's advantage, such as if this city is his goal, but he mistakenly thought that he had not yet reached its techum. However, if he wishes to retain the techum he had tacitly designated previously, he may do so (Rashba; Mishnah Berurah 400:2).

The halachah follows R' Yehudah (Rav; Orach Chaim 400).

אָמַר רַבִּי יְהוּדָה: ,,מַעֲשֶׂה הָיָה וְנִכְנַס רַבִּי טַרְפוֹן בְּלֹא מִתְכַּוֵּן." — R' Yehudah said: 'It once happened that R' Tarfon entered [a town] without [prior] intent.'

He had not been aware at the onset of the Sabbath of his proximity to the town and had consequently not intended that the town be his dwelling place (Rav; Rashi). [Nevertheless, upon realizing the truth, he entered the city and made full use of its techum. R' Yehudah cites this incident as proof that the Rabbis of the previous generation held his opinion.]

5.

If, during a journey, one found himself far from his intended goal and therefore decided to spend the Sabbath where he was, that place becomes his dwelling place and his techum is measured from there. No declaration to this effect is needed. The obvious, albeit unstated, desire to be allotted a 2,000 cubit techum can serve in lieu of an explicit declaration. However, if a traveler fell asleep on Friday before he had decided where he would spend the Sabbath, and slept through the onset of the Sabbath, this tacit intention and the automatic designation of a place of dwelling is not present.

מִי שֶׁיָּשַׁן בַּדֶּרֶךְ וְלֹא יָדַע שֶׁחֲשֵׁכָה, — One

who slept while on a journey and did not know that it had become dark

[When he awoke it was already after nightfall and too late to designate a dwelling place.]

יֵשׁ לוֹ אַלְפַּיִם אַמָּה לְכָל רוּחַ — דִּבְרֵי רַבִּי יוֹחָנָן בֶּן נוּרִי. — has two thousand cubits in every direction — [these are] the words of R' Yochanan ben Nuri.

R' Yochanan contends that the designation of a 2,000 cubit techum is automatic and not due to the subject's professed or tacit desire. His desire plays a role only where his place of dwelling is to be a place other than the one where he finds himself at the onset of the Sabbath (Rav, from Gem. 45b).

עירובין
ד/ו

רַבִּי אֱלִיעֶזֶר אוֹמֵר: וְהוּא בְּאֶמְצָעָן. רַבִּי יְהוּדָה אוֹמֵר: לְאֵיזֶה רוּחַ שֶׁיִּרְצֶה יֵלֵךְ. וּמוֹדֶה רַבִּי יְהוּדָה שֶׁאִם בֵּרַר לוֹ, שֶׁאֵינוֹ יָכֹל לַחֲזוֹר בּוֹ.

[ו] **הָיוּ** שְׁנַיִם, מִקְצָת אַמּוֹתָיו שֶׁל זֶה בְּתוֹךְ אַמּוֹתָיו שֶׁל זֶה, מְבִיאִין וְאוֹכְלִין בָּאֶמְצַע, וּבִלְבַד שֶׁלֹּא יוֹצִיא זֶה מִתּוֹךְ שֶׁלּוֹ לְתוֹךְ שֶׁל חֲבֵרוֹ. הָיוּ שְׁלֹשָׁה, וְהָאֶמְצָעִי מֻבְלָע בֵּינֵיהֶן, הוּא מֻתָּר

יד אברהם

[R' Yehudah agrees with R' Eliezer's basic premise that the total allotted area measures only four by four cubits. However, he maintains that the center of this area need not be the place of the individual. Rather, he may choose to have his location situated at the perimeter of the four cubit area, with the four cubits extended in whichever direction he chooses, thus allowing him to go a total of four cubits in one direction.]

וּמוֹדֶה רַבִּי יְהוּדָה שֶׁאִם בֵּרַר לוֹ, שֶׁאֵינוֹ יָכֹל לַחֲזוֹר בּוֹ. — Yet R' Yehudah agrees that once he chooses [lit. if he chose] for himself, he cannot retract.

Once he has chosen either by verbal designation or by action, e.g., by walking in a specific direction (Meiri), to have his allotted four cubits in one direction, he cannot change his mind and choose a different direction (Rav). Although the halachah is in accordance with R' Yochanan ben Nuri's view, the disagreement between R' Eliezer, R' Yehudah and the Sages is still relevant to us. There are many other instances where the individual is only allotted four cubits (e.g., mishnah 1) and the exact parameters of this minimal techum have to be defined (Meiri). This question is also relevant regarding the techum measurement of a person who made an eruv and places it in an open area, or one who at the onset of the Sabbath finds himself in such an area and must measure his techum from it. The 2,000 cubit techum is exclusive

— וַחֲכָמִים אוֹמְרִים: אֵין לוֹ אֶלָּא אַרְבַּע אַמּוֹת. But the Sages say: He has only four cubits.

The Sages are of the opinion that a two thousand cubit techum is allotted only where there is a conscious (even if unstated) designation of a dwelling place. Where this is lacking, one is allowed only the four cubits allotted to one who has left his techum (Rav from Gem. 45b).

The halachah is in accordance with R' Yochanan ben Nuri's view (Gem. 46a; Orach Chaim 401:1).

רַבִּי אֱלִיעֶזֶר אוֹמֵר: וְהוּא בְּאֶמְצָעָן. — R' Eliezer says: And he is in their midst.

R' Eliezer agrees with the Sages (Meiri), that in this instance the individual is granted only four cubits, but disagrees with them regarding the extent of these four cubits. The Sages maintain that an individual without a techum is granted four cubits in each direction, i.e., a square measuring eight by eight cubits, whereas R' Eliezer believes that the entire area should measure no more than four by four cubits, with the spot where the person was at the onset of the Sabbath being its center. Thus, this minimal techum extends no more than two cubits in each direction (Rav from Gem. 48a).

רַבִּי יְהוּדָה אוֹמֵר: לְאֵיזֶה רוּחַ שֶׁיִּרְצֶה יֵלֵךְ. — R' Yehudah says: He may go in any direction he wishes.

4
6

R' Eliezer says: And he is in their midst. R'
Yehudah says: He may go in any direction he wishes.
Yet R' Yehudah agrees that once he chooses for
himself, he cannot retract.

6. If there were two, some of the cubits of one
overlapping the cubits of the other, they may
bring [their food] and eat in the middle, provided that
one does not carry from his into his friend's.

If there were three and the middle one's [area] was
overlapped by the other two, he is permitted with

YAD AVRAHAM

of the four (or eight) cubit square and its
measurement begins from the square's
perimeter *(Orach Chaim* 397:1).

Several views as to how the halachah is

decided are given in *Orach Chaim* (396:1; see
commentaries there) but the later authorities
rule that one may go four cubits in every
direction *(Mishnah Berurah* 396:9).

6.

הָיוּ שְׁנַיִם, — *If there were two* [people],
This is a continuation of the previous
mishnah. Two people fell asleep and
were in the position of having only a
minimal *techum* of four cubits each
(Meiri).

The above probably reflects the view of
Rashi and *Rav* too, who, by offering no
comment regarding the situation in the
mishnah, leave the impression that it refers to
the instance just discussed in the previous
mishnah. *Rambam (Comm.)* comments that
this mishnah refers to any case where the
four cubit limit applies, not only *techumin.*
This would include two people standing in a
public domain or a *karmelis* where a person
may carry objects only within a four cubit
area (here the four cubit allowance is defined
by everyone as a four by four cubit area;
Gem. 48a, *Orach Chaim* 396:1). He adds that
the discussion of the mishnah would also
apply to two individuals having regular
2,000 cubit *techumin* which overlapped.

מִקְצָת אַמּוֹתָיו שֶׁל זֶה בְּתוֹךְ אַמּוֹתָיו שֶׁל זֶה,
some of the cubits of one overlapping
[some of] *the cubits of the other,*

For example, if Reuven is located six
cubits away from Shimon, so that the
two cubits to Reuven's right are
identical with the two cubits to
Shimon's left *(Rav; Rashi).*

מְבִיאִין וְאוֹכְלִין בָּאֶמְצַע, — *they may bring*
[*their food*] *and eat in the middle,*

We are not concerned that this
contact will cause Reuven to follow
Shimon into the area permitted to
Shimon but forbidden to Reuven or vice
versa *(Tif. Yis.;* see *Rambam's Comm.).*

וּבִלְבַד שֶׁלֹּא יוֹצִיא זֶה מִתּוֹךְ שֶׁלּוֹ לְתוֹךְ
שֶׁל חֲבֵרוֹ. — *provided that one does not
carry from his* [area; lit. *from between
his*] *into his friend's* [area; lit. *to
between his friend's*].

Each must be careful not to put his
belongings into the area permitted only
to the other, e.g., Reuven may not take
his food and place it in the area
forbidden to him even if he himself
remains in his allotted area. The
belongings of a person are also allotted
the same *techum* as their owner *(Beitzah*
5:3) and may not be transported outside
that *techum (Rashi).*

הָיוּ שְׁלֹשָׁה, וְהָאֶמְצָעִי מֻבְלָע בֵּינֵיהֶן, — *If
there were three* [people] *and the middle
one's* [area] *was overlapped by the other
two* [lit. *swallowed between them*],

Three people are situated in such a
way that the areas of Reuven and
Shimon do not overlap so that any

[91]   THE MISHNAH/ERUVIN—Chapter Four: *Mi Shehotziuhu*

עירוּבִין עִמָּהֶן, וְהֵן מֻתָּרִין עִמּוֹ; וּשְׁנַיִם הַחִיצוֹנִים אֲסוּרִים
ד/ו זֶה עִם זֶה.

אָמַר רַבִּי שִׁמְעוֹן: "לְמָה הַדָּבָר דּוֹמֶה? לְשָׁלֹשׁ
חֲצֵרוֹת הַפְּתוּחוֹת זוֹ לְזוֹ, וּפְתוּחוֹת לִרְשׁוּת
הָרַבִּים. עֵרְבוּ שְׁתֵּיהֶן עִם הָאֶמְצָעִית, הִיא מֻתֶּרֶת
עִמָּהֶם, וְהֵם מֻתָּרוֹת עִמָּהּ; וּשְׁתַּיִם הַחִיצוֹנוֹת
אֲסוּרוֹת זוֹ עִם זוֹ."

יד אברהם

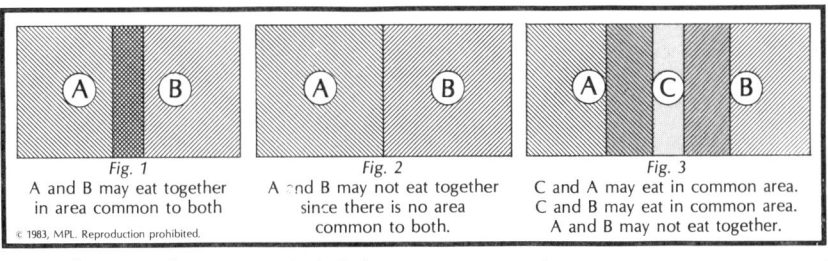

Fig. 1
A and B may eat together
in area common to both
© 1983, MPL. Reproduction prohibited.

Fig. 2
A and B may not eat together
since there is no area
common to both.

Fig. 3
C and A may eat in common area.
C and B may eat in common area.
A and B may not eat together.

contact between them is precluded; but the area of Levi is situated midway between them and so is partly accessible to both Reuven and Shimon, e.g., Levi is stationed in the middle with Reuven four cubits away on his right and Shimon four cubits away on his left, so that Reuven is eight cubits away from Shimon. Reuven has no common area with Shimon (even according to the Sages of the previous mishnah) but Levi has area in common with Reuven, to his right, and with Shimon, to his left (adapted from *Rav* and *Rashi* to reflect the view accepted by halachah).

הוּא מֻתָּר עִמָּהֶן, וְהֵן מֻתָּרִין עִמּוֹ; — *he is permitted* [to bring and eat] *with* [each of] *them, and they are* [each] *permitted with him;*

[We are not concerned that the middle person (Levi) will transport one's (Reuven's) belongings into the other's (Shimon's) area.]

וּשְׁנַיִם הַחִיצוֹנִים אֲסוּרִים זֶה עִם זֶה. — *but the outer two are forbidden* [to bring and eat] *with each other.*

[I.e., although the two outermost members — Reuven and Shimon — have no mutual area, each may bring his food

and eat with Levi. We are not concerned that the presence of Reuven and Shimon's belongings in Levi's area will cause Levi to transport these belongings to areas permitted to him but forbidden to their owner.]

אָמַר רַבִּי שִׁמְעוֹן: "לְמָה הַדָּבָר דּוֹמֶה? — *Said R' Shimon: 'To what is this comparable?*

R' Shimon finds a halachic parallel to the ruling permitting the middle person to eat with each of the outermost people while the outermost people themselves may not eat with one another.

To understand the comparison a few comments about the laws of *eruvei chatzeiros* are necessary.

As already explained (pref. to 1:1), in mishnaic times many houses opened into a common courtyard which, along with other courtyards, opened into a common alley that opened into the public street. The Sages prohibited carrying from an area belonging to one owner to that of another even if the concerned areas are properly partitioned private domains, unless the properties were merged by the setting of *eruvei chatzeiros.*

4
6
them, and they are permitted with him; but the outer two are forbidden with each other.

Said R' Shimon: 'To what is this comparable? To three courtyards which open one into the other and which open into the public domain. If the two made an *eruv* with the middle one, it is permitted to them, and they are permitted to it; but the two outer ones are forbidden one to another.'

YAD AVRAHAM

If two courtyards are situated one behind the other, so that the members of the inner courtyard must pass through the outer in order to pass into the street, the outer courtyard is considered the joint property of the members of both courtyards (since the residents of the inner courtyard also have the right to walk through it), and nobody may carry from his house into the outer courtyard unless the inhabitants of both courtyards have made an *eruvei chatzeiros* together (see 6:9-10). However, if the courtyards are arranged alongside each other so that each has its own access to the alley, each is viewed as a separate unit and the inhabitants of each may carry into their courtyard without incorporating the members of the adjoining courtyard into their *eruv*. They may not, however, carry into the adjoining courtyard. If they wish, they have the *option* of making a joint *eruv* with the neighboring courtyard (if there is a door between them) to permit them to carry from one courtyard to the other.

לְשָׁלֹשׁ חֲצֵרוֹת הַפְּתוּחוֹת זוֹ לְזוֹ, וּפְתוּחוֹת לִרְשׁוּת הָרַבִּים. — *To three courtyards which open one into the other and which* [also] *open into the public domain.*

Since each courtyard is open to the public domain, none is considered the joint property of its residents and the residents of another courtyard. Thus, an *eruv* may be set within each courtyard to permit its inhabitants to carry from their houses into it; no joint *eruv* with another courtyard is necessary. However, since they also open one into

another, they have the option of making a joint *eruv*, which would permit the carrying of objects from one courtyard to another *(Rav; Rashi).*

עֵרְבוּ שְׁתֵּיהֶן עִם הָאֶמְצָעִית, הִיא מֻתֶּרֶת עִמָּהֶם, וְהֵם מֻתָּרוֹת עִמָּה; וּשְׁתַּיִם הַחִיצוֹנוֹת אֲסוּרוֹת זוֹ עִם זוֹ.״ — *If the* [residents of the] *two* [outer ones] *made an* eruv *with the* [residents of the] *middle one, it* [i.e., the middle courtyard] *is permitted to them* [i.e., the residents of the outer courtyards], *and they* [i.e., the outer courtyards] *are permitted to it; but the* [residents of the] *two outer ones are forbidden one to another.'*

[If the residents of each of the two outer courtyards respectively made a joint *eruv* with the middle one, the inhabitants of the two outer courtyards may carry into the middle one (and vice versa), but they may not carry from one outer courtyard, across the middle one, and into the other outer courtyard.]

Objects from the middle courtyard may be carried to either of the outer courtyards and objects from the outer courtyards may be carried into the middle courtyard. However, no object

Objects may be transported between A and B and between C and B but not between A and C.

מִי שֶׁבָּא [ז] בַּדֶּרֶךְ וְחָשְׁכָה לוֹ, וְהָיָה מַכִּיר אִילָן אוֹ גָּדֵר, וְאָמַר: "שְׁבִיתָתִי תַחְתָּיו," לֹא אָמַר כְּלוּם. "שְׁבִיתָתִי בְעִקָּרוֹ,"

יד אברהם

which began the Sabbath in any of the houses[1] of the outer courtyards may be carried to the other outer courtyard even via the middle courtyard.[2]

The *Gemara* (48a) points out that the parallel drawn by R' Shimon is not given to clarify the law of *techum* but rather the reverse — the analogy is used to prove a halachic point in regard to the law of *eruvei chatzeiros*. R' Shimon infers from the law of *techum* that just as we allow the person whose *techum* area is to the right of center to carry into the central area (to the limit of his *techum*), and at the same time allow the person whose *techum* area is to the left of center to also carry into the central area — and we are not concerned that they will forget themselves and carry into each other's area — so, too, we need not be concerned that the inhabitants of the outer courtyards will emulate the inhabitants of the middle courtyard and

carry to the opposite outer courtyard. The *Gemara* adds that the Sages (R' Yehudah; see 46b) disagree and differentiate between the two cases. A courtyard contains many inhabitants and therefore the concern for error is greater (*Rashi* 48a). *Rambam* (*Comm.*) explains that in the case of *techum* the middle individual will remind his outer colleagues if they forget themselves and attempt to carry into areas forbidden to them. In the case of the courtyards, however, the residents of the middle courtyard cannot be relied upon to remind those of the outer courtyards because there are many people in the various courtyards and the people in the middle one may not know who lives where.

The halachah follows R' Shimon's view (*Rav* from *Gem.* 46b; *Orach Chaim* 378:1).

7.

מִי שֶׁבָּא בַּדֶּרֶךְ וְחָשְׁכָה לוֹ, — *One who was traveling as darkness approached* [lit. *and it became dark for him*],

[Late on Friday afternoon he realized that night was approaching and that he would not reach his destination before the onset of the Sabbath.]

וְהָיָה מַכִּיר אִילָן אוֹ גָּדֵר, — *and he knew [of] a tree or a fence*,

He knew of a landmark, in the direction he was headed, which he would be able to reach before nightfall if he would travel at his optimum speed, but he was too tired to travel at such a speed and consequently knew that he would not reach that place before nightfall (*Rav* from *Gem.* 51a).

If he would actually reach the landmark before nightfall there would be no problem in designating it as his place of dwelling. As already seen in mishnah 5, and more explicitly further in this mishnah, being in a specific location is a prime method of making an *eruvei techumin*. It is only if the designated site will not be reached by nightfall, and the designation must therefore be made verbally from a distance, that the halachic distinctions drawn in our mishnah need be discussed.

An example of this case is as follows: Close to nightfall a man found himself 4,000 cubits from his home. If the center point of his *techum*, i.e., his place of dwelling, were designated at his present site he would not be able to reach his home on the Sabbath. However, he

1. If the objects were in the courtyard at the beginning of the Sabbath they may be carried from one courtyard to another even without an *eruv*. See further 9:1.

2. Even if one puts the object down in the middle courtyard it is still prohibited to carry it out to the forbidden courtyard.

4
7

7. **O**ne who was traveling as darkness approached, and he knew [of] a tree or a fence, and said, 'My Sabbath dwelling place is beneath it,' has said nothing. [If, however, he said,] 'My Sabbath

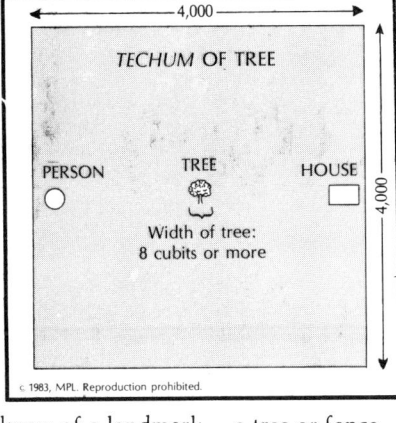

knew of a landmark — a tree or fence — midway between his present site and his home, which, if recognized as the center of his *techum* would include in that *techum* both his present location and his home, and thus enable him to reach his house *(Rashi).* [The tree, of course, must be within 2,000 cubits of his present location. If it were beyond that there would be no question of designating it as the center of his *techum* since he would then be left without (i.e., outside) any *techum* at all.[11]]

",שְׁבִיתָתִי תַחְתָּיו,, :וְאָמַר — *and said, 'My Sabbath dwelling place is beneath it,'*

[He designated from afar the entire area under the tree or next to the fence as the center point of his *techum.*]

לֹא אָמַר כְּלוּם. — *has said nothing* [i.e., his statement is invalid].

Because he did not designate a specific area of four by four cubits as his dwelling place, the area under the

tree cannot be regarded as such. The mishnah makes the point that a Sabbath dwelling place must be an identifiable area of four by four cubits and his *techum* is measured from there *(Rambam, Comm.* and *Hil. Eruvin* 7:5).

The mishnah assumes that the area under the tree is at least eight by eight cubits and thus the vague declaration, '*My Sabbath dwelling place is beneath it,'* cannot be construed as referring to a specific area. If the area was less than eight cubits in both dimensions, the declaration would be considered as referring to a specific area for at least a small strip would perforce be definitely designated *(Rav* from *Gem.* 50b). [There would thus be a definite point from which to measure and the declaration would then be valid.]

The view of the *Amora* Shmuel *(Gem.* 49b) that he is given 2,000 cubits from his present location is accepted by most authorities. The *Amora* Rav's view is that since he wanted his dwelling place to be under the tree and his intent was therefore *not* to establish a dwelling place at his present location, he has no dwelling place or 2,000 cubit *techum* at all since at his present location because he did not want it to be here, nor under the tree because he cannot legally make it there.

As stated, most authorities rule according to Shmuel. *Ravad* (quoted by *Rashba)* and *Rav* (the commentator) accept the opinion of Rav (the *Amora).*

Rashi interprets differently. Shmuel holds that the declaration of a dwelling place is valid even if its exact boundaries have not been specified. Therefore, in the case of the mishnah, he is given a dwelling place or new center point for his *techum* in the area beneath the tree. Since, however, this area is large and the exact location of the dwelling

1. There is a question as to whether the individual must be within the 2,000 cubit distance from the tree at the time of his verbal declaration, or it is good enough as long as he enters this area just before nightfall (even after his declaration). *Be'ur Halachah* (409:11) shows that *Rambam's* language *(Hil. Eruvin* 7:2) suggests the latter, more lenient view (see *Sfas Emes* here).

עירוּבִין מְהַלֵּךְ מִמְּקוֹם רַגְלָיו וְעַד עִקָּרוֹ אַלְפַּיִם אַמָּה,
ד/ח וּמֵעִקָּרוֹ וְעַד בֵּיתוֹ אַלְפַּיִם אַמָּה. נִמְצָא מְהַלֵּךְ
מִשֶּׁחֲשֵׁכָה אַרְבַּעַת אֲלָפִים אַמָּה.

[ח] **אִם** אֵינוֹ מַכִּיר, אוֹ שֶׁאֵינוֹ בָקִי בַּהֲלָכָה,
וְאָמַר: "שָׁבַתִּי בִמְקוֹמִי," זָכָה לוֹ
מְקוֹמוֹ אַלְפַּיִם אַמָּה לְכָל רוּחַ. עֲגֻלּוֹת — דִּבְרֵי
רַבִּי חֲנִינָא בֶּן אַנְטִיגְנוֹס. וַחֲכָמִים אוֹמְרִים:

יד אברהם

place is therefore indeterminate, the calculations of the *techum* must be made from the points which will yield the most stringent results. Thus the *techum* may only be extended 2,000 cubits from the point in the area which is furthest from the boundary being considered, thereby yielding a shorter limit. The area beneath the tree will, in effect, be subtracted from the regular *techum* area reducing its size. For example, if the area beneath the tree measures thirty by thirty cubits, the *techum*, as measured to the north, will have as its focal point the southernmost extremity of this area. When measuring to the south, one begins from the northernmost extremity, with the result that the distance between the north and south poles of the *techum*, instead of measuring 4,000 cubits as usual, will be only 3,970 cubits.

The mishnah, however, speaks of an instance in which the individual is 4,000 cubits away from his home and the tree is at the midpoint. He made his declaration with the expectation that it would allow him to walk 4,000 cubits in that direction and reach his house. Indeed, had he specified the exact location of his dwelling place he would have been able to do so. However, since he was not specific in his designation, he is not permitted to reach his objective. This is what the mishnah means by 'he has said nothing.' Although the declaration is (in this view) valid, it is nevertheless not enough to realize his objective (see *Orach Chaim* 409:11 where both views are presented).

שָׁבַתִּי בְעִקָּרוֹ, — [If, however, he said,] 'My Sabbath dwelling place is at

its trunk,'

This mode of designation avoids the indeterminacy presented by the previous one; it refers to a specific spot — the trunk of the tree (*Rav; Rashi*).

מְהַלֵּךְ מִמְּקוֹם רַגְלָיו וְעַד עִקָּרוֹ אַלְפַּיִם אַמָּה, וּמֵעִקָּרוֹ וְעַד בֵּיתוֹ אַלְפַּיִם אַמָּה. — *he may walk from his present location* [lit. *from the place of his feet*] *to the trunk* [a distance of] *two thousand cubits, and from the trunk to his house* [an additional] *two thousand cubits.*

In this formulation the declaration is valid and the individual's dwelling place is fixed at the site of the trunk. As a result, his *techum* extends 2,000 cubits in all directions from the tree trunk. Thus, for example, if the individual found himself 2,000 cubits to the north of the tree trunk and his house was situated 2,000 cubits south of it (i.e., he is 4,000 cubits away from his house), he may proceed to his house after making the above declaration (*Rav*).

נִמְצָא מְהַלֵּךְ מִשֶּׁחֲשֵׁכָה אַרְבַּעַת אֲלָפִים אַמָּה. — *Thus* [lit. *it is found*], *he may go four thousand cubits after dark.*

[If the individual stays at the site from which he made his declaration until it is dark, he may traverse the 4,000 cubit distance separating him from his home after dark.]

8.

אִם אֵינוֹ מַכִּיר — *If he does not know* [of any landmark],

He wishes to travel the maximum 4,000 cubit distance after dark but is not

4
8
dwelling place is at its trunk,' he may walk from his present location to the trunk two thousand cubits, and from the trunk to his house two thousand cubits. Thus, he may go four thousand cubits after dark.

8. If he does not know, or he is not conversant with the law, and he said: 'My Sabbath dwelling place is at my location,' his location acquires two thousand cubits for him in every direction. In a circle — [these are] the words of R' Chanina ben Antignos.

YAD AVRAHAM

familiar enough with the region to designate any far-off, unseen, site as his dwelling place.

אוֹ שֶׁאֵינוֹ בָּקִי בַּהֲלָכָה, — *or he is not conversant with the law,*

He does know of a potential site for designation but is not knowledgeable enough in the halachah to employ the stratagem described earlier.

This case, which the mishnah cites to make a halachic point, is not comparable to the one in mishnah 4. In that instance the designation made by a person who was unaware of his whereabouts is disregarded. Instead, he is given the designation we assume he would have made had he been informed. There it is evident that he would have designated the city as his place of dwelling had he known he was within its boundaries, whereas here it is not self-evident that he knows of a tree which he could have designated *(R' Yehonasan* and *Tos. Yom Tov).*

וְאָמַר: "שְׁבִיתָתִי בִמְקוֹמִי,, — *and he said: 'My Sabbath dwelling place is at my [present] location,'*

Tosafos (49b) demonstrates that the term *said* here is not used in its literal sense, since it is not necessary for him to actually declare his *techum* in order to have it measured from the site where he is at the onset of the Sabbath (see mishnah 5).

זָכָה לוֹ מְקוֹמוֹ אַלְפַּיִם אַמָּה לְכָל רוּחַ. — *his location acquires two thousand cubits for him in every direction.*

[His presence in that place at the onset of the Sabbath is sufficient to gain

the privileges of a 2,000 cubit *techum* for him, even though he has no food with which to make a formal *eruv.*]

[Although the regular *techum* extends 2,000 cubits from an individual's dwelling place (see *(Orach Chaim* 397:1), this dwelling place consists of the minimal four cubit *techum* allotted to each person. The 2,000 cubits are therefore measured from the perimeter of these four cubits. Thus, according to the halachically accepted view that the four cubits extend to every side of the individual (see above mishnah 5, s.v. וּמוֹדֶה רַבִּי יְהוּדָה, and *Orach Chaim* 396:1) and encompasses an area measuring eight by eight cubits, the exact extent of the *techum* from its center is 2,004 cubits and the entire length of the *techum* is 4,008 cubits. This fine point of halachah is indicated by the language of the mishnah. The mishnah does not say, זָכָה לוֹ אַלְפַּיִם אַמָּה, *he acquires 2,000 cubits,* but זָכָה לוֹ מְקוֹמוֹ אַלְפַּיִם אַמָּה, *his location,* i.e. the minimal four cubit dwelling place allotted to every person, *acquires for him 2,000 cubits ...* The 2,000 cubit *techum* is given in *addition* to the minimal four cubits. For purposes of simplification the *techum* is given as 2,000 instead of the more cumbersome 2,004.]

עֲגֻלוֹת — דִּבְרֵי רַבִּי חֲנִינָא בֶּן אַנְטִיגְנוֹס. — *In a circle — [these are] the words of R' Chanina ben Antignos.*

[The disagreement recorded here is not restricted to this context, but is relevant to all *techum* measurements. According to R' Chanina ben Antignos the 2,000 (or 2,004) cubits are taken as the radius of a circle with one's place of dwelling as the center.]

עֵירוּבִין מְרֻבָּעוֹת, כִּטַבְלָא מְרֻבַּעַת, כְּדֵי שֶׁיְּהֵא נִשְׂכָּר לַזָּוִיּוֹת.

[ט] **וְזוֹ** הִיא שֶׁאָמְרוּ: ,,הֶעָנִי מְעָרֵב בְּרַגְלָיו.'' אָמַר רַבִּי מֵאִיר: ,,אָנוּ אֵין לָנוּ אֶלָּא עָנִי.''

יד אברהם

וַחֲכָמִים אוֹמְרִים: מְרֻבָּעוֹת — *But the Sages say: In a square,*

A line measuring 2,000 cubits is drawn to each of the four directions of the compass[1] and a square is then drawn around it, so that the end point of each of these lines is perpendicular to, and bisects, a side of the square. The entire square then is reckoned as the area of the *techum*. The advantage to this system is the gain of additional distance at the corners, as the mishnah explains below.

The *Gemara* (51a) finds support for each of the views stated here in the verses describing the *open area* (מִגְרָשׁ) surrounding each of the cities of the Levites (*Numbers* 35:5). This area measured 2,000 cubits in each direction (similar to the Sabbath *techum*) and formed a square around the city. R' Chanina finds a hint in the language of the verse that the 2,000 cubits are to be arranged in a square only in the case of the Levites, whereas the Sages find hints

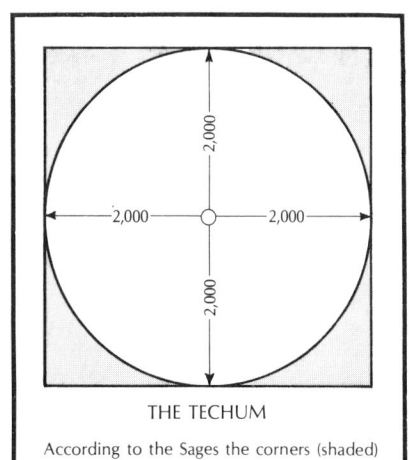

THE TECHUM

According to the Sages the corners (shaded) are incorporated into the *techum*.

© 1983, MPL. Reproduction prohibited.

indicating that the Sabbath *techum* also follows this pattern *(Rav)*.

כִּטַבְלָא מְרֻבַּעַת, — *like a square board,*

The *Tanna* mentions the square

1. In reference to the *techum* measurements of a town the *Gemara* (56a) states that the square's sides should face the points of the compass. However, *R' Yehonasan* (there) states that this directive is merely 'good advice' and not binding. *Noda BiYehudah* (v. 2, *Orach Chaim* 51) states that this view is unopposed and rules that townspeople may arrange the 'square' of the *techum* in any manner advantageous to them.

Although *Noda BiYehudah* does not clearly say so, it would seem to follow from this that an individual finding himself on the road at the onset of the Sabbath and confronted with the necessity of designating a *techum* area may arrange his *techum* square so that his present site is in one corner of the square and his destination in the corner diagonally opposite it, thus allowing him to traverse 5600 cubits. Indeed, this conclusion is reached (independently) by *Mirkeves HaMishneh* (Hil. Shabbos 27:2). However, *Chazon Ish* (Orach Chaim 110:23) vigorously opposes this view, asserting that it contradicts the apparent meaning of the *Gemara* cited earlier and of the *Poskim*. This opinion seems to be shared by *Mishnah Berurah* 398:7. A support for this view may be found in the previous mishnah which seemingly allows 2,000 cubits until the tree and 2,000 more cubits until his house as the maximum range possible. This is true according to *Chazon Ish* if the two points under discussion are situated due east and west or due north and south. According to the first view, however, a substantially greater distance is available by a judicious arrangement of the square.

But the Sages say: In a square, like a square board, so that he may gain the corners.

9. This is what they have said: 'The poor man may make an *eruv* with his feet.'

Said R' Meir: 'We can apply this only to a poor man'.

YAD AVRAHAM

board to indicate that in squaring the *techum* one need not be more precise than the average person's abilities allow. It is sufficient for it to be as square as what is commonly considered a square board, even though if the board were measured with precise instruments it would prove to be out of alignment (*Rambam, Comm.*).

כְּדֵי שֶׁיְּהֵא נִשְׂכָּר לַזָּוִיּוֹת. — *so that he may gain the corners.*

If the *techum* is plotted as a circle, one

may go only 2,000 cubits in any direction. If the circle is enclosed within a square, the 2,000 cubit restriction is true only at the four points where the square and circle make contact. Moving away from those points, the distance from the center to the parameters increases steadily until it reaches its maximum in the corners. The halachah accepts as a rule of thumb that the length of a square's diagonal measures one and two-fifths times the length of its side.

9.

וְזוֹ הִיא שֶׁאָמְרוּ: — *This is what they have said:*

The Sages of an earlier generation formulated a rule addressed to the case presented in the previous mishnah, in which the *techum* is assigned by a mere verbal declaration made at a great distance from the designated dwelling place (based on *Rambam's Comm.;* from *Gem.* 51b).

[The codex of the mishnah predates by many generations the Sages whose names figure in it most frequently (e.g., Beis Shammai and Beis Hillel, R' Meir and R' Yehudah, etc.). Most of the anonymous material in it was taken by Rabbi Yehudah HaNassi (the compiler and editor of Mishnah as we know it) from this earlier codex. Here the mishnah refers to this codex, explicitly stating, 'This [the cases brought in the previous mishnayos] is what the Sages [in the earlier codex meant when they] said ... The following segment of the mishnah cites the disagreement of R' Yehudah and R' Meir as to how to interpret the statement in the early codex. (See *Tos. R' Akiva, Pesachim* 1:1 and *Keilim* 30:4; *Yad Avraham* in ArtScroll

Pesachim 1:1; *Doros HaRishonim, v.* 1, pp. 206-310, Israeli ed.)]

„הֶעָנִי מְעָרֵב בְּרַגְלָיו." — *'The poor man may make an* eruv *with his feet.'*

[Ordinarily, establishing a Sabbath dwelling place outside of one's actual dwelling (for *techum* purposes) is done by placing food at the desired site prior to the Sabbath. However, the Sages taught that the poor man may make an *eruv* with his feet, i.e., his presence at the site, even without food, is as effective as placing food there.] In the situation described in the mishnah, a traveler stranded short of his destination on the eve of the Sabbath is considered *poor* even if he is rich (*Rav; Rashi*).

— אָמַר רַבִּי מֵאִיר: „אָנוּ אֵין לָנוּ אֶלָּא עָנִי." *Said R' Meir: 'We can apply this* [rule] *only to a poor man* [lit. *we do not have only a poor man*].'

[R' Meir takes the statement of the Sages at its face value. The mention of a

רַבִּי יְהוּדָה אוֹמֵר: ,,אֶחָד עָנִי וְאֶחָד עָשִׁיר; לֹא
אָמְרוּ: ,מְעָרְבִין בְּפַת,׳ אֶלָּא לְהָקֵל עַל הֶעָשִׁיר,
שֶׁלֹא יֵצֵא וִיעָרֵב בְּרַגְלָיו.׳׳

[יז] **מִי שֶׁיָּצָא** לֵילֵךְ בְּעִיר שֶׁמְעָרְבִין בָּהּ,
וְהֶחֱזִירוֹ חֲבֵרוֹ, הוּא מֻתָּר

יד אברהם

'poor man' in the statement allowing an *eruv* to be made with one's feet excludes a rich man.] R' Meir is of the opinion that the primary method of making an *eruv* is by placing food at the desired spot. The option of establishing an *eruv* with one's feet is a special dispensation granted only where placing food at the site is impractical, i.e., for a poor man (*Rav; Rambam;* from *Gem.* 51b citing R' Nachman).

As mentioned earlier, a stranded traveler is considered poor in this context no matter what his financial status is because he has no food to spare for the *eruv*. When an individual is at home and wishes to make an *eruv*, however, the question of whether he must place food at the desired spot is dependent on his economic status. Only a person so poor that he cannot spare the food for an *eruv* is allowed to make an *eruv* with his feet (*Ritva; Mishnah Berurah* 410:7 and *Be'ur Halachah* there).

רַבִּי יְהוּדָה אוֹמֵר: ,,אֶחָד עָנִי וְאֶחָד עָשִׁיר; — R' Yehudah says: 'Both [to] a poor man and [to] a rich man;

[Both may make an *eruv* 'with their feet.' The expression 'the poor man' does not exclude a rich man, it merely reflects the common usage — only the poor tend to use this provision. The rich ordinarily eschew this method, preferring in its place the more convenient method of placing food, either personally or through an agent, which does not require their presence at the spot at the onset of the Sabbath.] The *Gemara* 51b (R' Nachman's view) demonstrates that R' Yehudah's statement refers only to the verbal declaration, 'Let my Sabbath dwelling place be at my location.' When

the person is not at the designated spot at nightfall yet wishes to declare it as his dwelling place by saying, 'Let my Sabbath dwelling place be beneath that tree' (mishnah 7), even R' Yehudah agrees that the *eruv* takes effect only if the person is poor or on a journey. In this case, since the *eruv* is not effected even with his feet (he is not there), a special dispensation is necessary and this was granted only to the poor or to travelers (*Rav* based on *Rambam, Hil. Eruvin* 7:3).

Some authorities, however, maintain that even a poor man may not establish an *eruv* with a mere declaration as long as he is in his home and that the dispensation to establish an *eruv* by mere declaration is granted only to a traveler, whether poor or rich (see *Be'ur Halachah* to 410:1). Even a poor man, while at home, has the option to either establish an *eruv* with his feet or to send food to the designated location (*Orach Chaim* 409:13; see also *Be'ur Halachah* there).

לֹא אָמְרוּ: ,מְעָרְבִין בְּפַת,׳ אֶלָּא לְהָקֵל עַל הֶעָשִׁיר, שֶׁלֹא יֵצֵא וִיעָרֵב בְּרַגְלָיו.׳׳ — they did not say, "We may make an *eruv* with bread," except to make it easier for the rich man, so that he not [be forced to] go out and make an *eruv* with his feet.'

This segment is a continuation of R' Yehudah's statement. In his view the primary method of making an *eruv* is with one's feet, i.e., he should be at the desired loction before nightfall and remain there until it is definitely night (see *Mishnah Berurah* 409:26). However, the Sages, to make setting an *eruv* easier, allowed one to be represented by a token amount of food placed at that

R' Yehudah says: 'Both a poor man and a rich man; they did not say, "We may make an *eruv* with bread," except to make it easier for the rich man, so that he not go out and make an *eruv* with his feet.'

10. One who set out for a town for which they may make an *eruv*, but his friend turned him back, he may go, but all the townspeople are

YAD AVRAHAM

spot before the Sabbath. Nevertheless, anyone wishing to employ the basic method of 'making an *eruv* with his feet' may do so (*Rav* from *Gem.* 51b).

The *Gemara* explains in light of the above that the opening statement of the mishnah, 'This is what they have said ... which implies that the statement containing the ruling permitting making an *eruv* with one's feet refers only to specific instances and is not a general ruling, expresses the view of R' Meir.

The halachah is in accord with R' Yehudah's view (*Gem.* 94a; *Rambam, Hil. Eruvin* 7:1; *Orach Chaim* 409:7).

10.

מִי שֶׁיָּצָא לֵילֵךְ בְּעִיר שֶׁמְּעָרְבִין בָּהּ, — *One who set out* [on Friday] *for a town for which they may make an* eruv,

An individual who was appointed by his townspeople as their agent to set an *eruv* [of food] at a specific spot to enable them to go to a neighboring town which was accessible to them only through an *eruv* (*Rav; Rambam;* cf. *R' Chananel* to *Gem.* 51b).

The term שֶׁיָּצָא לֵילֵךְ, *who set out,* includes one who had moved even one step outside his house (*Rashi* 52b). Furthermore, even if he merely descended from the attic and was stopped before he left the courtyard, he is considered to have set out (see *Gem.* 52a; *Orach Chaim* 410:2).

וְהֶחֱזִירוֹ חֲבֵרוֹ, — *but his friend turned him back,*

His friend convinced him, for example, that it was too hot or too cold a day to exert oneself by going out to place an *eruv*. But the agent did not explicitly repudiate his original plan to go to the next town on the Sabbath (*Tos. Yom Tov;* see *Milchamos*).

הוּא מֻתָּר לֵילֵךְ, — *he may go* [on the Sabbath],

He may go to the next town on the Sabbath because he is considered to have established his Sabbath dwelling place at the designated site. Because he clearly intended to establish his dwelling place there, it is considered as if he had said, 'My Sabbath dwelling place is at that spot,' and it is judged under the rules governing such declarations. As outlined in mishnayos 7 and 9, all *Tannaim* agree that only a poor man is privileged to establish his dwelling place by intention alone without staying there at the onset of the Sabbath or placing food at the designated spot. This ruling of R' Yehudah postulates that the agent is considered as a traveler (mishnah 7) because he had set out to the designated spot, and he is therefore granted the privileges of a poor man regardless of his economic standing (*Rav; Rambam*).

The implication of the statement, 'but his friend turned him back,' is that if he turned back on his own initiative, he is considered to have changed his mind about going to the next town and is not awarded the *techum* that would allow him to go there (*Ritva* 52b, *Meiri*). *Shulchan Aruch (Orach Chaim* 410:1; see *Be'ur HaGra* there) makes no such distinction. However, if the individual did, in his mind, retract his avowed intention to go to the next town, he is classed with the other townsmen and may not depart from their *techum* (*Mishnah Berurah* 410:4).

עירובין לֵילֵךְ, וְכָל בְּנֵי הָעִיר אֲסוּרִין — דִּבְרֵי רַבִּי יְהוּדָה.
ד/י רַבִּי מֵאִיר אוֹמֵר: כָּל שֶׁהוּא יָכוֹל לְעָרֵב וְלֹא עֵרֵב,
הֲרֵי זֶה חַמָּר גַּמָּל.

יד אברהם

וְכָל בְּנֵי הָעִיר אֲסוּרִין — דִּבְרֵי רַבִּי יְהוּדָה.
but all the [other] townspeople are
prohibited — [these are] the words of R'
Yehudah.

They are not considered to have
established their dwelling place at the
designated spot. The intention of their
agent to go there, or even his and their
explicit declaration to establish their
Sabbath dwelling place at that location,
is insufficient to establish that dwelling
place for them. They are judged to be
rich men in this context and not eligible
to establish their Sabbath dwelling place
with a mere statement of intent (Gem.
52a).

Some authorities, however, maintain that
even a poor man may not establish an eruv
with a mere declaration as long as he is in his
home and that the dispensation to establish
an eruv by mere declaration is granted only
to a traveler, in which case it is effective even
for a rich man (see comm. to mish. 9). In this
view, it must be assumed that the
terminology 'poor man' and 'rich man' used
by the Gemara here is a mere figure of speech
influenced by the use of these terms in mishnah 9.

רַבִּי מֵאִיר אוֹמֵר: כָּל שֶׁהוּא יָכוֹל לְעָרֵב וְלֹא
עֵרֵב, — R' Meir says: Whoever is able to
make an eruv and does not,

Whoever is able to make an eruv with
food, e.g., the individual in the mishnah
who actually set out to make an eruv
and did not do so (Rav; Rambam).

הֲרֵי זֶה חַמָּר גַּמָּל. — he is caught in
between [lit. he is a donkey driver who
is also a camel driver].

R' Meir is in doubt as to whether one
who set out to place an eruv is

considered a poor man and granted the
dispensation of designating a techum
without actually being there or, because
he had the food with which to make an
eruv but allowed himself to be
dissuaded from going to place it, he is
considered a rich man and denied this
dispensation. Since the legality of an
eruv established by mere intent is open
to question, he is restricted to the area
common to both the contemplated
techum (since it is possibly valid) and to
the techum as measured from his home
(where his techum would be if the
designated techum were invalid). He
may not go to the next town (since it is
not within the techum of his home), nor
may he go beyond where the contemplated eruv techum ends (Rav; Rashi).
[The idiom חַמָּר גַּמָּל is explained in
commentary to 3:4.]

The above is the interpretation of
Rambam, Rif and Rosh and is based on a
similar commentary in Talmud Yerushalmi
and the commentaries of the Geonim (see
Milchamos). The pertinent fact that the
person who set out was sent by his townspeople to make an eruv must be assumed,
since otherwise the statement of the mishnah
that the townspeople may not go has no
meaning. (Since they did not even attempt to
place an eruv, why would anyone imagine
they should be allowed to go?) Most
commentators (Rashi, R' Yehonasan, Baal
HaMaor, Rashba, Ritva, et al.; see Sha'ar
HaTziyun 410:2)[1] do not accept this
assumption and assert that our mishnah
speaks of a case in which a verbal declaration
designating a specific location as the Sabbath
dwelling place had been made by everyone —
both the one who set out and these who sent
him.[2]. This, if judged effective, would

1. Ramban, however, points out (in Milchamos) that a comment in the Talmud Bavli indicates
that it does not interpret the mishnah in the manner presented by Talmud Yerushalmi
[although the commentary expounded by Ramban and attributed to Rif and the Geonim is not
contradicted by our Gemara].

2. The above commentary is based on the second view expressed by Rashi (52a) and is

4

10

prohibited — [these are] the words of R' Yehudah. R' Meir says: Whoever is able to make an *eruv* and does not, he is caught in between.

YAD AVRAHAM

enable them to go the next town. The phrase 'one who set out' refers to someone who had set out with the intention of actually arriving in the next town before the onset of the Sabbath but was turned back after he had set out. At that point, he made an oral declaration in lieu of a food *eruv*.[1] The individual who set out is put in the category of a poor man, in R' Yehudah's view, by virtue of his being underway (although he turned back midway) and his declaration is effective. Thus, his residence is established at the designated location and he may go to the neighboring town on the Sabbath. An additional restriction applied by the *Gemara* (52a) is that the one who set out also have a house in the neighboring town, so that we may consider him as a citizen of that town who has been stranded outside of his home and as such requires the dispensation of an oral declaration in order to be able to reach his home. Without this, there is no justification to consider him traveling since he is actually still near his own home or even in it (see above, s.v. מִי שֶׁיָּצָא). The townspeople's declaration, however, is not deemed valid because they had not set out[2] and, like all well-to-do people sitting in their homes, they

are not privileged to establish a dwelling place with a mere declaration.

Shulchan Aruch (Orach Chaim 410:1,3) accepts *Rambam's* view as halachah. See *Mishnah Berurah* there.

R' Meir's view is explained as above; there is a question as to whether to consider him a poor man or a rich man. The explicit declaration designating a site other than one's home as his dwelling place does not automatically disqualify the home even according to R' Meir, and on the possibility that he is judged a rich man he remains with the *techum* belonging to his house *(Tos.* 49b). Thus only the area common to both *techumin* is permitted to the one who set out *(Rashba; Ritva).*[3] [The statement, 'Whoever is able to make an *eruv* and does not ...,' in reference to the one who set out alludes to his ability to return to the town and to make a food *eruv* at the designated spot.]

The townspeople, however, are permitted the town's *techum* area in its entirety. There is no question as to their status as 'rich men.' Thus their Sabbath dwelling automatically reverts to their actual residence, their explicit declaration to the contrary notwithstanding.

accepted by most of the commentators. According to this view the case discussed in the mishnah presupposes an oral declaration on everyone's part.

1. According to this view, it is assumed that one who sets out merely to put down an *eruv* and is turned back may not establish a dwelling place with a mere declaration (see R' Yehonasan and *Avodas HaKodesh* 15; *Mishnah Berurah* 410:2). As R' Yehonasan explains, one who sets out with the idea of reaching the next town before the Sabbath cannot be faulted for not taking along food for an *eruv* since he had not intended to make an *eruv*. Thus, when he subsequently returns and is forced to make an oral declaration, he has no food with which to make an *eruv*, and he can be considered poor in this context. Someone who set out with food to make an *eruv* but failed to do so cannot be judged poor by this criterion.

2. In this view, there are two reasons for disqualifying the townspeople's declaration: (a) they had not set out and so cannot be considered travelers; (b) they do not possess residences in the neighboring town. Either of these reasons is sufficient to disqualify their declaration *(Rashba, Ritva, Ran).* Rambam *(Hil. Eruvin* 7:8) does not mention this last restriction at all and it is not a factor according to his view (see *Maggid Mishneh* there).

3. *Rashi* (52a, s.v. ורב יוסף, in the second view) has a different explanation for R' Meir's view. See also *Rashi* 51b s.v. איהו ביון דנפיק; *Maharshal* and *Maharsha* et. al. to the above cited *Rashi.*

עירובין [יא] **מִי שֶׁיָּצָא** חוּץ לַתְּחוּם, אֲפִלּוּ אַמָּה
אַחַת, לֹא יִכָּנֵס. רַבִּי אֱלִיעֶזֶר
אוֹמֵר: שְׁתַּיִם, יִכָּנֵס; שָׁלֹשׁ, לֹא יִכָּנֵס.
מִי שֶׁהֶחְשִׁיךְ חוּץ לַתְּחוּם, אֲפִלּוּ אַמָּה אַחַת,

יד אברהם

11.

מִי שֶׁיָּצָא חוּץ לַתְּחוּם, — *One who went out of the* techum,

He thus forfeits his original 2,000 cubit *techum* and is allotted a minimal *techum* of four cubits, as explained in mishnah 1 of this chapter.

אֲפִלּוּ אַמָּה אַחַת, — *even one cubit*,

In this case his four cubit *techum* allows him to return to · within the boundaries of his original 2,000 cubit *techum* (*Rav*).

לֹא יִכָּנֵס. — *may not return* [lit. *enter*].

By going one cubit beyond the 2,000 cubit limit, he forfeits his rights to that *techum*. Although he may re-enter his old *techum* as far as his new four cubit limit allows, he may not progress further into the *techum*; we do not reason that having (legally) re-entered his old *techum* it now reverts back to him and he may traverse its entirety. [Re-entry into the *techum* is a basis for allowing one to traverse the entire *techum* only where the exit had been forced or accidental. See comm. to mishnah 1.]

The fact that the four cubit minimal *techum* and the original 2,000 cubit *techum* overlap is also of no significance; we do not view this convergence as merging the two *techumin* (*Rav*).

רַבִּי אֱלִיעֶזֶר אוֹמֵר: שְׁתַּיִם, יִכָּנֵס; — *R' Eliezer says: Two cubits, he may return;*

If he had moved only two cubits or less beyond the old *techum* he may re-enter that *techum* and regain his rights to it. R' Eliezer is of the opinion that in a case such as this, where an individual has two *techumin* — his original 2,000 cubit *techum* and the new four cubit *techum* — and the two *techumin* converge, they are to be considered as one contiguous *techum* (*Rav* from *Gem.* 45a).

The Sages dispute this view and hold that the concept of convergence of *techumin* is operative only when the individual was allowed to leave the *techum*,[1] as in mishnah 3 (*Gem.* 45a).

שָׁלֹשׁ, לֹא יִכָּנֵס. — *three cubits, he may not return*.

If he went three cubits (or two cubits and a fraction — *Yerushalmi*) beyond his orginal *techum*, he may not return. R' Eliezer's present ruling is based on his own previous ruling (mishnah 5) that the four cubit *techum* extends only two cubits to each side of the individual. Therefore, once he moves more than two cubits beyond his orginal *techum*, the two *techumin* no longer overlap.

The above is the interpretation accepted by many commentators and based on the *Gemara* (45a). *Rambam* (*Hil. Shabbos* 27:11) and others maintain that even the *Tanna kamma* is of the opinion that the convergence of *techumin* permits us to consider both *techumin* as one.[2] Theoretically, then, if the

---

1. The differences between the similar concepts of הַבְלָעַת תְּחוּמִין, convergence of *techumin*, and the principle of כֵּיוָן דְּעַל עָל, *since he has come, he has come*, which allows one to traverse a *techum* he had left and subsequently re-entered, are complex and cannot be discussed here. See *Rashi* 44b, s.v. רב שימי, *Tos.*, *Ritva*, et al. there; *Rambam* and *Ravad*, *Hil. Shabbos* 27:1; *N'har Shalom*, *Orach Chaim* 396:1.

2. Those holding this view assume that the interpretation given in the *Gemara* 45a (as cited above) is not accepted halachically. *Magen Avraham* (405:1) asserts that even these authorities

11. **O**ne who went out of the *techum,* even one cubit, may not return. R' Eliezer says: Two cubits, he may return; three cubits, he may not return.

One who was overtaken by darkness outside the *techum,* even one cubit, may not enter. R' Shimon

YAD AVRAHAM

four cubit *techum* were to be extended to overlap the original *techum,* he would be permitted to re-enter the *techum.* The *Tanna kamma,* however, holds like R' Yehudah (above in mishnah 5) that the person has the option to choose the direction in which his four cubit *techum* should be allocated. In this case, it is assumed that he wants his four cubits in the direction he had been proceeding, i.e., in the direction away from the original *techum.* Thus, his four cubits are reckoned entirely in that direction, with the result that he may not traverse even the one cubit separating him from his original *techum (Maggid Mishneh;* see *Ravad* there, *Orach Chaim* 405:1).

The halachah is in accord with the view of the *Tanna kamma* (*Rav; Rambam*). However an individual who is permitted to leave the *techum* (as in mishnah 3) is, according to all opinions, allowed to re-enter his old *techum* and regain its use if it converges with the new *techum* assigned to him (*Orach Chaim* 405:1, 407:2).

מִי שֶׁהֶחְשִׁיךְ חוּץ לַתְּחוּם, אֲפִלּוּ אַמָּה אַחַת, — *One who was overtaken by darkness outside the* techum, *even one cubit,*

[Night fell while he was still outside the *techum of his destination.*]

לֹא יִכָּנֵס. — *may not enter.*

He is not considered as having a dwelling place in the city and may consequently not traverse the entire *techum* of the city. He is allowed only the *techum* as measured from the location in which he finds himself at nightfall (*Rambam, Hil. Shabbos* 27:11).[1]

Rambam (ibid.) takes this further (probably because, as stated, the mishnah's ruling would be self-evident and superfluous), and states that the mishnah's ruling refers even to a case where the *techum,* as measured from the individual's location, will have its boundary at the beginning of the town (which is considered as only four cubits). In this case he may still go in the town only as far as his personal *techum* extends (see 5:9).[2]

Other commentators understand the term 'he may not enter' as referring to the town's *techum* (as it is understood in the first passage of the mishnah) and not to the town itself, i.e., he is not granted the right to traverse the town's *techum* in its entirety. He may go into that *techum* only so far as his

hold this view only for one who exited the *techum* against his will or accidentally. They agree, however, that for one who exited the *techum* willfully, the principle of convergence is not applicable.

1. We have not given *Rav's* interpretation which allows him only a four cubit minimal *techum* because of the many difficulties raised by *Tosefos Yom Tov.*

2. The commentators are puzzled by *Rambam's* ruling. How is it possible for one's *techum* to extend into the town, when his location is outside that town's *techum* (see *Maggid Mishneh*)? *Beur HaGra* (to *Orach Chaim* 405:3) suggests the following: The *techum* of a person extends 2,000 cubits from the four cubits automatically allotted every person (see comm. to mishnah 8, s.v. זָכָה לוֹ). In the case of a town, the entire town is considered as four cubits and the *techum* measurement of the town begins at the town's perimeter. The individual finding himself just outside of the town's *techum,* however, is given a four cubit area at his present location and his 2,000 cubit *techum* is, in essence, 2,004 cubits. Thus his *techum* extends beyond the town perimeter (see *Mishneh Berurah* 405:4). Despite this, the mishnah teaches that he does not gain the town's *techum* and can enter only until the point where his 2,004 cubits end.

עֵירוּבִין לֹא יִכָּנֵס. רַבִּי שִׁמְעוֹן אוֹמֵר: אֲפִלּוּ חֲמֵשׁ עֶשְׂרֵה
ה/א אַמּוֹת, יִכָּנֵס; שֶׁאֵין הַמָּשׁוֹחוֹת מְמַצִּין אֶת הַמִּדּוֹת
מִפְּנֵי הַטוֹעִין.

[א] כֵּיצַד מְעַבְּרִין אֶת הֶעָרִים? בַּיִת נִכְנָס בַּיִת
יוֹצֵא, פָּגוּם נִכְנָס פָּגוּם יוֹצֵא, הָיוּ
שָׁם גְּדוּדִיּוֹת גְּבוֹהוֹת עֲשָׂרָה טְפָחִים, וּגְשָׁרִים

יד אברהם

techum, with its center outside of the town, extends. R' Yehonasan maintains that the individual discussed here mistakenly declared his Sabbath dwelling place to be in the town and as a result has neither the town *techum* [he is outside it] nor the *techum* of his location [his declaration established his dwelling place in the town]. He may walk only within the four cubit minimal *techum* allotted in any case. *Meiri* asserts that the individual discussed here has no regular *techum* awarded because he did not stop before night to formally establish a dwelling place. It is *Meiri's* view (not shared by other authorities) that a person may not establish a dwelling place while walking. The result is the same as that described in R' Yehonasan's view.

רַבִּי שִׁמְעוֹן אוֹמֵר: אֲפִלּוּ חֲמֵשׁ עֶשְׂרֵה אַמּוֹת, יִכָּנֵס; — *R' Shimon says: Even* [if he is] *fifteen cubits* [away], *he may enter;*

The fifteen cubit figure is an approximation. The same ruling applies to distances even slightly more than fifteen cubits (*Rav; Rashi*).

שֶׁאֵין הַמָּשׁוֹחוֹת מְמַצִּין אֶת הַמִּדּוֹת מִפְּנֵי הַטּוֹעִין. — *for the surveyors do not give the full measure* [lit. *do not exhaust the measure*], *because of those who err.*

The surveyors who measure the *techum* do not put the markers at the precise limit of the *techum* but place it nearer to the town, as a safeguard against those who wander out of the *techum* by error and would then not be able to return. By drawing in the markers there is leeway for allowing the wanderer to return (*Rav, Rashi*).

R' Shimon agrees that one who deliberately left the marked *techum* is not permitted to return because the leeway was granted only for those who err. Although the person described in our mishnah was never actually in the *techum*, R' Shimon permits him to enter because the circumstance was unavoidable (*Rav*).

In an alternative view, *Rashi* explains that the fifteen cubit figure is based on an exact calculation. The *techum* was, as a rule, measured with ropes measuring fifty cubits (see 5:4). The surveyors would not count the part of the rope being held in the fist of each surveyor. Thus the rope was, in effect, shortened by just over a fist at each end or two fists and one finger per rope. Thus a 2,000 cubit *techum*, which would be calculated as forty such ropes, would be eighty fists and forty fingers, equal to ninety fists (4 fingers = 1 fist) or fifteen cubits (6 fists = 1 cubit) short.

Chapter 5

1.

כֵּיצַד מְעַבְּרִין אֶת הֶעָרִים? — *How does one extend the towns?*

[In order to establish the *techum* of a town, the boundaries of the town must first be defined. The mishnah assumes as common knowledge the provision

that certain areas not strictly part of the town are considered part of it with regard to *techum* measurements. The mishnah opens the discussion of this extension with the rhetorical question, 'How does one extend the towns?']

says: Even fifteen cubits, he may enter; for the surveyors do not give the full measure, because of those who err.

1. **H**ow does one extend the towns? A house is recessed [or] a house protrudes, a tower is recessed [or] a tower protrudes, there were ruins ten fists high, or bridges or mausoleums in which there is

YAD AVRAHAM

בַּיִת נִכְנָס בַּיִת יוֹצֵא, — [If] *a house is recessed [or] a house protrudes,*

If the houses forming the outer perimeter of a town are not laid out in a straight line but, for example, a house is recessed towards the center of the town, the empty area resulting from this is considered to be part of the town. When the mark showing the boundary of the town is drawn, it is drawn as a straight line parallel to the rest of the houses (as stated further in the mishnah) with the unbuilt area included in the borders of the town. Moreover, even if only one house protrudes, the line is drawn parallel to that protruding house and the empty space between it and the rest of the houses is considered within the borders of the town *(Rav; Rashi).*

פָּגוּם נִכְנָס פָּגוּם יוֹצֵא, — *a tower is recessed [or] a tower protrudes*

[The same rule applies even to uninhabited towers which were built into the walls around the (ancient) towns.]

The translation is based on *Rashi*. R' *Chananel* renders *a cooplike structure.*[1] Even such structures are considered houses with regard to the boundaries of a town. *Rambam (Comm.)* interprets פָּגוּם as the ruins of a house.

הָיוּ שָׁם גְּדוֹדִיּוֹת גְּבוֹהוֹת עֲשָׂרָה טְפָחִים, — [or] *there were ruins ten fists high,*

If there were remnants of the walls of houses [that had previously been used for human habitation *(Mishnah Berurah* 398:31; cf. *Meiri* here)] on the perimeter

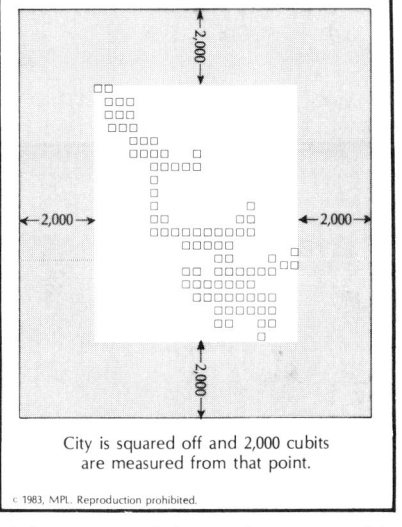

City is squared off and 2,000 cubits are measured from that point.

© 1983, MPL. Reproduction prohibited.

of the town, and these ruins were within seventy cubits of the town *(Rav; Rashi* from *Gem.* 55b, 57b).

The *Gemara* (55b) defines this further and stipulates that an unroofed ruin must have at least three walls. Although the *Gemara* does not determine the status of a roofed walled ruin, *Rambam (Hil. Shabbos* 28:3) and *Shulchan Aruch* (398:6) rule that such a ruin must have at least two walls to qualify as a house in regard to *techum* measurement.

וּגְשָׁרִים — *or bridges*

Covered bridges which are fit for habitation *(R' Yehonasan),* or uncovered bridges which have a cubicle for the toll collector to live in *(Meiri).*

וּנְפָשׁוֹת — *or mausoleums*

---

1. *Tosafos* (52b) comments that an ordinary coop is not considered a house for this purpose (see *Gem.* 55b), only a cooplike structure used for some form for human habitation.

עֵירוּבִין וּנְפָשׁוֹת שֶׁיֵּשׁ בָּהֶן בֵּית דִּירָה, מוֹצִיאִין אֶת הַמִּדָּה ה/ב כְּנֶגְדָּן, וְעוֹשִׂין אוֹתָהּ כְּמִין טַבְלָא מְרֻבַּעַת, כְּדֵי שֶׁיְּהֵא נִשְׂכָּר אֶת הַזָּוִיּוֹת.

[ב] **נוֹתְנִין** קַרְפֵּף לָעִיר — דִּבְרֵי רַבִּי מֵאִיר. וַחֲכָמִים אוֹמְרִים: לֹא אָמְרוּ קַרְפֵּף אֶלָּא בֵּין שְׁתֵּי עֲיָרוֹת; אִם יֵשׁ לָזוֹ שִׁבְעִים אַמָּה וְשִׁירַיִם וְלָזוֹ שִׁבְעִים אַמָּה וְשִׁירַיִם, עוֹשֶׂה קַרְפֵּף לִשְׁתֵּיהֶן לִהְיוֹת כְּאַחַת.

יד אברהם

A room built over a grave in which candles are lit and which contains a dwelling place for a watchman (*R' Yehonasan*).

שֶׁיֵּשׁ בָּהֶן בֵּית דִּירָה, — *in which there is a dwelling,*

The necessity of stating this condition is with regard to bridges; the mausoleums alluded to here customarily served as dwellings for the watchmen (*Tos.* 53a).

מוֹצִיאִין אֶת הַמִּדָּה כְּנֶגְדָּן, — *they extend the boundary* [lit. *the measure*] *opposite them,*

The *Gemara* (55a) adds that if the lines drawn as the town boundaries were not parallel, e.g., one side of the town was narrower than the other, the boundary is extended so that the area within the town boundaries forms a rectangle. Thus, for example, if a house at the northeastern corner of the town juts out ten cubits, the boundary is extended along the entire northern border as if a house jutted out at the northwestern corner as well (*Rav; Rashi*).

וְעוֹשִׂין אוֹתָהּ כְּמִין טַבְלָא מְרֻבַּעַת, — *and they make it as a square tablet,*

If the perimeter of a town was circular, the boundaries are drawn to form a square enclosing that circle (*Rambam* from *Gem.* 55a). Similarly, if the shape of the town was triangular or irregular it is squared off (*Rambam, Hil. Shabbos* 28:7). Square, as used here, refers to right-angled corners. It does not mean, however, that even rectangular shapes be made square (*Gem.* 55a).

כְּדֵי שֶׁיְּהֵא נִשְׂכָּר אֶת הַזָּוִיּוֹת. — *so that one may gain the corners.*

The mishnah here restates anonymously the premise advanced by the Sages previously (4:8). [There is an inconsequential difference, however, for here the mishnah refers to the boundaries of the town, whereas in 4:8 the discussion is about the shape of the *techum*.] *Kol HaRemez* suggests that it is repeated to show that even though the town has already been granted a leniency by having its boundaries extended opposite the protruding house (tower, ruin), as stated in this mishnah, further leniency in measuring the *techum* in a rectangular form is still granted (cf. *Tos. Yom Tov* and *Shoshanim l'David*).

2.

נוֹתְנִין קַרְפֵּף לָעִיר — דִּבְרֵי רַבִּי מֵאִיר. — *We grant a* karpeif *to* [i.e., around] *a town* — [these are] *the words of R' Meir.*

A *karpeif* is an area seventy and two-thirds cubits wide (see above 2:3). R' Meir maintains that the open area

a dwelling, they extend the boundary opposite them, and they make it as a square tablet, so that one may gain the corners.

2. We grant a *karpeif* to a town — [these are] the words of R' Meir. But the Sages say: They did not say [the rule of] *karpeif*, except between two towns; if this one has seventy cubits and a fraction and that one has seventy cubits and a fraction, a *karpeif* is granted to the two of them to become as one.

YAD AVRAHAM

extending seventy and two-thirds cubits beyond the town boundary is also regarded as part of that town and the *techum* measurement begins beyond that area *(Rav; Rashi)*. He bases this upon inferences from Scriptural provisions *(Numbers 35:4)* for the towns to be given to the Levites *(Gem. 57a)*.

וַחֲכָמִים אוֹמְרִים: לֹא אָמְרוּ קַרְפֵּף אֶלָּא בֵּין שְׁתֵּי עֲיָרוֹת; — *But the Sages say: They did not say [the rule of] karpeif, except [with regard to the separation] between two towns;*

[The provision allowing a space to be added to a town is applicable only if two towns were situated so close to each other that the additional spaces allotted to each town abut, and thus allow us to consider the two towns as one, as explained further in the mishnah. If only one town is concerned, so that the additional space would serve merely to enlarge the *techum*, this provision does not apply.]

אִם יֶשׁ לָזוֹ שִׁבְעִים אַמָּה וְשִׁירַיִם וְלָזוֹ שִׁבְעִים אַמָּה וְשִׁירַיִם, — *if this one has* [a space of] *seventy cubits and a fraction and that one has* [a space of] *seventy cubits and a fraction,*

[If the space between them is 141 1/3 cubits or less it can be divided so that each will receive no more than 70 2/3 around it.]

As explained above (2:3), this measurement is derived from the courtyard of the

Towns A and B that are within 141⅓ cubits (according to *Rashi* and *Rambam;* 70⅔ cubits according to *Raavad* and *Rashba)* of each other are considered as one town and share a common *eruv.*

Tabernacle. *Rashba* (citing *Ravad)* explains that this figure was chosen by the Sages because of the similarity in concept between the space granted to a town and the courtyard of the Tabernacle. The empty space is to the town as the courtyard is to the Tabernacle.

עוֹשֶׂה קַרְפֵּף לִשְׁתֵּיהֶן לִהְיוֹת כְּאַחַת. — *a karpeif is granted* [lit. *he makes a karpeif] to the two of them to become as* [i.e., to merge into] *one.*

In such a case the rule of *karpeif* is employed to enlarge the size of each

יד אברהם

town by 70 2/3 cubits, thereby causing them to merge into one (Rav).

[Two adjoining towns are not considered separate unless there is a gap between them. Where their boundaries overlap or meet, they are considered one town, halachically.] Thus, an inhabitant of the northern town, for example, would not measure his techum from the southern edge of his town but from the southern edge of the neighboring town; the entire area of the two towns and the space dividing them would be con-

sidered as four cubits and not be included in the 2,000 cubits allowed for the techum (Rav; Rashi).

Rav and Rambam (Hil. Shabbos 28:5) state that the halachah does not follow R' Meir. However, many authorities (R' Meir of Rothenburg, Rosh, et al.) rule with R' Meir in accordance with the dictum (Gem. 46a): In matters of eruv the halachah follows the one who is lenient. Shulchan Aruch (Orach Chaim 398:5) follows the former view, whereas Rama accepts the latter.

3.

וְכֵן שְׁלֹשָׁה כְּפָרִים הַמְשֻׁלָּשִׁין, — Similarly, three villages forming a triangle [lit. situated at equal intervals],

The translation is based on the Gemara (57b) which explains that the three villages are laid out not in a straight line but in a triangle. The mishnah teaches that for techum measurement purposes the middle village is considered as if situated in a straight line drawn between the two outer villages. To be considered in this way the middle village must lie within 2,000 cubits of each of the outer ones.

אִם יֵשׁ בֵּין שְׁנֵי הַחִיצוֹנִים מֵאָה וְאַרְבָּעִים וְאֶחָד וּשְׁלִישׁ, — if there are one hundred forty-one and a third [cubits] between the two outer ones,

If after the middle village has imaginarily been inserted between the outer two the distance from it to each of the others does not exceed 141 1/3 cubits, then all three villages can be considered as one. The actual open space between the two outer ones is considerably more than the 141 1/3 cubits alluded to in the mishnah; it is as large as the entire width of the middle

village plus 282 2/3 cubits (Rav; Rashi 57b; Rambam, Comm and Hil. Shabbos 28:5).

Rashba and Ravad reject this view and allow only a total of 141 1/3 cubits between the middle village and the two outer ones. Although two villages are usually given 70 2/3 cubits each, so that the distance between them may be as great as 141 1/3 cubits, in our case the middle village is not allotted this space because the real distance between it and the other is much greater than 141 1/3. Our mishnah refers to the total of the two spaces separating the towns after the middle town has been inserted between them. Thus, although the law is lenient considering the middle town as if it were directly between the outer ones, the additional leniency of giving it 141 1/3 extra cubits on each side of its imaginary site is not granted. In this view, after inserting the width of the middle town between the two outer ones only a total of 141 1/3 cubits additional empty space is allowed.

Shulchan Aruch (Orach Chaim 398:8) rules like Rashi and Rambam.

עָשָׂה אֶמְצָעִי אֶת שְׁלָשְׁתָּן לִהְיוֹתָן כְּאֶחָד. — the middle one causes all three of them to become as one.

5
3

3. **S**imilarly, three villages forming a triangle, if there are one hundred forty-one and a third [cubits] between the two outer ones, the middle one causes all three of them to become as one.

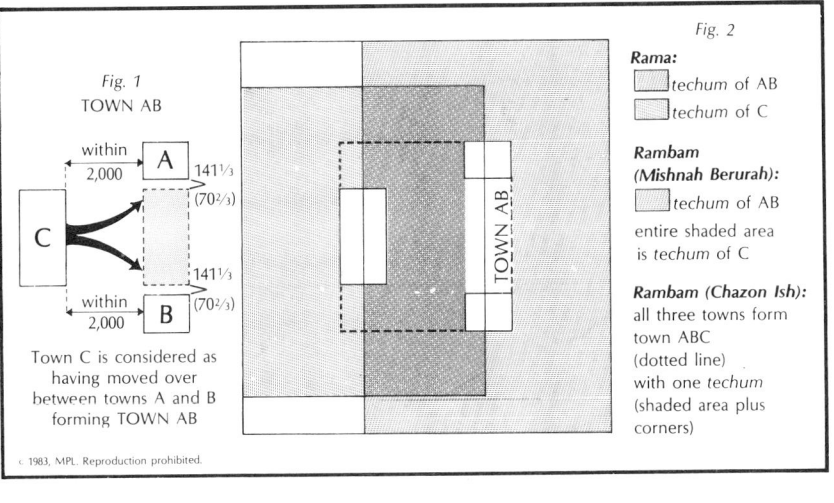

Fig. 2

Rama:
☐ techum of AB
☐ techum of C

Rambam
(Mishnah Berurah):
☐ techum of AB
entire shaded area
is techum of C

Rambam (Chazon Ish):
all three towns form
town ABC
(dotted line)
with one techum
(shaded area plus
corners)

Fig. 1
TOWN AB

within 2,000 → A 141⅓ (70⅔)

C

within 2,000 → B 141⅓ (70⅔)

TOWN AB

Town C is considered as
having moved over
between towns A and B
forming TOWN AB

© 1983, MPL. Reproduction prohibited.

All three villages are considered to be one extended village and they all share one *techum,* which is measured from the furthest point of each of them.

Thus, the inhabitant of one village may go to the next one and two thousand cubits beyond it; neither the area occupied by the villages nor the space between them is subtracted from the 2,000 cubit *techum (Rashi).*[1]

There is a disagreement regarding the middle village. *Rambam (Hil. Shabbos* 28:5) states that the three villages and the space between them are to be considered as one town and one *techum* is to be drawn around them. *Mishnah Berurah* (398:42; see *Be'ur Halachah* there) cites other anonymous authorities who understand *Rambam* to

mean the middle village has its own *techum,* plus the *techum* of the two outer villages. However, the two outer villages are limited to their own *techum. Chazon Ish* (110:9), however, interprets *Rambam* as considering all three villages as one village to be squared off just as is done to any other village.[2] This latter view is also cited by *Meiri* as the opinion of *Ravad.*

Rama (398:8), however, basing his view on one interpretation in *Tosafos* (57b), states that the rule allowing us to consider the middle village as directly between the two outer ones is operable only with regard to the two outer villages. The middle village has its *techum* drawn without regard to the other villages. *Mishnah Berurah* 398:44 rules in accordance with the first, more lenient opinion.

1. The two outer villages are considered one even if the size of the middle one exceeds 2,000 cubits so that the distance between the two outer ones is more than 2,000 cubits *(Gem.* 57b; *Mishnah Berurah* 398:42).

2. The later authorities do not cite this view nor do they contradict it. This is not surprising since this view is known only from *Meiri,* whose work on *Eruvin* was not published until relatively recent times (Warsaw, 5673/1913).

עירובין [ד] **אֵין** מוֹדְדִין אֶלָּא בְּחֶבֶל שֶׁל חֲמִשִּׁים אַמָּה,
ה/ד לֹא פָחוֹת וְלֹא יוֹתֵר.

וְלֹא יִמְדּוֹד אֶלָּא כְּנֶגֶד לִבּוֹ.

הָיָה מוֹדֵד וְהִגִּיעַ לְגַיְא אוֹ לְגֶדֶר, מַבְלִיעוֹ וְחוֹזֵר
לְמִדָּתוֹ; הִגִּיעַ לְהַר, מַבְלִיעוֹ וְחוֹזֵר לְמִדָּתוֹ; וּבִלְבַד

יד אברהם

4.

אֵין מוֹדְדִין אֶלָּא בְּחֶבֶל שֶׁל חֲמִשִּׁים אַמָּה, — *We may not measure except with a fifty cubit rope,*

Rambam (Comm.) notes that every measurement must, by its very nature, have a margin of inaccuracy. The mishnah sets down rules to minimize that margin.

As the mishnah goes on to explain, a fifty cubit rope measures with the greatest accuracy. The Gemara adds that the rope should be made of linen (Rav from Gem. 58a).

לֹא פָחוֹת — *neither shorter*

A shorter rope will give considerably when pulled taut, and thus lengthen the techum (Rav from Gem. 58a).

וְלֹא יוֹתֵר. — *nor longer.*

A longer rope would sag and unnecessarily shorten the techum (Rav from Gem. 58a).

וְלֹא יִמְדּוֹד אֶלָּא כְּנֶגֶד לִבּוֹ. — *One may not measure except [with the rope] opposite his heart.*

[I.e., the rope must be held level with the chest while measuring.] The Sages designated a standard part of the body against which the rope was to be held. Otherwise, one surveyor might hold his end of the rope level with his head while his colleague held the other end near his feet, thus diminishing the techum (Rav; Rashi). [This rule only applies when practical; as will be seen below there are many exceptions to it.]

Ritva adds that the most exact method of measuring is to measure upon the ground. The mishnah refers to surveyors who do not wish to use this more laborious method. The possible difference in height of the two

surveyors is not taken into account. It is assumed that they will be people of average stature and no substantial inaccuracy will result from their slight differences in height (Meiri).

הָיָה מוֹדֵד וְהִגִּיעַ לְגַיְא אוֹ לְגֶדֶר, — *If he was measuring and reached a valley or a mound,*

גֶדֶר means, literally, *a fence.* The mishnah refers here to a mound created by the collapse of a stone fence (Rav). Its slope is sufficiently gradual to accommodate the passage of people (Rashi 57b). [This is based on the Gemara's explanation on 58a (as understood by Rashi). In the case of an ordinary vertical fence, the measurement is taken directly over the top of the fence.]

מַבְלִיעוֹ — *he should span* [lit. *swallow*] *it*

If the valley or mound is fifty cubits or less across he may measure it as if it were level; the greater measurement resulting from the incline of the terrain may be discounted. One surveyor stands at one rim of the valley and another at the opposite rim and they measure straight across the valley (Rav; Rashi).

The spanning of a mound is accomplished in a similar manner. The two surveyors stand on opposite sides of the mound holding poles in their hands and measure the distance between the tops of the poles with the rope stretched from one pole to the other (Tos. 58a; Orach Chaim 399:4). [Obviously, the rule stated earlier that the rope must be held at chest level does not apply in this situation.]

In a case where the valley or mound cannot

5
4

4. **W**e may not measure except with a fifty cubit rope, neither shorter nor longer.

One may not measure except [with the rope] opposite his heart.

If he was measuring and reached a valley or a mound, he should span it and return to his measuring; if he reached a mountain, he should span

YAD AVRAHAM

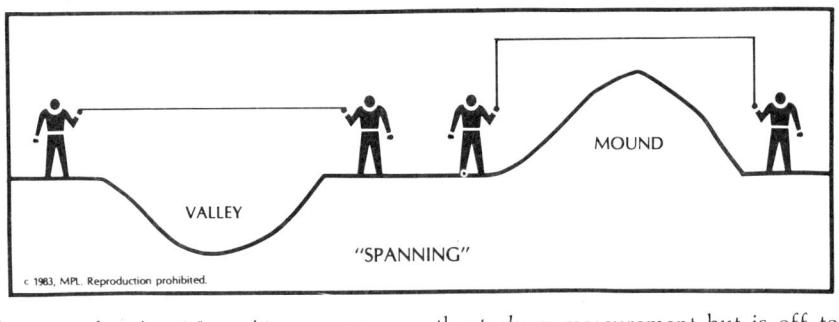

MOUND

VALLEY

"SPANNING"

c 1983, MPL. Reproduction prohibited.

be spanned with a fifty cubit rope, a rope longer than fifty cubits may not be used, but the *techum* must be measured using the more laborious method of 'piercing' (see below) with a four cubit rope.

וְחוֹזֵר לְמִדָּתוֹ; — *and return to his measuring;*

He resumes measuring in the normal fashion. However, by the use of the word *return* the mishnah seems to indicate that it is discussing even a case in which, while spanning the valley or mound, the measurement had to be interrupted. The *Gemara* explains this case as follows: The width of the mound or valley is not uniform — in some places it measures more than 50 cubits while in others it measures less. In the place where it faces the side of the town where the *techum* is being measured it measures more than fifty cubits across, but facing another part of the town its span is less than fifty cubits. The mishnah implies that the mound or valley may be surveyed by measuring a corresponding span at its narrow point on a line parallel to the original measurement. This may be done even if the second span is not opposite the town boundary, which is the starting point of

the *techum* measurement but is off to the side of that boundary. However, when the measurement of the area corresponding to the mound or valley has been finished the surveyor *returns* to the place where he had been measuring (*Rav; Rashi*).

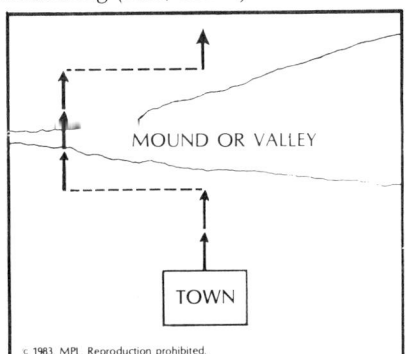

MOUND OR VALLEY

TOWN

c 1983, MPL. Reproduction prohibited.

הִגִּיעַ לְהָר, מַבְלִיעוֹ — *if he reached a mountain, he should span it*

The mountain may be measured either by spanning as described above for a mound, or by measuring the level ground to the side of the mountain. Either way, the additional distance resulting from the slope of the mountain is not taken into consideration (*Meiri*).

[113]   **THE MISHNAH/ERUVIN** — Chapter Five: *Keitzad M'abrin*

עֵירוּבִין שֶׁלֹּא יֵצֵא חוּץ לַתְּחוּם.
ה/ה אִם אֵינוֹ יָכוֹל לְהַבְלִיעוֹ — בָּזוֹ אָמַר רַבִּי
דּוֹסְתַּאי בַּר רַבִּי יַנַּאי מִשּׁוּם רַבִּי מֵאִיר: "שָׁמַעְתִּי
שֶׁמְּקַדְּרִין בֶּהָרִים."

[ה] **אֵין** מוֹדְדִין אֶלָּא מִן הַמֻּמְחֶה.
רִבָּה לְמָקוֹם אֶחָד וּמִעֵט לְמָקוֹם
אַחֵר, שׁוֹמְעִין לַמָּקוֹם שֶׁרִבָּה.

יד אברהם

וְחוֹזֵר לְמִדָּתוֹ; — *and return to his measuring;*

[As above in the case of the valley or mound.]

Tosafos (58a) queries why the mishnah separates the ruling about a mountain from that of a valley or mound since the law regarding them seems to be the same. *Tosafos* proposes that this is done because the following segment of the mishnah discusses the provision of 'piercing' which refers only to a mountain. *Tosefos HaRosh* elaborates further and explains that although the provision of 'piercing' applies to valleys and mounds as well, nevertheless, the use of this provision is more prevalent for mountains since it is usually impossible to span a mountain in the manner set forth above with poles.

וּבִלְבַד שֶׁלֹּא יֵצֵא חוּץ לַתְּחוּם. — *provided he does not go out of the* techum.

If the place where the valley narrows and can be spanned is beyond the *techum*, the surveyor may not go there to measure, because onlookers [who recognize the surveyors and realize that they are involved in measuring the town's *techum*] may be misled into assuming that the *techum* extended to the site the surveyors were measuring (*Rav; Rashi* in second interpretation 58a).

אִם אֵינוֹ יָכוֹל לְהַבְלִיעוֹ — בָּזוֹ אָמַר רַבִּי דּוֹסְתַּאי בַּר רַבִּי יַנַּאי מִשּׁוּם רַבִּי מֵאִיר: "שָׁמַעְתִּי שֶׁמְּקַדְּרִין בֶּהָרִים." — *If he is unable to span it — regarding this R' Dostai bar R' Yannai stated in R' Meir's name: 'I have heard that we pierce mountains.'*

"PIERCING MOUNTAINS"

© 1983, MPL. Reproduction prohibited.

If the width of the mountain is greater than fifty cubits and so cannot be spanned with the standard fifty cubit rope (*Tur Orach Chaim* 399 cited by *Tos. Yom Tov; Gem.* 58a), it is measured as though a tunnel had been drilled through it enabling one to measure the level distance from one side to the other. The *Gemara* (58b) explains how this is accomplished: Two surveyors stand at the foot of the slope, one higher than the other. The lower surveyor holds a four cubit rope to his chest while the surveyor who is higher up holds the other end of the rope to his feet. The lower one then moves to the point at which the four cubits end, while his colleague moves up the hillside. This procedure is then repeated over and over until the width of the mountain is measured (*Rav; Rambam*).

it and return to his measuring; provided he does not go out of the *techum*.

If he is unable to span it — regarding this R' Dostai bar R' Yannai stated in R' Meir's name: 'I have heard that we pierce mountains.'

5. **W**e may not [accept] measure[ments] except from an expert.

If he extended [the *techum*] at one point and shortened it at another, the extended [*techum*] is followed.

YAD AVRAHAM

[If we are to assume that the lower surveyor holds the rope two cubits above the ground, then on an upgrade rising at a ratio of two cubits for approximately every four and a half cubits of horizontal distance the string would be held on a plane parallel to the ground and only the horizontal would be measured. On any incline steeper or more gradual than this the rope would of necessity be held at an angle. It seems that one may not hold the rope high in the air in order to adjust it to a horizontal plane (see *Rashi*). The reason may be that this would lead to errors in measurement because the person may hold his hand at an angle from his body thereby shortening the measured span. Therefore the Sages stipulated that the rope be held at a fixed place — the heart for the lower surveyor and the feet for the upper one *(R' Y. Danziger).*]

The *Gemara* (ibid.) points out that the reservation expressed in the word בְזוּ, *regarding this*, stresses that the dispensation to measure by piercing is granted only for the purpose of *techum* measurement, because it only concerns a Rabbinic prohibition. When measuring in regard to עֶגְלָה עֲרוּפָה, *eglah arufah* (see *Deut.* 21:1-9), or עִיר מִקְלָט, *city of refuge* (see *Deut.* 19:3), the terrain must be measured as it is. Only because *techum* is a Rabbinic law is the lenient provision made for piercing *(Rav; Gem.* 58b).

5.

אֵין מוֹדְדִין אֶלָּא מִן הַמֻּמְחֶה. — *We may not [accept] measure[ments] except from an expert.*

The surveyor employed [to draw the *techum* boundaries around the city] must be an expert *(Rav; Rashi; Rambam, Comm.* and *Hil. Shabbos* 28:17). *Rashi's* version of the mishnah reads: אֶלָּא מְמֻמְחֶה, *except an expert.* Although *Rav* and *Rambam* follow the standard text, their interpretation follows *Rashi's.*

The *Geonim* (see *Rav, Rashba;* cf. *R' Chananel* in *Tos.* 58b) interpret the word מְמֻמְחֶה as *an accessible area* and see the mishnah as instructing the surveyors to choose a level area for measuring the *techum* so that piercing or spanning (see previous mishnah) not be necessary. The word מְמֻחֶה is related to *(Numbers* 34:11), וּמָחָה עַל כֶּתֶף יָם כִּנֶּרֶת, *and it* [the borders of *Eretz Yisrael*] *shall reach the edge of the Sea of Kinneres;* i.e., one should measure only where the measurement will *reach* without impediment.[1] *Rashba* points out that the first interpretation is clearly indicated in *Yerushalmi.*

רִבָּה לְמָקוֹם אֶחָד וּמֵעַט לְמָקוֹם אַחֵר. שׁוֹמְעִין לַמָּקוֹם שֶׁרִבָּה. — *If he extended* [the techum] *at one point and shortened it at another, the extended* [techum] *is followed.*

If after surveying it was found that

1. In order to designate the *techum* boundary it is not necessary to measure the distance from the town at every point. It is sufficient to measure from one point along each of the four squared off sides rather than to construct a line at right angles to the end point.

רַבָּה לְאֶחָד וּמְעַט לְאַחֵר, שׁוֹמְעִין לַמְּרֻבֶּה.
אֲפִלּוּ עֶבֶד, אֲפִלּוּ שִׁפְחָה, נֶאֱמָנִין לוֹמַר: ,,עַד
כָּאן תְּחוּם שַׁבָּת.'' שֶׁלֹּא אָמְרוּ חֲכָמִים אֶת הַדָּבָר
לְהַחֲמִיר, אֶלָּא לְהָקֵל.

יד אברהם

the *techum* boundary at one corner extended further than that at the opposite corner of the same side, the longer measure is followed. The discrepancy is attributed to the sag of the measuring rope which probably was not tautened sufficiently at the spot where the short *techum* measurement occurred (*Rav; Rashi*).

A different approach to this mishnah is taken by *Rambam* (*Comm.*). The town had traditionally accepted certain boundaries for their *techum*. But when an expert surveyor was commissioned to verify these boundaries, his report conflicted with them. In some places his survey added to the previously accepted *techum*, while in other places he diminished it. Just as they accept his more stringent measure and rely on it to repudiate the previously accepted longer *techum*, so may they rely on his lenient measure to extend their *techum* accordingly. In *Hilchos Shabbos* (28:17), *Rambam* writes merely that we accept the surveyor's leniency, but omits any mention about accepting his stringency.

רַבָּה לְאֶחָד וּמְעַט לְאַחֵר, שׁוֹמְעִין לַמְּרֻבֶּה. — *If one* [surveyor] *extended* [*it*] *while another shortened* [*it*]*, the one who extended* [*it*] *is followed* [lit. *we listen to the extended one*].

If two surveyors made separate surveys and came up with different results, the more lenient *techum* is followed. רַבָּה לְאֶחָד, lit. *he extended to one*, is to be understood as if it read רַבָּה אֶחָד, *one extended* (*Rav; Gem. 59a*).

Ramban extends this to include even a case where is conflicting testimony concerning the place of the *techum* boundary.[1] *Ritva* (59a) adds that although one should be

stringent in doubtful cases even in regard to a Rabbinical law, if it is possible to ascertain the truth, the case of *techum* is considered as not ascertainable. Because another survey would involve great difficulty, it is not considered a viable option.

אֲפִלּוּ עֶבֶד, אֲפִלּוּ שִׁפְחָה, נֶאֱמָנִין לוֹמַר: ,,עַד כָּאן תְּחוּם שַׁבָּת.'' שֶׁלֹּא אָמְרוּ חֲכָמִים אֶת הַדָּבָר לְהַחֲמִיר, אֶלָּא לְהָקֵל. — *Even a male slave, even a female slave is believed to say, 'Until here is the Sabbath* techum.' *For the Sages did not state this law* [lit. *matter*] *to be stringent, but rather to be lenient.*

[When the Sages enacted the laws of *techum* (or other Rabbinic laws; see below) they did not make them subject to all of the stringencies applicable to Biblical matters.]

It is evident from here that slaves are not relied upon concerning Biblical prohibitions. They fall into the category of those whose testimony is not accepted in such matters as financial affairs, capital offenses, laws pertaining to marriage or any matter where the testimony of two witnesses is required. Thus the validity of a slave's testimony is due the special leniency instituted by the Sages only in regard to the laws of *techum*. It would seem, however, that there is yet another reason why the testimony of a slave should be accepted here. The rule is that wherever a matter pertains only to a simple question of prohibition or permissibility, where the testimony of a single witness is sufficient (עֵד אֶחָד נֶאֱמָן בְּאִסּוּרִין), even the testimony of those normally disqualified, such as slaves, is accepted. This is true even for Biblical questions such as whether a piece of meat is kosher or not. Since *techum* is such a matter, the testimony of a slave should be valid even if it were a Biblical prohibition. *Tosafos* (59a)

---

1. [This facet of *Ramban's* ruling would probably be accepted as halachah by all authorities for the contradiction in testimony would render this a case of doubt concerning a Rabbinical law and would be decided for leniency (סְפֵיקָא דְרַבָּנָן לְקוּלָא).]

If one extended [it] while another shortened [it], the one who extended [it] is followed.

Even a male slave, even a female slave is believed to say, 'Until here is the Sabbath *techum.*' For the Sages did not state this law to be stringent but rather to be lenient.

YAD AVRAHAM

explains that this latter general rule applies only if the prohibition in question is one which the witness himself could have found a way to render permissible, such as the *kashrus* of a piece of meat from an animal that the witness himself could have properly slaughtered, thus insuring that it was kosher. The question of *techum* however, is not one over which any individual has control; it is merely a matter of determining where it is. Therefore, had it been a Biblical prohibition the testimony of a slave would not have been acceptable and it is only because it is

Rabbinic that it is acceptable.

Many other authorities dispute this restriction of *Tosafos.* As they see it, a slave's testimony is always acceptable in questions of permissibility or prohibition unless the matter under question is very complex. Since the question of *techum* involves complexities (e.g., mishnayos 1-4 here) they would be disqualified, if not for the fact that *techum* is only Rabbinic (*Rashba* in *Toras HaBayis* 1:1 (pp.13-4) in prevalent ed.); *Ramban, Chullin* 10b, ed. Reichman; cf. *Mishmeres HaBayis* 1:1).

6.

The mishnah now digresses from the topic of *techum* measurement to the subject of *shitufei mevo'os* — the *eruv* made to permit carrying within and to the alleys into which the courtyards open (see Gen. Intro. and prefatory note to ch 6). After the conclusion of this mishnah the mishnah returns to the topic of *techumin.* A *shitufei mevo'os* can be made, not only for the alleys of the town but, if the town is properly enclosed by walls, for the streets as well. Thus, if a *shitufei mevo'os* is made in an enclosed city, carrying should be permitted throughout the town. In practice, however, in order that the people recognize that carrying on the Sabbath is really prohibited and that it is permissible in this town only because of the *eruv* and *shituf*, the Sages prohi-

bited incorporating the entire town in one *shituf.* If the entire town were incorporated in one *shituf*, the prohibition against carrying would, in effect, be removed and, in the course of time, many might conclude that indeed no such prohibition exists.

This is true, however, only for a publicly owned town. A town entirely owned by an individual is not subject to this rule because its streets do not qualify as true public domains. As the name suggests, one of the qualifications of a public domain is that it be public property; a highway owned by an individual is not considered a public domain on a Biblical level, and is not Biblically subject to the prohibitions against carrying[1] (it is however, Rabbinically subject to these prohibi-

1. Most of the commentators (see *Rambam; Comm.* and *Hil. Eruvin* 5:19; *Rashba, R' Yehonasan;* et al.) agree that the terms private and public are to be understood as referring to ownership, but give no indication whether they agree with *Ramban's* premise that the mishnah's ruling is based on the fact that a privately owned street is not a public domain on a Biblical level. Indeed, it can be demonstrated that *Rashba* (see his *Chiddushim* to 22, s.v. מעלות, and *Ritva* there) disagrees.

עִיר שֶׁל יָחִיד וְנַעֲשֵׂית שֶׁל רַבִּים, מְעָרְבִין
ה/ו
אֶת כֻּלָּהּ; וְשֶׁל רַבִּים וְנַעֲשֵׂית שֶׁל יָחִיד,
אֵין מְעָרְבִין אֶת כֻּלָּהּ, אֶלָּא אִם כֵּן עָשָׂה חוּצָה לָהּ,

יד אברהם

tions). This distinction, having its roots in the very term public domain, is so well understood by everyone that there is no need to impose the safeguard of prohibiting one *shituf* for the whole town. We can safely assume that permission to carry in a privately owned town will not lead to the erroneous conclusion that one may also carry in the public domain of a public town (*Ramban; Ritva*). The mishnah now discusses the rule for towns which change from private to public or vice versa as well as various details of these rules.

עִיר שֶׁל יָחִיד — *If a town of an individual*
One person owned the real estate constituting an entire town and leased the houses to the inhabitants (*Rav* based on *Rambam, Hil. Eruvin* 5:19; *Ramban; Ritva*; et al.; *Rashi's* interpretation will be given below).

וְנַעֲשֵׂית שֶׁל רַבִּים, — *became public property,*
I.e., the owner of the town sold the houses to various people. The town, however, is still commonly referred to by the name of the original owner (*Rashba*).

According to other authorities, the law set forth here applies only where the individual retains ownership of the town, i.e., he originally built the town for his personal use, and later made it public, either by leasing the houses or

by selling them, nevertheless, he retained ownership of the streets (*Ramban; Ritva;* see *Mishnah Berurah* 392:1).

Rashi interprets this mishnah in a novel way, based on his view that, on a Biblical level, a public domain is defined as a street in a town to which 600,000 people have access.[1] [This number is derived from the number of people recorded in the Torah as having been in the Israelite camp in the wilderness. Although the number included only men between the ages of twenty and sixty and there were certainly a great many more people there, since the Torah does not specify how many there were, the number 600,000 is used, it being the only clearly stated number (*Tos.* 6a).]

The term עִיר שֶׁל יָחִיד is defined as a town to which less than 600,000 people have access and whose streets are, as a result, not public domains on a Biblical level. An עִיר שֶׁל רַבִּים, on the other hand, is a city to which 600,000 have access.

מְעָרְבִין אֶת כֻּלָּהּ; — *we may make an* eruv *for its entirety;*
The town is still considered to be a private town and its residents may therefore still make one communal *eruv* for all the streets of the town. The status granted to the town when it actually was privately owned remains (*Rav*).

The *eruv* referred to here is the שִׁתּוּפֵי מְבוֹאוֹת, *shitufei mevo'os*, which permits carrying into the alleys and streets. This is made after all the courtyards have made their respective *eruvei*

---

1. There are various opinions on how to interpret *Rashi's* view. Some hold that it is sufficient for the town to have 600,000 people in it, thus making the public domain accessible to this multitude, while others maintain that in order to qualify as a Biblical public domain, the domain itself must have 600,000 people passing through it on one day. See *Be'ur Halachah* to *Orach Chaim* 345:4, *Teshuvos Beis Ephraim Orach Chaim* 26, *Teshuvos Maharsham* 3:188. This question has a great bearing on the practical halachah, because many lenient rulings in regard to carrying on the Sabbath are based on *Rashi's* view. The most notable of these is the reliance on the device called the form of a doorway (צוּרַת הַפֶּתַח, colloquially referred to as *eruv*) around a city to render its streets a private domain and permit carrying within their confines on the Sabbath.

6. **I**f a town of an individual became public property, we may make an *eruv* for its entirety; but if a
public [town] became an individual's, we may not
make an *eruv* for its entirety, unless we exclude [an

YAD AVRAHAM

chatzeiros to permit their residents to carry from the houses to the courtyards. [The *eruvei chatzeiros* is unaffected by the status of the town.] The communal *shitufei mevo'os* for the entire town is instituted so that objects may be carried from one part of the town to another (*Rambam, Hil. Eruvin* 5:19).

Clearly, in the case under discussion the streets of the town and its courtyards have been so prepared that there is no problem concerning their certification as private domains with regard to their walls (*Gem.* 59a), i.e., they are surrounded by walls (or partitions) on three sides and the fourth, open side has been supplied with a pole or crossbeam or whatever other adjustment is applicable (as outlined in 1:2).

According to *Rashi's* interpretation of this mishnah (see above), a town to which less than 600,000 people have access may make one *eruv* for the entire town because even the unlearned do not consider the streets to be bona fide public domains. Even if the town subsequently[1] becomes a 'public town,' i.e. its population swells to 600,000, an *eruv* may be made. Since in the public mind the town is still thought of as a private town, we are still not concerned that permission to carry in its *shituf*-incorporated streets will lead to the mistaken notion that carrying in any public domain is permissible. In the case of a public town which becomes a private town (see below) this consideration operates in the reverse fashion and necessitates the setting aside of an area not to be included in the *eruv*.

וְשֶׁל רַבִּים וְנַעֲשֵׂית שֶׁל יָחִיד, — *but if a public [town] became an individual's,*

[The entire town was sold[2] to one individual (thereby making it a private town). This individual then leased the houses to others (thus necessitating the institution of an *eruv*).]

אֵין מְעָרְבִין אֶת כֻּלָּה, — *we may not make an* eruv *for its entirety,*

A number of households (specified further in the mishnah), concentrated in one area, must be excluded from the communal *shitufei mevo'os*. This ruling is true for any public town. Our mishnah adds only that a town's categorization as a public town is not removed by its sale to an individual. As explained in the prefatory note to this mishnah, the reason this ruling was instituted was so that the public not forget that carrying in public places on the Sabbath is generally prohibited, but in this town it is permitted through the establishment of an *eruv* and *shituf*.

אֶלָּא אִם כֵּן עָשָׂה חוּצָה לָהּ, — *unless we exclude [an area] from it* [lit. *we make outside it*]

[A nominal area must be excluded from the *shituf*.] Thus, the townspeople may carry objects anywhere within the town except in the area excluded from the *shituf*. The inhabitants of that area may also make a *shituf* permitting them

1. *Tosefos HaRosh* (see also *Tos. R' Peretz*) points out that any town inhabited by 600,000 people should qualify for an *eruv* because it once had less than that number. The only instance in which an *eruv* is disallowed is if 600,000 people settle in one place simultaneously — a virtual impossibility. *Tos. HaRosh* concludes that the determination of whether or not a town is public or private is made not at its initial settlement but when the first communal *eruv* is instituted (cf. *Ritva*).

2. *Mishnah Berurah* (*Sha'ar HaTziyun* 392:6) reasons that in this case everyone (see above, s.v. וְנַעֲשֵׂית) concedes that even total sale to an individual and complete removal of the public's control does not grant the town the lenient status of a private town as long as it is still known as a public town.

עֵירוּבִין כְּעִיר חֲדָשָׁה שֶׁבִּיהוּדָה, שֶׁיֵּשׁ בָּהּ חֲמִשִּׁים דִּיּוּרִין ה/ז
— דִּבְרֵי רַבִּי יְהוּדָה. רַבִּי שִׁמְעוֹן אוֹמֵר: שָׁלֹשׁ
חֲצֵרוֹת שֶׁל שְׁנֵי בָתִּים.

[ז] **מִי שֶׁהָיָה** בַּמִּזְרָח וְאָמַר לִבְנוֹ: "עָרֵב לִי
בַּמַּעֲרָב;" בַּמַּעֲרָב וְאָמַר
לִבְנוֹ: "עָרֵב לִי בַּמִּזְרָח" — אִם יֵשׁ הֵימֶנּוּ וּלְבֵיתוֹ
אַלְפַּיִם אַמּוֹת וּלְעֵרוּבוֹ יוֹתֵר מִכָּאן, מֻתָּר לְבֵיתוֹ
וְאָסוּר לְעֵרוּבוֹ; לְעֵרוּבוֹ אַלְפַּיִם אַמָּה וּלְבֵיתוֹ
יוֹתֵר מִכָּאן, אָסוּר לְבֵיתוֹ וּמֻתָּר לְעֵרוּבוֹ.

יד אברהם

to carry anywhere within their area but they may not carry into the rest of the town (Rambam, Hil. Eruvin 5:20).

כְּעִיר חֲדָשָׁה שֶׁבִּיהוּדָה, שֶׁיֵּשׁ בָּהּ חֲמִשִּׁים דִּיּוּרִין — דִּבְרֵי רַבִּי יְהוּדָה. — *equivalent to the town of Chadashah in Judea, which has fifty inhabitants* — [these are] the words of R' Yehudah.

The town Chadashah [mentioned in Joshua 15:37 among the towns belonging to the territory of the tribe of Judah (Tos. 60a)] was the smallest town in Judea and had been built as an extension or suburb of a larger, adjoining town. Therefore, the Sages made this town the prototype and criterion for measuring

the minimum area to be left out of the communal *shituf* (Rav from Gem. 60a).

רַבִּי שִׁמְעוֹן אוֹמֵר: שָׁלֹשׁ חֲצֵרוֹת שֶׁל שְׁנֵי בָתִּים. — *R' Shimon says: Three courtyards containing two dwellings* [each, must be excluded].

[R' Shimon is more lenient than R' Yehudah and rules that it is not necessary for the excluded area to contain fifty inhabitants; six households are sufficient.]

The Gemara (60a) sets forth the view of the Amora R' Yitzchak [based on a baraisa (Tos. 60a)] that it is sufficient to exclude one courtyard containing even only one household. The halachah is in accord with this view (see Orach Chaim 392:1).

7.

[After digressing in the previous mishnah, the topic of *techumin* is now resumed.]

מִי שֶׁהָיָה בַּמִּזְרָח — *One who was to the east* [of his town]

Before the onset of the Sabbath a person found himself in an open area east of his hometown (Rav; Rashi).

וְאָמַר לִבְנוֹ: "עָרֵב לִי בַּמַּעֲרָב;" — *and had told his son, 'Make an eruv for me in the west;'*

He had previously told his son (or any other agent) to make an *eruv* for him to the west (Rashi).

בַּמַּעֲרָב וְאָמַר לִבְנוֹ: "עָרֵב לִי בַּמִּזְרָח" — אִם יֵשׁ הֵימֶנּוּ וּלְבֵיתוֹ אַלְפַּיִם אַמּוֹת וּלְעֵרוּבוֹ יוֹתֵר מִכָּאן, — [or he was] *to the west and had told his son, 'Make an eruv for me in the east' — if the distance from him to his house is two thousand cubits* [or less] *and* [from him] *to his eruv more than that,*

[Thus, if the *eruv* took effect he would find himself outside his *techum*, since he is more than 2,000 cubits away from it. As a result, he would be prohibited to move outside the minimal four cubit *techum* given to anyone in a similar situation (as in 4:5).]

area] from it equivalent to the town of Chadashah in Judea, which has fifty inhabitants — [these are] the words of R' Yehudah. R' Shimon says: Three court-yards containing two dwellings.

7. **O**ne who was to the east and had told his son, 'Make an *eruv* for me in the west;' to the west and had told his son, 'Make an *eruv* for me in the east' — if the distance from him to his house is two thousand cubits and to his *eruv* more than that, he is permitted [the *techum* of] his house but forbidden [the *techum* of] his *eruv*; if to his *eruv* is two thousand cubits and to his house more than that, he is forbidden [the *techum* of] his house but permitted [the *techum* of] his *eruv*.

YAD AVRAHAM

מֻתָּר לְבֵיתוֹ וְאָסוּר לְעֵרוּבוֹ; — *he is permitted* [*the* techum *of*] *his house but forbidden* [*the* techum *of*] *his* eruv;

Since the *eruv* is inaccessible to him at the onset of the Sabbath it can have no validity. Therefore, the *techum* of his house is automatically in effect (*Rashi*).

[The statement that he is *forbidden* the *techum* of his *eruv* is unnecessary here. Surely if he is given the *techum* of his house the *eruv* must be judged invalid. It is inserted here merely to preserve the symmetry of the statements, for in the opposite case the mishnah will state that he is *forbidden* the *techum of his house but permitted the techum of his eruv.*]

Rashi explains that his avowed intention to make an *eruv* is not construed as a repudiation of his house as the centerpoint of the *techum*. It is to be assumed that the person's avowed intention is based on the mistaken premise that the *eruv* will be valid. Since, however, he is certainly satisfied to have his house considered as the center point of his *techum* if the *eruv* for some reason is not valid, the halachah grants him that *techum*, based on this unexpressed will. (See R' Yehonasan and *Mishnah Berurah* 411:3.)

לְעֵרוּבוֹ אֲלָפַּיִם אַמָּה וּלְבֵיתוֹ יוֹתֵר מִכָּאן, — *if* [*the distance*] *to his* eruv *is two thousand cubits* [*or less*] *and to his*

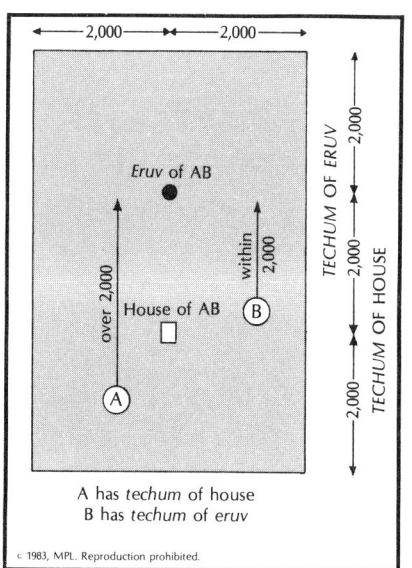

2,000 — 2,000

Eruv of AB

TECHUM OF ERUV

within 2,000

over 2,000

2,000

2,000

TECHUM OF HOUSE

House of AB — B

A

2,000

A has techum of house
B has techum of eruv

© 1983, MPL. Reproduction prohibited.

house more than that,

I.e., the reverse of the previous case.

אָסוּר לְבֵיתוֹ וּמֻתָּר לְעֵרוּבוֹ. — *he is forbidden* [*the* techum *of*] *his house but permitted* [*the* techum *of*] *his* eruv.

[Since his *eruv* is accessible to him at the onset of the Sabbath, it is effective

הַנּוֹתֵן אֶת עֵרוּבוֹ בְּעִבּוּרָהּ שֶׁל עִיר לֹא עָשָׂה
וְלֹא כְלוּם. נְתָנוֹ חוּץ לַתְּחוּם, אֲפִלּוּ אַמָּה אַחַת,
מַה שֶׁנִּשְׂכָּר הוּא מַפְסִיד.

[ח] **אַנְשֵׁי** עִיר גְּדוֹלָה מְהַלְּכִין אֶת כָּל עִיר
קְטַנָּה, וְאֵין אַנְשֵׁי עִיר קְטַנָּה
מְהַלְּכִין אֶת כָּל עִיר גְּדוֹלָה.

יד אברהם

and as a result his *techum* is designated using the *eruv* location as the centerpoint.] As a consequence, he may traverse only those parts of the *techum* of his house which overlap the *techum* of his *eruv* (*Rav; Rashi*).

Even if both the *eruv* and the town are within 2,000 cubits, the *eruv* takes effect and the ruling stated here is applicable. The *Tanna* states the condition that the house is beyond 2,000 cubits only to preserve the symmetry of the mishnah. The first case dealt with a circumstance where the person was within 2,000 cubits from one location (his house) and beyond 2,000 from another (the *eruv*); therefore when the mishnah states the circumstances of the opposite case the same format is used (*Tos. HaRosh and Tos. R' Peretz*).

הַנּוֹתֵן אֶת עֵרוּבוֹ בְּעִבּוּרָהּ שֶׁל עִיר — *One who places his* eruv *in the extension of a town*

A person wished to go beyond the *techum* of the town and made an *eruv* for this purpose. However, he placed the *eruv* in one of those areas beyond the town proper which is considered an *extension of the town* for the purpose of *techum* calculation, as specified in mishnah 1 (*Rambam*). Or he placed the *eruv* in one of the houses within seventy (and a fraction) cubits of the town (see mishnah 2), which is also considered part of the town (*Rav; Rashi*).[1]

לֹא עָשָׂה וְלֹא כְלוּם — *has accomplished nothing* [lit. *he has not done and it is nothing*].

Since, as explained above, the *techum*

of the town in any case is measured from beyond the *extension*, therefore, placing the *eruv* within the area considered to be part of the town cannot gain any extension of the *techum* beyond its regular boundaries (*Rav; Rashi*).

נְתָנוֹ חוּץ לַתְּחוּם, אֲפִלּוּ אַמָּה אַחַת, — *If he placed it beyond the* techum, *even one cubit*,

The word *techum* refers to the town boundaries as they are defined for *techum* measurement (*Rav from Gem.* 60b). [If the word *techum* were taken in its usual sense, the *eruv* would be invalid and the individual would be entitled to the regular town *techum* (see 3:4).]

מַה שֶׁנִּשְׂכָּר הוּא מַפְסִיד. — *whatever he gains he loses.*

The making of an *eruv* does not actually extend the *techum* area; it merely changes the point from which it is measured. Its effect, then, is to shift the entire *techum* area. As a result, for every cubit one extends the *techum* boundaries in one direction, one must necessarily subtract the same amount from the opposite direction. For example, if one places his *eruv* 1,000 cubits east of the town boundary, his personal *techum* now ends 2,000 cubits from that place in every direction. Thus, as a result of the *eruv*, he may go 3,000 cubits beyond the eastern border of the town but only 1,000 cubits beyond the western border of the town and he has

1. *Rashi* assumes that the mishnah accepts R' Meir's view (see mish. 2) which allows a *karpeif* to be added to every town.

One who places his *eruv* in the extension of a town has accomplished nothing. If he placed it beyond the *techum*, even one cubit, whatever he gains he loses.

8. The residents of a large town may traverse an entire small town, but the residents of a small town may not traverse an entire large town.

YAD AVRAHAM

lost in the east whatever he has gained in the west *(Rav; Rashi)*.

In fact, he may actually lose more than the corresponding 1,000 cubits to the west. By reckoning his place of dwelling as the town, he benefits by having the *whole* town considered as his place of dwelling, which results in his 2,000 cubits being measured from the town's boundaries. Thus, he does not use up any of those 2,000 cubits on the area of the town itself. However, when an

eruv (or an actual dwelling) is beyond the town boundaries, the *techum* is measured from that point. The area of the town is included in the 2,000 cubit limit and is not, in this case, considered as the equivalent of four cubits[1] *(Rav; Rashi)*.

However, if the *entire* town is within the *techum* of the *eruv* it is reckoned only as four cubits (see mishnah 8). In that case he would have 996 cubits (1000 minus 4) beyond the western border of the town (see *Orach Chaim* 408:1).

8.

אַנְשֵׁי עִיר גְּדוֹלָה מְהַלְכִין אֶת כָּל עִיר קְטַנָּה, — *The residents of a large town may traverse an entire small town,*

A large town and a small one are situated close to one another [but are separated by at least 141⅓ cubits or else they would be considered as one town for *techum* purposes]. The entire small town falls within the 2,000 cubit *techum* of the large town, whereas the 2,000 cubit *techum* of the smaller town ends in the middle of the larger town. As a consequence, the inhabitants of the large town may traverse the entire smaller town. This statement if taken at face value is obvious and superfluous. The *Gemara* (61a) therefore explains that the term *may traverse* here implies that practically the entire area of the small town is discounted in the *techum*

calculations of the larger town; it is counted as only four cubits. For example, if the small town is 1,000 cubits away from the large town and is itself 500 cubits wide, the inhabitants of the large town may walk yet another 996 cubits beyond the boundary of the small town. This allows them in effect a total of 2,496 cubits in this direction.

וְאֵין אַנְשֵׁי עִיר קְטַנָּה מְהַלְכִין אֶת כָּל עִיר גְּדוֹלָה. — *but the residents of a small town may not traverse an entire large town.*

Because the larger town is not entirely within the *techum* area of the smaller town it is not considered as four cubits but is calculated in terms of its actual area *(Rav from Gem. 60b)*.

[The expressions *large town* and *small*

1. *Rav* states that if a person makes an *eruv* outside his town and the 2,000 cubits measured from that point end in the middle of the town in which he is actually living, he may not progress beyond that point. However, *Tosafos* (60b, s.v. אין); see also *Ritva*) proves that one may always traverse the entire town one actually inhabits at the onset of the Sabbath even if one's formal dwelling as per *eruv* is outside the town; i.e., this entire town is considered as four cubits. It differs in this respect from a town one encounters in measuring the *eruv* but is not in at the onset of the Sabbath (see mishnah 8). Such a town is not considered 'four cubits' in regard to the *techum* measurement and the 2,000 cubit limit is expended even in the middle of the town. *Rama* rules in accordance with this view *(Orach Chaim* 408:1).

כֵּיצַד? מִי שֶׁהָיָה בְּעִיר גְּדוֹלָה וְנָתַן אֶת עֵרוּבוֹ
בְּעִיר קְטַנָּה, בְּעִיר קְטַנָּה וְנָתַן אֶת עֵרוּבוֹ בְּעִיר
גְּדוֹלָה, מְהַלֵּךְ אֶת כֻּלָּהּ וְחוּצָה לָהּ אַלְפַּיִם אַמָּה.
וְרַבִּי עֲקִיבָא אוֹמֵר: אֵין לוֹ אֶלָּא מִמְּקוֹם עֵרוּבוֹ
אַלְפַּיִם אַמָּה.

[ט] **אָמַר** לָהֶן רַבִּי עֲקִיבָא: ,,אִי אַתֶּם מוֹדִים לִי
בְּנוֹתֵן עֵרוּבוֹ בִּמְעָרָה, שֶׁאֵין לוֹ
מִמְּקוֹם עֵרוּבוֹ אֶלָּא אַלְפַּיִם אַמָּה?״
אָמְרוּ לוֹ: ,,אֵימָתַי? בִּזְמַן שֶׁאֵין בָּהּ דִּיוּרִין; אֲבָל
יֵשׁ בָּהּ דִּיוּרִין, מְהַלֵּךְ אֶת כֻּלָּהּ, וְחוּצָה לָהּ אַלְפַּיִם

יד אברהם

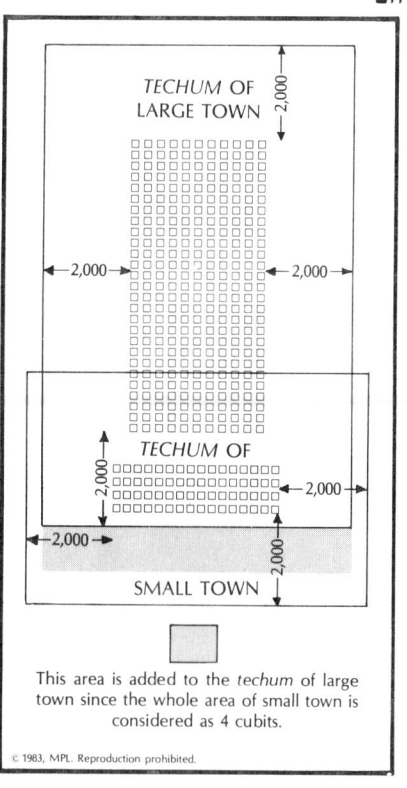

TECHUM OF
LARGE TOWN
2,000

←2,000→   ←2,000→

TECHUM OF
2,000   ←2,000→

←2,000→   2,000

SMALL TOWN

This area is added to the *techum* of large
town since the whole area of small town is
considered as 4 cubits.

© 1983, MPL. Reproduction prohibited.

the town which is not entirely within its
neighbor's *techum* is a *large town*.]

כֵּיצַד? — *How so?*

The *Gemara* (61a) observes that the
reply to this rhetorical question does not
elaborate on the preceding passage as
one would expect it to. The *Gemara*
concludes that this question is posed in
reference to an unstated passage
explaining the first passage. This
unstated passage says that the distinction drawn between the inhabitants of
the small and large town refers only to
the measurements of the *techumin* of
the towns. No distinction, however, is
drawn between inhabitants of a town
and individuals from the other town
who placed an *eruv* within this
neighboring town. It is to clarify this
law that this rhetorical question
addresses itself *(Rav)*.

מִי שֶׁהָיָה בְּעִיר גְּדוֹלָה וְנָתַן אֶת עֵרוּבוֹ בְּעִיר
קְטַנָּה, בְּעִיר קְטַנָּה וְנָתַן אֶת עֵרוּבוֹ בְּעִיר
גְּדוֹלָה, מְהַלֵּךְ אֶת כֻּלָּהּ וְחוּצָה לָהּ אַלְפַּיִם
אַמָּה. — *One who was in a large town
and placed his* eruv *in a small town,* [or
he was] *in a small town and placed his*
eruv *in a large town, may traverse its
entirety and two thousand cubits
beyond it.*

[The entire town in which he placed
his *eruv* is considered as four cubits and
the 2,000 cubit *techum* measurement is

town are defined here, not in absolute terms,
but according to their relative *techumin*. The
town which is entirely within the other
town's *techum* is called a *small town* whereas

How so? One who was in a large town and placed his *eruv* in a small town, [or] in a small town and placed his *eruv* in a large town, may traverse its entirety and two thousand cubits beyond it. But R' Akiva says: He has no more than two thousand cubits from the place of his *eruv*.

9. R' Akiva said to them: 'Do you not agree with me regarding one who placed his *eruv* in a cave, that he has no more than two thousand cubits?' They answered him: 'When is this so? Only when there are no inhabitants in it; but if it had inhabitants in it, he may traverse its entirety and beyond it for

YAD AVRAHAM

marked off from beyond the town perimeter. No distinction is made in this regard between the bona fide inhabitants of the town and the formal inhabitants as per *eruv*.]

וְרַבִּי עֲקִיבָא אוֹמֵר: אֵין לוֹ אֶלָּא מִמְּקוֹם עֵרוּבוֹ אַלְפַּיִם אַמָּה. — *But R' Akiva says: He has no more than two thousand cubits from the place of his* eruv.

The town wherein the *eruv* is placed is not considered as four cubits relative to the one making the *eruv*, according to R' Akiva. Accordingly, its area must be reckoned into the 2,000 cubit *techum* calculations. Only for bona fide inhabitants does the entire town figure as a four cubit area but not for those for whom the town is only a formal place of dwelling for *eruv* (Rav). The halachah is not in accord with R' Akiva's view (Rav; Rambam).

9.

אָמַר לָהֶן רַבִּי עֲקִיבָא: — *R' Akiva said to them:*

[I.e., to the Sages disagreeing with him in the previous mishnah.]

„אִי אַתֶּם מוֹדִים לִי בְּנוֹתֵן עֵרוּבוֹ בִּמְעָרָה, שֶׁאֵין לוֹ מִמְּקוֹם עֵרוּבוֹ אֶלָּא אַלְפַּיִם אַמָּה?" — *'Do you not agree with me regarding one who placed his* eruv *in a cave, that he has no more than two thousand cubits?'*

[R' Akiva seeks to prove his view from a case in which one placed his *eruv* in a cave. R' Akiva knew that the Sages agree that in this case the entire cave is not considered as four cubits although, technically, if an individual actually lived in the cave, his *techum* would begin outside its walls (just as in the case of a house). The conclusion is obvious — a distinction is to be drawn between

an actual home and a formal place of dwelling as proposed by R' Akiva.]

אָמְרוּ לוֹ: „אֵימָתַי? בִּזְמַן שֶׁאֵין בָּה דִּיוּרִין; אֲבָל יֵשׁ בָּה דִּיוּרִין, מְהַלֵּךְ אֶת כֻּלָּהּ, וְחוּצָה לָה אַלְפַּיִם אַמָּה." — *They answered him* [lit. said to him]: *'When is this so? Only when there are no inhabitants in it; but if it had inhabitants in it, he may traverse its entirety and beyond it for two thousand cubits.'*

The Sages feel that the cases are not analogous. When an *eruv* is placed in a town, there are inhabitants in the town for whom the town is regarded as four cubits. Consequently, the town is considered as four cubits even for one who is only placing an *eruv* there. In the case of the cave however, no inhabitants actually occupy it so that it is not, per se, regarded as an actual residential area

עֵירוּבִין אַמָּה.״ נִמְצָא קַל תּוֹכָהּ מֵעַל גַּבָּהּ. ו/א
וְלַמּוֹדֵד שֶׁאָמְרוּ: ,,נוֹתְנִין לוֹ אַלְפַּיִם,״ שֶׁאֲפִלּוּ
סוֹף מִדָּתוֹ כָּלָה בִּמְעָרָה.

[א] **הַדָּר** עִם הַנָּכְרִי בְּחָצֵר, אוֹ עִם מִי שֶׁאֵינוֹ
מוֹדֶה בְּעֵרוּב, הֲרֵי זֶה אוֹסֵר עָלָיו —

יד אברהם

which can be considered as four cubits. Merely placing an *eruv* at such a site does not convert it into a residence entitled to be considered as four cubits.

Furthermore, the Gemara (61b) states that if the cave is indeed habitable (see below), it is considered as having inhabitants even though none are actually living there. The Sages only accept R' Akiva's rule where the cave was uninhabitable because its walls had partially collapsed (Rav).

נִמְצָא קַל תּוֹכָהּ מֵעַל גַּבָּהּ. — *Thus it follows that its interior is more lenient than its roof.*

If one placed an *eruv* on top of the cave, the *techum* measurement would begin immediately after the four cubit area in which the *eruv* was deposited. Since the roof of the cave is not fit for habitation — it has no walls — its area is not qualified to be considered as four cubits. Therefore, by placing the *eruv* inside the cave one gains more space than by placing it on the roof (Rav).

וְלַמּוֹדֵד שֶׁאָמְרוּ: — *And concerning the surveyor, about whom they said,*

[This segment of the mishnah refers to the statement in mishnah 8: '... but the inhabitants of the small town may not traverse the entire large town,' and differentiates between an inhabitant of a

town for whom the entire town is discounted in regard to *techum* measurement, and a resident of the neighboring town, who has already begun his *techum* measurement and must calculate the town area in his measurement. The latter is here called 'the surveyor' because he must measure the town under discussion here.]

נוֹתְנִין לוֹ אַלְפַּיִם,,״ — 'We give him [only] two thousand cubits,'

[I.e., he has only 2,000 cubits and may not reckon the towns or houses that fall within that area as merely four cubits.]

שֶׁאֲפִלּוּ סוֹף מִדָּתוֹ כָּלָה בִּמְעָרָה. — *even if his measurement ended in the middle of a cave [it is so].*

Even if the 2,000 cubit boundary occurred in the midst of an inhabited cave (or house or town), the cave is not considered to be four cubits and he may not go beyond the actual boundary (Rav; Rashi, see Gem. 61a and Ritva there; cf. Sfas Emes). [Although an inhabited cave is considered to be only four cubits according to all views, this is only relative to where the 2,000 cubit measurement should begin; it is not viewed in this light concerning where the *techum* measurement ends.]

Chapter 6

◄§ Eruvei Chatzeiros and Nullification of Rights

The laws of *eruvei chatzeiros* and *shitufei mevo'os* form the major portion of the discussion in the next four chapters (6-9). Both of these institutions and peripheral topics are discussed at length in the General Introduction (which see). The primary provision of the laws of *eruvei chatzeiros* is based on the Rabbinical prohibition against carrying objects from one's house into a courtyard which he and the residents of the other houses in that courtyard use jointly. For this reason, in the

two thousand cubits.' Thus it follows that its interior is more lenient than its roof.

And concerning the surveyor, about whom they said, 'We give him two thousand cubits,' even if his measurement ended in the middle of a cave [it is so].

1. **O**ne who lives together with a gentile in a [single] courtyard, or with one who does not

terminology of this chapter, people living jointly in a courtyard are said to *restrict* (אוסרין) each other, i.e., they each restrict the other's use of the courtyard by disallowing the carrying of objects between the houses and the courtyard.

Along with the prohibition, the Rabbis provided two procedures by which it can be rendered inapplicable: (a) עֵרוּבֵי חֲצֵירוֹת [*eruvei chatzeiros*], *merging of the courtyards*, through which all the inhabitants are considered to be one unit or household; and (b) בִּיטוּל רְשׁוּת, *nullification of rights*, a formal renunciation of one's rights to use the courtyard or his rights to his house. This renunciation is accomplished with an oral declaration which may be made even on the Sabbath; *eruvei chatzeiros*, on the other hand, may only be made before the Sabbath.

By nullification, one gives up his rights to carry objects from his house into the courtyard (for that Sabbath) and is therefore no longer reckoned a partner in it. Consequently, if there is only one other resident in the courtyard it becomes, in effect, the sole domain of that resident and carrying between his house and the courtyard is permitted. It follows that if all the residents except one merged their interests with an *eruvei chatzeiros*, the one person who did not join in the *eruv* — and who therefore restricts everybody else — can nullify his rights, thereby leaving only those who joined in the *eruv* as legal owners of the courtyard and therefore permitted to carry into it.

A gentile who lives in a courtyard also restricts it under certain circumstances. However, neither of the two methods just outlined can remove that restriction. The only way to remove the restriction of a gentile is to rent his rights to the courtyard. The terms of this rental need not imply that the Jew actually takes away the gentile's rights and can prevent him from using the courtyard. Rather, it is a [symbolic (*Rambam, Hil. Eruvin* 2:12)] legal act, made solely for the purposes of *eruv*, and does not deprive the gentile of anything (*Gem.* 62a).

1.

הַדָּר עִם הַנָּכְרִי בְּחָצֵר, — *One who lives together with a gentile in a [single] courtyard,*

Since neither *eruvei chatzeiros* nor nullification of rights — applies to gentiles, carrying from one's house into a courtyard which he shares with a gentile is prohibited unless one rents the gentile's rights to the courtyard. The rental is merely symbolic (*Rambam, Hil. Eruvin* 2:12) and does not deprive the gentile of any of his former rights. It can

even be effected with a rental fee of less than the value of a *perutah* (*Gem.* 62a; for other rules concerning this commonly used device, see *Orach Chaim* 382:4-14 and 391:1.) The mishnah now discusses the circumstances under which a gentile's residence creates a prohibition against carrying (*Rav; Rashi*).

[The reason an *eruv* is not effective for a gentile is obvious. Since *eruv* is a purely Rabbinical and religious procedure its use is

עֵירוּבִין דִּבְרֵי רַבִּי מֵאִיר. רַבִּי אֱלִיעֶזֶר בֶּן יַעֲקֹב אוֹמֵר:
ו/א לְעוֹלָם אֵינוֹ אוֹסֵר עַד שֶׁיְּהוּ שְׁנֵי יִשְׂרְאֵלִים אוֹסְרִין
זֶה עַל זֶה.

יד אברהם

restricted to those who recognize the authority of the Rabbis, and as such excludes even Jews who are members of heretical sects.] However, the exclusion of gentiles from nullification of rights, which has legal aspects also, is based on other considerations. *Meiri* explains that according to the *Gemara's* conclusion (62a), 'A gentile's dwelling is not considered a dwelling' [i.e., it is not included in the legal definition of the term *dwelling* as it applies to the laws of *eruv*], the fact of the gentile's residency in the courtyard should not restrict the activities of the Jews living there. Nevertheless, to prevent Jews from living together with gentiles, whose ways they would learn to imitate, the Sages decreed that a gentile's residence should restrict. The great inconvenience of being denied the use of one's courtyard (which in Mishnaic times was a virtual extension of the home) would deter Jews from living in one courtyard with gentiles. [Although the Sages allowed the option of renting the gentile's dwelling, this could not, in most cases, be implemented. The gentiles, as a rule, were reluctant to agree to this procedure because they thought it was some form of witchcraft.] Had the Sages permitted the nullification of a gentile's rights, the inconvenience of living with a gentile would be greatly alleviated and the purpose of the Sages' decree would be defeated.

אוֹ עִם מִי שֶׁאֵינוֹ מוֹדֶה בְּעֵרוּב, — *or with one who does not accept* [the laws of] eruv,

I.e., a Cuthite (*Rav; Rashi;* from *Gem.* 31b), or any member of the heretical sects of Mishnaic times, e.g., a Sadducee, et al. (*Tos.* 61b). [See commentary to 3:2, s.v. בְּיַד מִי שֶׁאֵינוֹ; the status of modern-day heretics is discussed in a footnote at the end of mish. 2.]

The Cuthites were a motley group sent by the Assyrian king Shalmanessar to colonize the area of *Eretz Yisrael* left desolate by the exile of the Ten Tribes. An outbreak of attacks by wild animals convinced the Cuthites to convert to Judaism. However, although they adopted the Jewish religion

and practiced many facets of it, they did not relinquish all their heathen beliefs and practices, as related in *I Kings* 17:24-41. Because of the ambiguity of the circumstances surrounding their conversion to Judaism there is disagreement among the *Tannaim* as to the legality of their conversion, i.e., whether the Cuthites are legally gentiles or Jews. However, their attitude vis-a-vis the Sages was unequivocal — they repudiated their authority and consequently did not recognize the institution of *eruv*.

The Sadducees were a powerful heretical group which acknowledged only the written Torah but repudiated the Oral Law and the authority of the Sages. *Rambam (Comm.* to *Avos* 1:3) maintains that their alleged adherence to the written Torah was not sincere and was intended merely as an ideological ploy to attract adherents. The group was named for its founder, the heretic Tzadok who had been a disciple of Antigonus of Socho, the eminent spiritual heir to Shimon HaTzaddik [approx. 3500/third cent. CE] (*Avos* 1:3; see also *Avos d'R' Nassan* ch. 6).

הֲרֵי זֶה אוֹסֵר עָלָיו — דִּבְרֵי רַבִּי מֵאִיר. — *that person places a restriction upon* [the use of the courtyard for] *him* — [*these are*] *the words of R' Meir.*

[I.e., the presence of a gentile or Cuthite resident in the courtyard prohibits any Jew living there from carrying into the courtyard and precludes the effectiveness of an *eruvei chatzeiros* or nullification of rights.]

The reason for our mishnah's disqualification of Cuthites is a point of issue between the commentaries. *R' Yehonasan* (see *Tos.* and *Maharsha*) suggests that the *Tanna* of our mishnah is of the opinion that legally the Cuthites are to be regarded as gentiles, and as such neither their inclusion in an *eruv* nor the nullification of their rights is valid. This, however, leaves unexplained why the other individuals — bona fide Jews — included in the term 'one who does not recognize *eruv*' have this rule applied to them. Furthermore, *Tosafos* (61a) demonstrates that in fact the *Tanna* of this mishnah subscribes to the view

6
1

accept [the laws of] *eruv*, that person places a restriction upon him — [these are] the words of R' Meir. R' Eliezer ben Yaakov says: He never restricts, unless there are two Jews restricting each other.

YAD AVRAHAM

that the Cuthites are legally Jews.

Accordingly, the reason our mishnah disqualifies Cuthites is based on the premise that anyone who does not recognize the authority of the Sages is treated as a gentile in this context, although he is in reality a Jew and is judged a Jew with regard to all other matters *(Rashba, Ritva, et al., based on Tos.)*.

Rashba (cf. *Tos. R' Peretz*), based on the principle enunciated in the *Gemara* (see below) that the reason that a gentile restricts the use of a courtyard is so that a Jew not elect to live in close proximity to a gentile and thus not be led to imitate his neighbor's lifestyle, explains further. Anyone about whom the Sages were concerned lest a Jew learn from his improper life style is given the status of a gentile in regard to this law, although he is legally regarded as a Jew in regard to other Torah laws. [As explained above, the *eruv* law peculiar to a gentile was legislated as a safeguard against this same concern.]

רַבִּי אֱלִיעֶזֶר בֶּן יַעֲקֹב אוֹמֵר: לְעוֹלָם אֵינוֹ אוֹסֵר עַד שֶׁיִּהְיוּ שְׁנֵי יִשְׂרְאֵלִים אוֹסְרִין זֶה עַל זֶה. — *R' Eliezer ben Yaakov says: He* [i.e., the gentile] *never restricts unless there are* [also] *two Jews restricting each other.*

Only if there are two Jews residing in the courtyard, and thereby restrict each other, does the gentile's presence also restrict. Consequently, where only one Jew lives in the courtyard with the gentile no *eruv* is necessary at all. However, where two Jews live in that courtyard — the gentile's presence also restricts. Since an *eruv* is ineffective for a gentile, the effect of this restriction is to prohibit carrying even after the two Jews make an *eruv* with each other *(Rashi)*.

The reason for this ruling is that, as

explained above (s.v. הַדָּר), the residence of a gentile is essentially exempt from the laws of *eruv* and cannot affect the restriction of carrying. As formulated by the *Gemara* (62a): 'A gentile's dwelling is not considered a dwelling,' [i.e., it is not included in the legal definition of the term *dwelling* as it applies to the laws of *eruv*]. It was only to prevent Jews from living together with gentiles and thereby learning to imitate their ways that the Sages decreed that the presence of a gentile should restrict. R' Eliezer ben Yaakov, however, reasons that since it was extremely rare, at least in Mishnaic times, for a solitary Jew to share a courtyard with one or more gentiles, for fear of being murdered, the Sages did not include such a case in the decree that a gentile's residence restricts. This follows the general principle that the Sages did not decree for highly unusual situations.[1] Since this case is not included in the decree and since the gentile's dwelling does not inherently restrict, there is no reason to prohibit carrying in a courtyard in which only one Jew lives with gentiles.

The *Tanna kamma*, however, states that a gentile restricts under all circumstances — even if only one Jew lives in the courtyard. Although he agrees that a gentile's dwelling is not considered a *dwelling*, he argues that the instance of a solitary Jew living with a gentile is not such a rare occurrence as to merit being exempted from the decree *(Rav from Gem. 62a)*.

The halachah follows R' Eliezer ben Yaakov's view *(Rav; Rambam)*.

1. Although it would not be unusual for a solitary Jew to live in a courtyard with a Cuthite (or Sadducee), the decree, nevertheless, does not apply to such a situation, and the Jew is not restricted. The Sages did not create any special legal status for these groups, but merely assigned them the [already existing] status of gentiles. Consequently, their presence cannot restrict except where a gentile's presence restricts *(Tos.)*.

[129]   THE MISHNAH/ERUVIN —Chapter Six: *HaDar*

עירובין [ב] **אָמַר** רַבָּן גַּמְלִיאֵל: „מַעֲשֶׂה בִּצְדוֹקִי אֶחָד
ו/ב
שֶׁהָיָה דָר עִמָּנוּ בְּמָבוֹי בִּירוּשָׁלַיִם,
וְאָמַר לָנוּ אַבָּא: ,מַהֲרוּ וְהוֹצִיאוּ אֶת כָּל הַכֵּלִים
לַמָּבוֹי עַד שֶׁלֹּא יוֹצִיא וְיֶאֱסֹר עֲלֵיכֶם.' "
רַבִּי יְהוּדָה אוֹמֵר בְּלָשׁוֹן אַחֵר: „מַהֲרוּ וַעֲשׂוּ
צָרְכֵיכֶם בַּמָּבוֹי עַד שֶׁלֹּא יוֹצִיא וְיֶאֱסֹר עֲלֵיכֶם."

יד אברהם

2.

אָמַר רַבָּן גַּמְלִיאֵל: „מַעֲשֶׂה בִּצְדוֹקִי אֶחָד שֶׁהָיָה דָר עִמָּנוּ בְּמָבוֹי בִּירוּשָׁלַיִם, — Rabban Gamliel said: 'It once happened that a Sadducee lived with us in an alley in Jerusalem,

[The rules governing restriction of a courtyard apply to alleys as well (see General Introduction concerning shitufei mevo'os). A Sadducee lived in a courtyard opening into the same alley as Rabban Gamliel's courtyard. In addition to the shitufei mevo'os collected from the other Jewish residents, the Sadducee had been asked to nullify his rights (Rav; Rashi). [The question arose whether the Sadducee's nullification was valid, i.e., whether Sadducees, because of their heretical views in regard to the oral law, are put in the category of gentiles with regard to the provision of nullification of rights, (as held by the first Tanna), and thus their nullification is not valid; or whether they are to be judged as Jews concerning this provision (see Gem. 68b).

Generally, if an incident is recorded in a mishnah, it has been adduced to support a previously stated ruling. Here, since no ruling concerning the validity of a Sadducee's nullification of rights has previously been stated, the Gemara (68b) questions the reason for relating the incident and concludes that

this mishnah is incomplete and should read: צָדוֹקִי הֲרֵי הוּא כְּנָכְרִי, וְרַבָּן גַּמְלִיאֵל אוֹמֵר: צָדוֹקִי אֵינוֹ כְּנָכְרִי. וּמַעֲשֶׂה ... A Sadducee is to be judged as a gentile [i.e. his nullification is not valid]. Rabban Gamliel says: A Sadducee is not to be judged as a gentile [and to prove his point he cites the following episode]: it once happened ...

Tosafos (62a) postulates that Rabban Gamliel means to dispute the entire ruling applied to those classified by the Tanna kamma as 'those who do not accept eruv.' Accordingly, his ruling also concerns the legal status of the Cuthites. In Rabban Gamliel's opinion those who do not accept eruv are not to be treated as gentiles with regard to the laws of eruv, but as Jews. Accordingly, their nullification is valid. However, they cannot join in an eruv because they do not accept it.

Thus, in Rabban Gamliel's view, there are three classifications: (a) A Jew — his restriction of a courtyard can be removed either by his joining an eruv or by his nullifying his rights; (b) one who does not accept eruv — his restriction can be removed only by his nullifying his rights [rental of his rights is not an option because this method is effective only for gentiles, but this person is judged a Jew]; (c) a gentile — his restriction is removed through rental of his rights. The Tanna kamma, on the other hand, treats those who do not accept eruv as gentiles, and thus eliminates the second classification.[1]

1. As explained above (first footnote to mish. 1), Rashba and Ritva maintain that Sadducees are not included in the term 'one who does not accept eruv.' Accordingly, it may be that Rabban Gamliel does not dispute the Tanna kamma's ruling concerning a Cuthite but is merely stating a new ruling concerning a Sadducee to which the Tanna kamma may actually agree.

2. Rabban Gamliel said: 'It once happened that a Sadducee lived with us in an alley in Jerusalem, and Father told us, "Hurry and carry out all your utensils into the alley before he carries out and restricts you." '

R' Yehudah related [this] in different terms: 'Hurry and attend to your needs in the alley before it passes and he restricts you.'

YAD AVRAHAM

וְאָמַר לָנוּ אַבָּא: — *and Father told us,*

[The Rabban Gamliel of this mishnah is Rabban Gamliel II who was *Nassi* of the post-Destruction Sanhedrin which sat in Yavneh (see *Tos.* 61b). His father was Rabban Shimon ben Gamliel I, the great-grandson of Hillel, who lived in Jerusalem and held the post of *Nassi* (president of the Sanhedrin) just prior to the destruction of the Second Temple. The Rabban Shimon ben Gamliel usually encountered in Mishnah is Rabban Shimon ben Gamliel II, the son of the Rabban Gamliel mentioned here.]

Rabban Gamliel adduces a ruling made by his father to support his position that a Sadducee is to be treated as a Jew in regard to nullification.

מַהֲרוּ וְהוֹצִיאוּ אֶת כָּל הַכֵּלִים לַמָּבוֹי עַד שֶׁלֹּא יוֹצִיא וְיֶאֱסֹר עֲלֵיכֶם — *"Hurry and carry out all your utensils into the alley before he carries out and restricts you." '*

If one who has nullified his rights to a courtyard nevertheless carries from his house into that courtyard, his act is tantamount to a retraction of his nullification. Thus, Rabban Gamliel's father admonished his household to carry their belongings out into the alley before the Sadducee carried his utensils out. They would thereby legally formalize the Sadducees's nullification by taking possession, as it were, of his part of the alley, and the Sadducee's further acts would have no effect on them. If, however, the Sadducee would carry into the alley before the other Jews had done so, his nullification would be

voided and his renewed presence would restrict them (*Rashi* from *Gem.* 68b).

רַבִּי יְהוּדָה אוֹמֵר בְּלָשׁוֹן אַחֵר: — *R' Yehudah related [this] in different terms:*

There is a difference of opinion as to exactly what Rabban Gamliel had quoted in the name of his father. The version cited anonymously is that of R' Meir, according to whom Rabban Gamliel attempted to prove that a Sadducee is not judged as a gentile. R' Yehudah's version of the story differs and consequently the conclusions drawn from it also differ (*R' Yehonasan*).

„מַהֲרוּ וַעֲשׂוּ צָרְכֵיכֶם בַּמָּבוֹי עַד שֶׁלֹּא יוֹצִיא וְיֶאֱסֹר עֲלֵיכֶם.'' — *'Hurry and attend to your needs in the alley before it [i.e., Friday] passes and he restricts you.'*

According to R' Yehudah's version of the story, Rabban Gamliel's father instructed them to make sure to take care of all of their needs prior to the Sabbath so that they would not need to carry anything out on the Sabbath itself. In this version, they would be prohibited to carry out into the courtyard regardless of what the Sadducee did. According to this view, a Sadducee has the status of a gentile and nullification is not effective for him (*Rav; Rambam*). [The only alternative is to rent his property.]

In this version, יוֹצִיא refers to the day, not to the Sadducee. The mishnah should be understood as if it read עַד שֶׁלֹּא יֵצֵא הַיּוֹם, *before the day is carried out* (*Gem.* 69a, as emended by *Hagahos HaBach*).

חָצֵר שֶׁשָּׁכַח אֶחָד מֵהֶם וְלֹא עֵרֵב,
בֵּיתוֹ אָסוּר מִלְהַכְנִיס וּמִלְהוֹצִיא לוֹ
וְלָהֶם; וְשֶׁלָּהֶם מֻתָּרִין לוֹ וְלָהֶם.
נָתְנוּ לוֹ רְשׁוּתָן, הוּא מֻתָּר וְהֵן אֲסוּרִין. הָיוּ

יד אברהם

In an alternative view in the *Gemara* (69a),
R' Yehudah is also understood to hold that a
Sadducee is not to be considered a gentile and
that his nullification is valid. However, R'
Yehudah disagrees only with that aspect of
the previous version which holds that 'taking
possession' of the nullification precludes its
being retracted. R' Yehudah maintains that
retraction of the nullification is always
effective and because of this Rabban Gamliel
cautioned them to take care of their needs as
soon as possible so that they not be left in a
difficult situation once the Sadducee carries
out to the courtyard (a likely occurrence),
thereby legally retracting his nullification. In
this interpretation the phrase עַד שֶׁלֹּא יוֹצִיא is
taken in its simple meaning and rendered,
before he carries out.

The halachah rules that a heretic who
does not recognize the authority of the
Sages is not regarded as a gentile (even
in regard to *eruv*). He may nullify his
rights but cannot participate in an *eruv*.

This is so, however, only if his heretical
views do not lead to blatant desecration
of the Sabbath. One who desecrates the
Sabbath publicly (in the presence of or
with the knowledge of ten Jews) is
treated (where this is a stringency) as a
gentile in regard to all laws of the Torah.
However, if the desecration is performed surreptitiously, the violator is
treated as a Jew (*Gem.* 69a; *Rambam,
Hil. Eruvin* 2:16). Cuthites were
excluded from Jewry by special
legislation enacted by Rabban Gamliel
and his *beis din* and later in the days of
the *Amoraim* R' Ammi and R' Assi
(*Chullin* 5b-6a), and they have the
status of gentiles (*Orach Chaim* 385:1-
2). Nullification is formalized when the
residents carry out from their houses to
the courtyard (*Hil. Eruvin* 2:6; *Orach
Chaim* 381:1).[1]

3.

— אַנְשֵׁי חָצֵר שֶׁשָּׁכַח אֶחָד מֵהֶם וְלֹא עֵרֵב,
*The residents of a courtyard, one of
whom forgot to participate in the* eruv,
Since one of the inhabitants of the
courtyard forgot to contribute to the
eruvei chatzeiros before the Sabbath, he
restricts all those who did contribute. To
permit the others to carry between their
houses and the courtyard, this individual

nullified his rights (although once the
Sabbath has begun it is too late to join
the *eruv*, nullification is valid even after
the onset of the Sabbath). The mishnah
now delineates the halachic situation
created by this nullification. The
Gemara (69a) explains that the case
discussed in our mishnah refers to a
specific type of nullification — the

1. Nowadays, when a large area is enclosed to allow carrying on the Sabbath, an *eruvei
chatzeiros* is made to include all the Jews in the area and rental is made to remove the
restricting power of the gentile inhabitants. Nothing is done to provide for the eventuality that
one of the inhabitants may be a heretic (for whom the *eruv* is not effective) who refrains from
blatant desecration of the Sabbath and who would as a consequence be judged a Jew (for
whom rental is not effective).

Chazon Ish (*Orach Chaim* 87:13) explains that the peculiar type of heretic discussed in the
mishnah no longer exists and we do not need to provide for him. He reasons that a heretic who
denies the validity of the Torah as directly given to Israel is regarded as a gentile, and that
accordingly, one has to assume that the Sadducees did believe in the Written Torah and denied
only the Oral Torah and the authority of the Sages. This is not true of present-day heretics
who either accept the Torah in its entirety — Written and Oral — or reject its God-given status
entirely.

3. The residents of a courtyard, one of whom forgot to participate in the *eruv*, his house is restricted with regard to carrying in and carrying out, to him and to them; but theirs are permitted to him and to them.

If they ceded their rights to him, he is permitted, but they are restricted. If there were two, they restrict

individual nullified only his rights in the courtyard while retaining his rights in his house (*Rav*).

The *Gemara* comments that our mishnah holds that nullification of one's rights in the courtyard does not automatically entail nullification of one's rights in his house, even though it opens into that courtyard. On this point they disagree with R' Eliezer (above in 2:6).

בֵּיתוֹ אָסוּר מִלְהַכְנִיס וּמִלְהוֹצִיא לוֹ וְלָהֶם; — *his house is restricted with regard to carrying in* [from the courtyard] *and carrying out* [to the courtyard, both] *to him and to them;*

Since the individual nullified his rights in the courtyard, the other residents, whose houses are considered through their *eruv* to be the property of one corporation, are now in sole possession of the courtyard. Therefore, carrying objects from their houses into the courtyard or vice versa is permitted. However, since the one who forgot to join the *eruv* has nullified his rights to the courtyard while retaining his rights to his house, his house is under different ownership than the courtyard. Consequently, no one may carry from the courtyard to this individual's house since they would then be carrying from property owned by the corporation of *eruv* participants to the house owned by this individual (*Rav*).

Had he nullified his rights in his house too, it would be permitted for the *eruv* participants to carry between the courtyard and this individual's house. However, the individual would be prohibited from carrying out from his house to the courtyard because such an act, if performed deliberately, would be construed as a retraction of the nullification and would restrict the others.

וְשֶׁלָהֶם מֻתָּרִין לוֹ וְלָהֶם. — *but theirs are permitted to him and to them.*

Both the *eruv* participants and the individual may carry between the courtyard and the houses of the *eruv* participants. Because the *eruv* and the nullification render the houses and the courtyards the sole property of the corporation of *eruv* participants, carrying between them is considered carrying within one property, which is permitted. The presence of the individual who nullified his rights does not restrict because when he enters their houses he is considered their guest. A guest need not be included in an *eruv* because he has no rights in the courtyard and therefore does not restrict anyone (*Rav*).

נָתְנוּ לוֹ רְשׁוּתָן, — *If they ceded their rights to him,*

If the participants in the *eruv* nullified their rights in the courtyard in favor of the individual who forgot to participate in the *eruv* (*Rav; Rashi*).

הוּא מֻתָּר — *he is permitted* [to carry between his house and the courtyard],

Because of their nullification, the individual not participating in the *eruv* is now the sole remaining owner of the courtyard and he may therefore carry between his house and the courtyard freely (*Rav*). However, he may not carry from their houses into the courtyard because, as in the previous case, the mishnah refers to an instance in which only the rights in the courtyard have been nullified, not those to the houses (*Tif. Yis.*).

וְהֵן אֲסוּרִין. — *but they are restricted.*

They are prohibited from carrying even between his house and the court-

עירוּבִין שְׁנַיִם, אוֹסְרִין זֶה עַל זֶה; שֶׁאֶחָד נוֹתֵן רְשׁוּת וְנוֹטֵל

ו/ד רְשׁוּת, שְׁנַיִם נוֹתְנִים רְשׁוּת וְאֵין נוֹטְלִין רְשׁוּת.

[ד] **מֵאֵימָתַי** נוֹתְנִין רְשׁוּת? בֵּית שַׁמַּאי אוֹמְרִים: מִבְּעוֹד יוֹם. וּבֵית הִלֵּל אוֹמְרִים: מִשֶּׁחֲשֵׁכָה.

מִי שֶׁנָּתַן רְשׁוּתוֹ וְהוֹצִיא, בֵּין בְּשׁוֹגֵג בֵּין בְּמֵזִיד, הֲרֵי זֶה אוֹסֵר — דִּבְרֵי רַבִּי מֵאִיר. רַבִּי יְהוּדָה

יד אברהם

yard. Since they have nullified their rights in the courtyard there is no longer any justification for their carrying between their houses and the courtyard. The only way to allow carrying between his house and the courtyard would be to consider all the residents as guests of the individual not participating in the *eruv*. However, giving them this designation would be incongruous since five families, for example, are rarely the guests of one. Only in the reverse case, where the individual nullified his rights in favor of the majority, can the designation of 'guest' be reasonably applied to the nullifier — an individual (*Rav* from *Gem.* 69b).[1] Accordingly, if the participants in the *eruv* were to carry even from the individual's house to the courtyard this would be construed as a retraction of their nullification (*Rashi*).

הָיוּ שְׁנַיִם, — *If there were two,*

[If two individuals forgot to participate in the *eruv* and the participants in the *eruv* nullified their rights in favor of these two.]

אוֹסְרִין זֶה עַל זֶה; — *they restrict each other* [lit. *one upon the other*];

Although all of the *eruv* participants

nullified their rights this does not remove the restriction against carrying, since even after the nullification the courtyard is still in the possession of two individuals who did not make an *eruv*. The result is that they restrict each other. Moreover, even if one of these two now nullifies his rights in favor of the other, it is of no avail. This is because the nullification of the *eruv* participants in favor of two unincorporated people is considered invalid, as the mishnah proceeds to explain (*Rav* from *Gem.* 69b).

שֶׁאֶחָד נוֹתֵן רְשׁוּת — *because an individual can cede [his] rights*

[An individual may nullify his rights in the courtyard, or even in his house, in favor of another individual or corporation of *eruv* participants, as outlined above.]

וְנוֹטֵל רְשׁוּת, — *and acquire rights,*

[An individual may acquire the rights of others through nullification.]

שְׁנַיִם נוֹתְנִים רְשׁוּת — [while] *two* [people] *can cede* [their] *rights*

[Two individuals may cede their rights through nullification to one individual (or to one corporation of *eruv* participants).]

1. If there are only two houses in a courtyard and one nullified in favor of the other, there is disagreement among the *Poskim* as to whether the nullifier can be considered the other's guest. Some understand the *Gemara* to mean that the guest designation can only be assigned to an individual relative to a group, but that in a one to one situation he cannot be designated a guest (*Rashba* in *Avodas HaKodesh* 28). Others, however, accord the status of guest even where one individual nullifies in favor of another individual (*Meiri*). *Shulchan Aruch* (380:4) accepts the first view but some later authorities dispute this ruling (cf. *Beur Halachah*).

each other; because an individual can cede rights and acquire rights, two can cede rights but cannot acquire rights.

4. **W**hen may rights be ceded? Beis Shammai say: While it is yet day. But Beis Hillel say: When it is dark.

One who ceded his rights then carried out, whether unintentionally or deliberately, restricts — [these are] the words of R' Meir. R' Yehudah says: Deliberately,

YAD AVRAHAM

וְאֵין נוֹטְלִין רְשׁוּת. — *but cannot acquire rights.*

Two people cannot acquire these rights for one to pass them to the other by further nullifying them. Acquisition of nullified rights to a restricted courtyard is only effective when such acquisition is sufficient to remove the restriction. If rights are nullified and passed on to two people who have no *eruv* between them, their acquisition of these rights does not remove any

restrictions. [Even if it were valid, this would still not permit carrying between houses and courtyard for each house is the property of an individual, while the courtyard belongs jointly to the two of them.] Consequently, since neither of the two can acquire the nullified rights, one cannot pass those rights on to the other.[1] Therefore, even after one of the two remaining owners nullifies in favor of the last one, carrying is still prohibited (*Rav, Rashi; see Ritva*).

4.

מֵאֵימָתַי נוֹתְנִין רְשׁוּת? — *When may rights be ceded?*

[Until this point we have assumed that one may nullify his rights to the courtyard even after the onset of the Sabbath. This is not, however, universally accepted. The mishnah now discusses whether one may only nullify his rights before the Sabbath has begun, or if he may do so even during the Sabbath day itself.]

בֵּית שַׁמַּאי אוֹמְרִים: מִבְּעוֹד יוֹם. — *Beis Shammai say: While it is yet day.*

[I.e., rights may only be nullified before the Sabbath begins.] Beis Shammai regard nullification as a transfer of ownership, an act prohibited on the Sabbath under the general ban on business transactions and activities (see

Beitzah 5:2; Rav from Gem. 71a).

וּבֵית הִלֵּל אוֹמְרִים: מִשֶּׁחֲשֵׁכָה. — *But Beis Hillel say:* [Even] *when it is* [already] *dark.*

[Beis Hillel permit nullification even on the Sabbath.] They hold that nullification is merely a giving up of one's rights of usage and not a transference of ownership. It is therefore not included in the ban on transactions (*ibid.*).

מִי שֶׁנָּתַן רְשׁוּתוֹ וְהוֹצִיא, בֵּין בְּשׁוֹגֵג בֵּין בְּמֵזִיד, הֲרֵי זֶה אוֹסֵר — דִּבְרֵי רַבִּי מֵאִיר. — *One who ceded his rights then carried out, whether* [he did so] *unintentionally or deliberately,* [he] *restricts — [these are] the words of R' Meir.*

As explained above, if, after nullify-

1. If those joined by an *eruv* and one of the two individuals all nullified their rights to the other individual, the nullification and acquisition is valid and carrying is permitted (*Mishnah Berurah* 380:24).

עֵירוּבִין אוֹמֵר: בְּמֵזִיד אוֹסֵר; בְּשׁוֹגֵג אֵינוֹ אוֹסֵר.

ו/ה

[ה] **בַּעַל** הַבַּיִת שֶׁהָיָה שֻׁתָּף לִשְׁכֵנִים, לָזֶה בְּיַיִן
וְלָזֶה בְּיַיִן, אֵינָם צְרִיכִים לְעָרֵב; לָזֶה
בְּיַיִן וְלָזֶה בְּשֶׁמֶן, צְרִיכִים לְעָרֵב. רַבִּי שִׁמְעוֹן
אוֹמֵר: אֶחָד זֶה וְאֶחָד זֶה, אֵינָם צְרִיכִים לְעָרֵב.

יד אברהם

ing his rights, the nullifier carried an object from his house to the courtyard (or vice versa) on the Sabbath, he is considered to have retracted his nullification and he now restricts the use of the courtyard. R' Meir maintains that this is so even if he did so unintentionally and no conscious retraction was indicated. In R' Meir's view, we must deal strictly with even unintentional violations in order to prevent deliberate ones *(Rav from Gem. 68b; see Mishnah Berurah 381:3).* [R' Meir's view in regard to penalizing unintentional violations is well known from other cases in the mishnah. (See, e.g., *Terumos* 2:3, *Gittin* 53b.)]

רַבִּי יְהוּדָה אוֹמֵר: בְּמֵזִיד אוֹסֵר; בְּשׁוֹגֵג אֵינוֹ אוֹסֵר. — *R' Yehudah says:* [If he did so] *deliberately, he restricts;* [but if he did so] *unintentionally, he does not restrict.*

[R' Yehudah does not subscribe to the view that unintentional violations should be penalized to prevent deliberate ones. Therefore, only if the individual deliberately carried out, so that his actions constitute a retraction of his previous nullification, does he restrict.]

5.

The next mishnah discusses an aspect of the laws of *shitufei mevo'os* (the incorporation of the alleys; see General Introduction). As mentioned above (comm. to 3:1), an *eruvei chatzeiros* may be made only with a loaf of bread, so that this mishnah, which discusses the validity of an *eruv* made of liquids, must of necessity refer to *shitufei mevo'os (Rav; Rambam).* [The mishnah commonly refers to *shituf* as *eruv.* See, for example, above 5:6.]

בַּעַל הַבַּיִת שֶׁהָיָה שֻׁתָּף לִשְׁכֵנִים, לָזֶה בְּיַיִן וְלָזֶה בְּיַיִן, — *If a houseowner was a partner with* [his] *neighbors, with this one in wine and with that one in wine,*

Ordinarily a *shituf* is made by placing a quantity of commonly owned food or drink in a protected spot in one of the courtyards of the alley. This is accomplished in either of two ways: (a)

Every courtyard contributes an amount of food or drink (see 7:8) which is placed together with that contributed by the other courtyards *(Orach Chaim 366:4, 386:1);* or (b) a person living in one of the courtyards takes his own food or drink and transfers possession of the requisite amount to the residents of the other courtyards. In the case under discussion, neither of these actions was taken to effect a *shituf,* but the members of the courtyards involved happened to be partners in foodstuffs or liquids *(Rav; Rashi).*

אֵינָם צְרִיכִים לְעָרֵב; — *they need not make an* eruv;

[The term *eruv* here means *shituf* which is really an *eruv (merging)* of the courtyards and the alleys, just as *eruvei chatzeiros* is a merging of the houses and courtyards (see end of mish. 8).][1]

he restricts; unintentionally, he does not restrict.

5. **I**f a houseowner was a partner with neighbors, with this one in wine and with that one in wine, they need not make an *eruv;* with this one in wine and with that one in oil, they must make an *eruv.* R' Shimon says: In either case they need not make an *eruv.*

YAD AVRAHAM

The *Gemara* (71a) adds that the *shituf* is valid only if everyone's wine is held in the same container. If each partner's share is in a separate container, or if he had wine in partnership with one neighbor in one container and with the other neighbor in another container, it is not valid[2] *(Rambam Comm.; Mishnah Berurah* 386:16).

לָזֶה בְּיַיִן וְלָזֶה בְּשֶׁמֶן, צְרִיכִים לְעָרֵב. — [if he was a partner] *with this one in wine and with that one in oil, they must make an* eruv.

[I.e., they are not exempted from a *shitufei mevo'os.*] If the partnerships were in different foodstuffs, the *shituf* is not valid even if they were placed in one utensil *(Rashba; Ritva* to 71b).

רַבִּי שִׁמְעוֹן אוֹמֵר: אֶחָד זֶה וְאֶחָד זֶה, אֵינָם צְרִיכִים לְעָרֵב. — *R' Shimon says: In either case* [lit. *whether this one or that one*] *they need not make an* eruv.

R' Shimon holds that even such liquids as wine and oil which do not mix are considered as one unit when placed together in one utensil. This is consistent with his view elsewhere *(Tevul Yom* 2:5) concerning the laws of *tumah*-contamination *(Gem.* 71b, as understood by *Ritva* and *Meiri;* cf. *Tos. R' Akiva* here).[3]

It follows, then, that R' Shimon disagrees only in the case of two different liquids. If the householder was a partner with his neighbors in two different solid foodstuffs the *eruv* is not valid, since in this case each substance must be considered an entity to itself.[4]

According to *Rambam* and *Rav* the halachah follows the first *Tanna's* view. However, *Tur (Orach Chaim* 366 as explained by *Beis Yosef)* and *Rama*

1. According to *Rama* (*Orach Chaim* 387:1), once courtyards have incorporated themselves in a *shitufei mevo'os* there is no longer any necessity for them to make individual *eruvei chatzeiros,* i.e., the *shituf* serves in lieu of the separate *eruvin* as well. Furthermore, this is true even if the *shituf* is made with wine or other foodstuffs not valid for use in an *eruvei chatzeiros.* According to this, the mishnah can be taken literally. Because the partnership serves as a *shituf,* they need not even make an *eruvei chatzeiros (Tif. Yis.).*

2. Where foodstuffs have been designated and collected specifically for an *eruv,* there is no absolute requirement that all the portions be in one container; when one container has been filled with the *eruv* or *shituf* portions, a second one can be used for the additional contributions *(Gem.* 49a). In our case, however, where the foodstuffs have not been collected for the purpose of *shituf,* even if one barrel is full, the *shituf* is not valid unless all the partners own wine in it *(Rashi* 71a).

3. The above interpretation follows the view of R' Yosef in the *Gemara.* Rabbah's view, which has not been presented here, is extremely complex. Moreover, as *Ritva* comments, there are no halachic differences between the two views; they differ only in interpretation.

4. However, this is so only in the case of the mishnah, for the foodstuffs have not been collected and deposited with the intent that they serve as a *shituf.* If they are collected specifically for the purpose of *shituf* they are valid. *(Tosafos* cited by *Rashba;* cf. *Orach Chaim* 386:4 and *Ravad* in *Hil. Eruvin* 1:11.)

חָמֵשׁ חֲבוּרוֹת שֶׁשָּׁבְתוּ בְּטְרַקְלִין אֶחָד —
בֵּית שַׁמַּאי אוֹמְרִים: עֵרוּב לְכָל
חֲבוּרָה וַחֲבוּרָה. וּבֵית הַלֵּל אוֹמְרִים: עֵרוּב אֶחָד
לְכֻלָּן. וּמוֹדִים בִּזְמַן שֶׁמִּקְצָתָן שְׁרוּיִין בַּחֲדָרִים אוֹ
בַּעֲלִיּוֹת שֶׁהֵן צְרִיכִין עֵרוּב לְכָל חֲבוּרָה וַחֲבוּרָה.

[ז] הָאַחִין וְהַשֻּׁתָּפִין שֶׁהָיוּ אוֹכְלִין עַל שֻׁלְחַן
אֲבִיהֶם, וִישֵׁנִים בְּבָתֵּיהֶם, צְרִיכִין

יד אברהם

(386:3; see *Beur HaGra*) seem to rule like R' Shimon in accord with the general rule (*Gem.* 46a) that the halachah follows the more lenient view with regard to the laws of *eruv* (cf. *Bach* to *Tur Orach Chaim* 366).

6.

חָמֵשׁ חֲבוּרוֹת שֶׁשָּׁבְתוּ בְּטְרַקְלִין אֶחָד — *If five groups spent the Sabbath in one mansion —*

A large mansion that opened into a courtyard was occupied by five different groups. Each group lived in a different part of the mansion and each had its own door to the courtyard. Additionally, other houses opened into this courtyard, thereby necessitating an *eruv* to permit carrying there. The question now arises whether to consider all five groups as one large group (with regard to the *eruvei chatzeiros* necessary for this courtyard) since they are all staying in the same hall. If they are considered one group, only one contribution towards the *eruv* of this courtyard will be required (as in the case of a house occupied by one family). If they are considered five separate groups, each group will have to make its own contribution.

The *Gemara* (72a) concludes that in the case under discussion the groups had erected makeshift partitions measuring at least ten fists high between each group but that these partitions did not reach the ceiling. If the partitions reached the ceiling there is no question that each group would be considered separate, even if the partitions were

made of the flimsiest cloth (*Mishnah Berurah* 370:23). Similarly, if the partitions were of a sturdy construction, such as boards, everyone would agree that even if they did not reach the ceiling they must be considered separate groups. Obviously, then, if no partitions were made at all there is no question that the groups would be considered as one. In the case in question makeshift partitions of cloth were put up, but they did not reach the ceiling of the hall.

בֵּית שַׁמַּאי אוֹמְרִים: עֵרוּב לְכָל חֲבוּרָה וַחֲבוּרָה. — *Beis Shammai say: An* eruv *for each group* [i.e., each group must contribute to the *eruv*].

Beis Shammai maintain that even flimsy partitions set the groups apart and they are considered five different groups or families living in one house. Consequently, each must contribute individually to the *eruv* of the courtyard (*Rav*; *Rashi*).

According to one view in the *Gemara* (72a), Beis Shammai's ruling applies even to a partition less than ten fists high. Another view disputes this and maintains that Beis Shammai requires that the partition be at least ten fists high.

וּבֵית הַלֵּל אוֹמְרִים: עֵרוּב אֶחָד לְכֻלָּן. — *But Beis Hillel say: One* eruv [contribution

6. **I**f five groups spent the Sabbath in one mansion — Beis Shammai say: An *eruv* for each group. But Beis Hillel say: One *eruv* for all of them. They agree, however, that when some of them are quartered in rooms or upper stories, they need an *eruv* for each group.

7. **B**rothers or partners who eat at their father's table, but who sleep in their own homes, need

YAD AVRAHAM

suffices] *for all of them.*

Because of their flimsiness [they are made of cloth *(Tos.)*] and the fact that they do not totally separate the different groups [they do not reach to the ceiling] *(Gem.* 72a), the partitions are not significant enough to separate the groups. Consequently, the groups are considered one (just as one big family would be), and one contribution towards the *eruv* joining the hall with all the other houses in the courtyard suffices for all the groups *(Rav; Rashi).*

וּמוֹדִים בְּזְמַן שֶׁמְּקְצָתָן שְׁרוּיִין בַּחֲדָרִים אוֹ בַּעֲלִיּוֹת שֶׁהֵן צְרִיכִין עֵרוּב לְכָל חֲבוּרָה וַחֲבוּרָה. — *They* [i.e., Beis Hillel and Beis Shammai] *agree, however, that when some of them are quartered in rooms or upper stories, they need an eruv*

[contribution] *for each group* [respectively].

In this case, each room, by virtue of its sturdy walls which also reach the ceiling, separates its occupants from the others and necessitates their contributing separately to the *eruv.* As explained above, the *Gemara* (72b) proves that even where they are not in bona fide rooms, but in areas separated by ceiling-high partitions, they are considered separate groups.

The phrase *each group* refers only to those groups quartered in the rooms. The groups quartered in the hall are considered to be one unit *(Rashba; Ritva; Meiri).* [Thus, if three groups were quartered in rooms and two in the hall in the manner described in the mishnah, the room dwellers would contribute three portions to the *eruv* and the hall dwellers only one.]

7.

הָאַחִין וְהַשְׁתָּפִין שֶׁהָיוּ אוֹכְלִין עַל שֻׁלְחָן אֲבִיהֶם, — *Brothers or partners who eat at their father's table,*

The mishnah means brothers who eat at their father's table, or partners [i.e., workers who labor together] who eat together at one table [i.e., at the table of their employer]. The *Gemara* (72b) explains that this does not refer to actually eating together at one table; the idiom 'eating at their father's table' is merely used to indicate that all their food comes from a common source — either from their father on whom they are dependent, or their employer in the

case of fellow workers [see below] *(Rav; Rambam).*

The text presented here is that of *Rambam* (see ed. Kafich) and is compatible with his interpretation of the mishnah. The version found in most editions of the Mishnah reads הַשְׁתָּפִין (minus the prefix וְ; *Shinuyei Nuschaos*). Nevertheless, the meaning of the mishnah is the same (see *Rav*). *Rashi* (and the present edition of the Talmud) deletes the word וְהַשְׁתָּפִין, *and partners,* entirely, because of the obvious difficulty presented by the concluding phrase *who eat at their father's table.*

וִישֵׁנִים בְּבָתֵּיהֶם, — *but who sleep in their own homes,*

עֵירוּבִין עֵרוּב לְכָל אֶחָד וְאֶחָד. לְפִיכָךְ, אִם שָׁכַח אֶחָד
מֵהֶם וְלֹא עֵרַב, מְבַטֵּל אֶת רְשׁוּתוֹ. אֵימָתַי? בִּזְמַן
שֶׁמּוֹלִיכִין עֵרוּבָן בְּמָקוֹם אַחֵר; אֲבָל אִם הָיָה עֵרוּב
בָּא אֶצְלָן, אוֹ שֶׁאֵין עִמָּהֶן דִּיּוּרִין בֶּחָצֵר, אֵינָן
צְרִיכִין לְעָרֵב.

[ח] **חָמֵשׁ** חֲצֵרוֹת פְּתוּחוֹת זוֹ לְזוֹ וּפְתוּחוֹת
לְמָבוֹי — עֵרְבוּ בַּחֲצֵרוֹת וְלֹא

יד אברהם

Each has his own house which opens into the same courtyard as their father's. Additionally, there are other houses opening into this courtyard thus necessitating an *eruvei chatzeiros* (Rav; Rashi). [According to the interpretation cited earlier that the brothers do not actually eat at their father's table, the term 'sleep' is used here to indicate that they live in their own homes and includes both eating and sleeping. In fact, the activity which determines whether a person is a resident of a place in regard to *eruv* purposes is, according to this view, eating and not sleeping. The question now arises whether to consider the brothers as part of their father's family (because they all eat his food) or whether to consider them separate family units (since each eats in his own house). If they are all regarded as part of their father's family, one contribution to the *eruv* suffices for all of them; if they are regarded as separate family units, each one must make a separate contribution.]

צְרִיכִין עֵרוּב לְכָל אֶחָד וְאֶחָד. — *need an eruv* [i.e., a separate contribution to the *eruv*] *for each one.*

The fact that they live in their own houses sets them apart as separate units.

The *Gemara* (72b), however, explains that this is so only if they do not actually eat with their father. The term 'eat at their father's table' is not literal and is only an idiom referring to their dependency upon him, i.e., he *supports* them with food but they eat it in their own houses.[1] If they actually eat at their father's table they need not contribute to the *eruv* since they are then included in their father's contribution.[2]

The above follows the halachically accepted interpretation of the mishnah of the *Amora* Rav who holds that one's power to restrict the use of a courtyard is determined by where he eats (see *Orach Chaim* 370:5). Thus one who has two residences, one for eating and one for sleeping, only restricts in the courtyard in which he eats. One who eats at another's table, however, is considered a guest and cannot restrict. It follows that sons 'eating at their father's table' do not retrict and the phrase must be understood idiomatically as referring to their dependence upon him.

The *Amora* Shmuel, on the other hand, maintains that the determining factor is not where one eats but where one sleeps. Thus, the phrases 'eat at their father's table' and 'sleep in their own homes' are taken literally.

לְפִיכָךְ, אִם שָׁכַח אֶחָד מֵהֶם וְלֹא עֵרַב, מְבַטֵּל אֶת רְשׁוּתוֹ. — *Therefore, if one of them*

---

1. No distinction is made whether this support takes the form of food or of money (see *Rashi* and *Mishnah Berurah* 370:44).

2. *Rambam* (*Comm.* and *Hil. Eruvin* 4:6) interprets this differently. The sons are independent of their father's support and are not constant guests at his table, but eat at his table occasionally in payment for services rendered to him. This does not automatically include them in the father's household. *Shulchan Aruch* (*Orach Chaim* 370:5) omits mention of this view.

6
8

an *eruv* for each one. Therefore, if one of them forgot to contribute to the *eruv*, he must nullify his rights. When is this so? When they bring their *eruv* to another place; but if the *eruv* was brought to them, or there are no other residents in the courtyard, they need not contribute to the *eruv*.

8. Five courtyards which open one into the other and into an alley — if they made an *eruv* in the

forgot to contribute to the eruv, *he must nullify his rights.*

[Since the brothers are viewed as separate families, each of which must contribute separately to the *eruv*, if one forgot to do so he restricts the other inhabitants of the courtyard.] In order to allow the others to carry into the courtyard, the forgetful brother must nullify his rights in the courtyard *(Rav).*

אֵימָתַי? — *When is this so?*

[In which instance are brothers who are supported by their father considered as separate families because they eat and sleep in their own houses?]

בִּזְמַן שֶׁמּוֹלִיכִין עֵרוּבָן בְּמָקוֹם אַחֵר; — *When they bring their* eruv *to another place;*

Only when the *eruv* is deposited with a party other than the brothers are they required to make separate contributions. Here the question is not *whether* this family must contribute towards the *eruv* but *how many* contributions they must make. With regard to this issue, the brothers are considered separate families *(Rav; Rashi).*

אֲבָל אִם הָיָה עֵרוּב בָּא אֶצְלָן, — *but if the* eruv *was brought to them,*

If the *eruv* is deposited with one of the brothers or the father, the question of the brothers' status is *whether* they need contribute at all, since if they are regarded as one household all of them

will fall under the exemption granted the household holding the *eruv (Rav; Rashi).* [The rule is that the household with which the *eruv* is deposited need not contribute to the *eruv*. The *eruv* is to symbolize that all its contributors are eating in the house where it is deposited. It follows, then, that the family which is actually eating there need not contribute.]

אוֹ שֶׁאֵין עִמָּהֶן דִּיּוּרִין בֶּחָצֵר, — *or there are no other residents in the courtyard,*

If the brothers and father are the sole occupants of the courtyard the question is again *whether* there is need for any *eruv* at all. If they are regarded as one household there is no need for any *eruv* since a single family then owns the whole courtyard *(Rav; Rashi).*

אֵינָן צְרִיכִין לְעָרֵב. — *they need not contribute to the* eruv.

Neither the father nor any of the brothers need contribute to the *eruv* *(Rav).*

[Because the brothers do receive their support from one source, namely, their father, they do, to some extent, qualify as part of their father's household. This partial relationship is reason enough to free them from the requirement of an *eruv*. Where, however, an *eruv* is necessary, it is insufficient to have them all included in one contribution, as explained above.]

8.

חָמֵשׁ חֲצֵרוֹת פְּתוּחוֹת זוֹ לְזוֹ וּפְתוּחוֹת לְמָבוֹי— — *Five courtyards which open one into the other and into an alley —*

There is a question whether the phrase 'which open one into the other' should be deleted from the mishnah.

יד אברהם

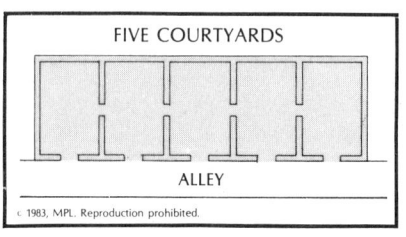

FIVE COURTYARDS

ALLEY

c 1983, MPL. Reproduction prohibited.

The *Amora* Rav concludes that it should be deleted. The mishnah as emended reads, חָמֵשׁ חֲצֵרוֹת הַפְּתוּחוֹת לַמָּבוֹי, *Five courtyards which open into an alley* (*Gem.* 73a).

The question of whether the mishnah must be emended is based on the following: As set forth above (1:2) an alley closed off on three sides requires only a pole or crossbeam on the fourth, open side to complete its partition requirements. [After this, it is eligible for *shitufei mevo'os* which will permit carrying in it.] This is *not* sufficient for a courtyard, which needs either two poles, one on each side of its open end, or a board measuring at least four fists on one side of its opening, to properly close the fourth side. A crossbeam or a single pole is not effective at all in a courtyard.

There are several characteristics which legally distinguish a courtyard from an alley. One of these is that to qualify as an alley the street must have courtyards (rather than just houses) opening into it. There is a dispute as to whether one courtyard opening into the alley is sufficient or two are required. The view accepted as halachah is that two are necessary. Thus, in order to qualify as an alley, and thus qualify for the more lenient partition requirement, the street must have at least two courtyards opening into it.

It is *Rav's* opinion that if the courtyards open into each other, they can make one *eruv* together and legally be considered one courtyard. Consequently, they are considered as one courtyard even if they do not actually

make one *eruv*. Accordingly, the street into which they open is legally considered to have only one courtyard and is thus deprived of its alley status. As a result, the street will require the more stringent adjustments of a courtyard[1] before a *shitufei mevo'os*[2] can be made (*Rav; Rambam*).

Many authorities accept Rav's conclusion as halachah. However, others assume that the *Gemara* means that *only* Rav emends the mishnah but that the majority opinion disputes it. According to the majority opinion, two courtyards opening into each other are to be considered as two separate courtyards in regard to *shituf*, even after having been merged through an *eruv*. Thus they rule that in the case of our mishnah, even if the five courtyards open into each other, they are considered separate courtyards and the street into which they open qualifies as an alley and the attendant leniency with regard to partition requirements (*Rosh* and *Ravad*). *Orach Chaim* (363:26) cites both views and *Mishnah Berurah* (363:103) rules that the latter, more lenient view, may be followed. According to this view there is no need to emend the mishnah.

עֵרְבוּ בַּחֲצֵרוֹת — *if they made an eruv in the courtyards*

The residents of each courtyard made an *eruv* to permit carrying from their houses into their courtyard, but no *eruv* was made to merge all the courtyards to permit carrying from one courtyard to another (*Rav; Rashi* to *Gem.* 73b; *Ritva*).

Many authorities (*Tosafos*, et al.) disagree with this explanation and understand the term 'made an *eruv*' to refer to both the *eruv* within each individual courtyard, and the *eruv* between the courtyards which merges them and permits carrying between the

1. Theoretically, the mishnah could be discussing a case where the adjustment to the open side of the street did meet the requirements of a courtyard. Nevertheless, the *Gemara* chooses to delete the words 'open into each other' because it is reasonable to suppose that when the term alley is used in the mishnah it refers to an alley fulfilling only the minimum partition requirements needed for an alley (*Tos.* 74a).

2. Although an alley not having courtyards opening into it is classified as a courtyard with regard to partition requirements, it is nevertheless regarded as an alley concerning the laws of *eruv*, and *shitufei mevo'os* is the method used to permit carrying in this alley.

courtyards but did not make a *shituf* in the alley, they
are permitted in the courtyards but prohibited in the

courtyards.

This is true even according to the opinion of the *Amora* Rav who, as explained above, holds that in the mishnah's case there are no doors between the courtyards. Although there is a clear rule that an *eruv* between two areas may be made only if they are accessible to each other, e.g., where there is a doorway between them (see 7:1), *Tosafos* (74a) suggests several ways of avoiding this problem. One is that the courtyards, although not accessible to each other by means of a doorway, are nevertheless connected to each other by means of windows which start within ten fists of the ground. These windows provide sufficient access from one courtyard to the other to permit making an *eruv* between them, as stated in 7:1. But since there is not complete access between them (because they lack doorways), they are still considered separate courtyards of the alley even after having been merged by an *eruv*. Rav, Rashi and Ritva (the first explanation) do not find this distinction acceptable. In their view, any form of access sufficient to merge the courtyards with an *eruv* is likewise sufficient to consider the courtyards as one, thus depriving the alley of the two courtyards required. Accordingly, the mishnah can only be speaking of courtyards which cannot be merged with an *eruv*, i.e. where there are neither doorways nor windows in the walls between the courtyards.

וְלֹא נִשְׁתַּתְּפוּ בַמָּבוֹי, — *but did not make a* shituf *in the alley,*

[The separate courtyards did not make a *shituf* to permit carrying into the alley.]

מֻתָּרִין בַּחֲצֵרוֹת — *they are permitted* [to carry] *in the courtyards*

They may carry from their houses into the courtyard fronting them (Rav). According to *Tosafos'* opinion (see above, s.v. עֵרְבוּ בַחֲצֵרוֹת) they may also carry from one courtyard to the other via the windows.

וַאֲסוּרִין בַּמָּבוֹי: — *but (they are) prohibited* [from carrying] *in the alley;*

[They are prohibited from carrying from the courtyards into the alleys or vice versa.]

According to those (Rav; Rashi; Ritva) who understand the mishnah to refer to courtyards which cannot make an *eruv* with each other, the reason they are prohibited from carrying into the alley is obvious — because no *shituf* has been made. However, according to those (Tos.) who explain that the courtyards did join together in one *eruv*, they should be allowed to carry into the alley because there is now legally one (merged) courtyard having access to this alley. As a result, it is entirely the domain of this one courtyard and should not require a *shituf* at all.

The *Gemara* (73b) [which, according to the simple reading] follows the latter explanation] explains that this mishnah is in accord with R' Meir's view that even where all of the courtyards of an alley have been merged with each other through an *eruv*, a *shituf* is still needed to permit carrying from the courtyards into the alley. *Eruvei chatzeiros* cannot, in R' Meir's view, serve in lieu of a *shituf*.[1] Consequently, where they made an *eruv* between themselves but no *shituf*, they are permitted to carry from one courtyard to another only via the doorways or windows between them but not via the alley.

This explanation is superfluous in light of Rav's commentary above (s.v. עֵרְבוּ בַחֲצֵרוֹת) that holds that no *eruvei chatzeiros* was ever made uniting all five courtyards, but the *eruv* mentioned in the mishnah refers to the separate *eruv* made by each courtyard to permit carrying within that courtyard itself. We are now left with five courtyards, unincorporated with each other, which open onto the alley. Since no *shituf* was made, it is

1. R' Meir's view is based on the concern that children growing up in these houses should know both the laws of *eruv* and *shituf*. For this reason, he does not consider either one to be valid in place of the other (Gem. 73b).

עירוּבִין וְאִם נִשְׁתַּתְּפוּ בַּמָּבוֹי, מֻתָּרִין כָּאן וְכָאן.
ו/ח עֵרְבוּ בַּחֲצֵרוֹת וְנִשְׁתַּתְּפוּ בַּמָּבוֹי, וְשָׁכַח אֶחָד
מִבְּנֵי חָצֵר וְלֹא עֵרֵב, מֻתָּרִין כָּאן וְכָאן; מִבְּנֵי מָבוֹי
וְלֹא נִשְׁתַּתָּף, מֻתָּרִין בַּחֲצֵרוֹת, וַאֲסוּרִין בַּמָּבוֹי;

יד אברהם

obvious that carrying from the courtyards into the alley is prohibited.

Ritva explains that the *Gemara's* interpretation is based on the unemended version of the mishnah and assumes that the courtyards *do* open into each other and thus an *eruv* between the courtyards is to be assumed. Once the *Gemara* emends the mishnah, however, this assumption is rendered untenable, since in the emended version the courtyards do not open into each other and thus no joint *eruv* is possible. (As explained above, *Ritva* rejects *Tosafos'* distinction between a doorway and a window. Accordingly, the mishnah must be speaking of a case in which no *eruv* at all is possible.) Thus, the ruling of the mishnah must be explained as above. *Beis Yosef* (to *Tur Orach Chaim* 387) assumes that *Rambam* also adheres to this view.

However, many authorities follow *Tosafos'* view, explaining that an *eruvei chatzeiros* between the courtyards was made via windows. Therefore, even after emending the mishnah, in the case under discussion a joint *eruv* had been made for all five courtyards and the *Gemara's* explanation of this segment of the mishnah remains intact. This view of *Tosafos* is endorsed by *Rashba* and *Meiri*, and seems to be the view of *Rif*, *R' Yehonasan* and *Rosh* as well.

וְאִם נִשְׁתַּתְּפוּ בַּמָּבוֹי, — *if they did make a* shituf *in the alley,*

If, in addition to the *eruv* already mentioned, a *shituf* was also made to permit carrying into the alley (*Rav* from *Gem.* 73b).

If only a *shituf* was made (as a superficial reading of the mishnah would suggest), carrying from the houses to the courtyards would also be prohibited according to the view of R' Meir that a *shituf* cannot serve in

lieu of an *eruvei chatzeiros*.[1] Since the *Gemara* maintains that our mishnah follows this view, and since the mishnah now states that carrying in the courtyards is also permissible, the mishnah must mean that a *shituf* was made in addition to the *eruv*.

מֻתָּרִין כָּאן וְכָאן. — *they are permitted* [both] *here and there.*

[They may carry both from their houses into the courtyards and from the courtyards into the alley.]

עֵרְבוּ בַּחֲצֵרוֹת וְנִשְׁתַּתְּפוּ בַּמָּבוֹי, — *If they made* [both] *an eruv for the courtyards and a shituf for the alley,*

[As in the previous case.]

וְשָׁכַח אֶחָד מִבְּנֵי חָצֵר וְלֹא עֵרֵב, — *but one of the residents of the courtyard forgot to contribute to the* eruv,

A resident of one of these five courtyards forgot to contribute to the *eruv* of his courtyard. He did, however, contribute to the *shituf* of the alley (*Rav*).

מֻתָּרִין כָּאן וְכָאן; — *they are permitted* [to carry both] *here and there;*

Carrying is permitted both from the houses to the courtyards and from the courtyards to the alley. The failure of one of the courtyard's residents to participate in the *eruv* does not cause him to restrict carrying from the houses to the courtyard. The reason for this is that intrinsically the *shituf*, which unites all of the inhabitants of the alley, accomplishes the objective of the *eruv* as well -- to merge all the residents into one household. Their being considered

1. Although, as explained above, *Rav* assumes that the *Gemara's* rendering of the mishnah according to the opinion of R' Meir is unnecessary once the mishnah has been emended, he nevertheless chooses to explain the mishnah according to R' Meir because the halachah seems to follow his opinion (see *Rambam, Hil. Eruvin* 1:19). Additionally, the following segment of the mishnah, which deals with the failure of one of the courtyard residents to participate in the *eruv*, appears to follow R' Meir's view.

alley; if they did make a *shituf* in the alley, they are permitted here and there.

If they made an *eruv* for the courtyards and a *shituf* for the alley, but one of the residents of the courtyard forgot to contribute to the *eruv*, they are permitted here and there; if one of the residents of the alley did not participate in the *shituf*, they are permitted in the courtyards, but are prohibited in the

YAD AVRAHAM

one household relative to the alley is equally effective for the courtyard. Consequently, where a *shituf* is made to incorporate the alley there should be no necessity for the individual courtyards to make an *eruv* even according to R' Meir (see footnote above, s.v. וַאֲסוּרִין בַּמָּבוֹי). Since the majority of the courtyard residents did participate in the *eruv*, the *shituf* may serve in lieu of an *eruv* for the one forgetful resident will not lead to the abandonment of *eruvei chatzeiros* (*Rav* from *Gem.* 73b).

מִבְּנֵי מָבוֹי וְלֹא נִשְׁתַּתַּף, — [but] *if one of the residents of the alley* [forgot] *(and) did not participate in the* shituf,

I.e., one of the residents of the courtyards who should have contributed to the *shituf* of the alley forgot to contribute *(Tif. Yis.)*. [He is called here one of the residents of the *alley* only in the context of his neglect to participate in the *shituf*.]

R' Yehonasan and *Meiri* maintain that מִבְּנֵי מָבוֹי refers to an entire courtyard which forgot to participate in the *shituf*. Thus this phrase is rendered *one of the members of the alley*, i.e., an entire courtyard (see below, s.v. וַאֲסוּרִין בַּמָּבוֹי). The Hebrew term בְּנֵי is amenable to either translation.

מְתָּרִין בַּחֲצֵרוֹת, — *they are permitted* [to carry] *in the courtyards,*

[Because all of them participated in the *eruv*, as stated.]

וַאֲסוּרִין בַּמָּבוֹי; — *but are prohibited* [from carrying] *in the alley;*

[I.e., from the courtyards to the alley.] The single householder who neglected to participate in the *shituf* restricts the rest who did. Here the *eruv* cannot serve in lieu of a *shituf*, because as explained earlier (s.v. עֵרְבוּ and וַאֲסוּרִין בַּמָּבוֹי), the *eruvei chatzeiros* made by the courtyards united only the residents of each individual courtyard, but did not incorporate the courtyards with each other as needed for *shituf* (*Tos. Yom Tov* in explanation of *Rav*).

According to the view that our mishnah discusses a case in which an *eruv* uniting the courtyards was made, the above explanation is untenable and the difference between forgetting to join the *eruv* and forgetting to join the *shituf* must be explained on a different basis. *R' Yehonasan* and *Meiri* (see also *Ritva*) explain that in the case of *eruv*, since only an individual is involved in the failure to join the *eruv*, there is no apprehension that this will lead to a weakening of the institution of *eruv*. By contrast, in the case of the failure to join the *shituf*, since an entire courtyard forgot to participate (see above, s.v. מִבְּנֵי מָבוֹי), there is greater concern that this will lead to a weakening of the observance of *eruv*. For this reason, R' Meir does not allow for the *eruv* to serve in lieu of the *shituf* even in such a case.

It follows from this that those who disagree with *Rav* and *Rashi's* view and assume that in the case of the mishnah an *eruv* was made to merge all the courtyards (see s.v. עֵרְבוּ בַּחֲצֵרוֹת at the beginning of the mishnah) and cannot as a result accept the explanation of *Tosefos Yom Tov*, must assume the interpretation suggested by *Meiri*. This observation is made by *Tosefos R' Akiva* in regard to another matter. Indeed only one commentator states explicitly that

עֵירוּבִין שֶׁהַמָּבוֹי לַחֲצֵרוֹת כֶּחָצֵר לַבָּתִּים.

[ט] שְׁתֵּי חֲצֵרוֹת זוֹ לִפְנִים מִזוֹ — עֵרְבָה
הַפְּנִימִית וְלֹא עֵרְבָה הַחִיצוֹנָה,
הַפְּנִימִית מֻתֶּרֶת וְהַחִיצוֹנָה אֲסוּרָה; הַחִיצוֹנָה וְלֹא
הַפְּנִימִית, שְׁתֵּיהֶן אֲסוּרוֹת; עֵרְבָה זוֹ לְעַצְמָהּ וְזוֹ
לְעַצְמָהּ, זוֹ מֻתֶּרֶת בִּפְנֵי עַצְמָהּ, וְזוֹ מֻתֶּרֶת בִּפְנֵי
עַצְמָהּ. רַבִּי עֲקִיבָא אוֹסֵר הַחִיצוֹנָה, שֶׁדְּרִיסַת

יד אברהם

the mishnah speaks of a case in which a common *eruv* uniting the courtyards was made — *Meiri* — and he is one of the authors of the second explanation here.

שֶׁהַמָּבוֹי לַחֲצֵרוֹת כֶּחָצֵר לַבָּתִּים. — *for an alley is to the courtyards as a courtyard is to the houses.*

The relationship between the alley and the courtyards parallels that of the courtyard to the houses. Just as a device, *eruvei chatzeiros*, is necessary to permit carrying from the houses to the courtyard, so is a similar device, *shitufei mevo'os*, needed to permit carrying from the courtyard to the alley. It would be erroneous to differentiate between the two relationships and to argue that

carrying from the house, a private residence, into the courtyard, a public area by comparison, resembles carrying from the private domain to the public domain and is therefore prohibited, whereas carrying from the courtyard to the alley should be permitted without any device since they both resemble public areas. It is to dispel this notion that the statement of the mishnah is made (*Rav; Rashi*). Because a courtyard is set aside primarily for the use of its residents, whereas the alley is for the use of all of the courtyards, [hence ownership of the two areas varies] carrying between the two is prohibited (*Meiri*).

9.

שְׁתֵּי חֲצֵרוֹת זוֹ לִפְנִים מִזוֹ — *Two court-yards* [which were arranged] *one behind the other* —

The inner courtyard has no independent outlet to an alley or a street. It opens only into the outer courtyard, which in turn opens to a street, and the residents of the inner courtyard have דְּרִיסַת הָרֶגֶל, *rights of passage*, through the outer courtyard (*Rav; Rashi*).

עֵרְבָה הַפְּנִימִית וְלֹא עֵרְבָה הַחִיצוֹנָה, — *if the inner* [courtyard] *made an* eruv *but the outer* [one] *did not,*

All the residents of the inner courtyard joined in an *eruv* which did not include the residents of the outer courtyard (*Rav; Rashi*).

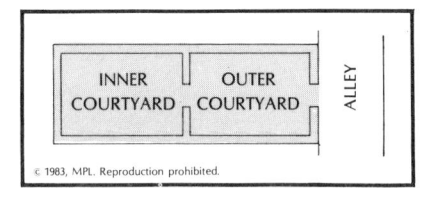

הַפְּנִימִית מֻתֶּרֶת וְהַחִיצוֹנָה אֲסוּרָה; — *the inner* [one] *is permitted* [to carry] *while the outer* [one] *is prohibited;*

[The outer courtyard is prohibited because its residents did not make an *eruv*. Their lack of an *eruv*, however, does not restrict the use of the inner courtyard because they have no rights in the inner courtyard.]

alley; for an alley is to the courtyards as a courtyard
is to the houses.

9. Two courtyards one behind the other — if the inner made an *eruv* but the outer did not, the inner is permitted while the outer is prohibited; the outer, but not the inner, both are prohibited; each courtyard made its own *eruv*, [then] each is individually permitted. R' Akiva prohibits the outer

YAD AVRAHAM

הַחִיצוֹנָה וְלֹא הַפְּנִימִית, שְׁתֵּיהֶן אֲסוּרוֹת; — [if] the outer [one made an *eruv*], but not the inner [one], both [courtyards] are prohibited;

The residents of both courtyards are prohibited to carry from their houses to the courtyard.' The residents of the inner courtyard may not carry because they did not make an *eruv*, and those of the outer courtyard may not carry because their *eruv* did not include the residents of the inner courtyard. Since the residents of the inner courtyard have the right of passage through the outer courtyard, they too are classified as residents of that courtyard and must be included in their *eruv*. If they are not, they restrict the bona fide residents just as if one of their own had not participated in the *eruv* (Rav; Rashi). [The right of passage through a courtyard makes one an owner' in that courtyard. He thus has the same status as those who actually own houses there.]

עֵרְבָה זוֹ לְעַצְמָהּ וְזוֹ לְעַצְמָהּ, — [if] each courtyard made its own eruv [lit. if this one made its own eruv and that one made its own eruv],

[The inner and outer courtyards each made an *eruv* for its own residents but the two courtyards did not join together in one *eruv*.]

זוֹ מֻתֶּרֶת בִּפְנֵי עַצְמָהּ, וְזוֹ מֻתֶּרֶת בִּפְנֵי עַצְמָהּ. — [then] each [courtyard] is individually permitted [lit. this one is permitted by

itself and that one is permitted by itself]

Each courtyard's *eruv* is valid for itself and it is permissible to carry from the houses in each courtyard to that courtyard but not from one courtyard to the other. Although residents of the inner courtyard have the right of passage through the outer one, and have not joined with them in a common *eruv*, they do not, in this case, restrict the outer courtyard. In the opinion of this *Tanna*, the right of passage through a courtyard is not entirely equal to the right to use a courtyard. The right of passage only restricts when those who possess that right are themselves restricted in their home courtyard. Or as phrased by the *Gemara* (75a): 'A foot which is permitted in its own place does not *restrict* out of its place.' When those having the right of passage may carry in their own courtyard, they do not restrict an area through which they merely have the right of passage. Thus, the right of passage does not restrict where its possessors participated in an *eruv* in their own courtyard, or where there is only one inhabitant in the inner courtyard who does not, therefore, need an *eruv* for his courtyard (Rav from Gem. 75a). [They may not, however, carry from one courtyard into the other because the two courtyards have not been merged with an *eruv*.]

רַבִּי עֲקִיבָא אוֹסֵר הַחִיצוֹנָה, שֶׁדְּרִיסַת הָרֶגֶל אוֹסַרְתָּהּ. — R' Akiva prohibits the outer

עֵירוּבִין הָרֶגֶל אוֹסַרְתָּה. וַחֲכָמִים אוֹמְרִים: אֵין דְּרִיסַת
הָרֶגֶל אוֹסַרְתָּה.

[י] שָׁכַח אֶחָד מִן הַחִיצוֹנָה וְלֹא עֵרֵב,
הַפְּנִימִית מֻתֶּרֶת וְהַחִיצוֹנָה אֲסוּרָה;
מִן הַפְּנִימִית וְלֹא עֵרֵב, שְׁתֵּיהֶן אֲסוּרוֹת.
נָתְנוּ עֵרוּבָן בְּמָקוֹם אֶחָד, וְשָׁכַח אֶחָד, בֵּין מִן
הַפְּנִימִית בֵּין מִן הַחִיצוֹנָה, וְלֹא עֵרֵב, שְׁתֵּיהֶן
אֲסוּרוֹת.
וְאִם הָיוּ שֶׁל יְחִידִים, אֵינָן צְרִיכִין לְעָרֵב.

יד אברהם

וַחֲכָמִים אוֹמְרִים: אֵין דְּרִיסַת הָרֶגֶל אוֹסַרְתָּה.
— *But the Sages say: The right of passage does not restrict it.*

The Sages maintain that the right of passage is not to be equated with the right of use in *any case* at all. In their opinion, the right of passage never restricts, even when the inner courtyard did not make any *eruv* (*Rav* from *Gem.*). [In this they dispute even the ruling of the *Tanna kamma.*]

The halachah is in accord with the *Tanna kamma* (*Rav; Rambam*).

[courtyard] *because the right of passage restricts it.*

R' Akiva does not accept the above distinction. In his opinion, just as the right of passage restricts the outer courtyard when no *eruv* was made in the inner courtyard (the first case of the mishnah), so, too, it restricts even when the inner courtyard did make an *eruv*. Only when the two courtyards are joined in one *eruv* can the outer courtyard be permitted (*Rav* from *Gem.* ibid.).

10.

שָׁכַח אֶחָד מִן הַחִיצוֹנָה וְלֹא עֵרֵב, הַפְּנִימִית מֻתֶּרֶת וְהַחִיצוֹנָה אֲסוּרָה; — *If one* [resident] *of the outer* [courtyard] *forgot to contribute to the* eruv, *the inner* [courtyard] *is permitted while the outer* [one] *is prohibited.*

[This is a repetition of the previous mishnah. As was explained there, the negligent resident of the outer courtyard restricts his colleagues but cannot restrict the members of the inner courtyard who are separated from them by a partition.]

מִן הַפְּנִימִית וְלֹא עֵרֵב, שְׁתֵּיהֶן אֲסוּרוֹת. — *If one from the inner* [courtyard forgot], *both* [courtyards] *are prohibited.*

[The inner courtyard is prohibited because of the failure of one of its members to participate in the *eruv*, thus

placing its residents in the category of a foot which is restricted in its place' (see previous mishnah). Consequently, their right of passage causes them to restrict the outer courtyard as well, in accord with the opinion of the *Tanna kamma* of the previous mishnah.]

It is difficult to see what the point of this segment of the mishnah is. The ruling in both cases parallels what is already known from the previous mishnah. R' Yehonasan suggests that the mishnah intends to give a definitive ruling on the three way controversy of the previous mishnah, making clear that the halachah follows the *Tanna kamma's* view.

נָתְנוּ עֵרוּבָן בְּמָקוֹם אֶחָד, — *If they placed their* eruv *in one place,*

The two courtyards made one communal *eruv* to permit carrying from

because the right of passage restricts it. But the Sages say: The right of passage does not restrict it.

10. If one [resident] of the outer forgot to contribute to the *eruv*, the inner is permitted while the outer is prohibited. If one from the inner [forgot], both are prohibited.

If they placed their *eruv* in one place, and one [resident] of either the inner or the outer forgot to contribute to the *eruv*, both are prohibited.

But if they were inhabited by individuals, they need not make an *eruv*.

YAD AVRAHAM

courtyard to courtyard and placed it in one of the houses belonging to the outer courtyard *(Rav)*.

The Gemara 75a explains that the outer courtyard is alluded to with the phrase *one place* because it is the area to which both courtyards have rights. [The word אֶחָד may mean either *one* or *together*.]

וְשָׁכַח אֶחָד, בֵּין מִן הַפְּנִימִית בֵּין מִן הַחִיצוֹנָה, וְלֹא עֵרַב, שְׁתֵּיהֶן אֲסוּרוֹת. — *and one [resident] of either the inner or the outer [courtyard] forgot to contribute to the* eruv, *both [courtyards] are prohibited.*

The communal *eruv* between the two courtyards unites them so that the participants in the *eruv* are now considered one big household whose residence is in the house where the *eruv* has been deposited. Therefore even if the negligent resident was a member of the outer courtyard, he restricts carrying even in the inner courtyard because their dispensation per *eruv* depends on their being considered as residing (with the negligent member) in the outer courtyard. Even if they were to disassociate themselves from the outer courtyard they would still be prohibited from carrying in the inner courtyard because they would then be left without any *eruv* at all. [This is based on the rule that the *eruv* food must be in one of the houses of the courtyard being merged in order to permit carrying within that courtyard.] Had the *eruv* been deposited

in the inner courtyard the ruling would be different. In that case the ability of the *eruv* to permit carrying in the inner courtyard does not depend on the residents of the inner courtyard being considered as residing in the outer courtyard. On the contrary, the residents of the outer courtyard are now considered as residing in the inner courtyard. Consequently, the members of the inner courtyard can now disassociate themselves from the outer courtyard and thereby permit carrying within the inner courtyard. The fact that the *eruv* allows us to consider both courtyards as one does not *force* us to consider the outer courtyard (and thus its negligent member) as residing in the inner courtyard. Thus, they may disassociate themselves from the outer group, or as put in the *Gemara* (75a): 'Close the door and use [the courtyard]' *(Rav)*. They may argue that their association was meant only to improve their situation [to allow them to carry from courtyard to courtyard], not to detract from it [to restrict them even in their own courtyard] *(Gem.* 75b). [The outer courtyard, however, is restricted by the non-participation of one of its members as it would in any other situation of non-participation.]

וְאִם הָיוּ שֶׁל יְחִידִים, — *But if they* [i.e., the courtyards] *were inhabited by individuals,*

עירוביןּ [א] **חַלּוֹן** שֶׁבֵּין שְׁתֵּי חֲצֵרוֹת — אַרְבָּעָה עַל
אַרְבָּעָה בְּתוֹךְ עֲשָׂרָה, מְעָרְבִין
שְׁנַיִם, וְאִם רָצוּ, מְעָרְבִין אֶחָד; פָּחוֹת מֵאַרְבָּעָה
עַל אַרְבָּעָה, אוֹ לְמַעְלָה מֵעֲשָׂרָה, מְעָרְבִין שְׁנַיִם,
וְאֵין מְעָרְבִין אֶחָד.

יד אברהם

Each courtyard was inhabited by only one individual so that no *eruv* was necessary to permit carrying within the inner courtyard (*Rav; Rashi*).

All the members of a family are counted as one person in this regard (*Rambam*).

אֵינָן צְרִיכִין לְעָרֵב. — **they need not make an eruv.**

The resident of the inner courtyard does not restrict the outer courtyard even if no joint *eruv* was made. Since he is the only resident of his courtyard, he is in the category of a foot which is permitted in its own place and, as a consequence, his right of passage cannot restrict the outer courtyard. Thus the mishnah, with this anonymous statement, concludes that the view of the first *Tanna* in the previous mishnah be accepted as halachah (*Rav; Rashi*).

Chapter 7

The previous chapter dealt with several cases of two or more courtyards joined together in one communal *eruv*. The first five mishnayos of this chapter now delineate when two or more courtyards cannot join in one *eruv* but may each make an *eruv* independent of the others; when they cannot each make independent *eruvin* but must join in one *eruv*; and when they are permitted their choice of an independent or a joint *eruv*. There are two main criteria to be considered: (a) the degree of separation between the courtyards; and (b) the degree of their access to each other.

(a) If two areas adjoin each other and are not adequately separated, they are considered one area and the residents of both areas *must* share one communal *eruv* before they may carry even into their respective areas. In such a case, it is not sufficient for the residents of each respective area to merely make an *eruv* among themselves.

(b) In the reverse situation, where both areas are totally separated from each other by means of a partition, the residents of one area *cannot* make an *eruv* with the residents of the other area for the purpose of passing objects over the partition to the adjoining area. The object of an *eruv* is to merge all of the participants into one unit or household. Where the participants are separated by a partition blocking off normal access to each other, they cannot reasonably be considered one unit. As a result, no *eruv* between them is possible.

As will be seen, there are instances where a partition is judged sufficient to separate two areas yet it does not preclude a mutual *eruv* being made between the two areas. Hence, it is possible for adjoining areas not to be *required* to have a mutual *eruv*, but nonetheless to be *allowed* a mutual *eruv*. This occurs where the partition, although valid, does not totally seal off access between the areas.

1. **A** window between two courtyards — [if it is] four by four [fists] within ten, they may make two *eruvin,* or, if they wish, they may make one *eruv;* less than four by four or higher than ten, they may make two *eruvin,* but may not make one *eruv.*

YAD AVRAHAM

1.

חַלּוֹן שֶׁבֵּין שְׁתֵּי חֲצֵרוֹת — — *A window between two courtyards —*

[The two courtyards are completely separated by a wall measuring at least ten fists high — the minimum height for any valid partition — but there is a window in the wall through which objects may be passed.]

אַרְבָּעָה עַל אַרְבָּעָה — [*if it is*] *four by four* [*fists*][1]

[The minimum size necessary for this window to qualify as an opening between the two courtyards is four fists by four fists.]

בְּתוֹךְ עֲשָׂרָה, — *within ten* [fists of the ground],

The window must begin at a point in the wall which is within ten fists of the ground. It is sufficient for even a minute portion of the opening of the window to be within these fists (*Rav* from *Gem.* 76a).

מְעָרְבִין שְׁנַיִם, — *they* [i.e., the two courtyards] *may make two* eruvin,

Each courtyard may make its own *eruv* and need not participate with the other courtyard. In this case, they may carry only from their houses into their courtyard, but not from one courtyard to the next (*Rav; Rashi*).

וְאִם רָצוּ, מְעָרְבִין אֶחָד; — *or, if they wish, they may make one* [joint] *eruv;*

They have the option of making one joint *eruv* with the residents of the neighboring courtyard. They then place the loaves collected from both courtyards in a house in either one of the courtyards (*Rav; Rashi*). [In this case, the residents of both courtyards will be permitted to pass objects to each other through the window or even over the partition.]

[The window does not invalidate the partition even though it breaches it within ten fists of the ground. A breach in a wall invalidates it as a partition only if it: (a) was breached in its entirety [if any minute part of the wall remained on each of the sides, or if a segment four cubits long remained on one side, the wall is not considered as breached in its entirety]; or (b) is wider than ten cubits (see *Orach Chaim* 362:8-9, 372:7). Therefore, in spite of the window, the two courtyards are still considered separate areas. At the same time, however, the window is considered a פֶּתַח, *entrance* (i.e., access point), so that the two courtyards may be united in one common *eruv.* It goes without saying that a door between the two courtyards would accomplish the same result.]

פָּחוֹת מֵאַרְבָּעָה עַל אַרְבָּעָה, — [*if it is*] *less than four by four*

If the window is not four fists by four fists it is not considered a legitimate opening (*Rav; Rashi*).

אוֹ לְמַעְלָה מֵעֲשָׂרָה, — *or higher than ten,*

If the window begins at a height of

---

1. [The use of the masculine form of the number — אַרְבָּעָה (and below עֲשָׂרָה) — denotes fists because טְפָחִים, fists, is a masculine word. If אַמּוֹת, cubits, were meant, the feminine form of the number — אַרְבַּע (and עֶשֶׂר) — would have been used. Thus, the gender used for the number makes clear which of the two common measures it refers to, and this obviates the need to specify.]

כּוֹתֶל שֶׁבֵּין שְׁתֵּי חֲצֵרוֹת, גָּבוֹהַּ עֲשָׂרָה וְרָחָב אַרְבָּעָה, מְעָרְבִין שְׁנַיִם, וְאֵין מְעָרְבִין אֶחָד.

הָיוּ בְרֹאשׁוֹ פֵרוֹת, אֵלּוּ עוֹלִין מִכָּאן וְאוֹכְלִין, וְאֵלּוּ עוֹלִין מִכָּאן וְאוֹכְלִין, וּבִלְבַד שֶׁלֹּא יוֹרִידוּ לְמַטָּה.

נִפְרְצָה הַכּוֹתֶל — עַד עֶשֶׂר אַמּוֹת, מְעָרְבִין שְׁנַיִם, וְאִם רָצוּ, מְעָרְבִין אֶחָד, מִפְּנֵי שֶׁהוּא כְּפֶתַח; יוֹתֵר מִכָּאן, מְעָרְבִין אֶחָד, וְאֵין מְעָרְבִין שְׁנַיִם.

יד אברהם

more than ten fists from the ground, so that there is a legal-sized partition of ten fists below it, the two courtyards are considered totally separated (Rav; Rashi).

מְעָרְבִין שְׁנַיִם, וְאֵין מְעָרְבִין אֶחָד — they may make two eruvin, but (they) may not make one eruv.

[If they wish to make an eruv, each courtyard must make its own separate eruv. Since without a legal opening between them the two courtyards are considered totally separated, a joint eruv is not feasible. Obviously then, even after each courtyard has made its own eruv, they cannot pass objects to each other through the invalid window or over the top of the wall.]

2.

כּוֹתֶל שֶׁבֵּין שְׁתֵּי חֲצֵרוֹת, גָּבוֹהַּ עֲשָׂרָה וְרָחָב אַרְבָּעָה, מְעָרְבִין שְׁנַיִם, וְאֵין מְעָרְבִין אֶחָד. — If a wall between two courtyards is ten [fists] high and four [fists] wide, they may make two eruvin, but may not make one eruv.

This ruling is not novel in itself; it can be derived from the previous mishnah. With regard to preventing the two courtyards from making one joint eruv the thickness of the wall is irrelevant; a valid partition of any thickness will necessitate two separate eruvin. This clause serves only to introduce the following one concerning the placing of objects on top of the wall (Rav; Rashi).

הָיוּ בְרֹאשׁוֹ פֵרוֹת, אֵלּוּ עוֹלִין מִכָּאן וְאוֹכְלִין, וְאֵלּוּ עוֹלִין מִכָּאן וְאוֹכְלִין, וּבִלְבַד שֶׁלֹּא יוֹרִידוּ לְמַטָּה. — If there was fruit on top of it [i.e., the wall], these ascend from here and eat, and those ascend from there and eat, provided they do not bring [any] down.

Because the top of the wall is four fists wide, it qualifies as a separate area belonging to both courtyards. [Four by four fists is the minimum size for a space to be considered a domain (רְשׁוּת).] Therefore, they may not carry from the top of the wall to the courtyard just as they may not carry from one courtyard to the other. If, however, the top of the wall is less than four fists wide, it does not qualify as a separate area and is classified as an exempt area (מָקוֹם פָּטוּר). In this case they may carry down from the top of the wall to the courtyards and

2. **I**f a wall between two courtyards is ten [fists] high and four wide, they may make two *eruvin*, but may not make one *eruv*.

If there was fruit on top of it, these ascend from here and eat, and those ascend from there and eat, provided they do not bring down.

If the wall was breached — up to ten cubits, they may make two *eruvin*, or, if they wish, one *eruv*, because it is like an entrance; greater than that, they may make one *eruv*, but may not make two *eruvin*.

YAD AVRAHAM

from there to their houses *(Rav, Rashi, based on R' Yochanan in Gem. 77a)*.

The *Gemara* (92a) explains that according to R' Shimon's (halachically accepted) view (see 9:1) that one may carry objects which were in the courtyard at the onset of the Sabbath from one courtyard to another without benefit of an *eruv*, and that *eruv* is necessary only to permit carrying objects from the houses to the courtyard (or vice versa), one may carry even from a wall top four fists wide to the courtyard. The prohibition of the mishnah refers (according to R' Shimon) only to carrying from the top of the wall to a house.

וְנִפְרְצָה הַכּוֹתֶל עַד עֶשֶׂר אַמּוֹת — *If the wall was breached — up to ten cubits,*
[A breach of up to ten cubits can be considered an entrance and does not therefore invalidate the partition that separates the two areas (see above 1:8).]

מְעָרְבִין שְׁנַיִם, וְאִם רָצוּ, מְעָרְבִין אֶחָד, — *they may make two* eruvin, *or, if they wish, one* [joint] *eruv,*
The two courtyards are now in the category of areas separated by the wall between them but which still have easy access to each other because of the entranceway in that wall. Therefore, they may elect to make two *eruvin* (one for each courtyard), in which case they will be prohibited from carrying from one courtyard to the other, or they may make one joint *eruv* and thus be

permitted to carry from one courtyard to the other.]

מִפְּנֵי שֶׁהוּא כְּפֶתַח; — *because it* [i.e., the breach] *is* [considered] *like an entrance;*
[Because the breach is considered only an entrance the separation is not invalidated. Since walls usually have doorways in them, a doorway does not diminish the wall's status as a partition. Even an open doorway is considered a partition (since it is an integral part of the wall) and the two areas may be considered completely separated from each other.]

יוֹתֵר מִכַּאן, מְעָרְבִין אֶחָד, וְאֵין מְעָרְבִין שְׁנַיִם. — [if the breach was] *greater than that, they make one* eruv, *but may not make two* eruvin.
[A breach wider than ten cubits is too wide to be considered an entrance (it being uncommon for a wall to have an entrance wider than ten cubits), so that the breached section of the wall cannot be considered a partition. Since a large section of the boundary between the two courtyards is completely open, the separation is invalid and the two courtyards are now legally considered one undivided area and, in effect, one courtyard. Consequently, all the residents of this enlarged courtyard must participate in one *eruv* in order for it to be effective.]

[ג] **חָרִיץ** שֶׁבֵּין שְׁתֵּי חֲצֵרוֹת, עָמֹק עֲשָׂרָה
וְרָחָב אַרְבָּעָה, מְעָרְבִין שְׁנַיִם, וְאֵין
מְעָרְבִין אֶחָד, אֲפִלּוּ מָלֵא קַשׁ אוֹ תֶבֶן. מָלֵא עָפָר
אוֹ צְרוֹרוֹת, מְעָרְבִין אֶחָד, וְאֵין מְעָרְבִין שְׁנַיִם.

[ד] **נָתַן** עָלָיו נֶסֶר שֶׁהוּא רָחָב אַרְבָּעָה טְפָחִים,
וְכֵן שְׁתֵּי גְזֻזְטְרָאוֹת זוֹ כְּנֶגֶד זוֹ, מְעָרְבִין

יד אברהם

3.

חָרִיץ שֶׁבֵּין שְׁתֵּי חֲצֵרוֹת, עָמֹק עֲשָׂרָה
וְרָחָב אַרְבָּעָה, — *If a trench between two
courtyards is ten* [fists] *deep and four*
[fists] *wide,*

Two adjoining courtyards are
separated by a trench ten fists deep and
four fists wide that runs the entire
length of their boundary (*Rav; Rashi*).[1]

If the trench does not extend along the
entire boundary, leaving a segment four fists
or more in width between the two courtyards
uncut by the trench, or if the trench itself
lacks the minimum dimensions listed here for
a span of four fists, that space is considered
an entrance between the two courtyards and
they may make either one *eruv* or two *eruvin*
(*Rama, Orach Chaim* 372:17; *Mishnah
Berurah* 372:118).

מְעָרְבִין שְׁנַיִם, וְאֵין מְעָרְבִין אֶחָד, — *they
may make two* eruvin, *but may not
make one* eruv.

[The trench separates the two areas
totally and precludes them from joining
in a common *eruv*.] If the trench's width
is less than four fists it is easy to step
over and for that reason it cannot be
considered a separation (*Rav; Rashi*). In
such a case, they may make one *eruv*,

but not two (*Ritva; Meiri; see Mishnah
Berurah* 372:128).

The depth of the trench must be at least
ten fists just as a partition must be at least ten
fists high (*Mishnah Berurah* 372:118). If it is
shallower than this minimum it is considered
as if it were level and they must make one
joint *eruv* (*ibid.; Ritva* here).

אֲפִלּוּ מָלֵא קַשׁ אוֹ תֶבֶן. — *even if it is filled
with stubble or straw.*[2]

The straw or stubble is not considered
a permanent feature of the trench
because it is assumed that the owner will
eventually remove it (to use as fodder).
Therefore, the separation effected by
the trench is still considered intact (*Rav;
Rashi*).

מָלֵא עָפָר אוֹ צְרוֹרוֹת, מְעָרְבִין אֶחָד, וְאֵין
מְעָרְבִין שְׁנַיִם. — *If it is filled with earth or
pebbles, they may make one* eruv, *but
may not make two* eruvin.

[Since the earth or pebbles will likely
remain in the ditch permanently, and
thus become a part of it, there is no
longer a partition between the two
courtyards and they must be considered
as one.]

---

1. Most prevalent editions of the mishnah read here אַרְבַּע [female gender] instead of אַרְבָּעָה
[male gender] as in the text. However, this seems to be an error since the former would refer to
אַמּוֹת, cubits [אַמָּה being feminine], with the result that the trench's width would have to be
four cubits. אַרְבָּעָה, however, being masculine, refers to טְפָחִים, fists. That the unit of measure
meant here is *fists* (and not *cubits*) is stated clearly by *Rashi, Tosefos Yom Tov* and *Mishnah
Berurah* 372:119 and is evident from the reason for the measurement given by *Rashi, R'
Yehonasan, Meiri* and *Ritva*. The reading אַרְבָּעָה is found in the mishnah versions of *Rambam*
(ed. Kafich) and *Meiri* and is indicated in *Rambam's* code (*Hil. Eruvin* 3:16).

2. The translation of קַשׁ and תֶבֶן is based on *Tosafos* in *Shabbos* 36b. According to *Rashi*
(there) קַשׁ is hay.

3. If a trench between two courtyards is ten deep and four wide, they may make two *eruvin*, but may not make one *eruv*, even if it is filled with stubble or straw. If it is filled with earth or pebbles, they may make one *eruv*, but may not make two *eruvin*.

4. If one placed a board which is four fists wide across it, similarly if two balconies are opposite each

YAD AVRAHAM

The mishnah must mean that the trench was filled in for more than ten cubits of its length. If it were filled in for less than that, the remaining unfilled part of the trench would serve as a separation with the filled in part being considered an entrance. They would then have the option of making either one *eruv* or two, as in the case of the breach in the wall in mishnah 2 *(Tos. R' Akiva)*.

The *Gemara* (78b) explains that unless the owner had specific intention to the contrary, the earth and the pebbles are assumed to have been placed in the trench permanently, while the stubble and the straw are assumed to have been placed only temporarily. As noted above, these assumptions are based on the fact that straw and hay are usually used as fodder and not as land fill, while earth and pebbles are generally placed in a trench to fill it in.

The question of how permanent or temporary the designation must be in this context is the subject of controversy among the *Poskim*. Some hold that *permanent* in this context means for the duration of that Sabbath. [Accordingly, temporary would mean an object which will be removed on that Sabbath, e.g., hay which can be used on the Sabbath as animal fodder. There are also instances in which even earth or pebbles, if properly designated, may be removed on the Sabbath. See *Orach Chaim* 308:38.] Others maintain that even in this context permanently means forever *(Orach Chaim* 372:16 and 358:2 *Mishnah Berurah*, ibid.).

4.

נָתַן עָלָיו נֶסֶר שֶׁהוּא רָחָב אַרְבָּעָה טְפָחִים, — *If one placed a board which is four fists wide across it,*

[He bridged the trench with a board four fists wide so that there is now an access point between the two courtyards measuring the minimum width of an entrance — four fists.]

וְכֵן שְׁתֵּי גְזוּזְטְרָאוֹת זוֹ כְנֶגֶד זוֹ, — *similarly if* [he did so in the case of] *two balconies* [which] *are opposite each other,*

The residents of two houses whose

only direct access to each other is through balconies facing each other and separated by a stretch of open space[1] cannot make an *eruv* to allow them to throw objects from balcony to balcony. If, however, they bridged the gap between them with a board measuring four fists in width ... *(Rav).*[2]

מְעָרְבִין שְׁנַיִם, — *they may make two* eruvin,

[The two areas are considered separated despite the bridge between

1. *Rav* mentions that the open space is a public domain but this is not meant to exclude *karmelis* or private domains. Indeed the formulation of this halachah in *Rambam (Hil. Eruvin* 3:14) amd *Shulchan Aruch* (373:1) makes no reference to the halachic status of the intervening domain.

2. *Rashi* (78b) understands that both balconies are on one side of a public domain. This raises a difficulty for, as stated in *Shabbos* 11:2, there is a Biblical prohibition against handing

עֵירוּבִין שְׁנַיִם, וְאִם רָצוּ מְעָרְבִין אֶחָד; פָּחוֹת מִכָּאן, מְעָרְבִין שְׁנַיִם, וְאֵין מְעָרְבִין אֶחָד. ז/ה

[ה] **מַתְבֵּן** שֶׁבֵּין שְׁתֵּי חֲצֵרוֹת, גָּבוֹהַּ עֲשָׂרָה טְפָחִים, מְעָרְבִין שְׁנַיִם, וְאֵין מְעָרְבִין אֶחָד. אֵלּוּ מַאֲכִילִין מִכָּאן, וְאֵלּוּ מַאֲכִילִין

יד אברהם

them. The bridge is only an entrance and consequently, they may make two eruvin.]

וְאִם רָצוּ מְעָרְבִין אֶחָד; — or, if they wish, they may make one [joint] eruv;

[The entrance provided by the bridge is sufficient to allow the two areas to merge in one eruv.]

פָּחוֹת מִכָּאן, מְעָרְבִין שְׁנַיִם, וְאֵין מְעָרְבִין אֶחָד. — [but if it is] less than this, they may make two eruvin, but (they) may not make one eruv.

If the board forming the bridge from one area to the other is narrower than four fists it is difficult to use and cannot be considered a proper entrance. Because of its narrowness people will be afraid to pass over on it (Rav; Rashi).

The Gemara (79a) derives from the specification in the mishnah one opposite the other that if the balconies did not face each other, e.g., one protruded from a house facing east and the other from one facing north [so that a bridge connecting them

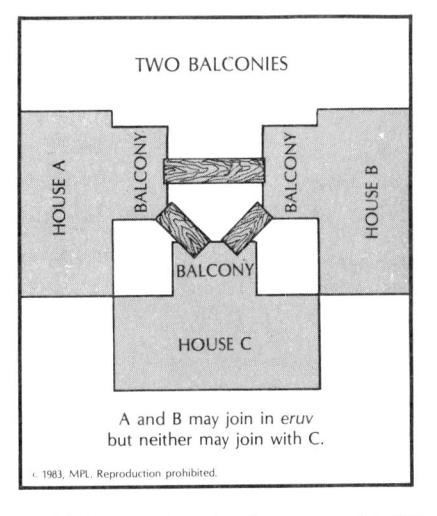

TWO BALCONIES

HOUSE A · BALCONY · BALCONY · HOUSE B

BALCONY

HOUSE C

A and B may join in eruv but neither may join with C.

c. 1983, MPL. Reproduction prohibited.

would have to be placed at an angle] (R' Yehonasan),[1] or if one was three fists or more higher than the other, the device of placing a bridge will not effect a change in the status of the balconies.[2] Ritva explains that because the bridge must serve as an

objects (מוּשִׁיט) from one balcony to another over the public domain under these circumstances. Furthermore, it is implied there that it is Rabbinically prohibited to carry objects in such a manner (see Rashash). Pri Megadim (Mishbetzos 373:1) suggests that in this case one may carry objects from balcony to balcony because the space over the connecting bridge is not considered to be 'over the public domain.' It follows then that one may not transfer objects through the air space between the balconies. R' Yehonasan and Meiri understand that the mishnah speaks about balconies facing each other on opposite sides of the public domain. (Ritva's version of Rashi concurs with this interpretation.) Thus this problem is averted for, as stated earlier, the prohibition against handing things from balcony to balcony is restricted to balconies situated on the same side of a public domain.

Pri Megadim points out, however, that for the point of halachah discussed in the mishnah it is not necessary for the intervening space to be a public domain; the same ruling applies to balconies separated by a courtyard (as implied in the comm. above).

1. Rashi (79a) describes the case of balconies not facing each other as follows: '[Two balconies on the same side of the public domain] one protruding further than the other.' (See glosses of Chavas Yair to Rif.)

2. The interpretation of the Gemara given here is Rashi's view. Tosafos (78b) has a different interpretation. Shulchan Aruch (Orach Chaim 372) accepts Rashi's view.

other, they may make two *eruvin*, or, if they wish, they may make one *eruv*; less than this, they may make two *eruvin*, but may not make one *eruv*.

5. **I**f a haystack between two courtyards is ten fists high, they may make two *eruvin*, but may not make one *eruv*. These may feed from this side and

YAD AVRAHAM

'entrance' from one balcony to another, it must be made in such a way that people are not afraid to walk on it. If one balcony is higher than the other or at an angle to the other, the danger of falling off will deter people from using it.

5.

מַתְבָּן שֶׁבֵּין שְׁתֵי חֲצֵרוֹת, גָּבוֹהַ עֲשָׂרָה טְפָחִים, מְעָרְבִין שְׁנַיִם, וְאֵין מְעָרְבִין אֶחָד. — *If a haystack between two courtyards is ten fists high, they may make two* eruvin, *but may not make one* eruv.

[Two courtyards had no permanent partition between them but were separated by a pile of hay ten fists high.]

[Although the haystack only separates the courtyards temporarily, it is nevertheless a valid partition since, at least for the present, the two courtyards are, in fact, separate. This is in contrast to mishnah 3 in which the hay, because it was placed in the trench on a temporary basis, does not invalidate the trench's status as a partition.]

אֵלוּ מַאֲכִילִין מִכַּאן, וְאֵלוּ מַאֲכִילִין מִכַּאן. — *These may* [let their livestock] *feed from this side and those may* [let their livestock] *feed from that side.*

We are not concerned over the possibility that the animals will eat so much of the hay as to invalidate the separation (resulting in a situation requiring one joint *eruv*) without anyone noticing. In order to invalidate the separation, the animals must lower the height of the partition to less than ten fists over a span measuring more than ten cubits (or the entire length of the boundary) and it is unusual for them to eat that much on one Sabbath (*Rav; Rashi*).

The translation is based on the *Gemara* (79a), which maintains that in fact one may not feed his animals directly from the pile or even lead them to it. It is only permitted to direct the animal to the pile.

Rashi gives two reasons for this prohibition: (a) Since the hay has been designated for use as a partition it is *muktzeh* and may not be used as fodder (see *Rashba*); (b) if it were permissible to take directly from the pile there would be a greater concern that the partition will be invalidated.

The *Gemara* (17a and 93b-94a) rules that once each courtyard has made a valid *eruvei chatzeiros*, carrying is permitted even if the partition between the two courtyards collapsed entirely (on the Sabbath). This is based on the principle that permissibility to carry in cases such as these is determined at the onset of the Sabbath and cannot be revoked even if the situation changes on the Sabbath. As the *Gemara* phrases it: 'Once the Sabbath is permitted it remains permitted.'[1] The commentators raise the question that here, too, we should not be concerned that he will take so much hay as to invalidate the partition since even if this were to happen the *eruv* (for this Sabbath) would remain valid for this Sabbath.

Ravad (cited by *Rashba*) answers that nevertheless it is prohibited to intentionally involve oneself in a situation which will lead to the removal of the partition and the reliance on the principle of 'once the Sabbath is

1. This is, of course, only in regard to the *eruvei chatzeiros*. If the walls making it a private domain were to collapse on the Sabbath, carrying would be immediately prohibited since the area is no longer a private domain.

עֵירוּבִין מִכָּאן. נִתְמַעֵט הַתֶּבֶן מֵעֲשָׂרָה טְפָחִים, מְעָרְבִין אֶחָד, וְאֵין מְעָרְבִין שְׁנַיִם.

[ו] **כֵּיצַד** מִשְׁתַּתְּפִין בְּמָבוֹי? מַנִּיחַ אֶת הֶחָבִית וְאוֹמֵר: ,,הֲרֵי זוֹ לְכָל בְּנֵי מָבוֹי.'' וּמְזַכֶּה לָהֶן עַל יְדֵי בְּנוֹ וּבִתּוֹ הַגְּדוֹלִים, וְעַל יְדֵי עַבְדּוֹ וְשִׁפְחָתוֹ הָעִבְרִים, וְעַל יְדֵי אִשְׁתּוֹ. אֲבָל אֵינוֹ מְזַכֶּה לֹא עַל יְדֵי בְּנוֹ וּבִתּוֹ הַקְּטַנִּים, וְלֹא עַל יְדֵי

יד אברהם

permitted ...' Ritva proposes that the prohibition is due to concern that residents will not learn of the invalidity of the partition even by the next Sabbath when the principle will not be operative. [For this reason Rosh maintains that this prohibition applies not only to the Sabbath but even to the weekdays (see Orach Chaim 372:19).]

נִתְמַעֵט הַתֶּבֶן מֵעֲשָׂרָה טְפָחִים, מְעָרְבִין אֶחָד, וְאֵין מְעָרְבִין שְׁנַיִם — If the hay was reduced to less than ten fists, they may make one eruv, but may not make two eruvin.

If the hay was reduced to below the

minimum ten fist height over a span measuring more than ten cubits or for the entire length of the courtyard boundary, the separation is invalidated and as a result the residents of the two courtyards must make one joint eruv (Rav; Rashi).

According to the view accepted as halachah, the ruling stated here applies only if the height of the haystack was reduced before the Sabbath. If it was reduced on the Sabbath, the eruv status of the courtyards is unaffected for the duration of that Sabbath (Gem. 79b, Orach Chaim 372:19).

6.

כֵּיצַד מִשְׁתַּתְּפִין בְּמָבוֹי? — How do we make a shituf for an alley?

The mishnah now discusses the particulars of making a shitufei mevo'os. One way to do this is to collect adequate amounts of food for this purpose from each household in each of the courtyards. Obviously, this would be a very cumbersome procedure and the mishnah therefore considers a more practical solution.

מַנִּיחַ אֶת הֶחָבִית וְאוֹמֵר: ,,הֲרֵי זוֹ לְכָל בְּנֵי מָבוֹי.'' — One places a barrel and declares, 'Let this belong to all the residents of the alley.'

[One of the inhabitants involved in the shituf may designate a barrel containing an amount of liquid (e.g., wine or oil) sufficient for everyone's

contribution as the shituf. In order to satisfy the requirement that each resident own a share of the shituf, he transfers ownership to them (this may be done in the case of an eruv as well) using the declaration set forth here.]

וּמְזַכֶּה לָהֶן עַל יְדֵי בְּנוֹ וּבִתּוֹ הַגְּדוֹלִים — He may confer possession to them through [lit. by the hand of] his adult son or daughter,

[The formal act of taking possession consists of transferring an object from the hand of the current owner to the hand of the recipient or his proxy. The current owner cannot be the proxy for the recipient since the physical placing of the object into his own hand could not be considered as a transfer from the hand of one person to the hand of

those may feed from that side. If the hay was reduced to less than ten fists, they may make one *eruv*, but may not make two *eruvin*.

6. **H**ow do we make a *shituf* for an alley? One places a barrel and declares, 'Let this belong to all the residents of the alley.' He may confer possession to them through his adult son or daughter, through his Jewish manservant or maidservant, or through his wife. But he may not confer possession through his minor son or daughter,

YAD AVRAHAM

another. As will be seen below, certain other people, such as the young children of the current owner who are still under their father's control, are also disqualified from acting as proxy, for their 'hand' is considered as the 'hand' of the owner. A man does not have legal control over his adult children or their possessions and thus they can act as proxies vis-a-vis their own father (see *Meiri*). Actually, anyone may serve as the proxy — not only the people mentioned here. These are mentioned only to contrast them with those mentioned in the second part of the mishnah as being disqualified.]

The act of taking posession with regard to *eruv* and *shituf* consists of the proxy raising the barrel at least one fist (*Rav; Gem.* 80a).

וְעַל יְדֵי עַבְדּוֹ וְשִׁפְחָתוֹ הָעִבְרִים, — *through his Jewish manservant or maidservant,*

[A Jew who sells himself as a servant to another Jew is not actually owned by him but is more in the nature of an indentured servant. Therefore, although one has placed himself in servitude, he nevertheless retains legal control over his own possessions.]

וְעַל יְדֵי אִשְׁתּוֹ. — *or through his wife.*

[Although the husband exercises

some control over his wife's possessions this is not sufficient to preclude her from acquiring the *eruv* food for others.]

The Talmud (*Nedarim* 88b) concludes that the status of a wife in regard to this law is the subject of a disagreement between R' Meir and the Sages. The halachah is also in question, as some authorities rule in accordance with R' Meir and others with the Sages. Both views are represented in *Shulchan Aruch* (*Orach Chaim* 366:10).

אֲבָל אֵינוֹ מְזַכֶּה לֹא עַל יְדֵי בְּנוֹ וּבִתּוֹ הַקְּטַנִּים, — *But he may not confer possession through his minor son or daughter,*

Minor sons are under the control of their father in that anything found or earned by them becomes the possession of the father.

There is question as to the definition of the terms *adult* and *minor* in our context. Some authorities assert that the term *adult* is literal, i.e., one who has reached legal maturity — thirteen years for a boy and twelve years for a girl (*Rif; Rambam; Ramban* in *Teshuvos HaMeyuchasos* 213).[1] Others (*Tosafos, Rosh*, et al.) maintain that the term *adult* means a son or daughter who is self-supporting (even, in the case of a

1. In this view, a further stringency is added in the case of a daughter. She cannot acquire possession for others (from her father) until she attains the status of *bogeres* [six months after her physical maturity] even if she is not dependent on her father (see *Tos.* 79b).

עֵירוּבִין עַבְדּוֹ וְשִׁפְחָתוֹ הַכְּנַעֲנִים, מִפְּנֵי שֶׁיָּדָן כְּיָדוֹ.

[ז] נִתְמָעֵט הָאֹכֶל, מוֹסִיף וּמְזַכֶּה, וְאֵין צָרִיךְ לְהוֹדִיעַ. נִתּוֹסְפוּ עֲלֵיהֶם, מוֹסִיף וּמְזַכֶּה, וְצָרִיךְ לְהוֹדִיעַ.

ז/ז

יד אברהם

son, if he is a minor in age).[1] If they are dependent on their father they are regarded as *minor* in this context (see *Tos., Bava Metzia* 12b and *Beis Yosef* to *Orach Chaim* 3966). Both views are presented in *Shulchan Aruch* (there).

However, all agree that a minor in age may serve as the proxy to transfer possession from someone who is not his father. This can be proven from the ruling of the mishnah that a Jewish maidservant, who is by definition a minor (she acquires her freedom upon maturity), may serve as the proxy (*Meiri; Tos. Yom Tov;* see *Gittin* 64b).

וְלֹא עַל יְדֵי עַבְדּוֹ וְשִׁפְחָתוֹ הַכְּנַעֲנִים, — *nor through his Canaanite slave or slavewoman,*

[The term 'Canaanite' embraces slaves of all nationalities. According to Torah law, the master owns all his slave's belongings. Since whatever the slave acquires automatically reverts to his master, the donor cannot use his own slave as the proxy since that is the equivalent of being the proxy himself.]

מִפְּנֵי שֶׁיָּדָן כְּיָדוֹ. — *because their hand is like his hand.*

[I.e., the physical transfer of the object from the donor's hand (or property) to that of the slave, etc., is not considered a transfer from the donor's hand to the proxy's, rather it is a mere passing of objects from the donor's right hand to his left. Consequently, this act is invalid to effect the transfer of ownership to a third party since it is considered as though the object had never left the control of the donor.]

7.

נִתְמָעֵט הָאֹכֶל, — *If the food* [designated for the *shituf*] *became diminished,*

If the quantity of food originally set aside for the *shituf* was adequate at the time but was later found to have diminished to less than the minimum amount specified in the next mishnah (*Rav; Rashi*).

In this case the deficiency was discovered before the onset of the Sabbath (*R' Yehonasan* as understood by *Bach* and *Karban Nesanel*). If it was discovered on the Sabbath [and it is possible for it to have occurred after the onset of the Sabbath], the *eruv* is valid for the remainder of that Sabbath and although it is presently deficient, it is not necessary to add to it (*Meiri*; see above 3:4).

מוֹסִיף וּמְזַכֶּה, וְאֵין צָרִיךְ לְהוֹדִיעַ. — *one may add* [to it] *and confer possession* [to the other participants], *but he does not have to notify* [them].

[When making a *shituf* one may not give the other residents possession of the *shituf* food and include them in the *shituf* without their express consent (as stated below and in mishnah 11) because one cannot always assume that the *shituf* is for their benefit (see below). However, once the *shituf* has been made with their consent, one does not have to

1. This view maintains that the validity of the act of transferring possession of an *eruv* is not dependent on the same criteria as established for objects found by a minor (see *Bava Metzia* 12a-12b). There the criterion is self-sufficiency (a self-sufficient minor may keep what he finds), whereas here only physical maturity is a criterion — even a self-sufficient minor is considered under the control of his father in this regard (see *Beis Meir, Orach Chaim* 366:10; *Meginei Shlomo, Kesubos* 47; *Keren Orah* here).

nor through his Canaanite slave or slavewoman, because their hand is like his hand.

7. If the food became diminished, one may add and confer possession, but he does not have to notify [them]. If more [residents] were added, he may add and confer possession, or he must notify [them].

obtain express consent to transfer possession of any additional foodstuffs to them.] Since they have given their consent the first time, it can be assumed that they agree to the addition of more food (Rashi).

The Gemara (80b) notes that the term diminished used in the mishnah points to a halachic distinction between a shituf which has merely become diminished to one which has been totally lost or destroyed. In this latter case, the other participants must be notified. Their previous assent cannot serve in lieu of the explicit agreement needed for the establishment of a new shituf because they may object to the use of their food at this time (Meiri). The Gemara adds that this is so only if the food added to the shituf differs from that used originally. If the same kind of food is used, no notification need be made even if the eruv has been destroyed entirely (Rav; Rambam). Since no change is made in the composition of the shituf, this is regarded as a mere extension of the original shituf, and the assent first given to it suffices for the re-establishment of the shituf as well (Meiri).

R' Yehonasan (see also Meiri) adds further that even where a new kind of food is being used to replace a shituf which was completely destroyed or lost, the residents of the alley only have to be notified when the one making the shituf is using their food to make the second shituf. If he uses his own food to make the replacement shituf and confers possession to the other residents, he need not notify them regardless of what kind of food he uses. This seems to be the opinion of Rashi as well. In light of this distinction, this segment of the mishnah should be rendered as follows: If the food became diminished he may add or confer possession. The distinction between a diminished shituf and one which was destroyed entirely is relevant only to the first suggested method — he may add (i.e., he may add food belonging to the

participants). Because the food used is taken without the owner's explicit permission this ruling is restricted to cases where the shituf was merely diminished or where the same type of food is used. The second method suggested by the mishnah — to confer possession of his own food — is not subject to any restrictions at all (Meiri).

נִתּוֹסְפוּ עֲלֵיהֶם, — If more [residents] were added [lit. there were added to them],

[If after the eruv or shituf was made new residents moved in, thus necessitating an adjustment in the eruv to include them.]

מוֹסִיף — he may add

The one making the shituf may add an amount adequate for the new residents.

וּמְזַכֶּה, — and confer possession,

I.e., if the food added to the shituf for the new residents is contributed by the maker of the shituf, he must give them possession, in which case he does not have to notify them. Since no contribution is taken from them, their participation in the shituf is a pure benefit (זְכוּת) without any negative aspects. Accordingly, it is valid without their explicit acquiescence in accordance with the dictum, זָכִין לְאָדָם שֶׁלֹּא בְּפָנָיו, we may benefit a person in his absence, i.e., one may act as proxy for another without his knowledge only if the other benefits from the act (Rashi).

וְצָרִיךְ לְהוֹדִיעַ. — or [else] he must notify [them].

If he takes the food for the shituf from the new residents, he must notify them (Rashi).

Rav and Rambam (Comm., Hil. Eruvin

[ח] **כַּמָּה** הוּא שִׁעוּרוֹ? בִּזְמַן שֶׁהֵן מְרוּבִּין, מָזוֹן
שְׁתֵּי סְעוּדוֹת לְכֻלָּם; בִּזְמַן שֶׁהֵן
מוּעָטִין, כִּגְרוֹגֶרֶת, לְהוֹצָאַת שַׁבָּת, לְכָל אֶחָד
וְאֶחָד.

[ט] **אָמַר** רַבִּי יוֹסֵי: בַּמֶּה דְבָרִים אֲמוּרִים?
בִּתְחִלַּת עֵרוּב, אֲבָל בִּשְׁיָרֵי עֵרוּב,

יד אברהם

5:6; see also *Rif*), basing themselves on a passage in the *Gemara* (81b), maintain that the *shituf* discussed here refers only to a particular case. In the case of the mishnah the courtyard opened into two alleys so that a choice has to be made by the courtyard's residents regarding which alley they want to merge with. It is because of this that one needs the residents' explicit permission for the *shituf* (see comm. to 7:11).[1] In this interpretation, ostensibly no distinction is

drawn between one who makes a *shituf* from his own food and confers possession, and a *shituf* made from the participant's own food. *Shulchan Aruch* (368:1-2) accepts *Rambam's* interpretation, but implies that if the *shituf* was destroyed the maker of the *shituf* can supply his own food and make the *shituf* without notifying the people. Some *Poskim* reason that the same is true in the case of additional inhabitants (*Mishnah Berurah* 368:9; see *Beur Halachah* there).

8.

כַּמָּה הוּא שִׁעוּרוֹ? — *What is its* [minimum] *quantity?*

[I.e., what is the minimum quantity of food required for a *shitufei mevo'os?*]

[The minimum quantity requirements for *eruvei chatzeiros* are the same as those of *shituf* (see *comm.* to mishnah 10). *Eruv* and *shituf* differ only in the types of food that may be used for them.]

בִּזְמַן שֶׁהֵן מְרוּבִּין, מָזוֹן שְׁתֵּי סְעוּדוֹת לְכֻלָּם; — *When they* [i.e., the participants] *are numerous, food* [enough] *for two meals* [suffices] *for all of them;*

[Food sufficient for two meals (for one person) is the largest amount ever required. This amount suffices even if there are hundreds of participants.] The

Gemara (80b) explains that this amounts to the volume of eighteen dried figs,[2] i.e., eighteen individual minimum contributions. Thus the term *numerous* is defined as eighteen or more participants. Because food sufficient for two meals is a significant amount, it is the maximum amount needed for *shituf* (R' Yehonasan).

There is disagreement among the *Poskim* how much eighteen dried figs, i.e. food for two meals, would be when measured by the egg volume system prevalent in the Talmud. Some maintain that food for two meals would be equivalent to the volume of six eggs while others hold eight eggs to be correct (see further 8:1). *Orach Chaim* (368:3) cites both views and *Mishnah Berurah* advises to

1. *Ravad* disagrees and points out that the halachah rules that one courtyard may merge with two alleys even if the alleys are not merged with each other, just as a courtyard may merge with courtyards to either side of it although these courtyards do not have a common *eruv* (see 4:6).

2. The quantity indicated here — *food for two meals*, i.e., eighteen dried figs — refers to foods which are eaten by themselves, e.g., bread, grains, etc. For foods eaten together with bread, e.g., roasted meat, etc. the maximum amount is not fixed at eighteen dried figs but as the amount of that food that would be eaten with bread during two meals (*Gem.* 29b; *Orach Chaim* 386:6-7).

8. **W**hat is its quantity? When they are numerous, food for two meals for all of them; when they are few, the volume of a dried fig, as in the case of transferring on the Sabbath, for each and every one.

9. **R′** Yose said: To what do these words apply? To the installation of the *eruv*, but for the remnants of the *eruv*, any amount. For they only

YAD AVRAHAM

conform with the more stringent view but rules that after the fact (בְּדִעֲבַד) the volume of six eggs may be relied upon.

בִּזְמַן שֶׁהֵן מוּעָטִין, — *when they are few,* [I.e., if there are eighteen or less participants.]

כִּגְרוֹגֶרֶת, לְהוֹצָאַת שַׁבָּת, לְכָל אֶחָד וְאֶחָד. — *the volume of a dried fig, as* [required for liability] *in the case of transferring on the Sabbath* [lit. *like the dried fig of transferring on the Sabbath*], *for each and every one.*

It is sufficient for each participant to contribute an amount of food equivalent to the volume of a dried fig, although the total will not add up to 'two meals.'

In order to be liable for a sin offering for inadvertently violating the Sabbath by carrying from a private domain to the public domain on the Sabbath, one

must carry a minimum quantity of that substance. For most foodstuffs the minimum is the volume of a dried fig (*Shabbos* 7:4).

[It can be conjectured that the mishnah uses this description to allude to the basis for the 'dried fig' minimum. The minimum quantities necessary for liability for desecrating the Sabbath are based on an evaluation of the respective substance's significance (see *Shabbos* 7:3). Thus the minimum quantity in regard to liability is also the smallest amount considered to have significance. The mishnah alludes to the reason for the designation of a 'dried fig' as a minimum *eruv* contribution by pointing out that in regard to liability for Sabbath desecration a dried fig is considered the smallest amount of food deemed to have significance.]

[The phrase לְהוֹצָאַת שַׁבָּת does not appear in the version of the mishnah with the *Gemara*, but is found in most editions of the Mishnah, as well as in *Rambam's* version (see *Comm.* to *Mishnah*, ed. Kafich; *Meleches Shlomo* and *Shinuyei Nuschaos*).]

9.

אָמַר רַבִּי יוֹסֵי: בַּמֶּה דְּבָרִים אֲמוּרִים? בִּתְחִלַּת עֵרוּב, — *R′ Yose said: To what do these words apply? To the installation of the eruv,*

The ruling in the previous mishnah providing for a minimum quantity for an *eruv* is true only in regard to making the *eruv* in the first place.

אֲבָל בִּשְׁיָרֵי עֵרוּב, כָּל שֶׁהוּא. — *but for the remnants of the* eruv, *any amount* [is sufficient].

Once the *eruv* has taken effect, i.e., any time after the onset of the Sabbath, it remains valid even if the designated

food has diminished to less than the required amount, as long as even a minute amount of it remains. Furthermore, it remains valid even for future Sabbaths, as well *(R′ Yehonasan; Meiri).*

From the reasoning given for this ruling in the concluding statement of the mishnah *(they only required an* eruv *in courtyards ...)* it seems that this segment of the mishnah refers to *eruvei chatzeiros,* and is a departure from the previous mishnayos which had discussed *shituf.* [Even so, some authorities maintain that the rule is true even for *shituf.* See below.] According to *Rambam's* view (see

עֵירוּבִין כָּל שֶׁהוּא. וְלֹא אָמְרוּ לְעָרֵב בַּחֲצֵרוֹת אֶלָּא כְּדֵי
שֶׁלֹא לִשְׁכַּח אֶת הַתִּינוֹקוֹת. ז/י

[י] **בַּכֹּל** מְעָרְבִין וּמִשְׁתַּתְּפִין, חוּץ מִן הַמַּיִם וּמִן
הַמֶּלַח — דִּבְרֵי רַבִּי אֱלִיעֶזֶר. רַבִּי
יְהוֹשֻׁעַ אוֹמֵר: כִּכָּר הוּא עֵרוּב. אֲפִלּוּ מַאֲפֵה סְאָה

יד אברהם

note to mishnah 10), however, there is no
minimum quantity required for *eruvei
chatzeiros*. Thus, it must be assumed that this
segment of the mishnah also refers to *shituf*
although the term *eruv* is used (*Tos. Yom
Tov* to mishnah 10). According to this view
the concluding statement *they only required
... is not part of R' Yose's ruling and refers to
eruvei chatzeiros rather than *shituf* (see
below).

וְלֹא אָמְרוּ לְעָרֵב בַּחֲצֵרוֹת אֶלָּא כְּדֵי שֶׁלֹא
לִשְׁכַּח אֶת הַתִּינוֹקוֹת. — For they only
required [lit. *for they only said to make*]
an eruv *in courtyards not to let the
children forget.*

When all the residents of an alley
have been incorporated by a *shituf* there
is really no need for the individual
courtyards to be merged with an *eruv*,
since they are already considered one
household as a result of the *shituf*. The
only reason the Sages decreed that an
eruv was still necessary was so that the
children not forget the function of *eruv*.
If *shituf* were relied upon in lieu of
eruv, children growing up in this area,
being unaware of the *shituf* food (which
is not necessarily kept in their
courtyard), might be misled into
thinking that carrying from the houses
into the courtyard is permitted without
benefit of any modifying procedure —
eruv or *shituf*. However, because in
essence *shituf* is effective in lieu of *eruv*,
the Sages were lenient and allowed the
continued validity of an *eruv* which had

originally been sufficient but had
become diminished later (*Rav; Rashi;
Rambam*). [Thus R' Yose's ruling is
confined solely to where a *shituf* was
made.]

Although the reason given by R' Yose
justifies only the use of the remnants of an
eruv and not the remnants of a *shituf*, there
are authorities (*R' Yehonasan; Meiri*) who
maintain that R' Yose's ruling also applies if
the *eruv* is intact but the *shituf* has been
diminished. Many *Poskim* (see *Beur
Halachah* to 368:4) maintain that the
remnants of an *eruv* or *shituf* are inherently
valid, because the minimum is required only
to establish the *eruv* — not to continue it.
They are consequently valid even if there is
no *shituf* to back up the *eruv*. The
concluding statement, 'they only required ...'
is not part of R' Yose's ruling but is a new
point. It is stated to clarify the necessity for
making any *eruv* at all when the residents of
the courtyard have already been incorporated
in a *shituf* and it is not meant to have any
halachic ramifications (*Or Zarua* 2:184).

In the opinion of *Tur* (*Orach Chaim*
368), R' Yose merely modifies the
statement of the previous mishnah
regarding the minimum amount required for an *eruv* and explains that the
Tanna kamma's ruling refers only to an
eruv found deficient before it had taken
effect. Thus there is no dispute between
him and the *Tanna kamma*, and the
halachah follows R' Yose's interpretation. This ruling is accepted by
Shulchan Aruch (368:4) as well.[1]

1. *Magen Avraham* (368:4) remarks that this ruling has no application nowadays, for the
custom is to make only an *eruv* which also serves in lieu of *shituf* (see *Rama* to *Orach Chaim*
387). Thus when the *eruv* is diminished, and consequently disqualified, the mitigating factor
of *shituf* is likewise lacking. However, *Mishnah Berurah* (*Beur Halachah* to 368:4) disputes
this conclusion and adduces the views of many early authorities that R' Yose's ruling is not

required an *eruv* in courtyards not to let the children forget.

10. **A**ny [food] may be used to make an *eruv* or a *shituf*, except water or salt — [these are] the words of R' Eliezer. R' Yehoshua says: A loaf is an *eruv*. Even if it is baked from a *se'ah* but it is broken,

Rambam and *Rav*, however, assume that the *Tanna kamma* holds that one must add even to an *eruv* found deficient before the Sabbath, and R' Yose disputes that view. *Rambam* and *Rav*

therefore rule that the halachah does not follow R' Yose and that even the remnants of an *eruv* must be increased to the minimum requirements before the next Sabbath begins.

10.

בְּכָל מְעָרְבִין וּמִשְׁתַּתְּפִין, — *Any [food] may be used to make an* eruv *or a* shituf,

The *eruv* referred to here is *eruvei chatzeiros* (R' Yehonasan; Meiri). Thus, although this statement seems identical to the anonymous statement in 3:1, its meaning is different since there the term *eruv* refers to *eruvei techumin*.

Rambam and *Rav*, however, interpret the term *eruv* here as referring primarily to *eruvei techumin* and only secondarily to *eruvei chatzeiros*. With regard to *eruvei techumin* the mishnah's statement is to be understood simply — it may be made with any kind of food. With regard to *eruvei chatzeiros* the term בְּכָל [lit. *with anything*] must be understood to mean any kind of bread, i.e., even with pieces of bread and not necessarily with whole loaves. R' Eliezer, however, concurs with R' Yehoshua that only bread is valid for *eruvei chatzeiros*. A similar interpretation is held by *Rashi, Tosafos,* and other commentators.

That the term *eruv* used here must refer to *eruvei chatzeiros* is clear from R' Yehoshua's disagreement, which would be completely out of place if the first *Tanna* did not discuss it (*Gem.* 81a).

חוּץ מִן הַמַּיִם וּמִן הַמֶּלַח — דִּבְרֵי רַבִּי אֱלִיעֶזֶר. — *except water or salt* — *[these are] the words of R' Eliezer.*

These substances are not considered foods at all. They also are given freely without compensation and are therefore not considered sufficiently significant to be used as the medium of exchange for *eruv* or *shituf* (R' Yehonasan; Meiri).

רַבִּי יְהוֹשֻׁעַ אוֹמֵר: כִּכָּר הוּא עֵרוּב. — R' *Yehoshua says:* [Only] a [whole] loaf [of bread] is [valid as] an eruv.

[R' Yehoshua states that (a) only bread, and (b) only *whole* loaves, can be used for *eruvei chatzeiros* (*Gem.* 81a). Regarding *eruvei techumin* or *shituf* R' Yehoshua agrees that any kind of food can be used. According to R' Yehonasan's explanation of R' Eliezer's opinion (see above), both of these are points of contention, for R' Eliezer permits any food, while R' Yehoshua requires whole loaves of bread. According to the opinion of *Rambam* and the other commentators, however, only the latter point is in dispute.

אֲפִלּוּ מַאֲפֵה סְאָה וְהִיא פְרוּסָה, אֵין מְעָרְבִין בָּהּ; — *Even if it is baked from a* se'ah [of

predicated on the presence of a *shituf* (as cited in the text). He concludes that preferably a diminished *eruv* should be augmented so that it meets the minimum requirements, but that *post facto* one can rely on such an *eruv* if it meets the guidelines set by R' Yose.

עֵירוּבִין וְהִיא פְרוּסָה, אֵין מְעָרְבִין בָּהּ; כִּכָּר בְּאִסָּר וְהוּא
ז/יא שָׁלֵם, מְעָרְבִין בּוֹ.

[יא] **נוֹתֵן** אָדָם מָעָה לְחֶנְוָנִי וּלְנַחְתּוֹם כְּדֵי
שֶׁיְּזַכֶּה לוֹ עֵרוּב — דִּבְרֵי רַבִּי
אֱלִיעֶזֶר. וַחֲכָמִים אוֹמְרִים: לֹא זָכוּ לוֹ מְעוֹתָיו.
וּמוֹדִים בִּשְׁאָר כָּל אָדָם שֶׁזָּכוּ לוֹ מְעוֹתָיו. שֶׁאֵין

יד אברהם

flour] *but it is broken, it may not be
used for an* eruv;

[A *seah* is the volume of 144 average
size chicken eggs.] The *Gemara* (81a)
explains that if broken loaves or slices
of bread were permitted for use in an
eruv this might lead to ill-feelings
among the contributors (who in the case
of *eruvei chatzeiros* are all neighbors).
The person contributing a whole loaf
would feel cheated if his neighbor
contributed only a slice (even if that
slice consisted of the minimum required
quantity and was as big as his whole
loaf). The disqualification of a slice
holds true, however, even if all the
participants wish to contribute slices.

כִּכָּר בְּאִסָּר וְהוּא שָׁלֵם, מְעָרְבִין בּוֹ. — [yet] a
loaf worth [only] *an* issar, *but which is*

whole, may be used for an eruv.

[An *issar* is a small copper coin.] Even
the smallest size loaf may be used for an
eruv provided enough of them are
contributed to meet the minimum
requirement. Thus, if a contribution the
size of a dried fig is called for (see above
mishnah 8) and one loaf does not fill
this minimum, a number of loaves can
be used (*Rav; Rashi*).[1]

Rambam's (Hil. Eruvin 1:8-9) understanding seems to be that R' Yehoshua
also disputes the rule requiring a minimum.
In his opinion, there is no fixed minimum
contribution required for an *eruv* — the only
requirement is that it be a whole loaf.
Accordingly all the previous mishnayos (7-9)
which refer to minimum quantities are
limited to *shituf* and do not apply to *eruv*.

11.

נוֹתֵן אָדָם מָעָה לְחֶנְוָנִי וּלְנַחְתּוֹם כְּדֵי שֶׁיְּזַכֶּה
לוֹ עֵרוּב — דִּבְרֵי רַבִּי אֱלִיעֶזֶר. — *A person
may give a* ma'ah [a small silver coin
worth 1/6th dinar] *to a grocer or to a
baker in order that he give him
possession in an* eruv — [these are] the
words of R' Eliezer.

A person, anticipating the collection
of foodstuffs for a *shituf*, may pay a
grocer in advance for foodstuffs to be
contributed to the *shituf* on his behalf.
Although he does not actually take
possession of the items he has paid for,
he can stipulate that when the *shituf*

collection is made and the residents of
the alley come to the grocer to buy food
for their *shituf*, that the grocer give
them a portion on his behalf. The same
is true for a person who prepays a baker
to give a loaf for an *eruvei chatzeiros* on
his behalf (*Rav, Rashi*). The *Gemara*
(82b) explains that since, as a rule,
payment of money is not a valid method
for acquiring formal possession of
movables (מְטַלְטְלִים; see *Bava Metzia*
4:1), the food or loaves for which this
person prepaid and which were
contributed on his behalf never legally

1. Some versions (see *Gemara, Rashi, Meiri, Rambam* ed. Kafich) have כִּכָּר כְּאִסָּר, *a loaf as big
as an issar.* The intent is the same — there are no requirements as to the loaf size as long as it is
whole.

it may not be used for an *eruv*; a loaf worth an *issar*,
but which is whole, may be used for an *eruv*.

11. A person may give a *ma'ah* to a grocer or to a baker in order that he give him possession in an *eruv* — [these are] the words of R' Eliezer. But the Sages say: His money does not effect possession. But they concur that in regard to other people his money gives him possession. And we cannot make an

YAD AVRAHAM

belonged to him. Thus the *eruv* should not be valid. Nevertheless, the non-validity of payment as a formal act of acquisition is only Rabbinic in origin, and the Sages waived this provision in certain instances, among them for the *mitzvos* of *eruv* and *shituf*.[1]

וַחֲכָמִים אוֹמְרִים: לֹא זָכוּ לוֹ מְעוֹתָיו. — *But the Sages say: His money does not effect possession.*

The Sages hold that even in the instance of *shituf* and *eruv* the Rabbinic decree invalidating payment as a method of formal acquisition was not waived. As a result, the food and loaf remain in the possession of the grocer or baker and are not valid as the person's contribution to the *eruv* or *shituf* (*Rav; Rashi*).

This is so even if the grocer or baker makes the *eruv* or *shituf* for the entire courtyard or alley from his own food and confers possession to all of the residents without any payment on their part (as in mishnah 6). Since the merchant has accepted money from this person and he does not want to return the money, he does not intend to give this

person a free share in the *eruv* (*Rav; Rashi*).[2] Alternatively, the buyer has demonstrated that he does not want to be given his portion gratis, but wishes to acquire it. Since his payment does not have the effect of acquiring the *eruv* portion, its acquisition for him by proxy would be equivalent of a gift by the merchant — an option explicitly rejected by the person (*Tos.*).

Rosh, however maintains that the mishnah's ruling does not invalidate the *eruv* where the storekeeper conferred possession.

וּמוֹדִים בִּשְׁאָר כָּל אָדָם — *But they* [the Sages] *concur that in regard to other people* [lit. *all the rest of people*]

The Sages agree that if he paid a person not engaged in the sale of food or bread to 'give him possession in an *eruv*' the *eruv* is valid (*Rav; Rashi*).

שֶׁזָּכוּ לוֹ מְעוֹתָיו. — *(that) his money gives him possession.*

Because the recipient of the money in this case is not a merchant, the term 'give possession' does not imply that the act of payment confers possession of the *eruv* upon the one giving the money, i.e., the term is not the equivalent of 'sell

1. Whether or not payment of money is valid as a formal act of acquisition on a Biblical level is the subject of disagreement between R' Yochanan, who holds it valid, and Resh Lakish, who holds that it is invalid (*Bava Metzia* 47b). However, even Resh Lakish can agree to the above interpretation because he concedes that some *Tannaim*, notably R' Shimon, uphold the Biblical validity of payment as a formal act of acquisition (see ibid.). Thus, our mishnah's ruling may be based on the opinion of those *Tannaim*.

2. The above is the interpretation given for *Rashi* by *Tosefos Yom Tov* and others (see *Sha'ar HaTziyun* 369:1,2). According to this, if the storekeeper specified that he was indeed conferring possession to the person who had prepaid, the *eruv* would be valid. However according to the view of *Tosafos* (cited further in the text) even in such an instance the *eruv* is not valid. See *Orach Chaim* 369 and *Mishnah Berurah* 2 there.

עֵירוּבִין מְעָרְבִין לְאָדָם אֶלָּא מִדַּעְתּוֹ.

ז/יא   אָמַר רַבִּי יְהוּדָה: בַּמֶּה דְבָרִים אֲמוּרִים? בְּעֵרוּבֵי
תְחוּמִין, אֲבָל בְּעֵרוּבֵי חֲצֵרוֹת מְעָרְבִין לְדַעְתּוֹ
וְשֶׁלֹּא לְדַעְתּוֹ; לְפִי שֶׁזָּכִין לְאָדָם שֶׁלֹּא בְּפָנָיו, וְאֵין
חָבִין לְאָדָם שֶׁלֹּא בְּפָנָיו.

יד אברהם

to me.' Rather, this term means 'make
an *eruv* for me' and I will pay you a
ma'ah (*Rav; Rashi*) [i.e., the *ma'ah* is
not a payment for the food but for the
service].

שֶׁאֵין מְעָרְבִין לְאָדָם אֶלָּא מִדַּעְתּוֹ. — *And we
cannot make an* eruv *for a person except
with his consent.*

This does not refer back to the
previous segment but is a new point.
One cannot make an *eruv* for someone
using that person's property without his
consent (*Tos. Yom Tov from Rosh*).
[Only when making the *eruv* from one's
own property can one do so for another
person even without his knowledge.]

The word שֶׁאֵין is used here as if it were
written וְאֵין. Although this usage is unusual it
is found elsewhere, too, e.g., *Beitzah* 1:2. *Rav*
and *Rashi*, however, take this word in its
usual sense — *for we cannot make an* eruv *for
a person except with his consent.* They
interpret this phrase as a reference to the first
case of the mishnah, added to explain the
Sages' invalidation of the *eruv*. There are
major difficulties involved with this explanation (see *Tos. Yom Tov*) and a discussion of
them is beyond the scope of this volume. A
solution to these problems is offered by
Chazon Ish (*Orach Chaim* 99:12).

אָמַר רַבִּי יְהוּדָה: בַּמֶּה דְבָרִים אֲמוּרִים?
בְּעֵרוּבֵי תְחוּמִין, — *R' Yehudah said: To
what do these words apply? To* eruvei
techumin,

[Normally any act performed for a
person by a proxy must first be
approved by that person; it can be done
only with his consent. The exception to
this rule is any action whose consequences are considered to be an

unqualified benefit (זְכוּת) to the person.
In such a case, a proxy may undertake
to act on behalf of another person even
without his prior consent, because the
consent may be assumed. Thus the
statement, 'we cannot make an *eruv* for
a person except with his consent' must
refer to a type of *eruv* whose halachic
consequences cannot be viewed as an
unqualified benefit but rather as one
which has disadvantages as well.] The
statement must then refer to *eruvei
techumin* which may be disadvan-
tageous to the person, due to the fact
that any area more than 2,000 cubits
from the *eruv* becomes prohibited even
if it had been within the *techum* as
measured from the person's home. Since
by placing an *eruv* one loses as well as
gains, the decision to exchange one
techum for another must be made by the
person himself (*Rav; Rashi*).

[In this instance even if possession of the
eruv food is conferred upon the person, the
eruv is invalid.]

אֲבָל בְּעֵרוּבֵי חֲצֵרוֹת מְעָרְבִין לְדַעְתּוֹ וְשֶׁלֹּא
לְדַעְתּוֹ; — *but in regard to* eruvei
chatzeiros, *we may make an eruv with
his consent or without his consent;*

The making of an *eruvei chatzeiros* is
regarded as an unqualified benefit for
which no prior consent is necessary. If
the *eruv* is not made, the person will not
be allowed to carry objects from his
house into the courtyard. Making an
eruv, on the other hand, in no way
limits him (*R' Yehonasan*). Therefore
someone may act as a proxy and confer
possession of *eruv* food to another or

eruv for a person except with his consent.

R' Yehudah said: To what do these words apply? To *eruvei techumin*, but in regard to *eruvei chatzeiros*, we may make an *eruv* with his consent or without his consent; for we may benefit a person in his absence, but we may not disadvantage a person except in his presence.

YAD AVRAHAM

even take the person's own food for this purpose[1] *(Meiri;* cf. *Mishnah Berurah* 368:9).

לְפִי שֶׁזָּכִין לְאָדָם שֶׁלֹּא בְּפָנָיו, — *for we may benefit a person in his absence,*

[I.e., we may perform a legal act for a person in his absence if it benefits him, even without his prior consent.]

וְאֵין חָבִין לְאָדָם שֶׁלֹּא בְּפָנָיו. — *but we may not disadvantage a person except in his presence.*

[An act which may be detrimental to a person may be performed for him only after his consent has been secured.]

The *Gemara* points out that in some cases even *eruvei chatzeiros* is not classified as a

benefit and prior consent is necessary even according to R' Yehudah. This is possible if one courtyard opens into two separate alleys so that it is questionable which alley the courtyard wants to be merged with. In that case one cannot confer possession in the *shituf* to the courtyard in question without the prior consent of the residents. The *Gemara* uses this circumstance to resolve an apparent contradiction to R' Yehudah's ruling in mishnah 7 where the mishnah clearly states that making a new *eruv* requires explicit consent from the parties involved. The *Gemara* concludes that that ruling refers exclusively to where making an *eruv* is not viewed as an unquestionable benefit.[2]

The *Gemara* (81b) states that the halachah is in accord with R' Yehudah's view.

1. The *Gemara* (81b) records a disagreement among the Amoraim whether R' Yehudah's statement is uncontested or whether other *Tannaim* dispute it. The reason for the view that *eruvei chatzeiros* is classified as a possible disadvantage is not discussed at length by the commentators. *Rosh* remarks tersely: Perhaps a reason deterring a person from participating in an *eruv* may be seen. R' Yehonasan indicates that the question is only about an *eruv* made by taking the person's food for an *eruv* without his knowledge. Then it may be argued that he may value the use of his food over the convenience provided by an *eruv*. Where the food used for the *eruv* is 'given to him,' however, everyone agrees that the *eruv* can be made for him without his prior consent (see *Meiri*). Other authorities, however, dispute R' Yehonasan's assumption, maintaining that taking the person's food is viewed as a disadvantage even by R' Yehudah and that R' Yehudah's statement refers only to an *eruv* made effective by conferring possession (see *Mishnah Berurah* 368:10).

2. Many authorities (*Rashba; Ritva; Ravad;* et al.) maintain that this distinction is predicated on the view (4:6) that a courtyard situated between two courtyards which do not themselves have a common *eruv* may not make an *eruv* with both of them. According to the halachically accepted view (*Rambam, Hil. Eruvin* 4:23; *Orach Chaim* 378:1) that it may indeed merge with both courtyards, making an *eruv* with one alley should not be classified as a disadvantage for this will not preclude the courtyard from making another *eruv* with the other courtyard. *Rambam,* however, rules that a courtyard between two alleys is an exception to the rule that *eruvei chatzeiros* is viewed as a 'benefit' and his view is accepted as halachah in *Shulchan Aruch* (368:1; see *Mishnah Berurah;* see also *Rosh*).

עירובין [א] **כֵּיצַד** מִשְׁתַּתְּפִין בִּתְחוּמִין? מַנִּיחַ אֶת הֶחָבִית, וְאוֹמֵר: ,,הֲרֵי זֶה לְכָל בְּנֵי עִירִי״ — לְכָל מִי שֶׁיֵּלֵךְ לְבֵית הָאָבֵל אוֹ לְבֵית הַמִּשְׁתֶּה. וְכָל שֶׁקִּבֵּל עָלָיו מִבְּעוֹד יוֹם, מֻתָּר; מִשֶּׁתֶּחְשַׁךְ, אָסוּר, שֶׁאֵין מְעָרְבִין מִשֶּׁתֶּחְשַׁךְ.

[ב] **כַּמָּה** הוּא שִׁעוּרוֹ? מְזוֹן שְׁתֵּי סְעוּדוֹת לְכָל אֶחָד; מְזוֹנוֹ לְחוֹל וְלֹא לַשַׁבָּת —

יד אברהם

Chapter 8

1.

כֵּיצַד מִשְׁתַּתְּפִין בִּתְחוּמִין? — *How do we make a communal* eruvei techumin [lit. *How can we participate in* techumin]?

[How can an *eruvei techumin* be set up so that anyone who wishes to establish his Sabbath place of dwelling at the spot where the *eruv* is to be deposited may do so?]

מַנִּיחַ אֶת הֶחָבִית, — *One places a barrel* [of food at the site],

[The one making the *eruv* deposits at the spot designated for the *eruv* a container holding enough food to meet the *eruv* needs of all the participants (see mishnah 2).]

וְאוֹמֵר: ,,הֲרֵי זֶה לְכָל בְּנֵי עִירִי״ — — *and declares: 'Let this be* [the eruv] *for all the people of my town'* —

If the food has been collected from each of the individuals concerned the simple declaration is sufficient. But if the food belongs to the person making the *eruv* he must also confer possession to the potential *eruv* participants in the manner described for *shitufei mevo'os* in 7:6 (*Tos. Yom Tov* from Gem. 80a).

לְכָל מִי שֶׁיֵּלֵךְ לְבֵית הָאָבֵל אוֹ לְבֵית הַמִּשְׁתֶּה. — *for whoever will go to a house of mourning or a house of rejoicing.*

[I.e., for whoever wishes to offer condolences to a mourner or to join in wedding festivities.]

This segment of the mishnah is not part of the declaration to be made for a communal *eruv* (see *Orach Chaim* 413:1). Rather it is the *Tanna's* elaboration regarding which people are eligible to be included. With these examples the mishnah teaches that the declaration and the *eruv* are limited to those engaged in mitzvah related activities. The mishnah thus states that an *eruvei techumin* may not be made if the activity for which one wishes to go beyond his regular *techum* is a purely personal one, having nothing to do with a mitzvah (*Rav* from Gem. 82a).

וְכָל שֶׁקִּבֵּל עָלָיו מִבְּעוֹד יוֹם, מֻתָּר; — *Whoever accepted this* [as his eruv] *while it was yet day* [i.e., before the onset of the Sabbath] *is permitted* [to make use of it].

The *Gemara* (82a) modifies this to include whoever has been notified about the *eruv* while it was yet day, whether or not he has already decided to accept it as his *eruv*. Accordingly, as long as one knew of the placement of the *eruv* before the Sabbath, he may defer his decision of whether to be included in the *eruv* until the Sabbath itself (*Rav*).

[This modification is based on the ruling that in Rabbinic matters (such as *techumin*) the principle of *bereirah* (בְּרֵירָה) may be relied upon. This principle states that under

1. **H**ow do we make a communal *eruvei techumin?* One places a barrel, and declares: 'Let this be for all the people of my town' — for whoever will go to a house of mourning or a house of rejoicing. Whoever accepted this while it was yet day is permitted; after dark, he is prohibited, because we cannot make an *eruv* after dark.

2. **W**hat is its quantity? Food for two meals for each person; of his food for a weekday, but not for the Sabbath — [these are] the words of R'

YAD AVRAHAM

certain conditions a decision may become effective retroactively (in Talmudic usage, הוּבְרַר הַדָּבָר לְמַפְרֵעַ, *the matter becomes clarified retroactively*) provided that at the earlier moment the ultimate decision was technically possible. For this reason, if the person did not know about the existence of the *eruv* before the Sabbath, and consequently could not have at that moment decided to opt for the *techum* provided by the *eruv*, this principle is not operable.]

מִשֶּׁתֶּחְשַׁךְ, אָסוּר, שֶׁאֵין מְעָרְבִין מִשֶּׁתֶּחְשַׁךְ. —

[but if] *after dark, he is prohibited, because we cannot make an* eruv *after dark.*

If he does not find out about the *eruv* until after the Sabbath began [and thus the earliest moment at which it could become valid for him is on the Sabbath proper], he may not make use of this *eruv*, because in order for an *eruv* to be valid it must take effect at the very beginning of the Sabbath (*Rav*).

2.

בַּמֶּה הוּא שִׁעוּרוֹ? — *What is its quantity?* [What is the minimum amount of food required per person for *eruvei techumin?*]

מְזוֹן שְׁתֵּי סְעוּדוֹת לְכָל אֶחָד; — [Enough] *food for two meals for each person;* [Food sufficient for two meals has to be placed on the spot designated as the *eruv* site for *each* eventual participant in the *eruv*.] The reason for this minimum (in contrast to *shituf* where food sufficient for just two meals for one individual is enough for everybody; see 7:8) is that the essence of *eruvei techumin* is that one (symbolically) establishes his place of dwelling at the *eruv* site for the Sabbath by depositing his food for the day there. Consequently, each person wishing to participate must have enough food for two meals at the *eruv* site (*Rambam*). [In the case of

shituf, however, the purpose of the food is to (symbolically) incorporate them into one unit. Consequently, as long as the total contribution amounts to a significant amount of food, it can serve to signify the incorporation of the membership in the combined unit.

מְזוֹנוֹ לְחוֹל וְלֹא לַשַּׁבָּת — דִּבְרֵי רַבִּי מֵאִיר. *of his food for a weekday, but not* [of his food] *for the Sabbath —* [these are] *the words of R' Meir.*

[The amount of bread eaten at a meal may vary from the Sabbath to the weekdays. R' Meir maintains that the weekday meal be used as the criterion.]

The amount of food involved is not determined by the amount of food consumed by an average person at a meal, but rather by the average meal of the participant in the *eruv* (*Gem*. 30b, *Keilim* 17:11). This is alluded to by the

עֵירוּבִין דִּבְרֵי רַבִּי מֵאִיר. רַבִּי יְהוּדָה אוֹמֵר: לַשַּׁבָּת וְלֹא

ח/ב לַחוֹל. וְזֶה וָזֶה מִתְכַּוְּנִין לְהָקֵל.

רַבִּי יוֹחָנָן בֶּן בְּרוֹקָה אוֹמֵר: מִכִּכָּר בְּפוּנְדְּיוֹן,

מֵאַרְבַּע סְאִין בְּסֶלַע. רַבִּי שִׁמְעוֹן אוֹמֵר: שְׁתֵּי יָדוֹת

לַכִּכָּר, מִשָּׁלֹשׁ לַקַּב.

יד אברהם

use of the word מְזוֹנוֹ, *his food*, rather than מָזוֹן, *food*.

רַבִּי יְהוּדָה אוֹמֵר: לַשַּׁבָּת וְלֹא לַחוֹל. — *R' Yehudah says: For the Sabbath, but not for a weekday.*

[R' Yehudah uses the Sabbath meals as the criterion.]

וְזֶה וָזֶה מִתְכַּוְּנִין לְהָקֵל. — *And both intend to rule leniently.*

Both R' Meir and R' Yehudah are of the opinion that the meal at which he eats less should be used as the criterion, thus reducing the size of the minimum *eruv* contribution. They disagree regarding at which meal people generally eat less. R' Meir maintains that people generally eat more bread on the Sabbath because the tastiness of the foods increases their appetite (*Rav from Gem.* 82b). R' Yehudah, however, thinks that people generally eat less per meal on the Sabbath because they must eat an additional (third) meal before nightfall (*Rav; Rashi*). Alternatively, R' Yehudah is of the opinion that on the Sabbath because a person usually eats more side dishes and has more to drink, he consequently eats less bread than on weekdays (*Rambam, Comm.* here and *Keilim* 17:11; *R' Yehonasan*).

It is difficult to understand how there can be a disagreement about this matter. *Meiri* explains that the disagreement is based on the principle set forth in the Gemara (30b and *Keilim* 17:11) that the minimum quantity is determined according to the individual and not according to a universal norm. Thus, he postulates, there is no real disagreement between R' Meir and R' Yehudah. Each one merely presents different situations and the

rulings pertaining to them. R' Meir rules that for a person who eats less on weekdays, the weekday meal serves as the criterion, whereas R' Yehudah considers the opposite situation and rules that a person who eats smaller meals on the Sabbath should use that as his yardstick.

רַבִּי יוֹחָנָן בֶּן בְּרוֹקָה אוֹמֵר: — *R' Yochanan ben Berokah says:*

There are different opinions as to what the relationship is between the views of R' Yochanan ben Berokah and R' Shimon (below) and the preceding views of R' Meir and R' Yehudah.

As explained (s.v. מְזוֹנוֹ לַחוֹל), the minimum quantity of food required for *eruvei techumin* (two meals per person) is determined by the individual's eating habits. The Gemara adds that this is true only when the individual eats less than the average person. If, however, he eats more, then the average-sized meal is used as the yardstick even for him. *Meiri* explains that all the *Tannaim* mentioned here agree to this in principle. R' Yochanan ben Berokah and R' Shimon argue as to how to define the universal norm, whereas R' Meir and R' Yehudah discuss how to determine the individual's minimum meal when that is less than the universal norm.[1]

A second view indicated in *Tosafos* (80b) is that we have here four different opinions as to how to determine the minimum quantity needed for *eruvei techumin*. It seems that according to this view R' Meir and R' Yehudah believe that the minimum is not determined separately for each individual but that

---

1. This is ascribed to *Rosh* by *Beis Yosef* (*Orach Chaim* 409) and is accepted as halachah by *Shulchan Aruch* (*Orach Chaim* 409:7 as emended by *Mishnah Berurah* there 30, 31).

משניות / עירובין — פרק ח: כיצד משתתפין [172]

Meir. R' Yehudah says: For the Sabbath, but not for a weekday. And both intend to rule leniently.

R' Yochanan ben Berokah says: A loaf worth a *pundyon*, when four *se'ah* cost a *sela*. R' Shimon says: Two-thirds of a loaf of which there are three to a *kav*.

YAD AVRAHAM

an average meal is used. They disagree only as to how to determine that average. R' Shimon and R' Yochanan ben Berokah on the other hand maintain that the minimum is less than the actual average but is statutory and is only considered a meal with regard to the law of *eruv*. They disagree as to what that statutory amount is.[1]

.מְכַבָר בְּפוּנְדְיוֹן, מֵאַרְבַּע סְאִין בְּסֶלַע — *A loaf worth a* pundyon, *when four* se'ah *cost a* sela.

Both R' Yochanan ben Berokah and R' Shimon give precise amounts for the general statement 'enough food for two meals.' Both state that this comes to one loaf. However, they disagree as to what size loaf is meant. According to R' Yochanan ben Berokah, a loaf containing the volume of six eggs is meant. This is arrived at by reckoning the amount of bread which can be bought for a *pundyon* (a small coin) when four *se'ah* (a volume measure) of flour cost a *sela* (a large coin).

The monetary system current at the time this mishnah was written was:

1 *sela* = 4 *dinar*;
1 *dinar* = 6 *me'ah*;
1 *me'ah* = 2 *pundyon*.

A *sela* therefore contained 48 *pundyon* (see *Kiddushin* 12a). Thus the loaf referred to here is 1/48th of four *se'ah*, the amount

which could be bought for a *sela*.

A *se'ah* is a measure of volume. The volume measures of those times were as follows:

1 *se'ah* = 6 *kav*;
1 *kav* = 4 *log*;
1 *log* = 6 average-sized chicken eggs.

Accordingly, one *se'ah* equals 144 eggs and the amount bought for a *sela* (4 *se'ah*) is 576 eggs (144 x 4). Thus, the amount bought for one *pundyon* (576 divided by 48) would be twelve eggs. However, the *Gemara* 82b demonstrates that half that amount — six eggs — is meant. The substance bought at four *se'ah* for a *sela* is grain, not bread. Generally, a loaf of bread cost twice as much as the grain used in it. Thus, if one *pundyon* could buy twelve eggs of flour it could only buy six eggs of bread — the amount needed for two meals. The mishnah must therefore be understood as 'a loaf of bread worth one *pundyon* when four *se'ah* of flour cost a *sela*' (*Rav* from *Gem.* 82b).

רַבִּי שִׁמְעוֹן אוֹמֵר: שְׁתֵּי יָדוֹת לְכִבָּר, מִשָּׁלִשׁ לְקַב. — *R' Shimon says: Two-thirds* [lit. *two parts*] *of a loaf of which there are three to a* kav.

[According to R' Shimon, the loaf used as a standard is one-third of a *kav*, or eight eggs and the minimum amount of bread needed for an *eruvei techumin* is two-thirds of that, or five and one-third eggs. The loaves described in this mishnah were probably standard sizes in Mishnaic times.]

1. *Rambam* in his commentary does not rule on the disagreement between R' Meir and R' Yehudah, indicating only that the halachah follows R' Yochanan ben Berokah. It appears from this that he too sees a four-way disagreement here in which he rules according to R' Yochanan ben Berokah. Similarly in *Hil. Eruvin* (1:9 and 6:7) he makes no ruling on the question of whether the two meals are measured by weekday or Sabbath consumption. Clearly, *Rambam* holds that R' Yochanan ben Berokah's view contradicts both R' Yehudah's and R' Meir's and that a ruling in favor of R' Yochanan ben Berokah is automatically a ruling against both of these *Tannaim*. Both interpretations outlined here encounter difficulties in interpreting the text of the *Gemara*, but these difficulties are beyond the scope of this volume (see *Geon Yaakov*).

חֶצְיָה לְבֵית הַמְנֻגָּע, וַחֲצִי חֶצְיָה לִפְסוֹל אֶת הַגְּוִיָּה.

[ג] **אַנְשֵׁי** חָצֵר וְאַנְשֵׁי מִרְפֶּסֶת שֶׁשָּׁכְחוּ וְלֹא עֵרְבוּ, כָּל שֶׁגָּבוֹהַּ עֲשָׂרָה טְפָחִים

יד אברהם

A *kav* consists of 24 eggs (see above). Thus a loaf measuring one third of a *kav* consists of eight egg volumes. The two meal requirement is met by two-thirds of such a loaf or five and one-third eggs. The disagreement in the mishnah refers only to the minimum as it applies to bread. As seen above (3:1), an *eruvei techumim*, like a *shituf*, can be made with any food substance; the minimum quantities of other foods are outlined in the *Gemara* (29-30) and *Shulchan Aruch* (*Orach Chaim* 381:6-7).

חֶצְיָה — *Half of it*

Half of the standard loaf used to define the minimum needed for *eruvei techumin* (i.e., a six egg loaf according to R' Yochanan ben Berokah or an eight egg loaf according to R' Shimon) (*Rav; Rashi*).

לְבֵית הַמְנֻגָּע, — [is the measure used] *for a house infected with* tzaraas,

The Torah states (*Lev.* 14:33 ff) that a stone house found infected with *tzaraas*, the symptoms of which are deep red or green splotches, be quarantined and placed under observation by a *Kohen* for a period of between one and three weeks. During this period the house is considered *tamei* (contaminated). One of the aspects of this *tumah* status is that anyone who enters the house during this period also becomes *tamei*. There are, however, different levels of

contamination to which the person is subject depending upon the length of his stay in the house. If the person exits immediately after entering, only he is *tamei* but not the clothing he is wearing.[1]

If, however, he stays in the house for the length of time necessary to eat a meal, the clothing also becomes *tamei*.[2]

Since the loaf under discussion here contains two meals, half of it suffices for one meal. Consequently, the length of time needed to eat half the loaf of our mishnah is the length of the stay in the tzaraas-infected house which causes a person's clothing to also become *tamei* (*Rav; Rashi*).

[According to R' Yochanan ben Berokah, then, the clothing become *tamei* if the person stays in the house long enough to eat a piece of bread the size of three eggs (in volume) while according to R' Shimon the clothing only become *tamei* if he tarries long enough to eat bread the volume of four eggs.[3]

Although R' Shimon ruled that in regard to *eruvei techumin* one-third of the loaf is sufficient for one meal (two-thirds of the loaf is considered 'food for two meals') this is so because the Sages were more lenient in regard to the Rabbinic institution of *eruv* (*Rav; Rashi*).

וַחֲצִי חֶצְיָה לִפְסוֹל אֶת הַגְּוִיָּה. — *and one-fourth of it* [lit. *half of its half*] to render one's [lit. *a*] *body* pasul.

1. The degree of *tumah* contracted by him is *rishon* which cannot per se pass on any *tumah* to clothing. However, this is true only for clothing he is wearing. If he carries clothing into the house, they are treated like utensils and become *tamei* immediately (*Negaim* 13:9).

2. This is based on the verse in *Lev.* (14:47) which states that, *one who eats in the house must cleanse his clothing* (by immersion in a *mikveh*). The Talmud (*Berachos* 41a and elsewhere) proves that this does not mean actually eating in the house but staying in the house the length of time necessary to eat a meal.

3. The half loaf as it is defined here in regard to a house infected with *tzaraas* is identical with the term פְּרָס, *pras* [lit. *a piece of a loaf*], i.e. a half loaf, which serves as the measure in כָּזַיִת בִּכְדֵי אֲכִילַת פְּרָס,[eating a piece of food] *the size of an olive in the time it takes to eat a pras.* Wherever the Torah forbids a substance to be eaten, the prohibition applies to even the least

Half of it for a house infected with *tzaraas*, and one-fourth of it to render one's body *pasul*.

3. If the residents of a courtyard and the residents of a gallery forgot to make an *eruv*, whatever is

YAD AVRAHAM

[The term *pasul* (lit. *unfit*) as used here refers to a weak degree of *tumah*-contamination in which the person himself is considered *tamei* but in which he cannot transmit *tumah* to any other object with which he comes in contact. Because he himself is *pasul*, he is prohibited to eat *terumah*.] In the circumstances discussed here, the person ate food substances contaminated with *tumah*, thereby rendering himself *pasul*, i.e., prohibited to eat *terumah* until he purifies himself by immersion in a *mikveh*. An amount of contaminated food equal in volume to one quarter [half of a half] of the loaf discussed here is sufficient to confer this *tumah* upon the body of the person eating it *(Rav; Rashi)*. [According to R' Shimon, therefore, the amount called for here is two egg volumes, whereas according to R' Yochanan ben Berokah it is one and one-half egg volumes.]

[*Tumah*-contaminated food substances cannot, as a rule, render a person *tamei* upon contact. However, the Sages decreed that a person eating *tumah*-contaminated food contracts a weak degree of *tumah*.]

Rambam (Comm. and *Hil. Eruvin* 1:9) rules in accord with R' Yochanan ben Berokah but *Rashi* here, *Tosafos* (80b) and others rule in accord with R' Shimon in regard to the definition of *pras* (the half loaf), and the minimum which makes a person *pasul*.

In regard to *eruv*, *Rambam* also rules that six eggs are necessary whereas *Tosafos* and others hold that five and one-third eggs are sufficient. *Tur* *(Orach Chaim* 409), however, rules that the two meals required for *eruv* total eight eggs (see *Beis Yosef, Bach* and *Turei Zahav* there; *Beur HaGra, Orach Chaim* 486:1). *Shulchan Aruch* 368:3 cites the views of *Rambam* and *Tur* (see *Beur HaGra* there) and the *Poskim* advise that preferably the more stringent ruling of *Tur* should be complied with, but rule that an *eruv* comprising only six eggs is, in the end, valid.

3.

Mishnayos 7:6-11 discussed the actual procedure of making a *shitufei mevo'os* [and *eruvei chatzeiros*]. The first two mishnayos of this chapter discuss the same topic in reference to the parallel institution of *eruvei techumin*. The rest of this chapter will dwell on certain ramifications of the laws of *eruv*, particularly the aspect of this law which prohibits carrying into

the courtyard when no *eruv* has been made. The mishnah will define when and where a non-participant in the *eruv* can cause the courtyard to be prohibited for carrying.

אַנְשֵׁי חָצֵר וְאַנְשֵׁי מַרְפֶּסֶת — *If the residents of a courtyard and the residents of a gallery*

Some of the apartments within a

amount of that food. However, if one violates that prohibition, the beis din cannot punish him unless he eats a certain minimum amount. The minimum one must eat in order to be liable for punishment is the volume of an olive (כְּזַיִת). The same minimum applies to substances which the Torah obligates us to eat, e.g., matzoh on the first night of *Pesach*. This amount must be eaten within a time span not longer than it takes to eat a *pras*. Thus, the disagreement between R' Yochanan and R' Shimon (and the subsequent difference of opinion on how to rule; see further) is pertinent to many areas of halachah.

עירובין לַמַּרְפֶּסֶת; פָּחוֹת מִכַּאן, לֶחָצֵר. ח/ג
חֻלְיַת הַבּוֹר וְהַסֶּלַע גְּבוֹהִים עֲשָׂרָה טְפָחִים,
לַמַּרְפֶּסֶת; פָּחוֹת מִכַּאן, לֶחָצֵר. בַּמֶּה דְבָרִים
אֲמוּרִים? בִּסְמוּכָה; אֲבָל בִּמְפֻלֶּגֶת, אֲפִלּוּ גָבוֹהַּ

יד אברהם

courtyard open directly onto it; their inhabitants are here termed *the residents of a courtyard.* Other apartments are located above ground level and open onto a long gallery at the end of which is a stairway leading down to the courtyard; the inhabitants are termed *the residents of a gallery (Rav; Rashi).*

שֶׁשָּׁכְחוּ וְלֹא עֵרְבוּ, — *forgot to make a* [joint] *eruv,*

The residents of the courtyard made an *eruv* among themselves, as did the residents of the gallery, but the two groups did not unite in a joint *eruv.* From a halachic viewpoint, if the gallery is at least ten fists above the courtyard, the two are considered separate areas so that each group's *eruv* suffices for its area. Carrying from the gallery to the courtyard and vice versa, however, is prohibited.

The fact that the inhabitants of the gallery have rights of passage (דְּרִיסַת הָרֶגֶל) through the courtyard does not restrict the courtyard, because, according to the halachically accepted view, mere right of passage does not restrict where those holding that right are permitted to carry into the area facing their houses [see above 6:9; s.v. רֶגֶל הַמֻּתֶּרֶת בִּמְקוֹמָהּ] *(Rav).*

כָּל שֶׁגָּבוֹהַּ עֲשָׂרָה טְפָחִים — *whatever is higher than ten fists*

I.e., any elevated area of the courtyard which is ten fists above the floor of the courtyard, e.g., a mound or post *(Rav; Rashi).*

לַמַּרְפֶּסֶת; — [belongs] *to the gallery;*

The area is considered to be part of the gallery area and only its residents may reach over to it and transfer objects to and from it; the residents of the courtyard may not carry to this area.

The underlying principle here is that any area near to but not halachically

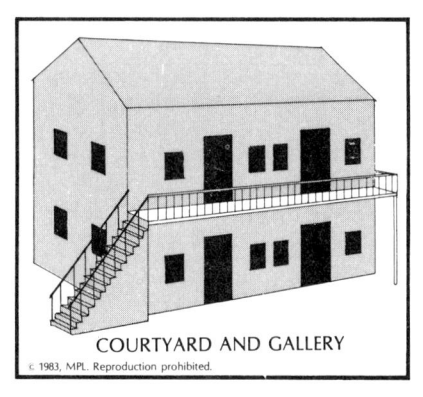

COURTYARD AND GALLERY
© 1983, MPL. Reproduction prohibited.

contiguous to two other areas is considered the province of the area to which it is more readily accessible. The *Gemara* (84a) explains that the area under discussion here is less than ten fists below the level of the gallery so that it is more readily accessible to the inhabitants of the gallery than to those of the courtyard.

If the level is ten fists or more below that of the gallery the area belongs to both the gallery and the courtyard, being that its use is equally inconvenient to all. Since it is equally the province of the courtyard and the gallery and they are not merged by an *eruv,* the area is prohibited to both *(Gem. 84a).*

The ruling stated here is also subject to the condition stated at the end of the mishnah, namely that the area under discussion be near the gallery *(Rav).*

The areas discussed here are owned jointly by both groups. Otherwise the area would be judged as belonging, for *eruv* purposes, to the group owning it regardless of its elevation or proximity *(Tos. R' Peretz; Tur* and *Shulchan Aruch, Orach Chaim* 375).

פָּחוֹת מִכַּאן — *less than that,*

[If the height of the area under discussion is less than ten fists above that of the courtyard.]

higher than ten fists [belongs] to the gallery; less than that, to the courtyard.

The embankment around a pit or a rock which is ten fists high[belongs]to the gallery; less than that, to the courtyard. To what do these words apply? To that which is near; but that which is at a distance,

YAD AVRAHAM

לְחָצֵר. — *[belongs] to the courtyard.*

The *Gemara* (84a) explains this to mean that the area belongs to the courtyard *also*, in addition to its association with the gallery. As a result the area is prohibited for use to the residents of both the courtyard and the gallery, since it is an area whose residents — i.e., those who have access to it, in this case both the people of the gallery and the courtyard — have not united in an *eruv*.

חֻלְיַת הַבּוֹר — *The embankment around a pit*

[It was customary to heap the earth dug from a pit around it to serve as a fence.]

וְהַסֶּלַע — *or a rock*

[Or a rock standing in a courtyard.]

גְּבוֹהִים עֲשָׂרָה טְפָחִים, לַמִּרְפֶּסֶת; — *which is ten fists high [belongs] to the gallery;*

Since the top of the embankment or rock is ten fists above the floor of the courtyard but within ten fists of the gallery, it is considered the province of the gallery as in the previous case *(Rav)*.

The *Gemara* (84a) proves that the ruling of the mishnah cannot refer to transferring objects [or water] between the floor of the pit and the gallery [e.g., by rope]. Since the embankment around the pit is itself ten fists high, the floor of the pit would be more than ten fists below the gallery. Consequently, the floor of the pit would belong equally to the courtyard and the gallery. [Because the ten

fist high embankment makes access to the floor of the pit as difficult to the people of the courtyard as it is to the gallery, both areas would be viewed as having equal access to it.] Since it would then belong to two areas not merged by an *eruv*, neither area would be permitted to use it, as explained above. The *Gemara*, therefore, concludes[1] that the pit is filled with objects which may not be moved on the Sabbath — because they are *muktzeh* — in such a manner that the surface of the pit's interior is within ten fists of the gallery. It is thus more accessible to the gallery than it is to the courtyard (which is still separated from it by the ten fist high embankment).

However, if the pit is filled with water (or any other object which may be moved on the Sabbath), residents of the gallery may not draw from it even if the water level is within ten fists. There is concern that if this were allowed, water would continue to be drawn even after the level fell to a point more than ten fists below the gallery.

פָּחוֹת מִכָּאן, לֶחָצֵר. — *less than that, to the courtyard.*

[I.e., if the rock or embankment is less than ten fists high, it belongs to both the courtyard and the gallery and the residents of both areas are prohibited from using it, as explained above.]

בַּמֶּה דְבָרִים אֲמוּרִים? בִּסְמוּכָה; — *To what do these words apply? To that which is near;*

[The ruling that an area within ten vertical fists of a gallery belongs to the gallery holds true only if it is also near the gallery horizontally.]

1. *Tosafos* (cited by *Ritva*) gives two reasons why the obvious alternative — that the mishnah refers just to the top of the embankment — is rejected by the *Gemara*. (a) Usually the thickness of the embankment is less than four fists, in which case that area should be judged as a מְקוֹם פְּטוּר, *exempt area*, and be permitted to both groups no matter what its height (see 7:2); (b) the embankment is a function of the pit and is automatically awarded the same status as its interior.

עֵירוּבִין עֲשָׂרָה טְפָחִים, לֶחָצֵר. וְאֵיזוֹ הִיא סְמוּכָה? כֹּל שֶׁאֵינָהּ רְחוֹקָה אַרְבָּעָה טְפָחִים. ח/ד

[ד] **הַנּוֹתֵן** אֶת עֵרוּבוֹ בְּבֵית שַׁעַר, אַכְסַדְרָה וּמִרְפֶּסֶת, אֵינוֹ עֵרוּב; וְהַדָּר שָׁם אֵינוֹ אוֹסֵר עָלָיו. בְּבֵית הַתֶּבֶן וּבְבֵית הַבָּקָר וּבְבֵית הָעֵצִים וּבְבֵית הָאוֹצָרוֹת, הֲרֵי זֶה עֵרוּב; וְהַדָּר שָׁם אוֹסֵר עָלָיו. רַבִּי יְהוּדָה אוֹמֵר: אִם יֵשׁ שָׁם תְּפִיסַת יָד שֶׁל בַּעַל הַבַּיִת, אֵינוֹ אוֹסֵר עָלָיו.

יד אברהם

אֲבָל בִּמְפֻלְגֶת, אֲפִלּוּ גָּבוֹהַּ עֲשָׂרָה טְפָחִים, לֶחָצֵר. — *but that which is at a distance, even if it is ten fists high, [belongs] to the courtyard.*

I.e., it is considered as belonging to the courtyard also (*Rav; Gem.* 84a). [Since it is at a distance from the gallery, access to it is not any easier from the gallery than from the courtyard. Consequently, both parties are prohibited to carry to and from it.]

וְאֵיזוֹ הִיא סְמוּכָה? כֹּל שֶׁאֵינָהּ רְחוֹקָה אַרְבָּעָה טְפָחִים. — *And what is [considered] near? Whatever is not four fists away.*

[Only if the area under discussion is within four horizontal fists of the gallery does it belong to the gallery (if it is within ten fists vertically).]

4.

[See previous mishnah.]

הַנּוֹתֵן אֶת עֵרוּבוֹ בְּבֵית שַׁעַר, — *If one places his eruv in a gatehouse,*

At the entrance to the courtyard there was often a small booth used by a watchman. The *eruvei chatzeiros* of this courtyard, which must be deposited in one of the houses of the courtyard in order to be valid, was deposited instead in this booth (*Rav*).

אַכְסַדְרָה — *a colonnade*

A structure consisting of a roof supported by columns with all the sides left open (*Rashi* 90b). *Tosafos* (94a) maintains that an אַכְסַדְרָה is closed on three sides and is open on only one side.

וּמַרְפֶּסֶת, — *or a gallery,*

אֵינוֹ עֵרוּב; — *the eruv is not valid* [lit. *it is not an eruv*];

An *eruvei chatzeiros* must be deposited in one of the dwellings of the courtyard, thus symbolizing the designation of that house as the common dwelling of all the residents of that courtyard.[1] A colonnade and gallery are not considered dwellings because they are not surrounded by walls, and a gatehouse, although it has sufficient walls, is not considered a dwelling because the residents of the courtyard are constantly passing through it on their way into and out of the courtyard (*R' Yehonasan; Meiri*).[2]

1. By the comparison made at the end of 6:8, a *shitufei mevo'os*, which is designed to symbolize the incorporation of many courtyards of an alley into one, may be placed in an open courtyard (*Gem.* 85b; *Orach Chaim* 386:1).

2. According to this interpretation, only a gatehouse through which the public passes is excluded; the gatehouse at the entrance to a private residence may have an *eruv* placed in it, as

even if it is ten fists high, [belongs] to the courtyard. And what is [considered] near? Whatever is not four fists away.

4. If one places his *eruv* in a gatehouse, a colonnade or a gallery, the *eruv* is not valid; and one who lives there does not restrict it. In a silo, barn, woodshed or storehouse, the *eruv* is valid; and one who lives there restricts it. R' Yehudah says: If the owner retains a holding there, he does not restrict him.

YAD AVRAHAM

וְהַדָּר שָׁם אֵינוֹ אוֹסֵר עָלָיו. — *and one who lives there does not restrict it* [i.e., the courtyard].

A person living in one of these structures who did not join in the *eruv* does not restrict the other residents of the courtyard from carrying into it. Only a person living in a proper dwelling in the courtyard restricts and these structures are not considered to be proper dwellings. Consequently, there is no need for him to join in the *eruv* at all (*Rav; Rashi*).[1]

בְּבֵית הַתֶּבֶן וּבְבֵית הַבָּקָר וּבְבֵית הָעֵצִים וּבְבֵית הָאוֹצָרוֹת, הֲרֵי זֶה עֵרוּב; — [If he placed the eruv] *in a silo* [used for straw], *barn, woodshed or storehouse, the* eruv *is valid* [lit. *indeed this is an* eruv];

These structures are considered fit for dwelling (*R' Yehonasan, Meiri*). Even if the construction of these structures is flimsy, e.g., they are made of twigs and reeds, they are considered dwellings (*ibid*).

וְהַדָּר שָׁם אוֹסֵר עָלָיו — *and one who lives there restricts it.*

If the owner of one of these structures permitted someone to live in them, that person restricts the other residents of the courtyard from carrying into the courtyard and he must therefore contribute to the *eruv* (*Rav; Rashi*).

However, in order to restrict, one must eat his meals at the location. A person who merely sleeps at a place does not restrict (*R' Yehonasan* from *Gem.* 73a; *Orach Chaim* 370:5).

Some versions of the mishnah omit the word עָלָיו here and in the ruling about a gatehouse, etc. (see *Shinuyei Nuschaos*). This seems to have been *Rav's* version as well (see below, s.v. אֵינוֹ אוֹסֵר).

רַבִּי יְהוּדָה אוֹמֵר: אִם יֶשׁ שָׁם תְּפִיסַת יָד שֶׁל בַּעַל הַבַּיִת, — *R' Yehudah says: If the owner retains* [lit. *has*] *a holding there,*

I.e., he retains the right to keep his belongings in the dwelling (*Rav; Rashi*) and he actually has belongings there (*Mishnah Berurah* 370:10) which can-

indicated by the *Gemara* (85b). However, *Rambam* (*Hil. Eruvin* 1:16) and *Tur* (*Orach Chaim* 366) do not draw this distinction (*Beis Yosef* 370; see *Be'ur Halachah* 366:3, s.v. לאפוקי).

1. Even those who permit an *eruv* to be placed in a private gatehouse agree that a person living in such a place does not restrict (*Gem.* 85b; see *Tos.* 75b) [because of the lack of privacy resulting from people passing through the house (*Magen Avraham* 370:2)]. However, *Rambam's* view (*Hil. Eruvin* 4:8) seems to be quite the reverse. As mentioned in the previous footnote he rules that an *eruv* may not be placed in a private gatehouse but intimates that a person living in a private gatehouse does restrict (*Maggid Mishneh*; cf. *Beis Yosef, Orach Chaim* 370).

[ה] **הַמַּנִּיחַ** בֵּיתוֹ וְהָלַךְ לִשְׁבֹּת בְּעִיר אַחֶרֶת,
אֶחָד נָכְרִי וְאֶחָד יִשְׂרָאֵל, הֲרֵי זֶה
אוֹסֵר — דִּבְרֵי רַבִּי מֵאִיר. רַבִּי יְהוּדָה אוֹמֵר: אֵינוֹ
אוֹסֵר. רַבִּי יוֹסֵי אוֹמֵר: נָכְרִי אוֹסֵר, יִשְׂרָאֵל אֵינוֹ
אוֹסֵר, שֶׁאֵין דֶּרֶךְ יִשְׂרָאֵל לָבֹא בַּשַּׁבָּת. רַבִּי שִׁמְעוֹן

יד אברהם

not be moved on the Sabbath because they are *muktzeh* or because they are too heavy (*Gem.* 86a; see *Tos. Yom Tov*).

אֵינוֹ אוֹסֵר עָלָיו. — *he does not restrict him.*

This section of the mishnah refers to any tenant (and not only to one who lives in a silo, barn, etc.) and states that a tenant does not restrict the landlord if the latter retains the right to hold his belongings in the tenant's domain (*R' Yehonasan; Meiri*). Since the landlord did not totally remove his presence from the residence, the tenant is considered as

though he were living with the landlord as a guest and consequently does not restrict, he does not necessitate an *eruv* (*Rashi*).

If, however, there are other people living in the courtyard, in which case an *eruv* must in any case be made, this tenant must also contribute and restricts as long as he did not. This is alluded to with the word *him* (he does not restrict 'him'), i.e., the tenant does not restrict the landlord — if they are the only two residents of the courtyard. This implies that he does restrict if there are other residents[1] (*Rav, R' Yehonasan; see Rama, Orach Chaim 370:2*).

The halachah is in accordance with R' Yehudah (*Rav; Rambam*).

5.

הַמַּנִּיחַ בֵּיתוֹ וְהָלַךְ לִשְׁבֹּת בְּעִיר אַחֶרֶת, — *One who left his house and went to spend the Sabbath in another town,*

[He left for another town without participating in the *eruvei chatzeiros*. The question now is whether an absentee resident restricts.]

אֶחָד נָכְרִי וְאֶחָד יִשְׂרָאֵל, הֲרֵי זֶה אוֹסֵר — דִּבְרֵי רַבִּי מֵאִיר. — *whether a gentile or a Jew, restricts* — [these are] *the words of R' Meir.*

In R' Meir's view, the residence of an

absent person is reckoned as a proper residence and his rights must also be merged by the *eruv*. If they are not, he restricts the other residents of the courtyard from carrying (*Rav; Rashi*). [A gentile also restricts. See above 6:1.]

The *Gemara* (62b) demonstrates that (according to R' Meir) a gentile restricts only when there is reason to assume that he will return on that Sabbath (e.g., he is in a nearby town), but a Jew restricts even where he cannot return (e.g., if the town to which he went is beyond the *techum*).[2]

1. Obviously *Rav's* version of the mishnah had the word עָלָיו only in this last segment. According to our versions which have it in each of the three segments of the mishnah no halachic insight can be gained from the use of the word עָלָיו here.

2. The reason for this distinction is as follows: In essence absentee residency is not to be reckoned as residence. However, an absent Jew restricts because of the Rabbinic safeguard (גְּזֵרָה) instituted out of concern that people will fail to distinguish between an absent resident and a present one, so that if an absent resident does not restrict they may be misled into ignoring the obligation to make an *eruv*. This applies, however, only to a Jew. A gentile's residence never restricts 'essentially' and his restricting status is itself due to a safeguard based

5. **O**ne who left his house and went to spend the Sabbath in another town, whether a gentile or a Jew, restricts — [these are] the words of R' Meir. R' Yehudah says: He does not restrict. R' Yose says: A gentile restricts, a Jew does not restrict, for it is unusual for a Jew to return on the Sabbath. R'

YAD AVRAHAM

Meiri and Maggid Mishneh (Hil. Eruvin 4:13) maintain that even according to R' Meir a Jewish absentee restricts only when he is still within one day's travel of his dwelling and it is thus at least physically possible — albeit halachically forbidden — for him to return. If he is so far away that it is physically impossible for him to return on that day, his residence is no longer considered a factor in this courtyard.

רַבִּי יְהוּדָה אוֹמֵר: אֵינוֹ אוֹסֵר. — R' Yehudah says: He does not restrict.

R' Yehudah maintains that the residence of an absent person is not reckoned a proper residence, i.e., that by his absence one nullifies his status as a resident of this courtyard with respect to eruv, and as a result he does not restrict (Rav; Rashi).

[As noted in the introduction to ch. 6, mere ownership of a house does not automatically confer restricting status; for this, actual dwelling is necessary.]

If the gentile has gone to another town, there is no reason to assume that he will return on the Sabbath, and even R' Meir will agree that the gentile does not restrict (see above, s.v. אֶחָד נָכְרִי). On the other hand, if we are aware of the gentile's intention to return on the Sabbath, then even R' Yehudah agrees that he restricts. They disagree only when the gentile's intentions are unknown (and he is near enough to return if he so desires). R' Meir holds that since he is able to return, he restricts. R' Yehudah maintains that since we do not know from certain that he wil return, we need not assume that he will, and so he does not restrict (Turei Zahav 371:1). Others understand that they disagree even when the gentile's intention to return are known. Only the gentile's actual presence

restricts; his intended presence does not (Chazon Ish, Orach Chaim 82:24, based on Rashi 62b).

רַבִּי יוֹסֵי אוֹמֵר: נָכְרִי אוֹסֵר, יִשְׂרָאֵל אֵינוֹ אוֹסֵר, — R' Yose says: A gentile restricts, a Jew does not restrict,

R' Yose concurs with R' Yehudah that the residence of an absent person is not reckoned a proper residence and it therefore cannot restrict. However, when the absentee is a gentile, one must take into consideration the likelihood that he will return to his home on the Sabbath, and thereby restrict (Rav; Rashi).

שֶׁאֵין דֶּרֶךְ יִשְׂרָאֵל לָבֹא בַּשַּׁבָּת. — for it is unusual for a Jew to return [lit. come] on the Sabbath.

Since it is assumed that the Jew will abide by his decision to celebrate the Sabbath in the next town, his residence is classified as an ownerless house in regard to the eruv law and he does not restrict. By contrast, a gentile's decision to this effect is not as binding upon him and he is not considered to have entirely ruled out the possibility of returning home on the Sabbath. Accordingly, it is classified as a proper residence and as a consequence the gentile restricts (from Rashi 47a).

Meiri assumes that the term 'another town' in the mishnah refers to a town outside the techum. Thus, the residence of a Jew, who is prohibited by the halachah to return to his town, is considered ownerless, and does not restrict. By contrast, a gentile, for whom the restriction of techum does not exist, restricts even when he is in another town.

on the concern that his Jewish neighbors will be influenced by his lifestyle. Therefore, the Sages felt it would be excessive to place one safeguard upon the other (גְּזֵירָה לִגְזֵירָה) by declaring that a gentile restricts even in his absence.

עֵירוּבִין אוֹמֵר: אֲפִלּוּ הִנִּיחַ בֵּיתוֹ וְהָלַךְ לִשְׁבּוֹת אֵצֶל בִּתּוֹ ח/ו
בְּאוֹתָהּ הָעִיר אֵינוֹ אוֹסֵר, שֶׁכְּבָר הִסִּיעַ מִלִּבּוֹ.

[ו] **בּוֹר** שֶׁבֵּין שְׁתֵּי חֲצֵרוֹת, אֵין מְמַלְּאִין מִמֶּנּוּ
בַּשַּׁבָּת, אֶלָּא אִם כֵּן עָשׂוּ לוֹ מְחִצָּה
גָּבוֹהַּ עֲשָׂרָה טְפָחִים, בֵּין מִלְמַעְלָה, בֵּין מִלְמַטָּה,
בֵּין מִתּוֹךְ אוֹגְנוֹ. רַבָּן שִׁמְעוֹן בֶּן גַּמְלִיאֵל אוֹמֵר:

יד אברהם

רַבִּי שִׁמְעוֹן אוֹמֵר: אֲפִלּוּ הִנִּיחַ בֵּיתוֹ וְהָלַךְ
לִשְׁבּוֹת אֵצֶל בִּתּוֹ בְּאוֹתָהּ הָעִיר אֵינוֹ אוֹסֵר,
שֶׁכְּבָר הִסִּיעַ מִלִּבּוֹ. — R' Shimon says:
Even one who left his house and went to
spend the Sabbath at his daughter's
[house] in the same town does not
restrict, for he has already dismissed
[any thought of returning] from his
mind [lit. heart].

[R' Shimon is the most lenient. He
concurs with R' Yehudah and R' Yose
that the residence of an absent person is
not reckoned a proper residence and
does not restrict, and he extends this
principle even to where it is permissible
for the resident to return on the
Sabbath. R' Shimon argues that even in
such an instance he does not restrict
where it is improbable that he will
return.]

The Gemara (86a) notes that R' Shimon's
ruling is specific and applies only to one who
went to his (married) daughter's house. If he

went to his married son's house (and it is
within the techum), he does not entirely
dismiss from his mind the possibility of
returning home, since he is apprehensive that
an altercation with his daughter-in-law may
force him to leave. (A daughter, however,
would not allow her father to leave on the
Sabbath, even under such circumstances; R'
Chananel.)[1]

The halachah is in accord with R'
Shimon (Rav from Gem. 86a). R'
Shimon does not rule in regard to an
absentee gentile and the halachah in
regard to this is the subject of a
disagreement among the Poskim. Rambam (Comm. and Hil. Eruvin 4:13) rules
in accordance with R' Yose that as long
as it is possible for him to return he
restricts. Whereas Rosh and Rashba
(Avodas HaKodesh) rule with R'
Yehudah that he does not restrict.
Shulchan Aruch (371:1) cites both
views and Rama (there) accepts the
latter, more lenient ruling.

6.

בּוֹר שֶׁבֵּין שְׁתֵּי חֲצֵרוֹת, — If a cistern is
between two courtyards,

[These two courtyards adjoin and are
properly separated by a partition. Each
courtyard has its own eruv but the two
do not have a joint eruv. Consequently,
the residents of one courtyard cannot
carry into the other courtyard. Between
the two courtyards is a cistern from
which both draw their water.]

In the case under discussion, the wall
separating the courtyards passes directly over the cistern (R' Yehonasan).
[Nevertheless, the wall is not considered
as a partition separating the two sides of
the cistern. See commentary at end of
this mishnah.]

אֵין מְמַלְּאִין מִמֶּנּוּ בַּשַּׁבָּת, — we may not
draw [water] from it on the Sabbath,

1. If he declared explicitly his intention not to return he does not restrict in any case (Rashba,
Avodas HaKodesh; cf. Rambam, Hil. Eruvin 4:13 with Maggid Mishneh; Orach Chaim 371:1
with Be'ur Halachah).

Shimon says: Even one who left his house and went to spend the Sabbath at his daughter's [house] in the same town does not restrict, for he has already dismissed [any thought of returning] from his mind.

6. If a cistern is between two courtyards, we may not draw [water] from it on the Sabbath, unless they made a partition for it ten fists high, whether above or below, or within its walls. Rabban Shimon

YAD AVRAHAM

Drawing water from such a cistern (even from one's own half of the cistern) is viewed as drawing water from the side of the neighboring courtyard (*Rav; Rashi*). [Water drawn from a cistern is governed by the principle: עֲרִיבֵי מַיָא, *the waters are mixed*, i.e., the water drawn cannot be said to be fixed in either courtyard. Consequently, the cistern is viewed as a separate area to which both courtyards have equal access, and it is prohibited to both courtyards until an acceptable partition is set up (cf. *Ritva; Meiri; Chazon Ish* 103:6).]

This does not mean that we are apprehensive that water will be removed from one courtyard to the other. The remedy of the mishnah in no way prevents this (*Tos.* 86a). [It means that the waters cannot be distinguished as belonging to one or the other courtyard.]

According to R' Chananel the mishnah is apprehensive that people from one courtyard will unwittingly allow their bucket to float to the side of the cistern which is in the other courtyard. This is prohibited because the two courtyards do not have a joint *eruv*. A partition placed in the water will remove this concern by preventing the water bucket from floating to the other side.

אֶלָּא אִם כֵּן עָשׂוּ לוֹ מְחִצָּה — *unless they made a partition for it*

This partition clearly defines the two sections of the cistern, thus making it evident that each courtyard is drawing from its own part of the cistern (*Tos.* 86a).

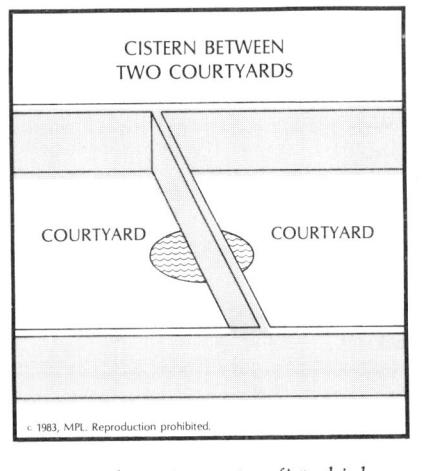

CISTERN BETWEEN TWO COURTYARDS

COURTYARD   COURTYARD

© 1983, MPL. Reproduction prohibited.

גָּבוֹהַּ עֲשָׂרָה טְפָחִים, — *ten fists high,*

[The partition need not extend the entire depth of the cistern; ten fists is sufficient.]

בֵּין מִלְמַעְלָה, בֵּין מִלְמַטָּה, — *whether above* [the water level] *or below* [it],

The partition may be placed either just above the surface of the water or just below. If it is situated below the water level, it must reach one fist above the water's surface. (*Rav* from *Gem.* 86a).

בֵּין מִתּוֹךְ אוֹגְנוֹ. — *or* [anywhere] *within its walls.*

The water level generally does not reach the rim of the cistern, often being considerably below it. The partition may be placed anywhere within these walls of the cistern, even at a distance

עֵירוּבִין בֵּית שַׁמַּאי אוֹמְרִים מִלְמַטָּה; וּבֵית הִלֵּל אוֹמְרִים
ח/ז מִלְמַעְלָה. אָמַר רַבִּי יְהוּדָה: לֹא תְהֵא מְחִצָּה
גְדוֹלָה מִן הַכֹּתֶל שֶׁבֵּינֵיהֶם.

[ז] **אַמַּת** הַמַּיִם שֶׁהִיא עוֹבֶרֶת בֶּחָצֵר, אֵין
מְמַלְאִין הֵימֶנָּה בַּשַּׁבָּת, אֶלָּא אִם כֵּן
עָשׂוּ לָהּ מְחִצָּה גָבוֹהַּ עֲשָׂרָה טְפָחִים בַּכְּנִיסָה
וּבַיְצִיאָה.

יד אברהם

above the surface of the water, as long as it is below the rim of the cistern (Rav; Rashi).

רַבָּן שִׁמְעוֹן בֶּן גַּמְלִיאֵל אוֹמֵר: — *Rabban Shimon ben Gamliel says:*

[Rabban Shimon ben Gamliel states that the ruling expressed in anonymous terms by the first *Tanna* is disputed by Beis Shammai (i.e., the first *Tanna's* ruling is that of Beis Hillel), and that some aspects of it are not accepted even by Beis Hillel (see *Ritva*).]

בֵּית שַׁמַּאי אוֹמְרִים מִלְמַטָּה; — *Beis Shammai say* [the partition must be placed] *below* [the water level];

Rabban Shimon ben Gamliel maintains that Beis Shammai permit only a partition which is primarily within the water, i.e., at least nine fists under water and one fist emerging from the water. They disqualify one which is placed above the water even if part of it extends below the water level (Gem. 86a as explained by Tos. there).

According to *Rashi*, however, Beis Shammai require the partition to extend from one fist above the water level to the floor of the cistern, thus effectively dividing the cistern in two.

וּבֵית הִלֵּל אוֹמְרִים מִלְמַעְלָה — *but Beis Hillel say* [even] *above* [it].

Beis Hillel state that the partition need not be within the water (although they agree with Beis Shammai that it is valid if it is) but may be placed even above the water level (*Rashi* and others). However, at least one fist of the

partition must extend below the water level (Gem.).

As explained above, Beis Hillel's view as presented by Rabban Shimon ben Gamliel is not totally identical with that of the first *Tanna*. They disagree on the matter of a partition that is above the water and does not extend into it at all. This is permitted according to the first *Tanna* but not according to Beis Shammai (*Rashba; Ritva* and *Meiri*).

The commentary until this point has followed the interpretation of the *Amora* R' Yehudah, the interpretation adopted by most of the commentators, as well as *Shulchan Aruch* (Orach Chaim 366:1). The *Gemara* (86a), however, also cites the interpretation of R' Huna who holds that the terms *above* and *below* refer to the cistern rather than the water. In this view, Beis Shammai requires that the partition be placed *below* [in the lower part of the cistern], i.e., at the surface of the water but not in it, while Beis Hillel say that it may be placed even *above*, i.e., at the rim of the cistern and extending ten fists down — even if it does not reach the surface of the water. [*Rashi* points out that R' Huna's understanding of the *below* coincides with R' Yehudah's interpretation of *above*.] According to this latter view, the opinion of Beis Hillel is identical with that of the *Tanna kamma*.

The *Poskim* (Rif; Rambam Hil. Eruvin 3:21; Orach Chaim 376:1) accept R' Yehudah's view and rule that a partition above the water which does not extend one fist into the water does not permit the drawing of water.

אָמַר רַבִּי יְהוּדָה: לֹא תְהֵא מְחִצָּה גְדוֹלָה מִן הַכֹּתֶל שֶׁבֵּינֵיהֶם. — *R' Yehudah said: A*

8
7

ben Gamliel says: Beis Shammai say below; but Beis Hillel say above. R' Yehudah said: A partition should not be more effective than the wall that is between them.

7. **I**f a canal passes through a courtyard, we may not draw [water] from it on the Sabbath, unless they made it a partition ten fists high at the inlet and at the outlet.

partition should not be more effective than the wall that is [already] *between them.*

R' Yehudah (the *Tanna*) argues that no partition at all is necessary. The wall separating the courtyard which passes over the rim of the cistern is itself sufficient to separate the water into its two parts *(Rav; Rashi)* even though it was not expressly erected to permit the drawing of water *(Meiri)*. The *Tanna kamma* and Rabban Shimon ben Gamliel, however, require that the partition be inside the cistern and that it be made expressly to serve as a separation for the water *(Mishnah Berurah 376:3)*.

R' Yehudah holds that a hanging partition, i.e., one not reaching the ground, is valid to serve as a halachic divider (מְחִצָּה תְּלוּיָה שְׁמָהּ מְחִצָּה). Thus, even that segment of the wall separating the two courtyards which passes over the rim of the cistern is considered a bona fide partition so that any additional partition would be superfluous *(Gem. 86b)*. The first *Tanna* disagrees because he holds that a hanging partition is not, as a rule, valid. However, the Sages granted a special dispensation by validating hanging partitions for water holes — but restricted this dispensation to partitions situated below the rim of the cistern [which make the separation obvious *(Rashi)*], in order to allow the drawing of water on the Sabbath, subject to the various restrictions outlined. According to Rabban Shimon ben Gamliel, the dispensation is restricted even further to partitions which physically separate the water in some way *(Tos. 86b)*.

7.

אַמַּת הַמַּיִם שֶׁהִיא עוֹבֶרֶת בֶּחָצֵר, אֵין מְמַלְּאִין הֵימֶנָּה בַּשַׁבָּת, — *If a canal passes through a courtyard, we may not draw [water] from it on the Sabbath,*

The canal is considered a *karmelis* (see General Introduction) even when it is situated in a private domain *(Rav; Rashi)*.

Ravad (Hil. Shabbos 15:11) explains that because the canal is ten fists deep and four fists wide — the measurements of a domain — it is not considered a part of the courtyard but must be judged independently. Since it is

completely open at two ends, it is considered to be completely breached to an area prohibited to it (נִפְרְצָה בִּמְלוֹאָהּ לְמָקוֹם הָאָסוּר לָהּ; see also *Tosafos* cited by *Ritva* to 12b). *Rashba (12b)* and R' Yehonasan maintain that because the water in the canal is part of a moving stream of water which does not remain within the confines of the courtyard, it is not considered as being part of the courtyard which it occupies presently and is consequently a *karmelis*.[1]

אֶלָּא אִם כֵּן עָשׂוּ לָהּ מְחִצָּה גָּבוֹהַּ עֲשָׂרָה טְפָחִים בַּכְּנִיסָה וּבַיְצִיאָה. — *unless they*

1. It would seem that on a Biblical level the canal is considered a private domain since it is within a private domain; its classification as a *karmelis* is only Rabbinic. Accordingly, one who threw from a public domain into the canal would be liable. A similar case of a private domain which is Rabbinically classified as a *karmelis* is that of an area not enclosed for purposes of daily living (see *Gem. 67b*; cf. *Chazon Ish 103:3*; see comm. to 2:3, and Gem. Intro.).

רַבִּי יְהוּדָה אוֹמֵר: כֹּתֶל שֶׁעַל גַּבָּה תִּדּוֹן מִשּׁוּם מְחִצָּה. אָמַר רַבִּי יְהוּדָה: "מַעֲשֶׂה בְּאַמָּה שֶׁל אָבֵל שֶׁהָיוּ מְמַלְּאִין מִמֶּנָּה עַל פִּי זְקֵנִים בַּשַׁבָּת." אָמְרוּ לוֹ: "מִפְּנֵי שֶׁלֹּא הָיָה בָהּ כַּשִּׁעוּר."

[ח] **גְּזֻזְטְרָא** שֶׁהִיא לְמַעְלָה מִן הַמַּיִם, אֵין מְמַלְּאִין הֵימֶנָּה בַּשַׁבָּת, אֶלָּא אִם כֵּן עָשׂוּ לָהּ מְחִצָּה גְּבוֹהַּ עֲשָׂרָה טְפָחִים, בֵּין

יד אברהם

made it a partition ten fists high at [both] the inlet and at the outlet.

The partition must be placed within the banks of the canal running across its width, so that the canal is clearly enclosed (Rav; Rashi).

Although a hanging partition suffices for the purpose of drawing water it must nevertheless be made in a manner which makes it obvious that its purpose is to enclose the canal. Therefore the courtyard wall passing over the canal is not effective (according to the first Tanna) and a special partition must be erected. Because the use of a hanging partition is a special dispensation granted by the Sages, its validity is made subject to special restrictions, namely that it clearly enclose the waterway by being within its banks (Rashi).

According to Rabban Shimon ben Gamliel in the previous mishnah (s.v. וּבֵית הִלֵּל אוֹמְרִים), Beis Hillel require that at least one fist's length of the partition extend below the water surface. This condition is included by Rambam (Hil. Shabbos 15:11, 13) and Shulchan Aruch (Orach Chaim 356:1) in their transcriptions of this halachah.

רַבִּי יְהוּדָה אוֹמֵר: כֹּתֶל שֶׁעַל גַּבָּה תִּדּוֹן מִשּׁוּם מְחִצָּה. — R' Yehudah says: The wall [which passes] over it is considered a partition.

[R' Yehudah maintains that a special partition is not necessary. The water in the courtyard is already separated from the water outside it by the wall suspended over the canal's banks. R' Yehudah is consistent with his view (see previous mishnah) that a hanging partition is generally valid and no special dispensation is needed for water.]

אָמַר רַבִּי יְהוּדָה: "מַעֲשֶׂה בְּאַמָּה שֶׁל אָבֵל — Said R' Yehudah: 'It happened that [there was] a canal in Avel

Avel is a town mentioned in II Samuel 20:14ff (Meleches Shlomo).

The brook supplying water to the area passed through the courtyards (Rav; Rashi).

שֶׁהָיוּ מְמַלְּאִין מִמֶּנָּה עַל פִּי זְקֵנִים בַּשַׁבָּת." — from which they drew [water] on the Sabbath upon the ruling of the Sages.'

R' Yehudah cites support for his position that the courtyard wall suffices from an actual decision of the Sages [of a previous generation] in which they relied on the courtyard wall to permit water to be drawn from a canal, but did not require a special partition (Rav; Rashi).

אָמְרוּ לוֹ: "מִפְּנֵי שֶׁלֹּא הָיָה בָהּ כַּשִּׁעוּר." — They answered him: '[It was permitted there] because it did not have the minimum dimensions.'

The Sages do not dispute the veracity of R' Yehudah's report. However, they maintain that the ruling given for the town of Avel was not based on the position that a hanging partition is generally considered a valid partition, but rather on circumstances peculiar to that situation. The canal in Avel did not possess the minimum dimensions (ten

R' Yehudah says: The wall over it is considered a partition. Said R' Yehudah: 'It happened that [there was] a canal in Avel from which they drew [water] on the Sabbath upon the ruling of the Sages.'

They answered him: 'Because it did not have the minimum dimensions.'

8. If a balcony is above the water, we may not draw [water] from it on the Sabbath, unless they made a partition ten fists high for it, either from above or

YAD AVRAHAM

fists deep, four fists wide) necessary to render an area within the bounds of a private domain a *karmelis* and for this reason no special partition was needed. Accordingly it was not subject to the strictures of a *karmelis*. However, a canal which does possess these minimum dimensions does require a special partition and the courtyard wall is not sufficient *(Rav; Rashi).*

8.

גְּזוּזְטְרָא שֶׁהִיא לְמַעְלָה מִן הַמַּיִם, — *If a balcony is above the water,*

A balcony protrudes from one of the walls of a house and extends over a body of water *(Rav)*. This balcony has a hole in its floor so that a bucket may be lowered through it to the water below *(Rambam, Comm., Hil. Shabbos 15:15).*

אֵין מְמַלְּאִין הֵימֶנָּה בַּשַּׁבָּת, — *we may not draw [water] from it on the Sabbath,*

A person standing by the window of the house may not lower a bucket through the hole in the balcony and draw water from a body of water below to the house, for that body has the status of a *karmelis (Shabbos 11:4, see Yad Avraham in ArtScroll edition)* so that one may not transfer objects (water) from it to the house which is a private domain (based on the simple reading of the mishnah; cf. *Tos. 86b, Rosh 9:2, Levush 355:1;* see also *Pri Megadim, Mishbetzos 355:1).*

Later authorities and commentaries *(Magen Avraham 355:1, Beis Meir* there, *Tiferes Yisrael)* understand that even if the person stands on the balcony (rather than in the house) while raising the bucket, this is prohibited because the balcony is itself a private domain. [If it were not, there would be no prohibition to raise water up to it from the river because this would constitute transferring from a *karmelis* to a *karmelis* which is permissible as long as one does not move four cubits horizontally *(Magen Avraham)*. It would still, however, be prohibited to take the water into the house (a private domain) from the balcony *(Beis Meir).*] The balcony is a private domain because it is within three fists of the window and thus qualifies as a *nook of the private domain* (חוֹרֵי רְשׁוּת הַיָּחִיד) which has all the laws of a private domain *(Tos. 86b, 89a; Rosh 89a).*

אֶלָּא אִם כֵּן עָשׂוּ לָהּ מְחִצָּה גָבוֹהַּ עֲשָׂרָה טְפָחִים, — *unless they made a partition ten fists high for it,*

If a ten fist high partition surrounds the balcony or the hole through which the water is drawn, then the water directly below the surrounded area is regarded as a private domain with regard to drawing water, as explained further *(Rav, Rashi).*

בֵּין מִלְמַעְלָה — *either from above*

The partition may start from the floor of the balcony or the rim of the hole and extend upward for ten fists *(Rav; Rashi).*

עֵירוּבִין מִלְמַעְלָה בֵּין מִלְמַטָּה.
ח/ח וְכֵן שְׁתֵּי גְּזֻזְטְרָאוֹת זוֹ לְמַעְלָה מִזּוֹ, עָשׂוּ לָעֶלְיוֹנָה וְלֹא עָשׂוּ לַתַּחְתּוֹנָה, שְׁתֵּיהֶן אֲסוּרוֹת עַד שֶׁיְּעָרְבוּ.

יד אברהם

בֵּין מִלְמַטָּה. — *or from below.*

Alternatively, the partition may start at the underside of the balcony and extend ten fists down (towards the water).

Rambam (*Comm., Hil. Shabbos* 15:15) interprets the term *above* as referring to a partition extending downward from the underside of the balcony while the term *below* is understood as referring to a partition erected in the water (as in Mishnah 6). *Rashba* and *Ritva* accept this latter view but *Shulchan Aruch* (*Orach Chaim* 355:1) accepts *Rashi's* opinion.

Whether the partition extends upward or downward the halachic

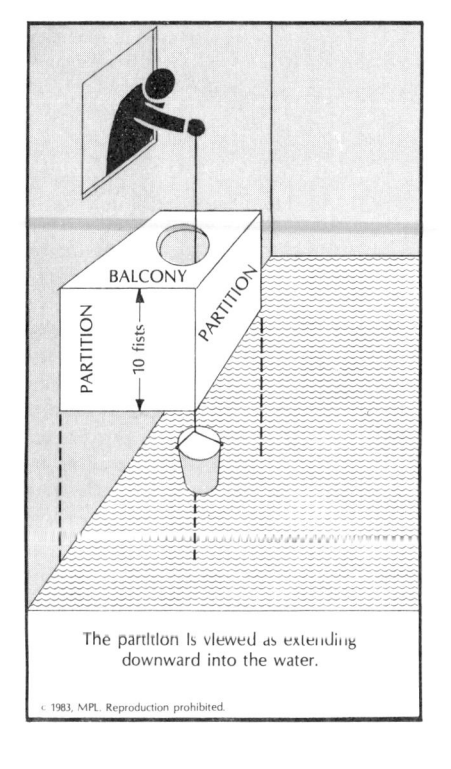

BALCONY

PARTITION

10 fists

PARTITION

The partition is viewed as extending downward into the water.

principle used is גּוּד אַחִית מְחִצָּתָא, *the partition is viewed as extending downward from its edge,* which allows us to view the valid wall which extends ten fists vertically as extending indefinitely below the actual physical space it occupies. Thus we can consider the area of the water below the balcony as surrounded by (halachic) partitions attached to the balcony (*Rav; Rashi*).

Rashi (87b) states that the partition may be placed either around the entire balcony or just around the rim of the hole. *Tosafos* (87b, s.v. בֵּין; see *Ritva*), however, implies that the partition must be erected around the hole where it is evident that its purpose is to permit the drawing of water. A partition around the entire balcony would be in the category of a courtyard wall which passes over a cistern (mish. 6) or canal (mish. 7), which is not valid according to the Sages. *Rashba* and *Ritva* concur with this and indicate that even *Rashi* subscribes to it (their version of *Rashi* evidently differed from ours). However, *Shulchan Aruch* (*Orach Chaim* 355:1) accepts *Rashi's* opinion and validates a partition surrounding the entire balcony (see *Geon Yaakov*).

וְכֵן שְׁתֵּי גְּזֻזְטְרָאוֹת זוֹ לְמַעְלָה מִזּוֹ, — *Similarly, two balconies* [situated] *one above the other,*

[The similarity of this case to the previous one is that it, too, deals with balconies jutting out above the water, although the problem involved is actually a different one. *Rashi* (84b) deletes the word וְכֵן, *similarly,* from the mishnah's text.]

The phrase *one above the other* does not necessarily mean that they are one directly above the other (with their holes aligned). Rather, the phrase means that one is at a higher point on the wall than the other — either overlapping or completely separate but within four

8 from below.

8 Similarly, two balconies one above the other, if they made [a partition] for the upper one, but did not make [one] for the lower one, both are prohibited unless they make an *eruv*.

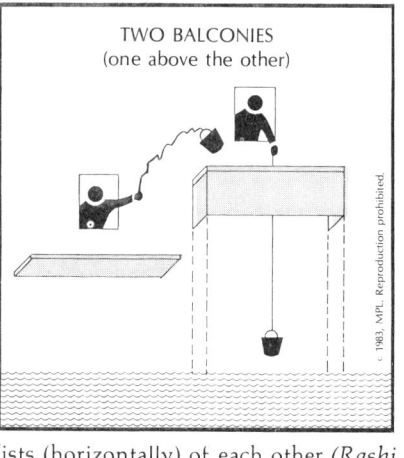

TWO BALCONIES
(one above the other)

© 1983, MPL. Reproduction prohibited.

fists (horizontally) of each other *(Rashi* based on *Gem.* 88a).

[If there were no partition at all, neither balcony would be allowed to draw water, as in the previous case.]

עָשׂוּ לָעֶלְיוֹנָה וְלֹא עָשׂוּ לַתַּחְתּוֹנָה, — *if they* [i.e., the residents of both balconies] *made [a partition] for the upper one, but did not make [one] for the lower one,*

The upper balcony made a partition, so that it should be able to draw water. However, the people of the lower balcony also draw water through the hole of the upper balcony to their balcony. Although this would not make them residents of the upper balcony, the *Gemara* (88a) explains that the mishnah speaks of a case where the people of the lower balcony contributed toward the cost of the partition so that they have the right of access to the drawing hole of

the upper balcony, thus creating a halachic problem in regard to *eruvei chatzeiros (Rav).*

The *Gemara* (88a) also adds that the two balconies have less than four fists (see *Rashi* there) of horizontal distance between them. If they are separated by four fists or more the people of the lower balcony cannot restrict those of the upper balcony.[1]

If the people of the lower balcony did not participate in the making of the upper balcony's partition they cannot restrict the upper balcony in any case. The *Gemara* (88a) derives this ruling from the principle that usage of an area in regard to restricting must be based on a legal right. Nonetheless, if the people of the lower balcony made their own partition they do not restrict in spite of their legal right to use the upper balcony. The erection of a partition on the lower balcony demonstrates their desire to refrain from using the upper balcony on the Sabbath.

שְׁתֵּיהֶן אֲסוּרוֹת עַד שֶׁיְעָרְבוּ. — *both are prohibited* [to draw water] *unless they make a* [joint] eruv.

The right to draw water (because of their participation in the partition) makes the people of the lower balcony bona fide users and 'residents' of the upper balcony, and necessitates an *eruv* between them and the people of the upper balcony. In the absence of such an *eruv*, both groups are prohibited from using the upper hole. The hole in the lower balcony may not be used, even if an *eruv* is made, because drawing water through it constitutes carrying from a *karmelis* (the sea) to a private domain *(Rashi).*

---

1. The above is based on the understanding of *Rashi* and most of the commentators. *Rav's* comments here are based on the view of *Rambam (Comm.* and *Hil. Eruvin* 4:24; see *Maggid Mishneh* and *Kessef Mishneh* there). We have not presented this view here because it is rejected as halachah (see *Orach Chaim* 355:5) and its complexity precludes its inclusion.

חָצֵר [ט] שֶׁהִיא פְּחוּתָה מֵאַרְבַּע אַמּוֹת, אֵין שׁוֹפְכִין בְּתוֹכָהּ מַיִם בַּשַּׁבָּת, אֶלָּא אִם כֵּן עָשׂוּ לָהּ עוּקָה מַחֲזֶקֶת סָאתַיִם, מִן הַנֶּקֶב וּלְמַטָּה, בֵּין מִבַּחוּץ בֵּין מִבִּפְנִים. אֶלָּא שֶׁמִּבַּחוּץ צָרִיךְ לִקְמוֹר, מִבִּפְנִים אֵין צָרִיךְ לִקְמוֹר.

יד אברהם

9.

חָצֵר שֶׁהִיא פְּחוּתָה מֵאַרְבַּע אַמּוֹת, — *If a courtyard is less than four cubits*

I.e., four cubits by four cubits (*Rashi*) or any other dimensions adding up to a minimum of sixteen square cubits (*Tos. Yom Tov* from *Gem.* 88b).

אֵין שׁוֹפְכִין בְּתוֹכָהּ מַיִם בַּשַּׁבָּת, — *we may not pour water into it on the Sabbath,*

In Mishnaic times it was customary to pour dirty water into the courtyard and from there it would flow into the street. Since in doing so one transfers the water from a private domain [the enclosed courtyard] to a public domain [the street], it is prohibited to pour the water into the courtyard unless one can reasonably expect the water to be absorbed by the ground of the courtyard.

The *Gemara* (88a,b) explains that a typical household used to pour two *se'ah* of water, and that this amount of water can be readily absorbed by an area equivalent to four by four cubits without making it muddy.

Thus, it can be assumed that a person pouring this amount of water into a courtyard of this size does not intend that the water pour over into the public domain. If, however, the area of the courtyard is less than sixteen square cubits, the person objects to the water remaining in the courtyard since it would make the ground muddy, and he intends that the water flow into the public domain. As a result, pouring the water into the courtyard is prohibited (*Rashi's* explanation of R' Zeira's view in *Gem.* 88a,b).

The fact that a sixteen square cubit area can absorb this amount of water does not mean that it will. If the ground of the courtyard is even slightly inclined towards the street it is clear that some of the water will flow out to the street before it can be absorbed. Yet the mishnah's permission is based entirely on the dimensions of the courtyard and therefore extends even to this case. Similarly, the dimensions are based on one person's water although the same dimensions are valid regardless of how many people live in the courtyard (*Gem.* 88b-89a). The fact that one does not intend the water to flow into the public domain is not in itself sufficient to remove the prohibition since all opinions agree that where an unintentional act must inevitably result in the violation of a *melachah* (פְּסִיק רֵישֵׁיהּ) it is forbidden (*Shabbos* 133a; see ArtScroll *Shabbos,* General Introduction).

It is obvious, therefore, that when one pours water in a private domain and that water flows automatically into the public domain one has not transgressed the Biblical prohibition against transferring from a private domain to a public domain (*Rashi* 88a,b). It seems that the natural movement of objects on the ground resulting from gravity is not legally considered the direct act of the person who set that force in motion and it is therefore not Biblically prohibited. The Sages, though, did prohibit one from pouring water in a private domain with the intent that it flow into a public domain out of concern that if this were allowed people might mistakenly conclude that even throwing the water directly into the street is permissible. Therefore pouring into the courtyard when it is obvious that one wants the water to flow to the street is prohibited (cf. R' Yosef Engel's *Gilyonei HaShas, Shabbos* 101b).

Chazon Ish (Orach Chaim 105:8) reasons that where one pours the water so close to the

9. If a courtyard is less than four cubits we may not pour water into it on the Sabbath, unless they made it a pit which can hold two *se'ah*, below the opening, whether on the outside or on the inside. Except that on the outside he must cover [it, whereas] on the inside he need not cover [it].

YAD AVRAHAM

public domain that the force of the pouring itself is sufficient to propel the water from the private to the public domain, a Biblical prohibition is violated and the leniencies set forth here (i.e., four cubits, a pit) do not apply.

אֶלָּא אִם כֵּן עָשׂוּ לָהּ עוּקָה מַחֲזֶקֶת סָאתַיִם, — *unless they made it a pit which can hold two* se'ah,

As explained earlier, two *se'ah* is the amount customarily poured out every day. Thus if the capacity of the pit is two *se'ah* it can hold the entire volume of water usually poured out on the Sabbath (*Rav; Rashi*).

If the required pit was made, water may be poured into it even if the pit is full and even if the volume of water exceeds two *se'ah*. Because the prohibition against pouring water in a courtyard of this size is only Rabbinic, the Sages were lenient in not placing any restrictions on spilling water once a pit was made (*Meiri; Mishnah Berurah 357:8*; c.f. *R' Yehonasan*).

מִן הַנֶּקֶב וּלְמַטָּה, — *below the opening,*

I.e., that it must be able to hold two *se'ah* without the water level reaching the opening of the pit so that none of the two *se'ah* flows out (*Rav, Rashi*).

בֵּין מִבַּחוּץ בֵּין מִבִּפְנִים. — *whether on the outside or on the inside.*

The pit may be dug either within the confines of the courtyard or outside it in the area of the public domain abutting the courtyard (*Rashi*).

[I.e., the pit may be situated in the public domain but it must be so positioned that the water can flow directly from the courtyard into it without passing through any other part of the public domain.]

אֶלָּא שֶׁמִּבַּחוּץ צָרִיךְ לִקְמוֹר, — *Except that on the outside he must cover [it],*

The pit must be covered so that it is marked off as an area separate from the public domain in which it is situated (*Rav; Rambam*). If the pit were not covered, people who saw it full of water next to the courtyard would suspect that the occupant of the courtyard had carried the water out of the courtyard into the public domain and poured it directly into the pit (*Beis Yosef, Orach Chaim 357; Tos. Yom Tov;* cf. *Rashbam* cited by *Ritva*).

Beis Meir explains that according to the dimensions given by *Rambam (Hil. Shabbos 15:16)* for the pit it is essentially an *exempt area* so that only the problem of suspicion remains.

Rashi explains that the covering is necessary so that the pit should be an exempt area.[1]

Rama (Darkei Moshe to *Orach Chaim 357)* suggests that the need for a covering is not related to the laws of *Shabbos,* but to the civic obligation to safeguard against people stumbling into the pit.

מִבִּפְנִים אֵין צָרִיךְ לִקְמוֹר. — *[whereas] on the inside he need not cover [it].*

[Since the pit is in the private domain.]

---

1. *Beis Meir (Orach Chaim 357;* see *Mishnah Berurah 357:7)* explains that although the pit may essentially be an *exempt area* (see above) it may, with the passage of time, become part of the public domain [i.e., debris from the public domain may accumulate in it and lessen its depth to less than three fists]. The cover over the pit will assure that it retains its exempt area status (cf. *Ritva).*

רַבִּי אֱלִיעֶזֶר [יז] בֶּן יַעֲקֹב אוֹמֵר: בִּיב
שֶׁהוּא קָמוּר אַרְבַּע
אַמּוֹת בִּרְשׁוּת הָרַבִּים, שׁוֹפְכִין לְתוֹכוֹ מַיִם בַּשַּׁבָּת.
וַחֲכָמִים אוֹמְרִים: אֲפִלּוּ גַּג אוֹ חָצֵר מֵאָה אַמָּה,
לֹא יִשְׁפֹּךְ עַל פִּי הַבִּיב; אֲבָל שׁוֹפֵךְ מִגַּג לְגַג,

יד אברהם

10.

רַבִּי אֱלִיעֶזֶר בֶּן יַעֲקֹב אוֹמֵר: בִּיב שֶׁהוּא קָמוּר
אַרְבַּע אַמּוֹת בִּרְשׁוּת הָרַבִּים, — R' Eliezer
ben Yaakov says: If a [drainage] conduit
is covered for four cubits in the public
domain,

If a conduit (or gutter) used to drain
water from the courtyard into the public
domain is covered for the first four
cubits of its length after it emerges into
the public domain ... (Rav; Rashi).
[Because of the covering, the conduit is
not considered a part of the public
domain.][1]

שׁוֹפְכִין לְתוֹכוֹ מַיִם בַּשַּׁבָּת. — we may pour
water into it on the Sabbath.

We may pour water into the part of
the conduit which is in the courtyard.
Because the conduit is four cubits long
(and is earthen) the water can be
absorbed by it before emptying into the
public domain (Rav; Rashi).
[Accordingly, the conduit must not only
be four cubits long but also four cubits
wide so that its area is sufficient to
absorb the usual daily two se'ah volume
of water as stated in the previous
mishnah (Tos. 88a).]

As in the previous mishnah, one may pour
water into the conduit even when the water
will not actually be absorbed (e.g., the
conduit is already full). Because water
overflowing from the conduit (which has the
status of a private domain) into the public
domain involves only a Rabbinic prohibition
(see previous mishnah), it is prohibited only
where the intent to pour the water into the
public domain is evident. In our case,
however, since in the normal course of events
the water is absorbed, it can be assumed that
his intent was that the water be absorbed
even where this is not the actual outcome
(Rashi).

[If the conduit is not covered for a four
cubit length one may not pour water into it
even if the courtyard has an area of sixteen
square cubits. The area of the courtyard is
irrelevant here because the water is poured
directly into the conduit.

Consequently, if the conduit is covered for
four cubits one may pour water onto it even
if the courtyard does not have a sixteen
square cubit area (Meiri, Beur Halachah to
357:2).

וַחֲכָמִים אוֹמְרִים: אֲפִלּוּ גַּג אוֹ חָצֵר מֵאָה
אַמָּה, — But the Sages say: Even if [it
runs along] a roof or courtyard [for] a

1. The dimensions of the part of the covered conduit within the public domain could,
however, render the area a karmelis. If so, the passage of wastes from that part of the conduit
within the courtyard and therefore a private domain to the part in the public domain would
entail transferring from a private domain to a karmelis. This problem is not dealt with in the
mishnah which only speaks of water passing from a private domain to the public domain.
Many authorities hold that causing the passage of liquids from a private domain to a karmelis
was not included in the Rabbinic ban against transferring between these domains (לֹא גָזְרוּ
כֹּחוֹ בְּכַרְמְלִית) but this view is not unanimous (see Orach Chaim 357:3 with Mishnah Berurah
23,24). Meiri, however, compares this to apertures in a wall facing a private domain (חוֹרֵי
רְשׁוּת הַיָּחִיד) which are halachically viewed as part of the private domain (see Shabbos 7b). This
solution depends upon the question of whether such apertures, if they are open to both a
public and a private domain, are classified as part of the private domain (see Mishnah Berurah
345:10). Meiri's view that the conduit discussed here spilled its wastes into a karmelis and
merely passed under the public domain is not accepted by the other commentators.

10. R' Eliezer ben Yaakov says: If a [drainage] conduit is covered for four cubits in the public domain, we may pour water into it on the Sabbath. But the Sages say: Even if [it runs along] a roof or courtyard [for] a hundred cubits, one may not pour into the opening of the conduit; but he pours

YAD AVRAHAM

hundred cubits,

Even if the conduit runs along on a roof or in a courtyard a distance of one hundred cubits before reaching the public domain ... *(Rashi).*

לֹא יִשְׁפֹּךְ עַל פִּי הַבִּיב; — *one may not pour* [water] *into the opening of the conduit;*

Although the area of the conduit is sufficient to absorb the usual amount of water — two *se'ah* — the Sages prohibit pouring water into it. They disagree with the view expressed in mishnah 9 according to which water may be poured into any courtyard having an area of sixteen square cubits. [That view expresses the view of R' Eliezer ben Yaakov and is disputed by the Sages here *(Meiri, Tos. Yom Tov;* based on the view of R' Zeira in *Gem.* 88a).] In their opinion only if the courtyard (or ditch) measures four cubits (or more) in both dimensions may water be poured into it. If it does not measure four cubits in one direction it is prohibited even if it has an area of sixteen square cubits (e.g., it is eight by two cubits).

The disagreement between the Sages and R' Eliezer centers on the reason for the dispensation to pour out water in a courtyard.

As explained in the previous mishnah, causing the water to flow out from the courtyard to the public domain is only Rabbinically prohibited (as long as one does not pour directly into the private domain) and the Rabbis permitted it wherever no intent to have it go into the public domain is evident. R' Eliezer ben Yaakov is of the opinion that this requirement is met wherever the two-*se'ah* measure of water is generally absorbed by the ground of the courtyard. He therefore permits water to be poured out in any courtyard or conduit having a total area equivalent to sixteen square cubits even though it measures less than four on one side.

The Sages, however, consider this insufficient and require yet another condition — that it appear as though the person pouring out the water has an interest in its remaining in the courtyard. Since the courtyards of those days were of dirt, it was common to spread water over them to keep the dust down and a person pouring out water into his courtyard would appear to be doing it for this purpose. However, this would only be done in a courtyard measuring at least four cubits square. A courtyard less than four cubits in width was too narrow [and too constricted in its use] for the proprietor to bother with spreading water over it. For this reason, one may not pour out water in such a courtyard according to the Sages, although it has an area of sixteen square cubits and is thus able to absorb the water. Similarly, a conduit, even if it measures four cubits in width, is not accorded this dispensation because no one is concerned with the level of dust in it.

The Sages do agree, however, that a pit is effective in removing the prohibition.

Most *Poskim* rule in accord with R' Eliezer ben Yaakov, and thus accept the ruling of mishnah 9, as explained above. However, *Rambam (Hil. Shabbos* 15:16, 18) rules according to the Sages. *Shulchan Aruch (Orach Chaim* 357:1-2) cites both views but the later authorities accept the more lenient ruling *(Mishnah Berurah* 357:21).

[In describing the circumstances of

[יא] **וְכֵן** שְׁתֵּי דְיוּטָאוֹת זוֹ כְנֶגֶד זוֹ. מִקְצָתָן עָשׂוּ
עוּקָה, וּמִקְצָתָן לֹא עָשׂוּ עוּקָה, אֶת

יד אברהם

the disagreement between R' Eliezer ben Yaakov and the Sages the mishnah stresses that it refers to the opening of the conduit. Even according to the Sages, one may pour out the water in the courtyard, close to the opening, as stated further in the mishnah.]

אֲבָל שׁוֹפֵךְ מִגַּג לְגַג, — *but he pours* [water] *from roof to roof*

I.e., he may pour the water upon the roof. [It is not necessary however to pour from one roof to the other.] The version of the mishnah printed in the Talmud reads אֲבָל שׁוֹפֵךְ הוּא לְגַג, *but he may spill onto a roof*. This seems to have been the version of the early commentators (see *Rashi* 88b; *Rambam* ed. Kafich; *Tos. Yom Tov; Shinuyei Nuschaos*).

וְהַמַּיִם יוֹרְדִין לַבִּיב. — *and the water descends into the conduit.*

The special prohibition stated by the Sages against pouring water onto a place from where it may flow into the public domain, and where the person has no interest to keep the dust down, does not apply when two areas must be crossed by the water before it reaches the public domain. Thus in this case, where the area in the conduit is sufficient to absorb the water — it is

four cubits square — one may pour water in the courtyard near the conduit even according to the Sages (*Geon Yaakov*; cf. *Ritva*). [The prohibition under discussion here is Rabbinic in origin and applies only to circumstances where it is evident that the person pouring wants the water to flow out to the public domain. Therefore where the flow to the public domain is less direct — there are more intermediate steps — the prohibition does not apply.]

הֶחָצֵר וְהָאַכְסַדְרָה — *A courtyard and a colonnade*

The אַכְסַדְרָה is an area closed off on three sides and open on the fourth (*Rambam*). [In this case the open side faces a courtyard.]

מִצְטָרְפִין לְאַרְבַּע אַמּוֹת. — *combine to* [*total*] *four cubits.*

This segment refers to mishnah 9 which states: 'If a courtyard is less than four cubits we may not pour water into it,' implying that one may pour water into a courtyard that is four cubit's square. The mishnah clarifies that two adjoining areas, although differing in their functions, may be measured together so that if their combined areas equal four cubits, water may be poured into them (*Rav; Rambam*).

11.

וְכֵן שְׁתֵּי דְיוּטָאוֹת זוֹ כְנֶגֶד זוֹ. — *Similarly, two balconies* [*that*] *are* directly] *opposite one another.*

The rule stated at the end of the previous mishnah applies as well to two second story apartments which face each other at the same elevation, each having a balcony in front of it. If the balconies are within four fists of each

other, the two balconies are considered as one area and if their combined area is four cubits wide they may pour their water upon the balconies without the benefit of a pit. It is assumed that the wooden beams of the balconies are covered with a soft, earthlike, mortar which absorbs water (*R' Yehonasan, Meiri*).

from roof to roof and the water descends into the conduit.

A courtyard and a colonnade combine to [total] four cubits.

11. **S**imilarly, two balconies [that] are opposite one another.

If some of them made a pit while others did not

YAD AVRAHAM

If the balconies are not directly opposite each other, either vertically or horizontally, pouring water from one to the other is impractical and their areas may not be combined *(Meiri)*.

[Some versions of the mishnah omit the word וְכֵן, *similarly*. The interpretation and halachic ramifications of this version are discussed below (s.v. מִקְצָתָן).]

מִקְצָתָן עָשׂוּ עוּקָה, וּמִקְצָתָן לֹא עָשׂוּ עוּקָה, — *If some of them made a pit while others did not make a pit,*

This clause refers to a different set of circumstances than that of above. A number of apartments opened into a courtyard which measured less than four cubits square. The residents of some of the facing apartments made a pit in the courtyard to catch their water but the residents of the other apartments did not *(Meiri; R' Yehonasan)*.

Since in the case under discussion the courtyard was less than four cubits, a pit is required in order to permit pouring the water into it (see mishnah 9; *Ritva; Rama, Orach Chaim* 377:1). Furthermore, the residents of the two apartments did not make an *eruv*, so that they may not carry into the courtyard *(Rav from Gem.* 89a). If an *eruv* was made water may be poured; one single pit suffices for all of the parties *(Tos. Yom Tov from Gem.* 88b). Similarly, if the courtyard had the required area all the parties may pour their water into it *(Rama* there). [As to why this is not prohibited because of the lack of an *eruv*, see below.]

The translation *balconies* in the previous segment follows *Meiri* and *R'*

Yehonasan. Rashi, Rav, et al., translate the word דִּיּוּטָאוֹת as *upper stories,* and explain that the residents of these upper apartments would pour their wastewater into the courtyard below. However, this courtyard did not measure four cubits square. *Tosefos Yom Tov* notes that the proponents of this translation did not have the word וְכֵן in their texts of the mishnah (see *Shinuyei Nuschaos*).

[According to this interpretation the mishnah reads: *Two upper stories are opposite one another; if some of them made a pit while others did not* ... The opening phrase is not a separate statement of halachah but serves to introduce the following statement. Since the halachic conclusions based upon the printed version of the mishnah do not follow necessarily from the halachah of the previous mishnah, but rest solely on the authority of this questionable text, it stands to reason that they are disputed by those possessing the text which deletes the word וְכֵן. The silence of *Shulchan Aruch* and the later *Poskim* on the matter of combining two balconies indicates that they do not accept the conclusion based on our text and probably did not have it.]

As explained previously, those who read וְכֵן treat the segment beginning with מִקְצָתָן, *If some ... as a new statement, separate from the preceding clause. R' Yehonasan and Meiri* comment that as a result there is no indication that the clause of the mishnah under discussion now refers to a case of two stories (or balconies)

[א] **כָּל גַּגוֹת** הָעִיר רְשׁוּת אַחַת, וּבִלְבַד
שֶׁלֹּא יְהֵא גַג גָּבוֹהַּ עֲשָׂרָה אוֹ
נָמוּךְ עֲשָׂרָה — דִּבְרֵי רַבִּי מֵאִיר. וַחֲכָמִים

יד אברהם

opposite each other; it can refer to any two apartments opening into a court-yard. However, even according to *R' Yehonasan* the law stated here will also apply to two stories opposite each other (see *Rashba* and *Ritva*).

אֶת שֶׁעָשׂוּ עוֹקָה מֻתָּרִין; — *those who made a pit are permitted* [to pour out their water];

[The pit they made is effective in removing the prohibition to pour out water, as stated in mishnah 9.]

Tosafos (89a) asks why they are not prohibited to pour out water because of the lack of an *eruv* just as they are prohibited to carry out any other objects into a courtyard lacking an *eruv*. *Tosafos'* answer to this question is based on the principle discussed several times above, that in pouring out water in a private domain one has not violated the labor of transferring from domain to domain on a Biblical level, even if the natural force of gravity propels the water to flow (along the ground) directly into the public domain. Although this is prohibited Rabbinically in transferring from private to public domains (or vice versa), the Sages permitted a flow from one private domain to another even though the two are not merged by an *eruv*. Since in such a case even pouring the water directly into the unmerged courtyard would involve no more than a Rabbinic prohibition, the Rabbis did not consider it necessary to ban *causing* the water to flow out there (itself only a Rabbinic

prohibition).

Tosafos adds that in our mishnah, too, the water may *not* be poured directly into the courtyard. It may only be poured onto the balcony facing the apartment and allowed to drip into the courtyard[1]

Tosafos is careful to differentiate between pouring into a courtyard and into a *karmelis*. Although in the case of a *karmelis* there can also be no Biblical violation of the *melachah* of transferring, nevertheless the Rabbinic prohibition regarding a *karmelis* may be more stringent than that of a courtyard lacking an *eruv*. The question of whether this dispensation applies to *karmelis* as well is the subject of debate among the authorities. (See *Tosafos* 88a; *Orach Chaim* 355:3 and 357:3; *Be'ur Halachah* to 355:1.)

וְאֶת שֶׁלֹּא עָשׂוּ עוֹקָה אֲסוּרִין. — *but those who did not make a pit are prohibited.*

Although the act of pouring water onto the balcony and allowing it to fall into the courtyard is not a violation of the law of *eruv*, the Sages prohibited those who did not make a pit to pour even in this manner. This was done lest they be led to carry the water directly into the courtyard in order to pour it into the pit, thus violating the *eruv* laws (*Rav* from *Gem.* 89a). *Tosafos* (89a; see also *Ritva*) explains that those who made a pit obviously placed it in such proximity to their balcony that the water will fall directly into the pit. Thus, this concern does not apply to them. It is only for those who did not make a pit that this concern is valid; because of the distance the water has to flow from their

1. Those who hold that the mishnah speaks about apartments facing directly onto the court-yard (see above, s.v. מִקְצָתָן) say similarly that the dispensation to pour water refers to water poured in the house, which will flow out to the courtyard (see *Meiri*).

make a pit, those who made a pit are permitted; but those who did not make a pit are prohibited.

1. **A**ll the roofs of a town are one domain, provided that one roof is not ten [fists] higher or lower [than the others] — [these are] the words of R' Meir.

YAD AVRAHAM

balcony to the pit we are afraid they may wish to avoid muddying the entire courtyard and will therefore carry the water to the pit.

It would seem that the law stated in the mishnah applies to a case of two houses opening directly onto a courtyard as well, yet the mishnah indicates that it refers specifically to *two upper stories opposite each other*. This difficulty is compounded according to those who do not have the word וְכֵן in their text. According to them the mishnah clearly refers only to such a case. *Ritva* suggests that the mishnah does not mean to say that this prohibition applies *only* to second story apartments, but that it

applies *even* to them. It might have been thought that this concern is not justified in the case of second story apartments since carrying the water down to the courtyard involves considerable bother. The later authorities, however, (*Bach, Orach Chaim 377; Magen Avraham 377:1*) assert that where a person has no balcony on which to pour out his water, he may not pour it in his house and let it flow into the courtyard even if he dug a pit. In this case, the concern is that he will not wish to dirty his house and that he will be led to carry his water out. This concern is so strong that it applies even to the maker of the pit (*Mishnah Berurah 377:5* cites this view).

Chapter 9

1.

The law of *eruvei chatzeiros* prohibits carrying objects from one private domain to another if the residents of the areas have not joined in an *eruv*. The mishnah now clarifies what constitutes 'another' domain.

כָּל גַּגּוֹת הָעִיר רְשׁוּת אַחַת, — *All the roofs of a town are* [considered] *one domain,*

I.e., one may carry objects from one roof to another[1] although the residents of the houses below these roofs have not been joined by an *eruv*. Houses are considered separate domains because they are constantly used by their owners as private areas. This exclusiveness marks them off as Rabbinically separate domains. Although roofs are also used as private areas, they are not used regularly. As a result, their level of exclusiveness is not significant enough to render them

separate domains. Since all roofs are considered part of one domain, objects which were on one roof at the onset of the Sabbath may be transferred to another roof on the Sabbath without benefit of an *eruv* (*Rav; Rashi*).

The *Gemara* (90b) explains that R' Meir also permits transfer of objects from one courtyard to another, or from one *karpeif* to another, but not the transfer of objects from a roof to a courtyard or *karpeif* (without benefit of an *eruv*, see below, s.v. רַבִּי שִׁמְעוֹן אוֹמֵר).

וּבִלְבַד שֶׁלֹּא יְהֵא גַּג גָּבוֹהַ עֲשָׂרָה אוֹ נָמוּךְ עֲשָׂרָה — דִּבְרֵי רַבִּי מֵאִיר. — *provided that one roof is not ten [fists] higher or lower [than the others] — [these are] the words of R' Meir.*

Although the roofs are considered one domain, R' Meir prohibits carrying from one roof to another when there is a ten fist difference in height between

---

1. This refers, simply, to roofs which adjoin. For the halachah regarding roofs which do not adjoin and one wishes to throw an object across the gap, see *Orach Chaim* 353:1.

עֵירוּבִין אוֹמְרִים: כָּל אֶחָד וְאֶחָד רְשׁוּת בִּפְנֵי עַצְמוֹ. רַבִּי
שִׁמְעוֹן אוֹמֵר: אֶחָד גַּגּוֹת, וְאֶחָד חֲצֵרוֹת, וְאֶחָד
קַרְפֵּיפוֹת, רְשׁוּת אֶחָד לְכֵלִים שֶׁשָּׁבְתוּ לְתוֹכָן,
וְלֹא לְכֵלִים שֶׁשָּׁבְתוּ בְּתוֹךְ הַבָּיִת.

[ב] גַּג גָּדוֹל סָמוּךְ לְקָטָן, הַגָּדוֹל מֻתָּר וְהַקָּטָן
אָסוּר. חָצֵר גְּדוֹלָה שֶׁנִּפְרְצָה לִקְטַנָּה,

יד אברהם

them. In his opinion, there is a general
prohibition against placing objects
down on a ten fist high, four fist wide
post or pedestal in a private domain.
Even though both the surrounding area
from which the object is taken and the
post onto which it is placed are both
private domains, R' Meir prohibits
because this situation could be confused
with a post of such dimensions situated
in a public domain. Since a post ten fists
high and four fists wide qualifies as a
private domain, taking an object from
the surrounding public domain and
placing it on the post would constitute
transferring from a public domain to a
private domain (Rav from Gem. 89a).

וַחֲכָמִים אוֹמְרִים: כָּל אֶחָד וְאֶחָד רְשׁוּת בִּפְנֵי
עַצְמוֹ. — But the Sages say: Each is a
domain for itself.

[The Sages dispute the distinction
made by R' Meir between houses and
roofs and maintain that the roofs of
houses belonging to different people are
considered separate domains just like
the houses below them.] Therefore, one
may not transfer objects from one roof
to another unless an eruv has been made
between the residents of the houses
below (Rav; Rashi).

רַבִּי שִׁמְעוֹן אוֹמֵר: אֶחָד גַּגּוֹת, וְאֶחָד חֲצֵרוֹת,
וְאֶחָד קַרְפֵּיפוֹת, רְשׁוּת אֶחָד — R' Shimon
says: Roofs, courtyards, and karpeifos
are all [considered] one domain

These three areas, because they are
not regularly used as private areas, are
all considered one domain according to
R' Shimon with regard to the laws of
eruvei chatzeiros. As a result, one may

carry from courtyard to courtyard even
without an eruv or from a courtyard to
a roof or to a karpeif (Rav; Rashi). [The
mishnah, however, grants this permission only to a certain group of utensils,
as it proceeds to explain.]

R' Shimon is in accord with R' Meir
on the basic premise that the separation
of domains in regard to the laws of eruv
is predicated on constant use and is
applicable, in the main, to houses only.
However, he disagrees with R' Meir on
two points; (a) he rejects R' Meir's
distinction between roofs that are level
with each other and those that are not,
and permits objects to be transferred
from one roof to another regardless of
the difference in their heights; and (b)
he permits objects to be transferred even
from roofs to courtyards and karpeifos
(enclosures) and vice versa (Rav).

The karpeifos referred to here must
conform with the guidelines established in
2:5 and must therefore be either: (a) enclosed
for living purposes or (b) have an area less
than 5,000 square cubits. Otherwise, the area
within the enclosure has many of the laws of
karmelis and one may not carry in it a
distance of four cubits (Rav). [Similarly, one
may not transfer objects from a courtyard to
such a karpeif even if the distance they are
carried is less than four cubits. Since the
karpeif is given karmelis status, this carrying
constitutes transferring from a private
domain to a karmelis and is prohibited even
where the strictures of eruv do not apply, i.e.,
even where both belong to one person (see
Tos. 90b; Mishnah Berurah 372:10). Thus
the dispensation outlined here by R' Shimon
can only refer to the type of karpeif described
earlier which is classified as a private domain
in all aspects.]

But the Sages say: Each is a domain for itself. R′ Shimon says: Roofs, courtyards and *karpeifos* are all one domain with respect to utensils which began the Sabbath in them, but not with respect to utensils which began the Sabbath in the house.

2. If a large roof is adjacent to a small one, the large one is permitted but the small one is prohibited. If a large courtyard was breached into a small one,

YAD AVRAHAM

לְכֵלִים שֶׁשָּׁבְתוּ לְתוֹכָן, — *with respect to utensils which began the Sabbath in them,*

These three areas are considered one domain only with respect to objects which were found within them at the onset of the Sabbath. Only these objects may be carried from roofs to courtyards to *karpeifos* (Rav; Rashi).

וְלֹא לְכֵלִים שֶׁשָּׁבְתוּ בְּתוֹךְ הַבָּיִת. — *but not with respect to utensils which began the Sabbath in the house.*

These objects may not be transferred from courtyard to courtyard (or roof) even if they were brought from the house into the courtyard legitimately. For example, if the residents of a courtyard made an *eruv*, they are permitted to carry objects from their houses into their courtyard. They may not, however, then carry those objects to another courtyard with which they have no *eruv*. However, if the objects were in the courtyard (rather than in the house) at the beginning of the Sabbath, they may be carried from one courtyard to another even if neither courtyard made an *eruv*. According to R′ Shimon then, the necessity of making an *eruv* is only for the sake of objects which begin the Sabbath in a house. If they are in the courtyard at the beginning of the Sabbath, they are exempt from the restriction of *eruv*[1] (Rav from Gem. 91a).

The halachah is in accord with R′ Shimon's view (Rav, Rambam from Gem. 91a).

2.

The following mishnah discusses aspects of the rule of נִפְרַץ בִּמְלֹאוֹ לְמָקוֹם הָאָסוּר לוֹ, [a place which is] *open entirely to an area which is prohibited to it*. This rule states that if an area in which carrying should be permitted is entirely open along one of its sides to an area which is prohibited to it (i.e., to an area into which one may not carry from here), the first area is also prohibited (i.e., one may not carry in the first area either).

גַּג גָּדוֹל סָמוּךְ לְקָטָן, — *If a large roof is adjacent to a small one,*

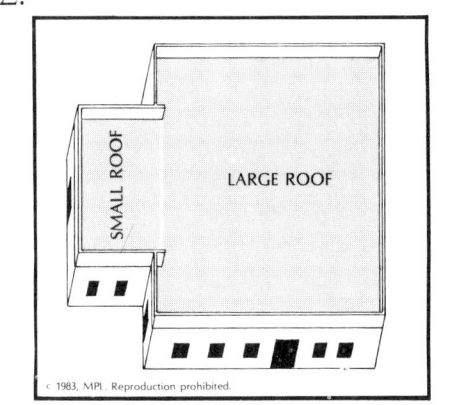

© 1983, MPL. Reproduction prohibited.

1. Actually, one restriction still applies. It is still prohibited to carry these objects from the courtyard into the house (*Mishnah Berurah* 372:3).

עֵירוּבִין גְּדוֹלָה מֻתֶּרֶת וּקְטַנָּה אֲסוּרָה, מִפְּנֵי שֶׁהִיא
ט/ב כְּפִתְחָהּ שֶׁל גְּדוֹלָה.
חָצֵר שֶׁנִּפְרְצָה לִרְשׁוּת הָרַבִּים, הַמַּכְנִיס מִתּוֹכָהּ

יד אברהם

The roofs are surrounded by a small fence[1] [ten fists high] but are open to each other along the entire line at which they adjoin (from *Rav* and *Rambam*; see *Tos. Yom Tov*).

[The residents of each house are permitted to carry from their house[2] to their *own* roof. However, since they did not make a joint *eruv*, they obviously cannot carry from one's house to the other's roof. Wherever two areas adjoin and are completely open to each other (נִפְרְצוּ בִּמְלוֹאָם), and there is a prohibition to carry from one to the other, each becomes itself prohibited. If the two roofs are the same width and consequently are entirely open along their common border, it should even be prohibited to carry from each house to its own roof. Our Mishnah, however, speaks of roofs of different widths. Although the narrower one is comple-

tely open to the wider one, the wider roof is not completely open to the narrower one.]

הַגָּדוֹל מֻתָּר — *the large one is permitted*

It is permissible to carry objects from the wider house to its roof and vice versa. Because the wider roof has segments of wall at the corners on both sides[3] of the place where the two roofs adjoin, the open space between the two roofs is considered as an entrance, in accordance with the ruling (1:8) that all open spaces of ten cubits or less in width in a wall are considered entrances and, as a consequence, do not nullify the separation (*Rav; Rashi*). (See diagram)

Accordingly, the mishnah must be speaking of a case where the line along which the two roofs adjoin is not more than ten cubits wide since if it were the area would be considered entirely open

1. *Rav* and *Rambam's* interpretation, which assumes that the roofs are surrounded by a wall, are presumably based on the opinion of R' Yosef in the *Gemara* (89b) who holds that in the absence of fences even the wider roof is considered to be open to the narrower one and, as a consequence, it too would be prohibited. Rav (the *Amora*) and Shmuel (ibid. and 92a) maintain that this is not necessary and that the outer walls of the houses beneath the roofs are considered to extend up infinitely (and serve the legal function of walls for the roof) based on the principle of גּוּד אַסִּיק מְחִיצָתָא, lit. *stretch upward the partition*. (The *Poskim* accept this view; see *Orach Chaim* 374:4.) However, the wall separating the two houses beneath the roofs at the point where they adjoin is not extended, so that the roofs are viewed as if they are surrounded by a wall but are open to each other. The reason for this is the subject of a disagreement between Rav and Shmuel (*Gem.* there). According to Rav, the principle of the upward extension of partitions does not apply to walls which are not discernible (מְחִצּוֹת שֶׁאֵינָן נִיכָּרוֹת) from the area to which they are to be extended. Shmuel holds that since the place where the imaginary, extended wall is to occupy is trod upon by the people using the roof (מְחִצָה הַנִּדְרֶסֶת) we cannot consider the wall as extending upward. The *Poskim* follow Rav in this matter (*Orach Chaim* 374:4).

2. As explained in the previous mishnah, objects which began the Sabbath on a roof may be carried to any roof (or courtyard). The issue, therefore, is only with regard to objects which began the Sabbath in the house and which one now wishes to take up to his roof (*Tos. Yom Tov*).

3. It is sufficient for the wider roof to be separated from the narrower one by two miniscule wall segments (or to merely exceed the narrower roof's width on both sides according to those who do not require an actual fence on the roof (see first footnote to this mishnah). If the wall is on only one side it must be four fists wide (*Pri Megadim* cited by *Be'ur Halachah* to 374:4, s.v. וקטנה).

the large one is permitted but the small one is prohibited, because it is like the entrance of the large one.

If a courtyard was breached into a public domain,

YAD AVRAHAM

despite the presence of wall segments at the corners (Rav).

וְהַקָטָן אָסוּר. — but the small one is prohibited.

It is prohibited to carry objects from the narrower house to the narrower roof or vice versa. Because the side of the narrower roof adjoining the wider roof is entirely open to it, the narrower roof has no separation setting it off from the wider roof. Since the residents of the two houses have not joined in an *eruv*, the narrower roof is entirely open to an area which is prohibited to it and as a result it, too, becomes prohibited. In order to permit carrying from the narrower house to its roof, its residents must join in an *eruv* with those of the wider one, in which case the wider roof is no longer an area prohibited to them, thus removing the prohibition from their own roof as well (Rav; Rashi).

חָצֵר גְּדוֹלָה שֶׁנִּפְרְצָה לִקְטַנָּה, — If [the wall of] a large courtyard was breached [so that it opened] into a small one,

[The entire wall separating a narrow courtyard from a wider one collapsed so that nothing[1] now separates the narrower courtyard from the large one. However, the segments of the wall of the wider courtyard which extend beyond the width of the narrower courtyard are still intact. [The layout of the two courtyards is now identical with that of the two roofs in the previous case.]

In the case under discussion, the breach was made before the beginning of the Sabbath. If at the onset of the Sabbath the wall was still standing, any breach made

subsequently may be disregarded for the duration of that Sabbath. As a general rule, the restrictions of *eruv* apply only if they were in effect at the onset of the Sabbath (Rav from Gem. 93b; see mishnah 3).

גְּדוֹלָה מֻתֶּרֶת וּקְטַנָּה אֲסוּרָה, — the large one is permitted but the small one is prohibited,

The explanation is the same as in the case of the roofs. The segments of the wall remaining from the wall of the wider courtyard bracket the narrower one, and set the wide courtyard off from the narrower one. But, as viewed from the narrower courtyard, no separation remains, so that the narrower courtyard is open in its entirety to an area prohibited to it. However, even to carry into the wider courtyard, the breach may be no larger than ten cubits (Rav).

מִפְּנֵי שֶׁהִיא כְּפִתְחָהּ שֶׁל גְּדוֹלָה — because it [i.e., the small courtyard] is like the entrance of the large one.

The small courtyard, since it is entirely open to the larger one, is considered a mere entranceway or appendage to the larger courtyard. In other words, the small courtyard is viewed as part of the larger one and in its domain (Rashi to 92a s.v. אסור לזרוע את הקטנה). Therefore, the residents of the small courtyard may not carry there unless they share an *eruv* with the residents of the larger one.

חָצֵר שֶׁנִּפְרְצָה לִרְשׁוּת הָרַבִּים, — If [the wall of] a courtyard was breached [so that it opened] into a public domain,

The entire wall separating the courtyard from the public domain facing it collapsed[2] without leaving any rem-

1. Any segment of wall not measuring ten fists in height is completely disregarded in this respect.

2. Where the breach opens the courtyard to the public domain and the concern is in respect to the status of the area itself, i.e., whether or not it is yet to be considered a private domain, there

עֵירוּבִין לִרְשׁוּת הַיָּחִיד, אוֹ מֵרְשׁוּת הַיָּחִיד לְתוֹכָהּ, חַיָּב —
דִּבְרֵי רַבִּי אֱלִיעֶזֶר. וַחֲכָמִים אוֹמְרִים: מִתּוֹכָהּ
לִרְשׁוּת הָרַבִּים, אוֹ מֵרְשׁוּת הָרַבִּים לְתוֹכָהּ, פָּטוּר,
מִפְּנֵי שֶׁהִיא כְּכַרְמְלִית.

יד אברהם

nant of a wall intact, or the breach was wider than the ten cubits, thereby nullifying the separating effect of any remaining sections of wall (Rav; see above 1:8).

[Carrying from the house into the courtyard, or in the courtyard itself for a distance of four cubits, is obviously prohibited in this case. As explained in the General Introduction, if the fourth side of a private domain is not adequately walled, it is Rabbinically prohibited to carry in it. This is the law requiring adjustments to the entrance of an alley (a pole or crossbeam) or a courtyard (a board four fists wide). The discussion concerns only the Biblical status of the courtyard described here.]

הַמֵּבִיא מִתּוֹכָהּ לִרְשׁוּת הַיָּחִיד, אוֹ מֵרְשׁוּת הַיָּחִיד לְתוֹכָהּ, חַיָּב — דִּבְרֵי רַבִּי אֱלִיעֶזֶר. one who brings [an object] from there [lit. inside it] into a private domain or from a private domain into it, is liable — [these are] the words of R' Eliezer.

R' Eliezer maintains that the breach renders the courtyard a part of the public domain (Rav from Gem. 94a). [As a consequence, the act of transferring an object from the courtyard to a private domain or vice versa is classified as transferring from a public domain to a private domain (or vice versa) — one of the 39 melachos (labors) listed in Shabbos 7:2 as Biblically forbidden on the Sabbath. A person guilty of this (or any other labor) is liable, i.e., obligated to bring a sin offering, if his offense was unintentional (see ArtScroll Mishnah Shabbos, General Introduction).]

R' Eliezer judges only the area

previously occupied by the wall as part of the public domain but agrees that the interior of the courtyard is not considered part of the public domain. The area of the wall is classified as צִדֵּי רְשׁוּת הָרַבִּים, the sides of a public domain, i.e., areas immediately adjacent to the public domain which are not as accessible to the public as the public domain proper. Although these areas do not in themselves meet the standards of a public domain, R' Eliezer considers them to be part of the public domain and subject to its laws (one opinion in Gem. 94a).

וַחֲכָמִים אוֹמְרִים: מִתּוֹכָהּ לִרְשׁוּת הָרַבִּים, אוֹ מֵרְשׁוּת הָרַבִּים לְתוֹכָהּ, פָּטוּר, מִפְּנֵי שֶׁהִיא כְּכַרְמְלִית. — But the Sages say: [One who brings] from it [i.e., the courtyard] into the public domain, or from the public domain into it, is not liable, because it is like a karmelis.

[The courtyard is neither a public domain nor a private domain but rather a karmelis. Consequently, carrying from it to either a private or public domain does not entail liability.]

The mishnah apparently states that an area surrounded by walls on three sides but open on the fourth is classified as a karmelis and even Biblically is not considered either a private or a public domain. This contradicts what most authorities understand to be the meaning of the Gemara on 12b that three walls are sufficient, Biblically speaking, to render an area a private domain (see Rashba and other comm. there; Rambam, Hil. Shabbos 17:9).[1] Tosafos (93b) suggests that the Sages' ruling refers only to segments of the side walls framing the area previously

is no distinction between a breach occurring on the Sabbath or before it. Such a distinction (see mishnah 3) can only be drawn with regard to the Rabbinic prohibitions of eruv. Even there, the halachah follows R' Yose who does not recognize such a distinction.

one who brings from there into a private domain, or from a private domain into it, is liable — [these are] the words of R' Eliezer. But the Sages say: From it into the public domain, or from the public domain into it, is not liable, because it is like a *karmelis*.

YAD AVRAHAM

occupied by the collapsed wall which were also breached, thus leaving this area open from all sides. The Sages hold that this area, although devoid of partitions, does not automatically become part of the public domain, because its status as private property hinders the public from using it. The Sages' reference to מִתוֹכָה, lit. *from inside it,* which obviously alludes to the inside of the courtyard, does not refer to the circumstance discussed here. The inside of the courtyard, being surrounded by three walls, retains its halachic status as a private domain, and carrying from it to a public domain does entail liability. Rather the Sages' statement seeks to prove from a parallel case that the area formerly occupied by the wall is a *karmelis,* and uses the situation of a courtyard which has had all of its walls breached as an illustration to prove their argument. (This is more analogous to the situation of the area left vacant by the collapse of the wall.) Such an area is certainly a *karmelis* since it is no longer enclosed at all and is not used by the public.

The Sages' classification of the area as a *karmelis* serves to express their dissent with R' Eliezer's position that it is a public domain. That being the case, it is strange that the Sages do not respond directly with a ruling concerning carrying from the courtyard to a private domain — the case discussed by R' Eliezer — and state that in contrast to R' Eliezer's opinion, there is no liability for doing so.[2]

Tosefos Yom Tov suggests that the Sages statement was not originally formulated to contrast with R' Eliezer's view. Rather, the reverse is true — R' Eliezer's statement was framed to illustrate his disagreement with the Sages. As their debate regarding the status of

the area of the wall began, the Sages pointed out to R' Eliezer, using the case of carrying from there to a public domain (i.e., from the inside of the courtyard to a public domain) as an illustration, that even he agreed that the inside of the courtyard was a *karmelis,* and that the same status should be accorded to the area previously occupied by the wall. [Later, this segment came to represent the Sages' view, as stated in our mishnah.] R' Eliezer responded to this by pointing out the difference between the wall area — which is now used by the public and therefore ought to be classified as a public domain — and the inside of the courtyard which is not accessible to them and is, as a result, a *karmelis* even according to R' Eliezer. In formulating R' Eliezer's position, an illustration using a case of carrying from the courtyard (the wall area) to a private domain had to be used since carrying from there to a public domain would not serve to illustrate their differences. According to R' Eliezer, this would constitute carrying from one public domain to another, which does not entail liability unless one carries a distance of four cubits, while according to the Sages one would be exempt because this would constitute carrying from a *karmelis* to a public domain. Since this case does not serve to illustrate the differences, R' Eliezer had to use an illustration involving carrying from the courtyard to a private domain to express his opinion that the courtyard is a public domain.

However, the editor of the mishnah, following usual procedure, placed R' Eliezer's view before that of the Sages, thus creating the impression that the Sages' statement was meant to counter R' Eliezer's (see also *Tos.* 93b and other commentators).

1. It is because of this difficulty that *Tosefos Rid* emends the mishnah to read *from there to a private domain ... is not liable because it is a karmelis.* On a Biblical level the area is a private domain but it is Rabbinically treated with the strictness of a *karmelis,* i.e., one may not carry from it to a private domain nor carry an object in the area itself a distance of four cubits.

2. This difficulty, too, is removed by *Tosefos Rid's* emendation.

חָצֵר שֶׁנִּפְרְצָה לִרְשׁוּת הָרַבִּים מִשְּׁתֵּי
רוּחוֹתֶיהָ, וְכֵן בַּיִת שֶׁנִּפְרַץ מִשְּׁתֵּי
רוּחוֹתָיו, וְכֵן מָבוֹי שֶׁנִּטְּלוּ קוֹרוֹתָיו אוֹ לְחָיָיו,
מֻתָּרִין בְּאוֹתוֹ שַׁבָּת, וַאֲסוּרִין לֶעָתִיד לָבֹא —
דִּבְרֵי רַבִּי יְהוּדָה. רַבִּי יוֹסֵי אוֹמֵר: אִם מֻתָּרִין
לְאוֹתוֹ שַׁבָּת, מֻתָּרִין לֶעָתִיד לָבֹא; וְאִם אֲסוּרִין
לֶעָתִיד לָבֹא, אֲסוּרִין לְאוֹתוֹ שַׁבָּת.

יד אברהם

3.

חָצֵר שֶׁנִּפְרְצָה לִרְשׁוּת הָרַבִּים מִשְּׁתֵּי רוּחוֹתֶיהָ,
— *If* [the wall of] *a courtyard was
breached* [so that it opened] *into a
public domain on two of its sides,*

[As above, the courtyard wall was
breached on the side facing the public
domain so that it is no longer a valid
partition, thus conferring upon the
courtyard the status of *karmelis*. The
Gemara explains that the breach
discussed here is less than ten cubits
wide and should ordinarily qualify as an
entrance (see 1:8) and not invalidate the
enclosure. However, the breach here is
on two sides, which the *Gemara*
explains as the collapse of a corner of
the wall, thus affecting two sides. Such
a breach cannot be considered an
entrance because people do not usually
make an entrance in a corner. Since it
cannot be legally classified as an
entrance, it invalidates the enclosure
(*Rav* from *Gem.* 94b).

וְכֵן בַּיִת שֶׁנִּפְרַץ מִשְּׁתֵּי רוּחוֹתָיו, — *or* [lit.
similarly] *if a house was breached on
two of its sides,*

Here, too, the walls at a corner of the
house were breached, causing them to
lose their validity as partitions (*Rav*
from *Gem.* 94b).

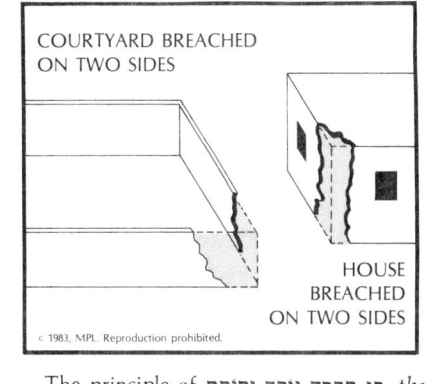

COURTYARD BREACHED
ON TWO SIDES

HOUSE
BREACHED
ON TWO SIDES

c 1983, MPL. Reproduction prohibited.

The principle of פִּי תִקְרָה יוֹרֵד וְסוֹתֵם, *the
edge of a roof is extended downward to be
considered a partition,* does not apply here
because in the mishnah's case the ceiling also
crumbled and fell in the corner and the edge
of the ceiling is now drawn at an angle to the
remaining walls (*Tos.* 94b).[1] The rationale
for this legal extension is that the open space
beneath the edge of the roof is considered an
entrance. Since, as already explained, a
corner cannot be viewed as an entrance, the
principle is of no avail to us in this case
(*Rosh*).

וְכֵן מָבוֹי שֶׁנִּטְּלוּ קוֹרוֹתָיו אוֹ לְחָיָיו, — *or an
alley whose crossbeams or poles were
removed;*

[I.e., the crossbeam or pole required

1. This is also *Rambam's* view as expressed in his Commentary (ed. Kafich) and in the
diagrams there (cf. *Maggid Mishnah, Hil. Shabbos* 17:35), and this may be what *Rav* means.
Tosefos Yom Tov understands the earlier translation of *Rambam's* Commentary in a different
manner. *Tosafos'* view is accepted as halachah by *Shulchan Aruch* (*Orach Chaim* 361:2).

3. If a courtyard was breached into a public domain on two of its sides, or if a house was breached on two of its sides, or an alley whose crossbeams or poles were removed; they are permitted on that Sabbath but prohibited in the future — [these are] the words of R' Yehudah. R' Yose says: If they are permitted on that Sabbath, they are permitted in the future; and if they are prohibited in the future, they are prohibited on that Sabbath.

YAD AVRAHAM

to adjust an alley (as explained in 1:2) was removed. Since the alley is no longer adjusted, it is treated with all the strictures of a *karmelis* even if a *shituf* has been made.]

Rashi comments that the text should be emended to read קוֹרָתוֹ אוֹ לֶחְיוֹ, *its beam* (singular) *or pole* (singular), because an alley needs only one beam or pole. This is indeed the version of the mishnah printed with the *Talmud Yerushalmi* (*Tos. Yom Tov*).

מֻתָּרִין בְּאוֹתוֹ שַׁבָּת, וַאֲסוּרִין לֶעָתִיד לָבֹא — .דִּבְרֵי רַבִּי יְהוּדָה — *they are permitted* [to be carried in] *on that Sabbath but (are) prohibited in the future* — [these are] *the words of R' Yehudah.*

If the wall became breached (or the crossbeam or pole was removed) on the Sabbath, they may continue carrying in that area for the rest of that Sabbath (*Rav; Rashi*). Once they were permitted to carry there for part of the Sabbath, the permission is not removed until the following week.

[Since the prohibition to carry involved here is Rabbinic in origin (the prohibition against carrying in a *karmelis* — see General Introduction), the Sages applied to this case the principle which states (in regard to other laws of carrying, see below) that the halachic status established at the onset of the Sabbath remains in force for that entire Sabbath day.]

רַבִּי יוֹסֵי אוֹמֵר: אִם מֻתָּרִין לְאוֹתוֹ שַׁבָּת, מֻתָּרִין לֶעָתִיד לָבֹא; וְאִם אֲסוּרִין לֶעָתִיד לָבֹא, אֲסוּרִין לְאוֹתוֹ שַׁבָּת. — *R' Yose says: If they are permitted* [to carry] *on that Sabbath, they are permitted in the future* [as well]; *and if they are prohibited in the future, they are prohibited on that Sabbath* [as well].

I.e., since carrying in the area can certainly not be permitted on the next Sabbath, it cannot be permitted on the Sabbath on which the breach occurred either. R' Yose rejects the application to this circumstance of the principle that the halachic status prevailing at the onset of the Sabbath remains for the rest of that Sabbath (*Rav* from *Gem.* 95a).

R' Yose admits to this principle only where the status of the area as a private domain remains unchanged (i.e., its partitions remain intact) but its status in regard to the laws of *eruvei chatzeiros* has changed (*Rav* from *Gem.* 17a), e.g., if two adjacent courtyards were connected by an entrance which enabled them to make a joint *eruv* and this entrance was boarded up on the Sabbath (thus removing their basis for making a joint *eruv*), they may nevertheless carry from courtyard to courtyard (by passing objects over the wall) on that Sabbath. Here the private domain status of the concerned areas is not affected, and only the *eruv* status is involved (*Gem.* 17a).

The halachah follows R' Yose (*Rav* from *Gem.* 95a).

עירובין [ד] **הַבּוֹנֶה** עֲלִיָּה עַל גַּבֵּי שְׁנֵי בָתִּים, וְכֵן
ט/ד גְשָׁרִים הַמֻּפְלָשִׁים, מְטַלְטְלִין
תַּחְתֵּיהֶן בַּשַׁבָּת — דִּבְרֵי רַבִּי יְהוּדָה. וַחֲכָמִים
אוֹסְרִין.
וְעוֹד אָמַר רַבִּי יְהוּדָה: מְעָרְבִין לְמָבוֹי הַמֻּפְלָשׁ.
וַחֲכָמִים אוֹסְרִין.

יד אברהם

4.

הַבּוֹנֶה עֲלִיָּה עַל גַּבֵּי שְׁנֵי בָתִּים, — *A second story built upon* [lit. *one who builds a second story upon*] *two houses*,

Two houses, situated on two opposite sides of a public domain, have another story built over them extending from one to the other and covering the public domain (*Rav; Rashi*).

וְכֵן גְשָׁרִים הַמֻּפְלָשִׁים, — *or bridges under which a road passes*,

I.e., overpasses.

מְטַלְטְלִין תַּחְתֵּיהֶן בַּשַׁבָּת — דִּבְרֵי רַבִּי יְהוּדָה. — *one may carry beneath them on the Sabbath* — [*these are*] *the words of R' Yehudah.*

The covered area has the status of a private domain and carrying under the covering is therefore permitted. The reasons for R' Yehudah's ruling are twofold: (a) The principle that the edge of a roof extends downward to be considered a partition allows us to view the area as closed off on all four sides (*Rav* from *Gem.* 95a); (b) R' Yehudah holds that any area closed off on two sides is considered a private domain (*Gem.* 95a; see *Rashi* there).

וַחֲכָמִים אוֹסְרִין. — *But the Sages prohibit* [this].

The Sages maintain that the principle of the downward extension of the roof's edge cannot be applied to two openings opposite each other where traffic passes freely under the roof (see *Meiri; Tosafos, Succah* 18b).

וְעוֹד אָמַר רַבִּי יְהוּדָה: מְעָרְבִין לְמָבוֹי הַמֻּפְלָשׁ. — *R' Yehudah also said: We may make an eruv for an open alley.*

The term *eruv* here refers to *shitufei mevo'os* (R' Yehonasan; *Tos. Yom Tov;* see also 6:5).

We may make a *shituf* for an alley which is open at both ends to public domains and has walls only along its two sides.

Before an alley can qualify for a *shitufei mevo'os* it must meet two conditions: (a) It must be a private domain on a Biblical level; (b) it must be properly adjusted (generally with a pole or crossbeam — see 1:2) to remove any Rabbinic prohibitions. That is, there must not be any restrictions against carrying in this area other than those arising from multiple ownership. Restrictions arising from the inadequacy of the partition are not removed by a *shituf*.

In R' Yehudah's opinion, an alley which has walls only along its sides but which is open to public domains at both ends is nevertheless a private domain on a Biblical level; two walls are sufficient to render an area a private domain. Thus, the alley fulfills the first condition and can fulfill the second by having *both* its open ends adjusted with poles or crossbeams. It is therefore possible, in his opinion, to make a *shitufei mevo'os* for an open alley and thereby permit carrying in it (*Rav* from *Gem.* 95a; *Gem.* 6a,b).

9
4

4. A second story built upon two houses, or bridges under which a road passes, one may carry beneath them on the Sabbath — [these are] the words of R' Yehudah. But the Sages prohibit. R' Yehudah also said: We may make an *eruv* for an open alley. But the Sages prohibit.

YAD AVRAHAM

The *Gemara* (95a) points out that the second clause of the mishnah clarifies a point in R' Yehudah's position which is not evident in the first case. It could be argued that R' Yehudah's lenient ruling in the cases of the second story or bridges is based on his view that the principle that the edge of a roof extends downward may be applied even to two openings opposite each other. Thus, R' Yehudah would admit that an area must have three proper walls before it can be adjusted with a pole or crossbeam. It would follow then that even R' Yehudah agrees that an open alley cannot be adjusted with a pole or crossbeam.[1] This misconception is rectified by the inclusion of the second clause which makes clear R' Yehudah's position that even two partitions render an alley a private domain on a Biblical level thus allowing it to be adjusted with a crossbeam or pole at both ends.

וַחֲכָמִים אוֹסְרִין. — *But the Sages prohibit* [this].

The Sages prohibit making a *shituf* here, i.e., a *shituf* is of no avail, because in their opinion an area enclosed on only two sides is not a private domain. [The adjustments of a pole or a crossbeam cannot make it a private domain because they are not actually walls *(Gem.* 6a, b).]

The halachah is in accord with the Sages' view[2] *(Rav; Rambam).*

The methods which are effective in rendering an open alley a private domain are given in the *Gem.* 6a-b and *Orach Chaim* 364:1.

Chapter 10

✒ The Melachah of Transferring from Domain to Domain

This chapter contains a variety of laws pertaining to the *melachah* (labor) of הוֹצָאָה, transferring objects from a private domain to a public domain and vice versa which have not been clarified in tractate *Shabbos.* Because the main part of our tractate deals with the problems of carrying in courtyards and alleys, as related to the laws of *eruv,* it is appropriate for these miscellaneous laws to be added here *(Meiri).*

Not every transfer of an object from place to place is considered a forbidden labor. The Scriptural injunction only applies to: (a) transferring from a public domain to a private domain, or vice versa; and (b) transferring an object over a distance of four *amos* within a public domain. Transfer between a public or private domain and a *karmelis* is only Rabbinically prohibited; transfer between these areas and an exempt area is permissible (see General Introduction).

Every act of *transferring* contains three elements: (a) עֲקִירָה [*akirah*], lit.

1. A crossbeam, whose width may be only one fist, cannot be effective under the principle of roof-edge extension; this principle specifies a minimum four fist width *(Tos.* 86a; see *Beur Halachah* 361:2).

2. According to the halachah, the ruling of the Sages refers even to an alley which is open to a public domain on one side and to a *karmelis* on the other, or to a *karmelis* on both sides (see *Gem.* 7a and *Orach Chaim* 364:1).

עירובין
י/א

[א] **הַמּוֹצֵא** תְּפִלִּין מַכְנִיסָן זוּג זוּג. רַבָּן
גַּמְלִיאֵל אוֹמֵר: שְׁנַיִם שְׁנָיִם.
בַּמֶּה דְּבָרִים אֲמוּרִים? בִּישָׁנוֹת, אֲבָל בַּחֲדָשׁוֹת
פָּטוּר.

יד אברהם

uprooting; i.e., removing an object from its present location; and (b) הַנָּחָה
[hanachah], placing; i.e., setting down the object in its new place; and (c) שִׁנּוּי
רְשׁוּת, change of domain. As regards a public domain, both the akirah and the
hanachah of the object must be from and to a place measuring at least four
handbreadths by four handbreadths. As regards a private domain, only the akirah
must be from a place of those dimensions.

1.

הַמּוֹצֵא תְּפִלִּין — *One who finds* tefillin

If someone finds *tefillin* in a field or
any other place where they are not safe
and may be desecrated he is not
permitted to leave them there *(Rav,
Rashi; Tos. Yom Tov)*. There is concern
they will be stolen by gentiles or that
animals will desecrate them (see *Beitzah*
15a and *Meiri*).

[The mishnah now discusses what he
should do if he finds them on the
Sabbath when he is not permitted to
carry them in.]

מַכְנִיסָן זוּג זוּג. — *should bring them in*
pair [by] pair.

He should don them as he would to
perform the *mitzvah* of *tefillin*, wear
them until he reached a place where he
could deposit them safely, remove them,
then return, put on a second pair, and
repeat this procedure until he has
brought in all the *tefillin*. He thereby
brings them pair by pair.

He may not, however, put on more
than one pair of *tefillin* at one time,
according to this opinion. This *Tanna*
holds that essentially *tefillin* should be
worn on the Sabbath (שַׁבָּת זְמַן תְּפִלִּין)
and the reason they are not worn is
because of a Rabbinic decree prohibiting

wearing *tefillin* in a public domain.[1]
[The decree was enacted because of the
concern that should a strap break the
person might then carry the *tefillin*
home in his hand *(Shabbos 61a)*.] This
decree was lifted for circumstances such
as those described here, so that the
person may put on a pair even in the
public domain. However, he may not
put on two pairs at one time for in doing
so he would be transgressing the
Scriptural precept of בַּל תּוֹסִיף, the
prohibition to add to the *mitzvos (Deut.
13:1) (Rav, Rambam, based on Gem.
96b-97a)*.

רַבָּן גַּמְלִיאֵל אוֹמֵר: שְׁנַיִם שְׁנָיִם. — *Rabban
Gamliel says: Two [by] two.*

Rabban Gamliel holds that the
mitzvah of *tefillin* does not apply to the
Sabbath. Thus, wearing two pairs of
tefillin does not violate the prohibition
against adding to the *mitzvos*, because
during a time period in which the
mitzvah itself cannot be fulfilled one
does not violate the prohibition against
adding unless he has clear intent to
perform the *mitzvah* anyway.[2] Since
his purpose here is to safeguard the
tefillin, this intent is not present and he
does not violate the prohibition (*Ritva;*

---

1. There is a question [independent of the dispute regarding whether 'the Sabbath is a time for
tefillin'] whether the wearing of *tefillin* is prohibited in a private domain. See *Magen Avraham*
29:1, 31:1, 308:11, *Be'ur Halachah* to *Orach Chaim* 31, *Sha'agas Aryeh* 41-2.

2. During a period in which the *mitzvah* can be fulfilled, one violates the prohibition even if
he does not specifically intend to perform an additional *mitzvah* (*Tos.* 96b).

1. One who finds *tefillin* should bring them in pair [by] pair. Rabban Gamliel says: Two [by] two. To what do these words apply? To old ones, but for new ones he is exempt.

YAD AVRAHAM

see *Tos.* 96b, s.v. אי).

Although the mitzvah of *tefillin* does not apply on the Sabbath, it is nevertheless permitted (on a Biblical level) to wear *tefillin* even in the public domain because they are considered an adornment (תַּכְשִׁיט) and wearing them is therefore not classified as transferring. Rabban Gamliel does not, however, permit wearing more than two pairs of *tefillin* at a time, because *tefillin* can only be considered an adornment if they are worn in the manner required for the performance of the *mitzvah*. The *Gemara* (96b) states that on each of the areas of the head and hand where the *tefillin* must be worn there is place for only two *tefillin* boxes.

The halachah is not in accord with Rabban Gamliel's view and only one pair of *tefillin* may be worn at one time (*Rambam, Comm.* and *Hil. Shabbos* 19:23, *Orach Chaim* 301:42).[1]

בַּמֶּה דְּבָרִים אֲמוּרִים? בִּישָׁנוֹת, אֲבָל בַּחֲדָשׁוֹת
פָּטוּר. — *To what do these words apply? To old ones, but for new ones he is exempt.*

The obligation to bring found *tefillin*

to a safe place applies only to old pairs. If the *tefillin* are 'new' (as defined below) one is neither obligated nor permitted to bring them in (see *Rav* and *Rashi*).

The *Gemara* (97a) defines 'old' *tefillin* as those that have their straps and knots in place so that they are ready to be worn. If there are no straps, or they are not knotted, he cannot be obligated to bring them in because it is impossible for him to put on these *tefillin* without making the requisite knots, and it is prohibited to make these knots on the Sabbath. [The making of knots is one of the 39 prohibited *melachos* — see *Shabbos* 7:2.] (*Gem.* as understood by *Rashi;* see *R' Betzalel Ranshberg's* gloss on 97a and *Ritva.*)[2]

Rambam (*Comm.* and *Hil. Shabbos* 19:24) and *Rif* understand the distinction between old and new *tefillin* as based on the consideration that what appears to be *tefillin* may actually be an amulet, which cannot be worn in a public domain (see *Shabbos* 6:2). Only those that are complete with straps and knots can be assumed to be bona fide *tefillin* (see *Milchemes* and *Beur HaGra Orach Chaim* 301:42, for explanations of this view).[3]

---

1. *Tosefos Yom Tov* notes that *Rambam's* ruling is contradictory for he also rules that the Sabbath is not a time for *tefillin*. See *Turei Zahav* to *Orach Chaim* 34:2, *Mirkeves HaMishneh*, and *Magen Avraham* 301:54.

2. *Tosafos* (97a) asks why he is not obligated to guard the *tefillin* until dark as in the case of bundles of *tefillin* outlined below. *Ritva* answers that 'new' *tefillin* in their uncompleted state may be invalid, in which case we need not be concerned with the possibility of their desecration. Although *tefillin* which have straps and knots may also be invalid (they must be checked before they may be used in the performance of the mitzvah of *tefillin*), since they are complete and seem ready for use, the Sages obligated one to safeguard their holiness despite the possibility of their being invalid.

3. We have omitted *Rav's* view, which defines old *tefillin* as those on which marks attesting to knots having once been in place are present (see *Tos. Yom Tov*). This contradicts the *baraisa* cited by the *Gemara* (97a) and the views of *Rif* and *Rambam*. It is based on the words of *Rashi* in the mishnah, but as seen from his commentary in the *Gemara* (97a, s.v. והשתא), this view is later rejected in the *Gemara's* conclusion (see *Tos.* 96b).

מְצָאָן צְבָתִים אוֹ כְּרִיכוֹת, מַחֲשִׁיךְ עֲלֵיהֶן וּמְבִיאָן. וּבְסַכָּנָה, מְכַסָּן וְהוֹלֵךְ לוֹ.

[ב] **רַבִּי שִׁמְעוֹן** אוֹמֵר: נוֹתְנָן לַחֲבֵרוֹ, וַחֲבֵרוֹ לַחֲבֵרוֹ, עַד שֶׁמַּגִּיעַ לֶחָצֵר הַחִיצוֹנָה. וְכֵן בְּנוֹ, נוֹתְנוֹ לַחֲבֵרוֹ,

יד אברהם

מְצָאָן צְבָתִים אוֹ כְּרִיכוֹת, — *If he found them tied in pairs or bundles,*

I.e., he found a large number of tefillin, either tied in pairs or all the tefillin tied in one bundle (*Rav* from *Gem.* 97a).

מַחֲשִׁיךְ עֲלֵיהֶן וּמְבִיאָן. — *he must wait near them until dark, then bring them in.*

If the number of tefillin is so great that he will be unable to bring all of them in before the Sabbath is over, he should stay there and guard them until dark and then bring them all in together (*Rav, Rashi* from *Gem.* 97a).

וּבְסַכָּנָה, — *But in a time of danger,*

During a time when mitzvah observance, specifically that of tefillin, is surpressed by the government and anyone safeguarding tefillin endangers himself ... (*Rav* from *Gem.* 97a).

מְכַסָּן וְהוֹלֵךְ לוֹ. — *he may* [merely] *cover them and leave.*

This ruling applies whether he found single pairs or bundles (*Rashi* 97b).

2.

רַבִּי שִׁמְעוֹן אוֹמֵר: נוֹתְנָן לַחֲבֵרוֹ, וַחֲבֵרוֹ לַחֲבֵרוֹ, — *R' Shimon says: He hands them* [i.e., the tefillin] *to his friend, and his friend to his friend,*

[R' Shimon's statement is a continuation of the previous mishnah.[11]] R' Shimon disagrees with the first *Tanna's* ruling that in times of danger one should merely cover the tefillin and leave them there. In his opinion, one should pass the tefillin to a friend who is standing within four cubits of him (thus avoiding the Biblical prohibition of carrying four cubits in a public domain), who then passes them to another person, with the process repeated until the tefillin have reached a place where they may be left safely.

The *Gemara* (97a-97b) notes that in light of the interpretation of the term

danger in the previous mishnah (s.v. וּבְסַכָּנָה) as referring to government surpression of Torah observance, it is difficult to understand R' Shimon's position. Surely anything more than a mere covering of the tefillin would be apt to attract attention and endanger the person. The method proposed by R' Shimon involves a number of people and the danger would therefore be multiplied.

The *Gemara* concludes that the mishnah must be emended and the following clause (found partly in a baraisa) must be inserted at the end of the first *Tanna's* statement: בַּמֶּה דְּבָרִים אֲמוּרִים? בְּסַכָּנַת עַכּוּ״ם, אֲבָל בְּסַכָּנַת לִסְטִים מוֹלִיכָן פָּחוֹת פָּחוֹת מֵאַרְבַּע אַמּוֹת, *To what does this* [the ruling that in times of danger he may merely cover them and

1. In the text of the mishnah found in the Talmud there is no separation between this statement and the previous mishnah. The breakup of the mishnah into segments does not rest upon any authority and may be disregarded wherever it causes difficulty.

If he found them tied in pairs or bundles, he must wait near them until dark, then bring them in.

But in a time of danger, he may cover them and leave.

2. **R'** Shimon says: He hands them to his friend, and his friend to his friend, until he reaches the outermost courtyard. So, too, his child, he hands

YAD AVRAHAM

leave] *apply? To a danger from gentiles* [i.e. a governmental decree prohibiting *mitzvah* performance] *but* [in a case of] *danger from bandits he should carry them in a series of moves of less than four cubits each.* Since in this case it is not dangerous for him to be discovered with *tefillin*, he cannot simply leave them in their place. However, since it is dangerous for him to stay there , he does not have to remain there until dark. Consequently, the Sages permitted him, in this case, to carry the *tefillin*, but only in a way that does not violate any Biblical prohibition — by carrying them less than four cubits,[1] stopping to rest for a moment (*Shabbos* 5b), again walking less than four cubits and repeating this process until the *tefillin* can be deposited in a safe place.

Although carrying in this manner is not Biblically prohibited, the Sages prohibited it. However, to protect *tefillin* from desecration, they lifted this prohibition where no other solution is possible.

It is with this solution that R' Shimon disagrees. R' Shimon maintains that one person carrying *tefillin* in this manner is in danger of forgetting himself and carrying more than four cubits at one time — thus violating the Sabbath. The more desirable solution, therefore, is to pass the *tefillin* from one person to another, thus avoiding the chance of

any one person carrying more than four cubits.

The first *Tanna*, however, holds that R' Shimon's method is not preferable because it involves many people and thus publicizes an ostensible desecration of the Sabbath (*Gem.* 97b).

R' Shimon agrees, however, where other people are not available that he may carry the *tefillin* in a series of moves less than four cubits each. His disagreement with the first *Tanna* is only regarding which of the two methods is preferable (*Tos.* 97b).

עַד שֶׁמַּגִּיעַ לֶחָצֵר הַחִיצוֹנָה. — *until he reaches the outermost courtyard.*

[The *tefillin* are given over from hand to hand until the first safe courtyard — the one at the outskirts of the town — is reached. Since the *tefillin* are safe there, and nothing is gained from transporting them further, all the strictures applicable to the transport of other objects apply to the *tefillin* as well, and they may not be transported further.]

Geon Yaakov adds that upon handing the *tefillin* into the courtyard, the person must be careful not to place them in the hand of the person receiving them for then he would be making both the *akirah* and the *hanachah*, thereby transgressing a Biblical law (see preface to this chapter). Nor may the person in the courtyard stretch his hand outside the courtyard and take the *tefillin* from the hand of the person holding them. This also involves a Biblical transgression of the *melachah* of transferring, for the person

1. The labor of transferring objects from one place in the public domain to another has a clause defining four cubits as the minimum distance which constitutes a transfer on a Biblical level. When transferring between a public and private domain there is no minimum distance requirement. It is only when an object was picked up in the public domain and put down there that this minimum applies.

עירוּבִין וַחֲבֵרוֹ לַחֲבֵרוֹ, אֲפִלּוּ מֵאָה.

י/ג　רַבִּי יְהוּדָה אוֹמֵר: נוֹתֵן אָדָם חָבִית לַחֲבֵרוֹ,
וַחֲבֵרוֹ לַחֲבֵרוֹ, אֲפִלּוּ חוּץ לַתְּחוּם.
אָמְרוּ לוֹ: ,,לֹא תְהַלֵּךְ זוֹ יוֹתֵר מֵרַגְלֵי בַּעֲלֶיהָ.''

[ג] **הָיָה** קוֹרֵא בְסֵפֶר עַל הָאַסְקֻפָּה, נִתְגַּלְגֵּל
הַסֵּפֶר מִיָּדוֹ, גּוֹלְלוֹ אֶצְלוֹ.

יד אברהם

receiving the tefillin has done both the akirah and the hanachah. The only way to avoid transgression of a Biblical law is for the person outside the courtyard to stretch his hand into the courtyard and allow the person inside to take the tefillin from his hand. In this manner, neither one performs an entire act of transfer since one is performing the akirah while the other performs the hanachah. Although this is normally forbidden by Rabbinic law,[1] it was permitted in this case to save the tefillin from desecration.

וְכֵן בְּנוֹ, — So, too, his child,
If a baby was born in the field and must subsequently be transported to the house (Rav from Gem. 97b).

נוֹתְנוּ לַחֲבֵרוֹ, וַחֲבֵרוֹ לַחֲבֵרוֹ, אֲפִלּוּ מֵאָה. — he hands him to his friend, and his friend to his friend, even if they are a hundred.

R' Shimon maintains his opinion even in regard to a baby, where it might be thought that out of regard to the newborn baby, for whom the passage through many hands could be discomforting, he would permit the first Tanna's method. R' Shimon's apprehension that the method proposed by the first Tanna could lead to Sabbath desecration overrides his concern for the child's comfort (Gem. 97b).

רַבִּי יְהוּדָה אוֹמֵר: נוֹתֵן אָדָם חָבִית לַחֲבֵרוֹ, וַחֲבֵרוֹ לַחֲבֵרוֹ, — R' Yehudah says: A

person may hand a barrel to his friend, and his friend to his friend,

R' Yehudah endorses the view of R' Shimon and goes even further. R' Shimon ruled that his method was merely preferable to that of the first Tanna, agreeing, however, that both methods are normally Rabbinically prohibited and are to be used only in certain extenuating circumstances. By contrast, R' Yehudah maintains that the method of handing from person to person is entirely permissible and may be used even for ordinary needs. Thus, even someone who finds a barrel of food or beverage in the street may pass it on to his friend (Ramban in Milchamos; Ravad cited there; Ritva; Rambam, Hil. Shabbos 12:17).

R' Yehonasan, however, is of the opinion that R' Yehudah agrees with R' Shimon that this method may be used only for special needs. He comments that the barrel discussed here contains water for which there is a critical need (such as for a person who has nothing to drink or for a sick person) so that this instance, too, represents a special need. R' Yehudah's statement (in this view) is novel only in regard to his opinion about techum (see below).

אֲפִלּוּ חוּץ לַתְּחוּם. — even beyond the techum.

R' Yehudah permits the barrel to be transported even beyond the techum. The Gemara (97b; in R' Ashi's view)

1. As in the case of all Sabbath labor, one is liable only if he performed the entire act himself; if two people share in an act that, by its nature, should be performed by one person, neither is liable — although the act is forbidden by Rabbinic law. Therefore, if one person effects the akirah and another effects the hanachah, the labor is considered as being performed by two people, and both are exempt from penalty (see Shabbos 1:1).

him to his friend, and his friend to his friend, even if they are a hundred.

R' Yehudah says: A person may hand a barrel to his friend, and his friend to his friend, even beyond the *techum.*

They said to him: 'This should not go further than the feet of its owners.'

3. **I**f one was reading a book [of Scripture] on the threshold [and] the book rolled from his hand,

YAD AVRAHAM

explains that the barrel under discussion (and its contents) was found under circumstances which render it ownerless. R' Yehudah follows the view (*Beitzah* 5:5) that ownerless objects do not have a *techum* limit imposed upon them,[1] for which reason there is no prohibition in passing them more than 2,000 cubits from their original place.[2] If, however, the barrel was owned by anyone, they would be limited to his *techum* and it would be prohibited to pass them beyond that *techum* (*Rav*).

אָמְרוּ לוֹ: ,,לֹא תְהַלֵּךְ זוֹ יוֹתֵר מֵרַגְלֵי בְעָלֶיהָ.'' — *They* [the Sages] *said to him: 'This should not* [be allowed to] *go further than the feet of its owners.'*

I.e., ownerless objects should not be allowed to be moved further than they would be if they had been owned by someone. This anonymous statement represents the opinion of R' Yochanan

ben Nuri (see 4:5; *Gem.* 45b), who asserts that even ownerless objects have a *techum* assigned to them (*Rav* from *Gem.* 97b).

The halachah follows R' Shimon and R' Yehudah (*Rambam, Comm.*). Thus it is preferable to pass the *tefillin* to one's friend, etc. Furthermore, this method is permitted even for ordinary needs. In his code, *Rambam* rules like R' Yehudah, permitting ordinary objects to be passed from hand to hand (*Hil. Shabbos* 12:17; *Orach Chaim* 349:3), but in regard to *tefillin* he rules that the two methods — carrying them in a series of moves less than four cubits each and passing them to one's friend — are equally acceptable (*Hil. Shabbos* 19:24). This view is accepted by *Shulchan Aruch* (*Orach Chaim* 301:42). See *Beis Yosef* and *Be'ur HaGra* there, and *Mirkeves HaMishneh.*

3.

הָיָה קוֹרֵא בְּסֵפֶר עַל הָאַסְקֻפָּה, נִתְגַּלְגֵּל הַסֵּפֶר מִיָּדוֹ, — *If one was reading a book* [*of Scripture* while] *on the threshold* [*and*] *the book rolled from his hand,*

An elevated threshold (similar to a stoop) fronted the entrance to a courtyard which was adjacent to a

public domain (*Gem.* 98a). The status of this platform is that of a *karmelis* [it is less than ten fists high and measures at least four by four fists (*Rav; Rashi*)].

The platform was also not within the walls of the courtyard, otherwise it would be considered a private domain. If this platform

1. However, if any of the people intended that his handling the barrel serve as a formal act of acquisition (קִנְיָן), it automatically acquires his *techum* and may not be carried outside it (*Tos.* 97b, see *Orach Chaim* 397:15 and 401:1; cf. *Ritva* citing *Ravad*).

2. Of course, each person must stay within his personal *techum.*

הָיָה קוֹרֵא בְּרֹאשׁ הַגַּג וְנִתְגַּלְגֵּל הַסֵּפֶר מִיָּדוֹ —
עַד שֶׁלֹּא הִגִּיעַ לַעֲשָׂרָה טְפָחִים, גּוֹלְלוֹ אֶצְלוֹ;
מִשֶּׁהִגִּיעַ לַעֲשָׂרָה טְפָחִים, הוֹפְכוֹ עַל הַכְּתָב. רַבִּי
יְהוּדָה אוֹמֵר: אֲפִלּוּ אֵין מְסֻלָּק מִן הָאָרֶץ אֶלָּא
כִּמְלֹא חוּט, גּוֹלְלוֹ אֶצְלוֹ. רַבִּי שִׁמְעוֹן אוֹמֵר: אֲפִלּוּ

יד אברהם

were a private domain, it would not qualify for the ruling mentioned below (see *Gem.* 97b,98a).

The books of Mishnaic times were written on scrolls. In the case under discussion, one end of the scroll unrolled and fell to the public domain while the other end remained in the reader's hand (*Rav; Rashi*).

גּוֹלְלוֹ אֶצְלוֹ. — *he may roll it* [back] *to himself.*

Since he still holds one end of the scroll in his hand (*Rav; Rashi*), the scroll cannot be considered as resting in the public domain (*Meiri,* see *Shabbos* 91b). Consequently, its subsequent transport to the *karmelis* on which he is standing is not a case of transferring from a public domain to a *karmelis.* We also do not need to be concerned that permission to retrieve it in such a case might lead to his retrieving it even where the roll had left his hand entirely, because even if he did he would violate only a Rabbinic prohibition.

Although for a secular object even rolling it back to himself is prohibited (*Rama, Orach Chaim* 352:1; *Magen Avraham* 352:4; cf. *Tosafos* 98a, s.v. אלא and *Ritva*), the Sages relaxed this prohibition for the sake of retrieving books of Scripture. By contrast, the prohibition to transfer objects actually resting in a public domain to a *karmelis,* although also only a Rabbinic prohibition, is more stringent and is not relaxed even for books of Scripture. For this reason, if the scroll fell entirely from his hand he may not retrieve it.

If the threshold is a private domain, he is also prohibited to roll it back even if part of it is still in his hand because it might lead him to do so even when the scroll fell from his hand entirely — a Biblically prohibited act (*Gem.* 97b).

הָיָה קוֹרֵא בְּרֹאשׁ הַגַּג — *If he was reading on top of the roof*

[The roof is elevated ten fists above the public domain and has the status of a private domain.]

וְנִתְגַּלְגֵּל הַסֵּפֶר מִיָּדוֹ — *and the book rolled from his hand —*

[But one end remained in his hand, as described earlier. The commentary below discusses the resting place of the scroll.]

עַד שֶׁלֹּא הִגִּיעַ לַעֲשָׂרָה טְפָחִים, גּוֹלְלוֹ אֶצְלוֹ; — *as long as it has not yet reached within ten fists* [of the ground], *he may roll it* [back] *to himself;*

[In this case, even if he had dropped the entire scroll, no prohibition would have been involved in catching it above ten fists from the ground and returning it to the roof because the air-space ten fists above the level of the public domain has the status of a מָקוֹם פְּטוּר, *an exempt area.* Since retrieving the scroll in these circumstances would not violate any Biblical prohibition even if both ends of the scroll were dropped, the Sages permitted its retrieval as long as one end is still in his hands.]

מִשֶּׁהִגִּיעַ לַעֲשָׂרָה טְפָחִים, — [but] *once it has reached* [within] *ten fists* [of the ground],

The *Gemara* (98a) understands that the unrolled end 'rests' within ten fists of the ground. This is possible if the house slants down from the roof towards the street so that the scroll lies on it. Once the hanging part of the scroll reaches to within ten fists of the ground, the hanging end now 'rests' in the public domain[1] and its retrieval would involve the Biblically prohibited labor of

he may roll it to himself. If he was reading on top of the roof and the book rolled from his hand — as long as it has not yet reached within ten fists [of the ground], he may roll it to himself; once it has reached ten fists, he should turn it over on its writing. R' Yehudah says: Even if it is only removed from the ground by the width of a thread, he may roll it to

YAD AVRAHAM

transferring from a public to a private domain were it not for the fact that one end of the scroll still remains in his hand. The Sages were concerned that some would not grasp this subtle distinction and be led to retrieve even a scroll which had left the reader's hand entirely and had come to rest in the public domain below ten fists. To prevent this mistake, they prohibited retrieval of the scroll even when one end of the scroll is still in his hand (*Rav* from *Gem.* 98a).

הוֹפְכוֹ עַל הַכְּתָב — *he should turn it over on its writing.*

Although he may not roll it back up, it would be improper to just leave the scroll dangling in midair uncovered until the end of the Sabbath (*Rav* from *Gem.* 98a). [Therefore, he should at least twist the scroll so that its writing faces the wall (and is thus covered) rather than the street.]

רַבִּי יְהוּדָה אוֹמֵר: אֲפִלּוּ אֵין מְסֻלָּק מִן

הָאָרֶץ אֶלָּא כִּמְלֹא חוּט, — *R' Yehudah says: Even if it is only removed from the ground by the width of a thread,*

[Even if the scroll is hanging within a needle's width of the ground ...]

Although many editions of Mishnah read כִּמְלֹא מַחַט, a needle's width, we have followed *Bach* (glosses to *Gem.* 97b) who emends the text to read, (with *Yerushalmi, Rif*, and others,) כִּמְלֹא חוּט, *the width of a thread* (see also *Meleches Shlomo* and *Shinuyei Nuschaos*). This also seems to have been the reading in *Rav's* version.

גּוֹלְלוֹ אֶצְלוֹ. — *he may roll it* [back] *to himself.*

R' Yehudah does not disagree with the ruling set forth earlier in regard to a scroll coming to rest on a slanty wall below ten fists. Rather, he refers to a case where the scroll did not come to rest but was left dangling in the air and rules that, in contrast to the previous case, here the scroll may be rolled back. Because the scroll did not come to rest, retrieving it in these circumstances

---

1. For this reason, in the case of a straight wall, if the unrolled end is left dangling in the air one may roll it back to himself even if it is within ten fists of the ground. Since it is not 'resting' in the public domain, even snatching it out of midair and putting it down on the roof would not constitute a Biblical violation.

Tosafos (Shabbos 5b, s.v. בכותל) comments that the slanty wall has the status of public domain only if it is used by passersby to adjust their loads (רַבִּים מְכַתְּפִין) upon it or the like. Otherwise, it would be a *karmelis* and in regard to the matter discussed here the ruling should be that he is permitted to roll it back up, as in the previous case of the threshold. Consequently, this ruling is further restricted to where the unrolled end came to rest on the segment of wall nine fists above the ground (see *Magen Avraham* 352:5 with *Machatzis HaShekel; Beis Meir* there). The segment of wall below this is not considered usable by the public and is classified as a *karmelis* (see *Orach Chaim* 345:10). Some authorities *(Rambam, Shabbos* 5b; *Ritva* here) feel that the area facing a slanty wall is classified a public domain even if it cannot be used by the public; this requirement applies to a horizontal area only. See *Be'ur Halachah* to 352:2, s.v. בענין.

עירוּבִין בָּאָרֶץ עַצְמוֹ, גּוֹלְלוֹ אֶצְלוֹ; שֶׁאֵין לְךָ דָבָר מִשּׁוּם
י/ד   שְׁבוּת עוֹמֵד בִּפְנֵי כִתְבֵי הַקֹּדֶשׁ.

[ד] **זִיז** שֶׁלִּפְנֵי חַלּוֹן, נוֹתְנִין עָלָיו וְנוֹטְלִין מִמֶּנּוּ
בַּשַּׁבָּת.
עוֹמֵד אָדָם בִּרְשׁוּת הַיָּחִיד וּמְטַלְטֵל בִּרְשׁוּת

יד אברהם

would not involve a Biblical prohibition[1] even if the scroll had left his hand entirely. Accordingly, the Sages did not prohibit retrieving it as long as one end is still in his hand.

The *Gemara* explains that actually the entire mishnah is stating R' Yehudah's view and that a phrase is missing from the mishnah. The additional segment should be inserted after the words הוֹפְכוֹ בַּמֶּה דְבָרִים אֲמוּרִים? עַל הַכְּתָב and read: בְּכֹתֶל מִשְׁפָּע, אֲבָל בְּכֹתֶל שֶׁאֵינוֹ מִשְׁפָּע אֲפִלּוּ פָּחוֹת מִשְּׁלֹשָׁה טְפָחִים גּוֹלְלוֹ אֶצְלוֹ. שֶׁרַבִּי יְהוּדָה אוֹמֵר: ... *To what do these words apply? To a slanting wall, but for a straight wall even if* [the scroll is] *within three fists* [of the ground; i.e., it is close enough to the ground to be considered on it under the principle of lavud[2]] *he may roll it* [back] *to himself, for R' Yehudah says ...* (Rav from Gem. 98b).

Shulchan Aruch (and other *Poskim*) accept this as the halachah and rule that as long as the scroll is not actually touching the ground it may be rolled back up. *Gra* (to *Orach Chaim* 352:2),

however, maintains that R' Yehudah's ruling is not definitive and adduces proof that other *Tannaim* disagree and consider objects suspended within three fists of the ground as at 'rest.' *Mishnah Berurah* (352:16) records this dissenting opinion (see *Be'ur Halachah* there).

רַבִּי שִׁמְעוֹן אוֹמֵר: אֲפִלּוּ בָאָרֶץ עַצְמוֹ, גּוֹלְלוֹ אֶצְלוֹ; שֶׁאֵין לְךָ דָבָר מִשּׁוּם שְׁבוּת עוֹמֵד בִּפְנֵי כִתְבֵי הַקֹּדֶשׁ. — *R' Shimon says: Even* [if the scroll is] *on the very ground, he may roll it* [back] *to himself; for no Rabbinically prohibited matter may stand in the way of the Holy Scriptures.*

R' Shimon maintains that even if one end of the scroll is actually touching the ground it may be rolled back up to the roof because all Rabbinical prohibitions are to be waived to preserve the dignity of the books of Scripture. Since rolling back a scroll still partially in the hand of the reader is at worst a Rabbinical prohibition, it must give way for an act aimed at preserving the dignity and sacredness of Scriptures.

The halachah is not in accord with R' Shimon's view (*Rav; Rambam*).

4.

זִיז שֶׁלִּפְנֵי חַלּוֹן, — *A ledge which is in front of a window,*

A ledge juts out from the window over the public domain at an elevation

1. However, there is a Rabbinical prohibition against retrieving, to a private domain, an object flying through the air of a public domain within ten fists of the ground (see *Magen Avraham* and *Beur HaGra* to *Orach Chaim* 352:1).

2. As explained in the General Introduction, the principle of *lavud* states that any two surfaces separated by a gap of less than three fists are considered joined. Thus, the scroll dangling within three fists of the ground could halachically be considered resting on the ground of the public domain. Nevertheless, as long as it is not actually resting there, he may roll it back up.

himself. R' Shimon says: Even on the very ground, he may roll it to himself; for no Rabbinically prohibited matter may stand in the way of the Holy Scriptures.

4. **A** ledge which is in front of a window, one may put onto it and take from it on the Sabbath. A person may stand in a private domain and move

YAD AVRAHAM

of more than ten fists *(Rav* from *Gem.* 98b).[1]

A ledge situated within ten fists of the ground and measuring four by four fists is a *karmelis* and carrying objects between it and the private domain is prohibited. The *Poskim* (see *Magen Avraham* 353:6; *Mishnah Berurah* 353:12) rule that even if this ledge is less than four fists wide, in which case it should be considered an exempt area, it is still treated as a *karmelis* as long as it is within ten fists of the ground. *Meiri* suggests that the Sages promulgated a special decree for ledges, cancelling any leniencies based on exempt area status (see *Beis Yosef* to *Orach Chaim* 353 and *Geon Yaakov* here).

נוֹתְנִין עָלָיו וְנוֹטְלִין מִמֶּנּוּ בְּשַׁבָּת. — *one may put [things] onto it and take [things] from it on the Sabbath.*

One may take objects from the house, pass them through the window, and put them on the ledge or vice versa. The public domain extends for only ten fists above the ground. Therefore, a ledge jutting out above the ten fist limit is not in the public domain and one may transfer objects freely between it and a private domain.

The *Gemara* (98b) restricts this ruling to utensils which would break if they fell off the ledge. Unbreakable objects may not be placed on the ledge because if they fall down into the public domain their owner might forget and bring them back to the private domain *(Rav)*.

According to the ruling of *Tur* and

Shulchan Aruch (Orach Chaim 345:16), a ledge with an area of four by four fists is a *karmelis* even if it is more than ten fists off the ground, and it is prohibited to take objects from the house and put them on this ledge. Accordingly, the mishnah's ruling here refers only to this situation — a ledge in front of a window. In this case the ledge is considered an extension of the window and house and is classified as an aperture of a private domain (חוֹרֵי רְשׁוּת הַיָּחִיד) which (if it is above ten fists from the public domain) is treated as a private domain.

According to other authorities, however, a ledge more than ten fists above the ground is an exempt area even if it is greater than four by four. Accordingly, the mention of a window is not pertinent to the ruling per se, since it may be used from the house whether it is a private domain or an exempt area. It serves merely to explain how the ledge is reached from the house *(Be'ur Halachah* to 353:2, *Be'ur HaGra* there and to 353:3, 345:16).

עוֹמֵד אָדָם בִּרְשׁוּת הַיָּחִיד וּמְטַלְטֵל בִּרְשׁוּת הָרַבִּים, — *A person may stand in a private domain and move objects in a public domain,*

[A person may stand in a private domain, stretch his hand into a public domain and move objects there. We are not concerned that he will forget himself and bring the objects from the public domain into the private domain. The *Gemara* cites the opinion of R' Meir who disputes this.]

The prohibition to move objects in the

1. This restriction of the mishnah's ruling is based on *Rashi's* understanding of the *Gemara*. From *Tosafos* (98b) it would seem that a ledge with an area of less than four by four would be an exempt area and the mishnah's ruling would therefore apply to it.

עֵירוּבִין הָרַבִּים, בִּרְשׁוּת הָרַבִּים וּמְטַלְטֵל בִּרְשׁוּת הַיָּחִיד;

י/ה־ו וּבִלְבַד שֶׁלֹּא יוֹצִיא חוּץ מֵאַרְבַּע אַמּוֹת.

[ה] **לֹא** יַעֲמֹד אָדָם בִּרְשׁוּת הַיָּחִיד וְיַשְׁתִּין בִּרְשׁוּת הָרַבִּים, בִּרְשׁוּת הָרַבִּים וְיַשְׁתִּין בִּרְשׁוּת הַיָּחִיד; וְכֵן לֹא יָרֹק. רַבִּי יְהוּדָה אוֹמֵר: אַף מִשֶּׁנִּתְלַשׁ רֻקּוֹ בְּפִיו, לֹא יְהַלֵּךְ אַרְבַּע אַמּוֹת עַד שֶׁיָּרֹק.

[ו] **לֹא** יַעֲמֹד אָדָם בִּרְשׁוּת הַיָּחִיד וְיִשְׁתֶּה בִּרְשׁוּת הָרַבִּים, בִּרְשׁוּת הָרַבִּים

יד אברהם

public domain set forth in mishnah 6 applies only to cases similar to the circumstances described there, where the object being moved is needed by the person (see below; *Tos. Yom Tov* from *Gem.* 99a).

בִּרְשׁוּת הָרַבִּים וּמְטַלְטֵל בִּרְשׁוּת הַיָּחִיד; — [or] *in a public domain and move objects in a private domain;*

[Similarly, he may stand in the public domain and move objects in the private domain.]

וּבִלְבַד שֶׁלֹּא יוֹצִיא חוּץ מֵאַרְבַּע אַמּוֹת. — *provided he does not take* [them] *beyond four cubits.*

This segment of the mishnah refers

back to the first case[1] mentioned here where the person was in the private domain and moved objects in the public domain (*Tos. Yom Tov*). He must take care not to move the objects more than four cubits from their original places in the public domain (*Rav*).

The Biblical prohibition not to move objects four cubits in the public domain is more closely defined here. Note that the mishnah does not say, 'provided he does not take them four cubits' but rather it says, 'take them *beyond* four cubits.' When one moves an object exactly four cubits he has not transgressed (see *Rambam, Hil. Shabbos* 12:19; *Mishnah Berurah* 349:9).

5.

לֹא יַעֲמֹד אָדָם בִּרְשׁוּת הַיָּחִיד וְיַשְׁתִּין בִּרְשׁוּת הָרַבִּים, בִּרְשׁוּת הָרַבִּים וְיַשְׁתִּין בִּרְשׁוּת הַיָּחִיד; — *A person may not stand in a private domain and urinate into a public domain,* [or] *in a public domain and urinate into a private domain.*

Urinating from the private to the public domain or vice versa falls into the category of the *melachah* of transferring from one domain to another on a Biblical level (*Rav* from *Gem.* 99a).

The *Gemara* explains that although the Biblical labor of transferring requires that the object being transferred be taken from a place measuring four by four fists (see preface to this chapter), urinating from one domain to another is still considered transferring. The exemption for taking an object from a surface of less than four by four fists applies only when the object is on such an under-sized surface incidentally, i.e., it is taken from there merely because that is where the object happens to be at that moment. However,

1. In some versions the order of the mishnah is reversed so that the case of a person in the private domain moving objects in the public domain immediately precedes this clause which modifies it (*Shinuyei Nuschaos*).

מִשְׁנָיוֹת / עֵירוּבִין — פֶּרֶק י: הַמּוֹצֵא תְּפִלִּין [218]

objects in a public domain, [or] in a public domain and move objects in a private domain; provided he does not take [them] beyond four cubits.

5. **A** person may not stand in a private domain and urinate into a public domain, [or] in a public domain and urinate into a private domain. Similarly, he may not expectorate.

R' Yehudah says: Even when one's saliva has become detached in his mouth, he may not walk four cubits until he expectorates.

6. **A** person may not stand in a private domain and drink in a public domain, [or] in a public domain and drink in a private domain, unless he

YAD AVRAHAM

where an object is on such a surface because that is where it should be and no other surface will do, that surface is considered the equivalent of four by four fists. Consequently, one who takes the object from that surface (or places it there) can be liable for transferring. In the case of our mishnah, therefore, the urine is considered coming from a place the equivalent of four by four fists (*Rav* from *Gem.* 99a; see *Tos.* s.v. מחשבתו).

וְכֵן לֹא יָרֹק. — *Similarly, he may not expectorate.*

[A person may not stand in a public domain and spit into a private domain or vice versa for the reasons outlined above.]

רַבִּי יְהוּדָה אוֹמֵר: אַף מִשֶּׁנִּתְלַשׁ רֻקּוֹ בְּפִיו, לֹא יְהַלֵּךְ אַרְבַּע אַמּוֹת עַד שֶׁיָּרֹק. — *R' Yehudah says: Even when one's saliva has become detached in his mouth, he may not walk four cubits until he*

expectorates.

R' Yehudah asserts that saliva, after it has accumulated in the mouth and is ready to be spit out, is no longer considered part of the body but is viewed as something being carried in the mouth. Thus, if one were to walk four cubits in a public domain with the saliva in his mouth he would have transferred it four cubits in the public domain.

According to *Rav* and *Rambam*, the halachah is not in accord with R' Yehudah. *Rambam* obviously takes R' Yehudah's statement about saliva to be an individual view disputed by other *Tannaim* (see *Maggid Mishneh, Hil. Shabbos* 13:3). *Tur* (*Orach Chaim* 350), however, seems to hold that R' Yehudah's ruling is undisputed and therefore accepted as halachah (see *Beis Yosef*). This view is reflected in *Shulchan Aruch* (350:3).

6.

לֹא יַעֲמֹד אָדָם בִּרְשׁוּת הַיָּחִיד וְיִשְׁתֶּה בִּרְשׁוּת הָרַבִּים, בִּרְשׁוּת הָרַבִּים וְיִשְׁתֶּה בִּרְשׁוּת הַיָּחִיד, — *A person may not stand in a private domain and drink in a public domain, [or] in a public domain and drink in a private domain,*

A person standing in a private domain may not bend over into the

public domain (and vice versa) to drink water or beverages which are in the other domain. We are concerned that he may forget himself while drinking and transfer the liquid into his domain (*Rav; Rashi*).

This is not comparable to mishnah 4 where a person is permitted to move objects in the

עירוּבִין וְיִשְׁתֶּה בִּרְשׁוּת הַיָּחִיד, אֶלָּא אִם כֵּן הִכְנִיס רֹאשׁוֹ
י/ו וְרֻבּוֹ לְמָקוֹם שֶׁהוּא שׁוֹתֶה; וְכֵן בַּגַּת.
קוֹלֵט אָדָם מִן הַמַּזְחֵילָה לְמַטָּה מֵעֲשָׂרָה

יד אברהם

public domain although he himself remains in the private domain. The ruling in that mishnah refers only to objects which are not presently needed by the person, thus there is little reason to fear that he may transfer them to his own domain. In our case, however, he needs the water in the public domain now, so that we are concerned that he will bring it into the private domain (Gem. 99a).[1]

אֶלָּא אִם כֵּן הִכְנִיס רֹאשׁוֹ וְרֻבּוֹ לְמָקוֹם שֶׁהוּא שׁוֹתֶה; — unless he brings his head and most of his body into the domain in which he drinks;

[By bringing most of his body into the domain of the water, the concern that he may forget and bring the water to his domain is removed, since the person is now mostly in the same domain as the water.]

וְכֵן בַּגַּת. — similarly regarding a wine pit.

[Wine used to be pressed into a pit lined with a leak-proof substance. The mishnah states that a ruling similar to

that set forth earlier in regard to a person standing in a public domain applies to drinking wine from a wine pit.] The Gemara (99a) explains that the ruling regarding a wine pit does not refer to the Sabbath,[2] but refers to drinking untithed wine. Untithed foodstuffs are termed tevel [see comm. to 3:2] and may not be consumed. Biblically, the obligation to tithe only applies after the food has been completely processed. Therefore, one may not consume fully processed food in any circumstance before tithing. However, foodstuffs not completely processed may be taken as a snack but not eaten in a formal manner. This is a Rabbinical decree. The wine discussed in the mishnah is still in the upper pit[3] and is thus not completely processed (Rashi, Shabbos 11b). Since it is still not completely processed, it may be drunk in an informal manner, i.e. in small quantities. The mishnah rules[4] that

1. The above is the interpretation of the Gemara according to Rashi and most commentators. Rambam (Comm. and Hil. Shabbos 15:2) understands that the Gemara distinguishes between expensive and ornate utensils (for there is concern lest the person transfer them) and inexpensive, inconsequential vessels (regarding which there is no such concern). In Rambam's view, mishnah 4 refers to inexpensive vessels whereas our mishnah refers to a person drinking water from an expensive one. Shulchan Aruch (Orach Chaim 350:1) cites both views but indicates his preference for Rashi's opinion (see Mishnah Berurah 350:8).

2. This is the opinion of Rava. The Gemara also quotes Abaye who suggests that the phrase, 'similarly regarding a wine pit,' refers to the laws of the Sabbath and that the wine pit has dimensions which render it a karmelis (it is four by four fists wide and less than ten fists deep). Thus the mishnah rules that the stringency recorded here regarding drinking from a water source in a domain other than the one in which the drinker stands applies even to a karmelis. However, Rava disagrees with this view, arguing that this would be a safeguard to a safeguard. He therefore rules that one may drink in any manner from a karmelis. Rava's opinion is accepted as halachah and is therefore presented in the commentary.

3. The Mishnah (Ma'asros 1:7) rules that wine is considered completely processed after it has gone through two phases: (a) The scum (consisting of the pits and peels) has been skimmed off; (b) the wine has been syphoned from the upper wine pit (גַּת הָעֶלְיוֹנָה) to the lower wine pit (בּוֹר) for storage. The wine under discussion here has (according to Rashi) already been skimmed off but is still in the upper pit (גַּת). Thus it may be drunk in an informal manner before it flows into the lower pit.

4. This ruling follows R' Meir's opinion in Ma'asros 4:4. The Sages there disagree with the distinction between wine drunk over the pit and outside it (see Yerushalmi and Meleches Shlomo there).

10
6

brings his head and most of his body into the domain
in which he drinks; similarly regarding a wine pit.
A person may catch [water] from a gutter lower

YAD AVRAHAM

drinking over the pit is considered
'snacking' and permitted, whereas
drinking outside the pit is considered
drinking in a formal manner and
prohibited before tithing. Therefore a
person may stand with his head and
most of his body over the wine pit and
drink without tithing, but he may not
stand outside of it and drink, because
we are concerned that he may bring the
wine to himself, in which case he would
be prohibited to drink it without first
tithing it *(Rav; Rashi).*

קוֹלֵט אָדָם מִן הַמַּזְחֵילָה — *A person may
catch [water] from a gutter*

A person standing in a public domain
may catch water running down from a
gutter. In Mishnaic times roofs were, as
a rule, flat. The rainwater accumulating
on the roof would be channeled toward
the side of the roof [and would drain off
through holes in the wall surrounding
the roof *(Meiri)].* The water would spill
from the roof onto a board (gutter)
which is attached along the length of the
house and which directed the water
away from the house *(Rashi).*

לְמַטָּה מֵעֲשָׂרָה טְפָחִים. — *[which is] lower
than ten fists* [above the ground].

I.e., a person may catch water from a

gutter whose open end is within ten fists
of the ground of a public domain *(Tos.
Yom Tov).*

He may catch this water since it is
already in the public domain and in
doing so he is not transferring the water
from domain to domain *(Meiri).* He may
not, however, place his mouth or a container directly[1] to the open end of the
gutter because the gutter, being within
three fists of the roof,[2] is considered an
extension of it and as a result, a private
domain. [This is so even for a gutter
within ten fists of the ground, e.g., the
roof is ten fists high and the gutter is
two fists below it *(Meiri).*] Thus, taking
the water directly from the gutter would
constitute transferring from a private
domain (the gutter) to a public domain
(where the person is standing) *(Rav;
Rashi).*[3]

Actually, since in the case of the gutter one
may only catch water in midair, there is no
difference whether he does so within ten fists
of the ground or above. The air-space more
than ten fists above the ground ranks as an
exempt area and one may surely transfer
objects from there to a public domain. The
mishnah specifies *within ten fists* because of
the concluding case of this mishnah, as will
be explained below.

1. There is disagreement as to how to define the term 'place directly' (מְצָרֵף) in this regard. *R'
Yehonasan* and *Meiri* maintain that if one's mouth or container are within three fists of the
gutter the principle of *lavud* (see footnote end of mishnah 3) applies and this is classified as
'directly.' Others *(Tur, Orach Chaim* 351) dispute this and restrict the exclusion of the
mishnah to cases in which the person's mouth or container is in actual contact with the gutter.
Shulchan Aruch (351) rules in accordance with *Tur* (see *Be'ur Halachah,* s.v. תוך).

2. *Meiri* adds that the open end of the gutter (from which the water is caught) also does not jut
out three fists from the house. If it did, the part of the gutter would not have private domain
status and one would be permitted to take water directly from it. One may also infer that the
gutter's width does not measure three fists for then its outer edge would be three fists removed
from the roof and it, too, would not have private domain status. Indeed, *Shulchan Aruch
HaRav (Orach Chaim* 351) states this clearly.

3. It would seem that the same ruling applies to a slanty roof which is primarily ten fists high
(thus classifying it as a private domain) but whose eaves dip to below ten fists so that gutters
running alongside them are below ten fists. However, see *Orach Chaim* 374:4 and 346:16 with
Mishnah Berurah about the halachic status of such roofs.

עירובין טְפָחִים. וּמִן הַצִּנּוֹר, מִכָּל מָקוֹם שׁוֹתֶה.
י/ז

[ז] **בּוֹר** בִּרְשׁוּת הָרַבִּים וְחֻלְיָתוֹ גְּבוֹהָה עֲשָׂרָה
טְפָחִים, חַלּוֹן שֶׁעַל גַּבָּיו מְמַלְּאִין הֵימֶנּוּ
בַּשַּׁבָּת.

יד אברהם

וּמִן הַצִּנּוֹר, — But from a pipe.

Drain pipes did not, as a rule, run alongside the roof as did a gutter but were perpendicular to the roof and ended at a point at least three fists away from its edge (Rav). The essential difference between a pipe and a gutter is not in their shape but their proximity to the roof (Meiri; Tos. Yom Tov).

מִכָּל מָקוֹם שׁוֹתֶה. — he may drink in any manner.

I.e., he may even place his mouth directly to the pipe and drink. This is in contrast to a gutter from which the mishnah only permits one to catch the water in midair. Because a pipe of this kind invariably ends three or more fists away from the house it cannot be considered an extension of the house, and it is therefore an exempt area even when it is below ten fists. Since it is not an extension of the roof, its status is determined by (a) its width and length; and (b) its height above the ground. Thus, if it is less than four by four fists, then regardless of its elevation it is an exempt area. If it is more than four by

four fists, within ten fists of the ground, it is a *karmelis*; above ten fists of the ground it is a private domain (because it is reckoned a cranny of the private domain[1]).

Accordingly, the *Gemara* (99b) adds that only when the pipe's dimensions are less than four by four fists may one place his mouth or container directly to the pipe. If it is four by four fists and within ten fists of the ground it is a *karmelis* and taking water from it to the public domain is prohibited (Rashi).

Furthermore, where the pipe is above ten fists, one may not place a container in direct contact with it even if its dimensions are less than four by four fists. This is because above ten fists from the ground it is possible for the pipe to be a private domain, i.e., if the pipe measures four by four.[2] Since taking water from such a pipe in this manner would constitute transferring from a private to a public domain,[3] the Sages prohibited taking water in this manner even if the pipe does not measure four by four, lest people not differentiate between pipes of differing

1. This commentary follows the view that crannies of a private domain which connect with a public domain are accorded private domain status only if they satisfy two conditions: (a) they measure four by four fists; and (b) they are situated ten fists or more from the ground. Both of these conditions are subject to debate. Some authorities argue that such nooks are given private domain status whether they meet these conditions or not (see *Mishnah Berurah* 345:9-10).

2. The private domain status conferred in this case is due to the principle that the crannies of a private domain have private domain status. The pipe cannot attain this status on its own because it lacks the prerequisite partition requirements. A board jutting out over a land area is not a private domain unless the land under it is also partitioned off with walls ten fists high (Magen Avraham 351:5).

3. It is not clear whether doing so would result in a Biblical transgression of the Sabbath. *Rambam* (Hil. Shabbos 15:4) reasons that no transgression is present since the water had not come to 'rest' in the private domain prior to it being transferred to the public domain. R' Yehonasan (see also Meiri) demonstrates from the Talmud (Shabbos 5a) that someone allowing the water to flow into his mouth or container, even if he places it directly to the pipe, cannot be said to have made an *akirah* (see Be'ur Halachah to 351 s.v. תוך).

than ten fists. But from a pipe he may drink in any manner.

7. **I**f a cistern is in a public domain and its embankment is ten fists high, the window above it may [be used to] draw from it on the Sabbath.

YAD AVRAHAM

sizes. Only when the pipe is below ten fists may one place his container directly to it if the pipe is less than four by four fists. Here, even if someone failed to grasp this distinction and placed his container directly to a pipe measuring four by four fists he would still only be transferring from a *karmelis* to a public domain — a Rabbinic violation. [A surface four by four but less than ten fists high cannot be a private domain unless it is enclosed by ten fist high partitions.] Catching water after it has left the pipe, however, is always permitted. Once the water has left the pipe and is falling through the air it is no longer in a private domain

regardless of the status of the pipe.

Thus, the specification *below ten fists* which is stated, ostensibly, in regard to the case of a gutter, really refers to the case of a pipe. Instead of restricting the dispensation to catch from a gutter to the area below ten fists, it restricts only the dispensation to *drink in any manner*, i.e., to place a container directly to the pipe. To catch water is permitted at any height.

The above is the interpretation of the mishnah as it is understood in our versions of *Rashi*.[1] There are, however, different readings of the mishnah (see *Rif, R' Yehonasan, Rambam Hil. Shabbos* 15:4, et al.). *Shulchan Aruch (Orach Chaim* 351) accepts the version of *Rashi* presented here.

7.

בּוֹר בִּרְשׁוּת הָרַבִּים וְחֻלְיָתוֹ גְּבוֹהָה עֲשָׂרָה טְפָחִים, — *If a cistern is in a public domain and its embankment is ten fists high,*

A cistern which is ten fists deep and four by four fists wide is a private domain even if it is located in the middle of a public domain. If a public domain passing in front of a house has a cistern in it, a person standing at the window of the house may not draw water from the cistern to the house on the Sabbath. Although both the house and cistern are private domains, the area between them

is a public domain and, by Rabbinical decree, one may not transfer between one private domain and another through a public domain (*Gem.* 99b). The *Gemara* explains that the mishnah discusses a case where the cistern is at least four fists away from the wall of the house; otherwise the area between the cistern and the house would not qualify as a public domain (since it is too narrow for people to pass through it) (*Rav*).

[The mishnah, however, discusses a case where there is a ten fist high

1. Our version of *Rashi* seems to have been before *Tosafos* (99b, s.v. מן) and *Tur (Orach Chaim* 351) and is accepted as halachah in *Shulchan Aruch* (there). However, it appears from *Ritva, Meiri* and *Tosefos HaRosh* that their versions of *Rashi* indicated that the specification 'below ten fists' refers to a gutter and clarifies that the inferred prohibition against placing a container directly to a gutter applies *even* to *below ten fists*. Thus there is no basis to restrict the dispensation stated in regard to a pipe to one placed below ten fists, as set forth by *Meiri* (see also *Geon Yaakov*). This latter view seems to have been held by *Rav* who makes no attempt to explain the difference between below and above ten fists in regard to a pipe.

אַשְׁפָּה בִּרְשׁוּת הָרַבִּים גְּבוֹהָה עֲשָׂרָה טְפָחִים,
חַלּוֹן שֶׁעַל גַּבָּיו שׁוֹפְכִין לְתוֹכָהּ מַיִם בַּשַּׁבָּת.

[ח] אִילָן שֶׁהוּא מֵסַךְ עַל הָאָרֶץ, אִם אֵין נוֹפוֹ
גָּבוֹהַ מִן הָאָרֶץ שְׁלֹשָׁה טְפָחִים,
מְטַלְטְלִין תַּחְתָּיו. שָׁרָשָׁיו גְּבוֹהִין מִן הָאָרֶץ
שְׁלֹשָׁה טְפָחִים, לֹא יֵשֵׁב עֲלֵיהֶן.
הַדֶּלֶת שֶׁבְּמֻקְצֶה, וַחֲדָקִים שֶׁבְּפִרְצָה, וּמַחְצָלוֹת
— אֵין נוֹעֲלִין בָּהֶן, אֶלָּא אִם כֵּן גְּבוֹהִים מִן הָאָרֶץ.

יד אברהם

embankment around the cistern, which changes the ruling.]

חַלּוֹן שֶׁעַל גַּבָּיו מְמַלְּאִין הֵימֶנּוּ בַּשַּׁבָּת. — *the window above it may [be used to] draw [water] from it [lit. we may fill from it] on the Sabbath.*

Since the embankment is ten fists high, the water-bucket will never pass over the public domain within ten fists of the ground. Since a public domain rises to a height of only ten fists, and anything above that is considered an exempt area (*Shabbos* 11:3, 100a), the person drawing water to the window will be transferring from one private domain to another through an exempt area rather than a public domain (*Rav*).

אַשְׁפָּה בִּרְשׁוּת הָרַבִּים גְּבוֹהָה עֲשָׂרָה טְפָחִים, חַלּוֹן שֶׁעַל גַּבָּיו שׁוֹפְכִין לְתוֹכָהּ מַיִם בַּשַּׁבָּת. — *If a rubbish heap in a public domain is*

ten fists high, the window above it may [be used to] pour water into it on the Sabbath.

The ruling regarding the garbage dump is identical with that concerning the cistern. Furthermore, we are not concerned that the garbage will someday be removed, thereby transforming the area into a public domain — and result in people desecrating the Sabbath as they continue to spill out their water from this window. The *Gemara* (99b) explains that the garbage dump under discussion is a public facility, which is therefore unlikely to be cleared. If it is a private dump, we are concerned that the individual responsible for the dump will one day remove it, causing people to desecrate the Sabbath by continuing to spill water in their customary manner (*Rav*).

8.

אִילָן שֶׁהוּא מֵסַךְ עַל הָאָרֶץ, אִם אֵין נוֹפוֹ גָּבוֹהַ מִן הָאָרֶץ שְׁלֹשָׁה טְפָחִים, מְטַלְטְלִין תַּחְתָּיו. — *A tree which droops over the ground — if its branches are not three fists higher than the ground, we may carry beneath it.*

Since the branches are within three fists of the ground the principle of *lavud*[1] can be applied and the branches are considered to extend to the ground. Thus they form a partition between the

area under the tree and the area outside it. The area under the tree is therefore considered a private domain (*Rav; Rashi*).

This ruling, however, is conditional upon a number of provisions: (a) The branches must be secured so that they do not sway in an ordinary wind; (b) the spaces between the branches must be filled in so that the remaining gaps measuring three fists or more do not exceed the closed sections (the basic requirement of any partition; see General

1. This principle states that any open space between two solid objects which measures less than three fists is considered closed. See General Introduction.

If a rubbish heap in a public domain is ten fists high, the window above it may [be used to] pour water into it on the Sabbath.

8. A tree which droops over the ground — if its branches are not three fists higher than the ground, we may carry beneath it. If its roots are higher than three fists above the ground, one may not sit on them.

The door of a backyard, thorns which are in a breach, and mats — we may not close with them unless they are above the ground.

YAD AVRAHAM

Introduction); c) the area beneath the tree may not be larger than two *beis-se'ah* (5,000 square cubits) because, as explained above (2:3), one may not carry objects in an area that exceeds two *beis-se'ah* even after it has been partitioned off, unless the partition was intended for purposes of human habitation[1] (*Rav* from *Gem.* 100a, and *Succah* 24b).

שָׁרָשָׁיו גְּבוֹהִין מִן הָאָרֶץ שְׁלֹשָׁה טְפָחִים, — *If its roots are higher than three fists above the ground,*

The tree's roots emerge from the ground as is often the case with old trees (*R' Yehonasan*).

לֹא יֵשֵׁב עֲלֵיהֶן. — *one may not sit on them.*

It is prohibited to make use of a tree on the Sabbath, because of the concern that one may be led to desecrate the Sabbath by breaking off a twig.[2] However, if the roots rise less than three fists above the ground they are considered part of the ground and are not included in this ban on sitting (*Rav; Rambam*).

הַדֶּלֶת שֶׁבְּמַקְצָה, — *The door of a backyard,*

In mishnaic times the area in back of a house was generally used as a storage

area [hence the name מַקְצָה, lit. *set aside*, i.e., an area for the long-term storage of objects which have been 'set aside' for future use]. Because this area was not used frequently, the door leading to it would not be attached to the door frame by means of hinges, but merely jammed into the frame. When one wished to enter the backyard, he would remove the door and place it on the ground and replace it when he left (*Rav; Rashi*).

וַחֲדָקִים שֶׁבְּפִרְצָה, — *(and)* [bunches of] *thorns which are in a breach,*

A breach in a fence was closed up by bunches of thorns. Whenever there is a need to do so, the thorns are removed to provide access through the breach; the breach is later resealed with the same thorns (*Rashi*). *Rambam* explains that they would attach thorns to [a framework of] poles and make something similar to a board from them, to seal breaches in garden fences.

וּמַחֲצָלוֹת — *and mats* —

Similarly, a mat made of reeds which is used to close a doorway and is removed when one wishes to enter (*Rav*).

1. Even if the tree was planted with the express purpose that it serve as a partition, the above limitation applies (*Rashi* 99b).

2. This prohibition is included in the ban against climbing a tree which is stated in *Beitzah* 5:2 (*Rambam;* see *Gem.* 100a).

יַעֲמֹד אָדָם בִּרְשׁוּת הַיָּחִיד וְיִפְתַּח בִּרְשׁוּת הָרַבִּים, בִּרְשׁוּת הָרַבִּים וְיִפְתַּח בִּרְשׁוּת הַיָּחִיד, אֶלָּא אִם כֵּן עָשָׂה מְחִצָּה גְּבוֹהַּ עֲשָׂרָה טְפָחִים — דִּבְרֵי רַבִּי מֵאִיר. אָמְרוּ לוֹ: "מַעֲשֶׂה בַּשּׁוּק שֶׁל פַּטָּמִין שֶׁהָיָה בִּירוּשָׁלַיִם, שֶׁהָיוּ נוֹעֲלִין וּמַנִּיחִין אֶת הַמַּפְתֵּחַ בְּחַלּוֹן שֶׁעַל גַּבֵּי הַפֶּתַח."

יד אברהם

אֵין נוֹעֲלִין בָּהֶן — **we may not close** [up an opening] **with them**

Closing an opening with them on the Sabbath resembles building and is therefore [Rabbinically] prohibited (Rav; Rashi).

אֶלָּא אִם כֵּן גְּבוֹהִים מִן הָאָרֶץ — **unless they are** [suspended] **above the ground.**

Unless they are tied to the partition which they serve, so that even when they are removed they do not touch the ground but dangle in midair (see Ritva).[1]

Even a minute elevation [i.e., even less than three fists] suffices (Rambam; Gem. 101a).[2]

Ba'al HaMaor points out that the ruling in our mishnah parallels R' Eliezer's ruling in

regard to a removable window shutter as set forth in Shabbos 17:7. Thus it follows that the Sages who dispute R' Eliezer's ruling there and permit the shutter to be replaced even if it is not tied at all (so that it must be placed on the ground when removed) will dispute the ruling of this mishnah as well and permit replacing the door, etc., even if it is not elevated above the ground. Ravad and R' Yeshayah of Trani (see Ritva; Rosh §15) assert that the ruling of our mishnah, which refers to entranceways which are seldom opened, resembles building to a greater degree (because of the semi-permanence of the sealing) than does replacement of a removable window shutter. Thus, even the Sages who rule leniently with regard to a window shutter will agree to the ruling set forth here. This view is endorsed by Shulchan Aruch (Orach Chaim 313:3; see also Milchamos and Ritva).

9.

לֹא יַעֲמֹד אָדָם בִּרְשׁוּת הַיָּחִיד וְיִפְתַּח בִּרְשׁוּת הָרַבִּים, בִּרְשׁוּת הָרַבִּים וְיִפְתַּח בִּרְשׁוּת הַיָּחִיד, — **A person may not stand in a private domain while unlocking** [a lock which is] **in a public domain,** [or] **in a public domain while unlocking in a private domain,**

A person standing in a private domain may not pick up a key from a spot in a public domain and open the lock of a building in a public domain, or vice versa. R' Meir prohibits this lest the person forget and bring the key to himself, thereby performing the labor of

1. This commentary, attributed to Ritva, is assumed by Mishnah Berurah (Be'ur Halachah to 313:3, s.v. גבוהים) to be held by most of the early authorities (see Mirkeves HaMishneh to Hil. Shabbos 26:8). However, Meiri explains that elevated refers to the door frame, i.e., the door step is elevated so that the door, after insertion, is elevated. Meiri cites the commentary adopted above in the text in the name of 'some commentators.' Chaye Adam (Nishmas Adam to Hil. Shabbos 39) arrives at this interpretation independently, but Mishnah Berurah (ibid.) rejects it vigorously (without alluding to Meiri).

2. Meiri and R' Yehonasan's version of the mishnah reads גְּבוֹהִין שְׁלֹשָׁה טְפָחִים, but it seems that the other Rishonim were not aware of such a reading. Meiri allows for the possibility that the halachah may not be in accord with the mishnah even according to this reading. See Mishnah Berurah 313:27.

9. **A** person may not stand in a private domain while unlocking in a public domain, [or] in a public domain while unlocking in a private domain, unless he makes a partition ten fists high — [these are] the words of R' Meir.

They said to him: 'It happened that in the butchers' market in Jerusalem they would lock and place the key in a window above the door.'

YAD AVRAHAM

transferring from domain to domain (*Rav; Rashi*).

R' Meir disputes the ruling set forth earlier (in mishnah 4) permitting one to stand in a private domain while moving objects (less than four cubits) in the public domain. That mishnah rules in accordance with the view of the Sages here (*Gem.* 98b).

[The concern here is that he may bring the key to himself *before* inserting it in the keyhole. The keyhole itself has (in the case discussed here) the status of an exempt area and no Biblical transgression would be involved were he to bring the key to himself after unlocking the lock.]

אֶלָא אִם כֵּן עָשָׂה מְחִצָּה גְּבוֹהַּ עֲשָׂרָה טְפָחִים — דְּבְרֵי רַבִּי מֵאִיר. — *unless he makes a partition ten fists high — [these are] the words of R' Meir.*

If a partition ten fists high is put up around the place in the public domain where the person is standing then that area is rendered a private domain, thus removing the basis of the prohibition. Even if he were now to bring the key to himself he would merely be transferring from one private domain to another, which is not Biblically prohibited even if a public domain is passed en route. The adjustment proposed by R' Meir is also applicable to the reverse situation, if a partition is put up around the door and

the location of the key in the public domain (*R' Yehonasan*).

אָמְרוּ לוֹ: ,,מַעֲשֶׂה שֶׁל פַּטָמִין שֶׁהָיָה בִּירוּשָׁלַיִם, שֶׁהָיוּ נוֹעֲלִין וּמַנִּיחִין אֶת הַמַּפְתֵּחַ בְּחַלּוֹן שֶׁעַל גַּבֵּי הַפֶּתַח.'' — *They* [the Sages] *said to him: 'It happened that in the butchers'* [lit. *animal fatteners'*[11]] *market in Jerusalem they would lock* [their stalls] *and place the key in a window above the door.'*

In this case, too, the market area in which the people were standing was a public domain and the window in which the key was deposited was a private domain (it was situated ten fists above the ground and measured four by four fists). Consequently, when people placed the key in the window they were standing in a public domain while placing an object in the private domain. The fact that this was done by the people of Jerusalem is proof that it is permitted and contradicts R' Meir's view (*Rashi*).

The *Gemara* (101a) elaborates that, on a Biblical level, Jerusalem was a private domain because it was surrounded by walls. The only barrier to carrying on the Sabbath was the fact that no *eruvei chatzeiros* was made[2] — so that it had to be treated as a *karmelis*, i.e., carrying was only Rabbinically

1. The translation follows *Rashi*. *Rambam (Comm.)* and *Rav* define פַּטָּמִין as bird breeders who fatten their fowl for slaughter. *Aruch* (s.v. פטם) and *Rif* translate this term as bird merchants. *Rav* follows *Rashi* in rendering butchers, but explains that they are called by this name because they fatten animals for slaughter.

2. The fact that no *eruvei chatzeiros* was made in Jerusalem (see *Gem.* 68a and *Orach Chaim* 366:13 that it is a *mitzvah* to make an *eruv*) needs explanation. *Rambam (Comm.)* remarks

רַבִּי יוֹסֵי אוֹמֵר: ,,שׁוּק שֶׁל צַמָּרִים הָיָה.''

[י] **נֶגֶר** שֶׁיֵּשׁ בְּרֹאשׁוֹ גְלוּסְטְרָא — רַבִּי אֱלִיעֶזֶר אוֹסֵר; וְרַבִּי יוֹסֵי מַתִּיר.

אָמַר רַבִּי אֱלִיעֶזֶר: ,,מַעֲשֶׂה בַּכְּנֶסֶת שֶׁבִּטְבֶרְיָא שֶׁהָיוּ נוֹהֲגִין בּוֹ הֶתֵּר, עַד שֶׁבָּא רַבָּן גַּמְלִיאֵל וְהַזְּקֵנִים וְאָסְרוּ לָהֶן.''

רַבִּי יוֹסֵי אוֹמֵר: ,,אִסּוּר נָהֲגוּ בָהּ; בָּא רַבָּן גַּמְלִיאֵל וְהַזְּקֵנִים וְהִתִּירוּ לָהֶן.''

יד אברהם

prohibited. Since this is not really analogous to R' Meir's case (where carrying is Biblically prohibited), the *Gemara* reconstructs from the argument of the Sages that R' Meir had prohibited even to stand in a *karmelis* and unlock in a private domain (or vice versa) and that it is to contradict this facet of R' Meir's view that the Sages adduced the custom of Jerusalem.[1]

Ritva explains that R' Meir's view in regard to a *karmelis* can be deduced from the statement, 'unless one erects a partition ten fists high.' If it were permitted to unlock in a private domain while standing in a *karmelis*, even a wall less than ten fists high would suffice, for even such a wall would render the enclosed area a *karmelis*.

רַבִּי יוֹסֵי אוֹמֵר: ,,שׁוּק שֶׁל צַמָּרִים הָיָה.'' — R' Yose says: 'It was the wool merchants' market.'

R' Yose agrees with the Sages on the legal point, disagreeing only as to where the event took place *(R' Yehonasan).*

The halachah is not in accord with R' Meir's view *(Rav; Rambam).*

that this is in accord with the ruling in 5:6 that in a public city an *eruv* which includes the entire town may not be made. R' Yaakov Emden *(Lechem Shamayim)* adds that, in keeping with this ruling, probably an *eruv* was made (cf. *Tos. Yom Tov)* leaving out only this market, because even in a public city an *eruv* may be made as long as a section of the town is excluded from the *eruv* (see there). Even so, however, a separate *eruv* could conceivably have been made for the market *(Kol HaRemez).* It is possible that at the time of this occurrence the inhabitants of this market had neglected to make an *eruv*. [Such a supposition is impossible, though, if a common *eruv* for the entire city were feasible, for then the *beis din* of the city would surely have seen to it that an *eruv* was made.]

Tiferes Yisrael suggests a plausible alternative. Jerusalem included among its many inhabitants many Sadducees who, as explained in 6:2, could not be included in an *eruv* because they fall into the category of one who does not accept the institution of *eruv*. The device of renting, which is effective for gentiles, is also not effective (because they are actually Jews). [Indeed, the ruling in 6:2 in regard to Sadducees is deduced from an occurrence with a member of this group in Jerusalem.] Only the option of nullification would be effective for Sadducees, and it may be assumed that they refused to comply with this requirement in a permanent manner.

A novel approach to this question is posed by R' Moshe Feinstein, *Igros Moshe, Orach Chaim I,* 139:5. See also *Yad Avraham* in ArtScroll edition of *Pesachim* 5:10.

1. The Sages disagree with R' Meir's ruling and permit one to stand in a bona fide public domain while unlocking in a private domain. This can be seen from their ruling in mishnah 4. They were, however, able to adduce proof contradicting R' Meir's view only in regard to a *karmelis* (*Rashbam* cited by *Ohr Zarua*).

R' Yose says: 'It was the wool merchants' market.'

10. A door bolt which has a knob at its end — R'
Eliezer prohibits [its use]; but R' Yose
permits. Said R' Eliezer: 'It happened that in the
synagogue in Tiberias they were accustomed to
permit this, until Rabban Gamliel and the Sages came
and forbade it to them.'

R' Yose says: 'They were accustomed to forbid
this; Rabban Gamliel and the Sages came and
permitted it to them.'

YAD AVRAHAM

10.

The next three mishnayos deal with the prohibition of *building* on the Sabbath. Closing or locking doors is not considered building because they are intended to be opened and closed and one is thus not adding to the structure of the house by closing or locking the door. However, the Sages forbade certain types of locks because they *appear* to be building, similar to the prohibition described above in mishnah 8. The following two mishnayos discuss this decree as it applies to door bolts.

נֶגֶר שֶׁיֵּשׁ בְּרֹאשׁוֹ גְלוֹסְטְרָא — — *A door bolt which has a knob at its end —*

A bolt which is not attached to the door but is re-inserted into the door each time and then jammed into the doorstep or jamb to secure the door (*Rav; Rashi*).

[A bolt without a knob does not resemble a utensil. Rather, it seems like an ordinary piece of lumber or metal and, as such, using it to secure the door gives the *appearance* of building, a Biblically forbidden labor. Its use is therefore Rabbinically forbidden. By contrast, if a utensil is used to secure the door it is apparent that the utensil's usage in this manner is temporary. It therefore does not resemble building and is permissible.]

A bolt with a knob at its end,

although not a regular utensil, is a utensil of sorts because it can be used as a pestle to pound pepper and other spices. It is therefore subject to the following dispute (*Rav; Rashi*).

רַבִּי אֱלִיעֶזֶר אוֹסֵר; — *R' Eliezer prohibits [its use];*

R' Eliezer prohibits this bolt to be used to secure a door because this would resemble building. Although the bolt is classified as a utensil, R' Eliezer prohibits its use in a door unless it always remains attached to it (*Rav; Rashi*; based on *Gem.* 101b-102a).

R' Eliezer does not dispute the rule that a utensil may be used to secure a door. He disagrees here because, although the bolt can be used as a pestle, it is not generally used as such and the resemblance to building is therefore not removed (*Ritva* citing *Yerushalmi*; see *Rashi* 102a, s.v. כשאין for a different explanation of R' Eliezer's view).

וְרַבִּי יוֹסֵי מַתִּיר. — *but R' Yose permits [it].*

Because the knob makes the bolt a usable utensil, its use does not resemble the labor of building (*Rashi*).

אָמַר רַבִּי אֱלִיעֶזֶר: ,,מַעֲשֶׂה בַכְּנֶסֶת שֶׁבִּטְבֶרְיָא שֶׁהָיוּ נוֹהֲגִין בּוֹ הֶתֵּר, עַד שֶׁבָּא רַבָּן גַּמְלִיאֵל וְהַזְּקֵנִים וְאָסְרוּ לָהֶן.'' — *Said R' Eliezer: 'It happened that in the synagogue in*

עירובין [יא] **נֶגֶר** הַנִּגְרָר, נוֹעֲלִים בּוֹ בַּמִּקְדָּשׁ, אֲבָל לֹא
בַּמְּדִינָה; וְהַמֻּנָּח, כָּאן וְכָאן אָסוּר.
רַבִּי יְהוּדָה אוֹמֵר: הַמֻּנָּח, מֻתָּר בַּמִּקְדָּשׁ, וְהַנִּגְרָר
בַּמְּדִינָה.

[יב] **מַחֲזִירִין** צִיר הַתַּחְתּוֹן בַּמִּקְדָּשׁ, אֲבָל
לֹא בַּמְּדִינָה; וְהָעֶלְיוֹן, כָּאן

יד אברהם

Tiberias they were accustomed to permit this, until Rabban Gamliel and the Sages came and forbade it to them.'

[The custom of the Jews of Tiberias was to secure their synagogue door with a knobbed bolt which was not permanently attached to the door. One time Rabban Gamliel and the Sages saw them doing this and forbade the practice, in accordance with the view expressed here by R' Eliezer.]

רַבִּי יוֹסֵי אוֹמֵר: "אָסוּר נָהֲגוּ בָהּ; בָּא רַבָּן גַּמְלִיאֵל וְהַזְּקֵנִים וְהִתִּירוּ לָהֶן." — *R' Yose says: 'They were accustomed to forbid this; [then] Rabban Gamliel and the Sages came and permitted it to them.'*

[R' Yose disputes R' Eliezer's version of the story about the synagogue in

Tiberias, maintaining that the reverse took place.]

Rashash (see also *Dikdukei Soferim* and *Shinuyei Nuschaos*) points out that probably we should read here R' Elazar [ben Shamua] who was a contemporary of R' Yose (both were disciples of R' Akiva; *Yevamos* 62b) instead of R' Eliezer [ben Horkenos] who preceded R' Yose by two generations (he was the mentor of R' Akiva). This version is, in fact, found in *Yevamos* 96b and in citations of this mishnah by some *Rishonim*. Thus the Rabban Gamliel mentioned here may be the Rabban Gamliel who lived after the destruction of the Temple (i.e., Rabban Gamliel of Yavneh; see comm. to 6:2, s.v. וְאָמַר לָנוּ אַבָּא).

11.

נֶגֶר הַנִּגְרָר, — *A door bolt which drags [on the ground],*

The bolt is attached to the door by means of a long cord so that when it is removed from the lock it drags on the ground when the door is moved. The bolt under discussion does not have a knob. If it had, one would be permitted to use it to secure the door even if it was not tied to the door at all [according to the Sages of the previous mishnah] (*Rav; Rashi*).

נוֹעֲלִים בּוֹ בַּמִּקְדָּשׁ, — *we may lock [a door] with it in the Temple,*

The use of such a bolt is not Biblically prohibited here because the bolt is attached to the door. However, because

the bolt drags when the door is opened, the fact that it is indeed a permanent part of the door is not sufficiently apparent and the use of such a bolt is, therefore, Rabbinically prohibited. Despite this it is permitted to be used in the Temple in accord with the dictum that Rabbinical edicts pertaining to the Sabbath do not (generally) apply in the Temple (*Rav; Rashi*).

אֲבָל לֹא בַּמְּדִינָה; — *but not in the provinces;*

It is Rabbinically prohibited to use such a bolt anywhere outside the Temple because it still bears some resemblance to the labor of building (*Rav; Rashi*).

11. **A** door bolt which drags [on the ground], we may lock with it in the Temple, but not in the provinces; but one which rests [on the ground] is prohibited here and there. R' Yehudah says: One which rests, is permitted in the Temple; but one which drags [even] in the provinces.

12. **W**e may reinsert the lower pivot in the Temple, but not in the provinces; but the upper

YAD AVRAHAM

וְהַמֻּנָּח, — *but one which rests [on the ground]*

I.e., a bolt (without a knob) which is not attached to the door at all but which is taken out of the door and placed on the ground (*Rav*; *Rashi*).

כַּאן וְכַאן אָסוּר. — *is prohibited* [both] *here and there*.

I.e., it is prohibited even in the Temple. Because the bolt is not tied (nor does it have a knob), its usage would constitute an act of building on a Biblical level, and such a prohibition cannot be waived even in the Temple (*Rav*; *Rashi*).

Ritva, however, maintains that the provisional nature of the bolt's use precludes its being classified building on a Biblical level. Rather, although the prohibition against the usage of the bolt is Rabbinic, it is considered a more stringent level of the Rabbinic decree against such semblances of building. Because of its stringency, it is not waived even for the Temple. The dictum that the Sabbath Rabbinical decrees do not apply in the Temple is not categorical (see *Tosafos* 102b, who

uses the same reasoning in regard to another matter).

רַבִּי יְהוּדָה אוֹמֵר: הַמֻּנָּח, מֻתָּר בַּמִּקְדָּשׁ, — *R' Yehudah says: One which rests is permitted in the Temple;*

R' Yehudah maintains that the usage of even a completely unattached bolt is only Rabbinically prohibited and is thus waived for the Temple (*Rav*; *Rashi*). Alternatively, R' Yehudah holds that the Rabbinical decree in regard to this bolt is not especially stringent, so that the rule of Rabbinic decrees being waived for the Temple can be applied to it, too (*Ritva*).

וְהַנִּגְרָר בַּמְּדִינָה. — *but one which drags* [on the ground is permitted *even*] *in the provinces.*

R' Yehudah's view in regard to a bolt which is attached to the door but drags on the ground is also more lenient than that of the first *Tanna*. He holds that use of this type of bolt is not prohibited at all (*Rav*).

The halachah is in accord with R' Yehudah's view (*Rav*, *Rambam* from *Gem.* 102a).

12.

מַחֲזִירִין צִיר הַתַּחְתּוֹן בַּמִּקְדָּשׁ, — *We may reinsert the lower pivot in the Temple,*

If the contents of the closet are needed for the sacrificial service, e.g., the closet contained salt, incense, etc. (*Rashi* to *Gem.* 102b).

The doors of the stalls and closets

were held in place by means of pegs which were set into the top and bottom of the door. These were inserted into holes in the frame of the closet to hold the door in place. The lower pivot was relatively simple to restore, and doing so could not be classified as building (*Rav*;

עֵירוּבִין וְכָאן אָסוּר. רַבִּי יְהוּדָה אוֹמֵר: הָעֶלְיוֹן בַּמִּקְדָשׁ,
וְהַתַּחְתּוֹן בַּמְּדִינָה.

[יג] מַחֲזִירִין רְטִיָּה בַּמִּקְדָשׁ, אֲבָל לֹא בַּמְּדִינָה; אִם בַּתְּחִלָּה, כָּאן וְכָאן אָסוּר.

יד אברהם

Rashi). [Although there is a Rabbinic prohibition to replace even the lower pivot, as seen from the mishnah's ruling in regard to the provinces, this prohibition is waived in the Temple, as in the previous mishnah.][1]

אֲבָל לֹא בַּמְּדִינָה; — *but not in the provinces;*

There is concern that the person reinserting it may attempt to secure the loose pivot using a hammer or other tools (Rav; Rashi). [This would violate the Biblical labor of striking the final blow (see Shabbos 7:2; see ArtScroll commentary there and 12:1).]

וְהָעֶלְיוֹן, כָּאן וְכָאן אָסוּר. — *but the upper one is prohibited* [both] *here and there.*

If the upper pivot has slipped out the entire door is in danger of falling out. Consequently, reinserting it is considered building on a Biblical level (Rav; Rashi). The Tanna of this segment of mishnah holds that the classification of building is applicable to movables as well (Rashi; see Beitzah 2:6).

Tosafos (102b), however, argues that since the halachah is that the rules of the labor of building do not apply to utensils (אֵין בִּנְיָן וּסְתִירָה בְּכֵלִים), the prohibition of this mishnah must be based on the concern that while

reinserting the pivot he may secure it by means of a hammer. This concern is greater for the upper pivot than the lower one (Meiri) and is so acute that the prohibition applies even in the Temple. The rule that Rabbinic decrees do not apply to the Temple does not refer to the more stringent decrees.

רַבִּי יְהוּדָה אוֹמֵר: הָעֶלְיוֹן בַּמִּקְדָשׁ, — *R' Yehudah says: The upper one in the Temple,*

R' Yehudah agrees that there is a prohibition against reinserting the upper pivot but argues that even in the case of the upper one this is merely a Rabbinic decree (due to the concern that he may use a hammer to secure the pivot) and it is therefore not applied in the Temple. In his opinion, since the matter under discussion concerns movables, even reinserting a door which fell out completely is not to be categorized as building, in accord with the view that the classification of building is not applicable to utensils [i.e., movables] (Rav; Rashi).

According to Tosafos' view, R' Yehudah disputes the first Tanna's categorization of the ban in regard to the upper hinge as a stringent Rabbinic ban.

וְהַתַּחְתּוֹן בַּמְּדִינָה. — *and the lower one* [even] *in the provinces.*

1. The permission granted here is only for the doors of movable objects. Even such minor adjustments are. however, prohibited in regard to the doors of fixed structures, such as buildings (R' Yehonasan). [The halachic definition of the term building is more stringent in regard to fixed structures (i.e., those attached to the ground) than in regard to movable objects. This is so even according to those who maintain that the classification of building is applicable to movables (יֵשׁ בִּנְיָן וּסְתִירָה בְּכֵלִים) as well (see Gem. 35a; see ArtScroll Shabbos 22:3). Thus, the minor act of reinserting the lower pivot is not classified as building in regard to movables, but is Biblically forbidden under that classification for attached structures.]

one is prohibited here and there. R' Yehudah says: The upper one in the Temple and the lower one in the provinces.

13. We may replace a dressing in the Temple, but not in the provinces; if for the first time, it is prohibited here and there.

YAD AVRAHAM

[R' Yehudah's opinion is that reinserting the lower pivot is not even Rabbinically prohibited and that there is no concern, even with regard to the lower one, that the person may attempt to repair the pivot with a hammer.]

13.

מַחֲזִירִין רְטִיָּה — *We may replace a dressing* [on a wound]

A רְטִיָּה is a medicinal salve smeared on a bandage for placement on a wound (*Rambam*).

בַּמִּקְדָּשׁ, — *in the Temple,*

It is prohibited to dress a wound on the Sabbath or *Yom Tov* (as explained further, s.v. אֲבָל). However, if a *Kohen* has a wound on his hand and removes the dressing in order to perform the service, he may replace the dressing upon completing his service. [The dressing would constitute an interposition (חֲצִיצָה, *chatzitzah*) between his hand and the sacrificial utensils with which the service is performed, and thus disqualify the service (*Zevachim* 24a).] This is one of several exemptions granted by the Sages because of the problems which would result from strict enforcement of the Rabbinical prohibitions ordinarily in force. As phrased by the *Gemara* (*Beitzah* 11b); הִתִּירוּ סוֹפוֹ מִשּׁוּם תְּחִלָּתוֹ, *they permitted the end* (replacing the dressing) *because of its beginning*, for sometimes a *Kohen* might forgo the service were he not permitted to replace the dressing on his wound (*Rav; Rashi*).

אֲבָל לֹא בַּמְּדִינָה; — *but not in the provinces;*

The Sages prohibited the application or replacement of such a dressing because of the concern that one may attempt to smooth out the salve on the bandage, thereby performing the Biblically prohibited labor of *smoothing* (*Rav; Rashi*). Alternatively, replacing the dressing is a form of healing (רְפוּאָה) which is prohibited on the Sabbath unless the problem is severe (*Shabbos* 14:3; opinion of R' Yosef in *Tos.* 102b).

Tosafos explains that *Rashi's* view is that the prohibition against healing does not apply here because the dressing was already in use before the Sabbath. According to R' Yosef, returning the dressing involves two prohibitions: (a) Healing; and (b) concern that he may smooth out the salve. The mishnah uses this case to teach that both prohibitions are waived in the Temple. *Magen Avraham* (328:26) accepts *Rashi's* view as halachah, as does *Mishnah Berurah* (328:1).

אִם בַּתְּחִלָּה, כַּאן וְכַאן אָסוּר. — [but] *if* [it is being placed on the wound] *for the first time, it is prohibited here and there.*

If the *Kohen* had not yet worn the

עירובין
י/יג

קוֹשְׁרִין נִימָא בַּמִּקְדָּשׁ, אֲבָל לֹא בַמְּדִינָה; אִם בַּתְּחִלָּה, כָּאן וְכָאן אָסוּר. חוֹתְכִין יַבֶּלֶת בַּמִּקְדָּשׁ, אֲבָל לֹא בַמְּדִינָה; וְאִם בִּכְלִי, כָּאן וְכָאן אָסוּר.

dressing before performing the service he may not put it on afterwards even in the Temple. The dispensation was granted only for a *Kohen* who removed a dressing for the purpose of performing the service (*Rav; Rashi*).

The rule that Rabbinic decrees are waived in the Temple only applies to the Temple service and is not relevant in this case. The dressing is not put on for the sake of the sacrificial service, but for the personal benefit of the *Kohen* (*Rav; Rashi*).

קוֹשְׁרִין נִימָא בַּמִּקְדָּשׁ, אֲבָל לֹא בַמְּדִינָה; — *We may tie a string in the Temple, but not in the provinces;*

As part of the daily service in the Temple, it was incumbent upon the Levites to accompany the libation service (נְסָכִים) with music even if this necessitated tying a string onto an instrument on the Sabbath with a permanent knot — an act normally prohibited because of the labor of tying (see *Shabbos* 15:1). The *Gemara* (103a) explains that the *Tanna* of our mishnah agrees with R' Eliezer that preliminaries necessary for the performance of a mitzvah, [e.g., tying the string to the instrument is a preliminary to the Levites' music] supersede the laws of the Sabbath (see *Shabbos* 19:1; *Gem.* there 131; *Rashi*).

The *Gemara* (103a) adds a restriction. Even in the Temple, one may tie a knot only if tying a bow [which is not classified as a knot with regard to the labor of *tying*], will not serve the same purpose. Thus, if the string broke at the end where it is attached to the pegs of the instrument a knot may not be tied because a bow would suffice to attach the string properly. However, if the string broke in the middle a bow would not tighten the string sufficiently to produce the proper

musical sound. In this case a knot may be tied.

אִם בַּתְּחִלָּה, כָּאן וְכָאן אָסוּר. — [but] *if* [it is being tied] *for the first time, it is prohibited here and there.*

If the string in question had never been attached to the instrument, it may not be tied to it on the Sabbath even in the Temple. Since the string could have been attached before the Sabbath, the dispensation granted for preliminaries does not apply (*Rashi*).

[Furthermore, even inserting in this spot a broken string and tying it in the middle is also prohibited. This, in fact, is the case which the mishnah now states is prohibited. The mishnah cannot be referring to a knot which is not in the middle because that is prohibited even where one is repairing the string.]

The *Gemara* explains that the *Tanna* of this mishnah differs with R' Eliezer on this one essential point. Whereas R' Eliezer permits preliminaries to be attended to on the Sabbath in all cases, this *Tanna* restricts this dispensation to circumstances where this action could not have been performed prior to the Sabbath (*Rashi* 103a, s.v. אלא).

Meiri adds that replacing an old string with a new one is included in the prohibition of installing a string for the first time.

According to this interpretation, this mishnah does not follow the accepted halachah which prohibits preliminaries to be performed on the Sabbath in any case.

Rambam (Hil. *Shabbos* 10:6), *Rav* and *R' Yehonasan* understand the mishnah as referring not to a permanent, Biblically prohibited, knot but to a temporary knot (קֶשֶׁר שֶׁאֵינוֹ שֶׁל קַיָּמָא) which is only Rabbinically prohibited (see ArtScroll *Shabbos*, Preface to ch. 15). The *Tanna* of the mishnah permits making such a knot in the

10
13

We may tie a string in the Temple, but not in the provinces; if for the first time, it is prohibited here and there.

We may cut off a wart in the Temple, but not in the provinces; if with an instrument, it is prohibited here and there.

YAD AVRAHAM

Temple. These commentators differ on the reason for this dispensation. *Rambam* holds that this is yet another example of the rule that Rabbinical edicts do not apply in the Temple. *R' Yehonasan* and *Rav* believe that this dispensation is due to the rule held by this *Tanna* that preliminaries which cannot be attended to before the Sabbath supersede the Sabbath. Obviously, *R' Yehonasan* interprets the passage in the *Gemara* (103a) as restricting this dispensation to Rabbincial prohibitions only.[1] (See *Ohr Gadol* in margin of *Mishnayos* ed. Vilna.) The concluding phrase of the mishnah, 'If for the first time' means that if the string could have been tied prior to the Sabbath, it is prohibited even in the Temple although only a Rabbinical prohibition is involved. See *Tosafos Yom Tov* and *Ohr Gadol* for the difficulties inherent in this interpretation.

חוֹתְכִין יַבֶּלֶת בַּמִּקְדָּשׁ, — *We may cut off a wart in the Temple,*

A wart is considered a blemish (מום) and disqualifies a sacrifice [or a *Kohen*[2]] from the Temple service (see *Lev.* 22:22). Its removal is therefore necessary for the sacrificial service. Removal of a wart is considered a *toladah* (secondary labor) of the labor of גוזז, *shearing*. Although this is a Biblical transgression, if it is removed in an unusual manner (כִּלְאַחַר יָד), e.g., bitten off or pulled off by hand instead of with a surgical instrument, it is only a Rabbinic prohibition, as is any labor done in an unusual manner (see *Shabbos* 10:3 and General Introduction to ArtScroll *Shabbos*, pp. 14-15). Consequently, for the sake of the Temple service the Sages permitted removing it in this fashion *(Rav; Rashi).*

אֲבָל לֹא בַמְּדִינָה; — *but not in the provinces;*

[Although removing a wart in this manner is not Biblically prohibited, it is Rabbinically prohibited.]

וְאִם בִּכְלִי, כָּאן וְכָאן אָסוּר. — [but] if [it is cut off] *with an instrument, it is prohibited here and there.*

If one wants to use an instrument [such as a scalpel or knife] to remove the wart, he is prohibited to do so even in the Temple since this would involve a Biblical transgression *(Rav; Rashi).*[3]

1. *R' Yehonasan* bases his interpretation on the *Gemara* which restricts the dispensation of our mishnah to knots in the middle of the string, and understands this in a different manner than does *Rashi.* A knot in the middle is temporary by its very nature because after the Sabbath the instrument will certainly be repaired in a more appropriate fashion. Therefore, only a Rabbinical prohibition is involved and this is waived here. A knot at the end of the string would be permanent, and therefore Biblically prohibited, so that no dispensation is appropriate.

2. *Meiri.* See *Mirkeves HaMishneh* to *Hil. Shabbos* 9:8 who declares that in *Rambam's* view our mishnah refers exclusively to removal of a wart from a *Kohen* and bases this on *Rambam's* commentary to the mishnah. But, as can readily be seen from R' Y. Kafich's edition of this work, the pertinent passage is a later interpolation.

3. *Rambam (Hil. Shabbos* 9:8) rules that even when removed with an instrument there is no Biblical prohibition. See *Mirkeves HaMishneh* and other commentaries.

עירובין [יד] **כֹּהֵן** שֶׁלָּקָה בְּאֶצְבָּעוֹ, כּוֹרֵךְ עָלָיו גֶּמִי
י/יד
בַּמִּקְדָּשׁ, אֲבָל לֹא בַמְּדִינָה. אִם
לְהוֹצִיא דָם, כָּאן וְכָאן אָסוּר.
בּוֹזְקִין מֶלַח עַל גַּבֵּי כֶבֶשׁ בִּשְׁבִיל שֶׁלֹּא יַחֲלִיקוּ.
וּמְמַלְאִים מִבּוֹר הַגּוֹלָה וּמִבּוֹר הַגָּדוֹל בַּגַּלְגַּל

יד אברהם

14.

כֹּהֵן שֶׁלָּקָה בְּאֶצְבָּעוֹ, — *A Kohen who injured his finger*

A *Kohen* who is injured should cover his wound because it is unseemly for him to perform the service with a wound showing (*Rav; Rashi*).

כּוֹרֵךְ עָלָיו גֶּמִי בַּמִּקְדָּשׁ, — *may wrap reed-grass over it in the Temple,*

Treatment of minor ailments is Rabbinically forbidden on the Sabbath (*Shabbos* 14:3). Nevertheless, a *Kohen* may wrap reed-grass (which has a curative effect) around his wound, because it serves the additional function of concealing the wound. This concealment is considered a prerequisite of the sacrificial service and the Rabbinic prohibition against healing is therefore waived in the Temple (*Rav; Rashi*).

The injury referred to here is to the *Kohen's* left hand, or, if on his right hand, on a part of the hand where it does not come in contact with the sacrifical utensils and objects used in the course of the service. Otherwise, the reed-grass would constitute an interposition (חֲצִיצָה) between the *Kohen's* hand and these objects and would invalidate the service (*Gem.* 103b; see comm., beginning of mish. 13). Furthermore, the *Kohen* may not tie a bandage of three by three finger breadths or a valuable small garment of any dimension around the wound, for this would be considered an additional garment to the four *Kehunah* vestments (see *Exodus* 28:40), and the service performed by a *Kohen* wearing additional vestments (מְרֻבֶּה בְגָדִים) is invalid (*Gem.* 103b with *Rashi*).

אֲבָל לֹא בַמְּדִינָה. — *but not in the provinces.*

[Wrapping reed-grass over a wound is considered a form of healing and is Rabbinically prohibited on the Sabbath.]

אִם לְהוֹצִיא דָם, — *If [it was done] to force out blood,*

If the reed-grass was tied fast in order to express the blood from the wound (*Rav; Rashi*).

כָּאן וְכָאן אָסוּר. — *it is prohibited here and there.*

Expressing blood from a living creature is forbidden as a derivative of the *melachah* of *slaughtering* (שׁוֹחֵט) and is Biblically prohibited. Consequently, it is prohibited even for the Temple (*Rav; Rashi*). Alternatively, expressing blood from the wound is not necessary for the sacrificial service and it would therefore be prohibited even if it were only a Rabbinic prohibition (*Rashi*).

בּוֹזְקִין מֶלַח עַל גַּבֵּי כֶבֶשׁ בִּשְׁבִיל שֶׁלֹּא יַחֲלִיקוּ. — *We may spread salt on the [Altar] ramp so that they [i.e., the Kohanim] should not slip.*

The long ramp leading up to the top of the Altar was very smooth and tended to be slippery in rainy weather [or from the fatty meat which would be put on it (*Rambam*)]. Salt would be spread on it to prevent the *Kohanim* from slipping. This may be done even on the Sabbath (*Rav; Rashi*).

Rav and *R' Yehonasan* add that this is prohibited in the provinces because it is considered מְתַקֵּן, *repairing* (which is prohibited by Rabbinic decree). The *Gemara* (104a) deduces this prohibition from the fact that the mishnah mentions the dispensation to spread salt in reference to the Altar-ramp.

14. **A** *Kohen* who injured his finger may wrap reed-grass over it in the Temple, but not in the provinces. If to force out blood, it is prohibited here and there.

We may spread salt on the ramp so that they should not slip. And we may draw water from the Exile's Well and from the Great Well with a windlass

Rashi (104a) asserts that the ban on spreading salt in this manner in the provinces is due to its similarity to the *melachah* of building since the salt is destined to remain at the place where it was spread and dissolve into it. In the Temple, however, the salt had to be swept up because, as the *Gemara* (104a) points out, it is prohibited to add to the dimensions of the Altar and that even the insignificant addition of salt to this edifice would fall under this ban. Accordingly, it would seem that there is no halachic difference between the Temple and the provinces. In both cases one may not spread substances which will remain there permanently but may sread substances which will be removed later. The practice which is permitted in the Temple would be permitted in the provinces as well, were the salt was intended to be swept away (see *Gem.* 104a). However, it may be that in the province salt may not be spread even if it is intended to be swept away, because usually it is meant to remain in the place where it was spread (*Geon Yaakov*).

וּמְמַלְּאִים מִבּוֹר הַגּוֹלָה — *And we may draw water from the Exile's Well*

This well was situated in one of the chambers on the southern side of the Temple court called לִשְׁכַּת הַגּוֹלָה, *the Exile's Chamber* (see *Middos* 5:4). The translation is based on *Rav's* commentary to *Middos* in which he explains that this well was dug by the exiles returning from Babylon at the beginning of the Second Temple era.

R' Yehonasan (apparently) punctuates this

word בּוֹר הַגּוֹלָה. *the Well of the Pail*, because a pail was used to draw water from this well (see *Tos. Yom Tov* to *Middos* 5:4). *Ravyah* (cited by *Tos. Yom Tov* there) and *Vilna Gaon* (in the margin of the Mishnah ed. Vilna there) say the name was due to the windlass (גַּלְגַּל) used to draw water from the well, as stated by the mishnah there. The mishnah there informs us that this well supplied water for the entire Temple court.

וּמִבּוֹר הַגָּדוֹל — *and from the Great Well*

Both of these wells were in a chamber in the Temple Court (*Rav*; *Rashi*).[1]

[See *Rambam's* commentary at the end of the mishnah.]

R' Yehonasan suggests that it was into this well that the laver (כִּיּוֹר) was lowered, as described in *Yoma* 3:10. Because of the laver's size the well had to be very large. However, it appears from R' Chananel's comments on this mishnah that (in his view) the laver was lowered into the Exile's Well. The same opinion is expressed by *Ravyah* (cited by *Tos. Yom Tov*, *Middos* 5:4).

בְּגַלְגַּל בַּשַּׁבָּת; — *with a windlass on the Sabbath;*

In the provinces it is prohibited to draw water with a windlass. Because of the ease with which the water is drawn, a person may forget and draw to water his garden (*Rav, Rashi* from *Gem.* 104a).[2]

The noise generated by the use of the windlass is not a contributing factor in the prohibition. Only musical sound is banned on the Sabbath (ibid.).

1. *Meiri* states that both of these wells were in the same chamber. This is probably also what *Rashi* and *Rav* mean.

2. However, only windlasses set up to draw great amounts of water at one time are prohibited. Pulleys used for small amounts of water may be used even in the provinces (*Tos.* 104a).

עֵרוּבִין בַּשַּׁבָּת; וּמִבְּאֵר הַקַּר בְּיוֹם טוֹב.

[טו] **שֶׁרֶץ** שֶׁנִּמְצָא בַּמִּקְדָּשׁ, כֹּהֵן מוֹצִיאוֹ
בְּהֶמְיָנוֹ, שֶׁלֹּא לְשַׁהוֹת אֶת הַטֻּמְאָה
— דִּבְרֵי רַבִּי יוֹחָנָן בֶּן בְּרוֹקָה. רַבִּי יְהוּדָה אוֹמֵר:
בִּצְבָת שֶׁל עֵץ, שֶׁלֹּא לְרַבּוֹת אֶת הַטֻּמְאָה.

יד אברהם

וּמִבְּאֵר הַקַּר בְּיוֹם טוֹב. — *and from the Flowing Well on Yom Tov*

The name בְּאֵר הַקַּר can be applied to all flowing wells, but the dispensation to draw water with a windlass on Yom Tov refers to a specific well which received a special dispensation. This well was needed by the exiles on *Yom Tov* when they first returned from Babylon and the prophets among them — Chaggai, Zechariah, and Malachi — granted them a special dispensation even though this well was in the provinces (i.e., outside of the Temple area). The dispensation remained in force even later [when the need for it was not so acute]. Other flowing wells, however, remain under the ban even on *Yom Tov* (*Rav, Rambam; Gem.* 104b).

Rashi adds that the dispensation to draw water from the Flowing Well applies only on *Yom Tov*, not on the Sabbath, as indicated by the language of the mishnah.

Rambam's version (see ed. Kafich) reads וּמְמַלְּאִין מִבּוֹר הַגּוֹלָה בַּגַּלְגַּל בְּשַׁבָּת וּמִבּוֹר הַגָּדוֹל וּמִבּוֹר הַקַּר בְּיוֹם טוֹב, *We may draw water from the Exile's Well with a windlass on the Sabbath, and from the Great Well and the Flowing Well on Yom Tov.* Thus the Great Well is one of two wells outside the Temple for which the prophets granted a special dispensation but only for Yom Tov (the words חָקָר and הַקַּר are synonymous; see *Rambam's Comm.* and *Shinuyei Nuschaos*). This conflicts with *Rav's* and *Rashi's* view (see above) that the Great Well was within the Temple area.

15.

שֶׁרֶץ שֶׁנִּמְצָא בַּמִּקְדָּשׁ, — *If a sheretz was found in the Temple,*

[If one of the eight species of creeping creatures listed in *Leviticus* (11:29, 30) as transmitting *tumah*-contamination was found dead in the Temple, it is incumbent to remove this contaminant from the Temple.[1] On the Sabbath, however, this presents a problem, for the carcass is useless and therefore *muktzeh* (an object which is Rabbinically prohibited to be moved on the Sabbath; see ArtScroll *Shabbos,* introduction to ch. 17).

1. It could be assumed that the obligation to rid the Temple of any contaminant such as a *sheretz* is based on the *mitzvah* (*Numbers* 5:2, 3) to *send out from the camp any metzorah ... so that they not contaminate* (with tumah) *their camps, in which I dwell.* R' Yerucham F. Perla in *Sefer HaMitzvos* of R' Saadiah Gaon (v. 1 pp. 809-12) argues that in *Rambam's* view this *mitzvah* refers only to contaminated *persons.* [However, according to a *baraisa* in *Sifre,* which requires that a minor (who is not himself obligated to perform *mitzvos*) be sent out of the Temple when he is contaminated, and R' Saadiah Gaon (see also *Tos.* 105a), this *mitzvah* obligates the public at large and the *beis din.*] According to *Rambam,* therefore, the above cited *mitzvah* cannot be the source for the obligation to remove a *sheretz* from the Temple. Rather, this obligation is part of the greater duty (incumbent upon the public at large) to see to the upkeep of the Temple. The presence of a contaminant within that holy precinct is to be viewed as a deterioration and impediment, as outlined further (s.v. וּמִבְּין הָאוּלָם). *Rambam* will interpret the disagreement between R' Shimon ben Nanas and R' Akiva (below) and the *Gemara's* comments pertaining to it in a manner different than that set forth in this commentary (s.v. וּמִבְּין הָאוּלָם).

on the Sabbath; and from the Flowing Well on *Yom Tov.*

15. If a *sheretz* was found in the Temple, a *Kohen* may remove it with his sash, so as not to prolong the presence of the *tumah*-contamination — [these are] the words of R' Yochanan ben Berokah. R' Yehudah says: With wooden tongs, so as not to increase the contamination.

YAD AVRAHAM

כֹּהֵן מוֹצִיאוֹ — *a* Kohen *may remove it*

He need not be concerned about the *muktzeh* prohibition since Rabbinic decrees are relaxed for the sake of the Temple *(Rav; Rashi).*

בַּהֲמְיָנוֹ, — *with his sash,*

I.e., he may remove it even in the sash (אַבְנֵט) which is one of the four priestly vestments worn by the *Kohen* while performing the service, although the sash will thereby contract *tumah* (see below, s.v. שֶׁלֹא לְשַׁהוֹת).

He should not, however, handle the *sheretz* with his bare hands, for in doing so he would himself contract *tumah* and a contaminated person is forbidden to enter the Temple courtyard or to remain there. The *sheretz* has the status of a primary *tumah* (אַב הַטֻּמְאָה) and it confers *tumah* on the person touching it. If the *Kohen* picks it up with his sash, however, the sash acts as a barrier between the *sheretz* and the *Kohen*. The sash acquires secondary *tumah* status (וְלַד הַטֻּמְאָה), or differently expressed,

tumah of the first degree[1] (רִאשׁוֹן לְטֻמְאָה), a level of *tumah* which is not potent enough to contaminate a person *(Rav; Rashi).*[2]

[It is preferable to contaminate the sash rather than the *Kohen* because one who introduces a contaminated utensil into the Temple is liable, at most,[3] to lashes (מַלְקוּת), whereas a contaminated person who enters the Temple Courtyard is liable to *kares, spiritual excision,* which is more severe.

שֶׁלֹא לְשַׁהוֹת אֶת הַטֻּמְאָה — דִּבְרֵי רַבִּי יוֹחָנָן בֶּן בְּרוֹקָה. — *so as not to prolong the presence of the* tumah*-contamination — [these are] the words of R' Yochanan ben Berokah.*

[This is the rationale for the preference for the procedure outlined here to that proposed below by R' Yehudah — to wait until a utensil not susceptible to *tumah*-contamination is found. The consideration of time, i.e., the additional interval needed to procure such a utensil, is more weighty than the consideration of not contaminating yet another object in the Temple.]

1. The term 'tumah of the first degree' does not mean the highest degree of *tumah*. It means the first level of acquired *tumah* — the first level of *tumah* that an object which is not itself a source of *tumah* generally contracts from an object which is.

2. A *sheretz* cannot pass on *tumah* by being carried (מַשָּׂא) as do other forms of *tumah* (see *Kelim* 1:1).

3. It is *Rambam's* view that for introducing a contaminated utensil into the Temple area only lashes (not *kares*) are incurred. Furthermore, he maintains that this is so only for utensils contaminated with a primary degree of *tumah* (אַב הַטֻּמְאָה). If the degree of contamination of the utensil is secondary (וְלַד הַטֻּמְאָה), e.g., a utensil contaminated through contact with a *sheretz*, only a Rabbinic prohibition bars its introduction into the Temple area (see *Ravad*). According to our versions, *Rashi* (104b, s.v. המכניס and חייב) holds that even for such a utensil *kares* is incurred. However, *Vilna Gaon* emends *Rashi* to conform with the view that only lashes are incurred in this case.

מֵהֵיכָן מוֹצִיאִין אוֹתוֹ? מִן הַהֵיכָל, וּמִן הָאוּלָם, וּמִבֵּין הָאוּלָם וְלַמִּזְבֵּחַ — דִּבְרֵי רַבִּי שִׁמְעוֹן בֶּן נַנָּס. רַבִּי עֲקִיבָא אוֹמֵר: מָקוֹם שֶׁחַיָּיבִין עַל זְדוֹנוֹ כָּרֵת וְעַל שִׁגְגָתוֹ חַטָּאת, מִשָּׁם מוֹצִיאִין אוֹתוֹ; וּשְׁאָר כָּל הַמְּקוֹמוֹת, כּוֹפִין עָלָיו פְּסַכְתֵּר. רַבִּי שִׁמְעוֹן אוֹמֵר: מָקוֹם שֶׁהִתִּירוּ לְךָ חֲכָמִים, מִשֶּׁלְּךָ נָתְנוּ לָךְ, שֶׁלֹּא הִתִּירוּ לְךָ אֶלָּא מִשּׁוּם שְׁבוּת.

יד אברהם

רַבִּי יְהוּדָה אוֹמֵר: בִּצְבַת שֶׁל עֵץ, — R' Yehudah says: With wooden tongs,

The *Kohen* should not handle the *sheretz* with an article of clothing which will contract *tumah* upon contact, but should wait until a wooden utensil, such as a pair of tongs, which is immune to *tumah* contamination, can be brought. [Wooden utensils cannot, as a rule, contract *tumah* unless they are receptacles, i.e., that the utensil is fit to serve as a container (see *Keilim* 2:1).]

שֶׁלֹּא לְרַבּוֹת אֶת הַטֻּמְאָה. — so as not to increase the tumah-*contamination*.

R' Yehudah's opinion is that the consideration of not increasing the number of contaminated objects outweighs the consideration of not prolonging the presence of *tumah* in the Temple. Thus, it is preferable to wait until wooden tongs can be brought rather than to hurry the removal by contaminating an additional object — the sash (*Rav; Rashi*).

מֵהֵיכָן מוֹצִיאִין אוֹתוֹ? — From where do we remove it [the *sheretz*]?

I.e., in which areas of the Temple does the presence of a *sheretz* warrant suspension of the prohibition against transporting *muktzeh* on the Sabbath? (*Rav; Rashi*). [On the weekdays, of course, the *sheretz* should be removed no matter where it is found.]

מִן הַהֵיכָל, — From the Temple,

[From the building itself, i.e., the Holy and the Holy of Holies.]

וּמִן הָאוּלָם, — (and from) the Antechamber,

[In front of the Temple entrance there was a huge room sixteen cubits wide (from east to west — including the thickness of its walls), and one hundred cubits long (from north to south). This room was called the אוּלָם, Antechamber or Hall.]

וּמִבֵּין הָאוּלָם וְלַמִּזְבֵּחַ — דִּבְרֵי רַבִּי שִׁמְעוֹן בֶּן נַנָּס. — and (from) between the Antechamber and the Altar — [these are] the words of R' Shimon ben Nanas.

[Between the Antechamber and the Courtyard Altar there was an open space twenty-two cubits wide. This area had a special status of holiness as compared with the rest of the Temple Courtyard (see *Keilim* 1:9).] If the *sheretz* is found anywhere else in the Temple Courtyard it may not be removed on the Sabbath. Rather, it is to be covered with a pot until nightfall when it may be removed, as explained below (*Rav; Rashi*).

The *Gemara* (104b; see *Tos*. 105a) explains that in R' Shimon ben Nanas's view the commandment to remove contaminated objects from the Temple does not apply to a *sheretz*. However, as *Meromei HaSadeh* and *Mikdash David* (38:1) demonstrate, besides this commandment it is incumbent to remove the *sheretz* because of the obligation to see to the upkeep of the Temple. According to this *Tanna*, the presence of a *sheretz* in the area of the Temple beyond the Altar is not offensive enough to warrant the suspension of the prohibition of *muktzeh* under the obligation to maintain the Temple.

From where do we remove it? From the Temple, the Antechamber, and between the Antechamber and the Altar — [these are] the words of R' Shimon ben Nanas. R' Akiva says: The area for which one incurs *kares* for an intentional transgression and a sin offering for unintentional transgression — from there we must remove it; but all other areas, we cover it with a pot.

R' Shimon says: Wherever the Sages have granted a dispensation, they have given you what is yours, for they have not permitted except that which is a Rabbinical decree.

YAD AVRAHAM

רַבִּי עֲקִיבָא אוֹמֵר: מָקוֹם שֶׁחַיָּיבִין עַל זְדוֹנוֹ כָּרֵת וְעַל שִׁגְגָתוֹ חַטָּאת, — *R' Akiva says: The area for which one incurs* kares *for an intentional transgression and a sin offering for unintentional transgression* —

The area in which a contaminated person who enters is liable to these penalties namely, the Temple building itself and the *entire* courtyard (Rav; Rashi).

מִשָּׁם מוֹצִיאִין אוֹתוֹ; — *from there we must remove it;*

R' Akiva disagrees with R' Shimon ben Nanas' opinion that removal of a *sheretz* on the Sabbath is limited to a small portion of the Temple Courtyard. He rules that the entire Courtyard is to be accorded this treatment. The punishment for a contaminated person entering the Courtyard does not distinguish between the area beyond the Altar and that before it *(Rav; Rashi).*

R' Akiva holds that a *sheretz* does fall under the the commandment to remove contaminated objects from the Temple. Therefore, its removal from any part of the area for which one incurs *kares* if he enters while contaminated, i.e., the entire Temple Courtyard area, is mandated by this *mitzvah.* The positive *mitzvah* to remove and the negative *mitzvah* forbidding one to enter (with its punishment of *kares)* are governed by identical criteria (Gem. 104b).

וּשְׁאָר כָּל הַמְּקוֹמוֹת, — *but* [in] *all (the) other areas,*

According to R' Shimon ben Nanas, the Courtyard area beyond the Altar; according to R' Akiva, the Temple Mount area (including the Women's Courtyard).

כּוֹפִין עָלָיו פְּסָכְתֵּר. — *we cover it* [the sheretz] *with a pot.*

If a *sheretz* was found in any of these areas it should be covered and left there until nightfall and then removed *(Rav; Rashi).*

רַבִּי שִׁמְעוֹן אוֹמֵר: מָקוֹם שֶׁהִתִּירוּ לָךְ חֲכָמִים, מִשֶּׁלְּךָ נָתְנוּ לָךְ, — *R' Shimon says: Wherever the Sages have granted a dispensation, they have given you what is yours,*

I.e., the Sages permitted only that which should have been permitted without their dispensation. The *Gemara* (105a) explains that R' Shimon refers to his ruling in 4:11 that one who found himself at the onset of the Sabbath up to fifteen cubits beyond the *techum* may return to his dwelling. Although superficially it appears that the Sages extended the dimensions of the *techum,* in reality this is not so for, as explained by R' Shimon (there), it can be assumed that the surveyors of the *techum* did not mark the boundary exactly but drew it in at least fifteen cubits closer to the town (Rambam). [The reasons for the inclusion of this ruling here are explained below.]

שֶׁלֹּא הִתִּירוּ לְךָ אֶלָּא מִשּׁוּם שְׁבוּת. — for they have not permitted except that which is [prohibited by] a Rabbinical decree

This refers to yet another dispensation mentioned earlier in this chapter in connection with the repair of a musical instrument by tying one of its strings (mishnah 13). In reference to this, R' Shimon disagrees (as interpreted by the Gemara 105a), and maintains that in such a case no regular knot may be made, only a bow (R' Shimon's explicit ruling to this effect is found in a baraisa cited by the Gemara 103a). Even a knot of a temporary nature, which entails only a Rabbinic prohibition, is forbidden because he may be led to make a similar knot of a permanent nature.[1] Only such Rabbinic decrees prohibiting actions which cannot ever, in the manner they are performed now, lead to Biblically prohibited acts, may be waived in the Temple. Therefore, only the Rabbinic decree against making a bow[2] is waived, for this type of knot is not halachically considered a knot, and is Biblically permitted even if intended

to be permanent (Rambam, with addition of some details from Gem. 105a).

The rightful place for this remark would have been earlier in mishnah 13,[3] but the editor of the mishnah wished to list together all the cases where a distinction is drawn between the Temple and the provinces. Upon completion of this list, R' Shimon's opinion, which erases this particular distinction in the case under discussion, is stated (Tos. 105a).

Rav's commentary (based on Rashi) sees R' Shimon's statement as an argument resolving an implicit contradiction between the two rulings alluded to, and thus connects the two seemingly unrelated statements. R' Shimon was responding to a perceived inconsistency in his attitude toward Rabbinic decrees, in that he tended to extreme leniency in regard to the Rabbinic prohibition against going beyond the borders of the techum whereas he tended to undue stringency when he banned all knots except bows to be used in repairing an instrument. R' Shimon explains that in the former case the seeming leniency is specious for the ruling is based upon the assumption that the person is actually within the techum — 'they have given you what is yours!' In the latter case, however, stringency is called for in circumstances where Rabbinically prohibited actions can evolve into Biblically prohibited ones.

1. According to Rashi's view above (see mishnah 13) even a permanent, Biblically forbidden, knot is permitted for the purpose of the musical accompaniment to the service. Hence, R' Shimon's concern is that he may be led to make an identical knot in the provinces where this would be a Biblical transgression.

2. It must be presumed that R' Shimon prohibits the making of bows by Rabbinic decree. This is a view hypothetically attributed to R' Yehudah by the Talmud (Shabbos 113a, Pesachim 11a) but rejected later. The halachah is that a bow is not even Rabbinically prohibited. See Orach Chaim 317:5.

3. Our commentary above has followed Rambam's commentary in expaining R' Shimon's statement as referring to two previous rulings: The first segment (מָקוֹם ... מִשֶּׁלְּךָ) refers back to 4:2, and the second segment (שֶׁלֹּא ... שְׁבוּת) to mishnah 13. The solution suggested by Tosafos does not explain the inclusion here of the first part of R' Shimon's statement.

Mr. and Mrs. Herman Wouk

and the

Abe Wouk Foundation

lovingly dedicate this volume in memory

of their בכור *and* ילד שעשועים

אברהם יצחק ע״ה בן חיים אביעזר זעליג נ״י

born September 2, 1946 / ו אלול תשי״ו

died July 27, 1951 / כג תמוז תשי״א.

*Abe was plucked from life before he flowered,
but the fruits of his memory nourish Torah and
chessed in America and Israel.*

*May the Torah learned from this volume
be a source of merit to his soul
and consolation to his parents.*

בלע המות לנצח

ᓆ§ מסכת ביצה
Tractate Beitzah

Translation and anthologized commentary by
Rabbi Hersh Goldwurm

Contributing editors:
Rabbi Naftali Kempler / Rabbi Avie Gold

Mesorah Publications, ltd

❧ The Thirty-nine Melachos (from Shabbos 7:2)

[1]	*sowing	זוֹרֵעַ
[2]	*plowing	חוֹרֵשׁ
[3]	*reaping	קוֹצֵר
[4]	*gathering	מְעַמֵּר
[5]	*threshing	דָּשׁ
[6]	*winnowing	זוֹרֶה
[7]	*sorting (*separating)	בּוֹרֵר
[8]	*grinding	טוֹחֵן
[9]	*sifting	מְרַקֵּד
[10]	*kneading	לָשׁ
[11]	*baking (*cooking)	(אוֹפֶה (מְבַשֵּׁל
[12]	*shearing	גּוֹזֵז
[13]	*whitening	מְלַבֵּן
[14]	*combing	מְנַפֵּץ
[15]	*dyeing	צוֹבֵעַ
[16]	*spinning	טוֹוֶה
[17]	*mounting the warp	מֵסֵךְ
[18]	*setting two heddles	עוֹשֶׂה שְׁנֵי בָתֵּי נִירִין
[19]	*weaving	אוֹרֵג
[20]	*removing threads	פּוֹצֵעַ
[21]	*tying	קוֹשֵׁר
[22]	*untying	מַתִּיר
[23]	*sewing	תּוֹפֵר
[24]	*tearing	קוֹרֵעַ
[25]	*trapping	צָד
[26]	*slaughtering	שׁוֹחֵט
[27]	*skinning	מַפְשִׁיט
[28]	*salting/*tanning[1]	מוֹלֵחַ/מְעַבֵּד
[29]	[*tracing lines]	[שְׂרְטוּט]
[30]	*smoothing	[מוֹחֵק [עוֹר
[31]	*cutting	מְחַתֵּךְ
[32]	*writing	כּוֹתֵב
[33]	*erasing	[מוֹחֵק [כְּתָב
[34]	*building	בּוֹנֶה
[35]	*demolishing	סוֹתֵר
[36]	*extinguishing	מְכַבֶּה
[37]	*kindling	מַבְעִיר
[38]	*striking the final blow	מַכֶּה בַפַּטִּישׁ
[39]	*transferring (*transporting) from domain to domain	הוֹצָאָה

*Throughout the introduction and commentary we have used an asterisk and italics to indicate an *av melachah.*

1. The list of *melachos* in *Shabbos* 7:2 includes *salting hides* and *tanning* as separate *melachos.* The Talmud (*Shabbos* 75b) states that these two are really the same *melachah,* and emends the mishnah by inserting שְׂרְטוּט, *tracing lines,* as the twenty-ninth *melachah.*

General Introduction

Commonly called בֵּיצָה, *Beitzah*, after the word with which it commences, this tractate is also known as tractate יוֹם טוֹב, *Yom Tov* (see *Iggeres R' Sherira Gaon, Meiri*), for it discusses the halachos peculiar to *Yom Tov*. [As used throughout this tractate, the term *Yom Tov* refers to those festival days on which the Torah forbids מְלָאכָה, *labor*. These include the first (and, outside of *Eretz Yisrael*, the second) and seventh (and eighth) days of Pesach, Shavuos, the first (and second) day(s) of Succos, Shemini Atzeres (with Simchas Torah), and Rosh Hashanah. Not included are Yom Kippur, to which all the stringencies of the Sabbath apply, and חוֹל הַמּוֹעֵד, *Chol HaMoed*, (the intermediate days of Pesach and Succos) on which the labor restrictions are greatly relaxed. Tractate *Moed Katan*, literally, *Minor Festival*, is devoted to the laws governing *Chol HaMoed*.]

◆§ Categories of Melachah (Labor) Permitted on Yom Tov

Basically, the same thirty-nine categories of labor [*melachah*] listed in tractate *Shabbos* 7:2 [see chart on facing page] as prohibited on the Sabbath are prohibited on *Yom Tov* as well. However, there is one basic difference which distinguishes *Yom Tov* from Sabbath and gives rise to a set of circumstances which must be dealt with in a unique halachic context — namely, the permissibility of labors involved in the preparation of אוֹכֶל נֶפֶשׁ, *food for human consumption*. As stated in the Torah: *No labor may be performed on them* [the first and seventh day of Pesach], *however, that which is eaten by any person, that alone may be performed for you* (*Exodus* 12:16). This dispensation allows for labor to be performed in connection with the preparation of food on *Yom Tov*. Additionally, *Ramban* (*Leviticus* 23:7) points out that the term מְלֶאכֶת עֲבוֹדָה, *servile work*, used in the prohibition against labor on *Yom Tov*, excludes labor done for the preparation of food, which may be termed מְלֶאכֶת הֲנָאָה, *pleasurable work*. Thus, the ban against labor on *Yom Tov* carries within itself the dispensation for מְלֶאכֶת אוֹכֶל נֶפֶשׁ, *labor performed in the preparation of food*. Significantly, the prohibitions against labor on Sabbath (ibid. v. 3) and *Yom Kippur* (ibid. v. 28) are not modified with the word עֲבוֹדָה. On these days all labor, whether servile or pleasurable, is prohibited.

◆§ Exceptions to the Dispensation for Food Preparation

Since the Torah requires but one condition — food preparation — for allowing the performance of labors, on *Yom Tov*, it should follow that any of the thirty-nine categories of forbidden labor are permitted on *Yom Tov* if they be performed in connection with the preparation of food. Indeed, it is abundantly clear throughout this tractate that there are no restrictions on the *melachos* of *cooking, *slaughtering, *kindling or *transporting from domain to domain, provided they serve the purpose of preparing food for *Yom Tov*. Yet from other statements in the Mishnah and in the *Gemara* it is clear that some labors are excluded from this dispensation. Examples of such exclusion are *trapping (see 3:1) and *reaping (Gem. 3a). The *Gemara*, however, does not indicate clearly which labors are permitted for food preparation and which are not, nor does it provide guidelines by which such a determination can be made.

The *Rishonim* (early commentators) differ in explaining the source of the prohibition against certain labors and establishing the criteria for which labors may be performed on *Yom Tov* for food preparation.

Tosafos (3a and 23b) cites *Talmud Yerushalmi* that among the labors performed as part of the process of baking bread [i.e., the first eleven *melachos* enumerated in *Shabbos* 7:2; see chart] only those labors from *kneading, and onward are permitted. Consequently, labors such as *reaping, *threshing, or *grinding are not permitted even if they are performed in connection with food preparation (see *comm.* 1:8, *Maharil* cited in *Ba'er Hetev* 495:5, and *Yam Shel Shlomo* 1:42; *Yerushalmi* 1:10). Another version of the *Yerushalmi* has it that three labors are specifically excluded from the dispensation of food preparation: *reaping, *threshing and *sifting (see *Yerushalmi* 1:10).[1]

Rashi (23b) distinguishes between labor that could have been performed before *Yom Tov* and labor that could not. Thus, *trapping and *reaping are prohibited for there would be no appreciable difference in the quality of the result of these labors had they been performed before the onset of *Yom Tov*. *Cooking and *slaughtering, by contrast, are labors that yield fresher and tastier results if performed immediately prior to consumption and therefore no restrictions are placed on these labor categories in connection with food preparation (see *Rashi* 3a).

Rambam's opinion (*Hil. Yom Tov* 1:5-8) concurs with that of *Rashi*, differing only in that according to *Rambam* this distinction is Rabbinically ordained and as far as the Scriptural law is concerned all labors are permitted in connection with food preparation. *Rambam* explains the reason for the Rabbinical prohibition on labors that can be performed before *Yom Tov* is that the Sages were concerned that a person may spend most of the day involved in food preparation and thus be unable to properly enjoy the *Yom Tov*.

---

1. *Maharshal (Yam Shel Shlomo* 3:1; cf. *Shitah Mekubetzes* and *Tos. R' Peretz* 23b) suggests that the *Yerushalmi* does not mean to prohibit only these specific labors, but rather to single out these labors to enable us to formulate a criterion of labors that are prohibited. The general rule is that labors associated with preparation of food for storage purposes rather than immediate consumption are prohibited. This explains why *trapping is forbidden while *slaughtering is permitted. Thus (see further) *Tosafos'* opinion parallels the views of *Rosh* and *Ran* (see further); they only differ in whether the prohibition is Scriptural *(Tosafos)* or Rabbinical *(Rosh* and *Ran).

Rosh and *Ran* are of the opinion that the reason some labors are prohibited is a Rabbinical decree: the Sages did not permit any type of labor which ordinarily is used in connection with the preparation of large amounts of food. *Reaping, for example, is the type of labor that is ordinarily associated with large scale food preparation, an act that would bear (according to *Rosh)* the semblance of weekday activity. Even picking one fruit off a tree is prohibited, for the criterion is the category of labor — *reaping — which is ordinarily associated with food preparation of greater quantities. *Ran* explains that the Sages were apprehensive that if a person were to be permitted to reap, for example, then he would do it in his usual manner and harvest enough food for a number of days. This would be a violation of *Yom Tov*, for even food preparation is permitted only in the quantities necessary for consumption on *Yom Tov* (see preface to ch. 2 and comm. to 3:1).

For a discussion regarding the specific prohibition against *grinding, see 1:7; *trapping, see 3:1.

✑§ The Principle of Mitoch

This dispensation is considerably broadened by the principle of מִתּוֹךְ, *mitoch*, enunciated by Beis Hillel (see 1:5). This concept extends the permissibility of those labor categories that may be performed in the preparation of food (e.g., *transporting* food from one house to another) to other necessities of *Yom Tov* not involved with food preparation (e.g., *transporting* a Torah scroll from which they will read on that day of *Yom Tov)*.

✑§ מֻקְצָה — Muktzeh

The subject of *muktzeh* appears recurringly in this tractate and an understanding of the basic rules of *muktzeh* is necessary to an understanding of many of the forthcoming mishnayos.

The term מֻקְצָה, *muktzeh*, literally *set aside*, refers to a class of objects whose use on the Sabbath or *Yom Tov* was unanticipated. For example, sticks or stones are items which are essentially useless and, unless otherwise indicated, are considered מֻקְצָה מִדַּעַת, *mentally set aside*, as objects that will not be used on the Sabbath. Another example is figs or grapes spread on a roof to dry (גְּרוֹגְרוֹת וְצִימוּקִים). Once this process has begun, the fruits are unfit for consumption for many days, until they are completely dried. Since they are not fit to be eaten they are considered *muktzeh*.

✑§ The Categories of Muktzeh

Since there are several reasons for which an object may be declared *muktzeh*, such objects are classified into various categories. *Beis Yosef* (308) classifies the various types of *muktzeh*:

(a) מֻקְצָה מַחֲמַת חֶסְרוֹן כִּיס, *set aside for fear of monetary loss*. This category included any utensil whose general use is objected to by the owner for fear it will become damaged, e.g., a barber's razor. [Though the owner certainly uses the razor for its primary function, cutting hair, that function is prohibited on the Sabbath and *Yom Tov*. Since this blade must be kept perfectly sharp, the owner objects to its being used for any secondary, permissible function (e.g., as a table knife) for fear of damaging the cutting edge.]

(b) כְּלִי שֶׁמְּלַאכְתּוֹ לְאִסּוּר, *a utensil used primarily for work prohibited on the Sabbath*. This includes any utensil (such as a hammer) whose primary use (*building*) is forbidden on the Sabbath and *Yom Tov* but which is also occasionally used for permissible activities (cracking nuts). Since the items in this category are not easily damaged, the owner does not object to their being used for these secondary purposes.

(c) מֻקְצֶה מֵחֲמַת גּוּפוֹ, *set aside because of its intrinsic properties*. This refers to anything which is neither a utensil nor a food edible to humans, or animals, e.g., stones, money, reeds, wood, beams, earth, sand, a corpse, living animals, figs and raisins in the process of being dried, and anything else not fit for use on the Sabbath or *Yom Tov*.

(d) בָּסִיס לְדָבָר הָאָסוּר, *a base to a muktzeh object*. This group comprises all otherwise non-*muktzeh* articles upon which an item of *muktzeh* lies e.g., a barrel upon which a stone is lying, or a pillow upon which money is lying. Even after the *muktzeh* has been removed (e.g., by a non-Jew), the base remains *muktzeh* until the end of that Sabbath or *Yom Tov*. This rule applies only to utensils which served as a base to a *muktzeh* object at the onset of the day, i.e., at twilight.

(e) מְחֻבָּר וּמְחֻסָּר צֵידָה, *attached [to the ground] or lacking capture*. Included in this category are any animal which was not trapped [this is relevant primarily to *Yom Tov*, when animals may be slaughtered and their meat cooked, but when they may not be trapped] and any growing item, such as a fruit, vegetable, or wood, which had not been reaped as of twilight on the eve of the Sabbath or *Yom Tov*.

(f) מֻקְצֶה לְמִצְוָתוֹ, *set aside because of its mitzvah*. Such items as the wood of a *sukkah* and its ornaments fall into this classification.

There is yet a seventh category of *muktzeh* known as נוֹלָד, *nolad* [lit. *just born*]. *Nolad* is any otherwise non-*muktzeh* object which has first achieved its presently useful state on this Sabbath. Since it was not in a usable state prior to the Sabbath, it cannot be said to have been 'prepared' before the Sabbath. Consequently it is *muktzeh*. [See first footnote of commentary for an example of *nolad*.] As with many of the categories of *muktzeh*, the limits of the law of *nolad* are subject to a dispute between R' Yehudah and R' Shimon. R' Shimon limits the prohibition of *nolad* to only those items whose present form and function is radically different from their pre-Sabbath one (*Tos*. 2a, *Eruvin* 46a). R' Yehudah, however, prohibits even certain items whose function has changed on the Sabbath, though their form has not (*Shabbos* 124b).

Anything one is permitted to prepare on the Sabbath is not regarded as *nolad* since it is within one's power to ready it. For this reason, a pot left on the fire at the beginning of Shabbos, despite its being too hot to eat, is not *nolad* since one may at any time remove it from the fire, allow it to cool and thereby render it edible *(Gem.* 26b).

According to many authorities, the halachah with regard to the laws of the Sabbath follows the opinion of R' Shimon. With regard to Yom Tov, it follows the opinion of R' Yehudah *(Shulchan Aruch* and *Rama,* 495:4; see *Mishnah Berurah* 495:17).

◄§ The Laws of Muktzeh

In the main, the restrictions against *muktzeh* objects center on carrying or moving them (טִלְטוּל מֻקְצֶה). An object classified as *muktzeh* at the onset of the Sabbath or *Yom Tov* may not be moved from its place for the duration of the day (see *Orach Chaim* 308:3 with *Mishnah Berurah,* for laws concerning touching *muktzeh).* Although the prohibition against moving *muktzeh* is clearly Rabbinical in nature, it can, according to most authorities, be traced back to Biblical times. The Talmud *(Shabbos* 123b) reports that because of the rampant desecration of the Sabbath in Jerusalem in the days of Nechemiah (see *Nechemiah* 13:15), the Sages added extra stringencies to the laws of *muktzeh* which were relaxed at a later date.[1] According to *Rambam (Hil. Shabbos* 24:12-13), restrictions were placed against the handling of *muktzeh* objects to preserve the sanctity of the Sabbath, thereby creating a visible distinction between one's behavior on the Sabbath and on weekdays.

According to *Ravad* (ibid.) the laws of *muktzeh* were intended as a safeguard against the prohibition of *transporting objects into the street; limiting the number of objects that may be moved reduces the chances of inadvertent carrying.[2]

In addition to the prohibition against moving *muktzeh,* there is also a lesser known, yet more stringent, restriction against eating *muktzeh* (see *comm.* to 3:2), for this prohibition is rooted in the Torah admonition *(Exodus* 16:5), *on the sixth day they shall 'prepare' what they bring,* which implies that the Sabbath food must be prepared in advance. A *muktzeh* object, being mentally 'set aside' from use, is not considered מוּכָן, *prepared.*[3]

Although the basic restrictions of *muktzeh* are undisputed, there are differences of opinion about the extent of these restrictions. In particular R' Yehudah and R' Shimon disagree numerous times on this subject (see for

---

1. *Doros HaRishonim,* ed. Jerusalem, v. 1, p. 344-5, maintains that this passage of the Talmud proves that *muktzeh* was in fact enacted prior to Nechemiah; only the additional stringencies date to his time, cf. *Maggid Mishneh* to *Hil. Shabbos* 24:12.

2. *Ravad's* view is stated in the Talmud *(Shabbos* 122a, 124b; see *Rashi).* See also *Tosafos (Beitzah* 12a).

3. See *Shabbos* 128a and *Rashi, Pnei Yehoshua* and *Chasam Sofer I* and *II* to 2b; preface to *Chasam Sofer II. Rashba (Shabbos* 29b) includes the use of *muktzeh* (הִשְׁתַּמְּשׁוּת וַהֲנָאָה בְּיָדַיִם) as part of the prohibition against eating it. See *Magen Avraham* 501:12; *Chiddushei R' Akiva Eiger* to *Orach Chaim* 325:4; cf. *Magen Avraham* 325:9, 328:41, 507:3; *Beis HaLevi* 1:2.

example 2a,b and 40a,b). R' Shimon is more lenient and permits certain categories of *muktzeh* while R' Yehudah is more stringent in the application of the *muktzeh* restrictions.

◄§ Sequence of Topics in Tractate Beitzah

The differences between the Sabbath and *Yom Tov* form the basis of much of the discussion in this tractate, and help to explain the seemingly haphazard sequence in which the topics appear. The first two chapters are a collection of all the disagreements between the schools of Shammai and Hillel, pertaining to *Yom Tov*. It is difficult to discover the thread connecting all of these mishnayos, but it can readily be seen that clusters of mishnayos, related to one another, are placed together. In the first two mishnayos we find the only three instances pertaining to *Yom Tov* where the opinion of Beis Hillel is more stringent than that of Beis Shammai. The mishnah first discusses an egg laid on *Yom Tov*, a case that pertains to the Sabbath as well. Next a law specific to Pesach is mentioned. The third topic is that of *slaughtering, which is permitted only on *Yom Tov*. The subject of *slaughtering is then expanded to include birds set aside for use on *Yom Tov* (mishnayos 3-4). Mishnah 5 speaks of actions not intrinsic to food preparation *per se* but which, if prohibited, would deter people from preparing food for *Yom Tov*. This mishnah concludes with the basic disagreement of Beis Shammai with Beis Hillel concerning the principle of *mitoch* (see above). Since the example chosen for the dispute about *mitoch* is the *transporting of objects not needed for food purposes, mishnah 6 continues with the rules regarding *transporting various foodstuffs. Mishnayos 7 and 8 digress to discuss certain labors which may be performed, but not in the usual manner. The last two mishnayos discuss objects which may be sent to a friend on *Yom Tov*, and should seemingly have been grouped with mishnah 6. Perhaps, these mishnayos are grouped separately because the opinions of two later *Tannaim* (R' Yehudah and R' Shimon) are introduced.

The first two mishnayos in the second chapter deal with the problems arising when *Yom Tov* occurs immediately before or after the Sabbath: the setting of an עֵירוּב תַּבְשִׁילִין, *eruv tavshilin*, to permit Sabbath preparations to be performed on *Yom Tov*, and the immersion of people and utensils in a *mikveh*. The next two speak of the immersion on *Yom Tov* of utensils to be used with sanctified foods and sacrificial portions, and the permissibility of bringing personal Temple sacrifices on *Yom Tov*. Mishnah 5 presents the final dispute in this collection of points of contention between Beis Shammai and Beis Hillel regarding *Yom Tov*. Three matters pertaining to *Yom Tov* in which Rabban Gamliel seemingly ruled according to Beis Shammai's more stringent opinion and three instances where R' Gamliel's view was more lenient than that of his contemporaries are then presented (mishnayos 6-7). Mishnah 8 follows with three matters about which R' Elazar ben Azariah [who, like R' Gamliel, was president of the *Sanhedrin*] disagreed with his contemporaries and permitted what they prohibited (as did R' Gamliel in mishnah 7). Since one of these matters involved the law of a pepper mill as it pertains to *Yom Tov*, the mishnah digresses (as it often does) to discuss the status of the different parts of the pepper mill vis-a-vis the laws of *tumah*-contamination (mishnah 9), and concludes (mishnah 10) with a law that relates to both *tumah* and *muktzeh*.

The third chapter returns to the laws of *Yom Tov* as they pertain to the use of live animals for food: **trapping* of fish and animals (1-2); **slaughtering* animals for food (3-4); moving the carcass of an animal which has not been slaughtered (5); apportionment of the meat of an animal slaughtered on *Yom Tov* (6-7); and measuring of foodstuffs on *Yom Tov* (8).

The fourth chapter deals mainly with the use of fire on *Yom Tov*. The discussions include laws pertaining to **transporting* commodities on *Yom Tov*, among them loads of straw and wood (1); which stores of wood or straw are *muktzeh* and may not be used on *Yom Tov* (2); splitting wood for a fire (3); preparations of other accessories for burning, such as lamps, wicks, ovens, and stands for pots during cooking (4-5). This leads to a digression about using wood for purposes other than fire, such as to guide an animal (5), or as a toothpick (6). The final mishnah (7) returns to the topic of fire and concludes with a statement of R' Eliezer's view on *muktzeh*. This conclusion, though inconsistent with the subject matter, is inserted here because R' Eliezer's view concerning slivers of wood had been mentioned in mishnah 6.

The fifth chapter starts with an instance where a Rabbinical prohibition is waived in order to enhance the enjoyment of *Yom Tov*, but not for Sabbath. There follows a long list of rabbinical prohibitions which apply to *Yom Tov* as well as to Sabbath (2); and a discussion of the ramifications of the *techum* laws (3-7). This latter topic, though not peculiar to *Yom Tov*, is discussed here because of the wider possibilities offered by the provision that permits **transporting* foodstuffs on *Yom Tov*. The tractate ends (7) on the topic of *muktzeh* as it pertains to animals pasturing outside the *techum*.

ביצה [א] בֵּיצָה שֶׁנּוֹלְדָה בְּיוֹם טוֹב — בֵּית שַׁמַּאי אוֹמְרִים: תֵּאָכֵל. וּבֵית הִלֵּל אוֹמְרִים: לֹא תֵאָכֵל.

יד אברהם

Chapter 1

1.

בֵּיצָה שֶׁנּוֹלְדָה בְּיוֹם טוֹב — — *An egg that was laid* [lit. *born*] *on Yom Tov* [i.e., Pesach, Shavuos, Rosh Hashanah, Succos] —

This discussion, about an egg laid on *Yom Tov*, pertains to Sabbath as well. *Yom Tov* is chosen as the setting for this discussion because the egg would normally not be eaten on the Sabbath when it would have to be eaten raw (see *HaMaor*).

בֵּית שַׁמַּאי אוֹמְרִים: תֵּאָכֵל. וּבֵית הִלֵּל אוֹמְרִים: לֹא תֵאָכֵל. — *Beis Shammai* [lit. *the Academy* (i.e., the disciples) *of Shammai*] *say: It may be eaten. But Beis Hillel* [lit. *the Academy of Hillel*] *say: It may not be eaten.*

The *Gemara* proposes various reasons for Beis Hillel's prohibition.[1] Rabbah (2b) explains that an egg which is laid one day is always fully developed (within the chicken) on the previous day. Thus, if one eats an egg which was laid today he is eating something which was prepared yesterday. If that day

was the Sabbath (i.e., *Yom Tov* was on Sunday), and the egg were eaten on *Yom Tov*, this would result in preparation for *Yom Tov* having occurred on the Sabbath. Similarly, an egg laid on a Sabbath subsequent to *Yom Tov* (i.e., *Yom Tov* was on Friday) is considered to be prepared on *Yom Tov*.

Rabbah expounds the principle of הֲכָנָה, *hachanah* [lit. *preparation*], which forbids the preparation of food (or other articles) on *Yom Tov* for use on the Sabbath, or on the Sabbath for use on *Yom Tov*. Such preparation renders the prepared object prohibited for use on the Sabbath or *Yom Tov* for which it was prepared, even though no forbidden labor was involved in preparation. Rabbah derives this principle from *Exodus* (16:5) which states concerning the Sabbath: *And it shall be on the sixth day and they shall prepare what they bring in.* The intention of the verse cannot be simply that preparation involving a

---

1. An egg laid on *Yom Tov* could be considered *muktzeh* for since it was not in existence before *Yom Tov* it is נוֹלָד, *nolad* [see General Introduction] and it cannot be considered מוּכָן, *prepared*, prior to *Yom Tov*. Alternatively, a hen designated for egg laying (תַּרְנְגֹלֶת הָעוֹמֶדֶת לְגַדֵּל בֵּיצִים) is itself *muktzeh*. Consequently, an egg which had at the outset of *Yom Tov* been part of it must also be considered *muktzeh* (*Gem.* 2a). However, an egg laid by a chicken designated for slaughter (תַּרְנְגֹלֶת הָעוֹמֶדֶת לִשְׁחִיטָה) is not considered *muktzeh* because the hen itself is not *muktzeh* on *Yom Tov* when *slaughtering* is permitted and the unlaid egg is considered part of the hen and therefore permitted (אוֹכְלָא דְאַפְרָת).

The *Gemara* demonstrates that the disagreement between Beis Shammai and Beis Hillel concerning an egg laid on *Yom Tov* cannot be due to their differing views regarding *muktzeh* (they would have disagreed about the use of the hen as well), and that the egg under discussion is the issue of a hen designated for slaughter. Since in this case the problem of *muktzeh* has no application, Beis Hillel's prohibition must be based on other considerations as outlined in the *Gemara* (2b-3a) and discussed here in the commentary.

1. **A**n egg that was laid on *Yom Tov* — Beis Shammai say: It may be eaten. But Beis Hillel say: It may not be eaten.

YAD AVRAHAM

forbidden labor (such as **cooking* and **baking)* must be done before the Sabbath, for that is specified later in the chapter *(v.* 23): *That which you must bake, bake* [now], *and that which you must cook, cook* [now]. Therefore, Rabbah concludes that all forms of preparation, even those not involving human endeavor (such as the formation of an egg), must be done before the Sabbath or *Yom Tov.* [This explanation is accepted as halachah by most authorities *(Rif; Rosh; Rambam, Hil. Yom Tov* 1:19 et al.; see *HaMaor).*]

This reasoning would apply only to an egg laid on *Yom Tov* immediately preceding or following the Sabbath; an egg laid on a *Yom Tov* not bordering on the Sabbath should be permissible. However, the Sages prohibited such an egg too, for an egg laid on a regular *Yom Tov* or Sabbath would easily be confused with one laid on a *Yom Tov* in proximity to a Sabbath. Hence, the halachah according to Beis Hillel is that an egg laid on *Yom Tov* (or the Sabbath) is prohibited regardless of when in the week *Yom Tov* occurs.

Beis Shammai dispute this ruling either

because: (a) They do not agree with Rabbah's principle of *hachanah,* and rule that the egg is permissible even if it was laid on a *Yom Tov* following the Sabbath (see *Tos., Eruvin* 38a; *Rashba* and *Shitah Mekubetzes* here); or (b) while they agree with Beis Hillel on the principle of *hachanah* and hold that on *Yom Tov* after the Sabbath the egg is prohibited, they do not agree with the blanket prohibition which prohibits even an egg laid on a *Yom Tov* not following the Sabbath *(Shitah* cited in *Chasam Sofer I).*

Rashi (2b and *Rav)* notes that *hachanah* applies only to a *Yom Tov* which follows the Sabbath or vice versa, but does not prohibit an egg laid on an ordinary Sunday despite the fact that it was prepared on the Sabbath. This is because the concept of *hachanah* does not prohibit the act of preparing food on the Sabbath or *Yom Tov.* Rather, it stipulates that food consumed on *Yom Tov* and the Sabbath must be מוּכָן, *in a state of preparedness,* before *Yom Tov* or the Sabbath (similar to the concept of *muktzeh)* and that this state cannot be attained on the Sabbath or *Yom Tov.*[1] A weekday meal has no requirement stipulating that it must have prior preparation, and therefore the exact time when the egg became ready is immaterial.

Tosafos (2a) points out that according to Beis Hillel the egg may not even be moved. Why then is only the prohibition against eating the egg mentioned? *M'romei HaSadeh* answers that if the egg were suitable for food, it *could* be moved. Only the proscription against eating the egg renders it unfit for use on *Yom Tov,* consequently proscribing its movement. By mentioning its forbidden status as food, the mishnah stipulates the root cause of the egg's status on *Yom Tov.*

1. There are two distinct ways to understand the concept of *hachanah:* (a) *Hachanah* is synonymous with *muktzeh.* [Though the *Gemara* rules that an egg laid by a hen designated for slaughter would not be considered *muktzeh,* Rabbah formulates a new principle which renders the egg *muktzeh* — the concept that the Sabbath may not prepare for the *Yom Tov* (or vice versa).] Thus, something not in a state of preparedness before *Yom Tov* is *muktzeh* and even if it attains preparedness on *Yom Tov,* it would still remain in a state of *muktzeh. (Rashi* [see *Ran, Rashba* and *Shitah Mekubetzes* here]; *She'iltos* 47, see *Ha'amek Sha'alah).* Accordingly, if it were possible for an egg to be laid on the day of its completion, it would surely be prohibited because of this principle. The *Gemara's* statement that the egg is always completed on the preceding day means to stress that it cannot be assumed that the egg was already com-

בֵּית שַׁמַּאי אוֹמְרִים: שְׂאוֹר בְּכְזַיִת; וְחָמֵץ
בְּכְכוֹתֶבֶת. וּבֵית הִלֵּל אוֹמְרִים: זֶה וָזֶה בְּכְזַיִת.

[ב] **הַשּׁוֹחֵט** חַיָּה וְעוֹף בְּיוֹם טוֹב — בֵּית
שַׁמַּאי אוֹמְרִים: יַחְפֹּר בְּדֶקֶר

יד אברהם

בֵּית שַׁמַּאי אוֹמְרִים: שְׂאוֹר — *Beis Shammai say: Leavening*

The subject matter of the next segment of this mishnah pertains only to the festival of Pesach and as such should have been included in tractate *Pesachim.* Its inclusion in tractate *Beitzah* is based upon its similarity to the segments immediately preceding and following it. These three are the only instances in *Seder Moed* in which Beis Shammai rule more leniently than Beis Hillel (*Rashi*).

[There are two prohibitions which pertain to חָמֵץ, *chametz,* namely the restrictions against eating *chametz* and keeping *chametz* (בַּל יֵרָאֶה). These prohibitions apply to two substances: *chametz,* a foodstuff made of leavened dough; and שְׂאוֹר, *leavening,* i.e., dough which has fermented to the extent that it can be used as a leavening agent (yeast) for other doughs. The mishnah now discusses the minimum amounts of these substances to which the prohibitions apply.]

בְּכְזַיִת; — *the volume of an olive;*

[The minimum amount of leavening which is subject to the prohibition against keeping it in one's possession on Pesach is a quantity equivalent in volume to that of an olive.]

וְחָמֵץ בְּכְכוֹתֶבֶת. — *and chametz the volume of a date.*

The volume of a date is greater than that of an olive. The stringency of the law concerning leavening is due to its ability to leaven other dough, i.e., its concentration of leavening agent (חִימוּצוֹ קָשָׁה; *Gem.* 7b).

וּבֵית הִלֵּל אוֹמְרִים: זֶה וָזֶה בְּכְזַיִת. — *But Beis Hillel say: This or that the volume of an olive.*

The *Gemara* (7b) comments that Beis Shammai concur insofar as the prohibition against eating *chametz* is concerned, that the volume of an olive is sufficient to render one liable. It is only concerning the prohibition against having leavening in one's possession on Pesach that they differentiate between leavening and *chametz.* They hold that although in the case of leavening as little as an olive's volume may not be in one's possession, in the case of *chametz,* an amount the size of a date is required to transgress (*Rav*).[1]

pleted two days prior to its birth (i.e., a weekday) and consequently prepared and permissible (*Shitah Mekubetzes*). (b) The prohibition of *hachanah* is independent of *muktzeh,* i.e., even if *muktzeh,* i.e., even if *muktzeh* has no Scriptural standing the egg is prohibited. [This school of thought considers preparation for *Yom Tov* on the Sabbath a prohibited action even where no prohibited labor is involved. The natural completion of the egg on the Sabbath is inherently a prohibited action, although no person can be held responsible for it.] Thus, if it were possible for an egg to be laid on the day of its completion, it would be permitted (*Tos., Eruvin* 38b; *Rashba* and others here; see also *HaMaor* and *Pnei Yehoshua*).

1　　　Beis Shammai say: Leavening the volume of an
2　　　olive; and *chametz* the volume of a date. But Beis Hillel say: This or that the volume of an olive.

2. **O**ne who slaughters a beast or a fowl on *Yom Tov* — Beis Shammai say: He may dig with a

YAD AVRAHAM

2.

As mentioned previously, the following mishnah contains the third instance in which Beis Shammai are more lenient than Beis Hillel regarding *Yom Tov*.

Slaughtering, although one of thirty-nine categories of labor forbidden on the Sabbath, is permitted on *Yom Tov*. This exemption is based on the general rule of the Torah *(Exodus* 12:16) that labor necessary for the preparation of food is permitted on *Yom Tov* [see General Introduction]. The discussion in the mishnah centers on the performance of the *mitzvah* of בִּסּוּי הַדָּם, *covering the blood* with earth, that the Torah requires after slaughtering beasts or fowl as described in *Leviticus* (17:13). This may involve either prohibited labor, such as digging [which depending on its purpose and location is a subcategory of either *plowing* or

building] crumbling clods of earth [a subcategory of *grinding*], or the movement and use of *muktzeh* (see *Tos.* 8a, with *Maharsha* and *Karnei R'em; Tos. R' Akiva* to 1:5; *Magen Avraham* 509:15). Consequently, Beis Shammai and Beis Hillel disagree as to which modes of covering are permitted on *Yom Tov*.

הַשּׁוֹחֵט — *One who slaughters* [i.e., one who intends to slaughter]

Usually this form of expression is used to describe a *fait accompli*, i.e., one who has already completed the act of slaughtering. However, since Beis Hillel rules, 'He may not slaughter,' it is obvious that the mishnah refers to an intended act, namely the case of one who intends to slaughter but has not previously prepared non-*muktzeh* material for covering the blood on *Yom Tov*. Now, on *Yom Tov*, he consults a

---

1. The usual distinction drawn between a halachically proscribed minimum amount (כְּשִׁעוּר) of a forbidden substance and a smaller than minimum amount (חֲצִי שִׁעוּר) pertains only to the punishment of מַלְקוּת, *lashes.* Transgression of any Torah command is nevertheless prohibited even with lesser amounts (see *Yoma* 74a). But most authorities maintain that the sin of having *chametz* in one's possession during Pesach does not entail corporal punishment (see *Pesachim* 95a with *Rashi, Tos., R' Chananel; Rambam, Chametz Umatzah* 1:3). Consequently, the stipulation of a minimum amount with regard to possession of *chametz* seems unwarranted.

Pnei Yehoshua raises this question and explains that the general prohibitions against less than minimum amounts applies only to אִיסּוּרֵי אֲכִילָה, *prohibition against consumption.* Thus, possession of less than the minimum amount of *chametz* is not prohibited (cf. *Teshuvas Chacham Zvi* 86; *Rashi, Shabbos* 74a). Other reasons are given to explain why there is no prohibition against having less than the specified amount of *chametz (Pri Chadash, Sha'arei Teshuvah* and *Da'as Torah* to *Orach Chaim* 442:7-8; *Sha'agas Aryeh* 81). However, *Mishnah Berurah* (442:37) rules that the prohibition against owning *chametz* applies even to less than the specified amount.

וִיכַסֶּה. וּבֵית הִלֵּל אוֹמְרִים: לֹא יִשְׁחֹט אֶלָּא אִם
כֵּן הָיָה לוֹ עָפָר מוּכָן מִבְּעוֹד יוֹם. וּמוֹדִים שֶׁאִם

יד אברהם

halachic authority to ask if he may slaughter a beast or a bird (Rav, Gem. 7b).

חַיָּה וְעוֹף בְּיוֹם טוֹב — a beast or a fowl on Yom Tov —

The mitzvah of כִּסּוּי הַדָּם, covering the blood, pertains only to beasts (חַיָּה) and fowl (עוֹף) (see Leviticus 17:13 with Rashi). Thus the slaughtering of livestock (בְּהֵמָה) poses no halachic problem.[1]

בֵּית שַׁמַּאי אוֹמְרִים: יַחְפֹּר בְּדֶקֶר וִיכַסֶּה. — Beis Shammai say: He may dig with a spade [or similar instrument used for digging] and cover [the blood].

Although before slaughtering he had nothing with which to cover the blood, Beis Shammai allow him to slaughter and cover the blood with

earth that he will dig up later (Rav, Gem. 7b).

Beis Shammai's permission to dig earth on Yom Tov is contingent on two factors: (a) The spade must have been stuck into the earth before Yom Tov; this renders the earth מוּכָן, prepared for later use, and thus eliminates both the problem of muktzeh, and that of digging it on Yom Tov;[2] (b) the earth must be granulated before Yom Tov so that there is no question of crumbling on Yom Tov (Rav and most authorities; based on Gem. 7b and 9b).

וּבֵית הִלֵּל אוֹמְרִים: לֹא יִשְׁחֹט — But Beis Hillel say: He may not slaughter

Although no Scriptural prohibi-

---

1. It is generally thought that the term בְּהֵמָה refers to domesticated animals, and חַיָּה to wild animals. However, the domesticated dog is called a חַיָּה because it readily adopts to both living with people and living in the wild (Shnos Eliyahu to Kilayim 8:6). [See also Ramban to Genesis 1:24. As a practical matter only three species are exempt from the mitzvah of covering the blood: cows, sheep and goats.]

2. These two alternative explanations for the necessity of having a spade stuck into the ground (דֶּקֶר נָעוּץ) is the subject of a disagreement between the poskim, and one rooted in the various explanations given for the dispensation to cover the blood on Yom Tov. First it must be understood that three possible violations of the Yom Tov laws may be involved in 'covering': *plowing (or *building) by digging; muktzeh, by moving and using the soil; and, *grinding, by crumbling the clods of earth. The last prohibition is avoided, as noted above, through the requirement that only granulated earth (עָפָר תְּחוּחַ) be used so that the requirement to have a spade stuck into the ground addresses itself only to the first two prohibitions. Furthermore, the Gemara (8a with Rashi) remarks that concerning digging there are two ameliorating factors: (a) the essence of digging — making a hole or softening the earth — is not the purpose of the labor performed here (מְלָאכָה שֶׁאֵינָה צְרִיכָה לְגוּפָהּ); and, (b) because the hole which is created by digging is unnecessary, it is a case of destroying (מְקַלְקֵל) [both of which concepts are explained in detail in the General Introduction to Mishnah Shabbos, ArtScroll ed., pp. 8-9]. However, the poskim are divided as to the role of these ameliorating factors. Some maintain that they effect total removal of the prohibition, and that the purpose of having a spade stuck into the ground is to remove (or ameliorate; see below, s.v. ובית הלל with note) the prohibition of muktzeh, i.e., the act of sticking in a spade is a preparation of sorts (see Tos., Rashba, Shulchan Aruch 498:14 with Mishnah Berurah 75). Others contend that only the Scriptural prohibition is removed because of the two considerations detailed above. The Rabbinic prohibition against digging is removed (or ameliorated) by the spade being stuck into the ground; and the resulting loosening of the soil renders the soil prepared (Rashi 9b; Ran here; Tur 498 with Beis Yosef and Bach).

1
2

spade and cover [the blood]. But Beis Hillel say: He may not slaughter unless he had earth prepared from the day before. But they agree that if he already

tion need be transgressed in this case (as explained in the commentary on Beis Shammai), nevertheless Beis Hillel do not allow him to slaughter, because covering the blood in this manner involves the Rabbinical injunction of *muktzeh*. In Beis Hillel's view, the prior insertion of a spade does not remove the prohibition against *muktzeh* as long as the earth on the spade adheres even partially to the ground. Therefore, Beis Hillel do not allow him to slaughter for he would have to move and use *muktzeh* to cover the blood. Beis Shammai, however, permit this act in order to enhance שִׂמְחַת יוֹם טוֹב, *the enjoyment of Yom Tov (Rashba; cf. Tos. Rid).*

Alternatively: There is a Rabbinical prohibition involved in digging out this earth — that of digging a hole. [See previous footnote for reason why this is not considered labor on a Scriptural level.] The issue involved in the dispute between Beis Shammai and Beis Hillel is whether the Rabbis waived this injunction in the face of the enjoy-

ment of *Yom Tov (Rosh; Tos.).*[1]

אֶלָּא אִם כֵּן הָיָה לוֹ עָפָר מוּכָן מִבְּעוֹד יוֹם.
— *unless he had earth prepared* [i.e., totally detached earth designated for use] *from the day before* [lit. *from when it was still day*].

[It is evident from the *Gemara* (7b-8b) that the Torah's dispensation for the performance of labor needed to prepare food applies only to acts directly related to such preparation. It would not apply, however, to labor required to cover blood, since this does nothing to enhance the food being prepared. This deed is a positive command (מִצְוַת עֲשֵׂה), completely divorced from the food preparation process. Despite the fact that prohibiting the covering of the blood on *Yom Tov* will prevent the slaughtering and eating of the meat, this ultimate conclusion does not place this procedure under the category of food preparation. In other words, removal of an obstacle to the attainment of food does not constitute food preparation.]

וּמוֹדִים שֶׁאִם שָׁחַט, — *But they* [i.e., Beis Hillel] *agree that if he already slaughtered,*

[If he transgressed the Rabbinical injunctions forbidding him to slaughter and we now prohibit him from covering the blood, fulfillment of the *mitzvah* will be prevented.]

1. The text reflects the view that, according to both Beis Hillel and Beis Shammai, the mitigating circumstances outlined above (see previous footnote) suffice only to ameliorate the pertinent prohibitions, i.e., a spade that is stuck into the ground does not remove the prohibition of *muktzeh* or digging entirely. It merely ameliorates the prohibition to a degree where it can be waived in the face of the overriding (according to Beis Shammai) consideration of the enjoyment of *Yom Tov*. This point itself is the subject of the debate between Beis Hillel and Beis Shammai. Beis Shammai hold that the enjoyment of *Yom Tov* is an overriding factor in this situation, while Beis Hillel disagree. This conception of the dispute is only one of the views set forth in the *Gemara* (9b). Another view holds that Beis Shammai's dispensation is not based on the consideration of the enjoyment of *Yom Tov*, but on the merits of the situation itself. Beis Shammai hold that the conditions described above — granulated earth and a spade stuck into the ground — suffice in themselves to remove entirely the pertinent prohibitions, but Beis Hillel, while agreeing that these conditions can effect the amelioration of the prohibitions, maintain they cannot eradicate them entirely.

[ג] **בֵּית** שַׁמַּאי אוֹמְרִים: אֵין מוֹלִיכִין אֶת
הַסֻּלָּם מִשּׁוֹבָךְ לְשׁוֹבָךְ, אֲבָל מַטֵּהוּ
מֵחַלּוֹן לְחַלּוֹן. וּבֵית הִלֵּל מַתִּירִין.

יד אברהם

שֶׁיַּחְפֹּר בְּדֶקֶר וִיכַסֶּה — *he should
dig with a spade and cover* [*the
blood with earth*] —

Though Beis Hillel hold that the
enjoyment of *Yom Tov* is not sufficient reason to permit slaughtering initially in the absence of
material to cover the blood, they
agree that once the animal has been
slaughtered, and we are confronted
with the possibility of transgressing
the *mitzvah* of covering the blood,
the Rabbinical prohibition is waived
in the face of the *mitzvah* (*Maharsha*).

This dispensation, too, is contingent upon the spade having been
stuck into the earth before *Yom
Tov* and the earth having been
detached and granulated (see above,
s.v. בֵּית שַׁמַּאי; *Gem.* 7b).

שֶׁאֵפֶר כִּירָה מוּכָן הוּא. — *for the ashes
of a stove are* [*considered*] *prepared*
[i.e., not *muktzeh*].

Since the halachah allows the use
of ashes for the *mitzvah* of covering
the blood (*Chullin* 88b; *Yoreh Deah*
28:23), even according to Beis Hillel
one may slaughter on *Yom Tov* and
rely on ashes from the oven for the
mitzvah of covering the blood for
these ashes are not considered
muktzeh.

The *Gemara* (8a) emends the
word שֶׁאֵפֶר, '*because*' *the ashes*, to
read וְאֵפֶר, '*and*' *the ashes* (*Rav*), explaining that this part of the mishnah is an independent halachah,
and is not part of Beis Hillel's
reasoning concerning the use of
earth for covering the blood.[1]

The *Gemara* (ibid.) adds that only ashes
left over from before *Yom Tov* are considered prepared. Ashes produced by a fire lit
on *Yom Tov* are *muktzeh*. Despite the fact
that the wood from which they came was
considered prepared [non-*muktzeh*], nevertheless, the ashes are *muktzeh* because they
are regarded as objects which came into being
on *Yom Tov* (נוֹלָד), and as such had no

---

1. *Vilna Gaon* (cited by his son R' Avraham in *Rav Pa'alim*, p. 107; see also *Lechem
Shamayim*) interprets the mishnah in a manner removing the need for emendation. Indeed it is
his contention that even where the *Gemara* indicates the need for emendation with the familiar
formula, חַסּוֹרֵי מִיחַסְרָא וְהָכִי קָתָנֵי, *it* [*the mishnah*] *is deficient and it should read as follows*, this
is not meant literally. In each case the meaning contained in the emendation may be inferred
from the original version (cf. R' Yosef Verga, *She'eris Yosef*, Warsaw, 5669, p. 4-5). The
Gaon treats this passage of the mishnah as an ellipsis which is understood in the following
manner. The preposition inherent in the Hebrew prefix שׁ refers, not to the preceding clause
('that he should dig with a spade and cover'), but to the phrase, וּמוֹדִים, *they agree*, and is to be
interpreted not as *for*, but as *that* (= אֲשֶׁר), i.e., they agree that if he slaughtered ... and *that the
ashes of a stove* ... However *Rambam's* version in the mishnah was וְשֶׁאֵפֶר, lit. *and that ashes*,
(see ed. R' Y. Kafich and the regular editions) and implies (in his mishnah commentary) that
the *Gemara* objects to even this version because it cannot be said that Beis Hillel and Beis
Shammai *agree* concerning the matter of stove ashes since their disagreement centers about
digging up earth for covering and has nothing to do with stove ashes. [See also *Rashba* and
Shitah Mekubetzes.]

slaughtered, he should dig with a spade and cover [the blood with earth] — for the ashes of a stove are [considered] prepared.

3. Beis Shammai say: We may not move the ladder from one dovecote to another, but may lean it from one window to another. But Beis Hillel permit it.

YAD AVRAHAM

previous preparation. [But ashes that are still hot enough to roast an egg are not yet *muktzeh* and may be used for covering the blood. In this state they are not as yet considered a new object. Rather, they are considered to be in their original state, that of firewood — and as such, are not *muktzeh*.]

Tosafos and *Rosh* cite the opinion of *Yerushalmi*, that once the animal has been slaughtered, one may use ashes to cover its blood even if the ashes are *muktzeh*. To enable fulfillment of the *mitzvah* of covering the blood, the sages waived the prohibition against *muktzeh*. *Shulchan Aruch* concurs (*Orach Chayim* 498:15; cf. comm. above, s.v. שֶׁיַחְפֹּר).[1]

3.

We find many instances in the Talmud of acts which in themselves would be permitted, but are nevertheless prohibited lest people suspect that some forbidden act is being performed. This principle is called מַרְאִית הָעַיִן, *mistaken suspicion* [literally, *that which the eye sees*], and is based upon the phrase וִהְיִיתֶם נְקִיִּם מֵה' וּמִיִּשְׂרָאֵל, *You shall be clear* [of suspicion] *before Hashem and Israel* (*Numbers* 32:22; see *Pesachim* 13a; *Yoma* 38a). The discussion in this mishnah centers upon such a prohibition.

בֵּית שַׁמַּאי אוֹמְרִים: אֵין מוֹלִיכִין אֶת הַסֻּלָּם מִשּׁוֹבָךְ לְשׁוֹבָךְ, — *Beis Shammai say: We may not move the ladder from one dovecote to another* [on Yom Tov],

If one wished to take some doves from their dovecotes to slaughter for the *Yom Tov* meal, he should not remove the ladder from one dovecote to the next, because people might suspect that he is taking the ladder to repair his roof [an act included in the *melachah* of *building*] (*Rav*, *Gem.* 9a).

אֲבָל מַטֵּהוּ מֵחַלּוֹן לְחַלּוֹן. — *but may lean it from one window to another.*

Each dovecote had different compartments in it. Although he may not remove the ladder from its place, he may lean the ladder from the window of one compartment to the window of another [since he does not carry the ladder, no suspicion can fall on him] (*Rav*; *Rashi*).

וּבֵית הִלֵּל מַתִּירִין. — *But Beis Hillel permit it.*

[Beis Hillel even allow the ladder to be transported from one dovecote

1. If one has the option of covering the blood with either ashes that are *muktzeh* or with loose earth that has a spade stuck into it (דְּקַר נָעוּץ), and the animal has already been slaughtered, it is debatable which option is preferable. *Rama* (498:15) holds that the option of using earth, where there is no question of *muktzeh* (see above, s.v. וּבֵית הִלֵּל), is the better one. However, some later authorities (see *Mishnah Berurah* there) disagree, and hold that the option of using ashes is the better one, for no forbidden labor is involved, whereas using earth entails at the very least a Rabbinical prohibition against the proscribed labor of digging a hole on *Yom Tov*.

בֵּית שַׁמַּאי אוֹמְרִים: לֹא יִטֹּל אֶלָּא אִם כֵּן נְעֲנַע מִבְּעוֹד יוֹם. וּבֵית הִלֵּל אוֹמְרִים: עוֹמֵד וְאוֹמֵר, „זֶה וָזֶה אֲנִי נוֹטֵל.‟

בֵּיצָה
א/ג

יד אברהם

to another.] The *Gemara* (9a,b) concludes that even according to Beis Hillel, a large ladder which is normally used for repairing roofs may not be carried on *Yom Tov* (neither in the street nor in the privacy of the home). Furthermore, even if the ladder is small and by design more suited to dovecotes than for roofing, one is still not permitted to carry the ladder in the street or public domain, for such action will arouse suspicion in the mind of the observer. One may carry this ladder only in the privacy of one's house or courtyard, where there is less room for mistaken suspicion (Rav).

The explanation cited above is one of two interpretations of the mishnah found in the *Gemara* and is the one accepted by *Rambam* (Hil. Yom Tov 5:4 and comm.). The *Gemara* explains that according to this version the issue in dispute between Beis Shammai and Beis Hillel is whether anything the Sages prohibited because of the suspicion of onlookers is prohibited even בְּחַדְרֵי חֲדָרִים, *in an inner room*, i.e., in private where one cannot be seen by others. Beis Shammai adhere to this principle and therefore prohibit carrying the ladder even in private, while Beis Hillel takes a more lenient view pertaining to carrying in a private area. *Rambam* (ibid.) explains that though they accept the principle that anything forbidden because of the suspicion of onlookers is prohibited even in the utmost privacy, Beis Hillel waives this restriction and allows carrying the ladder in a private area so as to enhance שִׂמְחַת יוֹם טוֹב, *the enjoyment of Yom Tov* (see Maggid Mishneh there).

However, most authorities (Rosh, Tur, Ravad and others) cite the second interpretation of the mishnah stated in the *Gemara*. According to this view Beis Hillel permit the dovecote ladder to be carried even in the street, for its size and design makes it sufficiently obvious that he is not using it for his roof. This opinion is accepted in *Shulchan Aruch* (Orach Chaim 518:4).

A question pondered by halachic authorities is whether a small household ladder follows the same rules as a dovecote ladder (see Tos. 9b; and Sha'ar HaTziyun 518:41-5). *Mishnah Berurah* (518:28) rules that such a ladder may be carried in private (בִּרְשׁוּת הַיָּחִיד), but not in the public domain (בִּרְשׁוּת הָרַבִּים).

The *Gemara* (9b-10a) notes that although in the preceding mishnayos Beis Shammai's opinion is the more lenient one where the enjoyment of *Yom Tov* is concerned, nevertheless here (and in the rest of this chapter) they adopt the more stringent opinion, while Beis Hillel's rulings are the more lenient (Gem. according to Rif, Ramban and Shulchan Aruch; see HaMaor and Milchamos; Tos. 9b).

בֵּית שַׁמַּאי אוֹמְרִים: לֹא יִטֹּל — *Beis Shammai say: One should not take [doves out of the dovecote on Yom Tov]*

The mishnah now discusses the procedure necessary to designate doves for slaughter on the eve of *Yom Tov*. As indicated in this and in many subsequent mishnayos, doves and other undomesticated birds, even if they inhabit dovecotes, are considered *muktzeh*, and need explicit designation in order to render them prepared and thus permitted for consumption on *Yom Tov*. In this they differ from domesticated doves or birds (i.e., those residing in the courtyard or in the house) which are automatically considered prepared unless they are specifically designated for *muktzeh* purposes (e.g., a chicken designated for egg-laying). It is a cardinal rule that מִגּוֹ דְּאִתְקְצָאי לְבֵין הַשְּׁמָשׁוֹת אִתְקְצָאי לְכוּלֵּא יוֹמָא, *once an object*

1
3

Beis Shammai say: One should not take [doves out of the dovecote on *Yom Tov*] unless one had held them before *Yom Tov*. But Beis Hillel say: He may stand and say, "This one and that one I will take."

had been *muktzeh* at the onset of *Yom Tov* or the Sabbath, it remains *muktzeh* for the entire day even if its situation has now changed. It must, however, be stressed that only the problem of *muktzeh* is dealt with. In order that the doves be permitted one must first establish that the prohibited labor of *trapping is not involved, i.e., the doves are not yet mature enough to fly freely (see 3:1 with *comm.*; *Shulchan Aruch* 497:6-9 with *Mishnah Berurah*; *Gem.* 24a, 25a).

אֶלָּא אִם כֵּן גִּעֲגֵעַ מִבְּעוֹד יוֹם. — *unless one had held* [lit. *shaken*] *them before Yom Tov* [lit. *while it was still day*].

Beis Shammai fear that if one were permitted to designate the doves for *Yom Tov* solely by verbalizing, he is likely to change his mind upon taking them in his hand and scrutinizing them closely on *Yom Tov* itself. Thus, he will have moved the doves needlessly (*Rav; Rashi*).

It appears from *Rashi* that there is no question of *muktzeh* here. Rather the issue is one of *needless moving* (טִלְטוּל שֶׁלֹּא לְצוֹרֶךְ). Perhaps this is so because the prohibition of *muktzeh* can readily be removed by an oral pronouncement obviating the requirement to hold the doves before *Yom Tov*. However, without such oral designation the doves are *muktzeh* (see *Rashi* 10a; cf. *Beis Meir* to 497:9; *Sha'ar HaTziyun* 497:51).[1]

Rambam (comm.) holds that Beis Shammai fear that if a mere oral designation were deemed sufficient the person is likely to change his mind before *Yom Tov*, thereby returning the doves to their previous state of *muktzeh*. Then, after the advent of *Yom Tov* he might reconsider and take the doves after all, thus transgressing the prohibitions of moving and eating *muktzeh*.

וּבֵית הִלֵּל אוֹמְרִים: עוֹמֵד — *But Beis Hillel say: He may stand*

Even from afar (*Rashi* 10a; *Mishnah Berurah* 497:31).

וְאוֹמֵר, — *and say,*

Or even think (*Mishnah Berurah* and *Shulchan Aruch HaRav*, loc. cit.).

,,זֶה וָזֶה אֲנִי נוֹטֵל." — *"This one and that one I will take."*

It is not sufficient to state before *Yom Tov*, 'I will take from among this group of birds tomorrow.' He must designate (orally or mentally) the specific doves desired for *Yom Tov* (*Gem.* 10a). We are concerned lest he pick up a dove on *Yom Tov*, and, upon inspection, find it too lean and choose another dove instead. Consequently, the second dove would be the designated, non-*muktzeh* dove, while the first dove

1. [*Rashi* does not *explain the reason* that one may not move the doves. We may conjecture that *Rashi's* underlying reasoning is the principle enunciated in tractate *Shabbos* (123b; see *Orach Chaim* 308:4), that even utensils that are not *muktzeh* should not be moved needlessly.] However, *Rosh Yosef* states (cryptically) that the prohibition involved in moving the doves needlessly is טְרְחָא דְלֹא צָרִיךְ, *needless exertion*, on *Yom Tov*.

ביצה
א/ד

זְמַן [ד] שְׁחוֹרִים וּמָצָא לְבָנִים, לְבָנִים וּמָצָא
שְׁחוֹרִים, שְׁנַיִם וּמָצָא שְׁלֹשָׁה —
אֲסוּרִים. שְׁלֹשָׁה וּמָצָא שְׁנַיִם — מֻתָּרִים.
בְּתוֹךְ הַקֵּן וּמָצָא לִפְנֵי הַקֵּן, אֲסוּרִים; וְאִם אֵין
שָׁם אֶלָּא הֵם, הֲרֵי אֵלּוּ מֻתָּרִים.

יד אברהם

would revert to its original *muktzeh* status, and his handling of this dove would retroactively be considered moving *muktzeh* (*Rashi*).

Similarly, one may not designate the entire dovecote for *Yom Tov* when his intent is to take only a few birds from this group (*Orach Chaim* 497:11 based on *R' Yerucham; Or Zarua* 2:334).

The *Gemara* (10a) adds that Beis Shammai require the doves to be handled only if they are the first pair of doves born in the dovecote in that season. Because it is customary to leave this pair with the mother as long as possible, Beis Shammai fear that he may regret his initial decision to slaughter these doves. Only where he has gone to the extent of actually handling them, are we not apprehensive that he will change his mind. Where ordinary doves are concerned even Beis Shammai concede that oral (or mental) designation is sufficient.

4.

זְמַן שְׁחוֹרִים וּמָצָא לְבָנִים, לְבָנִים וּמָצָא שְׁחוֹרִים, — *If one designated [before Yom Tov] black [doves] but [on Yom Tov] found white [doves], [or if he designated] white [doves] but found black [doves],*

It goes without saying that if he prepared only black doves and found white ones or vice versa that these birds are not permitted, for the ones he found are obviously not those that he had set aside. The *Gemara* (10b) explains that the mishnah speaks of one who designated both black and white doves and placed them in separate compartments of the cote. On *Yom Tov* he found their positions reversed, white doves were in the compartment formerly occupied by the blacks, while blacks were found in the whites' former quarters. The question addressed by the mishnah is whether we can assume that these are the same birds with their positions changed, or must we suspect that the original birds flew away and were replaced by others.

However, if the black and white doves were originally in one compartment and were found to have switched their respective places, we assume that they are the original designated doves (*Magen Avraham* 497:15; *Or Zarua* 2:334).

שְׁנַיִם וּמָצָא שְׁלֹשָׁה — *— or [if he designated] two and found three —*

And he is unable to distinguish the two designated doves among the group of three (*Rav; Rashi*).

אֲסוּרִים. *— they are prohibited.*

[In the first two cases, we cannot make the assumption that the original occupants of the two compartments switched places. In the last case, the addition of a third dove makes it certain that there is at least one *muktzeh* dove among them.]

4. If one designated [before *Yom Tov*] black [doves] but [on *Yom Tov*] found white [doves], [or if he designated] white [doves] but found black [doves], or [if he designated] two and found three — they are prohibited. [If he had designated] three but found [only] two — they are permissible.

[If the designated doves had been] in the nest, but he found [doves] in front of the nest, they are prohibited; but if there were none there except these, then these are permitted [to be slaughtered].

YAD AVRAHAM

Since only one bird among the three is un-designated while two are designated, *Tosafos* (10b) asks why we do not apply the principle of בִּיטוּל בְּרוֹב, *nullification into the majority* [i.e., when a prohibited substance mingles with a greater amount of permissible matter and cannot be distinguished from it, the entire mixture (including the prohibited substance) is permissible, for the prohibited lesser amount is subsumed into the major portion]. *Tosafos* gives two reasons why this principle does not apply here: (a) בַּעֲלֵי חַיִּים, *living things*, are considered too significant (חָשׁוּב) to be subsumed; and (b) דָּבָר שֶׁיֵּשׁ לוֹ מַתִּירִין, *a thing which will become permissible albeit at a later time*, cannot be subsumed — since all the doves will be permitted after *Yom Tov*, the principle of majority does not apply to them.

שְׁלֹשָׁה וּמָצָא שְׁנַיִם — מֻתָּרִים. — [If he had designated] three but found [only] two — they are permissible.

We assume that only one dove flew away and that the remaining doves are the designated ones (*Rav, Gem.* 10b).

Even if the three doves had been bound together and the two doves found in the cote are not tied, we may assume that the doves extricated themselves from their bonds (*Orach Chaim* 497:13 based on *Gem.* 10b; cf. *Ramban, Hil. Yom Tov* 2:6; *Turei Zahav* 497:9).

בְּתוֹךְ הַקֵּן — [If the designated doves had been] in the nest,

The cotes are subdivided into compartments called קֵנִים, *nests* (*Rashi* 10b).

וּמָצָא לְפְנֵי הַקֵּן — but he found [doves] in front of the nest,

But found nothing in the nest (*Rav; Rashi*).

אֲסוּרִים; — they are prohibited;

We must suspect that these doves are not those that were designated.[1] This is so even if they were found on a ledge protruding directly from the nest, where the doves within usually go for air (*Mishnah Berurah* 497:42, based on *Rashi* 11a; *Sha'ar HaTziyun* there).

וְאִם אֵין שָׁם אֶלָּא אֵלּוּ הֵם, הֲרֵי אֵלּוּ מֻתָּרִים. — but if there were none there [in the dovecote (*Rav;* cf. *Rashi* 11a)] except these, then these are permitted [to be slaughtered].

[I.e., this is the only occupied nest in this dovecote.] The *Gemara* (11a) adds that if another cote of undesignated doves is located

1. The principle upon which the mishnah's decision is based is one which has broad implications. There are two principles which the halachah uses to determine the origin of a found object, namely: רוֹב, *majority*, i.e., it may be assumed that the object came from the same place as the majority of like objects found in that vicinity [e.g., if one finds a piece of meat on the street of a city in which most of the butchers sell kosher meat, he may assume that the found meat

[ה] **בֵּית** שַׁמַּאי אוֹמְרִים: אֵין מְסַלְּקִין אֶת הַתְּרִיסִין בְּיוֹם טוֹב. וּבֵית הִלֵּל מַתִּירִין אַף לְהַחֲזִיר.

יד אברהם

within fifty cubits of the nest in question, we may not assume that the doves found in front of the nest are the former occupants unless the undesignated cote is obscured from view of the nest [e.g., they were arranged along two sides of a house]. However, if the second cote was in full view of the nest, then only if it is more than fifty cubits away may we assume that the birds found in front of the original nest are the designated doves.

This is true only when the doves found in the nest are able to walk

out of the nest, but are unable to fly at all. Doves with even a slight ability to fly (Mishnah Berurah 497:45) may not be slaughtered on Yom Tov (if they were found out of their designated place) because we suspect that they are undesignated birds which flew into the nests on Yom Tov (Rav, Gem. 11a).

[Doves able to fly well can never be designated for slaughter on Yom Tov, because catching them involves the forbidden labor of *trapping. Consequently, they are always considered muktzeh (Orach Chayim 497:9; Mishnah Berurah 497:45).]

5.

בֵּית שַׁמַּאי אוֹמְרִים: אֵין מְסַלְּקִין אֶת הַתְּרִיסִין בְּיוֹם טוֹב. — Beis Shammai say: We may not remove the shutters on Yom Tov.

Beis Shammai do not allow vendors to remove the shutters of the stand from which they sell spices and sundries on Yom Tov. The shutters are used to close the stands at night; by day they are removed and set on the ground as trays for displaying the vendors' wares. The vendors are permitted to sell their merchandise even on Yom Tov (see further 3:8 and Orach Chaim 323:4

for all the restrictions governing this law) as long as they sell only to their acquaintances and do not specify a price (Rashi 10a; cf. Gem. 11b).

Beis Shammai prohibit the removal of these shutters despite the fact that these stands are not fixed (מְחוּבָּר), but are portable. Beis Shammai hold the principle of יֵשׁ בִּנְיָן וּסְתִירָה בְּכֵלִים, which states that the labors of בּוֹנֶה, *building, and, סוֹתֵר, *demolishing, apply also to utensils, and not only to that which is attached to the ground

came from a kosher butcher shop]; and קָרוֹב, proximity, i.e., it may be assumed that the object came from the nearest possible location [e.g., there were thirteen money chests in the Temple Courtyard into which donations designated for different purposes were placed; money found between these chests could be assumed to have come from the nearest chest (see Shekalim 7:1)]. In our mishnah these two principles create a conflict, for if we are guided by considerations of nearness, we should assume the doves had come from the nest in which they had been designated and are permitted. If, however, we follow the majority, since there are more non-designated birds from elsewhere (מֵעָלְמָא), then we must assume that these are not the original birds. The mishnah's stringent ruling demonstrates that the principle of majority is the dominating rule, and the principle of proximity is ignored when its outcome contradicts the majority. The Gemara (11a) attempts to attribute the mishnah's ruling to other considerations, but in the final analysis, since the halachah is that in cases of conflict the principle of majority prevails, this is unnecessary.

5. **B**eis Shammai say: We may not remove the shutters on *Yom Tov*. But Beis Hillel permit even their replacement.

YAD AVRAHAM

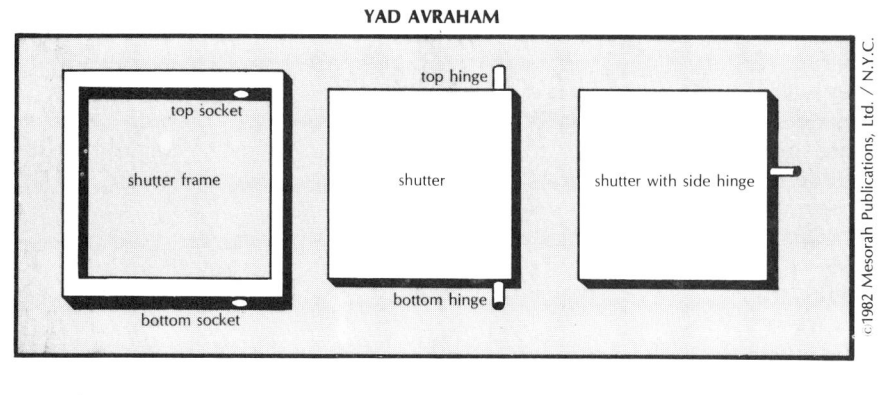

© 1982 Mesorah Publications, Ltd. / N.Y.C.

(מְחוּבָּר לְקַרְקַע), i.e., portable items. Thus, removing a shutter is similar to *demolishing* a wall, while replacing the shutter resembles *building* (Gem. 11b).

וּבֵית הֵלֵל מַתִּירִין אַף לְהַחֲזִיר. — *But Beis Hillel permit even their replacement.*

Beis Hillel permit not only the removal of the shutter at the day's start, but also their replacement at the end of the day. The *Gemara* (10a,11b) explains that Beis Hillel permit the removal of the shutters only to enhance the enjoyment of *Yom Tov* [i.e., the wares in the stand are needed on *Yom Tov*]. This reason suffices to explain Beis Hillel's approval of opening the stand on *Yom Tov*. It falls short, however, of clarifying the permissibility of replacing the shutters on *Yom Tov* — an act which is seemingly irrelevant to the enjoyment of *Yom Tov*. The latter deed is permitted by Beis Hillel because of the principle of הִתִּירוּ סוֹפָן מִשּׁוּם

תְּחִילָתָן, *they permitted their end because of their beginning,* i.e., if replacing the shutter were prohibited, the vendors would not remove the shutters in the first place, fearing that their wares would be stolen from the open stands. Therefore the Sages permitted even replacement of the shutters. Consequently, if the stand was located indoors, where the goods can be protected by locking the front door, replacement of the shutter is not permitted *(Gem. 11b).*

The *Gemara* adds that if the shutter had no hinge, no prohibition is involved and even Beis Shammai agree that reattachment of the shutter is permitted. In such a case one may remove and replace the shutter (or door) even of a structure which is attached to the ground *(Rav; Rambam, comm; Pnei Yehoshua;* cf. *Bach* to *Tur* 519). If the shutter had hinges on its upper and lower corners, even Beis Hillel agree that it may not be replaced (nor even removed).[1] The issue in the dispute between Beis Shammai and Beis Hillel involves a shutter which has its hinge in the middle of its side *(Rav, Gem. 11b).* [See diagrams.]

Shulchan Aruch (Orach Chaim 519:1) at-

---

1. There is disagreement as to why Beis Hillel agree that a shutter having one hinge on each corner is forbidden to be replaced. *Rav* holds that it is similar to *building* [whereas, when the hinge is in the middle the shutter is not secured well, therefore replacing such a shutter is not considered a form of *building* (see *Gem.* 47b)]. Although the Sages waived the Rabbinical

בֵּית שַׁמַּאי אוֹמְרִים: אֵין נוֹטְלִין אֶת הָעֱלִי
לְקַצֵּב עָלָיו בָּשָׂר. וּבֵית הִלֵּל מַתִּירִין.
בֵּית שַׁמַּאי אוֹמְרִים: אֵין נוֹתְנִין אֶת הָעוֹר לִפְנֵי
הַדּוֹרְסָן וְלֹא יַגְבִּיהֶנּוּ, אֶלָּא אִם כֵּן יֵשׁ עִמּוֹ כְזַיִת
בָּשָׂר. וּבֵית הִלֵּל מַתִּירִין.

יד אברהם

tributes the instances where replacing the shutters are prohibited to the apprehension that he may secure the hinges. Consequently since we conduct ourselves in accordance with Beis Hillel's rulings, removal of the shutters is always permitted on *Yom Tov* (*Mishnah Berurah* 519:5).

בֵּית שַׁמַּאי אוֹמְרִים: אֵין נוֹטְלִין אֶת הָעֱלִי — *Beis Shammai say: We may not take* [i.e., move] *the pestle*

A thick and heavy (circular) board with which grains are usually crushed (*Rambam, Kafich ed.;* see *Rashi* 11a, *R' Chananel, Aruch,* and *Radak, Shorashim,* s.v. עלל). [The question under discussion here is whether meat may be chopped

upon the board.] *Rav,* however, follows the standard edition of *Rambam's* commentary and interprets עֲלִי as the handle of the pestle.

Meiri (in his *Chidushim,* citing *Ravad*) explains that עֲלִי is a heavy wooden board with a concave surface which is used as a pestle. In our mishnah the issue is whether the board may be used as a weight to drive a knife, placed upon the meat, through the meat.

לְקַצֵּב עָלָיו בָּשָׂר. — *to chop meat upon it.*

The pestle is considered a כְּלִי שֶׁמְּלַאכְתּוֹ לְאִיסוּר, *utensil primarily reserved for forbidden labor* (i.e., grinding grain; see *Orach Chaim* 495:2) and consequently may not be

prohibition for the sake of the enjoyment of *Yom Tov* when the hinge is in the middle, they did not do so when the hinges are on the corners, because of the stronger resemblance to *building.

Ramban holds that the Rabbinical prohibition on shutters with hinges is based on the apprehension that שֶׁמָּא יִתְקַע, *he may secure the hinges with nails,* which would constitute *building even in regard to portable objects. This apprehension exists only when the hinges are located on the upper and lower corners and a nail can be driven through the hinge securing it to the frame of the stand without impairing the ability of the shutter to swing open and shut (the hinge is not of one piece with the shutter; it is only jammed into a groove on the shutter). When the hinge is on the middle of the panel a nail driven through the hinge and the frame would have to be removed before opening the shutter, thus greatly hindering the use of the stand. Nevertheless, where the stand is located indoors, the Rabbis prohibited closing even the latter type of shutter, fearing that people would fail to differentiate between the various types of hinges. This latter prohibition, being of a less stringent nature, is suspended to enhance the enjoyment of *Yom Tov* according to Beis Hillel. Thus, removal of this type of shutter is permitted by Beis Hillel, even where the consideration of enjoyment of *Yom Tov* does not apply because the act of removal does not engender apprehensions about driving nails (*Milchamos; Chiddushei HaRamban* 47, 102b; cf. *Rashi* 47b; *Rambam, Hil. Yom Tov* 4:12 and *Hil. Shabbos* 22:25).

The opinion of *Tosafos* is a variation on this theme: Anything attached snugly and securely (בְּחוֹזֶק), even to a portable object, is included in the category of *building and *demolishing. The controversy whether *building and *demolishing portable objects is forbidden labor centers only on objects that are attached loosely. The shutters discussed here are loosely attached and are therefore, according to Beis Hillel, permitted to be removed and replaced. However, Beis Hillel concur with Beis Shammai where there is apprehension that he may attach the hinge tightly (*Tos.* 102b; see *Chiddushei HuMeiri;* see also *Magen Avraham* 313:9, 314:10, 519:4).

Beis Shammai say: We may not take the pestle to chop meat upon it. But Beis Hillel permit it.

Beis Shammai say: We may not put the hide [of a freshly slaughtered animal] where it will be trampled, nor may we pick it up, unless meat the volume of an olive is on it. But Beis Hillel permit it.

YAD AVRAHAM

moved (according to Beis Shammai) even to be used for permissible labor *(Rashi).*[1]

וּבֵית הֶלֵּל מַתִּירִין. — *But Beis Hillel permit it.*

In tractate *Shabbos* (123-124) we find two interpretations of Beis Hillel's ruling. According to one interpretation the עֱלִי, pestle, is, as stated, a utensil primarily reserved for forbidden labor. Since a utensil of this sort is also used for other purposes (see *Tos., Shabbas* 36a), it is not (according to Beis Hillel and the halachah) classified as *muktzeh* whose movement is categorically prohibited. Rather, such a utensil may be moved לְצוֹרֶךְ גּוּפוֹ וּמְקוֹמוֹ, *for the purpose of using it* [the utensil] *or its place* [if the place the utensil occupies is needed (see *Shabbos* 124a; *Orach Chaim* 308:3)]. Thus, when Beis Hillel allow the pestle to be moved for the purpose of chopping meat upon it this is not, as is the case in the other parts of the mishnah, a special dispensation for the sake of the enjoyment of Yom Tov. It is, rather, part of the general principle which permits movement of such a utensil for the purpose of using it, or its place, even on the Sabbath.

Beis Shammai forbid movement of this type of *muktzeh* no matter what the purpose. *Meiri (Chidushim* citing *Ravad)* explains that Beis Shammai fear that people will suspect that the pestle was being used for its usual forbidden purpose — *grinding grain* (cf. *Rashi).*

According to another interpretation *(Shabbos* 123a), the pestle is a utensil which is normally handled with great care lest it warp. It, therefore, falls into the category of מוּקְצֶה מֵחֲמַת חֶסְרוֹן כִּיס, *muktzeh because of fear of monetary loss.* Ordinarily utensils in this category of *muktzeh* may not be moved for any purpose *(Shabbos* 17:4; *Orach Chaim* 301:1). Nevertheless, Beis Hillel allow the pestle to be moved and used because of the enjoyment of Yom Tov (cf. *Tos.,* 8a; *Maharsha* and *Karnei R'em* there; *comm.* to 1:2, s.v. וּבֵית הֶלֵּל אוֹמְרִים לֹא יִשָּׁחֵט).

Mishnah Berurah (499:19; see *Beur Halachah* there) leans toward the former interpretation, and postulates that a utensil which is *muktzeh* in the usual sense of the word may not be moved even for the enjoyment of Yom Tov.

בֵּית שַׁמַּאי אוֹמְרִים: אֵין נוֹתְנִין אֶת הָעוֹר לִפְנֵי הַדּוֹרְסָן — *Beis Shammai say: We may not put the hide* [of a freshly slaughtered animal] where it will be trampled [lit. before the one who tramples it; the translation reflects the alternative reading לִפְנֵי הַדְּרִיסָה, recorded in *Shinuyei Nuschaos; Rav's* version of the

1. *Rav* explains that the pestle, because of its excessive weight which precludes it from being carried around easily, loses its usefulness as a utensil (according to both Beis Hillel and Beis Shammai). Thus it is put in the category of an *object* (not a utensil) reserved for prohibited work which is *muktzeh* (מוּקְצֶה מֵחֲמַת אִיסוּר) and may not be moved for any purpose. *Tosafos Yom Tov* comments that this clearly contradicts the *Gemara* (10a). *Shulchan Aruch (Orach Chaim* 30:2) rules that heaviness or bulky size does not render any object *muktzeh* (see *Beis Yosef* loc. cit.; *Tos., Shabbos* 35a).

בֵּית שַׁמַּאי אוֹמְרִים: אֵין מוֹצִיאִין, לֹא אֶת
הַקָּטָן, וְלֹא אֶת הַלּוּלָב, וְלֹא אֶת סֵפֶר תּוֹרָה
לִרְשׁוּת הָרַבִּים. וּבֵית הִלֵּל מַתִּירִין.

יד אברהם

mishnah reads לִפְנֵי בֵּית הַדְּרִיסָה, *before the place where it will be trampled*],

Placing the hide where it will be trampled involves two prohibitions — moving *muktzeh* and the forbidden labor of *tanning* hides. The fresh hide of an animal, though sometimes used as a seating mat, is not ideally suited for this purpose. Thus, it is considered useless and is therefore *muktzeh*. Placing the hide where it will be stepped upon is the beginning of the *tanning* process (*Meiri*; cf. *Rashi* 10a), and as such is Rabbinically prohibited, because it appears as though he were *tanning* the hide (מֶחֱזֵי כִּמְעַבֵּד; *Meiri*).[1]

וְלֹא יַגְבִּיהֶנּוּ, — *nor may we pick it up*,

After the meat has been removed from the hide, the hide should be left lying where it is (*Rav*).

[The hide is now unfit for any use and is *muktzeh*.]

אֶלָא אִם כֵּן יֵשׁ עִמּוֹ כְזַיִת בָּשָׂר. — *unless meat the volume of an olive* [lit. *like an olive of meat*] *is on it*.

[In such a case the hide is not *muktzeh*, and he may pick it up.

But putting it in a place where it will be trampled is still forbidden because of the prohibition against *tanning*.]

וּבֵית הִלֵּל מַתִּירִין. — *But Beis Hillel permit it.*

[Beis Hillel permit the hide to be moved and to be placed where it will be trampled.]

If one would not be permitted to move the hide and put it where it would be trampled, the hide would be likely to spoil and one might refrain from slaughtering animals for consumption on *Yom Tov* (*Rav*; *Rashi* 11a; *Rambam, Hil. Yom Tov* 3:4) and as a result refrain from the enjoyment of *Yom Tov*. Thus, this is another instance where the Rabbis הִתִּירוּ סוֹפָן מִשּׁוּם תְּחִילָתָן, *permitted their end* (moving and placing the hide) *because of their beginning* (slaughtering the animal). Therefore this is only permitted if the animal was slaughtered on *Yom Tov*. If the animal was slaughtered before *Yom Tov* the above reason does not apply, and Beis Hillel concur with Beis Shammai (*Orach Chaim* 499:3).

⊷§ מִתּוֹךְ — Mitoch

כָּל־מְלָאכָה לֹא־יֵעָשֶׂה בָהֶם אַךְ אֲשֶׁר יֵאָכֵל לְכָל־נֶפֶשׁ הוּא לְבַדּוֹ יֵעָשֶׂה לָכֶם, *No labor may be performed on them* [i.e., the first and last day of the festival of Pesach], *however that which is eaten by any person, that alone may be performed for you* (Exodus 12:16).

אֵין בֵּין יוֹם טוֹב לַשַּׁבָּת אֶלָּא אֹכֶל נֶפֶשׁ בִּלְבָד, *There is no difference between* [the prohibited labors of] *Yom Tov and* [the prohibited labors of] *the Sabbath except* [in matters pertaining to] *the preparation of food* (Megillah 1:5).

Thirty-nine אֲבוֹת מְלָאכוֹת, *primary labors* [i.e., categories of labor], are

---

1. It is evident from the mishnah and *Gemara* (especially from Beis Hillel's opinion), that no Scripturally forbidden labor is involved in stepping upon the hide. This is difficult to understand in light of *Rambam's* statement (*Hil. Shabbos* 11:6): "He who stomps upon the hide till

1
5

Beis Shammai say: We may not carry out, neither a small child, nor a *lulav*, nor a Torah scroll to the public domain. But Beis Hillel permit it.

enumerated in *Shabbos* 7:2 as forbidden on the Sabbath (see General Introduction). These prohibitions apply to *Yom Tov* as well with one major exception — the dispensation of אוֹכֶל נֶפֶשׁ, *food for the soul*, i.e., certain labors involved in the preparation of food for human consumption are excluded from the general ban.

There is no question, then, that labors directly related to the preparation of food such as *cooking, *kindling a fire or *transporting food, are permitted on *Yom Tov*. It should be noted that there are some exceptions to this rule. These, as well as the other laws governing the dispensation of food preparation, are discussed in the General Introduction to this tractate. The subject of the following dispute between Beis Shammai and Beis Hillel is the extension of the permissibility of the labors involved in food preparation to situations where these labors are done for purposes unrelated to food.

Beis Hillel formulate the principle: מִתּוֹךְ שֶׁהוּתְּרָה לְצוֹרֶךְ הוּתְּרָה נַמִי שֶׁלֹּא לְצוֹרֶךְ, *since it is permitted for a purpose* [i.e., food preparation], *it is also permitted without a purpose* [i.e., not for food preparation]. This principle is generally termed מִתּוֹךְ, *mitoch*. Consequently, any labor which may be performed in the process of preparing food (e.g., *transporting foodstuffs into a public domain) is also permitted wherever there is any צוֹרֶךְ יוֹם טוֹב, *Yom Tov need.*[1]

בֵּית שַׁמַּאי אוֹמְרִים: אֵין מוֹצִיאִין, — *Beis Shammai say: We may not carry out,*

[*Transporting objects from a private[2] domain to the public domain is one of the thirty-nine prohibited labors enumerated in *Shabbos* 7:2.]

לֹא אֶת הַקָּטָן, וְלֹא אֶת הַלּוּלָב, וְלֹא אֶת סֵפֶר תּוֹרָה לִרְשׁוּת הָרַבִּים. — *neither a small child, nor a lulav, nor a Torah scroll* [although these are *mitzvos* needed to be performed on Yom

Tov] *to the public domain.*

Beis Shammai hold that the verse, *however that which is eaten by any person, that alone may be performed by you*, permits only labor performed in the preparation of food to be eaten on *Yom Tov*. Therefore *transporting objects other than food is prohibited.

וּבֵית הִלֵּל מַתִּירִין. — *But Beis Hillel permit it.*

Beis Hillel, however, applies the principle of *mitoch* [see prefatory

it becomes hard ... must bring a sin offering for inadvertently performing this labor on *Shabbos.*" *Yereim (HaShalem* 274) holds that treading upon a hide is a Rabbinical prohibition. *Tosafos R'em* (op. cit. 274:108) suggests that *Rambam's* rule refers to dried hide, whereas our mishnah speaks of fresh, moist hide (cf. *Pnei Yehoshua* here; see also *Mishnah Berurah* 499:5).

1. *Rosh Yosef* explains that according to Beis Hillel the verse in *Exodus* 12:16 is to be understood as follows: *But* [the type of labor which is (ordinarily) done for] *that which is eaten ... that alone may be performed* לָכֶם, *for your use* [i.e., if there is use for it on *Yom Tov*]. See *Or Zarua* 1:754 where a different reason for the rule of *mitoch* is given in the name of R' *Yeshayah of Trani*. See also R' Sh. Y. Zevin, *The Festivals in Halachah*, v. 1, pp. 12-16, for an extensive discussion on the principle of *mitoch*.

2. For a detailed explanation of these terms see *Orach Chaim* 345:2,7; *Shabbos* 6a; General Introduction to *Shabbos*, ArtScroll ed., pp. 11-13.

ביצה [ו] **בֵּית** שַׁמַאי אוֹמְרִים: אֵין מוֹלִיכִין חַלָּה וּמַתָּנוֹת לַכֹּהֵן בְּיוֹם טוֹב — בֵּין שֶׁהוּרְמוּ מֵאֶמֶשׁ בֵּין שֶׁהוּרְמוּ מֵהַיּוֹם. וּבֵית הִלֵּל מַתִּירִין.

יד אברהם

note] and permits carrying these items.

However, these labors are prohibited where there is no *Yom Tov* need (*Tosafos* 12a). [See *Yad Avraham* to *Megillah* 1:5, ArtScroll ed.]

R' Chananel restricts the dispensation even further and states that only labor performed for food needs, or for needs related to the performance of a *mitzvah*, is permitted. Therefore, the mishnah's dispensation [see text] is couched in terms of *mitzvah* per-

formance — a *lulav*, a Torah scroll. Likewise, the case of a small child refers to an infant being carried to his circumcision. *Tosafos*, *Rambam* (loc. cit.), and *Shulchan Aruch* (*Orach Chaim* 518:1), however, all disagree with R' Chananel's opinion.

Rashi (12a) holds that those labors used in preparation of food, and subject to the dispensation of *mitoch*, are permitted even where there is no *Yom Tov* need at all (see *Tos.*; *Pri Chadash* to *Orach Chaim* 495; *Rosh Yosef*).[1]

6.

בֵּית שַׁמַאי אוֹמְרִים: אֵין מוֹלִיכִין חַלָּה וּמַתָּנוֹת לַכֹּהֵן בְּיוֹם טוֹב — *Beis Shammai say: We may not deliver challah, or [the Kohen's] gifts, to a Kohen on Yom Tov —*

Numbers 15:17-21 stipulates that a portion *(challah)* must be separated from every batch of dough and given to the *Kohen*. The laws regarding *challah* are delineated in *Shulchan Aruch, Yoreh Deah* 322-330.

Deuteronomy 18:3 stipulates that from every ox, sheep or goat that is slaughtered one must give to a *Kohen* the (right) front foot, the cheeks (including the tongue) and the stomach. These are referred to in the mishnah as מַתָּנוֹת, *gifts*. The laws regarding these gifts are delineated in *Shulchan Aruch, Yoreh Deah* 61.

בֵּין שֶׁהוּרְמוּ מֵאֶמֶשׁ בֵּין שֶׁהוּרְמוּ מֵהַיּוֹם. — *whether they were separated yesterday* [and could have been given yesterday] *or they were separated today* [on Yom Tov, and could not have been given before Yom Tov].

Although it is permitted to separate *challah* on Yom Tov if the dough was mixed on Yom Tov [see *Gem.* 9a; *Orach Chayim* 506:3], nevertheless, one may not deliver it to the *Kohen* on Yom Tov (*Rav*).

[Separation of *terumah* and tithes from *tevel* (a name assigned to any commodity prior to the separation of the particular tithes applicable to that commodity) is a form of מְתַקֵּן, *perfecting* or *completing*. Since *tevel* may not be consumed, separation of tithes 'completes' the commodity, i.e., changes its status from forbidden to permitted. Such an act is Rabbinically prohibited on Yom Tov because of its similarity to the Scripturally prohibited labor of *striking the final blow*,

1. *Rambam's* opinion (*Hil. Yom Tov* 1:4) is not totally clear. *Meiri* understands him to hold that the dispensation of *mitoch* applies only to the labors of *transporting* and *kindling*. All other labors, including *slaughtering* and *baking*, do not fall under this dispensation, and are permitted only if needed for *Yom Tov* eating. *Maggid Mishneh* (loc. cit.) holds that all labors performed upon the food itself, such as *slaughtering* and *baking*, are permitted even when not needed for the purpose of eating on *Yom Tov* (see *Beis Yosef* 495; *Magen Avraham* at the beginning of 518; *Rosh Yosef*).

6. **B**eis Shammai say: We may not deliver *challah*, or [the *Kohen's*] gifts, to a *Kohen* on *Yom Tov* — whether they were separated yesterday or they were separated today. But Beis Hillel permit it.

YAD AVRAHAM

i.e., putting the finishing touch on a utensil (see below 5:2). Separating *challah* produces the same status change in dough, for until the *challah* is separated the dough may not be consumed. Thus, the Rabbinical prohibition against tithing on *Yom Tov* also applies to *challah*. However, in the case of dough first kneaded on *Yom Tov*, the Rabbis did not apply their restriction. In this instance the *challah* could not have been separated previously, for *challah* cannot be separated until after a dough has been formed (see *Gem.* 9a).]

The commentators advance two explanations for the prohibition against sending or delivering *terumah* [the portion separated and given the *Kohen* from produce] on *Yom Tov* (see below). Beis Shammai extends these reasons to *challah* and gifts. They are: (a) We are apprehensive that onlookers will suspect that the *Yom Tov* had been violated through the unlawful separation of *terumah* (see *Tos.* 12b with *Rosh Yosef*; *Yam shel Shlomo* 1:37); and (b) we are apprehensive that if delivery were permitted, people would be led to believe that separation of *terumah* (or of *challah* from a dough prepared before *Yom Tov*) was also permitted. According to these explanations even delivery not involving the labor of *transporting* is prohibited because of this apprehension[1] (see *Meiri*, *Chidushim*;

1. *Tosafos* (as cited by *Rashba*) contends that the prohibition against delivery in our mishnah refers to *transporting* the items through the public domain, thus involving the Scriptural labor of *transporting*. [Our versions of *Tosafos* holds the diametrically opposite view that even Beis Hillel permit the delivery of *challah*, etc., only in the giver's home — see *Tzlach*; this view is also held in a variant version of *Rashi* cited in *Or Zarua* 2:338.] Although carrying foodstuffs usually comes under the general dispensation of food preparation granted on *Yom Tov*, perhaps this instance is an exception because, for one, it is not known whether the recipient *Kohen* has need for the proferred portion (cf. *Tzlach* and R' A. L. Tzunz, *Simchas Yom Tov* on this mishnah); and, the intent of the sender is not to provide the *Kohen* with food for *Yom Tov*, but to perform a *mitzvah* (see *Riva* in *Tos.*, *Shabbos* 24b; *Pesachim* 46a; and *Ri* in *Tos.*, *Beitzah* 27b; *Tzlach* here; cf. *Turei Zahav* 506:5, and *Mishnah Berurah* 506:18). *Rashba* objects to this interpretation on the grounds that it is difficult to see how the argument advanced by Beis Hillel for leniency, namely that separation of *challah* and gifts are permitted on *Yom Tov*, has any bearing on the question of *transporting* on *Yom Tov*.

Tosefos R' Peretz (see also *Yam shel Shlomo* 1:37) attributes the prohibition to the concern about unnecessary exertion (טִירְחָא דְלֹא צָרִיךְ) on *Yom Tov*. The objection advanced by *Rashba* against *Tosafos'* interpretation would apply here too.

Meiri's view as presented in *Beis HaBechirah* (cf. *Chidushei HaMeiri*) basically concurs with that of *Tosafos* (that the prohibition of the mishnah refers to *transporting* into the public domain). However, he qualifies this and asserts that the primary, Scriptural prohibition applies only to *challah*, etc., already separated before *Yom Tov*. Since the requirement to give these portions was already in effect before *Yom Tov* they should have been given before *Yom Tov*, and as a result their delivery on *Yom Tov* is not considered a צוֹרֶךְ יוֹם טוֹב, *labor necessary for Yom Tov*. This differs, he argues, from portions of food which may be sent (see mishnah 9) for in general, a person does not know before *Yom Tov* exactly what he will eat and is given the option to decide on *Yom Tov*. However our mishnah discusses instances where separation took place on *Yom Tov* but delivery is prohibited because it may be suspected that the foodstuffs had already been separated prior to *Yom Tov*. In light of this, Beis Hillel's argument can be understood; the permissibility of separating *challah* and gifts on *Yom Tov* should remove the onus of suspicion.

אָמְרוּ לָהֶם בֵּית שַׁמַּאי: גְּזֵרָה שָׁוָה. חַלָּה
וּמַתָּנוֹת מַתָּנָה לַכֹּהֵן, וּתְרוּמָה מַתָּנָה לַכֹּהֵן. כְּשֵׁם
שֶׁאֵין מוֹלִיכִין אֶת הַתְּרוּמָה, כָּךְ אֵין מוֹלִיכִין אֶת
הַמַּתָּנוֹת.

אָמְרוּ לָהֶם בֵּית הַלֵּל: לֹא. אִם אֲמַרְתֶּם
בִּתְרוּמָה שֶׁאֵינוֹ זַכַּאי בַּהֲרָמָתָהּ, תֹּאמְרוּ בְמַתָּנוֹת
שֶׁזַּכַּאי בַּהֲרָמָתָן.

יד אברהם

Shitah Mekubetzes; Rashi 12b can be interpreted as holding this view[1]).

וּבֵית הַלֵּל מַתִּירִין. — *But Beis Hillel permit it.*

[Beis Hillel do not extend the prohibition against delivering *terumah* on *Yom Tov* to include *challah* and gifts. They feel that concern about: (a) misplaced suspicion; and (b) confusion leading to erroneous permitting of separation on *Yom Tov*, is unfounded. The underlying reasons for the disagreement between Beis Shammai and Beis Hillel are articulated in the discussion that follows.]

אָמְרוּ לָהֶם בֵּית שַׁמַּאי: גְּזֵרָה שָׁוָה. — *Beis Shammai said to them* [to Beis Hillel]: *There is an analogy.*

One of the י״ג מדות שהתורה נדרשת בהם, *thirteen hermeneutic principles by which the* [*written*] *Torah is expounded,* is called גְּזֵרָה שָׁוָה [*gezeirah shavah*], similar phraseology, and involves a comparison of Scriptural verses which contain identical [or

almost identical] wording as a basis for deriving a common law between them. In our mishnah the term *gezeirah shavah* is used as a borrowed phrase to connote similarity of halachos, as a basis of comparison (*Rashi*).

חַלָּה וּמַתָּנוֹת מַתָּנָה לַכֹּהֵן, וּתְרוּמָה מַתָּנָה לַכֹּהֵן. כְּשֵׁם שֶׁאֵין מוֹלִיכִין אֶת הַתְּרוּמָה, — *Challah and gifts are grants to the Kohen and terumah is a grant to the Kohen. Just as we may not bring the terumah* [*to the Kohen on Yom Tov*],

[Even Beis Hillel concur that *terumah* may not be delivered to a *Kohen* on *Yom Tov*, for the reasons given above.]

כָּךְ אֵין מוֹלִיכִין אֶת הַמַּתָּנוֹת. — *so may we not bring the gifts.*

The word מַתָּנוֹת is here used in a broader sense and includes *challah* also.

[Beis Shammai argue that since Beis Hillel concur that delivering is prohibited for *terumah*, they should extend this ban to the delivery of *challah* and gifts as well.][2]

1. However, a close reading of *Rashi* (see also *Ran*) suggests that he differs from this view and believes this prohibition to be included in the general prohibition against separating (see *Rosh Yosef*). An explanation of this view and the consequent re-interpretation of the *mishnah* can be found in *Pnei Yehoshua, Tzloch* and *Simchas Yom Tov*.

2. The commentators (see *Pnei Yehoshua, Rosh Yosef*, and *Simchas Yom Tov*) find difficulty with this analogy. They argue that none of the reasons given for the prohibition of delivering *terumah* apply to *challah* and gifts whose separation is permitted on *Yom Tov*. Although this appears to be Beis Hillel's rejoinder, nevertheless Beis Shammai's position needs to be clarified.

The simplest solution to this problem that suggests itself is to suppose that Beis Shammai's

1
6

Beis Shammai said to them: There is an analogy. *Challah* and gifts are grants to the *Kohen* and *terumah* is a grant to the *Kohen*. Just as we may not bring the *terumah* [to the *Kohen* on *Yom Tov*], so may we not bring the gifts.

Beis Hillel answered them: No [it is not analogous]. If you say so regarding *terumah* which one may not separate [on *Yom Tov*], will you also say the same thing regarding gifts which one may separate [on *Yom Tov*]?

YAD AVRAHAM

אָמְרוּ לָהֶם בֵּית הִלֵּל: לֹא. — *Beis Hillel answered* [lit. *said to*] *them* [Beis Shammai]: *No* [it is not analogous].

אִם אֲמַרְתֶּם בִּתְרוּמָה שֶׁאֵינוֹ זַכַּאי בַּהֲרָמָתָהּ, תֹּאמְרוּ בְמַתָּנוֹת שֶׁזַּכַּאי בַּהֲרָמָתָן. — *If you say so* [that delivering is prohibited on *Yom Tov*] *regarding terumah which one may not* [lit. *is not privileged to*] *separate* [on *Yom Tov*], *will you also say the same thing regarding gifts which one may* [lit. *is privileged to*] *separate* [on *Yom Tov*]?

Challah and the *Kohen's* gifts may be separated on *Yom Tov*,

because the obligation to separate these portions first takes effect on *Yom Tov*, when the dough is mixed and the animal slaughtered. This is unlike *terumah* which the owner is obligated to separate before *Yom Tov* (Rav). [Hence, none of the reasons advanced to explain the prohibition against sending *terumah* (see above, s.v. בֵּין שֶׁהוּרְמוּ) apply to sending gifts and *challah*.]

The halachah is not decided in accordance with this mishnah, for the *Gemara* (12b) cites a *baraisa* that states various versions of the dispute between Beis Shammai and Beis Hillel. Our mishnah contains only one version, that of אֲחֵרִים. R' Yose holds that Beis Sham-

disagreement with Beis Hillel is over this point itself; namely whether separation of *challah* from dough prepared on *Yom Tov* and gifts from an animal slaughtered on *Yom Tov* is permitted. The view in the *Gemara* (9a) permitting this may be based on Beis Hillel's explicit dispensation regarding this. However there is a difficulty here too. *Rashba* and *Meiri* assert that separation of gifts differs from that of *challah* in that it is permitted even from an animal slaughtered before *Yom Tov* (see also R' Yitzchak Aboab cited in *Beis Yosef* 506; *Bach* and *Prishah* there; *Turei Zahav* 506:5). Two reasons are given for this: (a) Separation of gifts cannot be considered an act of perfecting or completing because, unlike *terumah* and *challah*, there is no prohibition against eating the meat prior to separating the gifts; (b) the gifts are considered separated immediately upon slaughter, i.e., no formal act of separation is necessary. Since these considerations have no basis in the language of Beis Hillel and are based rather on Talmudic reasoning, the conclusions derived from them — permitting separation of gifts in all cases — must be imputed to Beis Shammai as well as to Beis Hillel. However, it can be deduced from *Rashi* (12b) that the separation of gifts should be viewed in the same light as separation of *challah*, i.e., it is intrinsically included in the ban against separating and is permitted only in order to allow one to eat meat on *Yom Tov*. Thus it should be concluded that *Rashi* disagrees with *Rashba* and *Meiri* and prohibits separation of gifts when the animal was slaughtered prior to *Yom Tov* and allows for the interpretation set forth above. *Rashba* and *Meiri* may interpret the mishnah in any of the ways proposed by the above cited commentators (except the view expounded jointly by *Pnei Yehoshua* and *Rosh Yosef*).

בֵּ֫ית [ז] שַׁמַאי אוֹמְרִים: תַּבְלִין נָדוֹכִין בְּמָדוֹךְ
שֶׁל עֵץ, וְהַמֶּלַח בְּפַךְ וּבְעֵץ הַפָּרוּר.
וּבֵית הִלֵּל אוֹמְרִים: תַּבְלִין נָדוֹכִין כְּדַרְכָּן בְּמָדוֹךְ
שֶׁל אֶבֶן, וְהַמֶּלַח בְּמָדוֹךְ שֶׁל עֵץ.

יד אברהם

mai concur with Beis Hillel in the matter of bringing *challah* and gifts. They disagree only about bringing *terumah* to the *Kohen*. The *Gemara* accepts R' Yose's version. Thus,

since we conduct ourselves in accordance with Beis Hillel, even *terumah* is permitted to be brought to the *Kohen* on *Yom Tov* (see *Orach Chaim* 506:3).

7.

Although the general rule is that otherwise forbidden labor is permitted on *Yom Tov* for the purpose of food preparation, there are some labors that are forbidden despite the fact that they involve the preparation of food. Examples of excluded labors are *trapping (see 3:1) and *reaping (Gem. 3a). [See General Introduction for a discussion of the reasons for excluding these labors.]

*Grinding grain is categorically prohibited on *Yom Tov*, for it is done in bulk and can be done before

Yom Tov with no difference in the quality of the food. *Grinding spices, the subject of the following mishnah, does not fall under this prohibition for it is usually done in small quantities and spices that are freshly ground taste better.[1]

Although grinding spices is permitted it must be done with a שִׁינּוּי, *change*, [i.e., the labor should be performed כְּלְאַחַר יָד, *in an unusual manner*] in the mode of *grinding, apparently to underscore the fact that not all *grinding is permitted.

1. [Some authorities hold that the labors excluded from the dispensation for food preparation are prohibited by the Torah (see *Tosafos*, 3a; *Yam shel Shlomo*, 3:1; *Sha'ar HaTziyun* 495:18). Since the prohibition of these labors is of Torah origin, they are forbidden to be performed even if a שִׁנּוּי, *change*, is effected in the mode of operation (e.g., tearing a fruit off a tree in an unusual manner, etc.). Therefore the permissibility of the *grinding of spices and salt (as is apparent in this mishnah) requires an explanation, in view of the fact that *grinding is one of the prohibited labors.

Maharshal (Yam shel Shlomo) suggests that determination of whether a certain act is accorded the dispensation for food preparation does not depend upon the *type* of labor done, but upon the specific food being prepared. The criterion to be followed is: If this act of preparation is used in preparing huge amounts of this type of food for storage, then the dispensation for food preparation does not apply, even if now only a small amount is being prepared. If a food which is not ordinarily prepared in large amounts (for storage) is being prepared, then the dispensation for food preparation does apply. Thus *grinding of even minute amounts of flour is prohibited (by the Torah), whereas even relatively large amounts of spices or salt may be ground, because these seasonings are usually prepared in small amounts.

This raises an interesting halachic question. Since most (if not all) spices are nowadays ground in huge amounts and stored, grinding even these substances should be prohibited on *Yom Tov*, and all the laws expounded in this mishnah (and *Orach Chaim* 504) should not apply. Thus, *grinding horseradish on *Yom Tov* even with a change should not be allowed *Beur Halachah* (to 504) suggests (concerning pepper) that not only the type of food being processed has to be taken into account, but also the type of utensil used. Thus horseradish may be grated on a grater (with a change) because one does not grate large amounts on this utensil (see also *Mishnah Berurah* 504:19 with *Sha'ar HaTziyun*).]

7. **B**eis Shammai say: Spices may be crushed [on *Yom Tov*] with a wooden pestle; but salt [should be crushed] with a flask or with a wooden mixing spoon. But Beis Hillel say: Spices may be crushed in their usual manner with a stone pestle, and salt [should be crushed] with a wooden pestle.

YAD AVRAHAM

The dispute between Beis Shammai and Beis Hillel in this mishnah concerns when the change should be performed and the form the change should take.

בֵּית שַׁמַּאי אוֹמְרִים: תַּבְלִין נִדּוֹכִין בְּמָדוֹךְ שֶׁל עֵץ, — *Beis Shammai say: Spices may be crushed* [*on Yom Tov*] *with a wooden pestle;*

Spices are usually crushed with a stone pestle. Beis Shammai require that on *Yom Tov* a change be made and a wooden pestle should be used. However, the spices may be crushed in their usual manner with the wooden pestle. The change from stone to wooden pestle is sufficient (*Rav*).

[As mentioned in the prefatory note, there is no Scripturally prohibited labor involved in grinding spices. Nevertheless, Beis Shammai hold that a change in the *modus operandi* should be made.]

[In other instances where the dispensation of food preparation applies (e.g., *cooking), no change is necessary even according to Beis Shammai. Perhaps *grinding is different because it is a labor which does not fall entirely under this dispensation (e.g., *grinding wheat is prohibited), therefore according to Beis Shammai a change must be made even in those instances where it is permitted.]

וְהַמֶּלַח — *but salt* [*should be crushed*]

In places where salt is mined in chunks it needs to be crushed before it can be used (*Rashi*).

בְּפַךְ — *with a flask*
He may tilt a flask and crush the salt with it (*Rav; Rashi*).

וּבְעֵץ הַפָּרוּר. — *or with a wooden mixing spoon.*

A greater degree of change than that required for spices is required for salt. In the former case a pestle, albeit a wooden one, is allowed, whereas for salt only a spoon may be used. According to one view in the *Gemara* (14a) the reason for requiring a more substantial change in the grinding of salt than in the grinding of spices is because the taste of salt does not fade with time and it could have been ground before *Yom Tov*. The taste of spices, however, fades, and delaying the grinding to *Yom Tov* can be justified (*Rav*).

וּבֵית הִלֵּל אוֹמְרִים: תַּבְלִין נִדּוֹכִין כְּדַרְכָּן, בְּמָדוֹךְ שֶׁל אֶבֶן, — *But Beis Hillel say: Spices may be crushed in their usual manner with a stone pestle,*

[Since we can justify the grinding of spices on *Yom Tov* on the grounds that their taste fades if ground earlier, the grinding need not be done in an unusual manner. According to Beis Hillel grinding spices meets the criteria of food preparation (see General Introduction to this tractate and prefatory remarks to this mishnah) and, like *cooking, is permitted without any change].

וְהַמֶּלַח בְּמָדוֹךְ שֶׁל עֵץ. — *and salt* [*should be crushed*] *with a wooden pestle.*

[Since salt could have been

[ח] **הַבּוֹרֵר** קִטְנִיּוֹת בְּיוֹם טוֹב — בֵּית
שַׁמַּאי אוֹמְרִים: בּוֹרֵר אֹכֶל
וְאוֹכֵל. וּבֵית הִלֵּל אוֹמְרִים: בּוֹרֵר כְּדַרְכּוֹ —
בְּחֵיקוֹ, בְּקָנוֹן וּבְתַמְחוּי; אֲבָל לֹא בְטַבְלָא, וְלֹא

יד אברהם

crushed before *Yom Tov* without
any ensuing loss of taste, an unusual manner is required. However,
Beis Hillel hold that the change
from a stone pestle to one of wood
is sufficient.]

According to the above explanation one
should be permitted to crush all kinds of
spices in the usual manner, and this is the
halachah according to *Shulchan Aruch*
(*Orach Chaim* 504:1). However, the *Gemara*
(14a) gives an additional difference between
salt and spices. Since every food is salted, the
need for salt was known before *Yom Tov* and
the salt should have been crushed then.
The use of spices, however, varies with the
type of dish prepared. Thus it is *possible* that
the person did not know he would need this
spice on *Yom Tov*. Therefore, if the person
knew before *Yom Tov* that he would need a
particular spice on *Yom Tov*, but he
nevertheless did not grind it, the grinding
may be performed on *Yom Tov*, but only in
an unusual manner, as specified pertaining
to salt. *Tosafos* (citing *Ri*) decides for this
opinion. *Rama* (504:1) testifies that the
custom is to make a change (albeit a small
one, e.g., holding the pestle on a slant) when
crushing spices. *Mishnah Berurah* (504:11)
cites authorities to the effect that the custom

extends even to cases where the need was not
known before *Yom Tov*.

The above discussion pertains to spices
that do not undergo a great loss of taste after
grinding. However, when cutting up onion
or garlic very fine (this too is included in
*grinding; see *Shabbos* 74b; *Orach Chaim*
321:2) no change need be made, for in such a
case an almost total loss of taste would result
if this were done before *Yom Tov* (ibid.).

However, all authorities concur that one
may not use a small grinder to grind pepper,
etc. (see *comm.* to 2:8) because use of such a
utensil is in the category of עוּבְדָּא דְחוֹל,
weekday activity (ibid.; cf. *Beur Halachah*).

Some authorities (*Semag, lavin* 70; *Or
Zarua* and *Maharil* quoted in *Darkei Moshe*
495; cf. *Beur Halachah* there) extend the ruling established in this mishnah (in regard to
spices) to all food preparation. Thus,
whatever *cooking or *baking can be done
before *Yom Tov* without adversely affecting
the quality of the food must be done prior to
the advent of the festival.

Rama (495:1) cites this opinion and seems
to rule in favor of it (see *Mishnah Berurah*
495:8). However, the authorities hold that, as
far as *cooking is concerned, almost all foods
are regarded as losing taste if left to stand
from before *Yom Tov*. Consequently, most
foods may be cooked on the *Yom Tov*, with
few exceptions (e.g., dried fruits).

$$8.$$

◄§ בּוֹרֵר — The Melachah of *Separating

*Separating inedible matter from food (or separating food not wanted at the mo-
ment from food one wishes to eat now, e.g., picking out and setting aside raisins
from a raisin-nut mixture in order to eat the nuts) by hand or with a sieve constitutes the forbidden labor of בּוֹרֵר, *sorting or *separating [lit. *clarifying*]. This
prohibition applies not only to unprocessed foodstuffs but even to ready-to-eat
food. The rules of this *melachah* are very complex and cannot be fully dealt with
within the limits of this work. The general rules as they apply to the Sabbath (taken
from *Orach Chaim* 319) are:

(a) Removing inedible matter — pebbles or spoiled parts of the food itself (or the
unwanted food) — from food is prohibited by Torah law under all circumstances,
regardless of whether the removal is done by hand or by special implement, either
before and during the meal.

8. **O**ne who separates pulse on *Yom Tov* — Beis Shammai say: He must separate the edible parts and eat. But Beis Hillel say: He may separate in his usual manner — into his lap, into a basket or into a large plate; but not on a board, nor with a fine

YAD AVRAHAM

(b) Removing food from inedible matter well in advance of a meal is prohibited, in any manner; but if the food is removed just before or during a meal it must be done by hand. Using an implement designed especially for separating the different substances (e.g., a sieve or sifter) is prohibited by Torah law; using a utensil not especially designed for such a task but whose use makes it easier (e.g., a funnel) is prohibited Rabbinically.

These are the rules of *separating* as they apply to the Sabbath. Most authorities hold that the labor of *separating* falls into the general exemption of work done in the preparation of food and is permitted on *Yom Tov* in any manner (according to Beis Hillel). However, in certain instances the Rabbis prohibited using a utensil, as stated below.

הַבּוֹרֵר קִטְנִיּוֹת בְּיוֹם טוֹב — בֵּית שַׁמַּאי אוֹמְרִים: בּוֹרֵר אֹכֶל וְאוֹכֵל. — *One who separates pulse* [from pebbles or other impurities found among them] *on Yom Tov — Beis Shammai say: He must separate the edible parts and eat.*

He must select single seeds and eat them as he selects. He may not separate a few seeds at a time *(Rav)* [nor pick out the inedible parts (see *Gemara* 14b)].

Beis Shammai hold that there is no dispensation for food preparation as far as *separating* is concerned. Thus *separating* may only be performed in the manner permitted on the Sabbath, i.e., separating the edible parts and eating them soon afterward. But Beis Hillel (see below) hold that *separating* is included in the dispensation for food preparation and one may separate in the usual manner as long as un-

necessary effort is avoided *(Rosh Yosef).*[1]

וּבֵית הִלֵּל אוֹמְרִים: בּוֹרֵר כְּדַרְכּוֹ — בְּחֵיקוֹ, בְּקָנוֹן וּבְתַמְחוּי; — *But Beis Hillel say: He may separate in his usual manner — into his lap, into a basket* [or *plate; see Mosaf HeAruch,* s.v. קָנוֹן] *or into a large plate;*

[*Aruch* explains that a תַמְחוּי is a large plate containing many compartments for different foods.]

He may separate more than one seed at a time, or he may even pick out the inedible parts *(Gem. 14b).*

The *Gemara* adds that Beis Hillel agree that when it is more troublesome to pick out the inedibles (e.g., if they are small particles), the edibles should be picked out so as not to cause needless labor on *Yom Tov.*

אֲבָל לֹא בְטַבְלָא, וְלֹא בְנָפָה, וְלֹא בִכְבָרָה. — *but not on a board, nor with a*

1. Some authorities hold that *separating* is not included in the exemption of work done in the preparation of food and that all *separating* forbidden by Torah law on the Sabbath is also forbidden on *Yom Tov.* According to this view our mishnah discusses only the instances of *separating* that are prohibited on the Sabbath by Rabbinic decree *(Rashba, Avodas HaKodesh* 1:5; see also *Maharil;* cf. *Pri Chadash* to *Orach Chaim* 495). However, this opinion is not accepted as halachah (see *Mishnah Berurah* 510:7).

בְּנָפָה, וְלֹא בִכְבָרָה.

רַבָּן גַּמְלִיאֵל אוֹמֵר: אַף מֵדִיחַ וְשׁוֹלֶה.

[ט] **בֵּית** שַׁמַּאי אוֹמְרִים: אֵין מְשַׁלְּחִין בְּיוֹם טוֹב אֶלָּא מָנוֹת. וּבֵית הִלֵּל אוֹמְרִים: מְשַׁלְּחִין בְּהֵמָה חַיָּה וְעוֹף, בֵּין חַיִּין, בֵּין שְׁחוּטִין. מְשַׁלְּחִין יֵינוֹת שְׁמָנִים וּסְלָתוֹת וְקִטְנִיּוֹת, אֲבָל לֹא תְבוּאָה. וְרַבִּי שִׁמְעוֹן מַתִּיר בִּתְבוּאָה.

יד אברהם

fine sieve, nor with a coarse sieve.

Because *separating with these utensils gives the appearance of separating more than the amount needed for Yom Tov (Maggid Mishneh, Hil. Yom Tov 3:16). Alternatively, *separating in this manner resembles weekday activity (Chidushei HaRitva).

רַבָּן גַּמְלִיאֵל אוֹמֵר: אַף מֵדִיחַ וְשׁוֹלֶה — Rabban Gamliel says: He may also rinse [the pulse] and skim [the chaff and other dirt which rises to the top].

He may put the pulse in a pot, fill it with water and let the inedible matter rise to the top or let it sink to the bottom (Rav; Gem. 14b).

[But Beis Hillel do not allow this. It seems that this method, too, is used in processing larger amounts of foodstuffs and is therefore similar to using a sieve, etc.]

The halachah does not follow Rabban Gamliel (Rav; Rambam, comm. to mishnah). Shulchan Aruch (Orach Chaim 510:2) makes no mention of Rabban Gamliel's method at all, nor does Rambam (Hil. Yom Tov 3:16). Magen Avraham (510:2) takes this omission as an indication that this method is prohibited (cf. Tif. Yisrael 49; Tif. Yaakov).

Meiri believes that the correct version is רַבָּן גַּמְלִיאֵל אוֹמֵר מֵדִיחַ וְשׁוֹלֶה, omitting אַף, also. Thus, Rabban Gamliel is understood as holding that only rinsing and skimming, steps which take less effort than Beis Hillel's method, should be permitted. According to Beis Hillel not only rinsing and skimming, but also *separating in the usual manner is permitted.

9.

בֵּית שַׁמַּאי אוֹמְרִים: אֵין מְשַׁלְּחִין בְּיוֹם טוֹב אֶלָּא מָנוֹת. — Beis Shammai say: We may not send [presents] on Yom Tov with the exception of [readied] portions.

Only portions of food ready to be eaten which are likely to be consumed by the recipient on Yom Tov may be sent to another person (Rashi; Rav).

The reason for this prohibition is so that one not do as he does on a weekday (Rambam, comm.) [i.e., we

are apprehensive, lest people keep themselves occupied with unnecessary tasks on Yom Tov (cf. Hil. Yom Tov 1:5-6)].

וּבֵית הִלֵּל אוֹמְרִים: מְשַׁלְּחִין בְּהֵמָה חַיָּה וְעוֹף, — But Beis Hillel say: We may send domestic animals, beasts or fowl,

If, however, the animals are muktzeh, e.g., fowl designated for breeding or producing eggs, they may not be sent (Mishnah Berurah 516:2).

sieve, nor with a coarse sieve.

Rabban Gamliel says: He may also rinse [the pulse] and skim [the chaff].

9. **B**eis Shammai say: We may not send [presents] on *Yom Tov* with the exception of [readied] portions. But Beis Hillel say: We may send domestic animals, beasts or fowl, whether alive or slaughtered.

We may send wines, oils, fine flours and pulse, but not grain. But R' Shimon permits grain [to be sent].

YAD AVRAHAM

בֵּין חַיִּין, בֵּין שְׁחוּטִין. — *whether alive or slaughtered.*

[Because even live animals may be slaughtered and used on *Yom Tov.*][1]

Although Beis Hillel permit sending presents on *Yom Tov,* nevertheless, they admit that certain restrictions apply. The present may not be delivered by a group of three (who present the gift to the recipient together or one after the other), for they would appear to be bringing goods to the market place (*Rav, Gem.* 14b).

מְשַׁלְּחִין יֵינוֹת שְׁמָנִים וּסְלָתוֹת וְקִטְנִיּוֹת, אֲבָל לֹא תְבוּאָה. — *We may send wines, oils, fine flours and pulse, but not grain.*

Because grain cannot [ordinarily] be used without *grinding, which is prohibited on *Yom Tov* (*Rav*). [Even salt and spices are only al-

lowed to be crushed (mishnah 7), not ground in a mill (see 2:8; *Orach Chaim* 504:1).]

וְרַבִּי שִׁמְעוֹן מַתִּיר בִּתְבוּאָה. — *But R' Shimon permits grain [to be sent].*

Because grain too can be used on *Yom Tov.* It can be crushed with a pestle [in an unusual manner, see mishnah 7] or cooked (*Rav, Gem.* 14b). [However, grain may not be ground into flour even if it is done in an unusual manner. See prefatory note to mishnah 7 and *Tosefos Yom Tov* here.]

The Sages do not accept this reason. A prohibition is promulgated against sending whenever there is a semblance of needless work or effort on *Yom Tov* (*Maggid Mishneh* 5:6). [Since most grain is ground in large quantity and used for flour, this semblance exists.]

[There is a question as to how far the prohibition against sending certain items ex-

---

1. *Shulchan Aruch HaRav* (516:1 cited by *Mishnah Berurah* 516:2) rules that even if the sender knows that the recipient will not use the animal on *Yom Tov* he is permitted to send the animal.

[No explanation for this is given. It is not clear why this case of *transporting* (the present) from domain to domain is not forbidden since there is no *Yom Tov* need. However, *Rashba* (*Avodas HaKodesh* 3:5) explains (concerning a similar matter) that a present, although not used on *Yom Tov,* is considered needed on *Yom Tov,* because there is enjoyment in the mere sending [and receipt] of presents. Perhaps this principle applies here too. Thus the only consideration is the unnecessary effort expended on *Yom Tov.* Therefore any present which might possibly be used on *Yom Tov,* or would enhance the sender's or the recipient's enjoyment of the day, may be sent.]

[י] מְשַׁלְּחִין כֵּלִים, בֵּין תְּפוּרִין בֵּין שֶׁאֵינָן תְּפוּרִין, וְאַף עַל פִּי שֶׁיֵּשׁ בָּהֶן כִּלְאָיִם, וְהֵן לְצֹרֶךְ הַמּוֹעֵד. אֲבָל לֹא סַנְדָּל הַמְסֻמָּר, וְלֹא מִנְעָל שֶׁאֵינוֹ תָפוּר. רַבִּי יְהוּדָה אוֹמֵר: אַף לֹא מִנְעָל לָבָן, מִפְּנֵי שֶׁצָּרִיךְ אֻמָּן.

יד אברהם

tends. Some authorities (Magen Avraham and Turei Zahav to 516; see also Meiri; cf. Chidushei Meiri) believe that only *transporting from domain to domain is prohibited, because where an item cannot be used on Yom Tov, *transporting it does not fall under the dispensation of food preparation. When it cannot be used even after Yom Tov without additional preparation, we cannot assume that there is enjoyment of Yom Tov to the sender in sending it. But where *transporting is not involved (e.g., there is an eruv), all presents are permitted. Mishnah Berurah (516:4), however, cites Maggid Mishneh and Chidushei Meiri that the mere semblance of unnecessary effort or work is reason enough to prohibit sending regardless of whether *transporting is involved. The same can be deduced from Rambam's commentary to Mishnah (here).]

10.

מְשַׁלְּחִין כֵּלִים, בֵּין תְּפוּרִין בֵּין שֶׁאֵינָן תְּפוּרִין, — We may send garments [lit. utensils], whether sewn up or not sewn up,

[This mishnah continues with an enumeration of the things permitted to be sent on Yom Tov according to Beis Hillel.][1]

The sewn-up garments can be used as apparel on Yom Tov, while the unsewn pieces of material can be used to cover oneself (Rav, Gem. 14b).

וְאַף עַל פִּי שֶׁיֵּשׁ בָּהֶן כִּלְאָיִם, — even if they contain a mixture of wool and linen,

Despite the fact that one may not even cover oneself with these garments they may be sent on Yom Tov because they can be used to sit upon. The Torah (Leviticus 19:19)

states, לֹא יַעֲלֶה עָלֶיךָ, It (i.e., a garment containing a mixture of wool and linen) shall not come onto you. The Sages forbade even sitting upon such garments lest a portion of the garment curl up and cover part of one's body. However, if the garment is hard and stiff one may sit upon it. Our mishnah speaks of this latter type of garment (Rav, Gem. 14b-15a).

וְהֵן לְצֹרֶךְ הַמּוֹעֵד. — because [lit. and] they enhance the [enjoyment of] Yom Tov.

Meiri, following the apparent meaning of the mishnah, takes this to be a conditional clause. Thus, One may send ... if they enhance the [enjoyment of] Yom Tov. Though even those things which cannot be used in their usual man-

1. Ravad (Hasagos to HaMaor 12a) maintains that clothing is given the status of food preparation and is consequently permitted to be sent even according to Beis Shammai. Razah (HaMaor, ibid.) holds that Beis Shammai disagree here as well as in the previous mishnah and prohibit sending clothing on Yom Tov (Tos. R' Akiva). [Evidently both Razah and Ravad understand that the mishnah permits sending presents even when this involves the labor of *transporting. See footnote to mishnah 9.]

10. **W**e may send garments, whether sewn up or not sewn up, even if they contain a mixture of wool and linen, because they enhance the [enjoyment of] *Yom Tov*. But [we may] not [send] a sandal with spikes, nor an unsewn shoe. Rabbi Yehudah says: Not even a white shoe [may be sent], because it requires a craftsman.

YAD AVRAHAM

ner on *Yom Tov* [e.g., *tefillin*, which are not worn on *Yom Tov*] may be sent (see below, s.v. בְּיוֹם טוֹב מְשַׁלְּחִין אוֹתוֹ), there must at least be some purpose for them on *Yom Tov* [e.g., *tefillin* may be sent if the recipient wishes to familiarize himself with the laws of *tefillin*]. However, the translation given here follows *Rashba* (*Avodas HaKodesh* 3:8), who holds that even if the gift serves no practical purpose on *Yom Tov* it may be sent, because the act of sending a present in itself enhances the enjoyment of *Yom Tov*. This latter interpretation is the halachah stated in *Shulchan Aruch* (*Orach Chaim* 516:3 with *Mishnah Berurah*). [Therefore, this clause of the mishnah must be understood in the manner given in the translation.]

אֲבָל לֹא סַנְדָּל הַמְסֻמָּר, — *But [we may] not [send] a sandal with spikes,*

This refers to a wooden sandal covered with spikes. The Sages prohibited this type of sandal to be worn on the Sabbath and *Yom Tov* in commemoration of a tragic episode in the martyrology of the Jewish people. A group of Jews had hidden themselves in a cave in order to escape religious persecution. According to one version of the story, they were discovered by the enemy. In the panic that ensued, many of the inhabitants of the cave were killed by the sharp spikes which they wore on their shoes (*Gem.* 60a). To commemorate this tragic episode which occurred on the Sabbath, the Rabbis decreed that no Jew should wear spiked shoes on the Sabbath or *Yom Tov* (*Rav*).

Spiked shoes, which may be worn on weekdays, are apparently an exception to the general rule stated at the end of this mishnah that anything which can be used on weekdays without requiring any modification may be sent on *Yom Tov* (see s.v. בְּיוֹם טוֹב מְשַׁלְּחִין אוֹתוֹ). Other objects which may not be utilized on *Yom Tov* may be sent because the sending (or receiving) of gifts in itself enhances enjoyment of *Yom Tov*. However, sending spiked shoes, which bring to mind such a sad episode in Jewish history, cannot be considered enjoyable, and is therefore prohibited on *Yom Tov* (*Tos.* 60a).

וְלֹא מִנְעָל שֶׁאֵינוֹ תָפוּר. — *nor an unsewn shoe.*

Even if it is partially attached with nails (*Rav, Gem.* 15a).

[Because it is not usable even on a weekday without further alteration.]

רַבִּי יְהוּדָה אוֹמֵר: אַף לֹא מִנְעָל לָבָן, מִפְּנֵי שֶׁצָּרִיךְ אֻמָּן. — *Rabbi Yehudah says: Not even a white shoe [may be sent], because it requires a craftsman.*

To blacken it (*Rav, Gem.* 15a). It was not customary to wear an unblackened shoe (*Rav; Rashi;* cf. *Tos., Bava Kama* 59b). [Thus, it is an item which cannot be used even

זֶה הַכְּלָל: כָּל שֶׁנֵּאוֹתִין בּוֹ בְּיוֹם טוֹב מְשַׁלְּחִין אוֹתוֹ.

[א] **יוֹם** טוֹב שֶׁחָל לִהְיוֹת עֶרֶב שַׁבָּת, לֹא יְבַשֵּׁל אָדָם בַּתְּחִלָּה מִיּוֹם טוֹב לַשַּׁבָּת; אֲבָל מְבַשֵּׁל הוּא לְיוֹם טוֹב, וְאִם הוֹתִיר, הוֹתִיר לַשַּׁבָּת.

וְעוֹשֶׂה תַבְשִׁיל מֵעֶרֶב יוֹם טוֹב וְסוֹמֵךְ עָלָיו

יד אברהם

on weekdays without change.]

זֶה הַכְּלָל: — *This is the rule:*
[To be followed in deciding what may or may not be sent on *Yom Tov*.]

כָּל שֶׁנֵּאוֹתִין בּוֹ — *Whatever can be used*
As is, without further change (*Rav; Gem.* 15a).

בְּיוֹם טוֹב מְשַׁלְּחִין אוֹתוֹ. — *may be sent on Yom Tov* [lit. *on Yom Tov we may send it*].
The *Gemara* (15a) comments that *tefillin* may be sent though they cannot be used on *Yom Tov*. The

Gemara concludes that the antecedent of the words 'on *Yom Tov*' in our mishnah is not כָּל שֶׁנֵּאוֹתִין בּוֹ, *whatever can be used*, but rather מְשַׁלְּחִין אוֹתוֹ, *it may be sent*. This commentary is reflected in the translation. Thus, the rule to be followed is that anything that can be used on a weekday without further modification may be sent on *Yom Tov*. That which cannot be used in its present state on weekdays may not be sent. However, that which can be used on *Yom Tov*, albeit with modification (e.g., live animals which must be slaughtered before they can be eaten), may be sent.

Chapter 2

1.

The dispensation permitting otherwise forbidden labors to be performed on *Yom Tov* when required for the preparation of food has been discussed in the General Introduction and in the commentary to chapter one. Exclusion from the prohibition, however, is only granted when the food prepared on *Yom Tov* is intended to be eaten on *Yom Tov*. Food may not be prepared for the next day [regardless of whether that day is *Chol HaMoed*

or a weekday]. Nevertheless, the Talmud (*Pesachim* 46b), based on the institution of *eruv tavshilin* which permits one to cook on *Yom Tov* for the Sabbath, notes that on a Scriptural level one may cook for the Sabbath. The Amoraim there differ regarding the reason that cooking on *Yom Tov* for the Sabbath is permitted while cooking for a weekday is forbidden. This dispute and its ramifications are discussed below (s.v. וְעוֹשֶׂה). Although

This is the rule: Whatever can be used may be sent on *Yom Tov.*

1. When a *Yom Tov* falls on Friday, a person may not cook on *Yom Tov* primarily for the Sabbath; but he may cook for *Yom Tov*, and if anything is left over, it may be left for the Sabbath.

But one should prepare a dish prior to *Yom Tov*

YAD AVRAHAM

on a Scriptural level the Sabbath preparations may take place on *Yom Tov*, the Sages (for reasons given below, s.v. וְעוֹשֶׂה) prohibited such preparations unless an עֵרוּב תַּבְשִׁילִין, *eruv tavshilin* (see below), has been made prior to *Yom Tov*. The mishnah now discusses the requirements of the *eruv tavshilin*, as well as some ramifications of the prohibition against preparing the Sabbath food on *Yom Tov*.

יוֹם טוֹב שֶׁחָל לִהְיוֹת עֶרֶב שַׁבָּת, לֹא יְבַשֵׁל אָדָם בַּתְּחִלָּה מִיּוֹם טוֹב לַשַּׁבָּת; — *When a Yom Tov falls* [lit. *a Yom Tov which fell*] *on Friday, a person may not cook on Yom Tov primarily for the Sabbath;*

He should not cook with the express purpose of preparing for the Sabbath *(Rav; Rashi).* [This is a Rabbinical injunction, for on a Scriptural level one may cook on *Yom Tov* (with certain restrictions) for Sabbath.] The reasons for this decree will be explained in connection with the explanation of *eruv tavshilin* [see prefatory note and commentary below, s.v. וְעוֹשֶׂה].

אֲבָל מְבַשֵׁל הוּא לְיוֹם טוֹב, וְאִם הוֹתִיר, הוֹתִיר לַשַּׁבָּת. — *but he may cook for Yom Tov, and if anything is left over, it may be left for the Sabbath* [lit. *and if he left over he left over*

for the Sabbath].

I.e., he may cook for *Yom Tov* and use the leftovers for Sabbath *(Rav; Rashi).*

[One may even cook a full pot of meat knowing that he needs only one piece of meat for *Yom Tov*. Since the labor of *cooking* consists of placing the pot on the fire, the same effort is expended in cooking one piece of meat as is expended in cooking ten pieces.

However, one must first fill the pot and then place it on the fire. If the pot is put on the fire first, then the addition of each slice is considered a separate performance of the *melachah* of *cooking*, and consequently one may only put in as much as is needed for *Yom Tov* (from *Gem.* 17a; *Orach Chaim* 503:1).

The *Gemara* (17b) warns that one should not resort to הַעֲרָמָה, *subterfuge*, i.e., to proclaim that one is cooking for *Yom Tov* and, at the conclusion of the cooking process "discover" that the food is not needed for *Yom Tov*.

[Some authorities hold that one may cook a pot of food on *Yom Tov* intended specifically for the next day, as long as care is taken to taste the food on the day it is cooked. However, this procedure is permitted only prior to the morning meal when it is still usual to cook for the *Yom Tov* meal. After the meal is eaten, this is not permitted even if the food is tasted on *Yom Tov* since the intention to cook for the next day is obvious (see *Mishnah Berurah* 503:7).]

וְעוֹשֶׂה תַבְשִׁיל מֵעֶרֶב יוֹם טוֹב וְסוֹמֵךְ עָלָיו לַשַּׁבָּת. — *But one should prepare a dish prior to Yom Tov and depend on it for the Sabbath.*

[This dish serves as the basis for

בֵּיצָה
ב/א

לַשַׁבָּת. בֵּית שַׁמַּאי אוֹמְרִים: שְׁנֵי תַבְשִׁילִין. וּבֵית
הִלֵּל אוֹמְרִים: תַּבְשִׁיל אֶחָד. וְשָׁוִין בְּדָג וּבֵיצָה
שֶׁעָלָיו, שֶׁהֵן שְׁנֵי תַבְשִׁילִין.

יד אברהם

his dispensation to cook for the Sabbath on *Yom Tov*.] In order to allow a person to prepare for the Sabbath during *Yom Tov*, the Rabbis required that a special dish be set aside before *Yom Tov*. This dish serves a symbolic function and is called עֵרוּב תַּבְשִׁילִין, *eruv tavshilin* [lit. *blending* or *mingling of dishes*].[1] The *eruv tavshilin* is a Rabbinic precept (מִצְוַת עֲשֵׂה מִדְרַבָּנָן) accompanied by the recitation of a בְּרָכָה, *blessing*, and a declaration of its purpose[2] (*Rav, Gem.* 15b).

The *Gemara* (15b) gives two reasons for the institution of *eruv tavshilin*: The first view, that of Rava, maintains that the *eruv tavshilin* was instituted to honor the Sabbath, i.e., one is forced to think of the Sabbath prior to *Yom Tov* and consequently he will set aside food in the quantity and of the quality appropriate for the Sabbath. The second opinion, that of Rav

Ashi, holds that the *mitzvah* of *eruv tavshilin* was instituted to preserve the sanctity of *Yom Tov*, by demonstrating that even preparations for the Sabbath may not be made on *Yom Tov* unless such preparations were *begun*, at least symbolically, prior to the holiday. This is done to make people realize that under no circumstances is one permitted to cook (or perform other labors) on *Yom Tov* for the week day.

The Talmud (*Pesachim* 46b) notes that the institution of *eruv tavshilin* presupposes that *cooking for the Sabbath *per se* involves no prohibition on the Scriptural level — surely the Rabbinical enactment of *eruv* would not be effective in removing such a prohibition. The Talmud, however, records a dispute concerning the origin of the prohibition against *cooking on *Yom Tov* for a weekday. According to R' Chisda it is considered a transgression of the Scriptural injunction against performing *melachah* on *Yom Tov* (since the dispensation for food preparation does not apply). This view holds that the permissibility of *cooking for the Sabbath is

1. *Rambam (Hil. Yom Tov* 6:2) says the term *eruv* is borrowed from *eruvei chatzeiros* which removes the Rabbinical prohibition of *transporting from one private domain to another. There, the name is quite appropriate since the *eruv* serves to merge the two areas (or their inhabitants) into a single unit.

Ravad (loc. cit.) states that the name *eruv* indicates the blending of the Sabbath and *Yom Tov* dishes (i.e., their preparation is done simultaneously).

2. The *eruv*-foods are held in the hand (*Orach Chaim* 527:12) and the blessing is recited:
בָּרוּךְ אַתָּה יהוה אֱלֹהֵינוּ מֶלֶךְ הָעוֹלָם, אֲשֶׁר קִדְּשָׁנוּ בְּמִצְוֹתָיו, וְצִוָּנוּ עַל מִצְוַת עֵרוּב.
Blessed are You, HASHEM, our God, King of the universe, Who has sanctified us with His commandments and has commanded us concerning the mitzvah of eruv.

Additionally, the rationale [see commentary] for the enactment of *eruv tavshilin* requires that the person setting the *eruv* must understand its purpose. For this reason, the accompanying declaration must be said in a language understood by that person. The text of the declaration is:

בְּהָדֵין עֵרוּבָא יְהֵא שָׁרֵא לָנָא לַאֲפוּיֵי וּלְבַשּׁוּלֵי וּלְאַטְמוּנֵי וּלְאַדְלוּקֵי שְׁרָגָא וּלְמֶעְבַּד כָּל צָרְכָנָא מִיּוֹמָא טָבָא לְשַׁבַּתָּא (לָנוּ וּלְכָל יִשְׂרָאֵל הַדָּרִים בָּעִיר הַזֹּאת).

Through this eruv may we be permitted to bake, cook, insulate (food), kindle flame, and do anything necessary on Yom Tov for the sake of the Sabbath (for ourselves and for all Jews who live in this city).

and depend on it for the Sabbath. Beis Shammai say: Two dishes. But Beis Hillel say: One dish. Yet they agree concerning a fish and the egg on it, because they are two dishes.

YAD AVRAHAM

based on the principle צָרְכֵי שַׁבָּת נַעֲשִׂים בְּיוֹם טוֹב, *the needs of the Sabbath may be performed on Yom Tov*, i.e., the needs of the Sabbath are equivalent to those of *Yom Tov* and therefore *cooking for the Sabbath is permitted by the same dispensation allowing *cooking for *Yom Tov* itself.

Rabbah, however, maintains that *cooking for the weekdays is not the same as performing a prohibited labor on *Yom Tov*. This opinion is based on the principle of הוֹאִיל, *ho'il* [lit. *because*], which states: הוֹאִיל וּמִיקְלְעֵי לֵיהּ אוֹרְחִים חֲזֵי לֵיהּ, *because, if* [unexpected] *guests should happen to arrive, it will be fit for him* [to serve his guests on *Yom Tov*]. By this reasoning, almost any food may be cooked on *Yom Tov*, since there is always the possibility that guests will arrive, obliging one to offer them the food he cooked for the weekdays. This is sufficient reason to qualify the food preparation as necessary for *Yom Tov* as far as Scriptural law is concerned. Only food prepared too late in the day to be ready for guests is considered unequivocally prepared for the weekday. Nevertheless, there is a Rabbinical injunction against any form of *cooking done on *Yom Tov* for the purpose of the weekdays. Accordingly, the Scriptural prohibition is removed by the principle of *ho'il*, while the Rabbinical prohibition is removed by the *eruv tavshilin*.

The first explanation, R' Chisda's, justifies *cooking for the Sabbath categorically, while the second, Rabbah's, permits it only where potential guests would be able to use the cooked food. Consequently, where the food will not be ready early enough for consumption on *Yom Tov*, the Scriptural prohibition would remain in force and *eruv tavshilin* would be ineffectual. *Mishnah Berurah* (527:3) rules that in deference to the second opinion cited here, care should be taken that food cooked on *Yom Tov* for the Sabbath be readied early enough to ensure the possibility of consumption on *Yom Tov*, especially so when the first, Scripturally mandated, day of *Yom Tov* falls on Friday.

בֵּית שַׁמַּאי אוֹמְרִים: שְׁנֵי תַבְשִׁילִין. — *Bais Shammai say: Two dishes.*

[One must prepare two dishes if one wishes to cook for the Sabbath, i.e., the *eruv* consists of two dishes.]

וּבֵית הֵלֵּל אוֹמְרִים: תַּבְשִׁיל אֶחָד. — *But Beis Hillel say: One dish.*

Beis Shammai hold that since it is not usual to eat only one dish on the Sabbath, one cannot consider the preparations for the Sabbath to have begun unless at least two dishes have been designated for the Sabbath. Beis Hillel disagree, on the grounds that since one dish is sometimes eaten, this is sufficient for this token preparation for the Sabbath.

Some authorities (see *Tur* 527) believe that one dish is sufficient only when the Sabbath meal consists exclusively of cooked food. If baked foods are also to be prepared, then one must add a baked item to the *eruv*. *Shulchan Aruch* (*Orach Chaim* 527:2) rules that this opinion should be deferred to. [Thus the prevalent custom is to use a loaf of *challah*, a matzah, or some other bread, along with a cooked food, such as fish or a hard egg.] However, if one has forgotten to add a baked item to the *eruv*, one may, nevertheless, bake for the Sabbath.

וְשָׁוִין בְּדָג וּבֵיצָה שֶׁעָלָיו, — *Yet they* [Beis Shammai and Beis Hillel] *agree concerning a fish and the egg on it* [that this dish is sufficient for *eruv tavshilin*],

Egg would be smeared over the fish when it was being broiled (*Rashi;* cf. *Lechem Mishneh* here).

שֶׁהֵן שְׁנֵי תַבְשִׁילִין. — *because they are two dishes.*

[The egg, though prepared and eaten together with the fish, is considered a separate dish.]

אֲכָלוֹ אוֹ שֶׁאָבַד, לֹא יְבַשֵּׁל עָלָיו בַּתְּחִלָּה. וְאִם
שִׁיֵּר מִמֶּנּוּ כָּל שֶׁהוּא, סוֹמֵךְ עָלָיו לַשַּׁבָּת.

[ב] חָל לִהְיוֹת אַחַר הַשַּׁבָּת — בֵּית שַׁמַּאי
אוֹמְרִים: מַטְבִּילִין אֶת הַכֹּל מִלִּפְנֵי
הַשַּׁבָּת. וּבֵית הִלֵּל אוֹמְרִים: כֵּלִים מִלִּפְנֵי הַשַּׁבָּת,
וְאָדָם בַּשַּׁבָּת.

יד אברהם

אֲכָלוֹ אוֹ שֶׁאָבַד, לֹא יְבַשֵּׁל עָלָיו בַּתְּחִלָּה.
— If one ate it [the dish designated
for the *eruv*] or it was lost [before
the preparations for the Sabbath
had been completed], *one may not
depend on it* [i.e., the *eruv*] to cook
primarily [for the *Sabbath*].

וְאִם שִׁיֵּר מִמֶּנּוּ כָּל שֶׁהוּא, סוֹמֵךְ עָלָיו
לַשַּׁבָּת. — *But if he left any of it over,*

he may depend on it [to cook] *for
the Sabbath.*

The *Gemara* (16b) indicates that a
minimum of a *kezayis* [the volume
of an olive] must be left over.

[The verb שִׁיֵּר, *he left*, indicates that the
mishnah refers to his having eaten the *eruv*.
Obviously, the same would hold true if part
of the *eruv* had been lost.]

2.

Having spoken (in the preceding
mishnah) of Sabbath preparations
performed on *Yom Tov*, the mishnah now turns to *Yom Tov* preparation made on the Sabbath, i.e.,
when *Yom Tov* falls on a Sunday.
The Talmud (*Rosh Hashanah*
16b) states: חַיָּב אָדָם לְטַהֵר עַצְמוֹ
בָּרֶגֶל, *a person is obligated to
cleanse himself before a Yom Tov.*
Therefore [especially in the times of
the *Beis HaMikdash*, when offerings were brought and ritual purity
was imperative], a necessary part of
the *Yom Tov* preparations was the
removal of *tumah*-contamination[1]
from people and their utensils by

immersion in a *mikveh* [ritual pool].
Our mishnah discusses the procedure to be followed when one
wants to make this preparation on
the Sabbath (*Rav; Rashi*).

חָל לִהְיוֹת אַחַר הַשַּׁבָּת — *When it falls
after the Sabbath* [i.e., *Yom Tov*
was on a Sunday],

בֵּית שַׁמַּאי אוֹמְרִים: מַטְבִּילִין אֶת הַכֹּל
מִלִּפְנֵי הַשַּׁבָּת. — *Beis Shammai say:
We must immerse everything* [i.e.,
utensils and people] *before the Sabbath.*

[While one is commanded to
cleanse oneself of all *tumah*-con-
tamination before *Yom Tov*, there

---

1. [טֻמְאָה, *tumah*, is a halachically defined contamination inherent in certain people (e.g., a
niddah) and objects (e.g., a corpse) that under specific conditions is transferred to another
person or object.]

2

2

If one ate it or it was lost, one may not depend on it to cook primarily [for the Sabbath]. But if he left any of it over, he may depend on it [to cook] for the Sabbath.

2. When it falls after the Sabbath, Beis Shammai say: We must immerse everything before the Sabbath. But Beis Hillel say: Utensils [must be immersed] before the Sabbath, but a person [may immerse himself] on the Sabbath.

YAD AVRAHAM

exists a Rabbinical ban on immersing in a *mikveh* on the Sabbath or *Yom Tov*. In the opinion of Beis Shammi this ban includes the immersion of human beings as well as inanimate objects. The reason for this restriction is that the objects that are immersed become cleansed of their prior contamination and are thus rendered suitable for uses from which they had previously been excluded (e.g., sacrifices or *terumah* may be placed in the cleansed vessels and consumed by the cleansed person). Such immersion resembles תִּקּוּן מָנָא, *repairing a utensil*, which is a subcategory of the forbidden labor of *striking the final blow*, i.e., putting the finishing touches on an object *(Gem.* 18a).]

וּבֵית הִלֵּל אוֹמְרִים: כֵּלִים מִלִּפְנֵי הַשַּׁבָּת, וְאָדָם בַּשַּׁבָּת. — *But Beis Hillel say: Utensils [must be immersed] before the Sabbath, but a person [may immerse himself] on the Sabbath.*

Beis Hillel hold that the Rab-

binical ban against immersion applies only to contaminated utensils because immersing them resembles repairing a utensil (i.e., making it suitable for use). Immersion of a person, however, would not necessarily appear to an onlooker to be an act of repair or improvement, for the person may immerse himself merely to cool off, or enjoy a bath. There is therefore no sufficient reason to prohibit this act.

Beis Hillel's reasoning in allowing people to immerse themselves on the Sabbath should not apply to us, for in our times it is not customary to bathe on the Sabbath for any reason.[1] Therefore, some authorities *(Rabbeinu Tam* cited by *Mordechai;* see *Beis Yosef* to *Yoreh Deah* 197) forbid a woman to immerse herself on Sabbath or *Yom Tov* to cleanse herself after menstruation, for this allows her to resume marital relations and therefore is considered an improvement. This opinion is rejected vigorously by *Beis Yosef* (see also *Nekudos HaKessef* there). Yet, *Rama* (*Yoreh Deah* 197:2) relates that in some places there is a custom that women perform the immersion on the Sabbath only if immersion was impossible previously.

1. The *poskim* stress that this custom is not predicated on an assumption that bathing in cold water is prohibited. Rather, it is based on the apprehension that bathing could result in transgression of such prohibited actions as wringing out the water in one's hair, etc. (see *Magen Avraham* 326:8; *Mishnah Berurah* 326:24), and on consideration of the view expounded above.

[ג] **וְשָׁוִין** שֶׁמַּשִׁיקִין אֶת הַמַּיִם בִּכְלִי אֶבֶן
לְטַהֲרָן. אֲבָל לֹא מַטְבִּילִין.
וּמַטְבִּילִין מִגַּב לְגַב, וּמֵחֲבוּרָה לַחֲבוּרָה.

יד אברהם

3.

וְשָׁוִין שֶׁמַּשִׁיקִין אֶת הַמַּיִם — *They* [Beis Shammai and Beis Hillel] *agree that we may make the waters contiguous* [*to the waters of a mikveh*]

The mishnah refers here to a procedure by which water that has contracted *tumah*-contamination may be cleansed. By placing the contaminated water in a utensil and lowering the utensil into a *mikveh* until the water in the utensil touches the water in the *mikveh* ever so slightly, the waters in the utensil are purified. The act of making the waters contiguous serves to fuse them into a single entity of *mikveh* water, freeing them of *tumah*. This method is effective only for water; no other contaminated food or drink can be cleansed, not even by immersion in a *mikveh* (see *Pesachim* 34b; *Rav*; *Rashi*).

בִּכְלִי אֶבֶן — *in a stone utensil*
The reason that a stone utensil should be used as a container for the waters is that a stone utensil is not susceptible to the laws of *tumah*. (See below, s.v. אֲבָל לֹא מַטְבִּילִין.)

לְטַהֲרָן. — *in order to cleanse them.*
There is no Rabbinical prohibition against removing *tumah* from water, because the concept of repairing utensils [see comm. to mishnah 2, s.v. בֵּית שַׁמַּאי אוֹמְרִים] is

not applicable to foodstuffs (*Shitah Mekubetzes*; cf. *Tzlach*; *Minchas Chinuch, Kuntres Mosech HaShabbos* 11; *Eglei Tal, HaOfeh* 37:1).

אֲבָל לֹא מַטְבִּילִין — *But we should not immerse* [*the water in a wooden container*].

One should not use a utensil susceptible to *tumah* (e.g., a wooden utensil) as a container for the water that is becoming contiguous to the *mikveh*, for the utensil would itself become contaminated and require immersion [i.e., in this case the procedure would not be considered הַשָׁקָה, *making the water contiguous*, but טְבִילָה, *immersion* of a utensil]. As previously mentioned [mishnah 2], utensils may not be immersed on *Yom Tov* (*Gem.* 18b).

וּמַטְבִּילִין מִגַּב לְגַב, — *We may immerse* [*utensils*] *from one purpose to another,*
If one immersed utensils with which to press olives for non-consecrated (חֻלִּין, *chullin*) oil and changed his mind and now wants these utensils for the purpose of pressing grapes[1] which have been designated as *terumah*, the utensils may be reimmersed on *Yom Tov*. One of the מַעֲלוֹת, *extraordinary safeguards*, promulgated by the

---

1. The change from olives to grapes has no bearing on the case discussed here because such a change *per se* does not require immersion. The *Gemara* inserts this particular only because it would be unusual for one to change his mind from *chullin* to *terumah* concerning the same substances [e.g., if he had olives of both *chullin* and *terumah* status his original immersion would have been with *terumah* in mind]. Only a change from *chullin* to *terumah* requires re-immersion, and it is regarding this that the mishnah rules here (*Tos. Yom Tov*).

3. They agree that we may make the waters contiguous [to the waters of a *mikveh*] in a stone utensil in order to cleanse them. But we should not immerse [the water in a wooden container].

We may immerse [utensils] from one purpose to another, and from one group to another.

YAD AVRAHAM

Sages pertaining to *terumah* and various levels of sanctity (see *Chagigah* 2:5, ArtScroll ed.) was that utensils to be used for specific levels of sanctity must be immersed with such purpose in mind (ibid. 2:6). If a utensil has been immersed for usage with non-sacred objects, and the person now wants to use this utensil for one of the varying levels of sanctity, it must be reimmersed. Since the purpose of the immersion is merely to comply with a מַעֲלָה דְּרַבָּנָן, *extraordinary safeguard instituted by the Sages*, such immersion is not considered an improvement which is prohibited on *Yom Tov*. In *Rambam's (Comm.)* words, we allow this immersion on *Yom Tov* because its purpose is not to remove *tumah*, but to add טהרה, *purity* (*Rav*; according to *Rambam's* version of *Gemara* 19a; cf. *Rashi* there).

וּמֵחֲבוּרָה לַחֲבוּרָה. — *and from one group to another.*

Another of the extraordinary Rabbinical safeguards is that if the utensils had been intended for a group eating *terumah* and are now to be used by a group eating sacrifices, a new immersion is required. Since such immersion is in compliance merely with a Rabbinical safeguard it may be performed on *Yom Tov* (*Rambam*; *R' Chananel* cited by *Maggid Mishneh, Hil. Yom Tov* 4:17).

Rav and *Rashi* understand this segment of the mishnah to refer to a case in which both groups were formed with the purpose of eating sacrifices (e.g., the *Pesach* lamb) but the members of the second group are more fastidious in their observance of the laws than the first, and require anyone joining them to immerse their utensils.

4.

◄§ Personal Temple Sacrifices on Yom Tov

שָׁלֹשׁ רְגָלִים תָּחֹג לִי בַּשָּׁנָה ... וְלֹא יֵרָאוּ פָנַי רֵיקָם ... שָׁלֹשׁ פְּעָמִים בַּשָּׁנָה יֵרָאֶה כָּל זְכוּרְךָ אֶל פְּנֵי הָאָדֹן ה'.

Three pilgrimages shall you celebrate to Me each year ... they shall not appear before Me empty-handed ... three times during the year all your males shall appear before the Lord, HASHEM (Exodus 23:14-17).

Pesach, Shavuos, and Succos are the שָׁלֹשׁ רְגָלִים, *three pilgrimage festivals*. Every Jewish male is commanded to appear at the בֵּית הַמִּקְדָּשׁ, *Holy Temple*, during these festivals. However, he must not appear with empty hands, but should bring an עוֹלָה, *burnt offering*, as a קָרְבָּן, *sacrifice*. This pilgrimage to the *Beis HaMikdash* is called רְאִיָּה, *appearance*, and the accompanying sacrifice is known as עוֹלַת רְאִיָּה, *the burnt offering of appearance*.

[ד] **בֵּית** שַׁמַּאי אוֹמְרִים: מְבִיאִין שְׁלָמִים וְאֵין סוֹמְכִין עֲלֵיהֶן, אֲבָל לֹא עוֹלוֹת. וּבֵית הִלֵּל אוֹמְרִים: מְבִיאִין שְׁלָמִים וְעוֹלוֹת, וְסוֹמְכִין עֲלֵיהֶם.

יד אברהם

Concomitant with the command of appearance is the command תָחֹג, *you shall celebrate* (Exodus 23:14). The Talmud (*Chagigah* 10b) cites various verses which indicate that celebration requires the bringing of שְׁלָמִים, *peace offerings*. Hence, along with his burnt offering each male must bring שַׁלְמֵי חֲגִיגָה, *peace offerings of celebration*, or *festival*. The name of this sacrifice is often shortened to just *chagigah*, and it is from here that tractate *Chagigah* gets its name.

There is yet another sacrifice to be offered alongside these two. The Jew is enjoined to be joyful before his God when he appears before Him during the festivals (*Deuteronomy* 16:14). But how is this joyfulness to be manifested? By slaughtering peace offerings and partaking of their meat (ibid. 27:7). These peace offerings are called שַׁלְמֵי שִׂמְחָה, *peace offerings of joy*, based on the verse (*Deut.* 16:14) *And you shall be joyful on your festivals*.

These latter offerings differ from the aforementioned two in that there is no obligation to offer them *per se*. Rather, one is obligated to eat the meat of peace offerings on *Yom Tov* (Rambam, Hil. Chagigah 2:10). If the *chagigah* does not supply enough meat, then these additional peace offerings should be brought.

Morever, this sacrifice differs from the aforementioned in that one need not offer a sacrifice designated for this specific purpose. It is sufficient to offer any sacrifice (e.g., מַעֲשֵׂר בְּהֵמָה, *the animal tithe*) for the purpose of joy (see *Turei Even*, *Chagigah* 7b).

Part of the preliminary procedure of every private sacrifice (קָרְבַּן יָחִיד) is the donor's leaning both his hands upon the head of the sacrificial animal בְּכָל כֹּחוֹ, *with all his might* (see *Chagigah* 2:2). This act is called סְמִיכָה, *leaning*, based on the verse: *And he shall lean his hands on the head of his sacrifice* (Leviticus 3:2). On *Yom Tov*, however, there is a Rabbinical injunction against using animals. Thus, leaning one's weight upon the head of an animal is prohibited for, since he leans 'with all his might,' in effect he is being supported by the animal and is thereby using it.

This mishnah deals with the following two questions: What types of sacrifices are permitted to be offered on *Yom Tov*? May leaning be performed on *Yom Tov*?

בֵּית שַׁמַּאי אוֹמְרִים: מְבִיאִין שְׁלָמִים — *Beis Shammai say: We may bring peace offerings* [on Yom Tov]

Though offering a sacrifice involves *melachah* (e.g., *slaughtering*), the peace offerings [see prefatory note] may be offered on *Yom Tov* because they are used for human consumption (*Rav; Rashi*),

in addition to their function as sacrifices.

וְאֵין סוֹמְכִין עֲלֵיהֶן. — *yet we may not lean on them,*

The usual preliminary procedure of leaning one's body upon the head of the sacrifice may not be performed because the Rabbinical prohibition against using animals is not waived in favor of the *mitzvah* of leaning. Beis Shammai hold that this *mitzvah* need not be performed immediately prior to slaughtering and can therefore be performed on

4. **B**eis Shammai say: We may bring peace offerings [on *Yom Tov*] yet we may not lean on them, but [we may] not bring burnt offerings. But Beis Hillel say: We may bring [both] peace and burnt offerings, and we may lean on them.

YAD AVRAHAM

the day before *Yom Tov* (*Rav* from *Gem.* 19a).

אֲבָל לֹא עוֹלוֹת. — *but [we may] not bring burnt offerings.*

The difference between peace offerings and burnt offerings is pointed out by *Rav* and *Rashi*. Peace offerings may be offered because portions of their meat are eaten either by the *Kohen* or by the owner and his household. Burnt offerings, on the other hand, are burned completely and leave nothing for human consumption. Thus the labor involved in their offering does not receive the dispensation granted for the preparation of food.

However, the public burnt offerings (עוֹלוֹת צִבּוּר; i.e., the daily burnt offering and the burnt offerings of the *Mussaf*) may be offered even on the Sabbath, for their sacrifice is fixed to a specific day and cannot be postponed. The mishnah refers only to private sacrifices such as the burnt offering of appearance which can be brought on any day during the festival (*Rav*).

וּבֵית הַלֵּל אוֹמְרִים: מְבִיאִין שְׁלָמִים וְעוֹלוֹת, — *But Beis Hillel say: We may bring [both] peace and burnt offerings,*

Using a hermeneutical interpretation of a Scriptural verse (כָּל — 'לַה; דְּלָה'; *Leviticus* 23:41) Beis Hillel derive that even burnt offerings are permitted, as long as they are relevant to *Yom Tov*. Therefore, even though burnt offerings of appearance can be brought at any time during the seven day festival period, one may choose to bring them on *Yom Tov*.

However, Beis Hillel admit that נְדָרִים וּנְדָבוֹת, *sacrifices vowed or donated*, and in no way connected to *Yom Tov*[1] may not be offered on the festival (*Rav; Gem.* 19a).

Private peace offerings may not be offered on the festival, despite the fact that almost all their edible meat is eaten. The offering of a sacrifice is considered to be an act performed solely for the purpose of fulfilling a commandment rather than for food purposes (*Tos. Yom Tov* citing *Tosafos* 27b).

[Because of this principle Beis Hillel are forced to derive the dispensation allowing the festival peace and burnt offerings from the hermeneutical interpretation mentioned above. They could have based their opinion on the principle of *mitoch* outlined previously (1:5) which would suffice to permit the offering of even burnt offerings. But because Temple sacrifices are considered only for their *mitzvah*, and not as food, the principle of *mitoch* does not apply to sacrifices. To qualify for the dispensation of *mitoch* there must at least be fulfillment of צוֹרֶךְ קְצָת, *minimal need* for *Yom Tov* (see *Tos.* 19a with *Maharsha* and *Pnei Yehoshua*).]

וְסוֹמְכִין עֲלֵיהֶם. — *and we may lean on them.*

Beis Hillel hold that leaning must

1. נְדָרִים וּנְדָבוֹת, *sacrifices vowed or donated*, are not permitted under the dispensation for festival peace offerings despite the fact that one can fulfill the *mitzvah* of joy with them, or with any sacrifice consumed by humans on *Yom Tov*. *Tosafos* (*Chagigah* 7b cited in *Tos. R' Akiva*) offers two solutions for this paradox: The prohibition against offering *vows and donations* applies only after one has already fulfilled the *mitzvah* of joy. Or, one can fulfill the *mitzvah* of joy only when one performs the sacrifice for the purpose of joy. When this inten-

[ה] **בֵּית** שַׁמַּאי אוֹמְרִים: לֹא יָחֵם אָדָם חַמִּין
לְרַגְלָיו אֶלָּא אִם כֵּן רְאוּיִין לִשְׁתִיָּה.
וּבֵית הִלֵּל מַתִּירִין.
עוֹשֶׂה אָדָם מְדוּרָה וּמִתְחַמֵּם כְּנֶגְדָּהּ.

יד אברהם

immediately precede slaughter
(תֵּיכֶף לִסְמִיכָה שְׁחִיטָה). Thus a sacrifice offered on *Yom Tov* must have
leaning performed on the same day.

Therefore, the Rabbinical prohibition against *using animals* is waived
in favor of the *mitzvah* of leaning
(*Tos. Yom Tov; Gem.* 20a).

5.

בֵּית שַׁמַּאי אוֹמְרִים: לֹא יָחֵם אָדָם
חַמִּין לְרַגְלָיו — *Beis Shammai say: A
person may not warm up hot water
for his feet* [i.e., to wash his feet]

Beis Shammai hold that the
Torah permitted work to be done on
Yom Tov only for the purpose of
food preparation, not for washing
(*Rav; Rashi*). [See comm. to 1:5,
s.v. מִתּוֹךְ.]

אֶלָּא אִם כֵּן רְאוּיִין לִשְׁתִיָּה. — *unless it
is fit for drinking.*

Beis Shammai permit cooking
water for washing only if the water
is fit for drinking and is put on the
fire with the intention of using at
least some of it for drinking. The
rest of the water may then be used
for washing (*Tos.* 21b citing *Yerushalmi*). [The labor of *cooking,
which consists of the simple act of
placing the pot on the fire, is needed
for food purposes — using the additional water in the pot for wash-

ing does not necessitate any additional labor. See *Gem.* 21a and
comm. to mishnah 1, s.v. אֲבָל מְבַשֵּׁל
הוּא.]

וּבֵית הִלֵּל מַתִּירִין. — *But Beis Hillel
permit it.*

Beis Hillel allow the cooking of
the water even if one has no intention of drinking it. This is consistent with Beis Hillel's opinion (1:5)
which accepts the principle of
mitoch, i.e., any labor that may be
performed for the sake of preparing
food, may also be performed where
no food preparation is involved,
provided it serves the needs of the
festival (*Rav; Ran*).

Rambam contends that Beis Hillel's ruling
here is not dependent on their view regarding
mitoch. They permit *cooking water for
bathing purposes because needs of the body
(צָרְכֵי הַגּוּף) are the equivalent of eating and
drinking and included in the dispensation
granted for the latter. *Rambam* finds allusion
to this in the phrase לְכָל נֶפֶשׁ, *by any person*

tion is absent one cannot discharge one's obligation with this sacrifice. It is only in such instances that the offering of *vows and donations* is prohibited. [Another solution suggests
itself. The major purpose of a sacrifice not specifically designated as a peace offering of joy
(e.g., the animal tithe), even if it is offered with the stated intention of using the meat for the
commandment of joy, is the purpose it was designated for (e.g., the *mitzvah* of the animal
tithe). Therefore, the secondary purpose of using the meat for joy must be discounted as a
basis for dispensation on *Yom Tov* (similar to the principle expounded by *Tosafos* cited
above).Thus, the offering of *vows and donations* would be prohibited under all conditions, as
the statement in the *Gemara* seems to suggest.]

5. **B**eis Shammai say: A person may not warm up hot water for his feet unless it is fit for drinking. But Beis Hillel permit it.

A person may make a bonfire and warm himself before it.

YAD AVRAHAM

(Exodus 12:16), in the passage of Torah stating this dispensation; the phrase לְכָל נֶפֶשׁ usually translated *by any person*, may also be interpreted by *the entire person*, i.e., any bodily need is included in the dispensation, and the explicit mention of eating in this passage [*that which is eaten by any person, that alone may be performed for you*] is meant only as an example (Comm. here and Hil. Yom Tov 1:16; see also Ramban, Shabbos 39b; Rashba in Avodas HaKodesh, Beis Moed 1:1 and 3:5; cf. Chiddushei HaRashba here; Sha'ar HaTziyun 511:2; see Sefer HaKovetz, and Sha'ar HaMelech, Hil. Yom Tov 1:4).

The mishnah specifies that the issue between Beis Shammai and Beis Hillel is the act of heating water to wash the feet (hands and/or face; see Orach Chaim 511:2 with Beur Halachah and Meiri here; cf. Lechem Shamayim here cited in Likutim in the margin of Mishnayos, ed. Vilna). Beis Hillel agree that water may not be heated to wash the entire body on Yom Tov (Tos. 21b; Rif). This is clearly evident in tractate Shabbos (40a; see Tos. there 39b). There is however disagreement about the severity of this prohibition. (A) Tosafos (ibid.) states that it is Scripturally prohibited to heat water on Yom Tov for washing the entire body. Tosafos finds a basis for this in the principle expounded in tractate Kesubos (7a) that no labor may be performed on Yom Tov for the sake of a need which is not common to most people (אֵינָהּ שָׁוָה לְכָל נֶפֶשׁ; see Pri Megadim, Eshel Avraham 511:4; i.e., a need shared only by epicures and the overly fastidious is not included). The need to bathe the entire body in hot water was not common at that time. (B) Rif and Rambam (Hil. Yom Tov 1:16) hold that warming water to wash on

Yom Tov is a Rabbinical injunction. Therefore, they deduce that if the water is heated before Yom Tov one may wash the entire body in such water (as opposed to the laws of Sabbath which proscribe bathing the entire body in hot water; see Orach Chaim 326:1). Shulchan Aruch rules in accordance with Rambam and Rif, whereas Rama accepts Tosafos' opinion (Orach Chaim 511:2).

עוֹשֶׂה אָדָם מְדוּרָה וּמִתְחַמֵּם כְּנֶגְדָהּ. — A person may make a bonfire and warm himself before it.

Beis Hillel also permit making a fire on Yom Tov to warm oneself. According to Beis Shammai this act is prohibited (Tos. Yom Tov; Gem. 21b).

[One might think that making a fire to warm oneself could be considered an enjoyment which is not common to all people and should therefore be prohibited on Yom Tov (see above, s.v. וּבֵית הִלֵּל מַתִּירִין). It stands to reason that in moderate weather (such weather is usually prevalent on Succos and Pesach) heating is not commonly needed (especially in Eretz Yisrael). Therefore the mishnah has to state that *a person may*, under all and any conditions, *make a bonfire and warm himself*. This act does not fall into the category of a need not common to all. Since heat is considered a common need under the specific circumstance of severe cold, it remains in this category regardless of the particular situation (see Beur HaGra, Orach Chaim 511:4). A similar explanation is found in the commentaries to Kesubos 7a (see Shitah Mekubetzes there) regarding the slaughter of deer on Yom Tov (see also Beur HaGra, Orach Chaim 511:4).

6.

This mishnah marks a departure from the pattern of the previous mishnayos, which are, in effect, an enumeration of the various in-

stances in which Beis Shammai and Beis Hillel disagreed concerning the laws of Yom Tov. Having completed this listing, R' Yehudah

[ו] **שְׁלֹשָׁה** דְבָרִים רַבָּן גַּמְלִיאֵל מַחְמִיר
כְּדִבְרֵי בֵית שַׁמַּאי: אֵין טוֹמְנִין
אֶת הַחַמִּין מִיּוֹם טוֹב לַשַּׁבָּת; וְאֵין זוֹקְפִין אֶת
הַמְּנוֹרָה בְּיוֹם טוֹב; וְאֵין אוֹפִין פִּתִּין גְּרִיצִין, אֶלָּא
רְקִיקִין.

יד אברהם

HaNasi, compiler and editor of the Mishnah, cites three instances in which his grandfather, Rabban Gamliel, ruled according to Beis Shammai.

[Perhaps, this mishnah has been juxtaposed with the preceding ones because it speaks of three instances in which the very existence of a disagreement between Beis Shammai and Beis Hillel is itself the subject of a dispute. Rabban Gamliel, a direct descendant of Hillel, sought to prove from the customs of his father's household that Beis Hillel never disagreed with Beis Shammai in these three cases (see commentary below, s.v. אָמַר רַבָּן גַּמְלִיאֵל). The Sages refuted this proof, maintaining that a disagreement between Beis Hillel and Beis Shammai did indeed exist in these matters. Thus the logic of the sequence of the mishnayos becomes apparent. First the instances in which there is a clear tradition of disagreement between Beis Shammai and Beis Hillel are set forth. This is followed by a description of those areas where the assertion that there was disagreement is challenged.]

שְׁלֹשָׁה דְבָרִים רַבָּן גַּמְלִיאֵל מַחְמִיר כְּדִבְרֵי בֵית שַׁמַּאי: — *In three matters* [pertaining to Yom Tov (Tos. R' Akiva; Ran)] *Rabban Gamliel ruled stringently in accordance with the opinion of Beis Shammai:*

Although Rabban Gamliel was a descendant of Hillel [he was the son of Rabban Shimon, son of Rabban Gamliel the elder (רַבָּן גַּמְלִיאֵל הַזָּקֵן), son of Shimon, son of Hillel (see *Shabbos* 15a with *Rashi*], he nevertheless accepted the opinion of Beis Shammai in these three matters (*Tos. Yom Tov*).

אֵין טוֹמְנִין אֶת הַחַמִּין — *We may not*

insulate the hot water

Since one may not boil water on the Sabbath, it becomes necessary to find a way to retain the heat of the water which was boiled on Friday throughout the Sabbath. This may be accomplished by removing the pot from the fire prior to the Sabbath and wrapping it snugly in insulating materials (e.g., wool). This procedure is called הַטְמָנָה, *insulating* [lit. *hiding*].

מִיּוֹם טוֹב לַשַּׁבָּת; — *on* [lit. *from*] *Yom Tov for* [lit. *to*] *the Sabbath;*

[I.e., on Yom Tov one may not insulate a pot of hot water for use on the Sabbath. Since insulating is Rabbinically prohibited on the Sabbath (see *Shabbos* 2:7) it should be prohibited on Yom Tov in situations to which the dispensation allowing for food preparation on Yom Tov cannot be applied. The cardinal rule concerning what is, or is not, permitted on Yom Tov is set forth in tractate *Megillah* (1:6): There is no difference between [the laws applying to] Yom Tov and [those applying to] the Sabbath except [in laws pertaining to] food.

Consequently one may insulate a pot for use on Yom Tov but not if the contents of the pot are intended for use on the weekday. Concerning insulating on Yom Tov for the Sabbath this would depend on whether an eruv tavshilin has been made. Surely if one neglected to make an eruv, he may not insulate for the

6. **I**n three matters Rabban Gamliel ruled stringently in accordance with the opinion of Beis Shammai: We may not insulate the hot water on *Yom Tov* for the Sabbath; we may not put together a candlestick on *Yom Tov*; and we may not bake thick loaves [of bread on *Yom Tov*], only thin wafers.

YAD AVRAHAM

Sabbath even if no other labor (e.g., *cooking)* is involved. The question of whether the *eruv tavshilin* applies to insulating is the subject of the disagreement between Beis Shammai and Beis Hillel in this mishnah.]

Beis Shammai hold that every type of food preparation must be separately represented in the *eruv tavshilin*. The cooked food in the *eruv* serves to permit *cooking* on *Yom Tov* for the Sabbath; baked goods are required to permit *baking*. By the same token insulating the pot for Sabbath is made permissible only by including a pot under wraps in the *eruv*. Beis Shammai's ruling against insulating refers to an instance where no insulating was included in the *eruv (Rav;* Abaye in *Gem.* 22a).

Beis Hillel hold that the *eruv* is all inclusive and insulating is permitted even if it is not specifically represented in the *eruv* (ibid.).

As mentioned previously (commentary to mishnah 1, s.v. שֶׁהֵן שְׁנֵי תַבְשִׁילִין), some authorities hold that Beis Hillel disagree with Beis Shammai only on the matter of insulating but agree that in order to permit *baking* for Sabbath, baked goods must be included in the *eruv*. This opinion is not shared by most authorities. Therefore, although one should preferably include a

baked item in the *eruv,* if one neglected to do so, one may still bake for the Sabbath.

וְאֵין זוֹקְפִין אֶת הַמְּנוֹרָה בְּיוֹם טוֹב; — *(And) we may not put together* [lit. *stand up*] *a candlestick on Yom Tov;*

The mishnah speaks of a candlestick composed of parts which have become separated from each other. Such a candlestick may not be reassembled on *Yom Tov.* Beis Shammai hold that assembling the parts of a utensil and putting them together is a subcategory of the prohibited labor of בּוֹנֶה, *building.* But Beis Hillel hold that the labor of *building* does not extend to assembling utensils *(Rav, Gem.* 22a).[1]

It must be added that assembling a candlestick is permitted only if this act does not require a forceful insertion of the parts being assembled *(Orach Chaim* 519:2). If the parts are screwed into each other, they may not be assembled on *Yom Tov (Sha'ar HaTziun* 519:2).

וְאֵין אוֹפִין פִּתִּין גְּרִיצִין, אֶלָּא רְקִיקִין. — *and we may not bake thick* [i.e., big] *loaves* [of bread on *Yom Tov*], only *thin wafers.*

The main concern here is not the thickness or thinness of the loaf, but rather the amount of dough involved. Beis Shammai proscribe

---

1. *Tosafos (22a; Shabbos* 46a) notes that the *Talmud (Shabbos* 46a) cites a *Baraisa* which prohibits assembling a candlestick, which is apparently at variance with Beis Hillel's ruling in this mishnah.

One of the resolutions of this contradiction offered by *Tosafos* is to differentiate between the Sabbath and the *Yom Tov.* Beis Hillel's lenient ruling in our mishnah pertains to *Yom Tov;* on the Sabbath even Beis Hillel concur that assembling a utensil is prohibited. *Rambam* (see *Hil. Shabbos* 26:11 and *Hil. Yom Tov* 4:13; *Magen Avraham* 519:4) and *Shulchan Aruch*

אָמַר רַבָּן גַּמְלִיאֵל: „מִימֵיהֶן שֶׁל בֵּית אַבָּא לֹא
הָיוּ אוֹפִין פִּתִּין גְּרִיצִין, אֶלָּא רְקִיקִין."
אָמְרוּ לוֹ: „מַה נַּעֲשֶׂה לְבֵית אָבִיךְ? שֶׁהָיוּ
מַחְמִירִין עַל עַצְמָן וּמְקִלִּין לְכָל יִשְׂרָאֵל לִהְיוֹת
אוֹפִין פִּתִּין גְּרִיצִין, וָחֲרִי."

יד אברהם

*baking large quantities of bread on Yom Tov while Beis Hillel permit this (Rambam, comm., according to Meleches Shlomo's interpretation; cf. Hil. Yom Tov 3:8 with Maggid Mishneh).

Beis Shammai's concern is not with the melachah involved per se, but with the unnecessary toil that is involved in baking such loaves (suggested by the language of the Gem. 22b; משום דקטרח טירחא דלא צריך).[1]

Tosafos (22b) understands that Beis Shammai's insistence on thin loaves (according to Tosafos this means small loaves) is due to the fear that if big loaves were per-

(Orach Chaim 279:7 and 519:2) seem to follow this opinion.

There is a difference of opinion as to the nature of this special dispensation granted on Yom Tov as opposed to the Sabbath. Vilna Gaon (519:5) cited by Mishnah Berurah assumes that the reason for allowing the assembling of a candlestick on Yom Tov is the need to enhance the enjoyment of Yom Tov (שמחת יום טוב). It should follow (although Mishnah Berurah does not clarify this) that where the absence of the candlestick does not affect the enjoyment of Yom Tov (e.g., it is not needed for light), its assembling should be prohibited (see similar restrictions in Orach Chaim 519:1 in the laws concerning removal and reinstallment of shutters).

Magen Avraham (ibid.) seems to assume that there is no ban on assembling a candlestick on Yom Tov at all (ביום טוב לא גזרו). However, it is not clear according to this how assembling a candlestick differs from reinstalling shutters onto booths (תריסי חנויות) which is permitted only if it enhances the enjoyment of Yom Tov (see above 1:5; Orach Chaim 519:1).

Meiri (Chiddushim and Beis HaBechirah) comments that booths, though essentially utensils, nevertheless resemble houses, and, therefore, are Rabbinically proscribed on Yom Tov to avoid confusion with the labor of *building. Assembling a candlestick, on the other hand, will not lead one to mistakenly perform the labor of *building even where enjoyment of Yom Tov is not involved.

1. The disagreement between Beis Shammai and Beis Hillel can (according to Rambam) be understood in two ways:

(a) Beis Shammai allows only a minimum of bread to be baked on the festival itself. Although the dispensation allowing work involved in food preparation generally does not oblige one to prepare only a bare minimum, the labor of *baking is singled out for greater stringency due to the great amount of physical work it requires.

(b) Even Beis Shammai agree that it is unnecessary to restrict oneself to a bare minimum when baking on the festival. As much leeway is allowed in *baking as is permitted in other melachos; as long as there is reason to believe that the dough to be baked will be used on the festival it may be baked on Yom Tov. What Beis Shammai object to is *baking bread on Yom Tov when that bread will surely not be used on Yom Tov. They might agree with Beis Hillel's logic (see below) divorcing such baking from the category of proscribed labors of Yom Tov. However, they prohibit this act because it is unnecessary toil on Yom Tov.

Beis Hillel hold that unnecessary toil is insufficient grounds to ban such *baking. In fact, Beis Hillel permit baking more bread on Yom Tov than is needed for the festival (see Rav; Rashi 22b). The additional work of *kneading which this dispensation implies is permitted 'because bread bakes better when the oven is full.' Thus, the extra loaves have a direct bearing on the quality of the bread being baked for Yom Tov itself, which are in the oven together with the superfluous loaves. Such baking is, therefore, still within the realm of baking for Yom Tov (see Gem. 17a). See Orach Chaim (507:6) where it is stated that this dispensation does not apply to our present-day mode of baking.

Said Rabban Gamliel: "In all the days of my father's household they would never bake thick loaves [of bread on *Yom Tov*], only thin wafers."

They said to him: "What shall we do with your father's household? They were stringent upon themselves, but allowed all of Israel to bake thick loaves [of bread], and coal baked bread."

YAD AVRAHAM

mitted one might make much larger loaves than are necessary for *Yom Tov* (see *Rosh* and *Rosh Yosef*). Beis Hillel, while concerned with the validity of this apprehension, hold that if only small loaves were baked people would bake only the bare minimum necessary for the holiday, resulting in the diminution of the enjoyment of *Yom Tov*. This commentary is reflected in the language of *Shulchan Aruch* (596:5). As usual, the halachah is in accordance with Beis Hillel.

אָמַר רַבָּן גַּמְלִיאֵל: ,,מִימֵיהֶן שֶׁל בֵּית אַבָּא לֹא הָיוּ אוֹפִין פִּתִּין גְּרִיצִין, אֶלָּא רְקִיקִין.״ — *Said Rabban Gamliel: "In all the days of my father's household they would never bake loaves [of bread on Yom Tov], only thin wafers."*

[Rabban Gamliel cites the custom of his father's household to demonstrate either that Beis Shammai's opinion should be accepted, or that Beis Hillel never really disagreed with Beis Shammai in this instance. As already mentioned, Rabban Gamliel was a direct descendant of Hillel.]

אָמְרוּ לוֹ: ,,מַה נַּעֲשֶׂה לְבֵית אָבִיךָ? *They* [the Sages who disagreed with Rabban Gamliel] *said to him: "What shall we do with your father's household?*

[The Sages reacted to Rabban Gamliel's citation of his father's

household with an exclamation of exasperation: 'What shall we do with your father's household? They exasperate us with their conduct which contradicts their own rulings, causing misconceptions of their opinions to arise.']

שֶׁהָיוּ מַחְמִירִין עַל עַצְמָן וּמְקִלִּין לְכָל — יִשְׂרָאֵל לִהְיוֹת אוֹפִין פִּתִּין גְּרִיצִין, *They were stringent upon themselves* [i.e., they conducted themselves with stringency concerning the baking of thick loaves], *but allowed* [lit. *were lenient to*] *all of Israel to* [lit. *that they should*] *bake thick loaves* [of bread],

The caution they exercised in not baking thick loaves of bread was a result of the stringent manner in which they conducted themselves personally. However, as far as the halachah is concerned, they too ruled like Beis Hillel.[1]

,,וָחֲרֵי.״ — *and coal baked bread."* I.e., large loaves baked on coals. This baking process requires much effort because the coals keep cooling off *(Rav; Rashi; Aruch s.v.* חר).

[*Ramban* (Genesis 41:15) seems to have חִיוָרֵי, *white*, here instead of חרי. Thus the word means *white bread*. However, he leaves unexplained what significance the whiteness of the bread has concerning *Yom Tov*.]

1. [It is evident from the Sages' reply that they knew with certainty that Rabban Gamliel's ancestors had adopted the more lenient ruling for others. How is it possible that Rabban Gamliel was unfamiliar with his father's rulings?

From the little we know of Rabban Gamliel's life we may deduce that he was very young when his father Rabban Shimon was killed (about the time of the Temple's destruction).

אַף הוּא אָמַר שְׁלֹשָׁה דְבָרִים לְהָקֵל: [ז]
מְכַבְּדִין בֵּין הַמִּטּוֹת; וּמַנִּיחִין
אֶת הַמֻּגְמָר בְּיוֹם טוֹב; וְעוֹשִׂין גְּדִי מְקֻלָּס בְּלֵילֵי
פְסָחִים. וַחֲכָמִים אוֹסְרִין.

יד אברהם

7.

Having mentioned three matters regarding which Rabban Gamliel's ruling had been more stringent than those of his colleagues, the mishnah goes on to list three matters where the reverse is true: Rabban Gamliel's ruling was more lenient than those of his colleagues (in matters pertaining to *Yom Tov*).

אַף הוּא אָמַר שְׁלֹשָׁה דְבָרִים לְהָקֵל: — *He also ruled leniently on three matters:*

[Rabban Gamliel ruled leniently regarding three matters which his colleagues had prohibited.]

מְכַבְּדִין בֵּין הַמִּטּוֹת; — *We may sweep between the couches;*

In those days people ate while reclining on couches or beds. Rabban Gamliel permitted them to sweep between the beds after the meal to clear away scraps of food which may have fallen there. The Talmud (*Shabbos* 95a) states that one may not sweep the floor on the Sabbath דִּילְמָא אָתֵי לְשַׁוּוּיֵי גוּמוֹת, *lest*

he try to even out some depressions, in the floor which, in the case of a house with an earthen floor, would be classified under the labor of *building*. Nevertheless, Rabban Gamliel permits sweeping between the beds because the area in question is usually small, thus minimizing the danger of desecrating the Sabbath or *Yom Tov* (Rav).

וּמַנִּיחִין אֶת הַמֻּגְמָר בְּיוֹם טוֹב; — *we may put incense [on coals] on Yom Tov;*

Incense was burnt to fill a room with a fragrant aroma. Although placing the incense involves *kindling*, Rabban Gamliel permitted it under the dispensation of food preparation (coupled with the principle of *mitoch*; see above 1:5).

וְעוֹשִׂין גְּדִי מְקֻלָּס בְּלֵילֵי פְסָחִים. — *and we may roast a kid in its entirety [lit. a helmeted kid] on Pesach eves.*

Although the kid was not a sacrifice, it was prepared in the special manner mandated for the

Although the office of נָשִׂיא, *prince of the nation*, had been hereditary since the incumbency of Hillel the Elder, Rabban Gamliel had not succeeded his father immediately and Rabban Yochanan ben Zakkai had filled the post. Only after Rabban Yochanan's death did Rabban Gamliel assume the princeship. *R' Menachem Azaryah of Fano (Ma'amar Chikur Din 2:12)* suggests that Rabban Gamliel had been too young at the time of his father's martyrdom to assume this post. It is therefore possible that although Rabban Gamliel was familiar with the customs of his father's household, he was not conversant with the actual rulings of his father.

However, *Seder HaDoros* (s.v. רבן גמליאל citing *Yad Yehudah*) proves that Rabban Gamliel had been at least in his twenties when his father was killed (see *Doros HaRishonom* ed. Israel, v. 3, p. 55ff). Nevertheless, when one considers that the years which Rabban Gamliel shared with his father were the tumultuous, strife-ridden years which preceded the destruction of the Temple, it is not at all unusual that he was not wholly familiar with his father's opinion concerning a matter relevant only three times a year.]

7. He also ruled leniently on three matters: We may sweep between the couches; we may put incense [on coals] on *Yom Tov;* and we may roast a kid in its entirety on Pesach eves. But the Sages prohibit [these].

Pesach offering, i.e., it was roasted with its entrails wound about the spit above the head, resembling a helmet, in conformance with the Torah's command that the *Pesach* be roasted, *its head with its knees and with its entrails ... (Exodus* 12:9; *Rav; Rashi;* see *Pesachim* 7:1 and 74a). [*Rambam* translates מְקֻלָּס, *ornate* or *decorated.* The meaning is the same — a kid roasted in the manner of the *Pesach* sacrifice.]

וַחֲכָמִים אוֹסְרִין. — *But the Sages prohibit* [*these* three matters permitted by Rabban Gamliel for the reasons outlined above].

[In the case of sweeping between the beds the Sages disagreed with Rabban Gamliel and refused to accept a distinction based on the size of the area to be swept.][1]

The Sages disagreed regarding incense since the dispensation for food preparation is limited to enjoy-

ments commonly enjoyed by the average person. Burning incense, however, is considered the indulgence of hypersensitive epicures (see *Kesubos* 7a; *comm.* to mishnah 5, s.v. וּבֵית הִלֵּל מַתִּירִין).

The *Gemara* (23a) notes that everyone agrees that one may not place a garment over a censer to impregnate the garment with a pleasant fragrance. This act is banned because it creates an aroma (אוֹלוּדֵי רֵיחָא) about the garment. Introducing a new quality into the garment on *Yom Tov* is Rabbinically prohibited. Therefore, one may not spray perfume onto a garment (or wig) on *Yom Tov* or Sabbath (see *Orach Chaim* 511:4 with *Ba'er Hetev*).

The Sages also prohibited the roasting of a kid in its entirety on Pesach eve because it would appear as though he had designated a kid for the *Pesach* sacrifice and was eating it without benefit of sacrifice in the Temple *(Rav, Gem.* 23a; cf. *Tzlach* to *Pesachim* 53a).

This prohibition applies equally to a kid and a lamb since both are equally valid for

1. *Shulchan Aruch (Orach Chaim* 337:2) cites three different opinions on this matter:

(a) *Behag* (and others; see *Beis Yosef* there) holds that the halachah is neither in accordance with Rabban Gamliel nor with the Sages who disagree with him: since the prohibition of sweeping is based on the fear that one may inadvertently even out depressions, it is therefore valid only according to R' Yehudah who considers a labor performed unintentionally (דָּבָר שֶׁאֵינוֹ מִתְכַּוֵּן) a violation of the Sabbath or *Yom Tov*. According to R' Shimon, whose opinion is the accepted one (see *Orach Chaim* 337:1), all unintentional work is permissible and therefore it follows that one may sweep even a large area on Sabbath or *Yom Tov*.

(b) *Rambam* maintains (accepted by R' *Yosef Karo*) that sweeping is prohibited even according to R' Shimon. For we fear that during the process of sweeping a person may forget himself and revert to his usual behavior and even out depressions intentionally. In this opinion however, this prohibition does not apply to a wooden or stone floor since the fear of evening out depressions is inapplicable in such cases.

(c) *Ri* and others state (see *Tur* and *Beis Yosef* there) that the Sages did not differentiate between types of floors but banned all sweeping. This is the opinion accepted by *Rama.* However, sweeping is only prohibited where a stiff broom is used; using a rag or feather broom is permitted, as they are usually incapable of removing enough dirt to smooth out a depression. [See *Beur Halachah* (ibid.) for a discussion on the use of a conventional 'soft' broom.]

שְׁלֹשָׁה [ח] דְּבָרִים רַבִּי אֶלְעָזָר בֶּן עֲזַרְיָה
מַתִּיר, וַחֲכָמִים אוֹסְרִין: פָּרָתוֹ
יוֹצְאָה בִּרְצוּעָה שֶׁבֵּין קַרְנֶיהָ; וּמְקָרְדִּין אֶת
הַבְּהֵמָה בְּיוֹם טוֹב; וְשׁוֹחֲקִין אֶת הַפִּלְפְּלִין בָּרֵחַיִם
שֶׁלָּהֶם.

רַבִּי יְהוּדָה אוֹמֵר: אֵין מְקָרְדִּין אֶת הַבְּהֵמָה
בְּיוֹם טוֹב מִפְּנֵי שֶׁעוֹשֶׂה חַבּוּרָה, אֲבָל מְקָרְצְפִין.
וַחֲכָמִים אוֹמְרִים: אֵין מְקָרְדִּין, אַף לֹא
מְקַרְצְפִין.

יד אברהם

the *Pesach* sacrifice. *Shulchan Aruch (Orach Chaim* 476:1) mentions שֶׂה, a term which includes the young of both sheep and goats. Perhaps the mishnah mentions גְּדִי, *a kid,* because it was the custom of the Roman Jews and their leader, Todos, to roast a whole kid on Pesach eve, as related in the *Gemara* (23a) and this may have occasioned the dispute between Rabban Gamliel and his colleagues as to the propriety of this custom.

[The mishnah *(Pesachim* 4:4) mentions that in some places it is customary to refrain from eating any roasted meat on Pesach eve. The halachic authorities *(Orach Chaim* 477:1) state that in *our countries* (eastern and central Europe) this is the custom. This custom seems to have become prevalent throughout world Jewry.]

8.

The next mishnah follows here because it lists three acts permitted by yet another *Tanna,* R' Elazar ben Azaryah, but prohibited by his colleagues.

שְׁלֹשָׁה דְּבָרִים רַבִּי אֶלְעָזָר בֶּן עֲזַרְיָה מַתִּיר, וַחֲכָמִים אוֹסְרִין: פָּרָתוֹ יוֹצְאָה בִּרְצוּעָה שֶׁבֵּין קַרְנֶיהָ; — *Three matters R' Elazar ben Azaryah permitted, but the Sages prohibited: His cow would go out* [into the public domain [i.e., the street] *with the strap which is between its horns;*

The strap was ornamental *(Rav; Rashi;* see *Shabbos* 52a).

Any labor which may not be performed by a person on Sabbath, may not be done by an animal for its owner on the Sabbath [see *Exodus* 20:10]. *Transporting from a private domain to a public domain is a labor. Since the strap is not part of the regular paraphernalia of a cow, it is considered a burden (see *Rashi* to *Shabbos* 51b, with *Pnei Yehoshua)* according to the Sages. R' Elazar held the strap to be an ornament, albeit an unusual one, and therefore permitted.

The *Gemara* (23a) comments that R' Elazar's own cows did not go out in this manner. It was his neighbor's cow that went out thus. However, since R' Elazar did not restrain his neighbor, it is considered as though he himself had transgressed. Actually, he had remained silent because he held it to be permissible, as stated previously.

וּמְקָרְדִּין אֶת הַבְּהֵמָה בְּיוֹם טוֹב; — *we may curry an animal on Yom Tov;*

A saw-like metal comb with thin teeth is used to groom animals, and due to the thinness of the teeth,

8. **T**hree matters R' Elazar ben Azaryah permitted, but the Sages prohibited: His cow would go out [into the public domain] with the strap which is between its horns; we may curry an animal on *Yom Tov*; and we may grind peppers in their grinder.

R' Yehudah says: We may not curry an animal on *Yom Tov* because it may make a wound, but we may curry with a wooden comb.

But the Sages say: We may not curry them [with an iron comb] and we may not even curry them with a wooden comb.

YAD AVRAHAM

blood is sometimes drawn. Drawing blood is prohibited because it is a subcategory of שׁוֹחֵט, *slaughtering* (*Rav; Rashi*). Nevertheless, R' Elazar ben Azaryah permits currying because the drawing of blood is unintentional and he holds (with R' Shimon) that unintended labor (דָּבָר שֶׁאֵינוֹ מִתְכַּוֵּן) is permitted [see footnote to mishnah 7]. The Sages hold (with R' Yehudah) that unintended labor is prohibited (*Gem.* 23a).

Rambam (comm. and *Hil. Yom Tov* 4:16) translates מְקָרְדִין, *removal of flies from the animal's coat*. These flies sometimes attach themselves to the animal's skin in such a way that their removal causes bleeding. The explanation of the argument is the same according to this translation as in the previous one. *Shulchan Aruch* (*Orach Chaim* 523:1) rules according to R' Elazar ben Azaryah.

וְשׁוֹחֲקִין אֶת הַפִּלְפְּלִין בָּרֵחַיִם שֶׁלָּהֶם. — *and we may grind peppers in their grinder.*

In the small grinders used for this purpose (*Rav*).

[It is permissible to grind spices on *Yom Tov* as explained above (1:7). Nevertheless, the Sages disagree with R' Elazar because employment of a grinder seems like a weekday activity (*Rashba* to 14a; *Orach Chaim* 504:1).

Rashba (*Shabbos* 141) and others (cited in *Beur Halachah* to 504) hold that using a grinder involves the Scripturally forbidden *melachah* of *grinding*. Crushing with a mortar, however, is permitted (1:7). Because this method is used when one is preparing for only a few meals it is included under the dispensation for food preparation. However, a method usually utilized in preparing great quantities for storage is not exempt as food preparation despite the fact that only a small amount is being prepared. The Sages hold that we must consider grinding pepper on a small grinder a method used for large quantities, for when one grinds even a small amount of pepper it suffices for a long time. They thus prohibit *grinding* pepper in any amount. The halachah accepts this view (*Orach Chaim* 504:1).

רַבִּי יְהוּדָה אוֹמֵר: אֵין מְקָרְדִין אֶת הַבְּהֵמָה בְּיוֹם טוֹב מִפְּנֵי שֶׁעוֹשֶׂה חַבּוּרָה, — R' *Yehudah says: We may not curry an animal on Yom Tov because it may make a wound,*

[For the reason outlined above (s.v. מְקָרְדִין). R' Yehudah prohibits even unintentional labor (see *Gemara* 23).]

אֲבָל מְקַרְצְפִין. — *but we may curry with a wooden comb.*

Since this comb has only dull wooden teeth there is no danger of wounding the animal (*Rav; Rashi*).

[*Rambam* understands מְקַרְצְפִין as *the removal of large flies* which do not attach

[ט] **הָרֵחַיִם** שֶׁל פִּלְפְּלִין טְמֵאָה מִשּׁוּם
שְׁלֹשָׁה כֵלִים: מִשּׁוּם כְּלִי קִבּוּל;
וּמִשּׁוּם כְּלִי מַתָּכוֹת; וּמִשּׁוּם כְּלִי כְבָרָה.

[י] **עֲגָלָה** שֶׁל קָטָן טְמֵאָה מִדְרָס, וְנִטֶּלֶת

יד אברהם

themselves to the animal's hide. Thus, their removal will not cause bleeding.]

וַחֲכָמִים אוֹמְרִים: אֵין מְקָרְדִין, אַף לֹא מְקָרְצְפִין. — *But the Sages say: We may not curry them [with an iron comb] and we may not even curry them with a wooden comb.*

The Sages hold that even currying with a wooden comb should be prohibited, as a safeguard (גְּזֵירָה). Some people may not perceive the fine distinction between employing

a wooden comb and using an iron comb and they might eventually use an iron comb as well (*Rav, Gem.* 23a).

[As already mentioned, the halachah is in accordance with the Sages except for their view on currying animals, which is based on R' Yehudah's opinion that unintentional labor is prohibited. Since in that matter we rule in accordance with R' Shimon that unintentional labor is permitted, it follows that in our case the ruling must be according to R' Elazar ben Azaryah.]

9.

Having made mention in the previous mishnah of a pepper grinder in connection with the laws of *Yom Tov*, the following mishnah digresses slightly to elaborate on the status of the pepper grinder in relation to the laws of *tumah*.

הָרֵחַיִם שֶׁל פִּלְפְּלִין טְמֵאָה מִשּׁוּם שְׁלֹשָׁה כֵלִים: — *The pepper grinder can contract tumah-contamination as* [lit. *is tamei because of*] *three utensils:*

Ordinarily, the laws of *tumah* do not apply to broken or disassembled utensils. The grinder however is composed of three parts, each of which is itself considered a complete utensil. Thus even if the grinder is taken apart, each individual part is susceptible to *tumah* (*Rav*; *Rashi*).

Tosafos (23b) adds that even in its assembled state the grinder is considered as a composite of its three parts and each component is considered an individual utensil. Thus, when one of these parts is touched by

a *tumah*, only that part contracts *tumah*. The other parts do not become contaminated and do not require immersion.

מִשּׁוּם כְּלִי קִבּוּל; — *as* [lit. *because of*] *a receptacle;*

The bottom (drawer-like) part into which the grindings fall is considered a receptacle (*Rav, Gem.* 23b).

[A wooden utensil can contract *tumah* only when it is a receptacle, e.g., a bowl. Wooden forks and knives, though considered utensils, cannot contract *tumah* (see *Keilim* 2:1). Our mishnah states that the bottom part of the grinder, though made of wood, is nevertheless susceptible to *tumah* because it is a receptacle.]

וּמִשּׁוּם כְּלִי מַתָּכוֹת; — *as* [lit. *because of*] *a metal utensil;*

The upper part of the utensil which does the grinding is not a receptacle and is therefore not

9. The pepper grinder can contract *tumah*-contamination as three utensils: as a receptacle; as a metal utensil; and as a sieve.

10. A child's [toy] wagon is susceptible to *midras*-contamination, and it may be moved on

YAD AVRAHAM

susceptible to *tumah* if made of wood. It can become *tamei* only if it is made of metal. Metal utensils are susceptible to *tumah* whether or not they are receptacles (see *Keilim* 11:1).

וּמִשּׁוּם כְּלִי כְבָרָה. — *and as* [lit. *because of*] *a sieve.*

It is susceptible to *tumah* even if it is of wood despite the fact that it is not a receptacle. A sieve, because it is woven, is considered, on a Rabbinical level (מִדְּרַבָּנָן), as a woven

cloth. Cloth is susceptible to *tumah* regardlesss of its composition *(Rav; Rashi;* see *Rambam, Hil. Keilim* 1:11).

Tosafos (23b) rejects this view and holds that the sieve contracts *tumah* because it is a receptacle for the bran which cannot fall through the holes of the sieve.

Rambam (Comm.) seems to understand that the sieve is composed of metal, in which case its susceptibility to *tumah* requires no special explanation. The mishnah merely stresses that the sieve itself is considered a utensil, not just part of a utensil, and as such is susceptible to *tumah* even when it is not attached to the grinder.

10.

This mishnah is placed here because of its concluding dispute regarding the issue of which utensils may be dragged upon the earth on the Sabbath, an argument predicated on the premise already outlined in mishnah 8, that unintentional labor is prohibited. In a digression similar to that in mishnah 9, this mishnah too elaborates upon the *tumah* status of the utensil under discussion.

עֲגָלָה שֶׁל קָטָן — *A child's* [toy] *wagon*

The translation reflects *Rashi* and *Rav's* opinion. *Tosafos* (23b) holds that עֲגָלָה שֶׁל קָטָן is *a stand placed upon wheels* (similar to a child's walker) and serves as a movable support for the child as he is learning to walk.

טְמֵאָה מִדְרָס, — *is susceptible to midras-contamination,*

Normally, *tumah* is contracted by direct contact with a contaminated object. However, *tumah* which originates as a result of a bodily function — e.g., *zav* (see *Leviticus* 15:1-15), or *metzora* (see ibid. 13:1-46) — can be contracted even without touching. In delineating the *tumah* of a *zav,* the Torah states: *And a person who touches his bed … or who sits on the seat* [lit. *utensil*] *upon which the zav sits shall wash his clothes* (ibid. 15:5-6). The wording used in the case of a menstruant is almost identical (ibid. 15:20-22). From these verses we see that such articles as the bed, couch or chair of the *zav* or *niddah* acquire the same level of contamination as the person from whom the *tumah*

בַּשַּׁבָּת, וְאֵינָה נִגְרֶרֶת אֶלָּא עַל גַּבֵּי כֵלִים.
רַבִּי יְהוּדָה אוֹמֵר: כָּל הַכֵּלִים אֵין נִגְרָרִין, חוּץ
מִן הָעֲגָלָה, מִפְּנֵי שֶׁהִיא כוֹבֶשֶׁת.

[א] אֵין צָדִין דָּגִים מִן הַבִּיבָרִין בְּיוֹם טוֹב, וְאֵין
נוֹתְנִין לִפְנֵיהֶם מְזוֹנוֹת. אֲבָל צָדִין

יד אברהם

emanates. One who touches any of these articles must immerse not only himself, but also his garments. The contamination of objects upon which one of these people rests or leans is called *midras*. One may contaminate through *midras* in any of five ways: by standing, sitting, or lying on objects, using leverage to move them (for example, a seesaw or balance scale), or leaning against them (*Zavim* 2:4; see *Chagigah* 2:7, ArtScroll ed., for a fuller discussion of *midras*-contamination).

וְנִטֶּלֶת בַּשַּׁבָּת, — *and it may be moved* [lit. *taken*] *on Sabbath,*

Because it is considered a utensil (*Rav; Rashi*).

[On Sabbath and *Yom Tov* one may move only utensils and consumables (food or firewood on *Yom Tov*; see *Rambam, Hil. Shabbos* 25:6 and 26:16). Everything else is termed *muktzeh* and may not be moved.]

וְאֵינָה נִגְרֶרֶת — *but it may not be dragged* [over the ground]

Because its wheels may dig out furrows, forbidden as a subcategory of חוֹרֵשׁ, *plowing*. This opinion is in accordance with R' Yehudah's that unintended labor is prohibited (*Rav, Gem.* 23b).

אֶלָּא עַל גַּבֵּי כֵלִים. — *except over cloth.*

If a piece of cloth (or rug) was

placed between the wheels and the ground so as to preclude the possibility of a furrow being carved in the ground, one may pull the wagon (*Rav; Rashi*). [The Hebrew noun כְּלִי includes *vessels, utensils, clothing* and *cloth*. The translation uses *cloth* because it best fits the context.]

רַבִּי יְהוּדָה אוֹמֵר: כָּל הַכֵּלִים אֵין נִגְרָרִין, — *R' Yehudah says: No utensil may be dragged* [over the ground, because a furrow may be dug],

חוּץ מִן הָעֲגָלָה, מִפְּנֵי שֶׁהִיא כוֹבֶשֶׁת. — *except the wagon because it* [only] *presses.*

The wagon does not remove any earth from its place. It only depresses the earth over which it passes and is therefore not to be considered *plowing* (*Rav; Rashi*). The first opinion in our mishnah agrees in principle, that making a depression in the earth is not considered *plowing*, but nevertheless prohibits the dragging of the wagon for fear that the wheels may get snagged and earth will be removed through dragging. R' Yehudah holds that this possibility is too remote to be considered (*Rashi*).

Shulchan Aruch (337:1) does not rule in accordance with either opinion expressed here. Both are based on R' Yehudah's unaccepted premise that unintentional work is prohibited.

Sabbath, but it may not be dragged [over the ground] except over cloth.

R' Yehudah says: No utensil may be dragged [over the ground], except the wagon because it [only] presses.

1. **W**e may not catch fish from a fish pond on Yom Tov, nor may we place food before

YAD AVRAHAM

Chapter 3

1.

Although the Torah clearly permits otherwise prohibited labor to be performed on Yom Tov when the labor is necessary in the preparation of food, not all *melachos* are granted this dispensation (see General Introduction). The mishnah now discusses **trapping* animals, fish and fowl to be eaten on Yom Tov.

אֵין צָדִין דָּגִים מִן הַבִּיבָרִין בְּיוֹם טוֹב, — *We may not catch fish from a fish pond on Yom Tov,*

In view of the general dispensation allowing labor involved in food preparation (אוֹכֶל נֶפֶשׁ), the prohibition against catching fish needs explanation. Most of the commentators agree that catching fish on Yom Tov is prohibited because it involves the labor of צָד, **trapping,* and this labor is not accorded the dispensation accorded food preparation in general. Numerous explanations for this exclusion are given (see General Introduction), some of which are outlined below.

Only those labors which, if per-

formed prior to Yom Tov, would diminish the enjoyment of the food, e.g., if **cooking* or **slaughtering* is done before Yom Tov there is apprehension that the food will spoil or lose some of its tastiness. Since, however, an animal trapped before Yom Tov will not taste different from one trapped on Yom Tov, **trapping* is excluded from the dispensation. Even fish caught prior to Yom Tov can be placed in a pail of water, where they will remain fresh until they are removed to be cooked (R aglei).[1]

Tosafos, holding to the view that certain labors, specifically **reaping,* are indicated to be prohibited by Scripture, explains that the labor of **trapping* is to be considered similar to **reaping* this matter. Shitah Mekubetzes explains this further and points out that the exclusion of **reaping* should not be viewed as specific to that labor, but as a model from which to develop a criterion applicable to all of the thirty-nine *melachos*. Only those preparatory labors close to the actual consumption of the food, e.g., **kneading,* **slaughtering,* **cooking,* are permitted, while those further away from the consumption, such as **reaping* and **trapping,* are prohibited [i.e., the labors involved in procuring the

1. *Tosefos Rid,* in a variation on this view, explains that the general nature of the labor must be considered. Since in general the labor of **trapping* is excluded from the dispensation (as in setting traps for animals, etc.), it is not granted even in the minority of cases which, if judged by the criterion of food deterioration, should be permitted.

ביצה חַיָּה וָעוֹף מִן הַבִּיבָרִין, וְנוֹתְנִין לִפְנֵיהֶם מְזוֹנוֹת.

ג/א

יד אברהם

food are prohibited, while those involved in the preparation are permitted].

According to *Rosh* and *Ran* (see General Introduction), *melachos* such as *trapping and *reaping are prohibited because they are usually done in the preparation of large food supplies to be consumed over an extended period of time.

Rambam (Hil. Yom Tov 2:7 and *Comm.;* also *Meiri)* has a totally different approach to this mishnah. In his view catching fish is not prohibited because of the labor involved (ostensibly this *melachah* falls under the general dispensation for food preparation), but rather because fish (or animals) which need to be caught or trapped cannot be considered מוּכָן, *prepared* [for *Yom Tov* use], and are *muktzeh* even if explicitly designated for consumption *(Meiri).* According to this view catching fish does not fall within the category of forbidden

labor for it, too, would be considered food preparation and would be granted dispensation.[1]

וְאֵין נוֹתְנִין לִפְנֵיהֶם מְזוֹנוֹת. — *nor may we place food before them.*

The fish can subsist on the food they find in the water *(Rav; Rashi).* A person may not feed animals that are not dependent on him. Such feeding is considered unnecessary effort and is consequently prohibited *(Rosh Yosef).*

Other commentators offer different reasons for the prohibition against feeding fish (or other animals not dependent on man). *Rambam (Comm.* and *Hil. Yom Tov* 2:17), *Tos.* (23b), and *Rashba (Avodas HaKodesh* 1:9) offer that we are apprehensive lest one forget and trap these animals[2] (see above the differing reasons given by *Rambam* and *Tosafos* for prohibiting *trapping on Yom Tov.*[3] *Meiri* (cf. *Ran)* adduces support for this view from *Yerushalmi (Shabbos* 13:7) and adds that *Rashi* himself *(Shabbos* 106b) ascribes to this view (cf., *Ran* and *Rosh Yosef).*

1. Although *Rambam* concurs with *Rashi* that labor which can be performed prior to *Yom Tov* does not fall under the dispensation for food preparation (see General Introduction), he nevertheless differs with him concerning this case and holds that catching fish is to be categorized as a labor necessary to be performed on *Yom Tov,* for upon being caught the fish will die and its taste will immediately begin to deteriorate. The possibility of evading this deterioration by placing the fish in water does not, according to *Rambam,* have the effect of prohibiting this labor (see *Mirkeves HaMishneh, Hil. Yom Tov* 1:6). Ultimately one is led to the conclusion that, in this view, catching fish entails only the prohibition of *muktzeh,* whereas the *trapping of animals (which can be done before *Yom Tov* without any loss of taste) carries with it the prohibition (Rabbinical in this case) against the labor of *trapping in addition to that of *muktzeh.*

2. According to *Rashi* the prohibition outlined here is identical in reason and scope to that applied to the Sabbath *(Shabbos* 24:3; see *Orach Chaim* 324:11), whereas according to the view presented by *Rambam* and *Tosafos,* the reason advanced here for this prohibition applies only to *Yom Tov* where, because of the dispensation allowing one to slaughter, there is apprehension he may forget and attempt to trap the animal while feeding it. Consequently, according to this view, one may not feed livestock which may not be trapped even if they are dependent upon man, whereas on the Sabbath this would be permitted (see *Meiri* in *Beis HaBechirah).*

3. The difference of opinions between *Tosefos* and *Rambam* concerning the prohibition against *trapping has halachic ramifications here (see *Tos., Shabbos* 106b), for according to *Tosafos* the ban, both against trapping and feeding, applies solely to fowl and animals whose apprehension would be categorized *trapping. Domesticated fowl and animals which regularly return to their nests (or stables) every night (see *Orach Chaim* 316:12 and 497:6), or those already confined in such a manner that further *trapping is not necessary (see *Orach Chaim*

3
1

them. But we may catch animals or fowl from
enclosures, and we may put food before them.

אֲבָל צָדִין חַיָּה וָעוֹף מִן הַבֵּיבָרִין, — *But
we may catch animals or fowl from
enclosures,* '

This refers to enclosures designed
for the purpose of stocking animals
(*Rambam, Comm.; Rashi on Rif*).

The בֵּיבָרִין mentioned here in connection
with fowl and animals differ from those for
fish (the former are corrals whereas the latter
are pools). The corrals for animals are usually called קַרְפִּיפִין, but the mishnah uses the
term בֵּיבָרִין here because it has already used it
earlier for fish. *Meiri* understands that these
corrals are stocked with wild animals such as
deer, antelopes, and large fowl in settings
that approximate their natural habitats.
There they multiply and raise their offspring
which are taken for food.

Animals and fowl contained in
these enclosures are considered
trapped, and the labor of *trapping
[or the prohibition of *muktzeh* applied to animals in their untrapped
state according to *Rambam's* view
above, s.v. אֵין צָדִין] does not apply.
Fish, by contrast, even when
stocked in a pond, can still elude
capture by hiding in crevices and
holes and are therefore considered
uncaptured. Therefore *trapping
them constitutes labor (*Rashi*).

The *Gemara* (24a) explains that even
animals may be caught only when in a small
enclosure, which is defined by the *Gemara* as
a place where the animal can be caught בְּחַד
שְׁחִיָא, *in one try* [lit. *with one bending*]. In
connection with feeding and catching birds

the *Gemara* states it is permitted only when
the [small] enclosure has a roof.[1]

Rav adds an important condition to the
permission given in the mishnah to catch
animals in an enclosure. They may be caught
only if they had been designated for
slaughter prior to *Yom Tov;* otherwise they
are *muktzeh*. Evidently *Rav's* position is
based upon a divergent version in *Rashi*
(23b) — which reads הַמּוּבָנִים, *which have
been prepared*, where prevalent text have
הַמְכוּנָסִים, *which have been ingathered —*
which was also in *Meiri's* (see notes there)
and *Or Zarua's* (2:352) copies of *Rashi's*
commentary. *Rambam's* paraphrase of our
mishnah (*Hil. Yom Tov* 2:7) clearly indicates
that wherever no *trapping* is necessary the
animals are automatically considered prepared (מוּבָן) [by virtue of their presence
within an enclosure erected for the purpose
of stocking animals for consumption]. *Meiri*,
too, disagrees with the view attributed by
him to *Rashi*. *Mishnah Berurah* (497:20)
rules in accordance with *Rav's* view without
indicating his source and without mention of
divergent opinions.

וְנוֹתְנִין לִפְנֵיהֶם מְזוֹנוֹת. — *and we may
put food before them.*

Because these animals depend
upon their owner for food during
the winter and sometimes even in
the summer if they can find no
pasture (*Rav; Rashi*).

The other reasons given for the
prohibition against feeding fish do
not apply here either. There is no
fear that he may violate the labor of
*trapping because the animals are

497:7) would not come under this ban. According to *Rambam*, however, the ban against
feeding applies to any animal considered *muktzeh*. For example, feeding a domesticated
chicken designated for egg-laying (and consequently *muktzeh;* see commentary and footnote
to 1:1, s.v. בֵּית שַׁמַּאי אוֹמְרִים תֵּאָכֵל) would be forbidden. *Mishnah Berurah* (497:4) decides the
halachah in accordance with *Tosafos'* view.

1. Thus, it may be inferred that the difference between animals and fish as delineated in the
mishnah refers to a small enclosure and a small pool. However, *Rambam's* opinion (*Hil. Yom
Tov* 2:7) is that even fish, if held in a small pool, may be caught. *Maggid Mishneh* (there) explains that *Rambam's* ruling is based on the view of Rabban Shimon ben Gamliel which allows such an inference to be drawn. [See commentary to end of this mishnah.]

רַבָּן שִׁמְעוֹן בֶּן גַּמְלִיאֵל אוֹמֵר: לֹא כָל הַבִּיבָרִין שָׁוִין. זֶה הַכְּלָל: כָּל הַמְחֻסָּר צֵידָה אָסוּר; וְשֶׁאֵינוֹ מְחֻסָּר צֵידָה מֻתָּר.

[ב] **מְצוּדוֹת** חַיָּה וָעוֹף וְדָגִים שֶׁעֲשָׂאָן מֵעֶרֶב יוֹם טוֹב, לֹא יִטּוֹל מֵהֶן בְּיוֹם טוֹב, אֶלָּא אִם כֵּן יוֹדֵעַ שֶׁנִּצּוֹדוּ מֵעֶרֶב יוֹם טוֹב.

considered previously trapped. *Muktzeh* does not apply because these animals may be slaughtered and eaten on *Yom Tov* (see above, s.v. אֲבָל).

רַבָּן שִׁמְעוֹן בֶּן גַּמְלִיאֵל אוֹמֵר: לֹא כָל הַבִּיבָרִין שָׁוִין. — *Rabban Shimon ben Gamliel says: Not all enclosures are the same.*

Rabban Shimon does not disagree with the previous *Tanna*. He is merely clarifying the law *(Rav)*. [Not all commentators agree with *Rav*. This will be explained below.]

זֶה הַכְּלָל: כָּל הַמְחֻסָּר צֵידָה אָסוּר; — *This is the general rule* [to be followed in determining whether an animal may be caught]: *Whatever* [animal] *requires* [lit. *lacks*] *trapping is prohibited* [to be caught or fed];

Whenever the animal cannot be caught without resorting to special tactics or strategies, as the *Gemara* (74a) puts it: Whenever one says הָבֵא מְצוּדָה וּנְצוּדֶנּוּ, *bring a trap* [or *net*] *and let us catch it.*

וְשֶׁאֵינוֹ מְחֻסָּר צֵידָה מֻתָּר. — *and whatever does not require trapping* [lit. *lack*] *is permitted* [to be caught and fed].

If it can be caught without any

special effort, it may be caught and fed *(Rav)*.

The *Gemara* (24a) questions whether there is disagreement between Rabban Shimon and the first *Tanna* for the latter, too, agrees that only those animals held in a small enclosure may be caught and fed (see above, s.v. צָדִין). The ambiguously worded text of the *Gemara* allows for *Rav's* understanding that it is concluded that they do not disagree. Hence his comment (as cited above). However, *Rashi* (24a) indicates that the passage can be understood as concluding that there is disagreement among the *Tannaim* (see *Maharsha; Maharam Shiff*). Assuming the premise that there is a disagreement, it centers about the criteria to be used in judging an animal trapped. According to the first *Tanna* one of the criteria (as stated in the *Gemara*) is that he be able to reach it with one lunge (דְּמָטֵי לֵיהּ בְּחַד שִׁחְיָא). If this requirement is met, the enclosure is considered small and the animals may (according to the first *Tanna*) be caught. But Rabban Shimon disagrees and prohibits catching the animal (even in the above case) as long as the person may ask for a trap with which to catch it *(Rashi* 24a) [i.e., although he can catch the animal with one lunge as he pleases, nevertheless, he will prefer to do so with a trap]. The halachah is as Rabban Shimon *(Gemara* 24a). In *Rav's* view the criteria presented by the first *Tanna* and Rabban Shimon are considered to be identical. *Rambam*, as explained by *Maggid Mishneh (Hil. Yom Tov* 2:7), holds that there is a disagreement, but interprets it differently. According to the first *Tanna* the criterion of being reachable with one lunge (or the identical, in this view, possibility of asking for a trap) applies only to animals and fowl, but

Rabban Shimon ben Gamliel says: Not all enclosures are the same. This is the general rule: Whatever requires trapping is prohibited; and whatever does not require trapping is permitted.

2. If traps for animals, birds, or fish were set prior to *Yom Tov*, one may not take from them on *Yom Tov*, unless he knows that they were trapped before *Yom Tov*.

YAD AVRAHAM

not to fish. Rabbi Shimon, however, applies this criterion categorically, to fish as well as to animal and fowl. *Rambam* decides the halachah according to Rabban Shimon and consequently one may catch fish from a small pool (see *Rama* in *Orach Chaim* 497:1).

2.

After clarifying questions related to *trapping and feeding animals, the mishnah follows with a discussion of the particulars of the laws governing using animals on *Yom Tov* in cases where *trapping is not involved.

As we have seen from the previous mishnah (s.v. וְאֵין נוֹתְנִין), animals, birds and fish which must be trapped on *Yom Tov* are muktzeh. The following mishnah discusses a case in which we are unsure whether the animal in question was caught prior to *Yom Tov*.

מְצוּדוֹת חַיָּה וָעוֹף וְדָגִים שֶׁעֲשָׂאָן מֵעֶרֶב יוֹם טוֹב, — *If traps for animals, birds, or fish were set prior to Yom Tov,*

[Upon returning on *Yom Tov*, one found animals caught in these traps.]

לֹא יִטּוֹל מֵהֶן בְּיוֹם טוֹב, — *one may not take [animals] from them on Yom Tov,*

Since the animals may have been trapped on *Yom Tov* they are

muktzeh and may not be eaten or even moved *(Rav).*

אֶלָּא אִם כֵּן יוֹדֵעַ שֶׁנִּצוֹדוּ מֵעֶרֶב יוֹם טוֹב. — *unless he knows that they were trapped before Yom Tov.*

This *Tanna* holds that the injunction of *muktzeh* applies even if there is only a suspicion of *muktzeh* (סָפֵק מוּכָן).

Muktzeh is a Rabbinical injunction, and Rabbinical injunctions do not apply in questionable circumstances (סְפֵיקָא דְרַבָּנָן לְקוּלָּא). Accordingly, the mere possibility of *muktzeh* should not prohibit the use of these animals.

Ramban proposes that this prohibition is based on the principle enunciated in the *Gemara* (4a) that דָּבָר שֶׁיֵּשׁ לוֹ מַתִּירִין, an object which will be permissible [e.g., an object prohibited because of the Sabbath, but which will become permissible after the Sabbath], is banned even under questionable circumstances, despite the fact that only a Rabbinical prohibition is involved. Thus, since *muktzeh* is a ban which will not apply after the Sabbath or *Yom Tov* it is forbidden even where the conditions are questionable *(Milchamos, Shabbos* 151a; cf. *Drush VeChiddush R' Akiva Eiger* 3b; *Tos. R' Akiva* here; see also *Tos. Yeshanim* 3b, *Meiri,* and *Ravyah* 3:763 for additional explanation for this stringency).

ביצה
ג/ג

וּמַעֲשֶׂה בְּנָכְרִי אֶחָד שֶׁהֵבִיא דָּגִים לְרַבָּן
גַּמְלִיאֵל, וְאָמַר: ,,מֻתָּרִין הֵן, אֶלָּא שֶׁאֵין רְצוֹנִי
לְקַבֵּל הֵימֶנּוּ.''

[ג] **בְּהֵמָה** מְסֻכֶּנֶת לֹא יִשְׁחֹט, אֶלָּא אִם כֵּן
יֵשׁ שָׁהוּת בַּיּוֹם לֶאֱכֹל מִמֶּנָּה
כְּזַיִת צָלִי.

יד אברהם

וּמַעֲשֶׂה בְּנָכְרִי אֶחָד שֶׁהֵבִיא דָּגִים לְרַבָּן
גַּמְלִיאֵל, — *There was an incident
with a certain gentile who brought
fish to Rabban Gamliel* [on Yom
Tov, and it was unknown whether
the fish had been caught before
Yom Tov].

וְאָמַר: ,,מֻתָּרִין הֵן, אֶלָּא שֶׁאֵין רְצוֹנִי
לְקַבֵּל הֵימֶנּוּ.'' — *He* [Rabban
Gamliel] *said, "They may be eaten,
but I do not want* [lit. *it is not my
desire*] *to accept* [a present] *from
him."*

Because I am not on friendly
terms with him (*Rav; Rashi*).

Lechem Mishneh suggests that the present
was given on a day which was a heathen
holiday, when it is forbidden to accept presents from or have any social contact with
heathens (*Avodah Zarah* 66b; *Yoreh Deah*
148:5).

[Evidently Rabban Gamliel offered this explanation because he did not want his refusal
of the present to be construed as an approval
of the first *Tanna's* decision prohibiting
questionable *muktzeh*.]

The *Gemara* (24a) explains that obviously
there is a segment missing in the text of the
mishnah. It should have said: סְפֵק מוּכָן אָסוּר,
*objects of questionable preparation are
prohibited* [as is evident from the words of
the first *Tanna*], וְרַבָּן גַּמְלִיאֵל מַתִּיר, *but Rabban Gamliel permits* [them]. The incident is
then cited to demonstrate Rabban Gamliel's
position.

According to this reading, Rabban Gamliel
disagrees with the first *Tanna* and permits
any *muktzeh* of questionable status.

The *Gemara* (24b) adds that Rabban

Gamliel agrees that questionable *muktzeh*
may not be eaten. He only permits it to be
moved (טלטול מוקצה). The *Gemara* (ibid.) rejects this opinion.

In light of this *Gemara*, Rabban Gamliel's
disagreement with the first *Tanna* must be
clarified. If Rabban Gamliel agrees that
eating the fish (which possibly is *muktzeh*) is
prohibited, one can assume that he agrees
with the first *Tanna's* reasoning as well.
Why then does he disagree on the question
of moving the fish?

Ramban (see above, s.v. אֶלָּא אִם כֵּן)
propose that the *Tanna kamma* applies the
injunction of *muktzeh* even if there is only a
suspicion of *muktzeh* because of the princi-
ple of דָּבָר שֶׁיֵּשׁ לוֹ מַתִּירִין, *an object which will
be permissible at a later time.* According to
Tzlach (24b; 3b) and *Tosefos R' Akiva* this
principle is only applied to eating. For eating,
an act which can be performed but once on
any object, may be deferred to a time when
no question of *muktzeh* exists. Moving an
object, on the other hand, by virtue of the
fact that it may be done repeatedly, is an act
which is irreplaceable when postponed. To
defer an act which may be repeated is to lose
the act. Its future performance is, by definition, an act other than the one contemplated
earlier. Thus, moving doubtful *muktzeh* on
Yom Tov is not an act which will become
permissible after Yom Tov when no question
of *muktzeh* exists. For the move of tomorrow
is separate and distinct from the move on
Yom Tov.

Following this logic we have two possible
explanations for Rabban Shimon's disagreement with the first *Tanna*: (a) Rabban
Shimon accepts this fine distinction between
eating and moving *muktzeh*, while the *Tanna kamma* rejects it; or (b) the first *Tanna*
agrees with the principle outlined above, but

3
3
There was an incident with a certain gentile who brought fish to Rabban Gamliel. He said, "They may be eaten, but I do not want to accept [a present] from him."

3. If an animal is dangerously ill, one may not slaughter [it], unless there is [enough] time — during the day — to eat an olive-sized [piece of its meat] roasted.

YAD AVRAHAM

he argues that the de facto prohibition against eating the questionable *muktzeh* in itself renders the object *muktzeh* concerning moving. This latter possibility is in accordance with the rule formulated by *Rosh* and *Rif* (here) that anything which may not be eaten is *muktzeh* regarding moving (*Tzlach, Rosh Yosef, Simchas Yom Tov*).

The *Gemara* (24b) also applies the logic of this mishnah to fruit brought by a gentile on *Yom Tov*. As long as there is a possibility that it was picked on *Yom Tov*, in which case it would be *muktzeh*, the fruit is prohibited.

3.

After discussing laws related to *trapping* animals on *Yom Tov*, the mishnah continues with laws related to the next step, *slaughtering*.

The discussion in this mishnah centers on the circumstances under which an animal may be slaughtered even if it is not really needed on *Yom Tov*, contrary to the general rule that labor performed on *Yom Tov* must be done for *Yom Tov* purposes only (see prefatory remarks and *commentary* to 2).

בְּהֵמָה מְסֻכֶּנֶת — *If an animal is dangerously ill* [lit. *An endangered animal*],

The animal is in danger of dying without undergoing *shechitah* (halachic slaughter), in which case it would, of course, not be permitted to be eaten. The owner, having already eaten, does not need the meat for *Yom Tov* but is anxious to slaughter the animal to prevent the

sizable financial loss that would ensue if the animal died of natural causes (*Rav; Rashi*).

לֹא יִשְׁחֹט, — *one may not slaughter [it],*

Slaughtering is permitted if the meat is needed on *Yom Tov*. In this case, however, slaughtering is not permitted, for its primary purpose is the prevention of monetary loss, a need which, in itself, does not qualify for the dispensation of food preparation.

אֶלָּא אִם כֵּן יֵשׁ שָׁהוּת בַּיּוֹם לֶאֱכוֹל מִמֶּנָּה כְּזַיִת צָלִי. — *unless there is [enough] time — during the day — to eat an olive-sized [piece of its meat] roasted.*

Since he can eat at least a small piece of the slaughtered animal on *Yom Tov*, even if there is only enough time for broiling the meat (rather than the lengthier process of cooking), he is permitted to slaugh-

רַבִּי עֲקִיבָא אוֹמֵר: אֲפִלּוּ כְזַיִת חַי מִבֵּית
טְבִיחָתָהּ. שְׁחָטָהּ בַּשָּׂדֶה, לֹא יְבִיאֶנָּה בְמוֹט
וּבְמוֹטָה. אֲבָל מֵבִיא בְיָדוֹ אֵבָרִים אֵבָרִים.

יד אברהם

ter the animal, for the possibility of using part of the meat for *Yom Tov* is sufficient reason to exempt the *slaughtering* as preparation of *Yom Tov* food.[1]

Although the need to eat does not include more than a minute amount, it is sufficient reason to permit the slaughter of an entire animal, since it is impossible for any of the meat to be eaten unless the entire animal is slaughtered (*Pesachim* 46b).

Although in this situation the need for food is no more than a transparent pretext, it is nonetheless permitted. The rule is that in the face of an imminent financial loss the Sages permitted the performance of labor, even if the need for food is contrived.[2] Ordinarily, however, this is not permitted. For example, one may not cook a meal

after one has already eaten under the pretext that he wants to eat another olive-sized piece, even if one actually intends to eat this amount of food, for this is considered a הַעֲרָמָה, *subterfuge*, which is only permitted under extraordinary circumstances such as those in our mishnah (*Orach Chaim* 503:1).

רַבִּי עֲקִיבָא אוֹמֵר: — *Rabbi Akiva says:*

[R' Akiva is more lenient than the first *Tanna* regarding the amount of time needed if *slaughtering* the animal is to be permitted.]

אֲפִלּוּ כְזַיִת חַי — *Even* [if there is time only for] *an olive-sized* [piece of] *raw* [meat]

[This eliminates the time required to roast the meat.]

1. The language of the mishnah suggests that the fact that there is time to eat an olive-sized portion is, in itself, sufficient reason to permit one to slaughter. There is no stipulation that the person actually eat the meat. The Talmud (*Pesachim* 46b) explains this on the basis of Rabbah's principle of *ho'il*, which permits labor, when, if guests were to come, the labor would be a holiday need, i.e., as long as there is even a remote possibility that a labor could be utilized for *Yom Tov* the labor is considered performed for the sake of *Yom Tov*, and, consequently, does not fall under the Scriptural prohibition of performing labor for the weekdays. The example cited there is the case of one who cooked on *Yom Tov* for the weekdays when there was still a possibility (though this is not the purpose of this work) of unexpected guests arriving and being served this food. According to Rabbah this is sufficient ground to remove the Scriptural prohibition.

Rav Chisda disagrees with the principle of *ho'il*. According to him, the mishnah takes it as a foregone conclusion that, where the possibility exists, the person will actually eat the meat, since only in this manner will he be permitted to slaughter the animal.

Rosh, Rif (*Pesachim* 46b) and *Rambam* (Hil. Yom Tov 1:15) accept Rabbah's opinion. Thus, slaughtering a dangerously ill animal is permitted even if one does not plan actually to eat its meat so long as the possibility of doing so exists (*Maggid Mishneh, Hil. Yom Tov* 1:12; *Be'er Hagolah* and *Mishnah Berurah* 498:6; *Beis Yosef*).

2. [Even if the need for food is merely a subterfuge, the dispensation allowing labors to be performed in preparing food applies on a Scriptural level. However, the Sages prohibited such application of the dispensation in ordinary circumstances. In the extraordinary instance described in our mishnah the Sages did not apply their prohibition.]

Rabbi Akiva says: Even an olive-sized [piece of] raw [meat] from the place of the incision.

If he slaughtered it in the field, he may not bring it [from the field to his house] on a pole or on a litter, but he may bring it in his hand, limb by limb.

YAD AVRAHAM

מִבֵּית טְבִיחָתָה. — *from the place of the incision* [i.e., from the part of the neck where the incision for the slaughter was made].

Eating from this part of the animal further reduces the amount of time needed for this dispensation, since one need not flay the animal in order to get at the meat *(Rav; Rashi).*

The first *Tanna* disagrees with R' Akiva and holds that if there was time only to eat the meat raw, one may not slaughter the animal because the subterfuge is too obvious *(Meiri).*

The halachah is not in accordance with R' Akiva on this point *(Orach Chaim* 498:6).

שְׁחָטָהּ בַּשָּׂדֶה, — *If he slaughtered it in the field*

Regardless of whether the animal is ill or healthy *(Tif. Yis.; cf. Meiri* and *Ran* cited below, s.v. לֹא וְיבִיאֶנָּה).

לֹא יְבִיאֶנָּה בְּמוֹט וּבְמוֹטָה. — *he may[1] not bring it [from the field to his house] on a pole or on a litter,*

This is forbidden because this manner of carrying attracts too much attention, and detracts from

the honor of the festival *(Rav; Rashi; cf. Tos. Yom Tov).*

Rambam (Hil. Yom Tov 5:5; see *Magen Avraham* 498:15) gives a slightly different reason for this prohibition. It is so that *he should not do as he does on weekdays,* i.e., certain permissible labor is considered antithetical to the festivity of *Yom Tov* and must be performed in an unusual manner on *Yom Tov* (even if done in private).

Meiri (see also *Ran*) holds that this mode of carrying the meat is prohibited because it draws attention to the fact that an animal had to be slaughtered suddenly [otherwise it would not have been slaughtered in a place from where it would have to be transported]. Consequently, it becomes known that the slaughter was not performed for a basic *Yom Tov* need. Thus, if in fact a healthy animal had been slaughtered, it may be carried on a pole or litter. However, he agrees that the words of *Rambam* and other authorities do not allow for such a distinction (see *Turei Zahav* to *Orach Chaim* 498:7; *Mishnah Berurah* there).

אֲבָל מֵבִיא בְּיָדוֹ אֵבָרִים אֵבָרִים. — *but he may bring it in his hand, limb by limb.*

Though this involves much more walking — an activity which should be curtailed as much as possible if unnecessary (see *Orach Chaim* 301:3 and 613:8) — this method is nevertheless preferable to the regular manner of carrying *(Magen Avraham* 498:15).

1. [It is not clear whether this injunction applies only when two people carry the animal. The reason given by *Rashi* and *Rav,* אוּשָׁא מִילְתָא, *it is a manner which attracts attention,* could be construed to prohibit only where two people are carrying. However, the advice tendered in the mishnah, *he may bring it … limb by limb,* suggests that even one person may not carry the whole animal himself. However, it is possible that this method is not mentioned because it is impractical for one person to carry an entire animal. Neither *Rambam (Hil. Yom Tov* 5:5) nor *Shulchan Aruch (Orach Chaim* 498:7) mention this restriction.]

[ד] **בְּכוֹר** שֶׁנָּפַל לְבוֹר, רַבִּי יְהוּדָה אוֹמֵר:
יֵרֵד מֻמְחֶה וְיִרְאֶה. אִם יֶשׁ בּוֹ מוּם,
יַעֲלֶה וְיִשָׁחֵט; וְאִם לָאו, לֹא יִשָׁחֵט.
רַבִּי שִׁמְעוֹן אוֹמֵר: כָּל שֶׁאֵין מוּמוֹ נִכָּר מִבְּעוֹד
יוֹם, אֵין זֶה מִן הַמּוּכָן.

יד אברהם

4.

◆§ בְּכוֹר בַּעַל מוּם — A Blemished First-born Animal

קַדֶּשׁ־לִי כָל־בְּכוֹר פֶּטֶר כָּל־רֶחֶם בִּבְנֵי יִשְׂרָאֵל בָּאָדָם וּבַבְּהֵמָה ..., *Sanctify unto Me every first-born — the one that opened each womb — among the Children of Israel, of the people and of the animals ... (Exodus* 13:12).

The Torah ordains that a בְּכוֹר [*bechor*], *first-born* [to his mother] *male*, of kosher domestic animals (cow, sheep, goat) be given to a *Kohen*. The *Kohen* must bring it to the Temple courtyard, slaughter it there, offer specified portions on the Temple altar, and only then eat the remaining meat of the animal *(Numbers* 18:17-18). The *bechor* may not be slaughtered outside the Temple courtyard unless it is a blemished animal, i.e., unless it is afflicted with a permanent מוּם, *blemish* or *imperfection*, which disqualifies it from being offered on the altar (see *Deuteronomy* 15:21-22). In this case the *bechor* may be slaughtered and eaten outside of the Temple.

The law stipulates that only a מֻמְחֶה, *an expert*, specifically ordained to judge these matters may determine whether a blemish found on the *bechor*, either at birth or at anytime thereafter, is considered a permanent blemish in the halachic sense, thus rendering it invalid for sacrifice and permitting its slaughter outside of the Temple.

The laws of *bechor* apply even in our post-Temple era, for although a *bechor* may not now be offered in the Temple, it is nevertheless considered a sacrifice and subject to the attendant law prohibiting its slaughter outside of the Temple unless pronounced blemished by an expert.

The mishnah now discusses the details of judging a blemish and slaughtering a *bechor* on *Yom Tov*.

בְּכוֹר שֶׁנָּפַל לְבוֹר, — *If a first-born fell into a pit* [lit. *a first-born which fell into a pit*],

The mishnah cannot be speaking of a blemish that was contracted on *Yom Tov*. Since the animal was unblemished before *Yom Tov*, its owner did not intend at that time to slaughter it on *Yom Tov*. Thus the animal was *muktzeh* at the onset of *Yom Tov* and remains *muktzeh* until the end of *Yom Tov* (Rashi 26a).

Rather the mishnah speaks of a *bechor* which is known to have been blemished before *Yom Tov*, but which had not yet been examined by an expert to determine the halachic status of the blemish. Now that the animal has fallen into a pit there is the possibility that it will suffocate there. To prevent total loss, the owner wishes to raise the animal and slaughter it for its meat. However, since it is a *bechor*, he may not do so until an expert has inspected the original blemish and declared it to be a permanent blemish which renders the animal

3
4

4. If a first-born fell into a pit, R' Yehudah says: An expert may go down and look [at the blemish]. If [the expert finds that] it has a blemish, he may bring it up and slaughter [it]; if not, he may not slaughter [it].

R' Shimon says: In any case where the blemish was not detected before *Yom Tov*, it is not considered to be prepared.

unfit for sacrifice *(Rav; Gem. 26a)*.

רַבִּי יְהוּדָה אוֹמֵר: יֵרֵד מֻמְחֶה וְיִרְאֶה. — *R' Yehudah says: An expert may go down* [into the pit] *and look* [at the blemish].

[As long as the blemish has not been declared permanent, we may not even hoist the animal out of the ditch, for in the event that the blemish is found to be temporary the animal may not be slaughtered. Thus raising the animal would constitute needless work or moving doubtful (סָפֵק) *muktzeh*. Thus, the expert must descend into the pit to examine the blemish (see *Gem.* 26a).]

אִם הָיָה בוֹ מוּם וְזָלַה וְיִשְׁחָטֶנּוּ — *If* [the expert finds that] *it has a blemish* [which will not heal], *he may bring it up and slaughter* [it];

If the expert finds that the blemish that had been contracted prior to the holiday was a permanent blemish, the animal is disqualified from the altar, and may be slaughtered *(Rav, Rashi)*.

וְאִם לָאו, לֹא יִשְׁחָט. — *if not* [i.e., the expert did not determine that it was a permanent blemish], *he may not slaughter* [it].

If the expert determines that the blemish that the animal contracted before *Yom Tov* does not disqualify the *bechor* as a sacrifice [i.e., it is a

temporary wound that will heal] then it may not be slaughtered.

The *Gemara* (26a) questions this last clause of the mishnah as superfluous: If the blemish was declared to be invalid then it goes without saying that the animal must be sacrificed as a *bechor* and may not be slaughtered outside of the Temple courtyard. The *Gemara* explains that the lesson of the mishnah is that even if the animal developed a new permanent blemish on *Yom Tov* it may not be slaughtered. Although the new blemish effectively removes the prohibition against slaughtering a *bechor* outside the Temple, one may still not slaughter it on *Yom Tov* because the new blemish was unanticipated before *Yom Tov*; thus the animal is still considered *muktzeh*.

רַבִּי שִׁמְעוֹן אוֹמֵר: כָּל שֶׁאֵין מוּמוֹ נִכָּר מִבְּעוֹד יוֹם, אֵין זֶה מִן הַמּוּכָן. — *R' Shimon says: In any case where the blemish was not detected* [by an expert] *before Yom Tov* [lit. *when it was yet day*], *it is not considered to be prepared.*

I.e., it is not ready to be designated as a blemished animal. R' Shimon holds that passing judgment on the validity of a blemish is equivalent to adjudicating a lawsuit (דָּן אֶת הַדִּין), an activity which is prohibited on *Yom Tov* (see below

[ה] **בְּהֵמָה** שֶׁמֵּתָה, לֹא יְזִיזֶנָּה מִמְּקוֹמָהּ.
וּמַעֲשֶׂה וְשָׁאֲלוּ אֶת רַבִּי טַרְפוֹן
עָלֶיהָ וְעַל הַחַלָּה שֶׁנִּטְמֵאָה. וְנִכְנַס לְבֵית הַמִּדְרָשׁ
וְשָׁאַל. וְאָמְרוּ לוֹ: ,,לֹא יְזִיזֵם מִמְּקוֹמָם."

יד אברהם

5:2). Therefore, if the blemish was not declared permanent before *Yom Tov*, it cannot be judged on *Yom Tov*.

The ruling against passing judgment on *Yom Tov* does not apply to other pronouncements in Rabbinical law. For example, if there is a question regarding the *kashrus* of a chicken, a rabbi may rule on it on *Yom Tov*. The rabbi's decision *per se* does not render the chicken kosher; it had been kosher all along. All the rabbi did was clarify the halachic status for the questioner who was not as well-versed in halachah as the rabbi. However, regarding a *bechor*, it is the expert's pronouncement which renders the animal unfit for sacrifice and, consequently, permissible for slaughter. If one slaughtered the animal before the pronouncement he is considered to have slaughtered an unblemished *bechor* and the meat may not be eaten (*Yoreh Deah* 310:1). Thus in effect the expert's ruling changes the status of the animal and is therefore prohibited on *Yom Tov* as adjudicating a lawsuit (*Mishnah*

Berurah 498:10 citing *Terumas HaDeshen* 54).

Tosafos (25b) comments that the phraseology אֵין זֶה מִן הַמּוּכָן, *it is not considered to be prepared*, suggests the concept of *muktzeh*. R' Shimon prohibits ruling on blemishes on *Yom Tov*. Therefore, if an expert were to examine a blemish on *Yom Tov* he would be transgressing a Rabbinical ban. And it is unreasonable to anticipate before *Yom Tov* that the expert will transgress this ban on the owner's behalf. Thus, the animal must be judged as unprepared, i.e., *muktzeh* because of a prohibition (מוּקְצֶה מֵחֲמַת אִיסּוּר), at the onset of *Yom Tov*. R' Yehudah, on the other hand, does not consider the *bechor* to be *muktzeh* since, in his opinion, ruling on the validity of a blemish is permissible on *Yom Tov*. Since the owner may have anticipated the expert's willingness to examine his animal on *Yom Tov*, the animal is considered prepared from before *Yom Tov*.

The halachah is in accordance with R' Shimon (*Orach Chaim* 498:8).

5.

בְּהֵמָה שֶׁמֵּתָה, לֹא יְזִיזֶנָּה מִמְּקוֹמָהּ. — *If an animal died* [lit. *an animal that died*], *one may not move it from its place* [on *Yom Tov*].

The carcass is considered *muktzeh* and therefore may not be moved.

The *Gemara* (27b) infers, from the juxtaposition of this case with that of *challah*, that the animal under discussion possessed some degree of sacredness, and that the ruling pronounced upon it here is

the consequence of its sacred status. The *Gemara* concludes that the mishnah refers to an animal that had been designated as a sacrifice. Now that it has died of natural causes it is considered totally useless, for as a consecrated object one may not derive any benefit from it; it cannot even be fed to dogs. Therefore it may not be moved, for like any object that has no use (e.g., sticks and stones) it is considered *muktzeh*.[1]

1. The option of redemption (פִּדְיוֹן) whereby the carcass will be rendered *chullin* (חוּלִין, *profane*) and fit for use as feed has no validity here: because (a) a sanctified animal can be redeemed only while it is alive; (b) one may not redeem sacred objects if the only use for these objects will be as animal food (אֵין פּוֹדִין אֶת הַקֳּדָשִׁים לְהַאֲכִילָן לִכְלָבִים); and (c) redeeming sacred objects is regarded as a business transaction and is forbidden on *Yom Tov* (*Rashi* 27b).

3
5

5. If an animal died, one may not move it from its place. There was an incident and they asked R' Tarfon about this matter and about *challah* which had contracted *tumah*-contamination. He entered the house of study and asked. They said to him, "He may not move them from their place."

YAD AVRAHAM

The *Gemara* (ibid.) adds that the inference forces one to conclude that if a non-sacred animal that was sick before *Yom Tov* and whose death was anticipated by its owner died on *Yom Tov*, it may be fed to the dogs. It is not considered *muktzeh* despite the fact that the animal had not been designated for this type of use before *Yom Tov* [when it had been reserved for human consumption] (see *Shabbos* 24:4). In the event that a healthy animal died unexpectedly on *Yom Tov*, its carcass is considered *muktzeh*, for as a healthy animal it was not considered designated for dog food at the onset of *Yom Tov*.[1]

וּמַעֲשֶׂה וְשָׁאֲלוּ אֶת רַבִּי טַרְפוֹן עָלֶיהָ
וְעַל הַחַלָּה שֶׁנִּטְמְאָה. — *There was an incident and they asked R' Tarfon about this matter and about challah which had contracted tumah-contamination.*

Challah is the portion which must be separated from the dough and given to a *Kohen* (*Numbers*

15:17-21; see above 1:6). *Challah* is subject to the same laws as *terumah*, the portion given to the *Kohen* from produce (*Challah* 1:9), and therefore it may not be eaten by a non-*Kohen*. If *challah* contracts *tumah*-contamination, it may not be eaten at all and must be burned.

Actually even *challah* which is *tamei* is not entirely useless, for since it must be burned it can be used as fuel. Nevertheless it is considered *muktzeh*, for the halachah states: אֵין שׂוֹרְפִין קָדָשִׁים בְּיוֹם טוֹב, *one may not burn consecrated objects* [such as contaminated *terumah* or *challah*] *on Yom Tov* (Rashi).[2]

וְנִכְנַס לְבֵית הַמִּדְרָשׁ וְשָׁאַל. וְאָמְרוּ לוֹ:
,,לֹא יְזִיזֵם מִמְּקוֹמָם.'' — *He entered the house of study and asked. They* [the Sages there] *said to him, "He may not move them* [the dead animal and the *challah*] *from their place."*

Tosafos Yeshanim (27b) explains

---

1. The opinion given above is one of two views presented in the *Gemara*. A conflicting opinion maintains that according to R' Shimon, whose rulings regarding *muktzeh* tend to be lenient (in comparison with those of R' Yehudah), even the carcass of an animal whose death was not anticipated is not *muktzeh*. Consequently the mishnah must not (in this view) refer exclusively to a deathly sick animal for it may represent R' Shimon's view (according to R' Yehudah such a carcass is surely *muktzeh*). Furthermore there is debate among the *Rishonim* (see *Rif* with *Ran*; *Rambam, Hil. Yom Tov* 2:16 and 1:17; *HaMaor, Rashba* and *Meiri*) whether R' Yehudah would consider the carcass of an animal deathly ill prior to *Yom Tov muktzeh*. If he does not consider it *muktzeh* the statement of the mishnah can be interpreted to agree with R' Yehudah's view. For a discussion of the halachah on these points see *Orach Chaim* 518:6 with *Mishnah Berurah* and *Beur Halachah*.

2. *Rashi* (27b) considers burning consecrated objects as הַבְעָרָה שֶׁלֹא לְצוֹרֶךְ, *burning without a* [Yom Tov] *need*.

Tosafos elaborates that the benefit that may be derived from the burning of *terumah* is considered secondary to the fulfillment of the precept that the burning accomplishes. Primarily this act is regarded as burning for sacred purposes rather than for the sake of the festival. Only a labor that fulfills a mundane holiday need is permitted on *Yom Tov*, but labor performed for the exclusive benefit of the sacred is not permitted. [See commentary to 2:4, s.v. וּבֵית הִלֵּל אוֹמְרִים.]

בֵּיצָה [ו] **אֵין** נִמְנִין עַל הַבְּהֵמָה לְכַתְּחִלָּה בְּיוֹם טוֹב.
אֲבָל נִמְנִין עָלֶיהָ מֵעֶרֶב יוֹם טוֹב
וְשׁוֹחֲטִין וּמְחַלְּקִין בֵּינֵיהֶן.

יד אברהם

that R' Tarfon thought that perhaps these two objects may be moved because of the reverence due holy objects. Leaving a dead sacrificial animal or contaminated *challah* in an open area might otherwise be considered a desecration of consecrated objects.

6.

Having completed the discussion of the *halachos* that apply to the various aspects of *trapping and *slaughtering animals on *Yom Tov*, the next three mishnayos speak of buying and selling the meat on *Yom Tov*. Although the purchase of meat is used as an illustration, the same laws apply to buying any article on the festival.

The basis of these laws, the prohibition against conducting business on *Yom Tov*, was apparently so well-known that there was no need to mention it. Only certain details of the law are touched upon. *Rashi* (27b) points out that this prohibition dates to ancient times, and is already mentioned in the Bible. At the end of *Nechemiah* (13:15-18) the Prophet is appalled at the desecration of the Sabbath in the Jerusalem of his times through commerce, and registers his strong protest. As a source for this prohibition, *Rashi* (37a) cites the verse in *Isaiah* (58:13) that states: *And you shall honor* [the Sabbath by] *not pursuing your business nor speaking about it*. In an alternate explanation, *Rashi* (loc. cit.) describes the prohibition against commerce on the Sabbath and festivals as a Rabbinical injunction, instituted lest a person may record business transactions in *writing.

Commerce is defined as the exchange of money or its equivalent for any commodity; buying on credit is permitted on *Yom Tov*. However, as the following mishnah makes clear, price may not be mentioned explicitly and the transaction must be based on mutual trust (see *Mishnah Berurah* 500:1; see also *comm.* to 3:7).

אֵין נִמְנִין עַל הַבְּהֵמָה — *We may not be counted ... for* [the meat of] *an animal*

The inference here is to a procedure, apparently commonplace in the times of the mishnah, whereby a number of people joined together [much the same as today's consumer cooperatives] to purchase the meat of an animal as a group. For example, a group of ten people would arrange for a butcher to slaughter an animal for their group.

The lesson of the mishnah is that such a group may not be formed on *Yom Tov*. The Gemara (27b) comments that this ban is in effect only if a price is specified, e.g., they say to the butcher, "We will take this animal which is worth so much and so much. Each of us will pay one tenth of the price" (from *Rav, Rambam*).

Tosefta (3:4 cited partially in *Gem.*) gives an illustration of the mishnah's law on an individual basis: A person may not approach a butcher and say, 'I will take [e.g.] ten dollars

6. **W**e may not be counted initially for [the meat of] an animal on *Yom Tov*. But we may be counted for it[s meat] prior to *Yom Tov*, and slaughter and apportion [it] among ourselves.

worth of meat from the animal you are going to slaughter.' The Tosefta adds that he may, however, say that he will take a third or any fraction of the animal, as long as money is not discussed. [Thus the mishnah's law simply stated is that one may not obtain meat from a butcher if a price is specified. Perhaps in the time of the mishnah, it was not practical to slaughter an animal unless one had advance commitments to purchase the meat of the entire animal. The mishnah chose the procedure then commonly used in meat purchasing to illustrate its central point — the ban on quoting prices on *Yom Tov* for any transaction performed on that day.]

Rashba (*Avodas HaKodesh* 2:4, and *Chiddushim*) understands that the mishnah prohibits forming a group for the purpose of purchasing an animal even where no price is mentioned. The mere forming of a group is a profane act (מַעֲשֶׂה חֹל) not in consonance with the spirit of the holiness and the festiveness which should pervade *Yom Tov* and is consequently banned. Thus our mishnah refers, not to commerce on *Yom Tov per se*, but to related activities. *Mishnah Berurah* (*Beur Halachah* to *Orach Chaim* 500:1) comments that although on the surface this appears to be the plain meaning of the mishnah, which is understood in this manner by the *Talmud Yerushalmi*, it is nevertheless not accepted as halachah by the *Poskim* because it contradicts the interpretation given this mishnah in the *Talmud Bavli* (here).

לְבַתְּחִלָּה בְּיוֹם טוֹב. — *initially ... on Yom Tov.*

[I.e., an agreement to participate

in a purchase specifying an amount of money may not be entered into on *Yom Tov.*]

[The commentaries do not explain what is added to the meaning of the mishnah with the word לְבַתְּחִלָּה (or בַּתְּחִלָּה in some versions), *initially*. Perhaps it excludes from the injunction an instance where the price (and the participants' share in it) had been agreed upon prior to *Yom Tov*. This exclusion is stated explicitly in the following clause of the mishnah: 'But we may be counted for it[s meat] prior to *Yom Tov*,' but it is within character for the mishnah to hint at a ruling which is stated explicitly further (see *Tos. Shabbos* 53a).][1]

אֲבָל נִמְנִין עָלֶיהָ מֵעֶרֶב יוֹם טוֹב — *But we may be counted for it[s meat] prior to Yom Tov,*

At first glance the statement that *we may be counted ... prior to Yom Tov* is puzzling. Surely, this act may be performed before *Yom Tov* (see *Tiferes Yisrael*, *Boaz* 2). However, it seems that the thrust of the statement lies in, *and slaughter and apportion ...* One might think that if the price has already been agreed upon, albeit before *Yom Tov*, then acquisition of the meat on *Yom Tov* is viewed as commerce, despite the fact that no mention of money is made at the time

---

1. According to those who omit the clause, 'But we may be counted for its meat prior to *Yom Tov*' (see below) the insertion of the word, 'initially,' assumes greater importance. It could have been thought that one may slaughter an animal on *Yom Tov* only if no previous agreement stipulating the price existed. Where such an agreement had been entered into, the subsequent slaughter and apportionment of the meat could be viewed as the consummation of a business deal and prohibited.

The Talmud *Yerushalmi* (here) deduces an additional point from the word לְבַתְּחִלָּה, *initially*. If five people had been counted prior to *Yom Tov* to participate in the purchase of an animal they may admit additional members to their group on *Yom Tov* (as long as money is not discussed; see *Chiddushei HaRashba* here). However, as pointed out by *Beur Halachah* (500:1) apparently the Talmud *Bavli* disagrees with this interpretation.

רַבִּי יְהוּדָה אוֹמֵר: שׁוֹקֵל אָדָם בָּשָׂר כְּנֶגֶד הַכְּלִי
אוֹ כְּנֶגֶד הַקּוֹפִיץ. וַחֲכָמִים אוֹמְרִים: אֵין מַשְׁגִּיחִין
בְּכַף מֹאזְנַיִם כָּל עִקָּר.

[ז] אֵין מַשְׁחִיזִין אֶת הַסַּכִּין בְּיוֹם טוֹב, אֲבָל
מַשִּׂיאָהּ עַל גַּבֵּי חֲבֶרְתָּהּ.

יד אברהם

of acquisition.[1]

It seems that many of the early commentators — Or Zarua (2:357), Rashi (27b; see Tif. Yis., Boaz 3), R' Betzalel Ashkenazi (cited by Meleches Shlomo) — did not have the phrase אֲבָל נִמְנִין עָלֶיהָ מֵעֶרֶב יוֹם טוֹב, But we may be counted for it prior to Yom Tov, in their texts. However, Rambam (see ed. Kafich) and Meiri include this phrase. It seems to have been in R' Chananel's version also.

וְשׁוֹחֲטִין וּמְחַלְּקִין בֵּינֵיהֶן. — and slaughter and apportion [it] among ourselves [lit. themselves].

The allocation of the portions of meat to the individual members of the group may take place on Yom Tov. We are not afraid that in the course of the apportionment they might measure, weigh, or assess the meat monetarily.

The Talmud (Shabbos 149a) states that group members who are not generous (הַמַּקְפִּידִים עַל זֶה) towards one another are in danger (see Tosafos there; Beis Yosef toward end of Orach Chaim 517) of transgressing [the prohibitions of] measuring, weighing, uniting, lending and repaying on Yom Tov … The mishnah teaches that in ordinary cases this apprehension is not relevant.

According to some early commentators (see above s.v. אֲבָל) the mishnah reads: אֵין נִמְנִין עַל הַבְּהֵמָה לְכַתְּחִלָּה בְּיוֹם טוֹב, אֲבָל שׁוֹחֲטִין וּמְחַלְּקִין בֵּינֵיהֶן, we may not be counted initially for [the meat of] an animal

on Yom Tov, but we may slaughter and apportion [it] among ourselves. The final clause (but … ourselves) takes on a new meaning in this version. It refers to the permissibility for a group to approach a butcher on Yom Tov and to arrange for him to slaughter an animal for them without mentioning any price. Instead, they rely upon the butcher's fairness in fixing the price after Yom Tov. This interpretation is reflected by Rashi (27b), whose comment on the word אֲבָל, but, reads: 'The butcher slaughters without fixing a price, and they [the group members] apportion [the meat] among themselves. On the next day, he [the butcher] will fix its price.'

רַבִּי יְהוּדָה אוֹמֵר: שׁוֹקֵל אָדָם בָּשָׂר כְּנֶגֶד הַכְּלִי אוֹ כְּנֶגֶד הַקּוֹפִיץ. — R' Yehudah says: A person may weigh meat against a utensil or against a chopper.

One may not use weights to weigh meat on Yom Tov in the ordinary fashion, because this is considered a weekday activity. One may, however, use some other object as a standard of weight. Thus, he can ascertain the exact weight of the meat by knowing the weight of the object against which it had been weighed (Rav; Rashi).

וַחֲכָמִים אוֹמְרִים: אֵין מַשְׁגִּיחִין בְּכַף מֹאזְנַיִם כָּל עִקָּר. — But the Sages say: We may not use [lit. pay attention

1. Tiferes Yisrael suggests that if the group was formed before Yom Tov the mishnah wishes to permit the mention of money at the time of acquisition (on Yom Tov) and even the calculation of each person's share in the payments, for the basic price has already been established before Yom Tov. However, the halachic implications of this interpretation, i.e., that one may make mention of a price on Yom Tov and the Sabbath if the price is already known and set, is the subject of disagreement between halachic authorities in Shulchan Aruch (Orach Chaim 323:4).

R' Yehudah says: A person may weigh meat against a utensil or against a chopper. But the Sages say: We may not use a scale at all.

7. **W**e may not sharpen the knife on *Yom Tov*, but we may sharpen one against the other.

YAD AVRAHAM

to] *a scale at all.*

Any form of weighing, even in the unusual and indirect manner permitted by R' Yehudah, is considered by the Sages as inconsistent with the sanctity of *Yom Tov*.

The *Gemara* (28a) comments that the

emphasis on the phrase כָּל עִקָּר, *at all*, indicates that not only is any manner of weighing prohibited, but if the scale is hanging on its p̄g, it may not even be used as a container to safeguard the meat from mice.

The opinion of the Sages is accepted as halachah (*Rambam, Hil. Yom Tov* 4:20; *Orach Chaim* 500:2).

7.

In a typical tangential discussion, the mishnah digresses from the purchase of meat to the sharpening of knives with which to slaughter the animal and butcher its meat.

Although the law applies to all cutting instruments, the mishnah states this law in a section dealing with butchers' knives, for butchers must sharpen their knives frequently. Thus this mishnah is not entirely out of place among the laws pertaining to purchases made on *Yom Tov*. The mishnah outlines how the knife to be used for slaughter may, or may not, be sharpened and then returns to the discussions about purchasing meat (*Rashba*).

אֵין מַשְׁחִיזִין אֶת הַסַּכִּין בְּיוֹם טוֹב, — *We may not sharpen the knife* [on a whetstone (*Rav*)] *on Yom Tov,*

The dispensation that allows otherwise forbidden labor to be performed for food preparation applies only to labor involved directly in

preparing the food itself (such as *slaughtering, *cooking). Labor related to the preliminary stages of food preparation, such as the ones involved in the repairing of utensils needed for food preparation, are considered מַכְשִׁירֵי אוֹכֶל נֶפֶשׁ, *preliminaries for food preparation*, and are forbidden. Sharpening a knife is an example of the latter category of labor and is prohibited on *Yom Tov*.[1]

The *Gemara* (28b) notes that R' Yehudah disagrees with the principle of the mishnah and permits even preliminary food preparation if they could not have been done before *Yom Tov* (אִי אֶפְשָׁר לַעֲשׂוֹתָן מֵעֶרֶב יוֹם טוֹב), e.g., fixing a utensil that was damaged on *Yom Tov*. Accordingly, R' Yehudah would permit sharpening a knife that became dulled or chipped on *Yom Tov*.

See *Shulchan Aruch, Orach Chaim* 509:1 (with *Beur Halachah*, s.v. אותו and וה׳ה) and 495:1 for a dispute concerning which opinion is the accepted halachah.

אֲבָל מַשִּׁיאָה עַל גַּבֵּי חֲבֶרְתָּה. — *but we may sharpen one against the other.*

---

1. *Rashi* (28a) and *Meiri* indicate that sharpening a knife is classified as מְתַקֵּן, *perfecting*, which is a subcategory of the *melachah* of *striking the final blow (see General Introduction). It is not clear, however, if it is labor on a Scriptural level or only on a Rabbinic level (*Rosh Yosef* vacillates on this question). *Pri Megadim* (*Mishbetzos Zahav* 323:8) suggests that

לֹא יֹאמַר אָדָם לְטַבָּח: „שְׁקֹל לִי בְּדִינָר בָּשָׂר."
אֲבָל שׁוֹחֵט וּמְחַלְּקִים בֵּינֵיהֶם.

[ח] **אוֹמֵר** אָדָם לַחֲבֵרוֹ: „מַלֵּא לִי כְלִי זֶה."
אֲבָל לֹא בְמִדָּה.
רַבִּי יְהוּדָה אוֹמֵר: אִם הָיָה כְּלִי שֶׁל מִדָּה, לֹא
יְמַלְאֶנּוּ.

יד אברהם

Because this is a deviation (שִׁנּוּי) from the usual method (Rav; Rashi).[1]

[The rendering מַשִׁיאָה, sharpen, is based on Rashi to Genesis 27:3 (see ArtScroll comm. there), and Bereishis Rabbah 65:13. However, in the Gemara (28a) there is a difference of opinion whether one may actually sharpen one knife upon another. According to one view he may only rub one knife against another to remove surface film (שְׁמֻנּוּנִית) from it. In this opinion one is permitted only to seemingly sharpen one against another (see also Chasam Sofer Chiddushim I; Teshuvos Yoreh Deah 15). See Shulchan Aruch (Orach Chaim 509:2).]

לֹא יֹאמַר אָדָם לְטַבָּח: „שְׁקֹל לִי בְּדִינָר בָּשָׂר." — *A person may not say to a*

butcher [on Yom Tov], "Weigh me out a dinar's worth of meat."

By specifying a *dinar's worth* he is mentioning money which is forbidden in a transaction taking place on Yom Tov (Rashi).

Apparently the mishnah is not concerned with the weighing, but rather with the mention of a price. In view of the statement in mishnah 6 that *they may not use a scale at all*, why is there no prohibition on the act of weighing?

Rosh Yosef suggests that here no scale or other device was used. The butcher merely estimates the weight of the meat by picking it up in his hand.[2]

אֲבָל שׁוֹחֵט וּמְחַלְּקִים בֵּינֵיהֶם. — *But he*

sharpening knives comes under *smoothing.

Pnei Yehoshua suggests a novel approach to *Rashi's* comments on the mishnah. Sharpening on a whetstone is prohibited because this is a weekday activity (עוֹבְדָא דְחוֹל). Consequently a knife may be sharpened upon another, because since this method is a departure from the usual procedure, it bears no semblance to weekday activities. However, this approach is incompatible with the understanding conveyed by most (or all) of the early commentators (see *Rif* and *Rosh*) who assume (based upon their understanding of the *Gemara*) that R' Yehudah (see below) does not concur with the ruling of the mishnah.

1. The language suggests that labor performed for utensils used in food preparation even where no Scriptural dispensation applies (e.g., it was possible to repair the utensil prior to Yom Tov, or according to the view of the Sages who prohibit all utensil repair), is nevertheless permitted when performed with a 'deviation' (see also in *Chiddushei HaRashba* and *Meiri*). However this writer has not found a blanket dispensation for utensil repair when performed with a 'deviation' mentioned in the codes or later authorities. According to *Pnei Yehoshua's* (cited in preceding footnote) interpretation of *Rashi's* view no such deduction can be made (but *Meiri* and *Rashba's* words are not amenable to *Pnei Yehoshua's* interpretation).

2. *Rosh Yosef* points out that *Ran* (28a) prohibits even this (see *Orach Chaim* 500:2). However *Ran's* version of the mishnah reads מָכוּר ... לֹא יֹאמַר אָדָם *a person may not say ... sell ...* (this is how the mishnah reads in *Yerushalmi* and in the Kafich edition of *Rambam's* commentary; see *Meleches Shlomo* and *Shinuyei Nuschaos*). *Rambam* (Hil. Yom Tov 4:21), in formulating this mishnah, says: *A person should not say to a butcher give me ...* In this version weighing is not mentioned in the mishnah at all.

3
8

A person may not say to a butcher, "Weigh me out a dinar's worth of meat." But he may slaughter [an animal] and they may apportion [the meat] among themselves.

8. **A** person may say to his friend, "Fill up this vessel for me." But not with a measure.

R' Yehudah says: If it is a measuring vessel, he may not fill it.

may slaughter [an animal] and they may apportion [the meat] among themselves.

The butcher may provide his customers with meat only in the manner mentioned in mishnah 6, i.e., to give the animal over to a group which is large enough to use a whole animal and, after slaughtering it, they may apportion it among themselves without mentioning the cost of each part.

[As already mentioned (mishnah 6), it was not practical for a butcher to slaughter an animal unless he had orders for all or most of its meat. It seems that the usual procedure was for the butchers to accept as many orders for meat on a monetary basis (e.g., a dinar's worth of meat) as he thought were sufficient to cover his investment. Thus, if people are not permitted to order on a monetary basis on *Yom Tov*, the butcher is deprived of his

usual method of calculation, and must seek other methods of apportionment if he is to slaughter at all. Although the mishnah gives the method mentioned previously (mishnah 6) as an alternative, this is, needless to say, not the only alternative available. Since the primary objection is the mention of money, a person may approach a butcher and order a quarter (or any fraction) of an animal (*Gem.* 28b) and avoid the mention of money (suggested by *Rashi* 28b).

Tosefos Yom Tov poses the obvious question: What is said in this mishnah that is not already included in mishnah 6? *Rosh Yosef* points out that in effect mishnah 6 only says that a group of people (or one person) may not approach a butcher and negotiate a price with him. But here a single person approaches the butcher and asks him to set aside a dinar's worth of meat. No price has been negotiated. Money has only been mentioned as a unit of measurement. This mishnah teaches that the mention of money is prohibited in this context too (see also *Shoshanim L'David*).

8.

אוֹמֵר אָדָם לַחֲבֵרוֹ: — *A person may say to his friend* [on Yom Tov],

[This refers to a grocer who trusts that he will be paid, though no mention of money has been made.]

"מַלֵּא לִי כְּלִי זֶה,, — *"Fill up this vessel for me."*

[Even if the volume of the vessel is known and it is usually used as a measure.]

אֲבָל לֹא בְמִדָּה. — *But not with a*

measure [i.e., he should not ask the grocer to give him a certain measure of an item (e.g., he may not ask for a quart of honey)].

רַבִּי יְהוּדָה אוֹמֵר: אִם הָיָה כְּלִי שֶׁל מִדָּה, לֹא יְמַלְאֶנּוּ. — *R' Yehudah says: If it is* [lit. *was*] *a measuring vessel, he may not fill it.*

[Even if he merely said to the grocer, "Fill up this vessel," without mentioning the amount it measures.]

מַעֲשֶׂה בְּאַבָּא שָׁאוּל בֶּן בָּטְנִית שֶׁהָיָה מְמַלֵּא מְדּוֹתָיו מֵעֶרֶב יוֹם טוֹב וְנוֹתְנָן לַלְּקוֹחוֹת בְּיוֹם טוֹב.

אַבָּא שָׁאוּל אוֹמֵר: אַף בַּמּוֹעֵד עוֹשֶׂה כֵן, מִפְּנֵי בֵּרוּרֵי הַמִּדּוֹת.

וַחֲכָמִים אוֹמְרִים: אַף בַּחֹל עוֹשֶׂה כֵן, מִפְּנֵי מִצּוּי הַמִּדּוֹת.

הוֹלֵךְ אָדָם אֵצֶל חֶנְוָנִי הָרָגִיל אֶצְלוֹ, וְאוֹמֵר לוֹ: ,,תֶּן לִי בֵיצִים וֶאֱגוֹזִים בְּמִנְיָן," שֶׁכֵּן דֶּרֶךְ בַּעַל הַבַּיִת לִהְיוֹת מוֹנֶה בְּתוֹךְ בֵּיתוֹ.

יד אברהם

R' Yehudah's opinion is not accepted as halachah (*Orach Chaim* 323:1; see also there, paragraph 4, with *Mishnah Berurah*).

The above commentary is based on the halachically accepted opinion of Rava (*Gem.* 29a). *Rav's* commentary here is based on Shmuel's (halachically unaccepted) opinion (ibid.). In this view the *Tanna kamma* forbids the use of a vessel which has already been used as a measure and only permits the use of a vessel that has been designated as a measure but has not yet been used in this way. The words of the *Tanna kamma* are interpreted as follows: *A person may say to his friend: 'Fill up this vessel* [a vessel whose volume is known and which has been designated as a measure but not yet used in this capacity] *for me.'* But not *with a measure* [he may not ask his friend to fill up a vessel which has already been used as a measure]. R' Yehudah disagrees and maintains that even *if it was* [only designated as] *a measuring vessel* although it has not yet been used for this purpose, one may not ask to have it filled.

מַעֲשֶׂה בְּאַבָּא שָׁאוּל בֶּן בָּטְנִית — *It happened that Abba Shaul ben Batnis*

[A *Tanna* mentioned elsewhere in the Talmud (see *Pesachim* 57a).]

שֶׁהָיָה מְמַלֵּא מְדּוֹתָיו מֵעֶרֶב יוֹם טוֹב — *filled his* וְנוֹתְנָן לַלְּקוֹחוֹת בְּיוֹם טוֹב.

measures before Yom Tov and gave them to his customers on Yom Tov.

[In so doing, he avoided the problem of measuring on Yom Tov. R' Yehudah cites Abba Shaul's conduct as support of his own opinion that measuring is prohibited on the festival (even when no mention is made of the quantity desired).]

-- אַבָּא שָׁאוּל אוֹמֵר: אַף בַּמּוֹעֵד עוֹשֶׂה כֵן, *Abba Shaul says: Even during Chol HaMoed* [when many labors may be performed] *he did so,*

Abba Shaul [not the same *Tanna* as Abba Shaul ben Batnis] disputes R' Yehudah's proof based upon Abba Shaul ben Batnis filling the measures before *Yom Tov*, noting that even during *Chol HaMoed* he would pre-fill his measures. [Therefore, his conduct cannot have been based on a prohibition against filling up a measure on *Yom Tov*, because on *Chol HaMoed* measuring is permitted.]

מִפְּנֵי בֵּרוּרֵי הַמִּדּוֹת. — *for the correctness* [lit. *clearness*] *of the measures.*

It happened that Abba Shaul ben Batnis filled his measures before *Yom Tov* and gave them to his customers on *Yom Tov*.

Abba Shaul says: Even during *Chol HaMoed* he did so, for the correctness of the measures.

The Sages say: Even on weekdays he did so, to drain the measures.

A person may go to a shopkeeper with whom he is familiar and say to him, "Give me a number of eggs or nuts," for this is the mode of a private person to count off in his home.

I.e., Abba Shaul's action was based on considerations of honesty rather than prohibitions of *Yom Tov*. When one spills from a large container into a measure, foam forms on top of the measure. In order to measure correctly, one must wait for the foam to subside. During *Chol HaMoed* when people did not work, many would come to Abba Shaul with their Torah questions. Thus, he could not spend as much time as was necessary to give an honest measure. To insure the accuracy of his measures, he would fill them the night before (*Rav; Gem.* 29b).

וַחֲכָמִים אוֹמְרִים: אַף בְּחֹל עוֹשֶׂה כֵן, מִפְּנֵי מִצּוּי הַמִּדּוֹת. — *The Sages say: Even on weekdays he did so, to drain the measures.*

It was the norm to use a measure to pour into the vessel in which the liquid was sold. Some liquids, such as oil, tend to cling to the walls of the measure because of their viscosity. In order to give an honest

measure, he suspended the measures overnight above the vessels to be sure to drain the last drops from the measures (*Rav; Rashi*).

הוֹלֵךְ אָדָם אֵצֶל חֶנְוָנִי הָרָגִיל אֶצְלוֹ, — *A person may go to a shopkeeper with whom he is familiar* [and who will trust him to pay after *Yom Tov*]

וְאוֹמֵר לוֹ: ,,תֶּן לִי בֵיצִים וֶאֱגוֹזִים בְּמִנְיָן,'' — *and say to him* [on *Yom Tov*], *"Give me a* [specific] *number of eggs or nuts,"*

[Although he specifies a quantity, this is not considered דֶּרֶךְ מֶקַח וּמִמְכָּר, *the usual manner of commerce.*]

שֶׁכֵּן דֶּרֶךְ בַּעַל הַבַּיִת לִהְיוֹת מוֹנֶה בְּתוֹךְ בֵּיתוֹ. — *for this is the mode of a private person* [lit. home owner] *to count off* [items] *in his home.*

[Even a private person counts his items in his home. Weighing or measuring food, by contrast, is a procedure that is associated with commerce and is therefore prohibited.]

[א] **הַמֵּבִיא** כַּדֵּי יַיִן מִמָּקוֹם לְמָקוֹם לֹא יְבִיאֵם בְּסַל וּבְקֻפָּה, אֲבָל מֵבִיא הוּא עַל כְּתֵפוֹ אוֹ לְפָנָיו. וְכֵן הַמּוֹלִיךְ אֶת הַתֶּבֶן לֹא יַפְשִׁיל אֶת הַקֻּפָּה לַאֲחוֹרָיו, אֲבָל מְבִיאָה הוּא בְּיָדוֹ.

וּמַתְחִילִין בַּעֲרֵמַת הַתֶּבֶן, אֲבָל לֹא בְּעֵצִים שֶׁבַּמֻּקְצֶה.

יד אברהם

Chapter 4

1.

As we have seen at the end of the preceding chapter, the Sages were concerned that activities on *Yom Tov* should not resemble the weekday manner of conducting commerce. The next mishnah begins with two illustrations of actions that must not be performed in their usual manner on *Yom Tov*, in order to distinguish them from weekday activities.

הַמֵּבִיא כַּדֵּי יַיִן — *One who carries* [lit. *brings*] *pitchers of wine*

Although one certainly is allowed to carry on *Yom Tov*, the moving of pitchers of wine must not be done in a manner that resembles the large scale transportation of the weekday. The mishnah refers to one who transports these pitchers on the street where his actions can readily be observed by others. Carrying pitchers indoors within the confines of the home is not subject to any restrictions *(Tos. Yom Tov, Beis Yosef, Orach Chaim 510; cf. Tosafos 29b; see Rama, Mishnah Berurah, Sha'ar HaTziyun 510:8; cf. Rosh Yosef).*

מִמָּקוֹם לְמָקוֹם — *from place to place*

Within the area that extends two thousand cubits in each direction from one's place of dwelling (תְּחוּם) within which one is permitted to walk on the Sabbath and *Yom Tov*[1] *(Rashi; Rav).*

לֹא יְבִיאֵם בְּסַל וּבְקֻפָּה, — *(he) may not carry them in a basket or in a hamper,*

Pitchers of wine were usually transported in large baskets that

---

1. One is Rabbinically prohibited from walking on the Sabbath or *Yom Tov* more than two thousand cubits away from his מְקוֹם שְׁבִיתָה, *place of dwelling.* This distance is known as the תְּחוּם שַׁבָּת, [techum] *Sabbath boundary.* The place of dwelling is defined as the place in which he found himself at the onset of the Sabbath regardless of whether or not that is his usual dwelling. If that place was: (a) a city, his place of dwelling is considered to be the entire city* and he may, therefore, walk two thousand cubits in any direction from the city limits; (b) a house out in the open* or any enclosed* encampment, his place of dwelling is considered to be the entire area within the walls and he may therefore walk two thousand cubits from the walls of his house or camp; (c) an unenclosed camp or open area in which he happened to be at the onset of the Sabbath, his place of dwelling is considered to be a square eight cubits by eight cubits with himself at the center and he may walk two thousand cubits from there. *For the halachic definitions of these terms, see *Shulchan Aruch, Orach Chaim* 397-398.

1. **O**ne who carries pitchers of wine from place to place may not carry them in a basket or in a hamper, but he may carry [them] upon his shoulder or in front of himself. Similarly, one who transports straw may not lower the hamper upon his back, but he may carry it in his hand.

We may begin using a stack of straw, but not wood which is in a backyard.

YAD AVRAHAM

held a quantity of small containers [a modern day parallel would be a case of bottles].

Carrying baskets of wine flasks in public appears to be a weekday activity and, therefore, is not compatible with the festivity of Yom Tov [even if the wine is actually needed for Yom Tov] (Rav; Rashi).

אֲבָל מֵבִיא הוּא עַל כְּתֵפוֹ אוֹ לְפָנָיו. — but he may carry [them] upon his shoulder or in front of himself [in his hand (Rashi)].

When one carries in this fashion, it is evident to the bystander that only food for the Yom Tov meal is being transported (Rav; Rashi).

The determining factor is the mode of carrying, not the amount of jars carried. Accordingly, one may not carry even one jar in a basket, but he can carry as many as possible in his hands (Tos. Yom Tov; see also Mishnah Berurah 510:28, Sha'ar HaTziyun; cf. Shitah Mekubetzes).

וְכֵן הַמּוֹלִיךְ אֶת הַתֶּבֶן — Similarly, one who transports straw

From the field to his house, for either animal feed or fuel (Rav; Rashi).

In the previous clause where the subject of discussion was the bringing of wine, the mishnah uses the verb הַמֵּבִיא, which connotes bringing something into the home. Here, in discussing straw, which is usually taken to a stable, the verb הַמּוֹלִיךְ, he who transports, is more appropriate (Shitah Mekubetzes).

לֹא יַפְשִׁיל אֶת הַקֻּפָּה לַאֲחוֹרָיו, — may not lower the hamper upon his back,

Because this would give the appearance of preparing to carry many loads or to carry this one for a long distance, in the manner that he would do on a weekday. This would debase the sanctity of Yom Tov (Rashi).

אֲבָל מְבִיאָהּ הוּא בְיָדוֹ. — but he may carry it in his hand.

Carrying in this unusual manner makes it clear that he is carrying a small amount for immediate use on Yom Tov.

[If the straw is to be used as fuel, there are no other restrictions on its transportation. However, if the straw is being transported for animal fodder then one may not perform the labor of *transporting from a private domain to a public domain (or a length of four cubits in a public domain) in moving it, for labor is permitted on Yom Tov only for human need and not for animals (see Gem. 21b; Tos.; Orach Chaim 512:3; cf. Yerushalmi; Ritva cited in Shitah Mekubetzes).

וּמַתְחִילִין בַּעֲרֵמַת הַתֶּבֶן, — (And) we may begin using a stack of straw,

I.e., we may take some straw from a stack which had been not been used before Yom Tov.

Even though this stack had not been designated for use before Yom Tov (i.e., it was kept in a storage area and was not intended for use in the near future), and the owner of

[ב] **אֵין** נוֹטְלִין עֵצִים מִן הַסֻּכָּה, אֶלָּא מִן הַסָּמוּךְ לָהּ. מְבִיאִין עֵצִים מִן הַשָּׂדֶה מִן הַמְכֻנָּס; וּמִן הַקַּרְפֵּף, אֲפִלּוּ מִן הַמְפֻזָּר.

this hay would not, usually, take hay for fuel from this stack, one may nevertheless use it for fuel on *Yom Tov (Rav; Rashi).*

This explanation of *Rav* and *Rashi* follows an interpretation mentioned in the *Gemara* (30a), according to which the haystack in our mishnah is of the type that would be considered *muktzeh* according to R' Yehudah, who regards any article not specifically designated for *Yom Tov* use as *muktzeh.* Accordingly, our mishnah, which allows the use of straw on *Yom Tov* from a previously unused and undesignated haystack, follows R' Shimon's opinion that this is not considered *muktzeh.* In citing this explanation of the mishnah *Rashi* is consistent with his view (33a) that on *Yom Tov* the halachah follows R' Shimon.

In another interpretation offered by the *Gemara* (cited by *Rambam* in his commentary), the straw in our mishnah was rotted and thorny and as a result was fit neither for animal fodder nor for use in cement for building. Therefore, it may be used for fuel even according to R' Yehudah, for it is not designated for storage and is not *muktzeh.* *Rambam,* too, is consistent with his view (*Hil. Yom Tov* 1:17) that on *Yom Tov* the halachah follows R' Yehudah regarding *muktzeh.*

Shulchan Aruch (Orach Chaim 517:7) rules that one may start on a haystack only if the straw is rotten and is mixed with thorns. However, *Mishnah Berurah* points out that this follows R' Yosef Karo's opinion elsewhere (ibid. 495:4) that on *Yom Tov* we rule in accordance with R' Yehudah. *Rama,* who disagrees and rules like R' Shimon, would surely disagree here as well.

אֲבָל לֹא בְּעֵצִים שֶׁבְּמֻקְצָה. — *but not wood which is in a backyard.*

The infrequently used space behind houses was called *muktzeh.* [In Talmudic times the entrance to a

house was generally through the חָצֵר, *courtyard,* an area which was also in constant use due to its convenient location. The backyard, however, because it was seldom entered was only suitable for storage.] Wood stored in this area is presumed to be intended for use in construction. This wood may not be used because it is considered מְקְצֶה מַחֲמַת חֶסְרוֹן כִּיס, *muktzeh due to monetary loss* [i.e., since lumber reserved for construction is generally too valuable to be used as fuel, using it on *Yom Tov* for firewood would constitute a financial loss]. Even R' Shimon agrees that such *muktzeh* is prohibited *(Rav).*

Here, as in the previous segment of the mishnah, two interpretations are given in the *Gemara* (30a). The interpretation cited by *Rav* follows R' Shimon's view according to which wood would not be considered *muktzeh* unless it was lumber designated for construction. According to the interpretation that our mishnah follows R' Yehudah's opinion, the wood referred to here may even be a regular pile of firewood, which, because it is stored in a place reserved for objects set aside for later use, is *muktzeh,* like anything kept in a storage place.

Rambam (Hil. Yom Tov 2:11), in consonance with his decision (ibid. 1:17) that on *Yom Tov* the halachah follows R' Yehudah, prohibits the use of any wood held in storage.

[Surprisingly, R' Yosef Karo fails to rule explicitly in this matter, although the prohibition against using stored materials is implicit in his words (see *Orach Chaim* 518:7, *Mishnah Berurah* 34; *Rama* 495:4). According to *Rama's* ruling, stored materials may be used (see *Mishnah Berurah* 495:18 and 518:35).]

2. We may not detach wood from a hut, except for what adjoins it.

We may carry in wood from a field from that which has been gathered; but from an enclosure, even from what is scattered.

2.

The mishnah continues to elaborate upon laws pertaining to the use of wood on *Yom Tov*.

אֵין נוֹטְלִין עֵצִים מִן הַסֻּכָּה, — *We may not detach wood from a hut* [on *Yom Tov*],

Detaching wood from the structure of a building is included in the *melachah* of *demolishing (Rav, Gem.* 30b).

The word סֻכָּה in the mishnah refers to a hut not used for the *mitzvah* of *sukkah*. Taking wood from the *sukkah* used on the festival is prohibited not only on *Yom Tov* but even on *Chol HaMoed Succos*. From the Torah's description of *Succos*, חַג הַסֻּכּוֹת שִׁבְעַת יָמִים לַה', *the festival of Succos, seven days to HASHEM (Leviticus* 23:34), the Gemara (30b) derives that just as the *Yom Tov* sacrifice (חָג = חֲגִיגָה) is sanctified and may not be used for other than its designated purpose, so is the *sukkah* — both the walls and the *schach* (roof or covering consisting of twigs and reeds) — sanctified and it may not be used for any other purpose *(Tos. Yom Tov;* see also *Meiri,* intro. to 2a).

אֶלָּא מִן הַסָּמוּךְ לָהּ. — *except for what adjoins it.*

The mishnah permits the use of wood which is next to, but not part of, the walls[1] of the hut. In this case, there is no problem of *demolishing,* because this wood is not attached to or interwoven with the walls of the hut *(Rav; Rashi).* Since its owner had intended to use it for *Yom Tov,* such wood is not [in the category of stored wood which is] *muktzeh* according to R' Yehudah (see comm. to mishnah 1, s.v. וּמַתְחִילִין); *Rashi, Shabbos* 45a).

מְבִיאִין עֵצִים מִן הַשָּׂדֶה מִן הַמְכֻנָּס; — *We may carry* [lit. *bring*] *in wood from a field* [only] *from that which has been* [previously] *gathered* [into a pile];

By gathering the wood before *Yom Tov,* the owner has demonstrated his intention of using it, thereby removing the status of *muktzeh (Rashi).* [But wood which is scattered over the field is considered *muktzeh* and may not be used.]

Although one may use a fire on *Yom Tov,* all wood, except that which has been specifically designated as firewood, is intrinsically *muktzeh.* Indeed, according to *Rashba* (33a), all wood including that designated as firewood is technically *muktzeh.* The Sages,

---

1. But if the wood is placed atop the roof then it may not be removed. The principle underlying this ruling is that anything placed upon a roof constructed of loosely strewn material may be deemed part and parcel of the roof; hence its removal constitutes *demolishing (Gem.* 30b, *Rashi;* see *Shulchan Aruch* 618:8, *Mishnah Berurah* 39-42, *Sha'ar HaTziyun* 66 and *Beur Halachah).*

אֵיזֶהוּ קַרְפֵּף? כָּל שֶׁסָּמוּךְ לָעִיר; דִּבְרֵי רַבִּי
יְהוּדָה. רַבִּי יוֹסֵי אוֹמֵר: כָּל שֶׁנִּכְנָסִין לוֹ בְּפוֹתַחַת,
וַאֲפִלּוּ בְּתוֹךְ תְּחוּם שַׁבָּת.

[ג] **אֵין** מְבַקְּעִין עֵצִים, לֹא מִן הַקּוֹרוֹת, וְלֹא
מִן הַקּוֹרָה שֶׁנִּשְׁבְּרָה בְּיוֹם טוֹב; וְאֵין

יד אברהם

however, lifted the restrictions of
muktzeh from wood that had
previously been designated as fuel.
The mishnah now specifies which
types of wood are or are not
muktzeh.

וּמִן הַקַּרְפֵּף, אֲפִלּוּ מִן הַמְפֻזָּר. — *but
from an enclosure, [we may carry
in] even from what is scattered.*

An enclosure surrounded by a
fence is considered a secure place,
therefore even wood which is scattered about within it is considered
prepared and is not *muktzeh*
(Rashi).

The *Gemara* (31a) states that the
opinion expressed in this mishnah
is that of R' Shimon ben Elazar, but
that most of his colleagues disagree
and consider scattered wood
muktzeh even if it is in an enclosed
area. Their opinion is accepted by
Rambam (*Hil. Yom Tov* 2:14) and
Shulchan Aruch (*Orach Chaim*
501:3), who rule that one may use
only the wood which has been
gathered into a pile in an enclosure;
neither a pile of wood in an open
field, nor scattered wood in an
enclosure may be used.

Ran cites the opinion of some authorities
that one may not bring in the wood scattered
on the field because collecting the wood is
classified under the labor of מְעַמֵּר, *gathering*. The Rabbis prohibited gathering wood
from the field even when necessary for *Yom
Tov* because it creates the appearance that
wood is being gathered for the weekdays

which would be a violation of *Yom Tov*. [See
Mishnah Berurah 501:11, *Sha'ar HaTziyun*
14.] In the halachically accepted opinion
cited in the *Gemara* (contrary to our mishnah), gathering wood even in an enclosure
(where it is normally not considered
gathering) is also prohibited on the ground
that this might be confused with gathering
scattered wood from the field.

Turei Zahav 501 suggests that according
to *Rashi* and *Rambam's* view, wood gathered
in the field may be used if before *Yom Tov*
the owner had explicitly declared his intention to use it on *Yom Tov*. (Cf. *Beur
Halachah* 501:3.)

אֵיזֶהוּ קַרְפֵּף? — *Which is [considered]
an enclosure* [to qualify under the
less stringent law as applied to
enclosures]?

כָּל שֶׁסָּמוּךְ לָעִיר; דִּבְרֵי רַבִּי יְהוּדָה. —
*Whichever [enclosure] is near to the
town; [these are] the words of R'
Yehudah.*

Anywhere within slightly more
than seventy cubits (שִׁבְעִים אַמָּה
וְשִׁירַיִים) of the town is considered
near (*Rashi; Ran; Rashba;* cf. *Maggid Mishneh, Hil. Yom Tov* 2:14).

The mishnah presumes that the enclosure
has a lock and therefore the wood is not considered *muktzeh* because it is in a safe place
(*Rav* from one view in the *Gem.* 31a). [Wood
in an unlocked enclosure is considered as if it
were in an open field and is *muktzeh*.] The
mishnah did not deem it necessary to mention this provision since it is assumed that
enclosures in general will have locks (*Rav*).

רַבִּי יוֹסֵי אוֹמֵר: כָּל שֶׁנִּכְנָסִין לוֹ בְּפוֹתַחַת,
וַאֲפִלּוּ בְּתוֹךְ תְּחוּם שַׁבָּת. — *[But] R'
Yose says: Whichever [enclosure]*

Which is [considered] an enclosure? Whichever is near to the town; [these are] the words of R' Yehudah. R' Yose says: Whichever they must enter with a key, even when it is [just] within the Sabbath boundary.

3. **W**e may not split wood, neither from beams, nor from a beam which was broken on *Yom*

they must enter with a key, even when it is [just] within the Sabbath boundary.

R' Yose holds that since the enclosure has a lock even if it is further than seventy cubits from the town as long as it is within the two thousand cubit *techum* (see footnote to mishnah 1) it is permitted (*Rav* based on one opinion in

the *Gem.* 31a).

The halachah follows R' Yose (*Rav; Gem.* 31a), but the *poskim* do not agree on whether R' Yose requires a lock even if the enclosure is near the town [i.e., within seventy cubits]. *Rambam* (Hil. *Yom Tov* 2:14) and *Shulchan Aruch* (Orach Chaim 501:3) do not make this distinction. However, many authorities hold that wood in an enclosure near the town is permitted even if there is no lock (*Ravad; Rashba; Turei Zahav* 501:4; *Mishneh Berurah* 501:15).

3.

אֵין מְבַקְּעִין עֵצִים, לֹא מִן הַקּוֹרוֹת, — *We may not split wood, neither from beams,*

[The use of a double negative occurs often in the Mishnah.]

The reference is to wood which has been set aside and stacked up to be used in construction (*Rav*, *Gem.* 31b). This wood may not be used because it is not prepared or intended for use as firewood (*Rav, Gem.* 31b).

Even R' Shimon, who holds the more lenient view in matters regarding *muktzeh*, concurs in prohibiting the category of *muktzeh* called מֻקְצֶה מַחֲמַת חֶסְרוֹן כִּיס, *muktzeh because of monetary loss* (Shabbos 157a), i.e., the owner has mentally removed the possibility that a specific object be used because such use would create financial loss [in our case the beams used for construction are ordinarily too valuable to be used for firewood] (*Tos.* 2b; cf. *Drush VeChiddush R' Akiva Eiger* there).

וְלֹא מִן הַקּוֹרָה שֶׁנִּשְׁבְּרָה בְיוֹם טוֹב; — *nor from a beam which was broken*

on Yom Tov;

Despite the fact that a broken beam can no longer be used for construction and its major use would now be for firewood, it is still considered *muktzeh* because at the onset of *Yom Tov* (בֵּין הַשְּׁמָשׁוֹת) it had been *muktzeh* (*Rav, Rashi* 31b). This is in accordance with the rule: that מִגּוֹ דְּאִתְקְצָאֵי בֵּין הַשְּׁמָשׁוֹת אִתְקְצָאֵי לְכוּלָא יוֹמָא, *since it was muktzeh at twilight* [i.e., the beginning of the Sabbath or *Yom Tov*] *it is muktzeh for the whole day*, even though the conditions which had rendered the object *muktzeh* no longer exist.

R' Shimon, however, does not agree with this principle. According to him, as soon as the beam breaks it is no longer *muktzeh* (*Gem.* 2b; see *Tos.*). Consequently, those who rule like R' Shimon on *Yom Tov* would not accept this segment of the mishnah as halachah (*Tur, Orach Chaim* 501). However, *Rama* is assumed to concur with the ruling of our mishnah, despite the fact that he rules

מְבַקְּעִין לֹא בְקַרְדֹם, וְלֹא בִמְגֵרָה, וְלֹא בְמַגָּל,
אֶלָא בְקוֹפִיץ.
בַּיִת שֶׁהוּא מָלֵא פֵרוֹת סָתוּם, וְנִפְחַת, נוֹטֵל
מִמְּקוֹם הַפָּחַת.
רַבִּי מֵאִיר אוֹמֵר: אַף פּוֹחֵת לְכַתְּחִלָה וְנוֹטֵל.

יד אברהם

like R' Shimon regarding *Yom Tov* (*Orach Chaim* 495:4; see *Magen Avraham* and *Mishnah Berurah* 501:1).

וְאֵין מְבַקְּעִין לֹא בְקַרְדֹם, וְלֹא בִמְגֵרָה, וְלֹא בְמַגָּל, — *nor may we split with an ax, nor with a saw, nor with a sickle,*

These are utensils used by an artisan and their use is considered a weekday procedure, and is therefore prohibited on *Yom Tov* (*Rashi; Meiri; Rambam, Hil. Yom Tov* 4:10).

The *Gemara* (31b) comments that the mishnah here obviously omits a pertinent detail (חַסּוּרֵי מְחַסְּרָא) [presumably because it is self-evident], namely that one *may* split beams that were broken *before Yom Tov*, as they are not considered *muktzeh* at the onset of the festival. It is to this type of wood that the mishnah's restrictions on the type of cutting instrument apply (*Rav*).

אֶלָא בְקוֹפִיץ. — *only with a kophitz.*
This tool, usually rendered *butcher's cleaver*, is designed for cutting meat and is not usually used for chopping wood. Therefore its use does not constitute a weekday procedure. The blade of the cleaver is (sometimes) broad at one side and tapers off to a point on the other. One may use only the narrow side for chopping wood, since the use of the broad side would resemble using a woodcutter's ax (*Rav; Rashi*).

Shulchan Aruch, Orach Chaim 501:1 (see also *Tos.* 31b), rules that today even a meat cleaver may not be used because the identification of the *kophitz* mentioned in our mishnah as a meat cleaver is uncertain. Therefore, only a knife may be used. *Shulchan Aruch* (501:2) also rules that one should not chop (or even break by hand) wood which can be burned as is.

The Talmud (*Shabbos* 74b) states that chopping wood into slivers is to be classified under the labor of *grinding*. If so, why is chopping wood permitted on *Yom Tov* at all? *Rosh* and *Or Zarua* (2:360) cite *Riva*, who asserts that one may only split wood into large pieces. Chopping wood into slivers, an activity which can be classified as *grinding*, is prohibited.

Ran reasons that when benefit is derived from the wood itself, e.g., when it is used to warm people, it may be chopped, just as food for human consumption may be chopped. Chopping wood for cooking, however, is classified as מַכְשִׁירֵי אוֹכֶל נֶפֶשׁ, *preliminary to food preparation* (cf. *Maggid Mishneh* to *Hil. Yom Tov* 1:4 and *Teshuvos Avnei Nezer, Orach Chaim* 408) and as such should be prohibited [according to all opinions; see comm. to 3:7], at least where this could have been done before *Yom Tov*. However, even this is permitted because of the principle of מִתּוֹךְ, *mitoch* (see comm. to 1:5; cf. *Tos., Kesubos* 7a; *Teshuvos Avnei Nezer, Orach Chaim* 406:11).

Ravad (*Hil. Yom Tov* 4:10; cited in *Rosh* and *Ran*) submits that the permitted manner of chopping wood is considered a deviation from the conventional manner of *grinding*, and is therefore prohibited only on a Rabbinical level [as are all labors done with a deviation from their usual manner]. The Sages lift their prohibition and permit labors to be done with a deviation when it is done for preliminary food preparation needed for *Yom Tov*, even where this labor could have been done before *Yom Tov* (see comm. to 3:7).

4
3

Tov; nor may we split with an ax, nor with a saw, nor with a sickle, only with a *kophitz.*

[If] a room that is full of produce is sealed, but is broken into, one may take from the place where the room is broken into.

R' Meir says: One may even break in initially and take.

בַּיִת שֶׁהוּא מָלֵא פֵּרוֹת סָתוּם, וְנִפְחַת, — [*If*] *a room that is full of produce is sealed* [before *Yom Tov*], *but is broken into* [on *Yom Tov*],

[Thus the produce could not be gotten to at the onset of *Yom Tov* because that would have involved *demolishing.* Now that the room has been broken into, making the produce accessible, we are confronted with the question whether the produce is considered *muktzeh.*]

נוֹטֵל מִמְּקוֹם הַפְּחָת. — *one may take* [produce] *from the place where the room is broken into* [lit. *from the place of the break*].

I.e., the produce is not considered *muktzeh* and may be used. Even though, in general, objects whose use is prohibited are classified as *muktzeh* (מֻקְצֶה מֵחֲמַת אִיסוּר), this rule does not apply to produce whose use is proscribed only by a Rabbinic decree. As explained in the *Gemara* (31b) in reference to R' Meir's view (see below, s.v. רַבִּי מֵאִיר), the wall enclosing the produce was formed by merely piling bricks one on top of another without using mortar or any other bonding agent. Because of this wall's weak construction, its demolition is not prohibited by Scriptural standards and only involves the violation of a Rabbinic law. But objects whose use is not Scripturally prohibited do not fall

under this classification of *muktzeh* (*Rav; Rashi*).

Tosafos (31b) and many others disagree with *Rashi's* basic premise that a Rabbinic law is not sufficient to render an object *muktzeh. Ramban* (*Milchamos,* end of this chapter; see also *Ran* here) presents a different explanation for the mishnah's ruling. The prohibition against *demolishing* has as its object, not the produce *per se,* but rather the wall. Thus the produce is to be considered a halachically permitted object whose use is restricted because of a physical barrier. Hence it does not fall under the classification of *muktzeh* because of prohibition (מֻקְצֶה מֵחֲמַת אִיסוּר). According to this explanation the produce is permitted even if the wall is solidly built and its demolition involves a labor of Scriptural standing. This seems to be the opinion of *Rif, Rambam* (*Hil. Yom Tov* 2:9; see *Maggid Mishneh*) and *Shulchan Aruch* (*Orach Chaim* 518:9). However, *Mishnah Berurah* (518:45) rules that the produce should not be used if the wall had been solid unless there is great need.

רַבִּי מֵאִיר אוֹמֵר: אַף פּוֹחֵת לְכַתְּחִלָּה וְנוֹטֵל. — *R' Meir says: One may even break in initially and take* [the produce].

I.e., not only may one use the produce if the room has already been broken into by others, but one may himself break into the room.

The *Gemara* (31b) explains that since the wall is formed by bricks that are not cemented into place, R' Meir permits even the intentional demolition of the wall. The halachah is not in accordance with R' Meir (*Rav; Rambam*).

Although bricks themselves are

[ד] **אֵין** פּוֹתְחִין אֶת הַנֵּר, מִפְּנֵי שֶׁהוּא עוֹשֶׂה
כְּלִי; וְאֵין עוֹשִׂין פֶּחָמִין בְּיוֹם טוֹב;
וְאֵין חוֹתְכִין אֶת הַפְּתִילָה לִשְׁנַיִם.
רַבִּי יְהוּדָה אוֹמֵר: חוֹתְכָה בָּאוּר לִשְׁתֵּי נֵרוֹת.

[ה] **אֵין** שׁוֹבְרִין אֶת הַחֶרֶס, וְאֵין חוֹתְכִין
הַנְּיָר, לִצְלוֹת בּוֹ מָלִיחַ; וְאֵין גּוֹרְפִין

יד אברהם

muktzeh, R' Meir permits them to
be removed because *muktzeh* may
be moved to procure food for *Yom
Tov*, just as other work is permitted
for food purposes *(Gem. 31b, Rashi
and Tos.)*.

[It appears from the *Gemara* as well as
from *Tosafos* that the *Tanna kamma's* disagreement with R' Meir is not on the point of
muktzeh. He would concur with R' Meir that

moving of *muktzeh* is permitted if needed to
enhance the enjoyment of *Yom Tov* (see
Orach Chaim 507:4 and 509:7). However,
the *Tanna kamma* holds that since by Rabbinic law even a wall erected without benefit
of cement may not be demolished, it may not
be broken on *Yom Tov* for any reason, for
*demolishing is not included in the categories
of labor permitted for preparation of food. R'
Meir, on the other hand, holds that since
only a Rabbinic ordinance against *demolishing is involved here, this too is permitted.]

4.

אֵין פּוֹתְחִין אֶת הַנֵּר, — *We may not
hollow out a lamp* [on *Yom Tov*],
I.e., one may not take a clump of
potter's clay and hollow out a cavity
in its middle to serve as a receptacle
for an oil lamp *(Rav; Rashi)*.

מִפְּנֵי שֶׁהוּא עוֹשֶׂה כְּלִי; — *because one
[thereby] makes a vessel;*
Making a vessel is classified as
either *building or as *striking the
final blow (see *Shabbos* 74b; *Rashi,
Tos.*, there).
An explanation is needed why the mishnah found it necessary to mention this
seemingly elementary prohibition. *Tosefos
Yom Tov* explains that one may think that
the lamp is not considered a vessel until it is
fired in a kiln, for according to the laws of
tumah contamination an earthenware vessel
is not considered completed and susceptible
to *tumah* until it has been fired. Therefore,
the mishnah has to point out that, as far as

the *Yom Tov* is concerned, the lamp is considered a vessel, even before it is fired.
Rambam (Comm. and *Hil. Yom Tov* 4:8)
interprets this segment of the mishnah in a
radically different way. A pair of lamps
would be formed from one piece of clay.
They would remain joined together until
ready for use at which time each pair was
broken up into its component parts. Unlike
our editions of Mishnah which read אֵין
פּוֹתְחִין, literally, *we may not hollow out* or
open, Rambam's version of this mishnah (ed.
Kafich) reads אֵין פּוֹחֲתִין, literally, *we may not
diminish* or *break*, a version that appears in
this mishnah as printed with the *Gemara*.
Consequently the translation of the mishnah
reads, *We may not break the lamp* [into two]
because one [thereby] *completes a vessel.*
Moreover *Rambam (Hil. Yom Tov* 4:8)
writes: Two vessels which are connected ...
may not be broken apart because this is
similar to perfecting a vessel (כִּמְתַקֵּן כְּלִי),
suggesting that this is only a Rabbinical
prohibition (cf. *Tos.* 32a.)
Mishnah Berurah 514:37 accepts all these
interpretations as halachically correct.

4

4-5

4. **W**e may not hollow out a lamp, because one [thereby] makes a vessel; nor may we make charcoal on *Yom Tov;* nor may we cut a wick in two.

R' Yehudah says: One may cut it with a flame for two lamps.

5. **W**e may not break a shard nor cut a [piece of] paper, to roast salted fish on it; nor may we rake out an oven or a double stove, but we may level

וְאֵין עוֹשִׂין פֶּחָמִין בְּיוֹם טוֹב; — *nor may we make charcoal on Yom Tov;*

Charcoals too are considered utensils in regard to the prohibitions of *Yom Tov* because goldsmiths make use of them when they purify gold. Therefore making charcoal is also prohibited because by so doing one makes a utensil (*Rav; Rashi*).

Ran holds that this is prohibited because making charcoal involves the labor of *extinguishing.

וְאֵין חוֹתְכִין אֶת הַפְּתִילָה לִשְׁנַיִם. — *nor may we cut a wick in two.*

Cutting a wick in half in effect creates a second wick. This is classified as תִּיקוּן מָנָא, *making a utensil,* for a wick, too, is considered a utensil (*Rav; Rashi*).

רַבִּי יְהוּדָה אוֹמֵר: חוֹתְכָהּ בָּאוּר לִשְׁתֵּי נֵרוֹת. — *R' Yehudah says: One may*

cut it with a flame for two lamps.

If one needs wicks for two lamps, he may place the two ends of a wick in the two lamps with the middle of the wick forming a bridge between them. He may then kindle the wick, thus effectively separating it into two wicks (*Rav; Gem. 32b*).

Since he intends to use both of the lamps his action does not have the appearance of creating an additional wick. Rather it appears as if he is simply lighting the lamps and it is therefore permitted (*Rav; Rashi 32b*).

[Apparently cutting the wick in two only has the appearance of or making a utensil and is prohibited only by Rabbinic law. Therefore when the appearance of creating a utensil is avoided it is permitted.]

The halachah is in accordance with R' Yehudah (*Rambam, Hil. Yom Tov* 4:8; *Orach Chaim* 515:8).

5.

אֵין שׁוֹבְרִין אֶת הַחֶרֶס, וְאֵין חוֹתְכִין הַנְּיָר, לִצְלוֹת בּוֹ מָלִיחַ; — *We may not break a shard nor cut a [piece of] paper, to roast salted fish* [e.g., herring] *on it* [i.e., on the shard or paper];

When roasting salt fish, shards or paper that had been soaked in water would be placed on the griddle so

that the hot bars of the griddle would not burn the fish (*Rav; Rashi*).

This too is considered making a utensil (*Gem. 32b*).

וְאֵין גּוֹרְפִין תַּנּוּר וְכִירַיִם, — *nor may we rake out an oven or a double stove* [i.e., a stove with place for two pots; see *Shabbos* 3:1],

תַּנּוּר וּכִירַיִם, אֲבָל מְכַבְּשִׁין; וְאֵין מַקִּיפִין שְׁתֵּי
חָבִיּוֹת לִשְׁפּוֹת עֲלֵיהֶן אֶת הַקְּדֵרָה; וְאֵין סוֹמְכִין
אֶת הַקְּדֵרָה בִּבְקַעַת, וְכֵן בְּדֶלֶת.
וְאֵין מַנְהִיגִין אֶת הַבְּהֵמָה בְּמַקֵּל בְּיוֹם טוֹב.
וְרַבִּי אֶלְעָזָר בְּרַבִּי שִׁמְעוֹן מַתִּיר.

יד אברהם

If plaster from the walls or ceiling of the oven or stove has fallen on its floor the removal of this debris is considered perfecting a utensil and is prohibited.

This mishnah apparently follows the views of the Sages who prohibit preliminary work to be done in connection with the preparation of food even if it was impossible to perform this work before *Yom Tov*. According to R' Yehudah it would be permitted to remove the plaster if it fell on *Yom Tov* (see *Gem.* 28b and comm. to 3:7; *Rav; Rashi*).

The *Gemara* (32b) cites a *baraisa* which states that if it is impossible to bake without removing the debris, it may be removed. *Rashi* explains that this ruling is in accordance with R' Yehudah who permits preliminary steps in food preparation if they were impossible to do before *Yom Tov*. Thus, as *Rashi* understands it, the mishnah disagrees with this *baraisa*.

Ran contends that the mishnah may follow R' Yehudah. The mishnah speaks only

of a case where it is possible to bake without removing the debris and even R' Yehudah would concur in such a case.[1]

Rosh, however, holds that perfecting a utensil is not the subject of our mishnah's discussion. The mishnah is only concerned with the prohibition against *muktzeh*. Since the debris is *muktzeh* the mishnah prohibits moving it. The *baraisa*, then, adds to this law, stating that where it is impossible to use the oven without removing the debris, the prohibition against moving *muktzeh* is waived because it is an obstacle to the preparation of food (see *comm.* to 4:3 and 1:2). *Shulchan Aruch (Orach Chaim* 507:4) reflects this view.

אֲבָל מְכַבְּשִׁין; — *but we may level it* [lit. *press down*];

We may spread out the ash and earth [or plaster *(Meiri)*] which has accumulated on the floor of the oven to keep the debris from touching the bread and burning it *(Rashi)*.[2]

According to *Rosh* who contends that the raking out of an oven is prohibited because it involves moving *muktzeh*, leveling it is per-

---

1. *Rambam (Hil. Yom Tov* 4:6 and 9; see *Maggid Mishneh)* rules contrary to R' Yehudah's view and yet permits removal of debris where it is impossible to bake without removing it (ibid. 3:10). Ostensibly he holds that removal of debris is merely a Rabbinic prohibition and that the Sages waived this ban where it poses an obstacle to food preparation *(Rosh Yosef; Beis Yosef* 509; cf. *Beur Halachah, Orach Chaim* 507:4).

2. In Talmudic times, bread was baked by pasting dough to the hot walls of the oven. Thus the mere presence of ashes and debris on the oven floor would not be an impediment. In our days, when bread is placed upon the oven floor itself, the presence of ashes would present an obstacle to baking, and raking is permitted *(Orach Chaim* 507:4).

Mishnah Berurah (Beur Halachah 507:5) points out that *Rashi* (cited above) implies that the permission to level the debris is granted because it constitutes food preparation, for if the debris is not leveled there is the possibility that any bread coming into contact with it will be spoiled. According to *Ran's* view (cited above) raking at the debris is banned only when it is not essential to baking. Thus it follows that leveling is permitted even when it is not essential. [Presumably, in his view, since in this case the debris remains in the oven, the act is not considered perfecting a utensil.]

4
5
it; nor may we position two barrels near each other [in order] to set a pot upon them; nor may we support a pot with a piece of wood, and the same applies to a door.

We may not drive an animal with a stick on *Yom Tov*. But R' Elazar ben R' Shimon permits [this].

YAD AVRAHAM

mitted because this action is assumed to involve only glowing coal and ashes which are not yet *muktzeh* (see *Beis Yosef, Orach Chaim* 507). Thus the distinction drawn between raking and leveling is not due to the nature of these actions, but to the objects they are performed upon; plaster may not be moved but glowing coal and embers may. In this view the prohibition refers not only to raking out plaster but also to merely leveling it out (see *Beur Halachah* to 507:4). By the same token one should be allowed to rake out the glowing coal or embers, but as observed by *Mishnah Berurah* (507:12) this may involve various other halachic transgressions.

וְאֵין מַקִּיפִין שְׁתֵּי חָבִיוֹת לִשְׁפוֹת עֲלֵיהֶן אֶת הַקְּדֵרָה; — *nor may we position two barrels near each other [in order] to set a pot upon them;*

A fire would then be kindled between the two barrels as a makeshift stove. This may not be done on *Yom Tov* because it is similar to *building (Rav; Rashi)

וְאֵין חוֹמְרִין אֶת הַקְּדֵרָה בִּבְקַעַת, — *may we support a pot with a piece of wood,*

[I.e., one may not prop up an unbalanced pot with a piece of wood.]

וְכֵן בְּדֶלֶת. — *and the same applies to a [sagging] door.*

Wood is considered to be exclusively designated for firewood and is therefore *muktzeh* for other uses *(Rav; Rashi).*

This represents a unique concept: an object may be *muktzeh* for some purposes and not *muktzeh* for others. *Rashi* (33a) adds that this prohibition is only according to R' Yehudah, whose rulings on *muktzeh* tend to be more stringent. It follows, then, that those who rule in accordance with R' Shimon with

regard to *Yom Tov* would permit one to support a door with a piece of firewood on *Yom Tov*. [On the Sabbath, when one may not make a fire, firewood is *muktzeh* even according to R' Shimon.] Therefore according to *Shulchan Aruch (Orach Chaim* 595:4) which rules in accordance with R' Shimon, this prohibition is not accepted halachically (see *Mishnah Berurah* 502:21, *Sha'ar HaTziyun).*

Rashba (33a), however, disagrees. He argues that although firewood is designated for a permissible purpose, it nevertheless can be considered neither a utensil nor food. Therefore even firewood must be considered basically *muktzeh.* The use of wood for a fire is permitted only by virtue of a special exception to the laws of *muktzeh* allowed by the Sages to facilitate cooking and heating on *Yom Tov*; insofar as other uses are concerned, the prohibition against *muktzeh* is still in effect. Thus even R' Shimon would concur with the laws of our mishnah. Apparently this is the view adopted by *Magen Avraham* 502:11.

Mishnah Berurah (ibid.) rules that in case of emergency (שְׁעַת הַדְּחָק) one may rely on the opinions of the former authorities.

וְאֵין מַנְהִיגִין אֶת הַבְּהֵמָה בְּמַקֵּל בְּיוֹם טוֹב. — *We may not drive [lit. lead] an animal with a stick on Yom Tov.*

Using a stick gives the appearance of driving the animal to the market to be sold and is therefore inconsistent with the sanctity of *Yom Tov* (Rav, Gem. 33a).

It is therefore even prohibited to use a stick that is not *muktzeh (Mishnah Berurah* 522:9 and others; from *Gem.* 33a).

וְרַבִּי אֶלְעָזָר בְּרַבִּי שִׁמְעוֹן מַתִּיר. — *But R' Elazar ben R' Shimon permits [this].*

Rambam (Hil. Yom Tov 5:3) and *Shulchan Aruch (Orach Chaim)* 522:4 rule according to the *Tanna kamma.*

[ו] **רַבִּי** אֱלִיעֶזֶר אוֹמֵר: נוֹטֵל אָדָם קֵיסָם
מִשֶּׁלְּפָנָיו לַחֲצוֹץ בּוֹ שִׁנָּיו; וּמְגַבֵּב מִן
הֶחָצֵר וּמַדְלִיק, שֶׁכָּל מַה שֶּׁבֶּחָצֵר מוּכָן הוּא.
וַחֲכָמִים אוֹמְרִים: מִגַבֵּב מִשֶּׁלְּפָנָיו וּמַדְלִיק.

יד אברהם

6.

רַבִּי אֱלִיעֶזֶר אוֹמֵר: נוֹטֵל אָדָם קֵיסָם
מִשֶּׁלְּפָנָיו לַחֲצוֹץ בּוֹ שִׁנָּיו; — *R' Eliezer
says: A person may take a sliver
from that which is* [lying] *before
him* [i.e., in his house] *in order to
clean his teeth;*

R' Eliezer holds that although the
wood is obviously designated mainly for firewood, it is not necessarily
restricted to this use. Since the
wood is not *muktzeh* it may be used
for other purposes, such as to pick
one's teeth;

The use of the word מִשֶּׁלְּפָנָיו,
from that which is before him, is
potentially misleading. It is para-
phrased from the statement made
by the Sages in the latter part of the
mishnah where they permit the
gathering of wood only 'from that
which is before him,' i.e., in the
house, but he may not gather from
what is strewn about in the courtyard. In R' Eliezer's statement,
however, there is no such restrictive
connotation, for he states quite
clearly that *one may gather from the
courtyard ... because everything
which is in the courtyard is considered prepared (Rav; Rashi).*

[*Tosafos* (33a) disagrees with this explanation and holds that even according to R'
Eliezer only wood lying about before him is
considered as prepared for all purposes and
consequently only such wood may be used
for cleaning one's teeth. Wood lying about in
the courtyard may be used only for firewood,
because it was never designated for any other
purpose. Thus, the word, מִשֶּׁלְּפָנָיו, *from that
which is before him,* has the same meaning in

R' Eliezer's statement as in that of the Sages.]

In the text cited by *R' Chananel, Rambam*
(see *Kafich* ed.) and *Rashba* the word
מִשֶּׁלְּפָנָיו does not appear in this stich of the
mishnah.

וּמְגַבֵּב מִן הֶחָצֵר וּמַדְלִיק, — *and one
may gather* [hay or splinters] *from
the courtyard and kindle* [a fire],

I.e., one may even take materials
strewn about in the courtyard to use
as kindling. In the view of *Rashi*
one may use splinters from the
courtyard for any purpose. According to *Tosafos* they can be used
only for a fire.

שֶׁכָּל מַה שֶּׁבֶּחָצֵר מוּכָן הוּא. — *because
everything which is in the court-
yard is considered prepared.*

Since the courtyard is adjacent to
the house, anything in it is not
muktzeh and is considered prepared
for use on *Yom Tov.*

[R' Eliezer's opinion does not contradict
the view (see above mishnah 2, s.v. וּמִן
הַקַּרְפֵּף; below, s.v. וַחֲכָמִים) which prohibits
wood strewn about an enclosure for use.
Surely materials in a courtyard (adjacent to a
domicile) should be considered in a greater
state of preparedness than those in an
enclosure (which may be some distance
away). Thus R' Eliezer can consider anything
in a courtyard prepared while viewing
materials strewn about an enclosure as
muktzeh. That objects in a yard are considered prepared has another halachic consequence. In such a place, R' Eliezer permits
the use of even hay and splinters whereas in
regard to an enclosure even the most lenient
view permits only wood strewn about (see
ibid.); all concur that hay or splinters strewn
about an enclosure may not be used (cf. *Tif.
Yis.*).]

6. **R'** Eliezer says: A person may take a sliver from that which is before him in order to clean his teeth; and one may gather [hay or splinters] from the courtyard and kindle [a fire], because everything which is in the courtyard is considered prepared.

But the Sages say: One may gather from that which is before him and kindle.

וַחֲכָמִים אוֹמְרִים: מִגַּבֵּב מִשֶּׁלְּפָנָיו וּמַדְלִיק. — *But the Sages say: One may gather* [only] *from that which is before him* [i.e., in the house (Rav; Rashi)] *and kindle* [a fire].

The Sages dispute R' Eliezer on two points. They maintain that: (a) one may gather only from that which is before him (i.e., in the house) and not from the courtyard; and (b) one may use these materials only for a fire, not for other purposes such as cleaning teeth.

Since hay and wood splinters are small objects, gathering then requires an expenditure of effort and so they cannot be considered prepared while they are in a courtyard. They, therefore, must be classified as *muktzeh*. In the house however they can be considered prepared.

Regarding the other point of their disagreement, the Sages hold that any wood is designated mainly for firewood and is considered *muktzeh* for any other purpose (Rav; Rashi)

Here again we have the situation mentioned previously that an object is considered prepared for one purpose, and yet *muktzeh* for other uses (see mishnah 5, s.v. וְכֵן בְּדֶלֶת). *Tosafos* (33a) comments that consequently the view of the Sages here would follow the halachically unaccepted view of R' Yehudah (cf. *HaMaor* here).

Tosafos therefore explains that *muktzeh* is not the basis of the Sages' prohibition of using wood for any purpose other than a fire. Rather, this ruling is based on the apprehen-

sion that allowing splinters to be used for cleaning teeth might lead one to form a toothpick from a sliver of wood. This would be considered making a utensil and be a violation of *Yom Tov*. This reason is, of course, applicable even according to R' Shimon.

Ran comments that even according to the Sages' view, only tiny objects such as hay and splinters which are strewn about in the courtyard are *muktzeh*. Moderately sized pieces of wood and twigs are permitted to be used for fire even according to the Sages. Thus the Sages' view does not contradict the opinion in mishnah 2 which permits the use of wood strewn about in an enclosure. [The Sages' opinion also does not contradict the halachically accepted opinion (in mishnah 2) which permits only wood gathered in a pile, because that ruling refers to wood held in an enclosure, whereas in our mishnah only wood and splinters scattered in the house are permitted for use.]

Rambam's (see *Comm.* in *Meiri* and ed. Kafich; see also *Hil. Yom Tov* 2:14; *Shinuyei Nuschaos* here) version of the Mishnah reads וַחֲכָמִים אוֹמְרִים, אַף, מִגַּבֵּב מִלְּפָנָיו (וּ)מַדְלִיק. *And the Sages say, he may* **also** *gather before him and make a fire.*

In this version the Sages are more *lenient* than R' Eliezer: not only may one gather splinters from the courtyard (adjacent to the house) but even wood scattered on the field may be used provided that it is used *before him*, i.e., the food is cooked near the area where the wood was gathered. Apparently the reason for this distinction is that gathering wood may give the impression that the wood is being gathered for some other use, and not exclusively for *Yom Tov*. Using the wood in the immediate area of its collection leaves no room for erroneous conclusions (see *Magen Avraham* 501:7).

ביצה
ד/ז

[ז] אֵין מוֹצִיאִין אֶת הָאוּר, לֹא מִן הָעֵצִים,
וְלֹא מִן הָאֲבָנִים, וְלֹא מִן הֶעָפָר, וְלֹא
מִן הַמַּיִם; וְאֵין מְלַבְּנִין אֶת הָרְעָפִים לִצְלוֹת בָּהֶן.
וְעוֹד אָמַר רַבִּי אֱלִיעֶזֶר: עוֹמֵד אָדָם עַל
הַמֻּקְצֶה עֶרֶב שַׁבָּת בַּשְּׁבִיעִית, וְאוֹמֵר: ,,מִכָּאן אֲנִי
אוֹכֵל לְמָחָר.''

יד אברהם

The Sages concur with R' Eliezer's statement that wood scattered about in a courtyard is considered prepared and may be used.

The halachah, as formulated by *Rambam* (ibid.) and *Shulchan Aruch (Orach Chaim* 501:3), does not reflect the view concurred to here by R' Eliezer and the Sages. One may gather wood in proximity to his fire and use it (as asserted by the Sages here). But one may not gather scattered wood even from one's yard to transport to a different location. Only wood piled in an enclosed area prior to *Yom Tov* may be used in this manner. Evidently *Rambam* assumed that on this point our mishnah contradicts the conclusion arrived at in mishnah 2 (see there, s.v. מִן הַקַּרְפֵּף) and is consequently unacceptable as halachah. For further elaboration on *Rambam's* view see in *Mishnah Berurah, Sha'ar HaTziyun* 501:14.

7.

אֵין מוֹצִיאִין אֶת הָאוּר, לֹא מִן הָעֵצִים,
וְלֹא מִן הָאֲבָנִים, — *We may not produce fire, neither from wood, nor from stones,*

[One may not produce fire by rubbing pieces of wood or stone against one another with the intent to produce sparks.]

וְלֹא מִן הֶעָפָר, — *nor from earth,*
Hardened earth, when dug, may produce sparks *(Rav; Rashi).*

[Perhaps this refers to earth containing an easily combustible element such as sulphur.] *Meiri* adds that when the digging tools strike hard earth or rocks, sparks are sometimes created. [It appears that *Rambam (Hil. Yom Tov* 4:1) understands the meaning of the word עָפָר as *ore.*]

וְלֹא מִן הַמַּיִם; — *nor from water;*
Water in a clear glass dish, when placed under the bright sun, will act as a lens and focus the sun's rays. Combustible materials placed near

the dish may, after some time, catch fire *(Rav; Rashi).*

[The lesson of the mishnah is that although one may utilize fire on *Yom Tov,* it is nevertheless prohibited to create *new* fire. One may ignite a fire only from an already existing fire.]

וְאֵין מְלַבְּנִין אֶת הָרְעָפִים לִצְלוֹת בָּהֶן. — *nor may we heat* [lit. whiten; i.e., heat them until they are white hot] *tiles in order to roast upon them.*

The *Gemara* (34a) explains that the mishnah refers to new tiles, which must be reheated to harden them and complete their manufacture. Heating the tiles in this manner is prohibited because it is considered making a utensil and a violation of the *melachah* of *striking the final blow.*

וְעוֹד אָמַר רַבִּי אֱלִיעֶזֶר: — *And R' Eliezer said yet another thing* [in addition to his statement in mishnah 6 *(Rav; Rashi)*]:

7. **W**e may not produce fire, neither from wood, nor from stones, nor from earth, nor from water; nor may we heat tiles in order to roast upon them.

And R' Eliezer said yet another thing: A person may stand next to [foodstuffs that are] *muktzeh* on Friday during the sabbatical year, and say, "From here I will eat tomorrow."

YAD AVRAHAM

Rashi comments that this segment of the mishnah actually should immediately follow mishnah 6 where R' Eliezer's first statement is cited. *Tosafos* (34a) explains that because the discussion in mishnah 6 centers around gathering wood for a fire, the *Tanna* wanted to complete all the laws pertaining to making a fire and so began this mishnah by stating that *one may not create a fire* before getting back to a continuation of R' Eliezer's statement.

עוֹמֵד אָדָם עַל הַמֻּקְצֶה עֶרֶב שַׁבָּת — *A person may stand next to [foodstuffs that are] muktzeh on Friday*

The term *muktzeh* in our mishnah refers to fruits such as figs and grapes which were set out in the sun to dry. The Talmud (*Shabbos* 45a) considers this the classic case of *muktzeh*, for they were literally set aside by the owner to be eaten only when the drying process — which takes many days — is completed. Even R' Shimon agrees that they are subject to the restrictions of *muktzeh* (Rav; Rashi).

[*Rambam* in his *commentary* interprets the word מֻקְצֶה as a *place* set aside for the drying of fruits.]

The fruits discussed in our mishnah have already been dried to the point where they are somewhat edible and some people would eat them while others would wait a little longer (see *Gem.* 26b). Therefore, if the owner declared his intention to eat them in their present state, they

are no longer *muktzeh*. The owner's oral declaration renders them prepared *(Rashi)*.

בַּשְּׁבִיעִית, — *during the sabbatical year*,

[As set forth in *Leviticus* 25:1-7] every seventh year is designated as a שַׁבָּת, *Sabbath*, for the earth and no sowing is to take place. The produce growing (by itself) in that year is to be הֶפְקֵר, *ownerless property*, which may be claimed by anyone. Ownerless produce is exempt from the obligations of *terumah* and tithes. Consequently produce grown on the sabbatical year may be eaten without the separation of *terumah* and tithes.]

People do not usually tithe produce before it is ready for consumption (לֹא נִגְמְרָה מְלַאכְתּוֹ). Thus the fruit set in the sun to dry has not yet been tithed. But untithed fruit (טֶבֶל, *tevel*) may not be eaten, and tithes may not be separated on the Sabbath or *Yom Tov* (see comm. to 1:6, s.v. בֵּין שֶׁהוּרְמוּ). Consequently the fruit is *muktzeh* and the question of its preparedness is academic. The mishnah specifies that the case of drying fruit refers to the sabbatical year, when *terumah* and tithes do not apply, to focus on the *muktzeh* status of produce during the drying process. The law would be the same

וַחֲכָמִים אוֹמְרִים: עַד שֶׁיִּרְשֹׁם וְיֹאמַר: ,,מִכָּאן
וְעַד כָּאן.''

[א] **מַשִׁילִין** פֵּרוֹת דֶּרֶךְ אֲרֻבָּה בְּיוֹם טוֹב,
אֲבָל לֹא בַּשַׁבָּת. וּמְכַסִּים
פֵּרוֹת בְּכֵלִים מִפְּנֵי הַדֶּלֶף, וְכֵן כַּדֵּי יַיִן וְכַדֵּי שֶׁמֶן;

יד אברהם

during any year in the sabbatical cycle if the *terumah* and tithes had previously been separated from the the drying fruit *(Rav; Rashi)*. Nevertheless, if the prohibition of *tevel* is removed (e.g., if someone transgressed the ban against separating *terumah* and tithes on *Yom Tov*) it is considered prepared and may be eaten *(Gem. 34b; Rashi)*.

וְאוֹמֵר: ,,מִכָּאן אֲנִי אוֹכֵל לְמָחָר.'' — *and say, "From here I will eat tomorrow."*

[An oral declaration is sufficient to remove the *muktzeh* status.]

He does not have to indicate specifically which fruit he will eat. The general statement, 'From here I will take,' is sufficient to remove the status of *muktzeh (Rav; Rashi)*.

[*Rashi, Tosafos* and *Rav* read אֲנִי נוֹטֵל, *I will take*, in place of אֲנִי אוֹכֵל, *I will eat*. This reading implies that he does not even have to state his purpose in "taking."]

This is not analogous to the case of doves (above 1:3) regarding which Beis Hillel ruled that the owner has to designate exactly which ones he wishes to slaughter. There we have reason to be apprehensive that upon handling a dove he will find it to be very lean, discard it for another, and thus have moved *muktzeh* needlessly. In contrast, any fruit which the owner has judged fit for consumption can be assumed to be edible and this fear does not apply *(Meiri)*.

וַחֲכָמִים אוֹמְרִים: עַד שֶׁיִּרְשֹׁם וְיֹאמַר: ,,מִכָּאן וְעַד כָּאן.'' — *But the Sages say: Only if* [lit. *until*] *he marks it off*

and says, "From here to here [*I will eat*]."

He has to make a mark to identify exactly which fruit he intends to use *(Rav; Rashi)*.

Unless he demarks exactly which fruit he wishes to eat, the declaration is not deemed to be based on sufficient resolve and it is possible that he will change his mind and not eat the fruit *(Meiri)*. [See comment of Rashi, above, s.v. עוֹמֵד.]

According to the view of the Sages, the procedure to render produce prepared is more stringent than that for designating birds for slaughter (above 1:3) where (according to Beis Hillel) a mere declaration indicating which birds he wishes to use is sufficient. Birds differ in that two or three will suffice and the owner will recognize them, whereas individual fruits are indistinguishable from one another. Also, the number he wishes to use on *Yom Tov* is not clearly fixed, therefore, he will not remember which fruits were designated if a mark is not made. However, if one is confident he will recognize the designated fruit a declaration is sufficient *(Meiri; cf. Beur Halachah 495:4 s.v.; Yerushalmi, cited in Tos. 34b)*.

Rambam (comm. and *Hil. Yom Tov 2:9)* and many other authorities (see *Sha'ar Ha-Tziyun 495:33*) rule like the Sages that a mark must be made. Although R' Yosef Karo omits overt discussion of this matter in *Shulchan Aruch, Magen Avraham 495:10* assumes that R' Yosef Karo rules in accordance with R' Eliezer that no mark need to be made, and *Rama 495:4* explicitly concurs. However *Mishnah Berurah 495:22* concludes that this opinion should not be depended on (see *Beur Halachah*).

But the Sages say: Only if he marks it off and says, "From here to here [I will eat]."

1. **W**e may lower produce through a skylight on *Yom Tov*, but not on the Sabbath. We may cover produce with cloths [to guard] against dripping water, and also pitchers of wine and pitchers of oil;

YAD AVRAHAM

Chapter Five

1.

מַשִּׁילִין פֵּרוֹת דֶּרֶךְ אֲרֻבָּה בְּיוֹם טוֹב, — **We may lower produce through a skylight on Yom Tov,**

If one had spread out fruit or grain on his roof to dry and, because of fear of oncoming rain, wishes to remove these crops from the roof, he may throw them through the skylight opening. The large scale moving of produce is usually considered excessive exertion which is prohibited on the Sabbath and *Yom Tov*. Nevertheless, in the face of financial loss the Sages permitted one to drop the produce through a skylight on *Yom Tov* because the amount of labor involved is minimal (i.e., the fruit need not be lifted but can be pushed to the open skylight through which it will fall).[1]

However the produce may not be tossed through a window in the wall. This would involve lifting the produce rather than merely dropping it through an opening in the roof, and is therefore considered excessive exertion (*Rav; Rashi*).

אֲבָל לֹא בַשַּׁבָּת. — **but not on the Sabbath.**

[The prohibition against excessive toil is more stringent on the Sabbath, so that even dropping produce through the skylight is not permitted on the Sabbath.]

In the event, however, that the produce is being moved to make room for the performance of a *mitzvah* (e.g., to make place for guests), it may even be lifted through a window on the Sabbath (*Orach Chaim* 333:1; *Mishnah Berurah*; see *Shabbos* 18:1).

וּמְכַסִּים פֵּרוֹת בְּכֵלִים מִפְּנֵי הַדֶּלֶף, — **(And) we may cover produce with cloths[1] [to guard] against dripping water,**

If the produce is exposed to a leak in the ceiling we may cover it with dropcloths to keep it dry. Although this activity is unnecessary for *Yom Tov*, it is nevertheless permitted because of the financial loss which would result if the produce were to come in contact with water (*Rav; Rashi*).

From the commentary of *Rav* and *Rashi* it appears that the dispensation for covering fruit applies only to *Yom Tov*. *Rosh*,

---

1. [Of course, financial loss is not sufficient grounds to permit violation of a Scriptural precept. Not even all Rabbinic decrees are waived in instances of financial loss. However, the Sages saw fit to waive certain aspects of Rabbinic decrees to prevent a financial loss. Thus, although produce may be lowered through a skylight on *Yom Tov*, in which case the Rabbinic decree against excessive exertion is lifted, one may not raise the produce to toss it through a window, in which case the Rabbinic decree remains in effect.]

..

[ב] **כָּל** שֶׁחַיָּבִין עָלָיו מִשׁוּם שְׁבוּת — מִשׁוּם רְשׁוּת, מִשׁוּם מִצְוָה — בַּשַּׁבָּת, חַיָּבִין עָלָיו בְּיוֹם טוֹב.

יד אברהם

however, cites *Ri*, who holds that this act is permitted even on the Sabbath. *Shulchan Aruch (Orach Chaim* 338:7; see *Mishnah Berurah* 26) accepts this ruling.

[The Hebrew noun כְּלִי includes *vessels, utensils, clothing* and *cloth*. The translation uses *cloth* because it best fits the context.]

וְכֵן כַּדֵּי יַיִן וְכַדֵּי שֶׁמֶן; — *and* [we may] *also* [cover] *pitchers of wine and pitchers of oil;*

The *Gemara* (36a) explains that the wine and oil in these pitchers are *tevel*, i.e., they may not be used because *terumah* and tithes have not been separated from them [see above 4:7, s.v. וּבַשְּׁבִיעִית]. They are consequently *muktzeh*.

If this segment referred to profane produce it would be a repetition of the first part of the mishnah. The mishnah teaches us that vessels and cloths (i.e., non-*muktzeh* objects) may be moved for the sake of *muktzeh* objects.

וְנוֹתְנִין כְּלִי תַחַת הַדֶּלֶף בַּשַּׁבָּת. — *and*

we may put a vessel under the dripping water on the Sabbath.

An empty container may be placed under a leak to prevent the house from getting wet. When the vessel fills up it may be emptied and replaced as necessary.

However, this applies only if the dripping water is fit for drinking or washing. If the water is not fit for such use it is *muktzeh* and when it drips into the vessel under the leak that vessel itself becomes unusable because of the *muktzeh* water in it. The Talmud (*Shabbos* 43a) calls this בִּיטוּל כְּלִי מֵהֵכָנוֹ, *nullification of a utensil from its availability.* Since the *muktzeh* in the utensil renders it unmovable, the vessel is locked in its place. The Rabbis found this similar to cementing of a utensil in place [which is a violation of the *melachah* of בוֹנֶה, *building* (*Meiri* ibid.)]. They therefore prohibited one to do anything to a utensil on the Sabbath or *Yom Tov* which would render it *muktzeh* (*Rav; Rashi,* ibid.). Others explain that *nullifying a utensil from its availability* is (since it becomes unusable) prohibited as a form of *demolishing* (*Rashi* to *Shabbos* 128b, 154b; *Rambam, Hil. Shabbos* 25:23). [See also *Orach Chaim* 338:7.]

2.

כָּל שֶׁחַיָּבִין עָלָיו מִשׁוּם שְׁבוּת — — *Any activity* [from] *which one is obliged* [to abstain] *because of a Rabbinical injunction —*

I.e., any action prohibited by the Sages because of its resemblance to a Scriptural category of labor (see *Rambam, Hil. Shabbos* 21:1).

[Use of the word חַיָּבִין in the context of a prohibited action is unusual; ordinarily it is

connected with a liability or obligation as in חַיָּב מָמוֹן, *liable for monetary payments,* or חַיָּב מִיתָה, *liable for the death penalty.* Our translation, *obliged to abstain from,* follows *Rashi's* commentary and is obviously an attempt to reconcile the normal usage of the word with its meaning in our mishnah. *Rambam's* view (*Hil. Shabbos* 1:3) that transgression of a Rabbinical injunction carries the punishment of מַכַּת מַרְדוּת, literally *lashes of rebelliousness,* would allow us to interpret חַיָּבִין in the ordinary sense of

and we may put a vessel under the dripping water on the Sabbath.

2. **A**ny activity [from] which one is obliged [to abstain] because of a Rabbinical injunction — [even] if it is a non-mandatory *mitzvah*, [or even] if it is a *mitzvah* — on the Sabbath, one is [also] obliged [to abstain from it] on *Yom Tov*.

YAD AVRAHAM

liability; i.e., any sin for which one is liable for the punishment of violating a Rabbinical injunction — namely, lashes.

[The term שְׁבוּת, used for Rabbinical injunctions of the Sabbath, is derived from the word שָׁבַת, *Shabbos,* or שְׁבִיתָה, *rest. Rambam (Comm.)* holds that שְׁבוּת, although Rabbinical in nature, is based on the Scriptural commandment, בֶּחָרִישׁ וּבַקָּצִיר תִּשְׁבֹּת, *from plowing and reaping shall you rest (Exodus* 34:21). The word תִּשְׁבֹּת, *you shall rest,* implies that one is to abstain even from actions which are not מְלָאכָה, *labor.* This is the basis of Rabbinical injunctions that prohibit actions which resemble the מְלָאכוֹת, *labors,* or may lead one to inadvertently violate a Scriptural precept *(Hil. Shabbos* 21:1).[1]

מִשׁוּם רְשׁוּת — [even] *if it is a non-mandatory mitzvah* [lit. *because of a voluntary act*],

This category includes actions that involve elements of a *mitzvah* but are not mandatory, (as illustrated in the examples provided by the mishnah) and which were nevertheless prohibited by the Sages *(Rav; Rashi).*

[This rendition of the word רְשׁוּת is a departure from its normal meaning which is a voluntary act not related to *mitzvah* performance. In the context of our mishnah this type of action would fall under the category of שְׁבוּת mentioned previously and therefore רְשׁוּת must refer to a quasi-*mitzvah* act, which by contrast to a *mitzvah* is considered voluntary.]

מִשׁוּם מִצְוָה — [or even] *if it is a mitzvah* [lit. *because of a mitzvah*] —

The category of Rabbinically prohibited actions that includes outright *mitzvos (Rav).*

בְּשַׁבָּת, — *on the Sabbath,*

[All of the above mentioned categories which are prohibited Rabbinically on the Sabbath.]

חַיָּבִין עָלָיו בְּיוֹם טוֹב. — *one is [also] obliged [to abstain from it] on Yom Tov.*

[Although the laws of *Yom Tov* are not as stringent as those of the Sabbath, the Rabbis did not waive any of their prohibitions.]

1. *Ramban* (to *Leviticus* 23:24; cited by *Maggid Mishneh, Hil. Shabbos* 21:1) remarks that if only the thirty-nine labors were banned, a person could occupy himself by toiling at tasks not included in these labors without finding a minute for rest (see *Lechem Mishneh; Mirkeves HaMishneh).*

Ritva (Rosh HaShonah 32b) qualifies this view. Included in the Scriptural precept of resting is the obligation to refrain from all activities banned by the Rabbis to keep from converting the Sabbath into a weekday. However, if one transgresses an individual Rabbinical prohibition but keeps the others, so that he does not transform the Sabbath into a weekday, then his act is only prohibited Rabbinically. *Chasam Sofer (Teshuvos, Choshen Mishpat* 195; see also vol. 6 §97) rules that the transgression of even a single Rabbinic prohibition, if committed continually so as to turn the Sabbath into a weekday — such as keeping a store open — constitutes a violation of the Scriptural precept of resting (cf. *Sefer HaMitzvos of R' Saadiah Gaon, v.* I, p. 377).

וְאֵלּוּ הֵן מִשּׁוּם שְׁבוּת: לֹא עוֹלִין בְּאִילָן, וְלֹא
רוֹכְבִין עַל גַּבֵּי בְהֵמָה, וְלֹא שָׁטִין עַל פְּנֵי הַמַּיִם,
וְלֹא מְטַפְּחִין, וְלֹא מְסַפְּקִין, וְלֹא מְרַקְּדִין.
וְאֵלּוּ הֵן מִשּׁוּם רְשׁוּת: לֹא דָנִין, וְלֹא מְקַדְּשִׁין,
וְלֹא חוֹלְצִין, וְלֹא מְיַבְּמִין.

יד אברהם

וְאֵלּוּ הֵן מִשּׁוּם שְׁבוּת: לֹא עוֹלִין בְּאִילָן,
— (And) these [i.e., the following] are
[to be abstained from] because of a
Rabbinical injunction: We may not
ascend a tree,

This act was prohibited by the
Sages lest, in the course of climbing
the tree, one may forget himself and
tear off branches (or fruit) which
would be a violation of the *melachah* of *reaping (Rav; Gem. 36b).

וְלֹא רוֹכְבִין עַל גַּבֵּי בְהֵמָה, — nor (may
we) ride upon an animal,

Lest one cut off a branch to use as
a whip (ibid.).

וְלֹא שָׁטִין עַל פְּנֵי הַמַּיִם, — nor (may
we) swim on the water,

Swimming is Rabbinically prohibited lest one make a raft or life
preserver. This construction would
be a Scriptural violation of the Sabbath or Yom Tov (ibid.).

וְלֹא מְטַפְּחִין, וְלֹא מְסַפְּקִין, וְלֹא מְרַקְּדִין. —
nor (may we) clap hands, nor (may
we) slap thighs, nor (may we)
dance.

These actions, which accompany
song, were prohibited so that one
would not be led to repair musical
instruments and thereby violate the
Sabbath or Yom Tov (ibid.). [See
Orach Chaim 339:3 for a justification of the prevalent custom that
places no restrictions on clapping
while singing or dancing, in apparent disregard to the prohibition
outlined here (see also Tos. 30a).]

וְאֵלּוּ הֵן מִשּׁוּם רְשׁוּת: — (And) these
are [lit. because of] non-mandatory
mitzvos:

[I.e., the following are included in
the category of Rabbinical prohibitions that involve *mitzvah* related
but not mandatory acts.]

לֹא דָנִין, — We may not adjudicate
[financial disputes],

One may not preside over a *din
Torah*, a financial lawsuit, on the
Sabbath or Yom Tov, for the reason
explained in the commentary below
(s.v. וְלֹא מְיַבְּמִין).

Although related to a *mitzvah*,
adjudicating is included in the
category of רְשׁוּת because it is not an
absolute obligation. There are times
that a judge should forgo ruling on
a case in order to allow someone
more qualified to adjudicate (Rav,
Gem. 36b).

וְלֹא מְקַדְּשִׁין, — nor (may we) betroth,

Throughout Talmudic literature,
discussion of the laws of marriage
center on two ceremonies which
create two distinct phases in the
status of the married couple. The
first, called קִידּוּשִׁין [kiddushin],
betrothal, occurs when a man con-
secrates (מְקַדֵּשׁ) his wife to himself
by any of three methods described
at the beginning of tractate Kiddushin, the most common of which
is giving the bride a ring or any object of monetary value. At this point
they are legally married in regard to
most aspects of Jewish law (e.g., she

These are [to be abstained from] because of a Rabbinical injunction: We may not ascend a tree, nor ride upon an animal, nor swim on the water, nor clap hands, nor slap thighs, nor dance.

These are non-mandatory *mitzvos:* We may not adjudicate, nor betroth, nor perform *chalitzah,* nor perform levirate marriage.

YAD AVRAHAM

is forbidden to other men), although the couple did not yet live together. The second phase of marriage is called נִישׂוּאִין [*nissuin*], *marriage,* and is effected by the *chupah* ceremony marking the completion of the marriage after which the bride and groom begin life together.

Although in our custom both phases of marriage take place simultaneously, in Talmudic times there was a lapse of up to a year between the *kiddushin* and the *nissuin* phases — during this period a woman was considered married but still lived with her parents.

[The use of the word *betrothed* for קִידּוּשִׁין is not exact, and is used only for want of a more accurate English expression for this phase of marriage. Betrothal as we know it, i.e., a commitment to enter into marriage, is known in Talmudic parlance as שִׁידּוּכִים, *shiduchim,* an agreement that may be made even on the Sabbath (see *Orach Chaim* 306:5; *Shabbos* 150a).]

The *kiddushin* ceremony is forbidden to take place on the Sabbath or *Yom Tov* because it is an act of legal implication and one may be led to writing documents (see below, s.v. וְלֹא מְיַבְּמִין).

The *Gemara* explains that *kiddushin* is not considered in the *mitzvah* category for it is not an absolute obligation; if a man already has children he is not bound to remarry. (See *Mishnah Berurah* 339:16.)

וְלֹא חוֹלְצִין, — *nor (may we) perform chalitzah,*

[As outlined in *Deuteronomy* (25:5-11), if a married man dies without children, his brother must

either marry the widow in what is known as יְבוּם [*yibum*], *levirate marriage,* or, through the rite of חֲלִיצָה, *chalitzah,* free her to marry another.]

The *Gemara* (37a) comments that this activity is classified here as non-mandatory because if there are more than one brother, the obligation to perform this *mitzvah* devolves primarily upon the oldest. Although if one of the younger brothers takes the initiative to perform either *chalitzah* or levirate marriage his act is valid, the original mandatory performance is not his responsibility. Thus the *mitzvos* of *chalitzah* and levirate marriage (see below) are considered non-mandatory in relation to all but the oldest brother.

וְלֹא מְיַבְּמִין. — *nor (may we) perform levirate marriage.*

Although under Rabbinic law *kiddushin* must precede the final phase of the levirate marriage as in any other marriage, the marriage is nevertheless not considered legal (in the specific context of *yibum*) by Scriptural law until it is consummated. Thus, a levirate marriage may not be consummated on Sabbath, for it is at this point that the marriage acquires legal status.

A normal marriage, by contrast, may be consummated on the Sab-

וְאֵלּוּ הֵן מִשּׁוּם מִצְוָה: לֹא מַקְדִּישִׁין, וְלֹא
מַעֲרִיכִין, וְלֹא מַחֲרִימִין, וְלֹא מַגְבִּיהִין תְּרוּמָה
וּמַעֲשֵׂר.

כָּל אֵלּוּ בְּיוֹם טוֹב אָמְרוּ, קַל וָחֹמֶר בַּשַּׁבָּת. אֵין
בֵּין יוֹם טוֹב לַשַּׁבָּת אֶלָּא אֹכֶל נֶפֶשׁ בִּלְבָד.

יד אברהם

bath if the *kiddushin* and *chupah* were performed prior to the Sabbath [see *Orach Chaim* 280:2].

All of these activities are prohibited on the Sabbath for fear that the course of their performance may lead to the labor of *writing. A judge may forget that it is Sabbath or *Yom Tov* and record the decision in writing; a *kesubah* (marriage contract) may be written; or a *chalitzah* document (שְׁטַר חֲלִיצָה; used to establish proof that a *chalitzah* has been performed) may be drawn up (*Gem.* 37a, *Rashi*).

וְאֵלּוּ הֵן מִשּׁוּם מִצְוָה: — *And these are mitzvos:*

The following are included in the category of *mitzvah* actions prohibited by the Sages on the Sabbath.

לֹא מַקְדִּישִׁין, — *We may not consecrate,*

[I.e., it is forbidden to designate an animal for sacrifice, or to donate an object to the Temple treasury (בֶּדֶק הַבַּיִת).]

וְלֹא מַעֲרִיכִין, — *nor (may we) make assessment vows,*

[The reference is to *Leviticus* 27:1-8 which states that if a person pledges the value of his own assessment (עֶרְכִּי עָלַי), or that of another person, he must donate to the Temple Treasury the amount established by the Torah as the

assessment of a person of that age and sex.]

וְלֹא מַחֲרִימִין, — *nor (may we) make a cherem,*

By Torah law a person may pronounce an object *cherem*, i.e., set aside or dedicated for priestly or Temple use. When he does not specify the exact nature of the *cherem*, it becomes the property of the Temple treasury (*Rav; Rashi*).

The reason for prohibiting these activities is that they resemble מֶקַח וּמִמְכָּר, *buying and selling,* because the ownership of an object is transferred from the individual to the Temple treasury (*Rav; Gem.* 37a).

The ban on doing business is found in Scripture (*Nechemiah* 13:15-22). It is also prohibited on the festival because it may lead to *writing. Talking about business activities is included in the command (*Isaiah* 58:13) to honor the Sabbath by refraining from speaking about weekday things (*Rashi* 37a and 27b; see prefatory note to 3:6).

וְלֹא מַגְבִּיהִין תְּרוּמָה וּמַעֲשֵׂר. — *nor (may we) separate terumah and tithes.*

[Terumah is the portion of the produce which by Torah law must be separated and given to the Kohanim. The Torah also requires tithes to be separated from crops. The first tithe (מַעֲשֵׂר רִאשׁוֹן) is given to the Levites and the second (מַעֲשֵׂר שֵׁנִי) is eaten by the owner in

5
2

And these are *mitzvos:* We may not consecrate, nor make assessment vows, nor make a *cherem,* nor separate *terumah* and tithes.

All these were promulgated regarding *Yom Tov,* surely they apply to the Sabbath. There is no difference between *Yom Tov* and the Sabbath except [in laws pertaining to] food preparation.

YAD AVRAHAM

Jerusalem. On the third and sixth year of the Sabbatical cycle the second tithe is replaced by מַעֲשַׂר עָנִי, *the tithe of the poor,* which is given to the needy.]

Since the produce may not be eaten prior to separating *terumah* and tithes, the separation is forbidden on the Sabbath because it is considered מְתַקֵּן, *perfecting and completing.* Moreover separation is prohibited even if the *terumah* is to be given a *Kohen* on *Yom Tov* and consumed by him on the same day (*Rav, Gem.* 37a with *Rashi;* see comm. to 1:6, s.v. בֵּין שֶׁהוּרְמוּ and 4:7, s.v. בַּשְּׁבִיעִית).

קָל אֵלּוּ הֵיוֹחַ נֶוֹב אַמְרוּ, 4 II *these* [aforementioned prohibitions] *were promulgated* [lit. *were said*] *regarding Yom Tov,*

[I.e., the original enactment of the prohibitions was intended for *Yom Tov.*]

קָל נָחֹמֶר בַּשַּׁבָּת. — *surely they apply* [lit. *a fortiori*] *to the Sabbath* [also].

[If these activities are prohibited on *Yom Tov* (on which dispensation is given for food preparation, and the punishment for violation is relatively mild), they are surely prohibited on Sabbath, where the laws are more stringent and the punishment more severe (see *Yad*

Avraham to *Megillah* 1:5, ArtScroll ed.).

Tosefos Yom Tov comments that, in light to this last statement, the opening phrase in the mishnah — *Any activity from which one is obliged to abstain ... on the Sabbath, one is also obliged to abstain from on Yom Tov* — must be referring to other prohibitions than the ones mentioned here, for the prohibitions mentioned here were originally promulgated for *Yom Tov.*

אֵין בֵּין יוֹם טוֹב לַשַּׁבָּת אֶלָּא אֹכֶל נֶפֶשׁ בִּלְבָד. — *There is no difference between* [the laws applying to] *Yom Tov and* [those applying to] *the Sabbath except* [in laws pertaining to] *food preparation.*

[The reference is of course to the law that labor required for the preparation of food is permitted on *Yom Tov.*]

The *Gemara* (37a) comments that the mishnah is in accordance with the view of *Beis Shammai* (above 1:5). According to *Beis Hillel* (ibid.), even labor not related to food preparation is permitted if the principle of *mitoch* (see ibid.) is applicable and the results of that labor are needed on *Yom Tov* (*Rav*).

The *Gemara* (ibid.) points out that the previous mishnah (5:1) also disagrees with our mishnah's statement, *there is no difference between Sabbath and Yom Tov except ...,* for there is another difference. The previous mishnah states, *We may lower produce through a skylight on Yom Tov, but not on the Sabbath.*

[107]   THE MISHNAH / BEITZAH — Chapter Five: *Mashilin*

לים. **הַבְּהֵמָה** [ג] וְהַכֵּלִים כְּרַגְלֵי הַבְּעָלִים.
הַמּוֹסֵר בְּהֶמְתּוֹ לִבְנוֹ אוֹ
לְרוֹעֶה, הֲרֵי אֵלּוּ כְּרַגְלֵי הַבְּעָלִים.

יד אברהם

3.

תְּחוּם — Techum ⏵⏴

One of the laws of Sabbath and *Yom Tov* limits the distance a person may walk to an area termed תְּחוּם, *techum* [lit. *border*]. Although the exact calculation of a person's *techum* is a complex matter, basically the law limits a person's walking to an area extending 2,000 cubits from his home or city in any direction. (A more detailed description of this halachah is available in the fourth and fifth chapters of *Eruvin* [see *Yad Avraham* in ArtScroll ed.] and in *Shulchan Aruch, Orach Chaim* 398, 399; see also footnote to 4:1.)

The basis of this prohibition is the verse: *Let none go out of his place on the seventh day* (Exodus 16:29; see *Eruvin* 51a). The term *his place* is defined as the area of the *techum*. There is controversy among the *Tannaim* as to whether this is a Scriptural prohibition or whether it is of Rabbinical origin (see *Sotah* 5:3; *Eruvin* 79b). The accepted majority opinion is that it is of Rabbinical origin (see *Mishnah Berurah* 397:1).

A lesser known aspect of the law extends the restrictions of *techum* to a person's property. Just as a person may not leave his *techum*, so may his belongings not leave the *techum*. The discussion in the following five mishnayos centers on this aspect of the law.

הַבְּהֵמָה וְהַכֵּלִים כְּרַגְלֵי הַבְּעָלִים. — *Animals and utensils are as the feet of the[ir] owners.*

Livestock and objects belonging to a person are restricted to his *techum*, and, as the mishnah phrases it, may be carried only to the point where *the feet of their owners* may go.

This restriction is not limited to the object's owner; no one is permitted to transport an object out of the *techum* allotted to its owner (*Rav; Rashi*). [For example, if A lives 1000 cubits south of B he may walk to a point 3000 cubits south of B's residence, but he may not carry B's possessions further than 2000 cubits from B's home.]

Although the mishnah specifies livestock and utensils, these are only used as common examples. Actually, every object is subject to this restriction (*Mishnah Berurah* 397:71; see also *Rambam, Hil. Yom Tov* 5:9).

2,000 — 2,000
2,000 | 2,000

Shimon's house

Reuven's house

southern border of Shimon's techum

Reuven's techum

Reuven may not move Shimon's possessions beyond the border of Shimon's techum.

©1982 Mesorah Publications, Ltd. / N.Y.C.

הַמּוֹסֵר בְּהֶמְתּוֹ לִבְנוֹ אוֹ לְרוֹעֶה, — *If one entrusts* [lit. *gives*] *his animals to his son or to a shepherd,*

One entrusted his animal to someone else's care on *Yom Tov.*

3. **A**nimals and utensils are as the feet of the[ir] owners. If one entrusts his animals to his son or to a shepherd, they are as the feet of the[ir] owners.

YAD AVRAHAM

The question is: which *techum* area shall we assign to the animal — that of its owner or that of the person presently responsible for its care?

[The *techum* is determined at the onset (בֵּין הַשְּׁמָשׁוֹת, *twilight)* of *Yom Tov*. Even if the ownership or association with an object changes on *Yom Tov*, the *techum* remains fixed as it was at the onset of *Yom Tov* (see mishnah 4, s.v. הַשּׁוֹאֵל כְּלִי).]

הֲרֵי אֵלוּ כְּרַגְלֵי הַבְּעָלִים. — *they are as the feet of the[ir] owners.*

Since they were not entrusted to the shepherd before *Yom Tov* they already had assumed the *techum* area of the owner at the onset of *Yom Tov*, and therefore they are subject to their owner's *techum* (*Rashi*).

The *Gemara* (37b) comments that the mishnah speaks of a case where there is more than one shepherd in the town who regularly care for people's flocks. Since the owner has a choice of shepherds, neither one of them can be assumed with certainty (before the onset of *Yom Tov*) to be the shepherd to whom the cattle will be assigned. The animals therefore cannot be considered as the shepherd's (concerning the law of *techum*) until they are actually assigned to him. If the assignation takes place on *Yom Tov* the livestock has already assumed their owner's *techum* at the onset of *Yom Tov* and this status will remain unchanged thereafter. The mishnah states, *If one entrusts his animals to his son or to a shepherd,* to highlight that the basis of the mishnah's

law is the fact that the owner here has a choice of shepherds (his son or the shepherd). If in fact there is only one shepherd to whom people regularly assign their animals, and the owner did not have the alternative of entrusting them to his son, then the animals can be assumed to have been assigned to the shepherd in advance, and would follow his *techum* area even if at the onset of *Yom Tov* they were still in the possession of the owner (see *Gem.* 37b, with *Rosh* and *Meiri*).

[The above interpretation is based on *Rashi's* (see also *Rosh, Rashba* and *Meiri*) comments to the *Gemara*. According to this interpretation, there is no basic difference between a son and a shepherd. *Rif* (see *HaMaor, Milchamos* and *Ran;* also *Rosh Yosef,* for the various renderings of *Rif's* opinion) and *Rambam* (Hil. Yom Tov 5:1) understand that the *Gemara* distinguishes between one's son and an outside shepherd. In the case of one's son to whom the cattle are sure to be assigned they are nevertheless considered to be in the owner's domain and their acquire his techum. This is true even where the animals were assigned to the son before *Yom Tov.* A child's domain is considered (vis-a-vis the parent) as an extension of the parent's jurisdiction, and not as a separate entity. But where there is only one (unrelated) shepherd, the cattle are considered to have been assigned to him before the onset of *Yom Tov,* and, being under his jurisdiction, assume his (the shepherd's) *techum* and are not 'like the feet of their owner.' However if the animals were assigned (even before *Yom Tov*) to the care of two shepherds, since we cannot consider the animals to be under the (sole) jurisdiction of any one of the shepherds, they are considered as not having left the jurisdiction of their owner for *techum* purposes. [The rendition of *Rif* given is that of *HaMaor* which coincides with *Maggid Mishneh's* understanding of *Rambam;* cf. *Milchamos, Ran, Rosh Yosef.*] Thus the mishnah tells us, *If*

כֵּלִים הַמְיֻחָדִין לְאֶחָד מִן הָאַחִין שֶׁבַּבַּיִת, הֲרֵי אֵלּוּ כְּרַגְלָיו. וְשֶׁאֵין מְיֻחָדִין, הֲרֵי אֵלּוּ כִּמְקוֹם שֶׁהוֹלְכִין.

[ד] **הַשּׁוֹאֵל** כְּלִי מֵחֲבֵרוֹ מֵעֶרֶב יוֹם טוֹב, כְּרַגְלֵי הַשּׁוֹאֵל. בְּיוֹם טוֹב, כְּרַגְלֵי הַמַּשְׁאִיל. הָאִשָּׁה שֶׁשָּׁאֲלָה מֵחֲבֶרְתָּהּ תַּבְלִין וּמַיִם וּמֶלַח

יד אברהם

one assigns his animals to his son (singular or plural) even before *Yom Tov*, or to a [consortium of] shepherd[s; plural], *they are as the feet of their owners*. If there is only one shepherd (or the animals have been assigned to one of many shepherds even on *Yom Tov*), they are·as the feet of the shepherd.

Shulchan Aruch's (*Orach Chaim* 397:4-5) ruling is in accordance with *Rambam* and *Rif*. However, many later authorities disagree with this and follow *Rashi's* opinion (see *Mishnah Berurah* 397:10-13).

כֵּלִים הַמְיֻחָדִין לְאֶחָד מִן הָאַחִין שֶׁבַּבַּיִת, — *Utensils which are reserved for one of the brothers in the house*

This case involves brothers who have inherited utensils from their parents but have not yet formally divided their inheritance. The mishnah states that if one brother is already using some of the utensils for himself, then those utensils follow his *techum* area.

[The word שֶׁבַּבַּיִת, *in 'the' house*, indicates that the brothers still reside in the house of their deceased parent. Otherwise, it would be inconceivable that one of the brothers would reserve the use of certain utensils before the inheritance had been divided.]

הֲרֵי אֵלּוּ כְּרַגְלָיו. — (*they*) *are as his feet*.

[His use of these utensils, coupled with the fact that he owns a share in them, is reason enough that the utensils be considered under his jurisdiction for *techum* purposes.]

וְשֶׁאֵין מְיֻחָדִין, — *But those* [utensils]

which are not reserved

Those utensils in the estate which are used by all the brothers equally (*Rav; Rashi*).

הֲרֵי אֵלּוּ כִּמְקוֹם שֶׁהוֹלְכִין. — *are to be carried only in the area where they* [all] *may go* [lit. *are as the place where they go*].

Reuven's house

Shimon's house

| Reuven's techum | common techum | Shimon's techum |

Utensils which are reserved for one of the brothers in the house are as his feet. But those which are not reserved are to be carried only in the area where they [all] may go.

4. If one borrows a utensil from his friend on the day before *Yom Tov*, [it is] as the feet of the borrower; if on *Yom Tov*, [it is] as the feet of the lender. If a woman borrowed from her friend spices, water

YAD AVRAHAM

The utensils assume the *techum* of all the brothers and are restricted to an area common to all of them.

Thus, if the brothers made *eruvei techumin* (see comm. to mishnah 6, s.v. וְעֵרְבוּ), and one placed his *eruv* 2000 cubits north of their residence, which thereby restricts his movements to the 4000 cubits north of their residence, and another brother placed his *eruv* 2000 cubits to the south, restricting his movements to an area 4,000 cubits south of the residence, then the utensils common to both of them may not be moved at all *(Rav; Rashi).*

4.

הַשׁוֹאֵל כְּלִי מֵחֲבֵרוֹ מֵעֶרֶב יוֹם טוֹב, כְּרַגְלֵי הַשׁוֹאֵל. — *If one borrows a utensil from his friend on the day before Yom Tov, [it is] as the feet of the borrower;*

[Since the utensil is under his jurisdiction it is considered his for *techum* purposes, even though he is not the actual owner.]

The *Gemara* (38a) adds that even if the lender merely promised the object to the borrower before *Yom Tov*, and the borrower first took the object home on *Yom Tov*, it is still considered under his jurisdiction and is *as the feet of the borrower.*

בְּיוֹם טוֹב, כְּרַגְלֵי הַמַּשְׁאִיל. — [But] *if* [the utensil was borrowed] *on Yom Tov, [it is] as the feet of the lender.*

Because the *techum* is determined at the onset of *Yom Tov* (at twilight), the *techum* assigned to an object depends upon its status at that moment *(Rav; Rashi).*

Rav adds (from *Gemara* 38a) that

even if the owner had been accustomed to lend this object to the same person every *Yom Tov*, it is nevertheless considered 'as the feet of the owner' as long as it was not borrowed (or promised) before *Yom Tov*.

הָאִשָּׁה שֶׁשָּׁאֲלָה מֵחֲבֶרְתָּהּ תְּבָלִין וּמַיִם וּמֶלַח לְעִסָּתָהּ, — *If a woman borrowed from her friend spices, water and salt for her dough,*

The woman borrowed spices for cooking, or water and salt for baking *(Rav; Rashi).* Since she borrowed these items on *Yom Tov*, the dish she cooks or bakes is actually a mixture of ingredients as far as *techum* is concerned: the woman's own ingredients would be assigned her *techum*, but those that she borrowed on *Yom Tov* would follow the *techum* of the person in whose possession they were at the onset of *Yom Tov*. The mishnah's question is: How are we to judge the *techum*

לְעִסָּתָהּ, הֲרֵי אֵלּוּ כְּרַגְלֵי שְׁתֵּיהֶן. רַבִּי יְהוּדָה פּוֹטֵר בְּמַיִם, מִפְּנֵי שֶׁאֵין בָּהֶן מַמָּשׁ.

[ה] **הַגַּחֶלֶת** כְּרַגְלֵי הַבְּעָלִים, וְשַׁלְהֶבֶת בְּכָל מָקוֹם.

גַּחֶלֶת שֶׁל הֶקְדֵּשׁ מוֹעֲלִין בָּהּ; וְשַׁלְהֶבֶת לֹא נֶהֱנִין, וְלֹא מוֹעֲלִין.

הַמּוֹצִיא גַחֶלֶת לִרְשׁוּת הָרַבִּים חַיָּב; וְשַׁלְהֶבֶת, פָּטוּר.

יד אברהם

of the dish or the dough which is composed of a combination of these ingredients?

הֲרֵי אֵלּוּ כְּרַגְלֵי שְׁתֵּיהֶן. — *they* [i.e., the dish and the dough] *are as the feet of both.*

Since the dish or the dough consist of ingredients with two incongruent *techum* areas they are limited to an area common to both women.

רַבִּי יְהוּדָה פּוֹטֵר בְּמַיִם, מִפְּנֵי שֶׁאֵין בָּהֶן מַמָּשׁ. — *R' Yehudah exempts water, because it has no substance.*

Since the substance of water cannot be discerned either in the dough or in the dish, R' Yehudah exempts the finished product from the limitations of *techum* imposed by the water. Thus if a woman borrowed water and added it to her flour, the dough would be assigned to her *techum* without any consideration of the water's original *techum*.

The *Gemara* (39a) says that the mishnah refers to a dish to which

water had been added but had cooked out. Since the mixture is now a dry solid food, the water is not considered as a separate ingredient. However, water that was used in a soup or other liquid dish is not exempt, for it is a discernible ingredient in the finished product. The *Gemara* adds that the salt referred to here is a thick salt which does not dissolve completely upon being mixed into the dish or dough. Otherwise it too, in R' Yehudah's opinion, would be exempt 'because it has no [distinguishable] substance.'

[The moisture in an object, though it can be chemically identified as water, is nevertheless considered non-existent as far as *techum* is concerned. Perhaps this is due to the principle of בִּטּוּל בְּרֹב, *subsumption into the majority*, i.e., when two unlike substances are combined, the substance forming the major part nullifies the second substance which is then halachically considered to be non-existent. Indeed the discussion in the *Gemara* concerning the ruling of the *Tanna kamma* (that the water, spices and salt are considered as distinct ingredients with their own *techum*) points to such an explanation.]

5.

The mishnah now mentions a distinction between a burning coal and its flame with regard to the *techum*,

then digresses briefly to two other instances where this distinction has halachic ramifications: (a) The law

5
5　　　and salt for her dough, they are as the feet of both. R'
　　　Yehudah exempts water, because it has no substance.

5. The burning coal is as the feet of its owner, but a
　　　flame can be taken everywhere.

[Using] a coal belonging to the Temple incurs a
me'ilah sacrifice; but concerning a flame, we may not
use it, yet we do not incur a *me'ilah* sacrifice.

One who takes a coal out [of a private domain] to a
public domain incurs a sin offering; but if [one carries out] a flame, he is exempt.

of מְעִילָה [*me'ilah*], *transgression*, the term used to describe the Torah's prohibition of the use of הֶקְדֵּשׁ, *sacred property*, for non-sacred, personal purposes. Under this law, described in *Leviticus* 5:14-16 (see *Rashi* ad loc.), anyone who unintentionally uses sacred property [sacrificial animals or objects belonging to the Temple treasury (בֶּדֶק הַבַּיִת)], must atone for his sin by bringing a קָרְבַּן מְעִילָה, *me'ilah sacrifice*. (b) The labor of *transporting from domain to domain* on the Sabbath.

The *Gemara* (39a) adds two more instances where this distinction has halachic ramifications.

הַגַּחֶלֶת כְּרַגְלֵי הַבְּעָלִים, וְשַׁלְהֶבֶת בְּכָל מָקוֹם. — *The burning coal is as the feet of its owner, but a flame can be taken everywhere* [lit. *the flame is in every place*].

If someone lit a candle from his friend's flame, he may transport the burning candle to outside of his friend's *techum* (*Rav; Rashi*). [Since the flame is not considered to be a tangible substance (דָּבָר שֶׁיֵּשׁ בּוֹ מַמָּשׁ) it is not subject to the restrictions of *techum*.]

גַּחֶלֶת שֶׁל הֶקְדֵּשׁ מוֹעֲלִין בָּהּ; — [*Using*]

a coal belonging to the Temple in-curs a *me'ilah* [lit. *transgression*] *sacrifice*;

Use of a burning coal belonging to the Temple treasury for personal benefit (e.g., cooking or heating) is a violation of Scriptural law and therefore incurs a *me'ilah* sacrifice (*Rav*).

וְשַׁלְהֶבֶת לֹא נֶהֱנִין, וְלֹא מוֹעֲלִין. — *but concerning a flame* [belonging to the Temple], *we may not use it, yet we do not incur a me'ilah sacrifice.*

[Since the flame does not have substance, it is not considered to be Temple property according to Scriptural law. Therefore, one does not incur a *me'ilah* sacrifice for this transgression.] Nevertheless there is a Rabbinical prohibition against us-ing the flame (*Rav; Rashi*).

[The flame (belonging to the Temple) referred to here is a flame detached from its source — the coal. While the flame is still attached to the coal the flame's use is con-sidered use of the coal (see *Rosh* here: *Turei Zahav, Yoreh Deah* 142:3).]

הַמּוֹצִיא גַחֶלֶת לִרְשׁוּת הָרַבִּים חַיָּב; — *One who takes a coal out* [of a private domain] *to a public domain*

בּוֹר שֶׁל יָחִיד כְּרַגְלֵי הַיָּחִיד; וְשֶׁל אַנְשֵׁי אוֹתָהּ
הָעִיר, כְּרַגְלֵי אַנְשֵׁי אוֹתָהּ הָעִיר; וְשֶׁל עוֹלֵי בָבֶל,
כְּרַגְלֵי הַמְמַלֵּא.

יד אברהם

incurs a sin offering;

[Carrying an object from a private domain into a public domain or vice versa on the Sabbath is a violation of *transporting*, which, if done unintentionally, must be atoned for with a sin offering.]

וְשַׁלְהֶבֶת, פָּטוּר. — *but if [one carries out] a flame, he is exempt [from bringing a sin offering].*

Since the flame itself has no substance, transporting it cannot be regarded as carrying.

The *Gemara* (39a) explains that a flame is considered substanceless only if the person, by blowing or waving at the flaming coal, detaches the flame from the coal. If one transports a flame which is still attached to its source, e.g., a flaming splint, he incurs liability for a sacrifice. [Even if the splint itself does not have the minimum size which is a prerequisite for incurring a sacrifice obligation, one is liable to a sin offering for *transporting* the flame, for a fire attached to its source is considered an item of substance.] The mishnah now returns to its discussion of various substances with regard to the laws of *techum.*

בּוֹר שֶׁל יָחִיד — *[The water in] a pit belonging to a private individual*

The water contained in a privately owned cistern was drawn on *Yom Tov* by someone other than the owner.

כְּרַגְלֵי הַיָּחִיד; — *is as the feet of that individual;*

The water drawn from this pit is limited to the *techum* of the pit's owner (Rav; Rashi).

וְשֶׁל אַנְשֵׁי אוֹתָהּ הָעִיר, כְּרַגְלֵי אַנְשֵׁי אוֹתָהּ הָעִיר; — *(and) [the water in] one belonging to the people of that*

town is as the feet of the people of that town;

Water drawn from a municipal water hole is limited to the *techum* of the town to which it belongs. The *techum* of the town extends two thousand cubits on every side of the town (see *Orach Chaim* 397 on how the *techum* of a town is determined). The ruling of the mishnah refers to a person living, for example, one thousand cubits outside of the town. His *techum* includes the water hole but extends for one thousand cubits past the limits of the town's *techum*. This person may not transport the water further than the town's *techum* (*Ran;* see *Tos. Yom Tov*).

The individual may not move the water out of the town's techum.

וְשֶׁל עוֹלֵי בָבֶל, — *but [the water in] those [set aside] for the Babylonian pilgrims*

Water holes were dug near the

5

5

[The water in] a pit belonging to a private individual is as the feet of that individual; [the water in] one belonging to the people of that town is as the feet of the people of that town; but [the water in] those [set aside] for the Babylonian pilgrims is as the feet of the one who draws [the water].

YAD AVRAHAM

roads to provide for the people making the pilgrimage from Babylon to the Holy Temple on the three festivals (Pesach, Shavuos, Succos) with water for themselves and their livestock (from *Rav* and *Rashi; Nedarim* 5:5 with *Rav; Tos. Yom Tov*).

כְּרַגְלֵי הַמְמַלֵּא. — *is as the feet of the one who draws* [*the water*].

These public cisterns are essentially ownerless, belonging neither to a private person nor to a specific municipality. Therefore the *techum* of the water contained in them was

not determined at the onset of *Yom Tov* and is first fixed when someone draws the water, thereby becoming its owner [and it becomes restricted to his *techum*] (*Rav; Rashi*).

The mishnah's distinction between a private or municipal water hole and one which is ownerless applies only to water stored in a cistern. Spring water, by contrast, is as 'the feet of the drawer' even if the spring flows from private property (*Gem.* 39a; *Orach Chaim* 397:15). Since spring water is perpetually moving, its *techum* cannot be determined (אֵינוּ קוֹנֶה שְׁבִיתָה) at the onset of the Sabbath. Only when the water is drawn and its movement arrested is its *techum* fixed (see *Eruvin* 46a with *Rashi*).

6.

עֵרוּבֵי תְּחוּמִין — Eruvei Techumin

עֵירוּבֵי תְּחוּמִין [*eruvei techumin*], literally, *blending of techum areas*, is a procedure instituted by the Sages to enable a person to modify the limits of his *techum*. More simply stated, this is accomplished by allowing a person to establish a legal residence at a location other than his regular home by putting a nominal amount of food at the desired location. This food constitutes the *eruv*, and the place where it lies symbolically becomes his residence for the duration of the Sabbath or *Yom Tov*. Thus, by placing an *eruv*, one alters the parameters of his *techum*, extending them in one direction, while shortening them in the other.

This is best explained by visualizing the *techum* of the Sabbath as an area whose center is the individual's residence and which extends two thousand cubits to all sides of the residence (see *Orach Chaim* 399:10). One who wishes to travel past the circumference of this circle on the Sabbath may do so by placing an *eruv* prior to the onset of the Sabbath, at the location within his *techum* closest to his destination. By establishing a symbolic residence at another point in the *techum* he shifts the center of the area, in effect lengthening in one direction the distance he may travel from his home. [See footnote to 4:1.]

For example, if he places his *eruv* two thousand cubits to the north of his regular residence, he thereby places his domicile at the southern extreme of the area at whose center he has placed his *eruv*. He therefore has the benefit of the entire length of the area of the circle to his north. However, as a consequence of shifting

[ו] מִי שֶׁהָיוּ פֵרוֹתָיו בְּעִיר אַחֶרֶת, וְעֵרְבוּ בְּנֵי
אוֹתָהּ הָעִיר לְהָבִיא אֶצְלוֹ מִפֵּרוֹתָיו,
לֹא יָבִיאוּ לוֹ. וְאִם עֵרֵב הוּא, פֵרוֹתָיו כָּמוֹהוּ.

[ז] מִי שֶׁזִּמֵן אֶצְלוֹ אוֹרְחִים, לֹא יוֹלִיכוּ בְּיָדָם
מָנוֹת, אֶלָּא אִם כֵּן זִכָּה לָהֶם מָנוֹתֵיהֶם
מֵעֶרֶב יוֹם טוֹב.

יד אברהם

his halachic 'place of dwelling' two thousand cubits north of his actual residence, he may not take even one step southward on the Sabbath.

techum as established by placement of eruv

מִי שֶׁהָיוּ פֵרוֹתָיו בְּעִיר אַחֶרֶת, — *If one's produce was in another town* [i.e., at the onset of *Yom Tov* his produce was in a town other than the one in which he was residing],

[The town where the produce was held was outside of the owner's *techum*, so that the produce could not be reached by him on *Yom Tov*.]

וְעֵרְבוּ בְּנֵי אוֹתָהּ הָעִיר לְהָבִיא אֶצְלוֹ מִפֵּרוֹתָיו, — *and the people of that town* [where the produce was held] *made an eruv* [in order] *to bring some of his produce to him,*

[As a result of the *eruv* made by the townspeople, they may go to where the owner resides, but the owner of the produce, who did not make an *eruv*, may not go to his produce.]

לֹא יָבִיאוּ לוֹ. — *they* [i.e., the townspeople] *may not bring* [the produce] *to him* [i.e., the owner].

The produce follows the *techum* of its owner (as in mishnah 3). Consequently, in the case under discussion, it is judged to be out of its own *techum*, and consequently may not be moved at all [just as a person who goes out of his *techum* may not move out of the four cubits in which he finds himself (Eruvin 4:1)] (Rav; Rashi).

וְאִם עֵרֵב הוּא, — *But if he* [the owner] *made an eruv,*

[And by means of the *eruv* he, too, can reach his produce.]

פֵרוֹתָיו כָּמוֹהוּ. — [then] *his produce is as himself.*

[And it may be brought to him by

6. If one's produce was in another town, and the people of that town made an *eruv* [in order] to bring some of his produce to him, they may not bring [the produce] to him. But if he made an *eruv*, his produce is as himself.

7. If one invited guests, they may not take portions with them, unless he had given them possession of their portions before *Yom Tov*.

YAD AVRAHAM

the townspeople.]

It would appear from the law in our mishnah that if a person entrusted his objects to someone else they follow the *techum* of the owner and not of the custodian, as illustrated by the fact that the produce does not follow the *techum* of the townspeople in whose custody it is found. The *Gemara* (40a), however, records a dispute on this matter, citing Shmuel's view that objects entrusted to another person are *as the feet of the custodian*. According to his view, the *Gemara* says that in the case of our mishnah the

produce should follow the *techum* of the townsman it was entrusted to and not that of its owner. Therefore, the *Gemara* contends that our mishnah refers to a situation where the trustee, when he had accepted its trusteeship, had designated a special place for the produce. In this case the *place* itself is considered to be loaned or leased to the produce's owner, and he is then considered to be holding the produce under his own jurisdiction. The halachah is in accordance with this view (*Orach Chaim* 398:17; *Mishnah Berurah* 41).

7.

מִי שֶׁזִּמֵּן אֶצְלוֹ אוֹרְחִים, — *If one invited guests* [lit. *if one summoned guests to himself*],

The guests lived outside of the host's *techum*, but had made an *eruv* which enabled them to come. The host, however, had not made an *eruv* and is thus restricted from going to his guests' places of residence (*Rav; Rashi*).

לֹא יוֹלִיכוּ בְּיָדָם מָנוֹת, — *they may not take portions with them,*

They may not take portions of food home with them because these portions belonged to the host at the onset of *Yom Tov* and had already had their *techum* determined 'as the feet of the host.' This status cannot be changed even when the ownership of these portions is transferred during *Yom Tov*.

אֶלָּא אִם כֵּן זִכָּה לָהֶם מָנוֹתֵיהֶם מֵעֶרֶב יוֹם טוֹב. — *unless he had given them possession of their portions before Yom Tov.*

[A present may officially be given to a recipient in absentia by having someone else take possession of the present for him. This transfer of ownership by proxy may be accomplished without the knowledge of the recipient, for the actions of the proxy are considered as those of the recipient himself. Once this is done, the recipient is the legal owner of the object, and the giver cannot renege on the gift. This act is called זְכוּת, *zechus.*] If the host had, by the process of *zechus*, given his guests possession of the portions before *Yom Tov*, they may take their portions home with them, because these portions

אֵין מַשְׁקִין וְשׁוֹחֲטִין אֶת הַמִּדְבָּרִיּוֹת, אֲבָל
מַשְׁקִין וְשׁוֹחֲטִין אֶת הַבַּיָּתוֹת. אֵלוּ הֵן בַּיָּתוֹת —
הַלָּנוֹת בָּעִיר; מִדְבָּרִיּוֹת — הַלָּנוֹת בָּאֲפָר.

יד אברהם

אֵין מַשְׁקִין וְשׁוֹחֲטִין אֶת הַמִּדְבָּרִיּוֹת, — *We may neither water nor slaughter (the) range animals,*

The reference is to animals which pasture freely and are not seen for an extended period of time. Since they are not always accessible to their owner at the onset of *Yom Tov*, they are considered *muktzeh*.

The *Gemara* (40a) explains that the primary intention of the mishnah is to prohibit **slaughtering* these animals. The remark about watering these animals is inserted here only incidentally, to teach that an animal should be watered before slaughter to loosen the hide to facilitate flaying.

Ran understands the *Gemara* to mean that merely watering these animals is permitted even though they are *muktzeh*. Only the watering which as a preliminary step in the slaughtering process is referred to here, and the words must be understood in context of the entire phrase — *one may not water and slaughter* [the] *pasturing animals*. Thus, the mishnah's lesson is that one may not water in anticipation of slaughtering, since these animals may not be slaughtered on *Yom Tov*.

However, there are those who maintain that *muktzeh* animals may not be fed nor watered (see Commentary to 3:1; *Beis Yosef*

already belonged to the guests at the onset of *Yom Tov* when the *techum* was determined, and the *techum* of the portions is 'as the feet of the guests' *(Rav; Rashi)*.

[The concluding segment of the mishnah deals with the prohibition of *muktzeh* and is not directly related to the previous discussion of the laws of *techum*. Perhaps it was placed here because the *muktzeh* status of an animal may be determined by whether or not its location at the advent of *Yom Tov* is within the *techum* (see below, s.v. הַלָּנוֹת בָּאֲפָר). *Meiri* maintains that this segment follows as part of the mishnah's previous discussion of guests and portions by mentioning other factors to be taken into consideration when preparing food for guests. In any event it is certainly appropriate that tractate *Beitzah* concludes with the topic with which it had commenced, and which occupies a sizeable portion of the tractate — *muktzeh*.]

We may neither water nor slaughter range animals,
but we may water and slaughter domesticated
animals. These are [considered] domesticated — those
that pass the night in the town; range animals —
those that pass the night on the pasture.

5
7

YAD AVRAHAM

to *Orach Chaim* 498; *Mishnah Berurah* 497:4).

אֲבָל מַשְׁקִין וְשׁוֹחֲטִין אֶת הַבַּיָּתוֹת. — *but we may water and slaughter (the) domesticated animals.*

These animals, because of their accessibility, are not considered *muktzeh*.

אֵלּוּ הֵן בַּיָּתוֹת ... וְהַלָּנוֹת **בָּעִיר**; — *These are [considered] domesticated — those that pass the night in the town;*

Animals which spend the night in the city or within the limits of its *techum* are considered domestic and not *muktzeh*, even if during the daytime they graze outside of the *techum* (Gem. 40a).

מִדְבָּרִיּוֹת — *range* — הַלָּנוֹת בָּאֲפָר.

animals — those that pass the night on the pasture.

[I.e., if they spend the night outside of the *techum*, they are *muktzeh*. If these animals happen to wander into the town of their own accord, so that no violation of *techum* was involved in their transport (they are *as the feet of their* owners), they are nevertheless *muktzeh* because of their inaccessibility at the onset of *Yom Tov*.

There is question in the *Gemara* (40b) whether *R' Shimon*, whose views on *muktzeh* tend to be lenient, classifies animals turned out to pasture as *muktzeh*. *Baal Haltur* (cited by *Tur Orach Chaim* 498) considers these animals *muktzeh* according to R' Shimon, while others (*Behag, Rosh*) do not. *Rama*, who rules according to R' Shimon with regard to *Yom Tov* (*Orach Chaim* 495:4), nevertheless agrees that these animals are *muktzeh*.

סליק מסכת ביצה

Glossary

Amora, pl. **Amoraim** (אֲמוֹרָאִים) אֲמוֹרָא: a Sage of the post-Mishnaic era quoted in the *Gemara* or other works of the same period

baraisa בְּרַיְיתָא: statements of the *Tannaim* not included in the Mishnah

beis din בֵּית דִין: Rabbinical court of law

Beis HaMikdash בֵּית הַמִקְדָשׁ: the Holy Temple in Jerusalem

Chol HaMoed חוֹל הַמוֹעֵד: see below, s.v., *Yom Tov*

Eretz Yisrael אֶרֶץ יִשְׂרָאֵל: the Land of Israel according to its halachically defined borders

Gemara גְמָרָא: the section of the Talmud that explains the Mishnah

halachah, pl. **halachos** (הֲלָכוֹת) הֲלָכָה: (1) a religious law; (2) [cap.] the body of Jewish law

ho'il הוֹאִיל: lit. *because*; the halachic principle which permits one to cook any food on *Yom Tov*, even if it is not certain that it will be needed for *Yom Tov*, 'because if guests should happen to arrive on *Yom Tov*, he would serve them that food'

Kohen כֹּהֵן: a member of the priestly family descended from Aaron

melachah מְלָאכָה: prohibited labor; see General Introduction

mikveh, pl. **mikvaos** (מִקְוָאוֹת) מִקְוֶה: ritualarium; pool of water for the halachic cleansing of one who is *tamei*

Mishkan מִשְׁכָּן: the Tabernacle which traveled with the Israelites in the wilderness

mitoch: see General Introduction

muktzeh: see General Introduction

posek, pl. **poskim** (פּוֹסְקִים) פּוֹסֵק: halachic authority

Rishon pl. **Rishonim** (רִאשׁוֹנִים) רִאשׁוֹן: early Torah authority of approximately 1000-1500 CE

taharah טָהֳרָה: a halachically defined state of ritual or spiritual purity, free of *tumah*-contamination

tahor טָהוֹר: in a state of *taharah*

Talmud Bavli תַּלְמוּד בַּבְלִי: the Babylonian recension of the Talmud, completed in the fifth century CE by R' Ashi

Talmud Yerushalmi תַּלְמוּד יְרוּשַׁלְמִי: the Jerusalem recension of the Talmud, completed in *Eretz Yisrael* at the end of the fourth century CE

tamei טָמֵא: in a halachically defined state of *tumah*-contamination

Tanna, pl. **Tannaim** (תַּנָאִים) תַּנָא: a Sage quoted in the Mishnah or in works of the same period

Tanna kamma תַּנָא קַמָא: unidentified speaker of first opinion stated in a mishnah or *baraisa*

terumah תְּרוּמָה: a portion of the crop sanctified and given to a *Kohen* who, together with his family, may eat it, but only if both the eater and the *terumah* are each in a state of *taharah*

tevel טֶבֶל: any commodity that requires that one or more tithes be removed from it is called *tevel* until the particular tithes have been set aside

tumah טֻמְאָה: a halachically defined contamination inherent in certain people (e.g., a *niddah*) or objects (e.g., a corpse) that under specific conditions is transferred to another person or object

Yom Tov יוֹם טוֹב: a festival or holiday, specifically, those days, other than the Sabbath, on which labor is forbidden; as used throughout this tractate, the term refers to the first (and, outside of *Eretz Yisrael*, also the second) and seventh (and eighth) days of Pesach, Shavuos, the first (and second) day(s) of Succos, Shemini Atzeres (with Simchas Torah), and Rosh Hashanah; not included are Yom Kippur, to which all the stringencies of Sabbath apply, and חוֹל הַמוֹעֵד, *Chol HaMoed*, (the intermediate days of Pesach and Succos) on which the labor restrictions are greatly relaxed

﴾ תפלה על הנפטר אחר למוד משניות ﴿

It is customary to recite this prayer whenever *Mishnayos* are studied in memory of a deceased.

אָנָּא יהוה מָלֵא רַחֲמִים, אֲשֶׁר בְּיָדְךָ נֶפֶשׁ כָּל חָי, וְרוּחַ כָּל בְּשַׂר אִישׁ. יִהְיֶה נָא לְרָצוֹן לְפָנֶיךָ תּוֹרָתֵנוּ וּתְפִלָּתֵנוּ בַּעֲבוּר נִשְׁמַת (deceased's Hebrew name) בֶּן/בַּת (father's Hebrew name) וּגְמֹל נָא עִמָּה בְּחַסְדְּךָ הַגָּדוֹל, לִפְתּוֹחַ לָהּ שַׁעֲרֵי רַחֲמִים וָחֶסֶד, וְשַׁעֲרֵי גַן עֵדֶן. וּתְקַבֵּל אוֹתָהּ בְּאַהֲבָה וּבְחִבָּה, וּשְׁלַח לָהּ מַלְאָכֶיךָ הַקְּדוֹשִׁים וְהַטְּהוֹרִים, לְהוֹלִיכָהּ וּלְהוֹשִׁיבָהּ תַּחַת עֵץ הַחַיִּים, אֵצֶל נִשְׁמַת הַצַּדִּיקִים וְהַצִּדְקָנִיּוֹת, חֲסִידִים וַחֲסִידוֹת, לֵהָנוֹת מִזִּיו שְׁכִינָתֶךָ, לְהַשְׂבִּיעָהּ מִטּוּבְךָ הַצָּפוּן לַצַּדִּיקִים. וְהַגּוּף יָנוּחַ בַּקֶּבֶר בִּמְנוּחָה נְכוֹנָה, בְּחֶדְוָה וּבְשִׂמְחָה וְשָׁלוֹם, כְּדִכְתִיב: יָבוֹא שָׁלוֹם, יָנוּחוּ עַל מִשְׁכְּבוֹתָם, הֹלֵךְ נְכֹחוֹ. וּכְתִיב: יַעַלְזוּ חֲסִידִים בְּכָבוֹד, יְרַנְּנוּ עַל מִשְׁכְּבוֹתָם. וּכְתִיב: אִם תִּשְׁכַּב לֹא תִפְחָד, וְשָׁכַבְתָּ וְעָרְבָה שְׁנָתֶךָ.

<table>
<tr><td>for a female:</td><td>for a male:</td></tr>
<tr><td>

וְתִשְׁמוֹר אוֹתָהּ מֵחִבּוּט הַקֶּבֶר, וּמֵרִמָּה וְתוֹלֵעָה. וְתִסְלַח וְתִמְחוֹל לָהּ עַל כָּל פְּשָׁעֶיהָ, כִּי אָדָם אֵין צַדִּיק בָּאָרֶץ, אֲשֶׁר יַעֲשֶׂה טּוֹב וְלֹא יֶחֱטָא. וְזִכוֹר לָהּ זְכִיּוֹתֶיהָ וְצִדְקוֹתֶיהָ אֲשֶׁר עָשָׂתָה. וְתַשְׁפִּיעַ לָהּ מִזְּהֲרָמָה לְדַשֵּׁן עַצְמוֹתֶיהָ בַּקֶּבֶר מֵרֹב טוּב הַצָּפוּן לַצַּדִּיקִים, דִּכְתִיב: מָה רַב טוּבְךָ אֲשֶׁר צָפַנְתָּ לִירֵאֶיךָ, וּכְתִיב: שֹׁמֵר כָּל עַצְמֹתָיו, אַחַת מֵהֵנָּה לֹא נִשְׁבָּרָה. וְתִשְׁכּוֹן בֶּטַח בָּדָד וְשַׁאֲנַן מִפַּחַד רָעָה, וְאַל תִּרְאֶה פְּנֵי גֵיהִנָּם. וְנִשְׁמָתָהּ תְּהֵא צְרוּרָה בִּצְרוֹר הַחַיִּים, וּלְהַחֲיוֹתָהּ בִּתְחִיַּת הַמֵּתִים עִם כָּל מֵתֵי עַמְּךָ יִשְׂרָאֵל בְּרַחֲמִים. אָמֵן.

</td><td>

וְתִשְׁמוֹר אוֹתוֹ מֵחִבּוּט הַקֶּבֶר, וּמֵרִמָּה וְתוֹלֵעָה. וְתִסְלַח וְתִמְחוֹל לוֹ עַל כָּל פְּשָׁעָיו, כִּי אָדָם אֵין צַדִּיק בָּאָרֶץ, אֲשֶׁר יַעֲשֶׂה טּוֹב וְלֹא יֶחֱטָא. וְזִכוֹר לוֹ זְכִיּוֹתָיו וְצִדְקוֹתָיו אֲשֶׁר עָשָׂה. וְתַשְׁפִּיעַ לוֹ נשפיעו לְדַשֵּׁן עַצְמוֹתָיו בַּקֶּבֶר מֵרֹב טוּב הַצָּפוּן לַצַּדִּיקִים, דִּכְתִיב: מָה רַב טוּבְךָ אֲשֶׁר צָפַנְתָּ לִירֵאֶיךָ. וּכְתִיב: שֹׁמֵר כָּל עַצְמֹתָיו, אַחַת מֵהֵנָּה לֹא נִשְׁבָּרָה. וְיִשְׁכּוֹן בֶּטַח בָּדָד וְשַׁאֲנַן מִפַּחַד רָעָה, וְאַל יִרְאֶה פְּנֵי גֵיהִנֹּם. וְנִשְׁמָתוֹ תְּהֵא צְרוּרָה בִּצְרוֹר הַחַיִּים, וּלְהַחֲיוֹתוֹ בִּתְחִיַּת הַמֵּתִים עִם כָּל מֵתֵי עַמְּךָ יִשְׂרָאֵל בְּרַחֲמִים. אָמֵן.

</td></tr>
</table>